ON RECORD 1984 G. BROWN

ON RECORD ENTRIES ARE NOT ORDERED ALPHABETICALLY, BUT ORGANIZED INTUITIVELY— A MIXTURE OF SEGUES BY MUSICAL GENRE OR STYLE.

CONTENTS

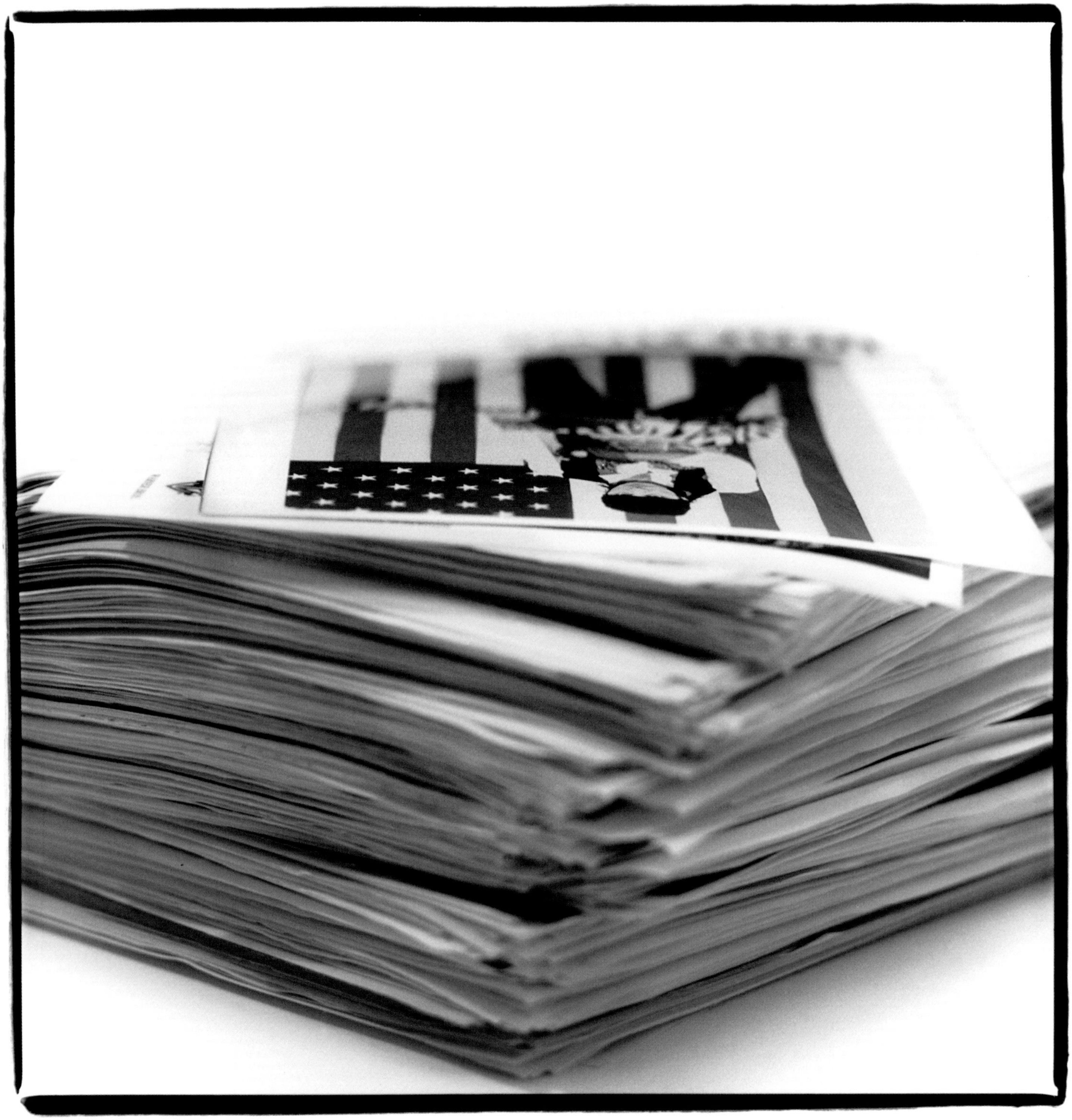

PHOTOGRAPH BY STEPHEN COLLECTOR

ON RECORD VOL. 2 1984

NO LONGER considered a fad by 1984, MTV ruled the cultural landscape and revolutionized the way people consumed music. With a music television station playing music videos 24 hours a day in nearly every American home, artists who previously just had to worry about creating great songs and albums and a concert experience, now had to get used to making short films—and looking good in them, too.

Newspapers were still a platform for artists to express and present themselves. Contracting with *The Denver Post*, I was the one of the few with access to something most fans didn't have—the opportunity to go to all the concerts and get all the new releases and press kits. To amplify my interviews and reviews, I strove to keep pace with the new influential visual communicators.

So I orchestrated exclusive photo shoots, working in tandem with the most gifted photographers in my purview: Stephen Collector, a mensch who carved out a striking freelance career for top national magazines and periodicals; Anthony Suau, who would soon win a Pulitzer Prize for Feature Photography for his images of the famine in Ethiopia; and the innovative photojournalist Brian Brainerd, a genius whose pre-production prep allowed him to snap a few frames of performers moments before a show—and make it look like the results of a daylong photo session.

We had memorable adventures taking rock stars' pictures. Cyndi Lauper endeared herself at a backstage meet-and-greet, working the entire room and posing for her portrait without saying a word—she had some sort of remedy in her mouth to keep her voice hydrated. A shuffling, sniffling Billy Idol took his mark, turned it on for the camera akin to a generator switch being thrown in an old science-fiction movie—and then turned it off just as abruptly. The spatting Daryl Hall & John Oates stood on opposite sides of the room until they ultimately stood back to back for a photo, not once making eye contact. Eurythmics proved challenging, but it wasn't the presumed diva Annie Lennox being obdurate—she was warm and cooperative in compensating for her petulant partner, Dave Stewart. Stevie Ray Vaughan was a distracted sweetheart of a guy looking to party. The girlish Go-Go's remained pert standing in the rain at Red Rocks Amphitheatre. The members of R.E.M. willingly sat on the fissured asphalt of a parking lot to provide a spontaneous backdrop.

My personal contribution was cracking a well-timed joke that resulted in the only picture extant of the sober-sided Don Henley laughing.

That year, I also stayed busy with more serious wordsmithing. I interviewed the "second British Invasion" of new wave bands who defined the music video aesthetic, from Depeche Mode to Wham! I reported on Prince's *Purple Rain*—his reply to Michael Jackson's dominance of the pop world—and on Billy Ocean, Lionel Richie and the other African American artists who were being added to the MTV playlist. I wrote about emerging stars such as Huey Lewis & the News and re-emerging ones such as Tina Turner. I covered the period's great up-and-coming bands—from Metallica to R.E.M. to Hüsker Dü—and the more established acts, including the Cars, Van Halen and maybe even Spinal Tap. And many, many others. I was and am a very lucky boy. Please allow me to share. — **G. Brown**

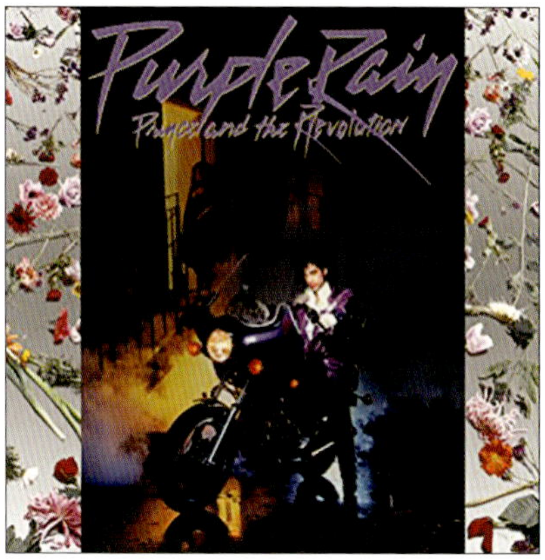

Purple Rain quickly became Prince's most critically acclaimed and commercially successful release.

Billboard 200: *Purple Rain* (No.1)
Billboard Hot 100: "When Doves Cry" (No.1);
"Let's Go Crazy" (No. 1); "Purple Rain" (#2);
"I Would Die 4 U" (#8); "Take Me With U" (#25)

HAVING SHOWCASED his talents on the groundbreaking albums *Dirty Mind*, *Controversy* and *1999*, Prince pursued a deal to star in a major motion picture. In *Purple Rain*, a dramatic film which contained several concert sequences, Prince portrayed "the Kid," a young musician from Minneapolis searching for artistic accomplishment, self-awareness and love; the character's magnetism played off a spunky but mysterious young singer-dancer (portrayed by Apollonia, Prince's latest discovery).

On the subject of the loosely autobiographical story about his career, Prince was rather soft-spoken. After all, his home state of Minnesota wasn't the usual training ground for pop stars.

"It was probably worse up there than you can even imagine," he said. "It was dead, and I found out early that there was no reason to listen to the radio—I knew I would be too far behind when I did my own music if that was all that was going on. Around 13 or 14, I started getting serious about composing and writing my own songs. The bands were real competitive—but I'm not saying we worked.

"I could always play several instruments, and I did out of fun, not necessity—until I got kicked out of the band I was in. I never thought I would be pursuing it, but then I graduated from high school and had to do something. I just stuck with music."

The *Purple Rain* studio album also served as the soundtrack to the film. Partially recorded with his touring band, the Revolution, it consolidated his funk and R&B roots while moving into pop, rock and heavy metal. "When Doves Cry" and "Let's Go Crazy" topped the charts, and the title track went to #2. The album spent 24 consecutive weeks at No. 1 and eventually sold more than 10 million copies in the US. ■

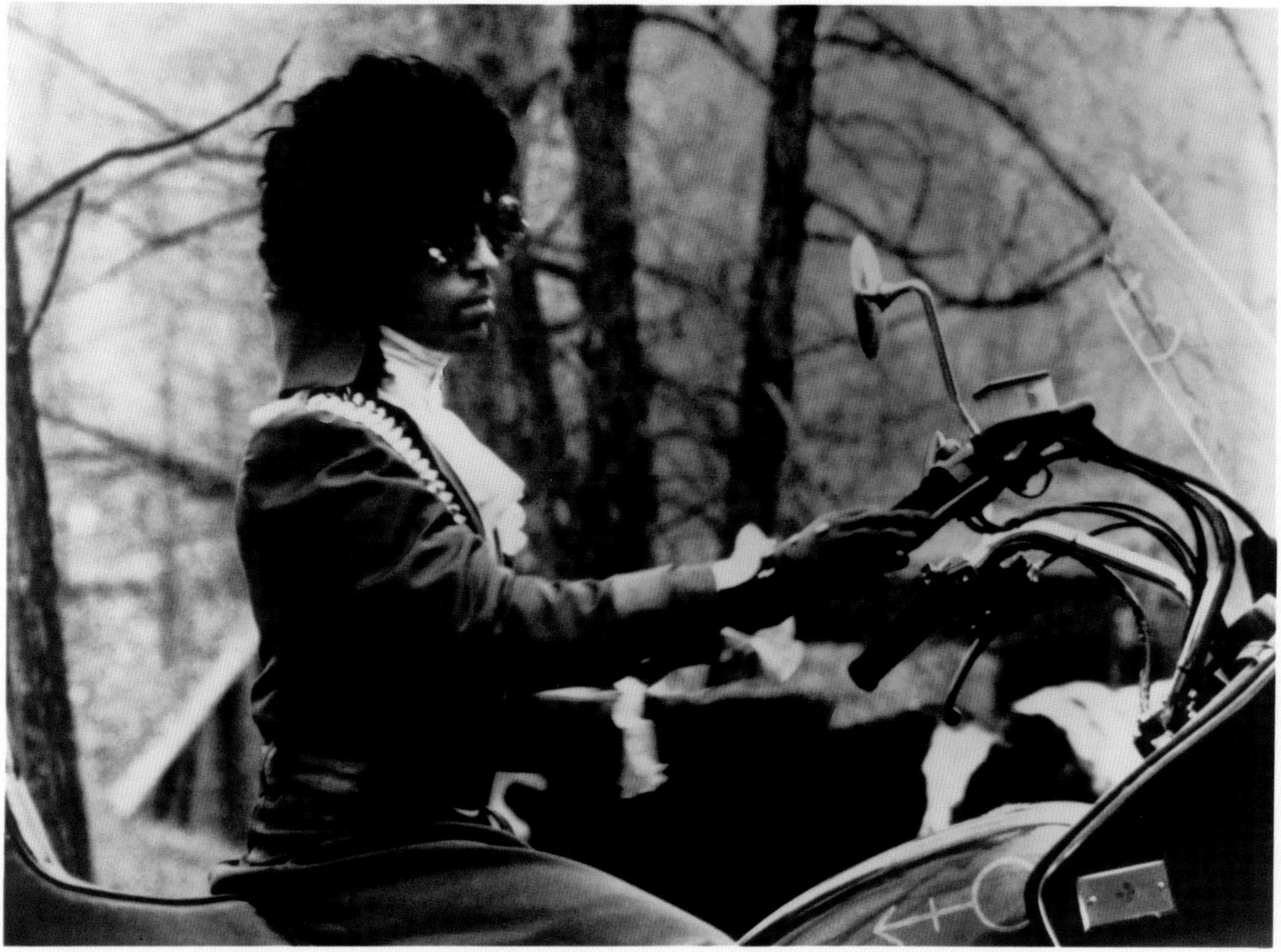

Prince stars in Purple Rain, a Warner Bros. release. The original soundtrack including the hit single "When Doves Cry," and eight other original songs from Prince and The Revolution, is available on Warner Bros. records and cassettes.

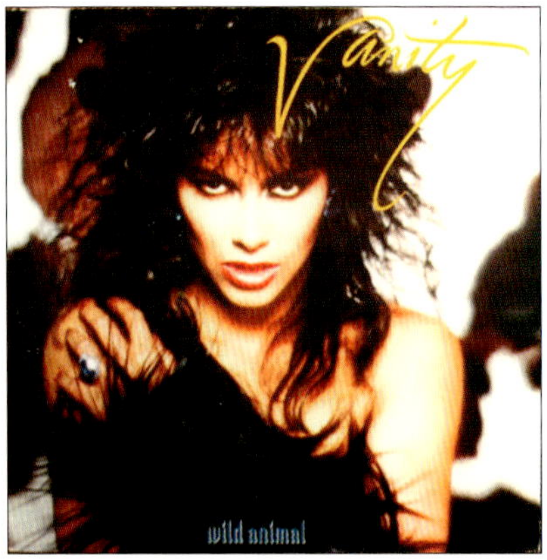

After turning down a role in Prince's *Purple Rain*, Vanity found mild success with the single "Pretty Mess."

Billboard 200: *Wild Animal* (#62)
Billboard Hot 100: "Pretty Mess" (#75)

THE MASSIVE success of the *Purple Rain* film and soundtrack catapulted Prince into the superstar stratosphere, and the benefits weren't his alone. By writing Minneapolis cohorts such as the Time into the storyline, he created personas for his entire camp. But where was Vanity of Vanity 6 fame?

Vanity 6 was Prince's steamy "girl group" creation, and Vanity sang the hit "Nasty Girls," which sold over a half-million copies. The ex-nudie actress made a name as part of Prince's touring revue by wearing lingerie onstage and mock-inserting candy canes before throwing them into the audience. She appeared to be a shoo-in for the part of Prince's girlfriend in *Purple Rain*—a role that, like many in the film, reportedly paralleled a real-life situation. But when the time came to shoot the film, the part went to Apollonia, played by 19-year-old Patty Kotero.

"I just wanted to go it on my own and try some solo things," the 23-year-old Vanity (real name Denise Matthews) pouted. "It wasn't any new decision. I thought it would be better not to do *Purple Rain* if I would be leaving afterwards—that wouldn't make much sense, would it? I still keep in touch with him."

Rumors took on a different tone; the rock press described the reasons for Vanity's departure as "ranging from money to ego to a faded relationship with the film's diminutive star." Whatever the circumstances, Vanity was stuck trying to attain fame without the sponsorship of Prince.

Thanks to Motown Records, the public got the chance to assess Vanity's talent. She collaborated on *Wild Animal*, her first solo album, with synthesizer player Bill Wolfer, producer of the Shalamar hit "Dancing in the Sheets." But Vanity didn't gamble by only relying on musical merits—"Pretty Mess," the single from the album, arrived at radio stations wrapped in black lace with five photos of the sultry singer.

Given her spacey demeanor, Vanity could have been dismissed as a joke, but she wasn't in on it, turning her aggressive sexuality into a legitimately hot property.

"That's what you work for," she concluded. "People see your face, they wonder what you can do, and then you have to prove yourself. That's what I'm doing now. I'm just doing it on my own, that's all." ■

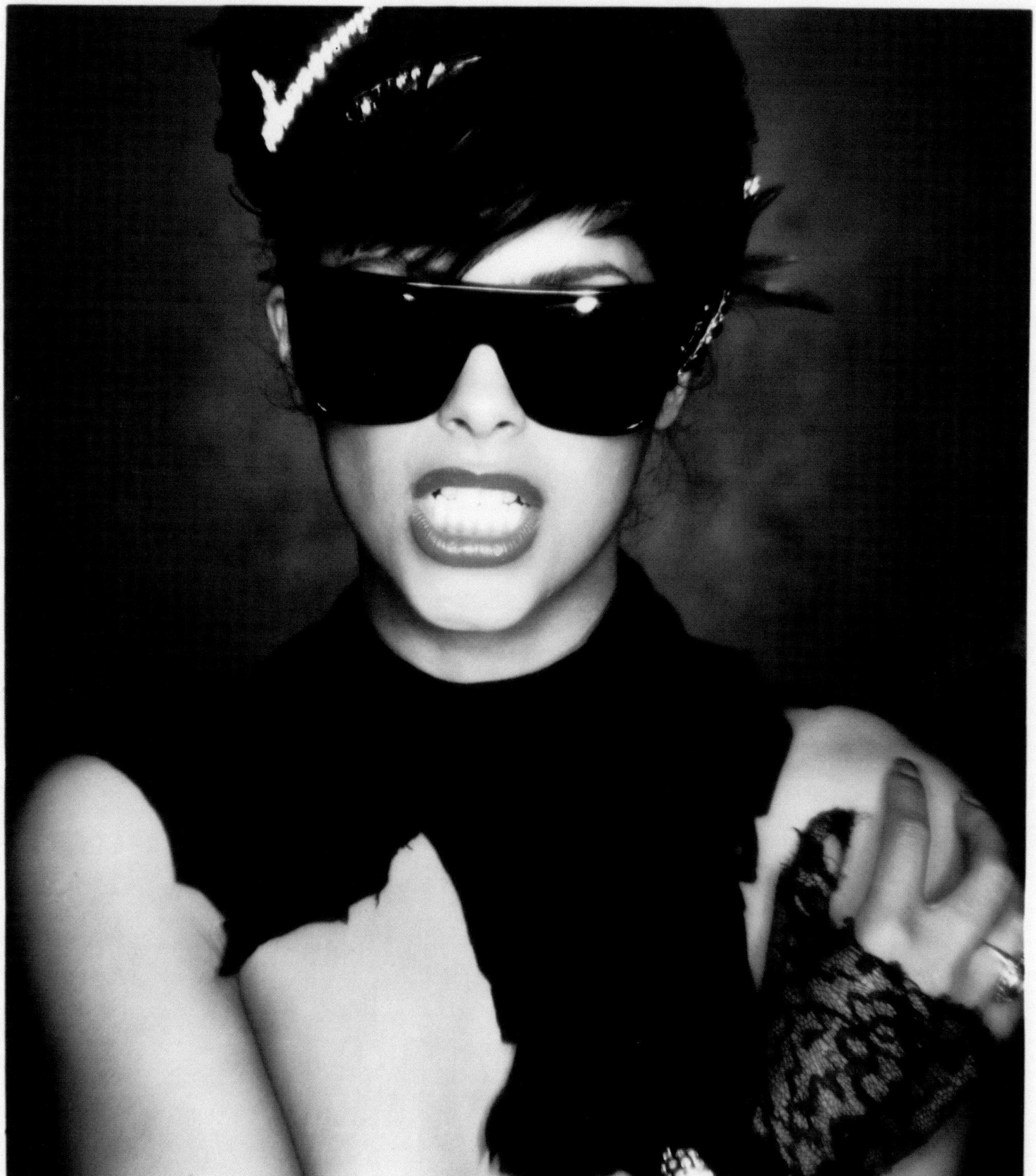

VANITY

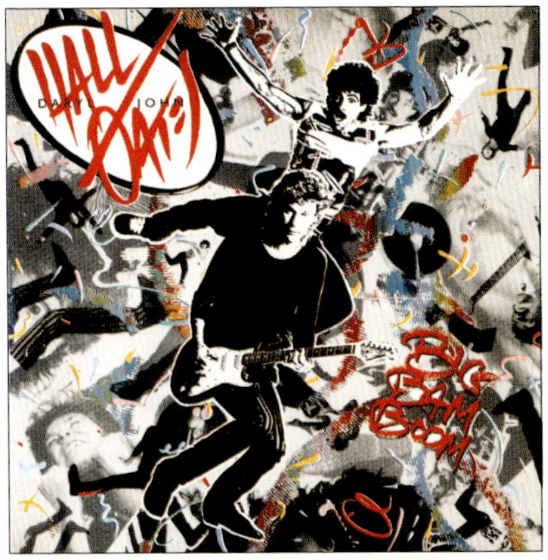

Billboard 200: *Big Bam Boom* (#5)
Billboard Hot 100: "Out of Touch" (No. 1); "Method of Modern Love" (#5); "Some Things Are Better Left Unsaid" (#18); "Possession Obsession" (#30)

Big Bam Boom gave a depth to Daryl Hall & John Oates' artistry that translated to a higher visibility.

DARYL HALL & John Oates had already earned a favorable mention in any discussion of rock's superstar acts, but the two singer-songwriters attained another plateau of popularity with *Big Bam Boom*. The album featured their usual quota of smash singles—the No. 1 pop hit "Out of Touch," "Method of Modern Love" and "Some Things Are Better Left Unsaid"—while exploring popular dance rhythms and emerging technology.

Those moves weren't premeditated. Hall & Oates' initial commercial success belied their early attempts at cracking Philadelphia's black music scene in the Sixties.

"Anybody that really knows our history realizes that dance music is what we do," Hall mused.

"Our roots are in East Coast urban music, and what's going on right now is just an Eighties version of it. I've never felt more comfortable with any supposed trend. This happened naturally, and we're just lucky enough to have certain technology that allows this kind of music to be put together."

Commercial success enabled the duo to experiment with the latest technical innovations in recording and playing (advanced polyphonic synthesizers and new sophisticated drum machines, for example). The hip-hop rhythms incorporated on *Big Bam Boom* reflected the scene in New York, Hall added.

"New York has been the hub of this music for about two years. It's regional—there are so many street people and little labels and small organizations putting out records. But I don't think anybody's missing out on the feeling that's going on—for the first time in a long time, that urban dance sound is getting played on radio across the country. I'm glad that's happening, because it was really segregated for so long."

Hall & Oates had finally outdistanced such restrictive labels as "blue-eyed soul."

"I do feel there's a different way of perceiving us now," Hall noted. "I think we're starting to get the kind of recognition that I've always wanted to have from people. Whatever it is, I'm happy about it!" ■

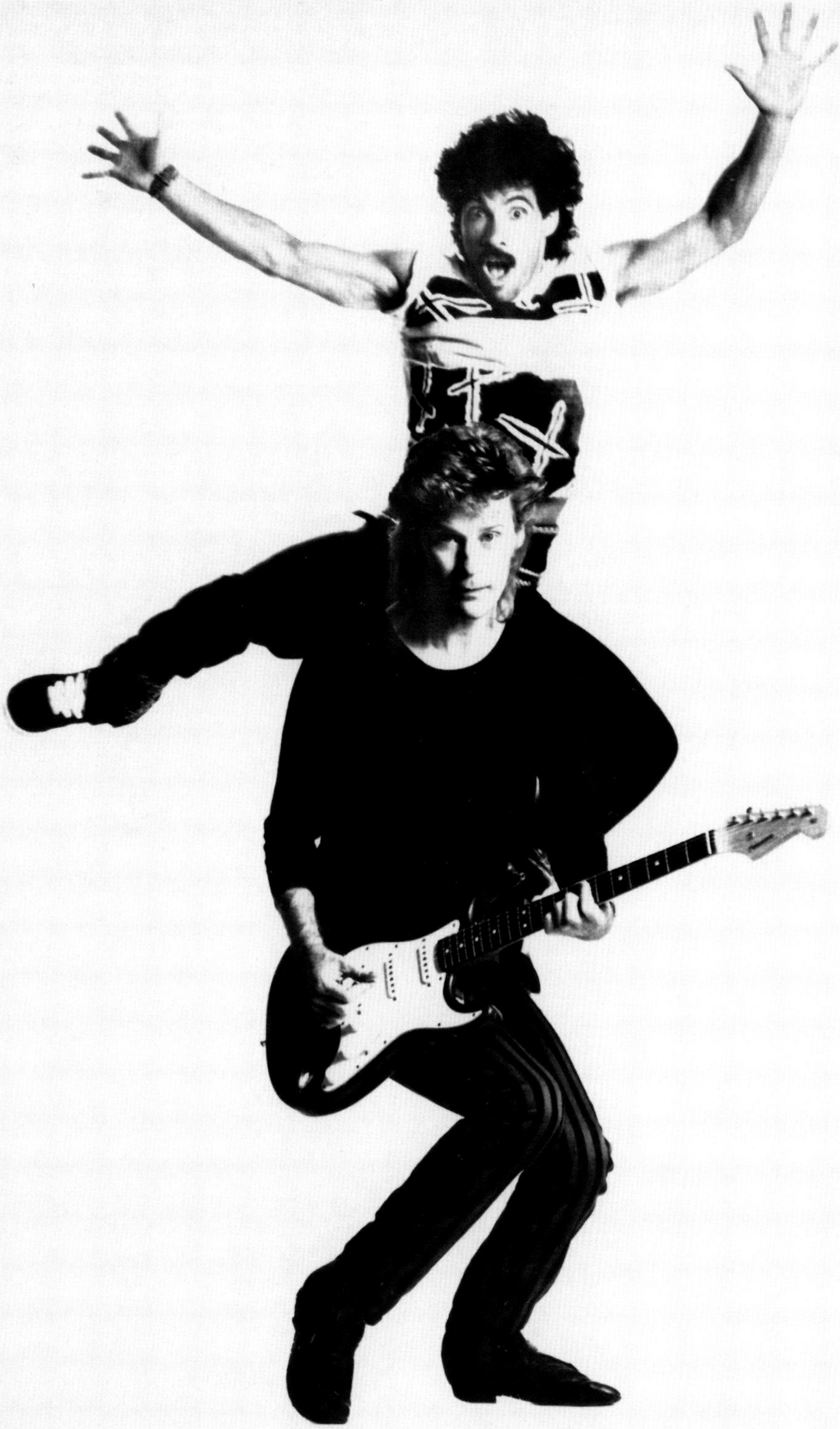

Photography by JEAN PAGLIUSO

DARYL HALL JOHN OATES

RCA
Records and Cassettes

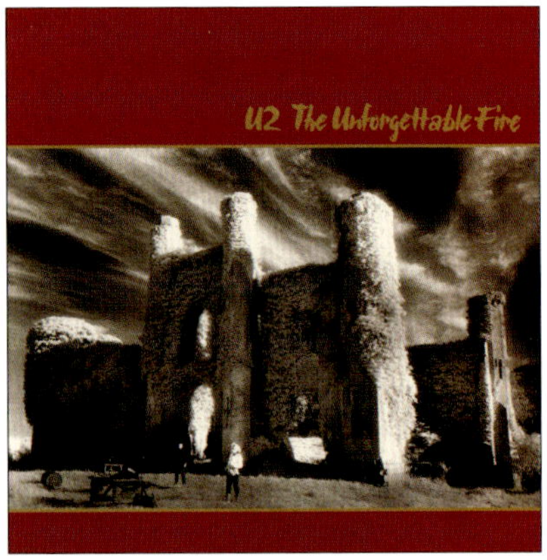

U2's *The Unforgettable Fire* generated "Pride (In the Name of Love)," the band's first US Top 40 song.

Billboard 200: *The Unforgettable Fire* (#12)
Billboard Hot 100: "Pride (In the Name of Love)" (#33)

IN 1977, four young musicians had banded together against the battle-zone backdrop of their native Ireland, committing themselves to a world vision. U2 built its reputation on live performances, dismantling the usual barriers between artist and audience. The special communion they formed with their devotees had propelled them from cult status to mainstream success at an early stage.

Called "the Band of the Eighties" by *Rolling Stone,* U2 may have been an important group, but its members weren't self-important. They tried to avoid the pitfalls of overkill. *The Unforgettable Fire*, U2's fourth album, was a dramatic change in direction, less rousing and more insinuating than past works. "Pride (In the Name of Love)" was inspired by Martin Luther King, Jr., the slain civil rights leader.

"We felt going into the record that we wanted to go for a European sort of atmosphere," bassist Adam Clayton explained. "And we had some difficulty trying to figure out a producer—a lot of Americans were high on the list, but we didn't want to go for that sort of record, not this time. Toward the eleventh hour, the name Brian Eno (of Talking Heads fame) jumped out of the hat. He wasn't keen to do it, but Bono talked him to death until he agreed."

Singer Bono, who had displayed an Irish gift of gab since his appearance on the music scene, had curbed his effusiveness to save his voice for shows, cultivating a more serious and intent image. In a live setting, Clayton, drummer Larry Mullen and guitarist The Edge provided a beat that transcended the band's politics, but U2's trademark urgency and commitment remained palpable.

"No matter how closely the media scrutinizes us, I don't think it will jeopardize our chemistry," Clayton admitted. "The thing that worries me is that Bono may find he doesn't have any time left to himself, and I wouldn't wish that on anyone. That's a difficult situation to find yourself in, to still keep ahold of what you are and the way you think. That's something we'll have to cope with, but we have a reasonably sensitive audience that's aware we need to have time on our own. I wouldn't want to be in Duran Duran. You wouldn't have an hour to yourself." ■

U2

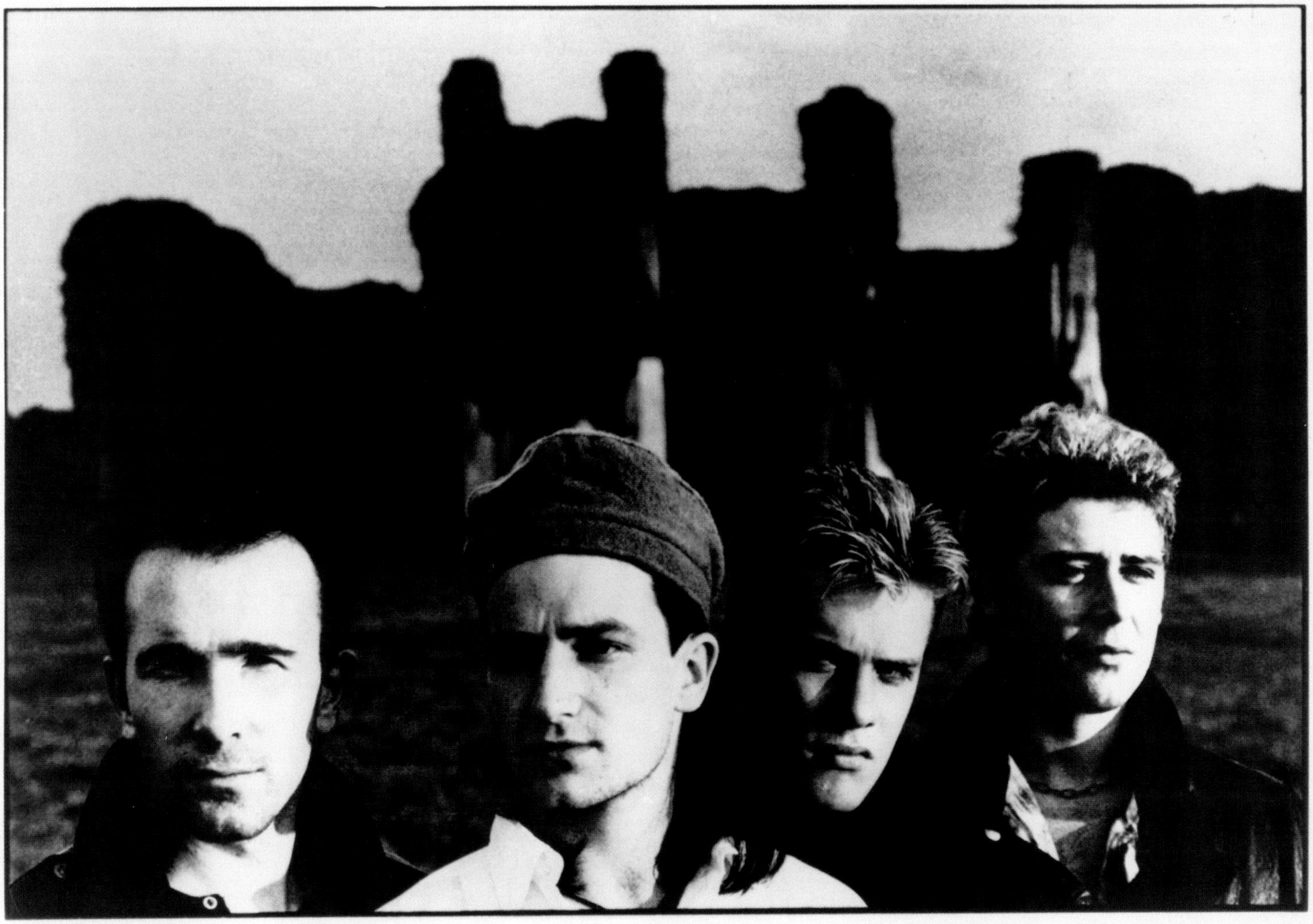

Photo Credit: ANTON CORBIJN 1984

ISLAND

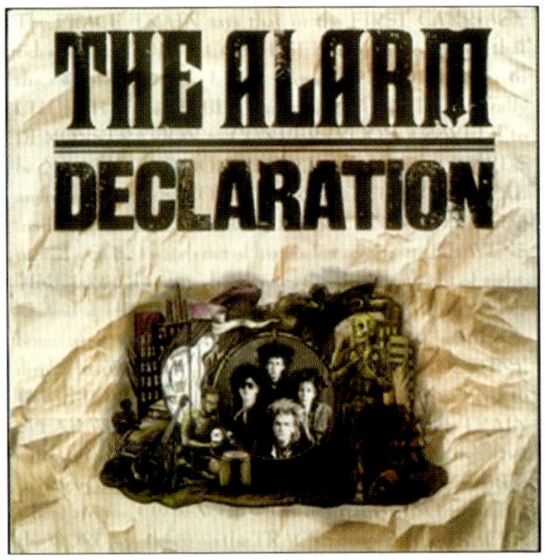

The Alarm's *Declaration* introduced the group's rousing anthems—and combed-with-egg-beaters hair.

Billboard 200: *Declaration* (#50)

THE INDIVIDUALS comprising the Alarm—vocalist Mike Peters, guitarist Dave Sharp, bassist Eddie MacDonald and drummer Nigel Twist—grew up together in northern Wales, and by the time they reached their teens they were ready to command the regional music scene.

"Ten miles across the water from Rhyl is Liverpool, and my friends and I were attracted there to find entertainment. We would go down in the basement of this club where the Beatles had started off, and it was there that we heard the Buzzcocks and the Jam in '76. That sort of music stopped me dead in my tracks. I was a computer operator, and I could see the straight line of the next 30 years. I just wanted to step off and see what I could do, go see the world, experiment. We all felt the same thing when we saw that music—shocked that we were so young, yet so old at the same time."

Taking their name from the first song they wrote, "Alarm Alarm," the members began playing to scrape up money for some time in a recording studio. The band drew comparisons to the Clash for its political fervor and to U2 for optimism-in-the-face-of-a-lost-world songs.

"We bought acoustic guitars, and it's turned into our trademark sound," Peters noted. "Anyway, we tried electric and it didn't work. With acoustic guitars, we've been able to rehearse in a flat, carry our own equipment and generally keep things within our own circle."

To an extent, *Declaration* was a collection of spirited singles the Alarm had been releasing since 1982—"68 Guns," "Marching On," "The Stand," "Where Were You Hiding When the Storm Broke?" and "The Deceiver."

On its first American tour, the quartet gained a reputation as a searing, passionate live band that communicated better in concert than on record.

"We picked up a loyal following of Americans that were staying in London," Peters enthused. "They've gone back happy and spread the word. We like a lot of American music, like Springsteen and Dylan. We're a live group, not like Culture Club or Human League, groups that don't tour a lot. We want to play every night of the week, every week of the year." ■

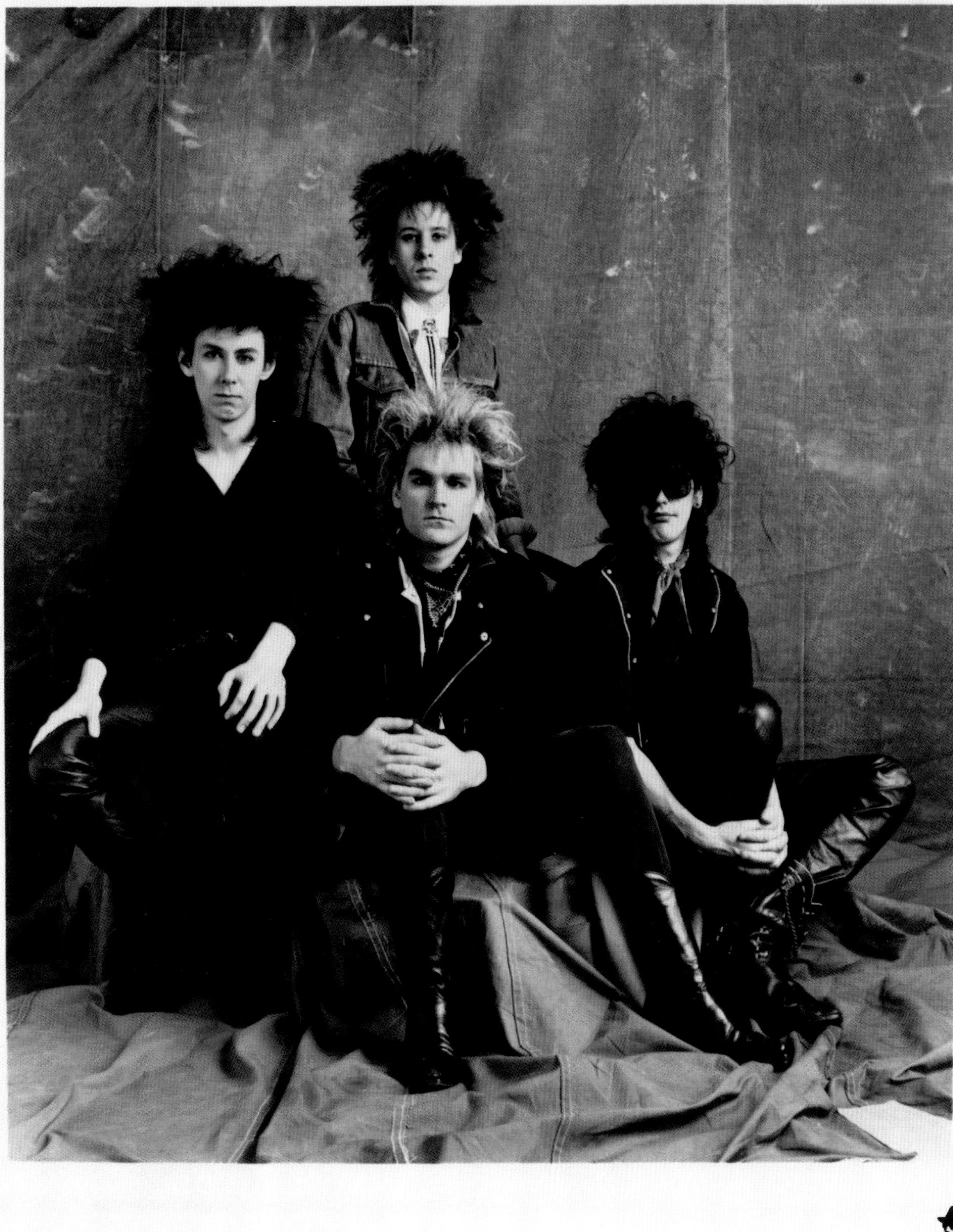

THE ALARM clockwise from top: **DAVE SHARP** **TWIST** **MIKE PETERS** **EDDIE MACDONALD**

I.R.S.

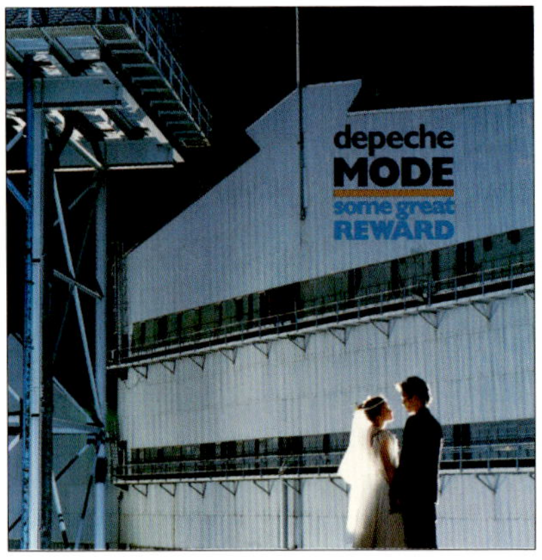

The synth-pop stylings of "People Are People" gave the UK's Depeche Mode its first American smash.

Billboard 200: *Some Great Reward* (#54)
Billboard Hot 100: "People Are People" (#13); "Master and Servant" (#87)

PEOPLE WHO swore by the guitar as the ultimate rock instrument were undoubtedly cringing at the crop of electro-pop bands in the early Eighties. Music fans called them a variety of things—cold, gloomy, distant, robotic—but there was no denying the success of a band like Depeche Mode, a British quartet that relied entirely on synthesizers for their sound.

"The fallacy is that electronic music is emotionless—as long as you can operate the equipment, you should be able to get some warmth to the music," founding member Martin Gore countered. "There are hardly any bands making music the way they should be in the Eighties. There are too many regressive bands."

Depeche Mode (the name, taken from a French clothing magazine, meant "fast fashion") came out of Britain's "new romantic" movement of the late Seventies.

"We were involved with that scene, but the 'new romantic' term didn't mean anything," Gore said. "For instance, Spandau Ballet had a regular instrumental lineup, and Duran Duran only had one keyboard. We were the only ones to be all electronic."

When Depeche Mode began making records in 1981, it seemed destined to become just another bright-sounding teeny-bop attraction. But after original frontman and synth player Vince Clarke left the band because he preferred the studio to touring, the group's songwriting responsibilities fell to Gore.

"We were young and naïve," Gore said, "so we didn't even consider what was going on. We just carried on."

The synth-pop quartet gradually gained a name for catchy, droll techno-dance singles such as "People Are People" and "Master and Servant." *Some Great Reward* was the band's artistic and commercial breakthrough, becoming the first Depeche Mode album to enter the US album charts. ■

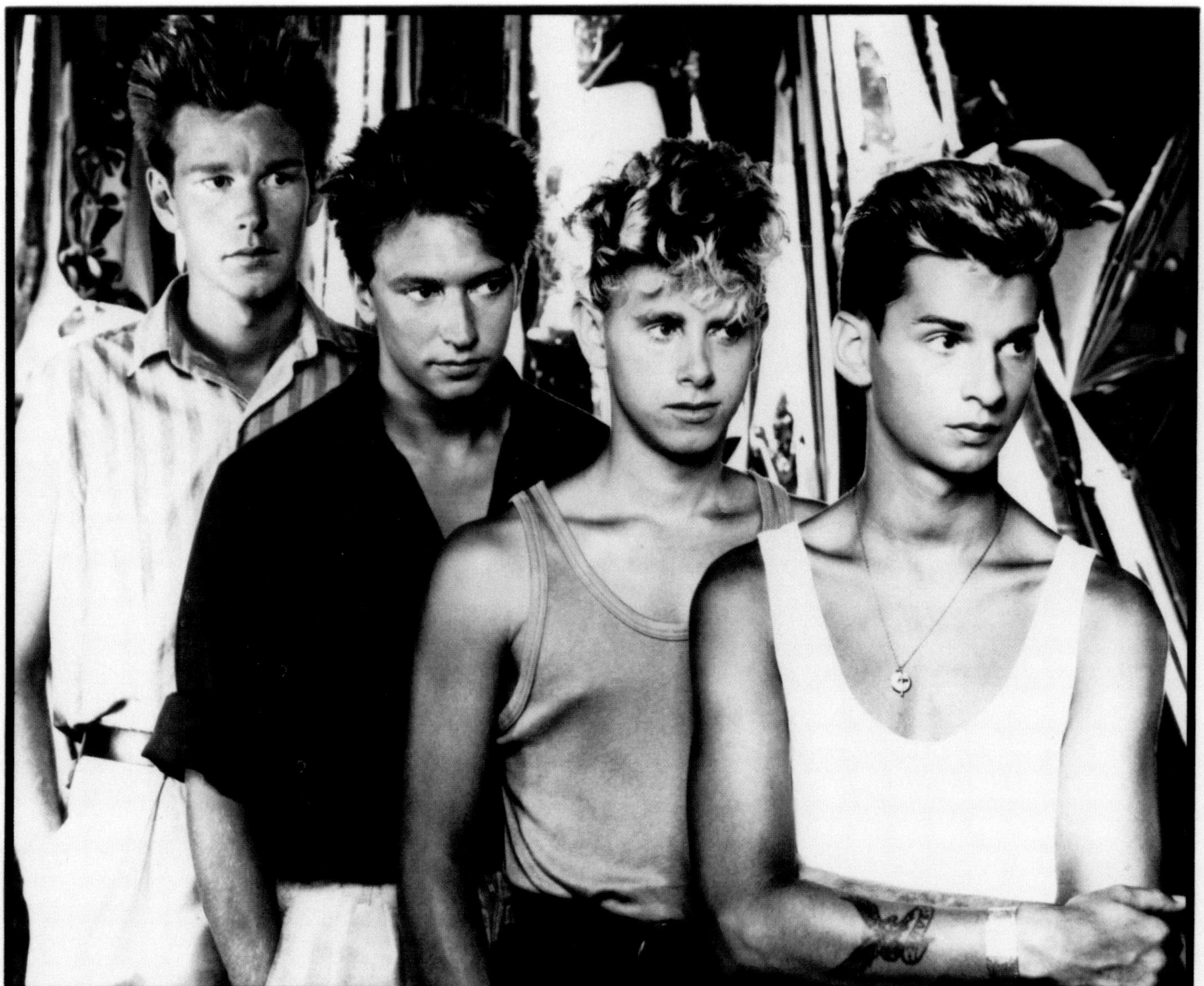

Photo credit: ALAN BALLARD

DEPECHE MODE

MUTE RECORDS

SIRE®

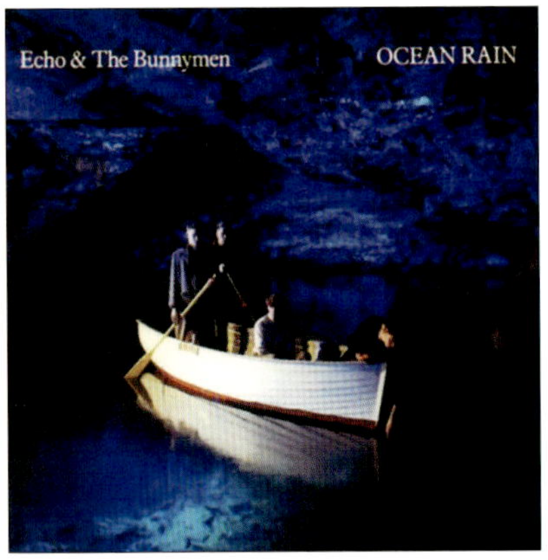

Echo & the Bunnymen reached the apogee of the British post-punk landscape with "The Killing Moon."

Billboard 200: *Ocean Rain* (#87)

AT THE beginning of the Eighties, a handful of British bands ostensibly created a Liverpool renaissance with a sound—termed the "new psychedelia" by the rock press—melding the stark themes of post-punk pop with a more ambitious musical sense. At the forefront of the movement was Echo & the Bunnymen, led by singer-guitarist Ian McCulloch.

"(David) Bowie had a lot to do with it—a lot of us of a certain age had grown up listening to him, (circa) 1972, '73," McCulloch said. "It wasn't normal music—it sounded like it came from outer space or somewhere weird. We were all drawn to this—not just having a beard standing on the monitor playing rock 'n' roll riffs. We wanted to do something else."

The group's original lineup included a drum machine until Pete de Freitas joined in.

"Echo the drum machine was what set us apart initially," McCulloch postulated. "People were either intrigued or wondered why we didn't have a drummer. It exposes the chordal guitar lines slightly. It also means you can play E to A over and over and it sounds great. It never sounded like just rock 'n' roll. It gave us a different slant on the way we rocked opposed to other groups."

On *Ocean Rain*, the foursome recalled the experimental sounds of late Sixties West Coast US bands, particularly the Doors. Decidedly surrealistic imagery and lush orchestration added to the psychedelic tag, while McCulloch was a cute, dour moptop with a supple croon and Jim Morrison fixation.

"Both groups have great singers, I suppose," McCulloch teased. "There must be a similarity somewhere, but it was never a particularly conscious one." ■

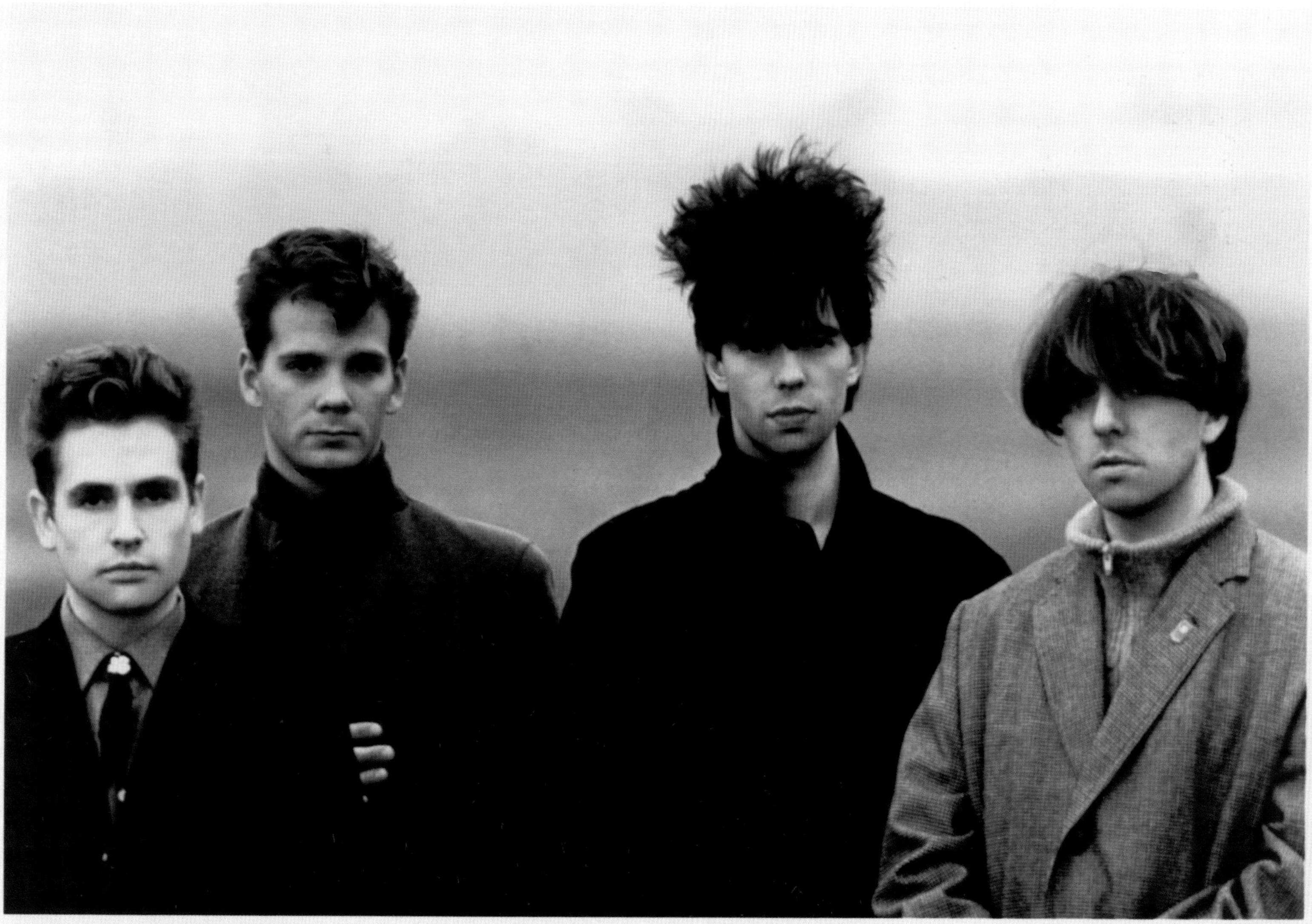

Photo Credit: Anton Corbijn/1984

LES PATTINSON PETE de FREITAS IAN McCULLOCH WILL SERGEANT

ECHO AND THE BUNNYMEN

SIRE™

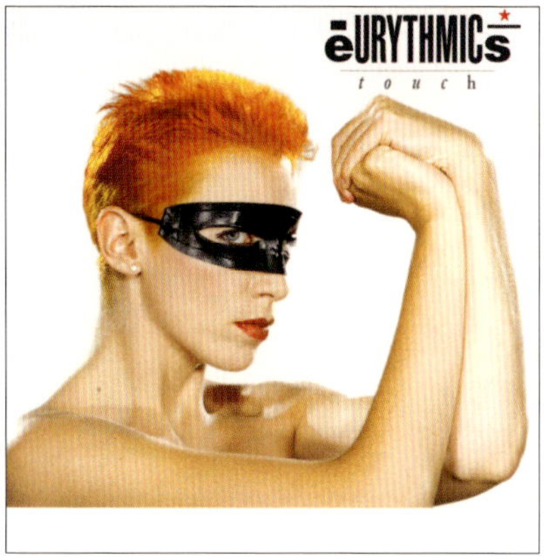

Billboard 200: *Touch* (#7)
Billboard Hot 100: "Here Comes the Rain Again" (#4); "Who's That Girl?" (#21); "Right by Your Side" (#29)

Touch by Eurythmics spawned three major hits, keeping the duo at the forefront of the MTV phenomenon.

IDENTIFYING THE elements that put Eurythmics above the competition in the British synth-pop genre, singer Annie Lennox said she and her partner Dave Stewart melded "the energy of the punk movement, the sweetness from soul music and the alienation of European mechanical rhythms."

"Here Comes the Rain Again" became the duo's second Top 10 US hit, following 1983's "Sweet Dreams (Are Made of This)." The music video for it and the other hits off Eurythmics' second album, *Touch*—"Who's That Girl" and "Right by Your Side"—showcased Lennox's penchant for striking costumes and gender-bending characters, but she was peeved by depictions of her and Stewart as being more fashion- than music-conscious.

"Dave and I don't see ourselves as a fashion group," she fumed. "It infers that you're trendy, that your popularity can shift with the wind. It makes us sound like we're struggling, having to constantly think of a new image. It's not like that at all."

Indeed, Lennox and Stewart were music business veterans, having survived a stint with the Tourists, a band whose UK hits in the late Seventies never made an impression in the States. Lennox and Stewart continued to establish themselves on their own terms.

"We don't have any particular grand plan," Lennox concluded. "We'll just see what comes out. It's not a formula—I don't know what to say about that; we just do what we can! Sometimes Dave plays keyboards, and he can't play keyboards. Sometimes I play something I can't play. It's just the way we work—anything for an interesting approach." ■

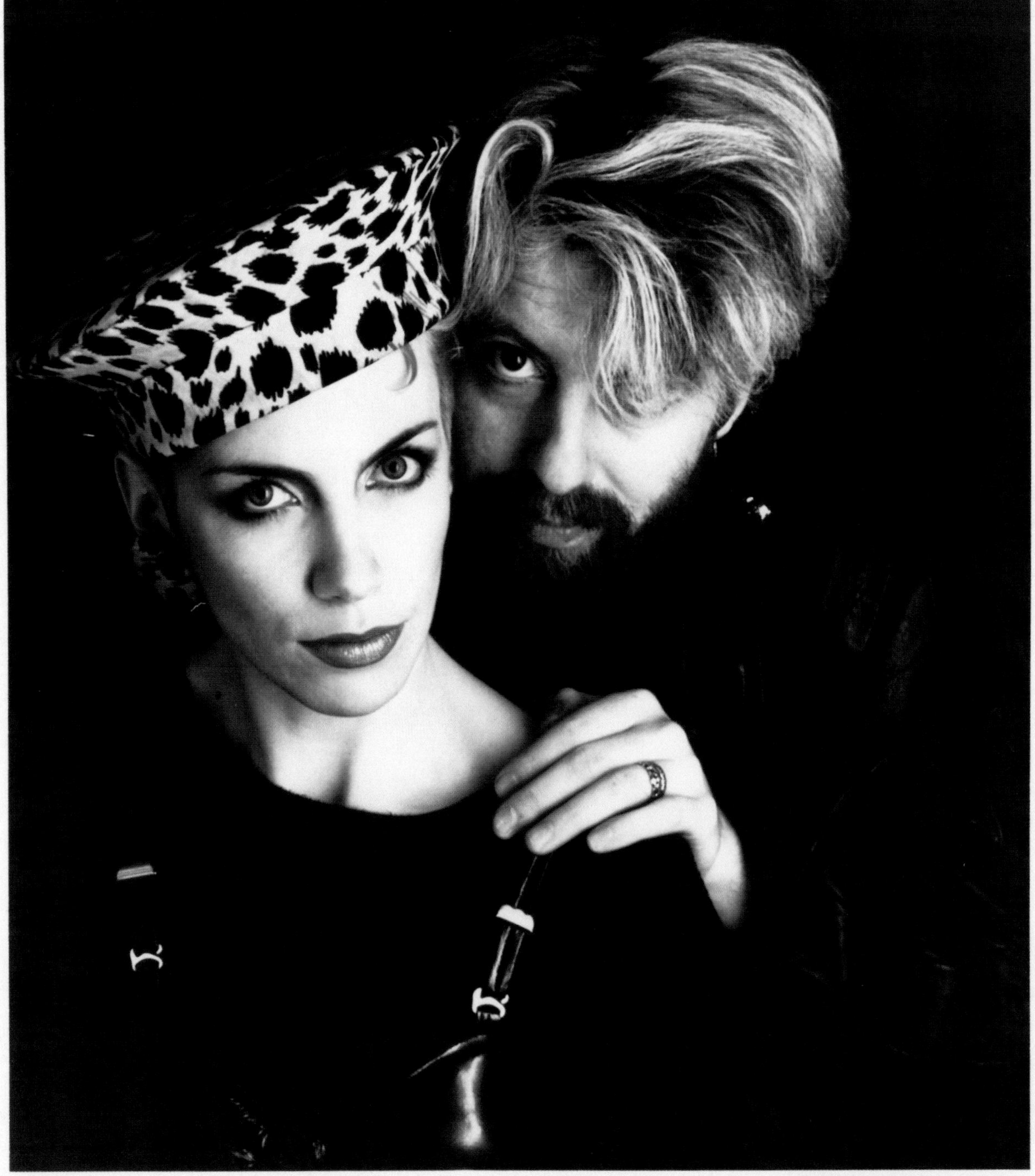

EURYTHMICS

RCA
Records and Cassettes

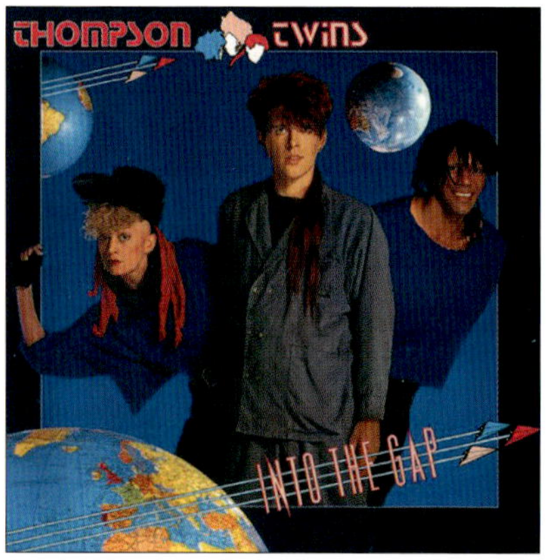

Thompson Twins' "Hold Me Now" emerged as the British synth-pop trio's most memorable American hit.

Billboard 200: *Into the Gap* (#10)
Billboard Hot 100: "Hold Me Now" (#3); "Doctor! Doctor!" (#11); "You Take Me Up" (#44); "The Gap" (#69)

STARTING OUT as a sizable London-based band, the distinctly unidentical Thompson Twins (there were no Thompsons or twins involved—the name came from a cartoon strip featuring two bumbling detectives) scored percussive dance-club hits with "In the Name of Love" and "Lies."

After scaling down to a threesome—guitarist and keyboardist Tom Bailey, girlfriend Alannah Currie and singer Joe Leeway—the Twins switched to a more mainstream synth-pop sound and secured a presence on radio and MTV with the album *Into the Gap*, featuring the chart smashes "Hold Me Now" and "Doctor! Doctor!"

But Bailey, who did most of the lead vocals and nearly all of the writing, was disconsolate on tour.

"This relentless chase to pursue fashion, money and being on top of the charts can take so much of your time," he said. "We're being forced to be less true to our real sentiments."

In concert, the group affected a slightly tatty yet glitzy look—fingerless gloves, neon socks and rhinestone appliques—and relied heavily on programmed sounds and synthesizer parts. Leeway got the stagecraft together for the tour, a stylishly striking high-tech affair that emphasized "the purely spectacular visual elements."

"It becomes too easy to walk on a stage knowing that all this big stuff will happen in its programmed way," Bailey mused. "That in itself can become the entertainment, almost as if the songs are fighting to keep up with it." ■

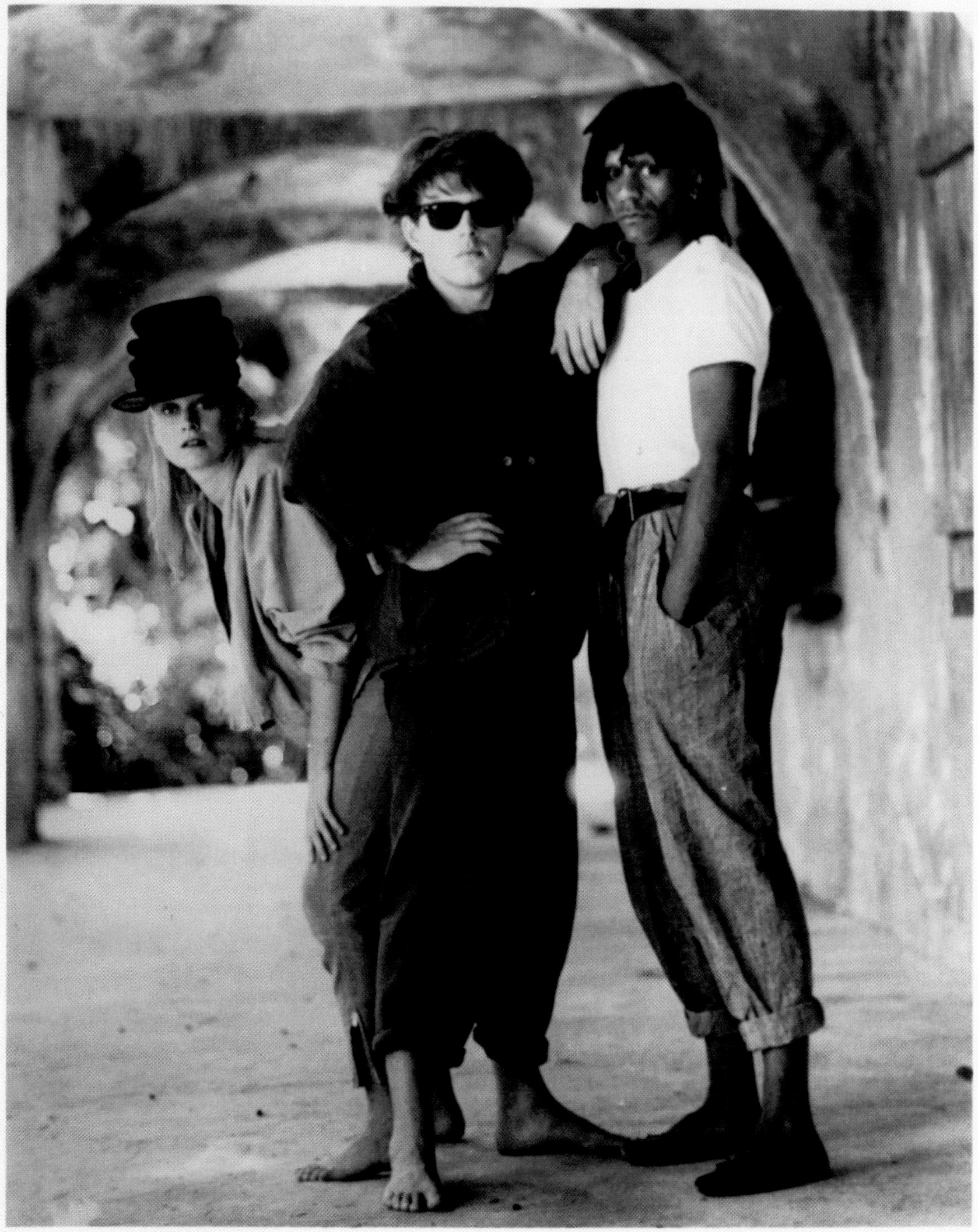

THOMPSON TWINS

ARISTA

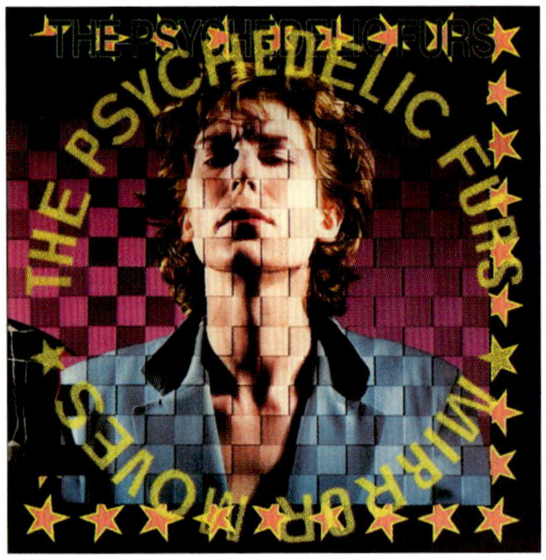

The Psychedelic Furs, reconstituted as a trio, enjoyed a breakthrough recording with *Mirror Moves*.

Billboard 200: *Mirror Moves* (#43)
Billboard Hot 100: "The Ghost in You" (#59)

THE PSYCHEDELIC Furs seemed destined to be a "critics' band." On the English group's first two albums, Richard Butler sang in an edgy drone, his lyrics purposefully elusive, and the swirling accompaniment of the six-piece band reflected such non-mainstream influences as mid-period David Bowie and Roxy Music.

But the Furs joined the ranks of commercially successful groups. *Mirror Moves*, the band's fourth album, spawned the radio hits "The Ghost in You" and "Heaven." Friendly and upbeat in discussing the evolution of the Furs' fortunes, Butler noted that his cynical lyrics were tempered by compassion, and he considered it important for rock musicians to be inspirational as well as rebellious.

"On the first albums I was writing about and projecting confusion, and I still do to a certain extent," he explained. "But I've learned that the best way to communicate confusion isn't necessarily confusion. I've become less confused in my personal life, which helps. The early lyrics still stand up—they were written in a very abstract, kind of collage style. It's a style that stands up as a way to work, but it's not easily understood. People come up and say, 'What's this song about?' I don't think that's important—it's the feel that's important."

The group had also made great strides in its record-making techniques. The producer of the first two records, Steve Lillywhite, wanted the sound of "in his words, a great live gig," Butler said. "But after that, we started developing ideas of what we wanted to do ourselves." When the Furs added cello to songs on their third album, *Forever Now*, they sought out Todd Rundgren to produce the tracks "because we wanted to get more melodic, and he's quite good at that." "Love My Way," the first Psychedelic Furs hit, resulted.

Mirror Moves featured the production expertise of Keith Forsey, best known for his work with Billy Idol. "We wanted to approach the rhythm section on this album," Butler noted. "Producers often have the reputation of just coming in and stamping their own sound all over albums, but we've never had a problem with that. A good producer can get the feel the band wants and suggest ideas in that framework like an extra member." Forsey's involvement on *Mirror Moves* reflected that ideal—he played percussion for the drummer-less trio, comprised of Butler, brother Tim on bass and guitarist John Ashton.

"We have a much clearer idea of what we're doing," Butler explained. "We're far more focused—on the first albums we didn't know what market we had, if we had any. The nature of what we do isn't immediately pop, and it's slow-building by necessity. Plus we're pretty uncompromising about what we do. I think we still have our integrity intact." ■

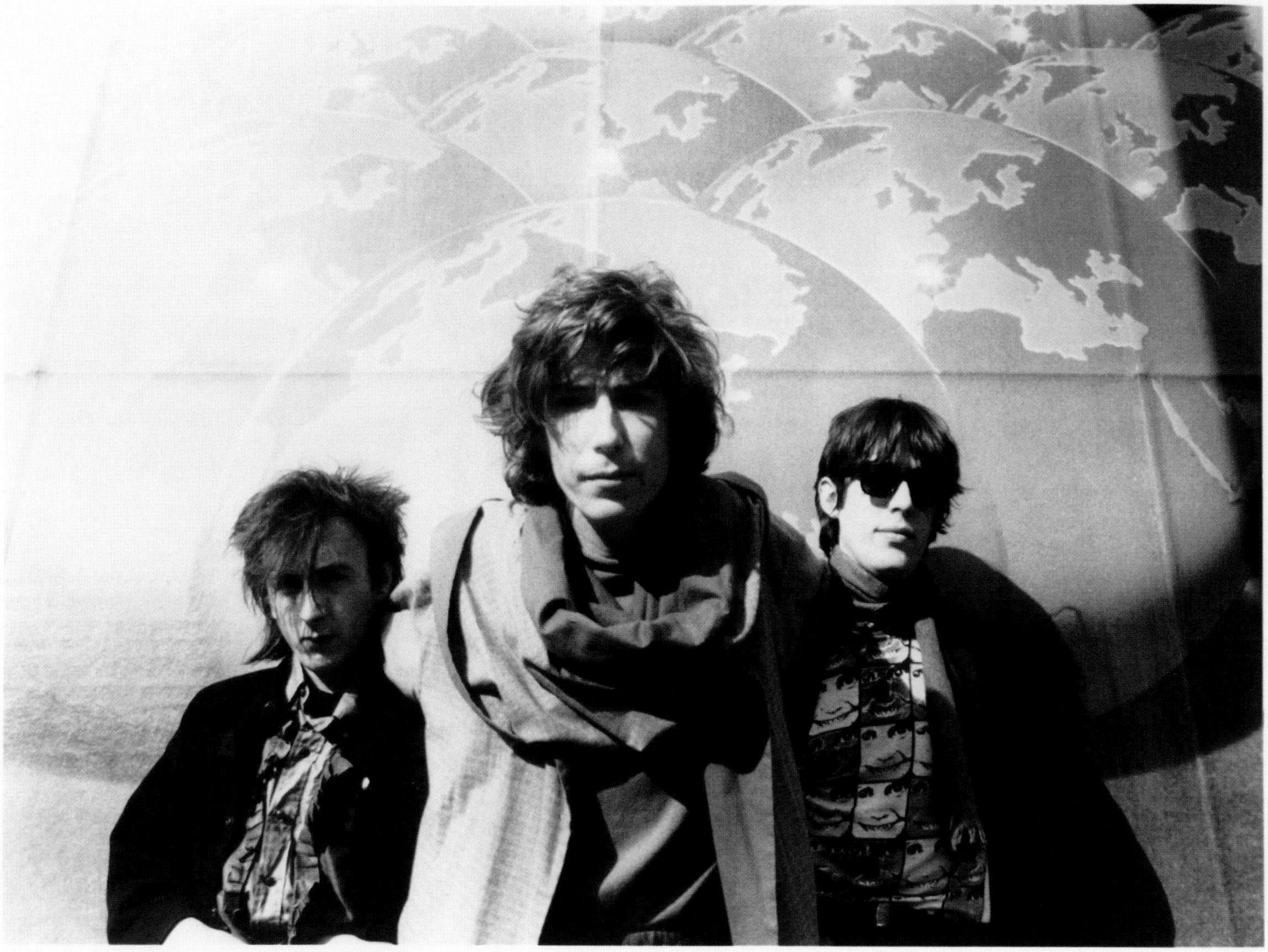

PHOTOGRAPH: TOM SHEEHAN

THE PSYCHEDELIC FURS

Columbia
8406

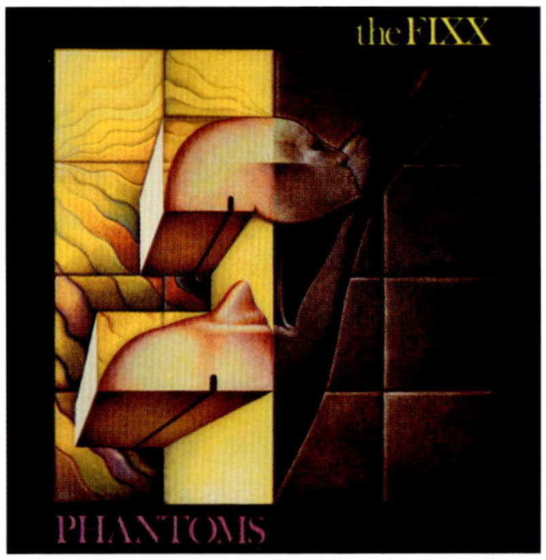

The Fixx issued *Phantoms*, the British band's third album, containing the hit single "Are We Ourselves?"

Billboard 200: *Phantoms* (#19)
Billboard Hot 100: "Are We Ourselves?" (#15); "Sunshine in the Shade" (#69)

HAVING ISSUED solid albums and benefiting from the novelty of MTV exposure early in the decade, a generation of post-new wave bands—among them Men at Work, Stray Cats and A Flock of Seagulls—found themselves trying to sustain métiers for the long haul. Another act in the same situation was the Fixx, founded by vocalist Cy Curnin and drummer Adam Woods.

"We're very competitive, and I think you have to be to survive all the ups and downs," Woods said. "You have to believe in what you're doing, and we think we're better than those other bands. It's a side of the band that the public doesn't see, but it's very much a part of us."

Fans had been more likely to notice the Fixx's dramatic yet accessible string of singles—"Red Skies," "Stand or Fall," "Saved by Zero," "One Thing Leads to Another." *Phantoms* added to that commercial legacy with "Are We Ourselves?" Assisted by a popular music video, the song hit No. 1 on *Billboard*'s Album Rock Tracks chart.

The studio touch of Rupert Hine established the band's bright rhythms and ringing guitar sound in a slick yet subtle setting. Hine had served as the sole producer on every Fixx album, a rarity in the ever-changing music industry.

"Once a band has had a hit, they might try to change the recipe," Curnin observed. "But with Rupert, we can change the recipe, but we're still in the same kitchen."

"It's a deeper relationship because he was the only guy who would believe in us at the beginning," Woods added. "We were rejected by every—and I mean every—recording contact in the world, except for him. So there's a sense of loyalty there."

"This group is the ideal of five people getting together to devote their lives to one thing," Curnin concluded. "You can drop your own values to take up the common community, and it's good for people to see that. And we thank God daily for the chance to do it." ■

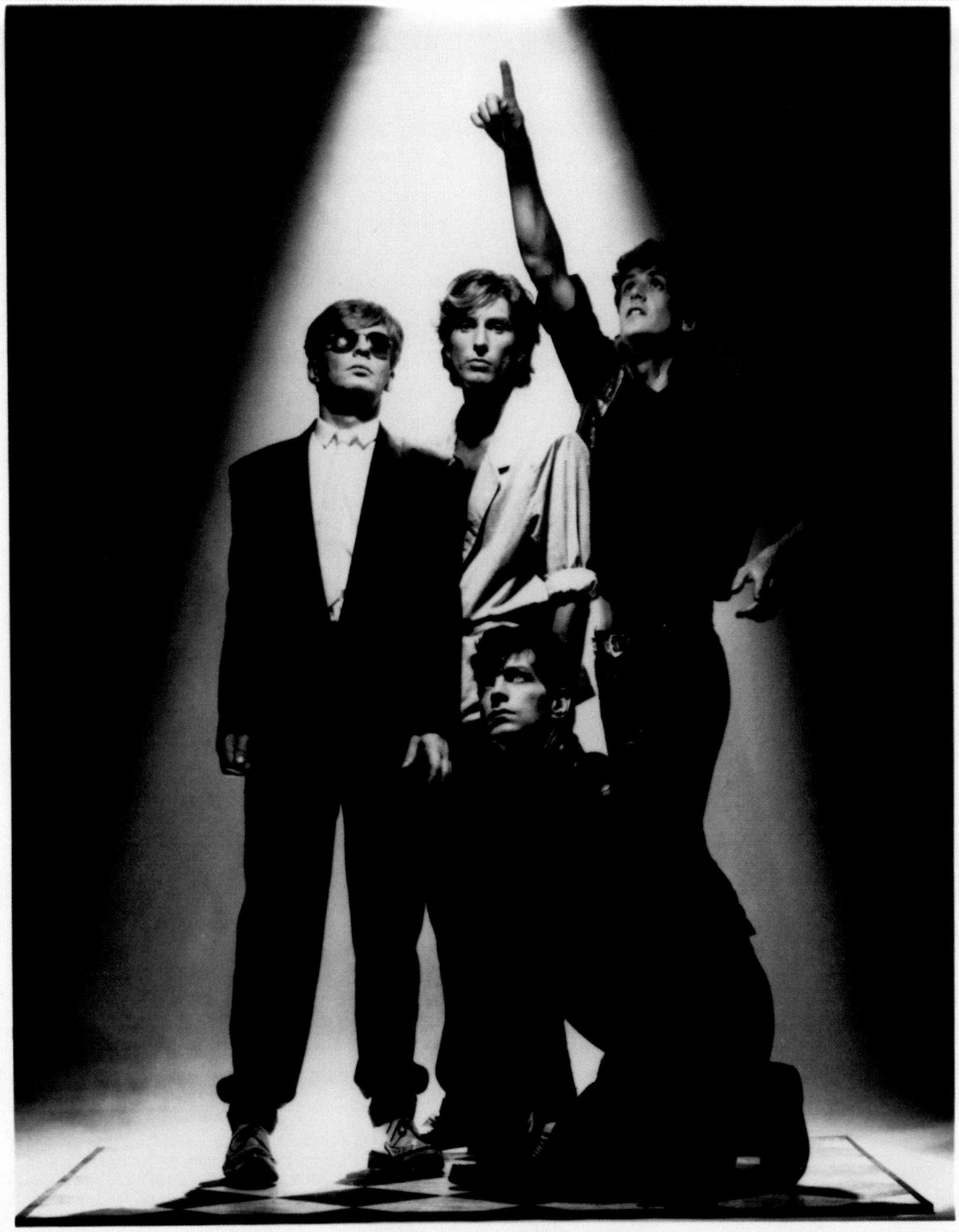

8/84

the FIXX

MCA RECORDS

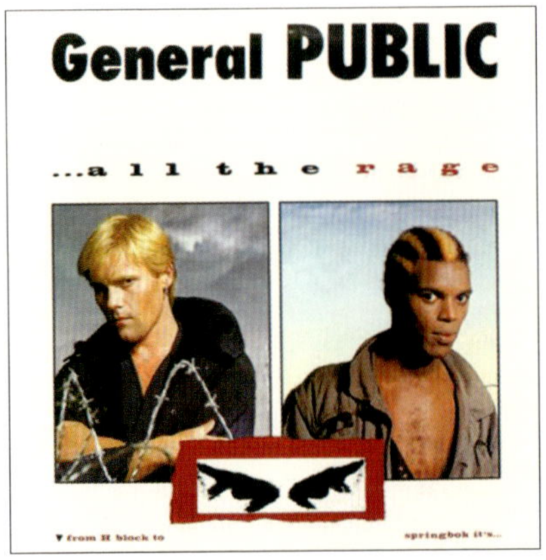

General Public rebounded from the English Beat's split-up, establishing a new peak with the hit "Tenderness."

Billboard 200: *All the Rage* (#26)
Billboard Hot 100: "Tenderness" (#27)

THE BEAT (known as the English Beat in the US) was one of ska pop's most promising British bands. So it came as quite a surprise when vocalists Dave Wakeling and Ranking Roger went on to work in a new enterprise.

"As people, we got along brilliantly—there were never any fights, we never argued," Roger explained. "But the Beat was on the verge of playing stadiums, which is where most bands start to lose it. When certain people did more than others, it wasn't equal anymore. There were loads of people going, 'You're mad! The English Beat is going to be huge!' But musically, it was turning into something effortless."

General Public was formed through auditions in Birmingham, England, where Wakeling and Roger lived. The band's debut album *All the Rage* continued in the diverse reggaefied-pop vein that made the English Beat popular. Ex-Clash guitarist Mick Jones contributed to the record, which listed him as a guest star rather than a full-fledged member.

"We spent over six months making the LP," Roger said. "It was a new group, and we were getting used to playing with each other. It could have been done better, but we did the best we could with what we knew. We had worked with producers before, and we thought it would be good to produce a record ourselves once. We learned from that—it's not as easy as it looks! So next time, I think we'll use a producer."

The band fared best in North America, where "Tenderness" was a hit. The song benefited from being featured in the John Hughes coming-of-age film *Sixteen Candles*. ■

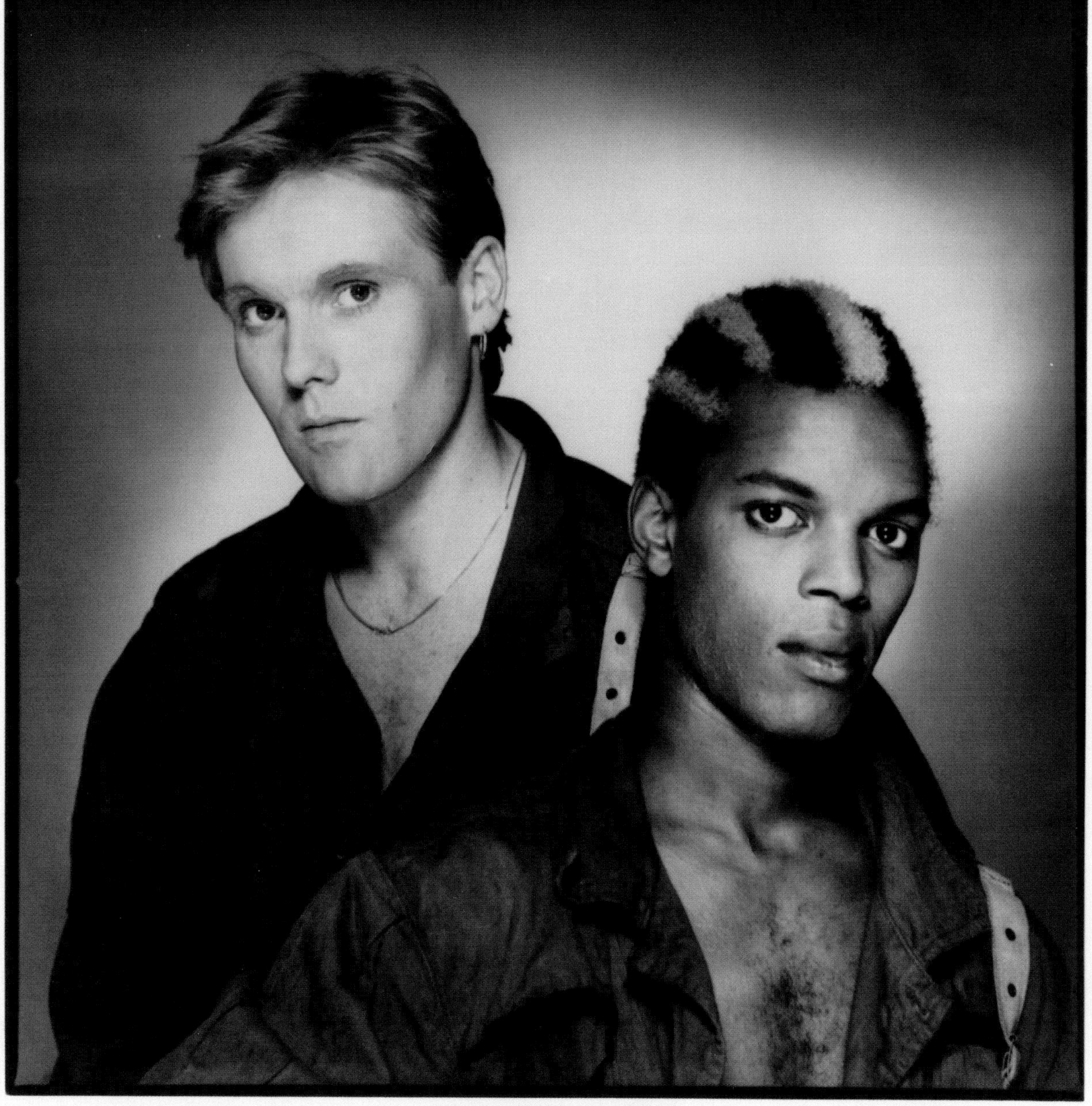

David Wakeling

Ranking Roger

General PUBLIC

I.R.S.

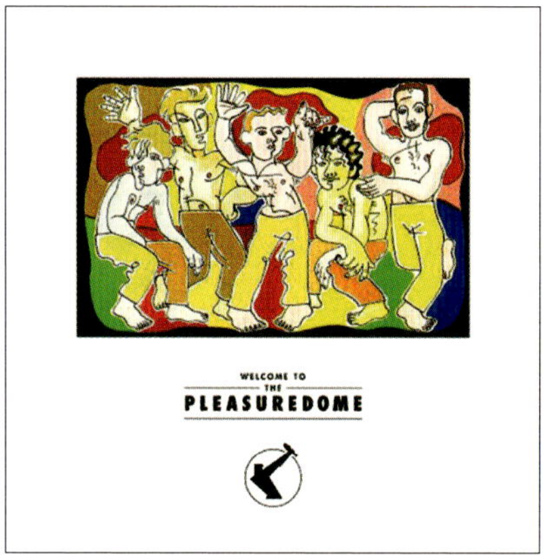

A wild reputation preceded Frankie Goes to Hollywood's debut album *Welcome to the Pleasuredome*.

Billboard 200: *Welcome to the Pleasuredome* (#33)
Billboard Hot 100: "Two Tribes" (#43); "Relax" (#10); "Welcome to the Pleasuredome" (#48)

AMERICANS GOT a chance to decide if Frankie Goes to Hollywood was the most exciting act to emerge in the early Eighties or a hype of massive proportions. Named after a Fifties article featuring Frank Sinatra, the British band first gained attention when the BBC in England banned its debut single "Relax" and its companion video. The lyrics, which were construed as a depiction of a gay encounter, came under further scrutiny when the two Frankie frontmen, singers Holly Johnson and Paul Rutherford, professed their homosexuality. "Relax" promptly jumped to No. 1 on the UK charts.

It was replaced by the six-man group from Liverpool's anti-war "Two Tribes" and its video showing lookalikes of President Reagan and Soviet President Konstantin Chernenko engaged in a bloody, winner-take-all fistfight. MTV asked that some violent content be removed before it would air the clip, but "Two Tribes" was No. 1 in the UK for weeks.

"We're the biggest band in Europe—you can't get any bigger," Johnson noted with stylish condescension. "We're here to stir things up, and even people that hate us have to admit that we're succeeding in doing that. That's all we want—a strong reaction."

Welcome to the Pleasuredome—a double LP, natch—stuck with an electronically enhanced heavy sound, and the bass-laden whomp that propelled "Relax" was hard to resist. The band's extramusical appeal was reinforced through its merchandising—white T-shirts with such mock slogans as "Frankie Say Arm the Unemployed" and "Frankie Say War! Hide Yourself" appeared throughout Britain and increasingly in America.

Frankie wasn't really a band in the traditional sense—it was more like a front, albeit a well-paid and highly visible one, for producer Trevor Horn. His studio work on *Welcome to the Pleasuredome* sounded like the Grand Canyon being formed through stereo speakers, with crunching, majestic bass lines and sophisticated engineering. With "Relax," he produced inventive, tribal dance rock—Frankie liked the bombastic song so much they released nine versions. Getting that kind of mileage out of a single didn't hinder Frankie's status as teenybopper sensations, even with the overtly suggestive nature of the band's presentation. It may have disconcerted older listeners to watch teenage girls screaming over "Krisco Kisses"—Frankie wasn't singing about flakier pie crusts—but sex sold. ■

FRANKIE GOES TO HOLLYWOOD

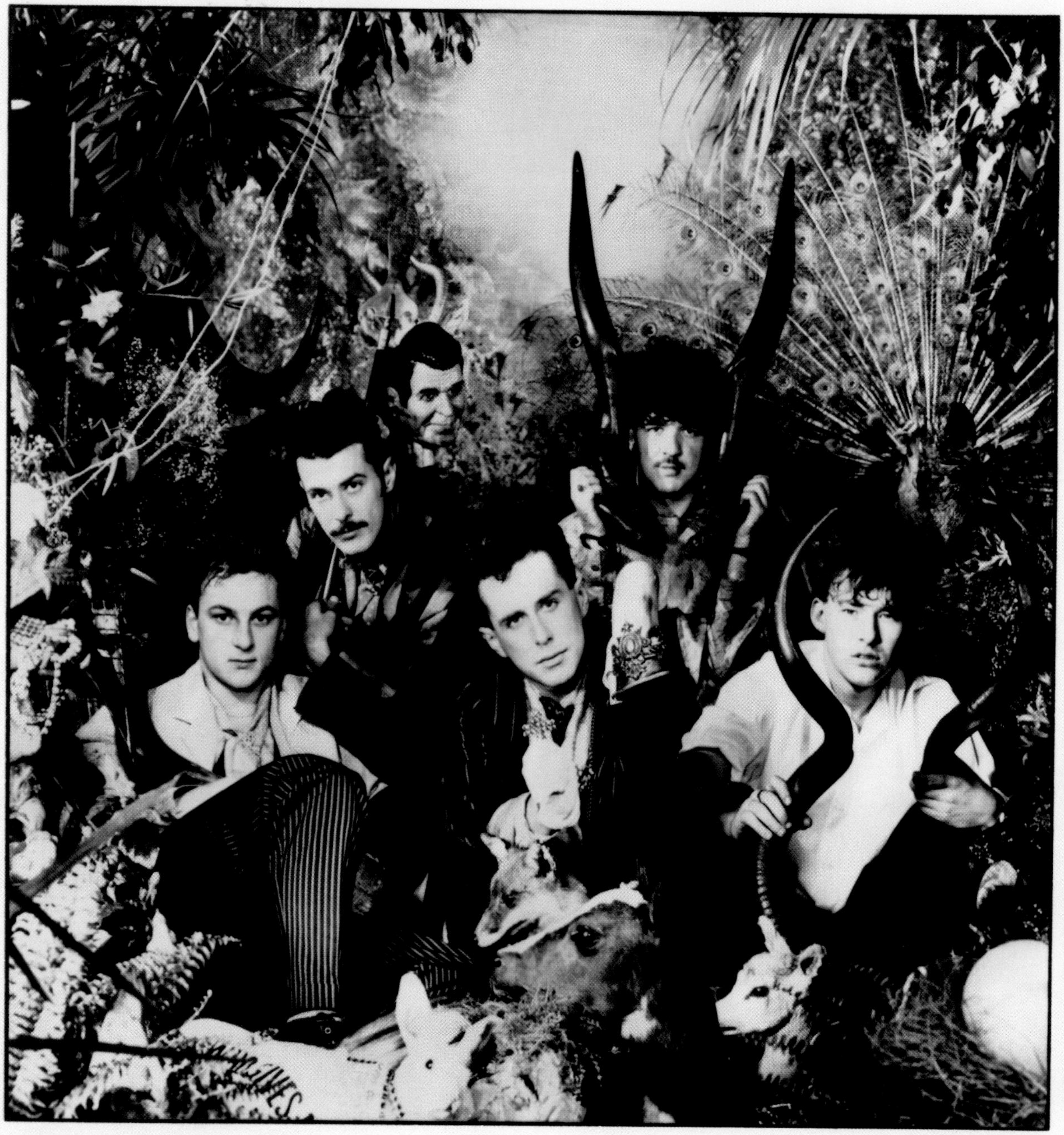

Photo Credit: PETER ASHWORTH 1984

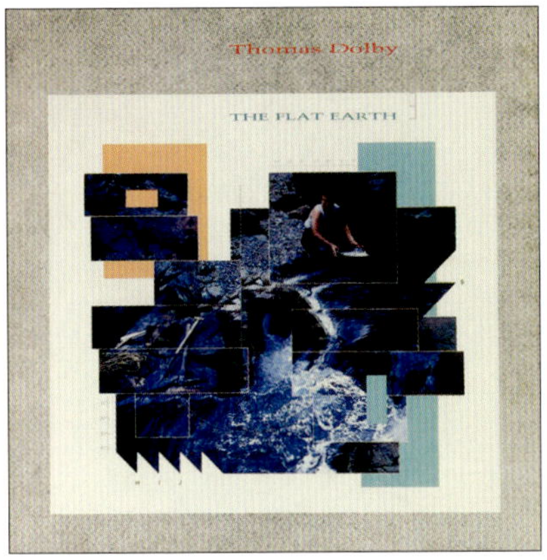

Techno-pop guru Thomas Dolby's *The Flat Earth* boasted the electroplated funk sound of "Hyperactive."

Billboard 200: *The Flat Earth* (#35)
Billboard Hot 100: "Hyperactive" (#62)

BEFORE LAUNCHING a solo career, Thomas Dolby's session résumé included keyboard work with Lene Lovich, Joan Armatrading and Bruce Wooley, as well as synthesizer tracks on Foreigner's *4* album. Dolby broke through with the 1982 hit single, "She Blinded Me with Science," championing himself as a slightly mad scientist of new wave.

"Oh, there's no doubt that the older musicians are intimidated by this technology revolution," Dolby smirked. "There's this attitude forming that's reacting to a natural evolution of the way we live—through electronics. Children take it for granted. I saw a couple of kids playing cowboys and Indians the other day—only instead of going 'bang, bang,' they were buzzing 'whrrrrt-whrrrt' like in a video game or something. It seems appropriate that they should have a kind of music to listen to that reflects that kind of life. What's been on their transistor radios has been a bunch of 40-year-old guys with shiny electric guitars."

The Flat Earth, Dolby's sophomore effort, was notable for an ensemble of supporting players and his interest in writing songs rather than grooves—"I've got more in common with Elton John than A Flock of Seagulls," he modestly admitted. The techno-pop artist was too intelligent to be dismissed as some smart-aleck Brit harnessing the power of synthesizers and samplers.

"When bands were able to use electric guitars and a P.A. system in the early Sixties, suddenly groups where whittled down to four pieces, where the popular music before that was big band-oriented. When multi-track recording became possible, we got things like *Sgt. Pepper*—suddenly the ethic of assembling good musicians and a good arranger and sticking them in the studio for three hours went out the window. That phase culminated in Fleetwood Mac taking eighteen months to make an album. So technology has always been important to popular music. I don't see the synthesizer as any more or less important than that."

Dolby figured that rock music's geriatric set would still carve out its slice of the pie.

"Rock 'n' roll as we know it is going to slip into a traditional form of music like jazz or folk—if Mick Jagger can do it when he's 40, he'll probably be doing it when he's 50," he said. "But there will always be a more up-to-date, state-of-the-art pop music—which at the moment is being made with synthesizers and computers. In another ten years, who knows?" ■

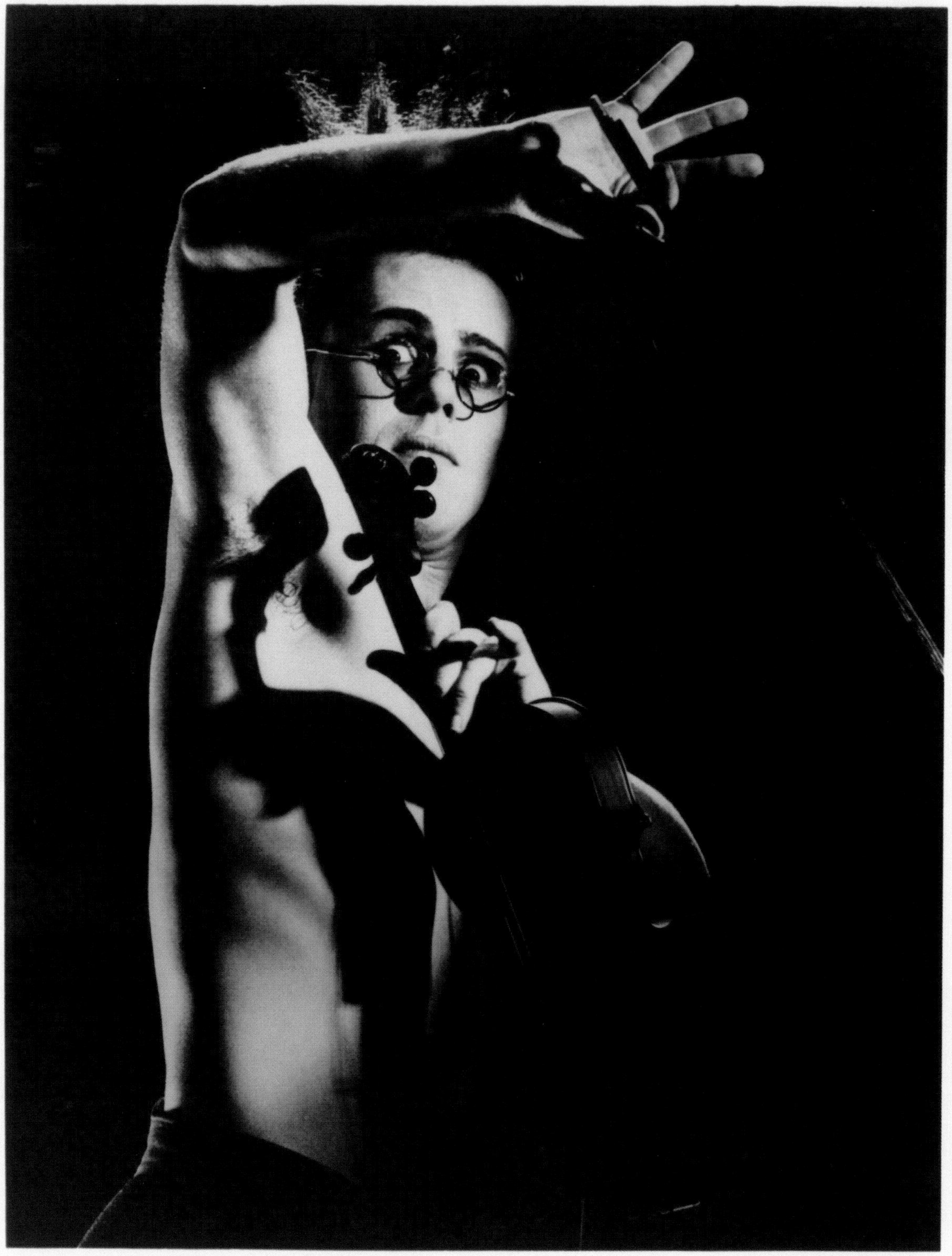

Photo: Richard Haughton / 1984

thomas dolby

Capitol RECORDS

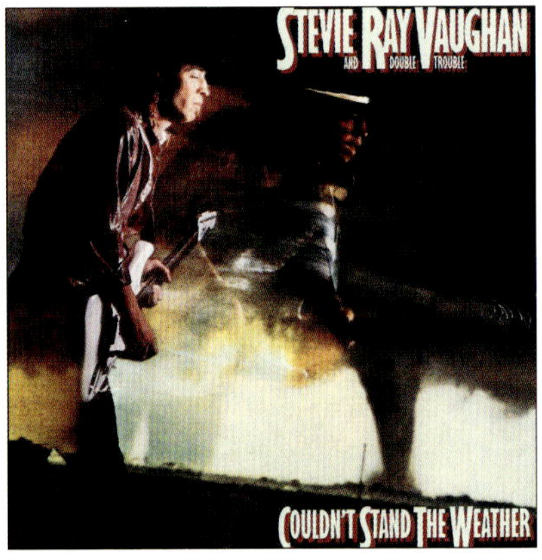

Billboard 200: *Couldn't Stand the Weather* (#31)

Stevie Ray Vaughan & Double Trouble's *Couldn't Stand the Weather* solidified the guitarist's eminence.

THE ACCLAIM hadn't stopped building for Stevie Ray Vaughan since the guitar whiz from Austin, Texas, exploded onto the scene with 1983's *Texas Flood* album. Since then, nearly every music-oriented publication in America had ordained him rock's "best new talent" or "best guitarist."

Vaughan seemed at ease with his sudden fame—he still sounded soft-spoken and anxious to share his success with others. He was always plugging other guitarists, spreading the word, hoping to get them a break. When he topped the bill over revered blues artists like B.B. King, he explained earnestly. "We're not headlining, we're just playing last."

After a performance in Canada, Vaughan felt embarrassed when promoters had billed him as the "World's Greatest Guitarist."

"There's not a 'World's Greatest Guitar Player,' and I damn sure don't think I'm it. There are so many musicians I've heard that just scare me to death, and they ain't even got a chance to play on a record—they're happy playing for 30 people in a club. I'm lucky—I haven't had to have a straight job since I was 12. I was a dishwasher and a paperboy for a couple of months. Since then, I've managed to play guitar and stay alive—and have a blast doin' it."

Vaughan dressed flashy but didn't act that way. He partied and had fun. He'd been happily married for six years. He didn't live the blues, he just played them like the dickens on his sophomore album *Couldn't Stand the Weather*. Radio jumped on the title track, "Cold Shot" and Vaughan's remake of Jimi Hendrix's "Voodoo Chile (Slight Return)" in a big way.

"Blues is like a flower to me—I don't see why you can't walk around it and look at it from different angles," he concluded. "People have compared me to Hendrix, but comparisons are for everybody else. We like his song, so we enjoy doing it. I think people are just getting back around to listening to guitar. There's been a lot of formulas going on, and using synthesizers has been a vehicle for a lot of people. But I never thought guitars would go by the wayside. There's nothing that sounds like a string, y'know?" ■

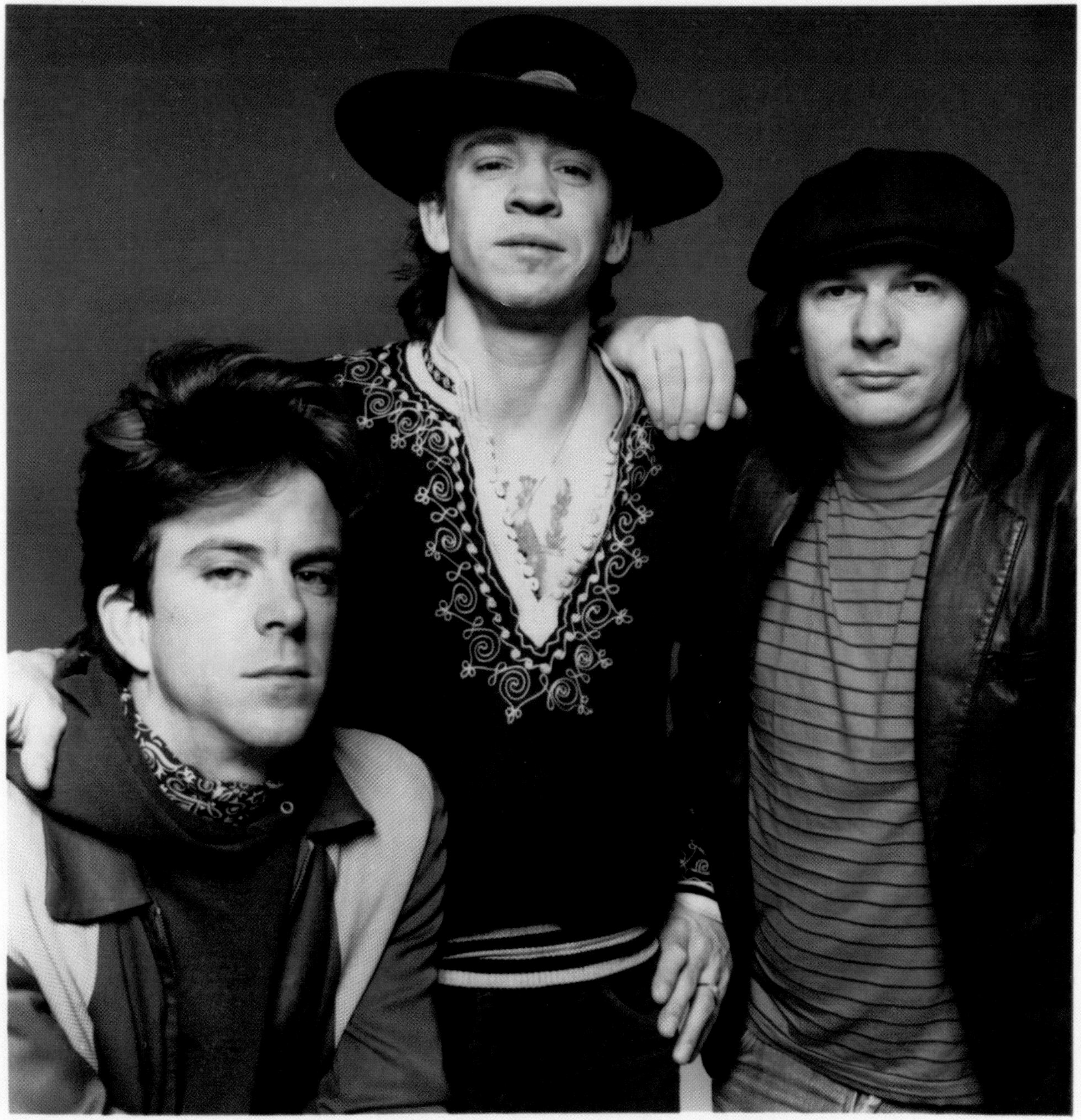

Photo: Don Hunstein

L-R: Chris Layton (Drums), Stevie Ray Vaughan(Guitars, Vocals),Tommy Shannon (Bass)

STEVIE RAY VAUGHAN AND DOUBLE TROUBLE

Epic

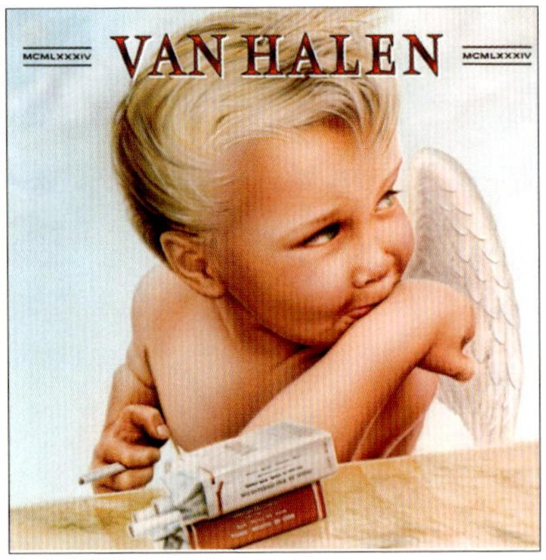

To all appearances, *1984* represented the pinnacle of Van Halen's reign as hard rock's top attraction.

Billboard 200: *1984* (#2)
Billboard Hot 100: "Jump" (No. 1); "I'll Wait" (#13); "Panama" (#13); "Hot for Teacher" (#56)

AFTER FIVE platinum-selling albums in the US, Van Halen outdid itself with *1984*, which went diamond, selling more than 10 million copies. Eddie Van Halen's repertory of ripping guitar lines had established him as a guitar deity, and singer David Lee Roth had mastered a swaggering, laughing-all-the-way-to-the-bank schtick. Some folks hated him because he never shut up, but he had a good time, made sure other people had a good time, and he made lots of money.

"We did title the album *1984* for a reason—I'm going to let you figure that out," Roth said. "Not too many people went up to Robert Frost when he wrote his poem about the two diverging roads and said, 'Bob, what's it all about?'"

Driven by Eddie Van Halen's prominent synthesizer riff, the exuberant "Jump" differed from earlier songs, but it became Van Halen's most successful single, reaching No. 1.

"It's not instead of, it's in addition to, the sound that came before," Roth said diplomatically.

Other singles included "I'll Wait," "Hot for Teacher" and "Panama." "'Panama' is about a car," Roth explained. "Always in the press they say, 'more of your traditional Van Halen—girls, cars, late Saturday nights,' and I thought, 'I never really did write a song about a car.'"

Eddie Van Halen continued to combine his electrifying technique with potent ideas. In addition, drummer Alex Van Halen and bassist Michael Anthony had developed over the years into a surprisingly sophisticated rhythm section.

"I think there is evidence that Van Halen has changed the face of rock music in two ways," Roth crowed. "One, because half the musicians try to copy the band—they grow their hair and play guitar lickety-split like Edward and they try to imitate Alex's drum sound. Two, because the other half is so revolted by our music and our pose and the way that I do interviews that they're forced to come up with alternatives, and that's where you get stuff like Kajagoogoo and Duran Duran."

1984, however, brought the band to its breaking point. Whereas Roth was flamboyant, the other members exhibited an increasing sullenness during the supporting tour. The next year, Van Halen replaced Roth with arena-rock veteran Sammy Hagar. ■

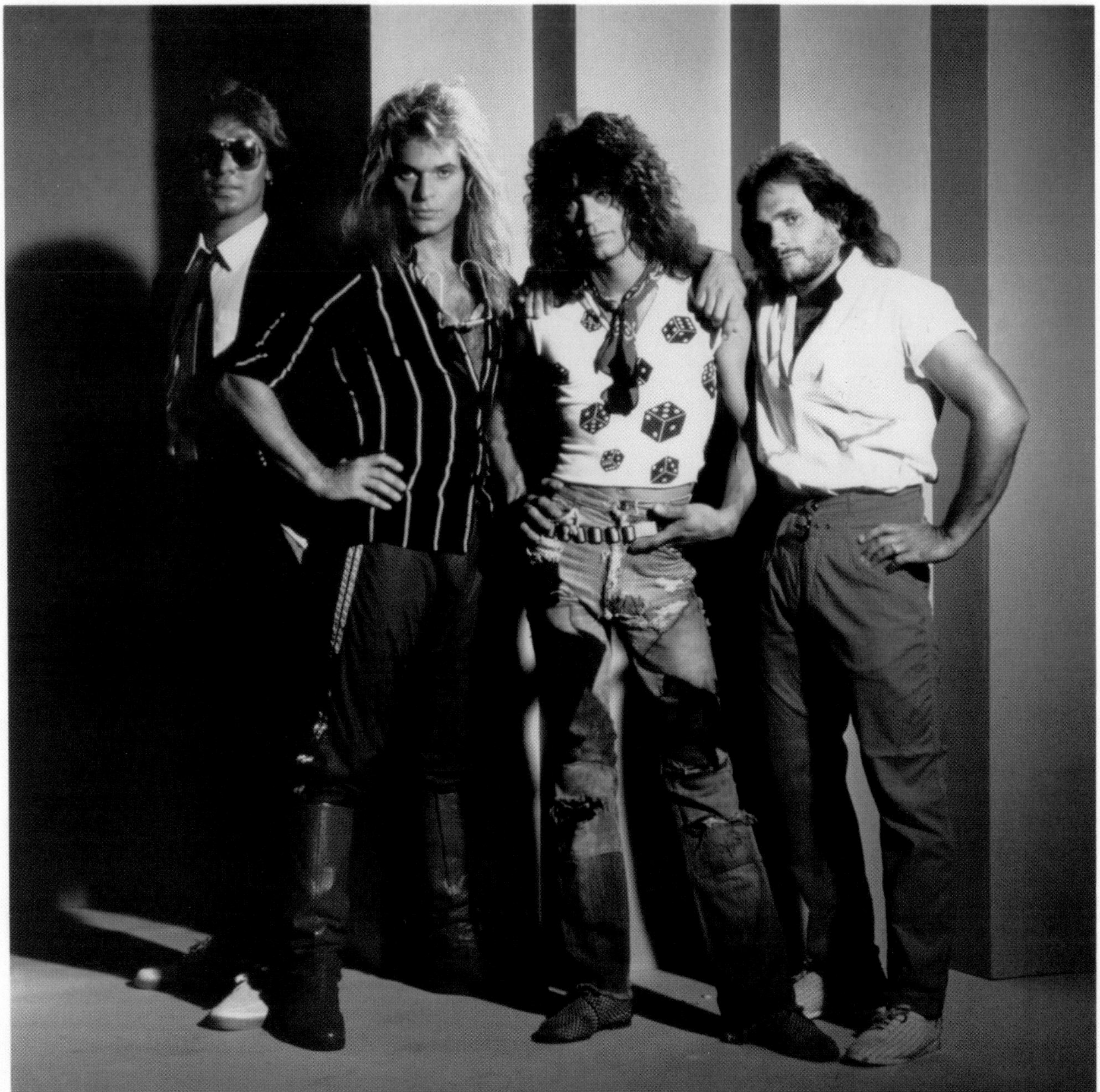

ALEX
VAN HALEN

DAVID
LEE ROTH

EDWARD
VAN HALEN

MICHAEL
ANTHONY

VAN HALEN

WARNER BROS.

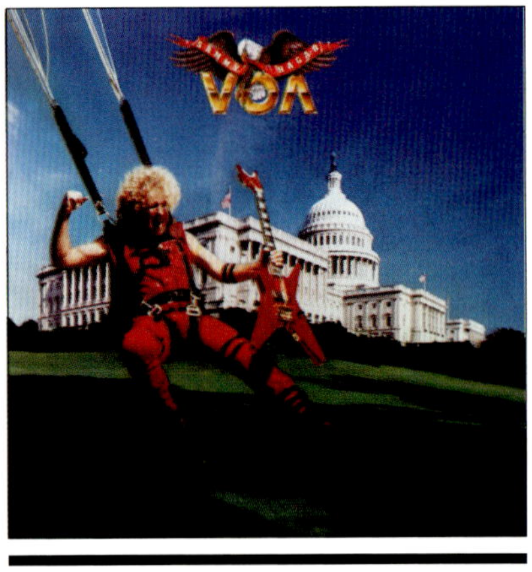

“Red Rocker” Sammy Hagar shifted his career into high gear with the abiding smash “I Can’t Drive 55.”

Billboard 200: *VOA* (#32)
Billboard Hot 100: “Two Sides of Love” (#38);
“I Can’t Drive 55” (#26)

SAMMY HAGAR’S appeal stemmed from the working-class sensibility he brought to hard rock, rather than the preening, all-Spandex posturing of the competition. Recognition came from a grueling tour schedule that began back in the early Seventies in the band Montrose; hit singles were a recent development.

“I Can’t Drive 55” protested the National Maximum Speed Law.

“I don’t try to aim for teenage stuff, but everything that I experienced that I look back on—to laugh at, to say ‘I don’t believe I did that’—happened when I was a teenager,” the affable “Red Rocker” explained. “I lead a responsible life now, so I don’t do as many radical things, but my teenage years were real influential, and I just write about that. It still impresses me when I look out there and see kids cruisin’ and boozin’ and having a great time.”

At 37, Hagar’s trademark remained energy, although that didn’t imply a lack of musical skills. Even if his eternal teenager shtick was as much choreography as spontaneity, he knew what worked and what didn’t; his cars-and-girls song themes lent themselves to a party atmosphere. The pro-US nature of “VOA,” the title track from his album (it stood for “Voice of America”), wasn’t lost on his fans.

“It’s not like Bruce Springsteen, though,” Hagar noted in a sedate moment. “People are out there raising American flags and screaming ‘Born in the U.S.A.,’ and I don’t think they’re listening to what he’s saying in between the chorus. He’s saying, ‘I lost my job and my brother was killed in Vietnam and my old lady’s leaving me and my car broke down…’

“I love Bruce, I’m such a fan, but that one really gets to me. I wish people understood that he’s putting such a negative approach on it. I don’t like that, myself. I think he’s a true-blooded American, so maybe he’s just talking artistically about that element in society. But I don’t like dwelling on that. I think there’s a real patriotic swing happening among younger kids. And it’s good, not a violent thing. They’re just proud to be American.” ■

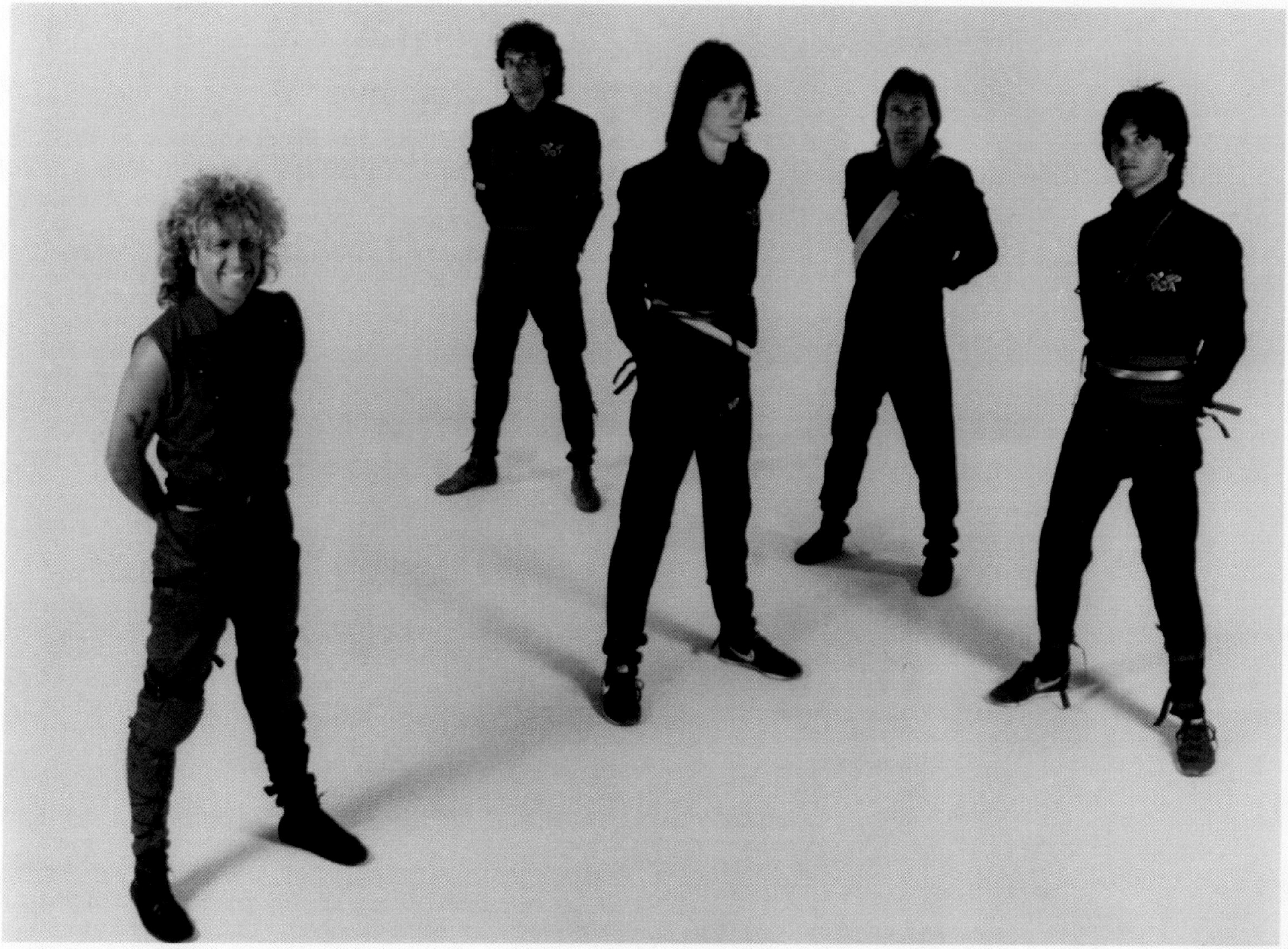

Photo Credit: Raúl Vega

JESSI HARMS GARY PIHL BILL CHURCH DAVID LAUSER

SAMMY HAGAR

GEFFEN RECORDS

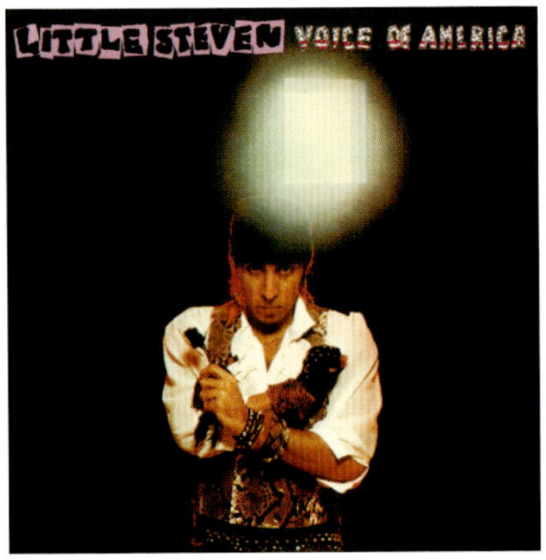

Little Steven found his niche as a political rocker after a decade in Bruce Springsteen's E Street Band.

Billboard 200: *Voice of America* (#55)

STEVEN VAN Zandt had made rock history by assuming various roles. In Bruce Springsteen's E Street Band, he functioned as the Boss' musical ace-in-the-hole as second guitarist, backing vocalist and co-producer. As co-founder of Southside Johnny & the Asbury Jukes, he elevated the archetypal Jersey bar-band sound of a group of Asbury Park cronies.

However, Van Zandt, aka Little Steven, revved up his streetwise activism on solo releases. With his bandana, skull rings and post-punk mode of dress, Little Steven didn't quite look like a spokesman for political commitment. But with *Voice of America*, he issued a hard-rocking plea to his audience—to wake up to the injustices that Reagan-era America was inflicting overseas.

Van Zandt got his first taste of anti-American sentiment on a European tour in 1982. "We are regarded as hypocrites all around the world," he noted. "We've lost most of our credibility. The old America is an identity we still cling to, which was the America at the end of World War II—being the most beloved nation, the good guy everybody loved for good reason.

"But the sad fact is, since then we have altered our modus operandi throughout the world to the detriment of our credibility. We do not carry the ideals of the Bill of Rights with us beyond our borders. I researched these things on my own, and there are good reasons most of these countries don't like us. I was very shocked, and I initially responded the way anyone would when they are accused of being a criminal—'Hey, what are you talking about? We're the ones who won your goddamn war, remember?' But on the street, it's not that way. God, it's ugly out there. And we're paying for it."

Voice in America dealt with world tensions and the betrayal of the nation's ideals, tempered with Van Zandt's own faith in the country. For all of his zeal, the guitar-laden music offset the rhetoric on tracks such as "Los Desaparecidos (The Disappeared Ones)," which detailed the casualties of South American politics, and "Out of the Darkness."

"Anytime you want to say something, it's hard—but saying it in rock 'n' roll, an artform where you have to know the rules, is particularly hard," he explained. "You have to keep it conversational; you can't use all the words you could if you were writing an article or an essay. I worked to make sure the music was equally as powerful, so the words would never become a diversion, because if you don't succeed there, you end up with folk music, an out-of-balance situation."

Van Zandt had to say goodbye to Springsteen, his close friend since they were teenagers, to work full-time on his own career. He helped with the production on Springsteen's *Born in the U.S.A.* album, but "near the end I just ran out of time. Unfortunately, that will probably be the last album I produce for anybody. Maybe I'll do a song for Bruce, but there's no more time for albums." ■

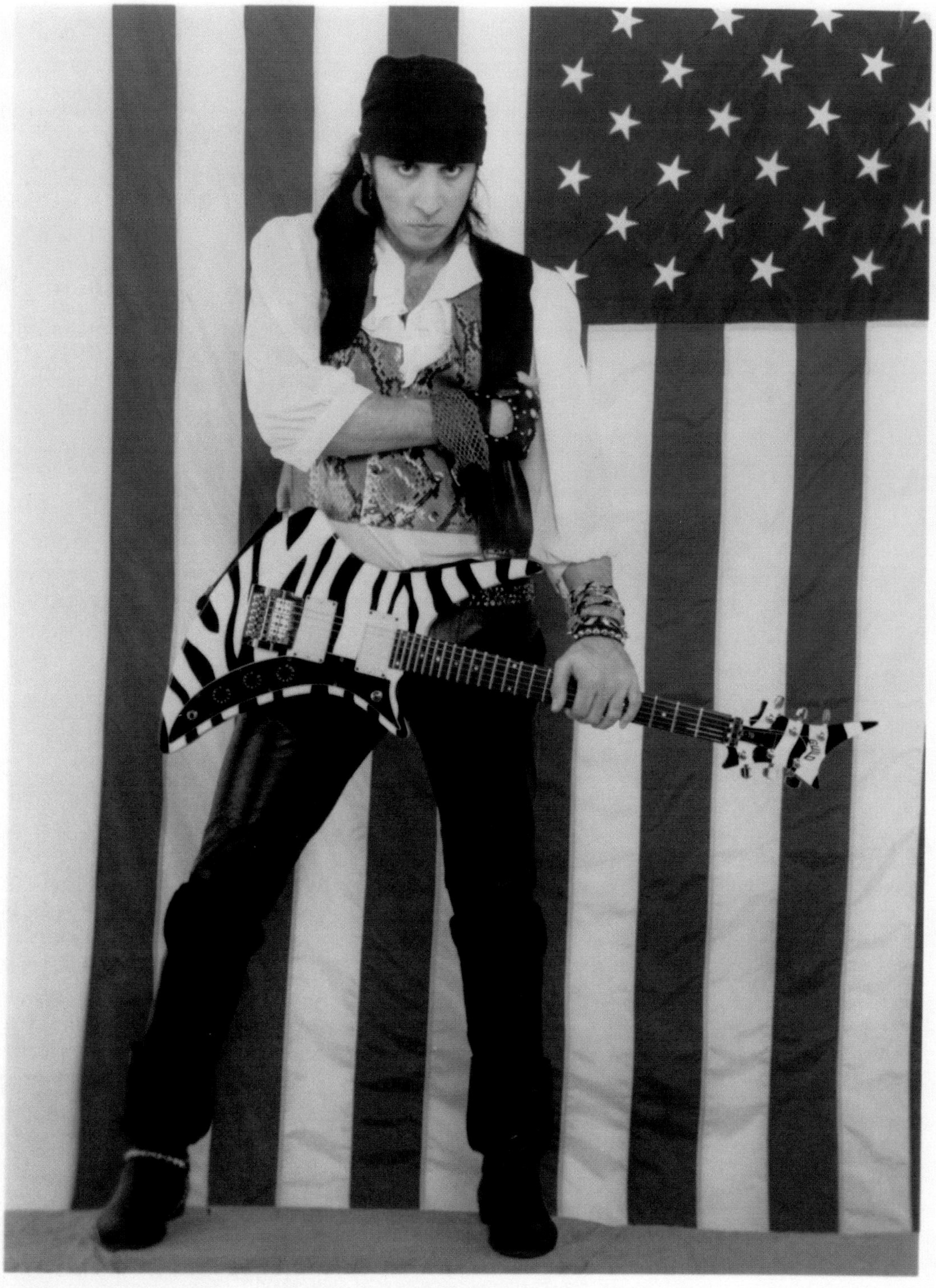

Photo: Mark Weiss

LITTLE STEVEN

EMI AMERICA

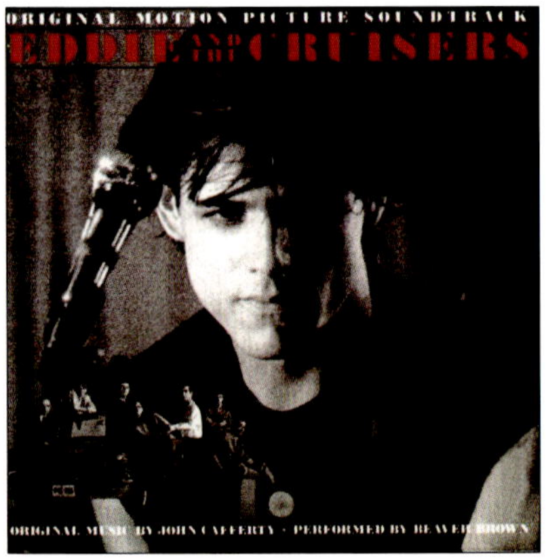

John Cafferty & the Beaver Brown Band rose to celebrity with the soundtrack to *Eddie and the Cruisers.*

Billboard 200: *Eddie and the Cruisers* (#9)
Billboard Hot 100: "On the Dark Side" (#7); "Tender Years" (#31)

MTV HAD given a boost to many new rock acts, but John Cafferty and his hard-working Beaver Brown Band preferred HBO.

After 12 years of honing their chops on the grueling East Coast bar circuit without a record deal—the music was tight, but music execs said Cafferty looked and sounded too much like Bruce Springsteen—the Rhode Island band finally achieved breakout success when producer Kenny Vance hired them to provide the music for a movie about a legendary bar band, *Eddie and the Cruisers.*

Cafferty was the voice of Eddie Wilson, the doomed rock star played by Michael Pare in the film; Beaver Brown provided the sound of the fictitious band. The film flopped, but thanks to ensuing airings of it on HBO, the soundtrack album rocketed up the charts without any more advertising or promotion.

"Things happened real fast," Cafferty exclaimed. "We were still playing in the same old places like this little bar in Connecticut when someone came backstage and said we had sold 30,000 that week. We said, 'Whaaa?' But it was from HBO. We knew the movie was going to be on, but we didn't have any idea sales would jump like that."

The soundtrack was re-launched centering around the Cafferty/Beaver Brown name. It reached the Top 10 on the charts and produced a hit single, "On the Dark Side." But Cafferty felt the song didn't represent his work.

"I was hired to write musical vehicles for scenes in the film. There was one scene where a guy sits rehearsing at the piano and sings a poem called 'On the Dark Side,' then the band leader comes over and shows him how to turn it into rock 'n' roll. The script called for something classical on the piano, and then a rock 'n' roll riff that worked on guitar as well. I came up with the song, but I was just trying to solve the scene."

"Tender Years," the movie's central song, was released as the soundtrack's second single. An old Beaver Brown tune, it meant a great deal to Cafferty. He fought hard to keep it out of the film and save it for his own career, but he finally gave in when no one else would give the song a shot.

"It was a 'Catch 22'—if I put the song in the film, we'd get a record deal. But if I get the deal, I'd lose the song for our album," he said. "We were way ahead of the game, no matter what happened. We got to go to Hollywood, write a score, make a record. All we can do now is keep on playing. If you do your best every time out, what goes around comes around. It seems to be coming around right now." ■

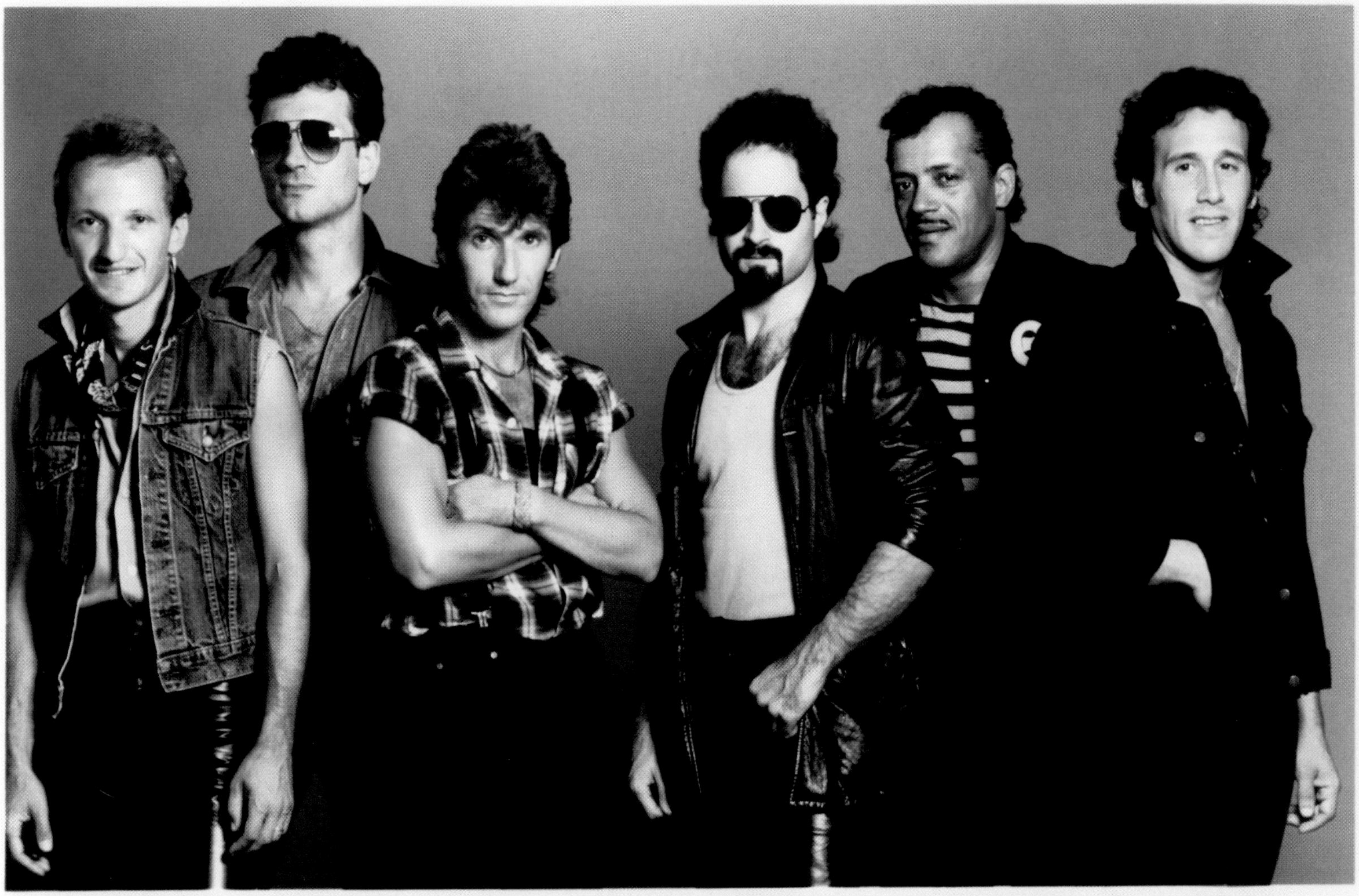

Photo Credit: David Gahr

Pat Lupo | Gary Gramolini | John Cafferty | Kenny Jo Silva | Michael "Tunes" Antunes | Robert Cotoia

Scotti Brothers ™

JOHN CAFFERTY AND THE BEAVER BROWN BAND

Epic

8411

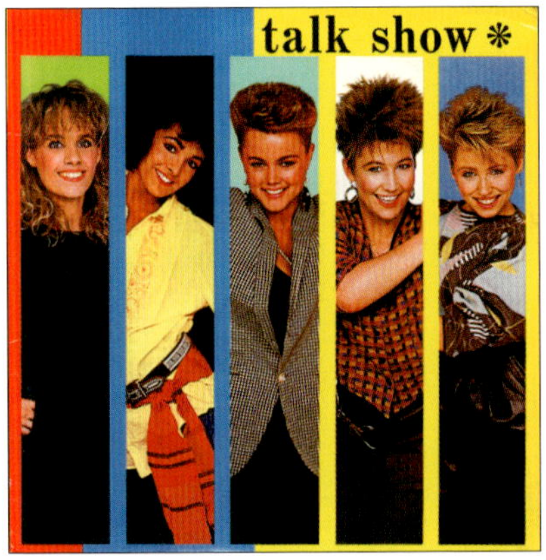

The Go-Go's returned with *Talk Show* and two bubbly singles, "Head Over Heels" and "Turn to You."

Billboard 200: *Talk Show* (#18)
Billboard Hot 100: "Head Over Heels" (#11); "Turn to You" (#32); "Yes or No" (#84)

THE GO-GO'S original success was as overwhelming as it was overnight. *Beauty and the Beat,* the 1981 debut release, proved that a female rock band in which all members played instruments and wrote original songs could sell lots of records. The album rose to No. 1 on the charts.

But *Vacation*, its inconsistent follow-up, ended up typecasting the band as disposable pop-rock cutie-pies.

"We knew that we had to come up with something different that showed some growth after *Vacation*, but we weren't really sure how we were going to go about it," lead singer Belinda Carlisle admitted. "A lot of people thought *Vacation* was musically invalid, and it isn't my personal favorite, either—I was very disappointed in the production, and we didn't have that much time to come up with songs."

The Go-Go's endured other trauma. Nerve trouble in guitarist Charlotte Caffey's right arm left her hand partially numb for several months. Drummer Gina Schock's open-heart surgery caused postponement of the group's summer tour. Business hassles developed with its record company for unpaid royalties.

For the third album, *Talk Show*, producer Martin Rushent imbued the Go-Go's with a harder-edged musical attack. The pulsating "Head Over Heels," the most successful of the album's three singles, just missed the Top 10. But even though the music was no longer lightweight, the Go-Go's still wanted to be known as an enthusiastic, fun band. To hear Carlisle tell it, those events in the last year were simply minor setbacks.

"Believe me, reading about it is a lot worse than when it actually happened," she explained. "It hasn't been exaggerated, but it seems to be an angle that people want to use now. But everybody has problems, and we don't particularly like to dwell on it or have it dramatized. Everybody's healthy and happy now, there's been no legal problems, and we've been out on tour. Everything's great!"

After completing the tour, the Go-Go's broke up in May of 1985. ■

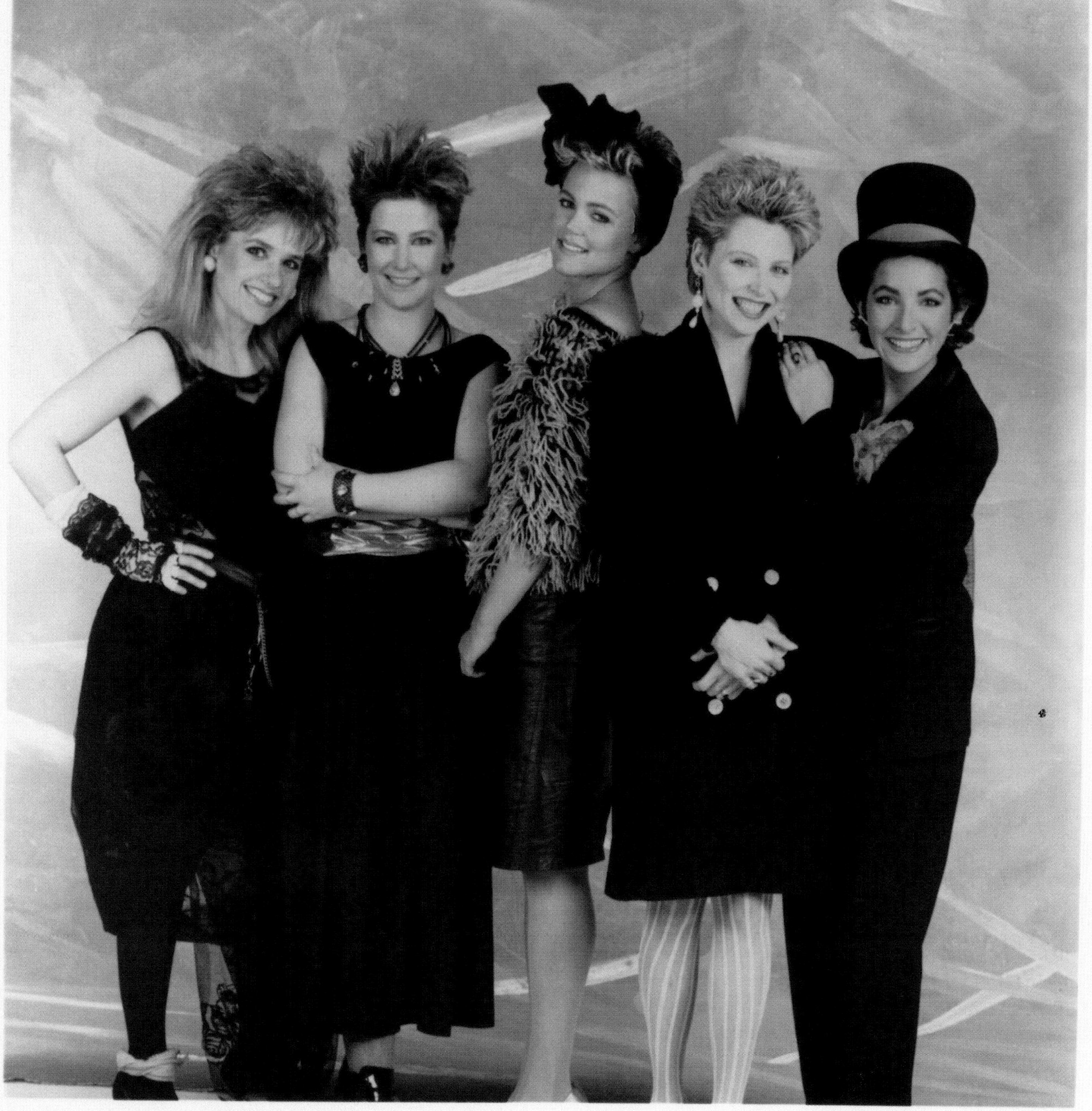

GO·GO'S *Charlotte Caffey Kathy Valentine Belinda Carlisle Gina Schock Jane Wiedlin*

I.R.S.

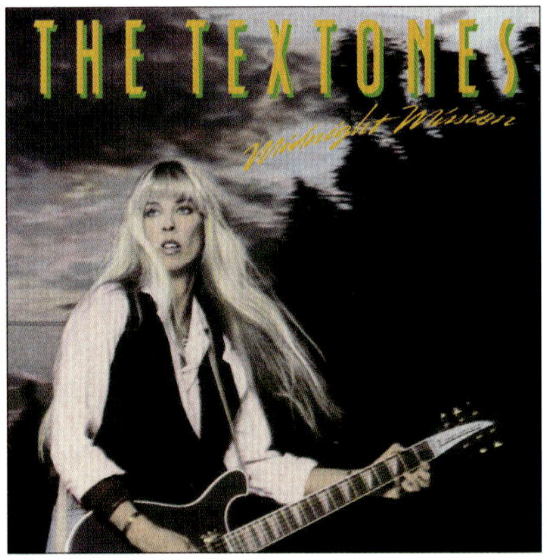

The Textones' debut release entered the charts, making Carla Olson an enduring SoCal musical presence.

Billboard 200: *Midnight Mission* (#176)

CARLA OLSON formed the first edition of the Textones in the late Seventies with Kathy Valentine, who went on to achieve short-lived fame as a member of the Go-Go's. As the group's sole remaining original member, Olson kept hipped into the music industry over the years by maintaining her day job with one of rock's biggest West Coast marketing concerns.

The Textones kept plugging away; power-pop singer and drummer Phil Seymour joined the roots-rock band, and Olson and her male cohorts had high hopes for the *Midnight Mission* album. It included help from Don Henley, Ry Cooder, Barry Goldberg and Gene Clark, and the title track was a featured video on MTV. But the record failed to translate the Textones' local reputation into national headlines.

"We were on a small label being distributed by a major label, and the small label didn't have the manpower to coerce the major to do the job," Olson said. "So our album got shelved."

The album made Olson one of the cult heroines of the Los Angeles roots-rock scene, singled out for her guitar playing skills. "A female Tom Petty" was the facile comparison. ■

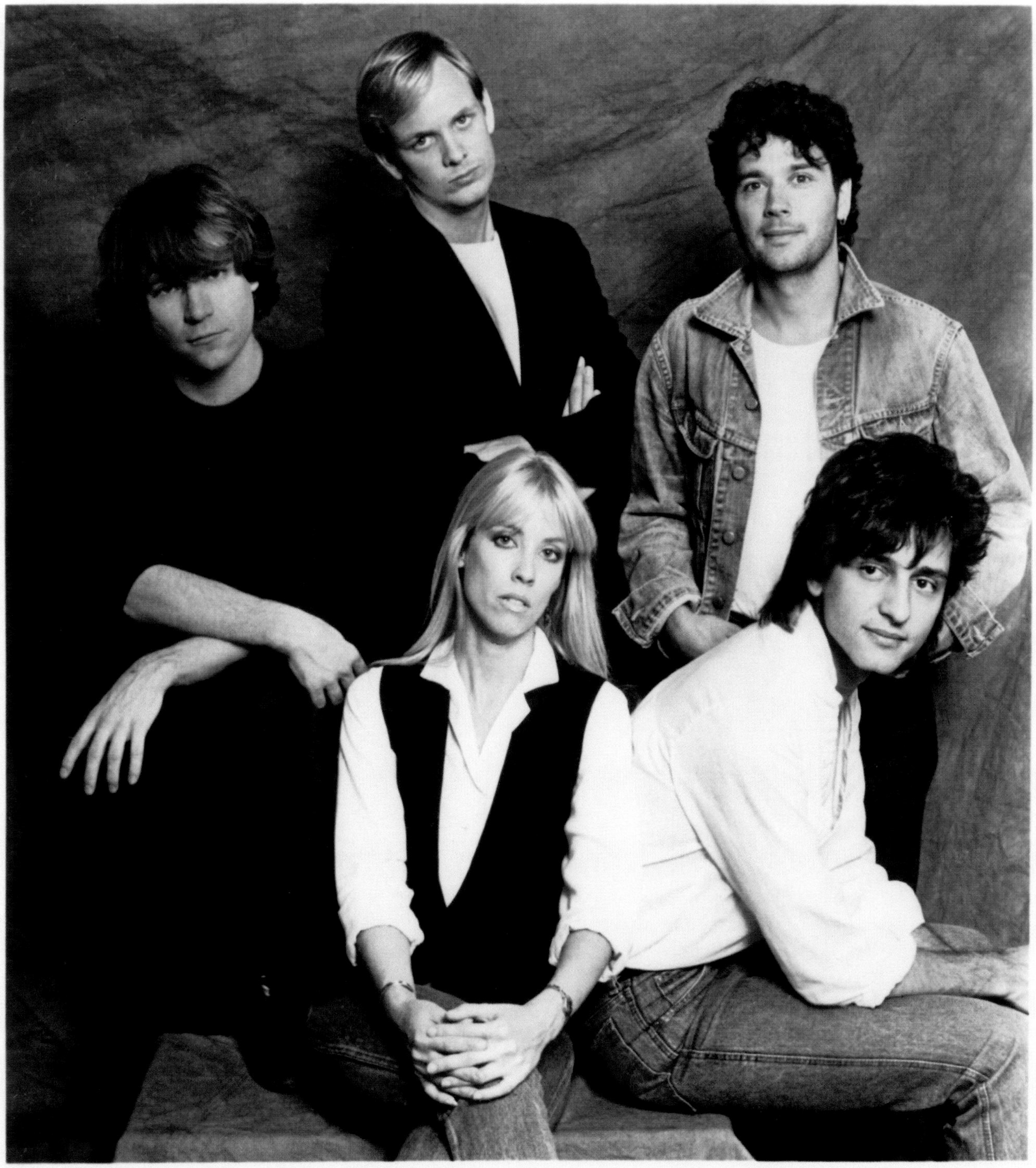

Phil Seymour Tom Junior Morgan Carla Olson Joe Read George Callins

THE TEXTONES

Management:
Saul Davis

A&M RECORDS

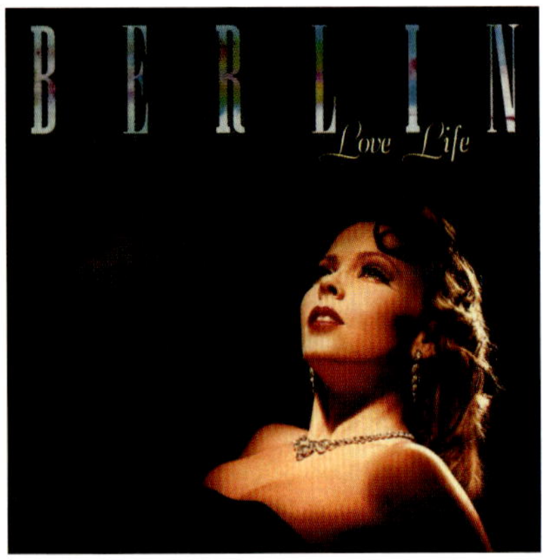

Billboard 200: *Love Life* (#28)
Billboard Hot 100: "No More Words" (#23); "Now It's My Turn" (#74)

Berlin broke down the wall to mainstream success as "No More Words" emerged as a Top 30 smash.

BERLIN HAD debuted auspiciously in 1982 with the independent EP *Pleasure Victim*, a sudden hit that only cost the Los Angeles-based band a total of $2,900 to produce and sold 25,000 copies before a major label signed the group. Audiences picked up on "Sex (I'm A…)," a salacious synth-driven tune which found lead singer Terri Nunn reciting a litany of moans and coolly despairing descriptors.

But "Sex (I'm A…)" wasn't played in Bible Belt areas. Berlin produced its first full album, *Love Life*, and "No More Words," an effervescent hit single co-produced by Giorgio Moroder, promoted a more orthodox image for the band; the video saw Nunn and bandmates act out a Bonnie and Clyde-style car chase and gunfight. And by adding Ric Olsen as a permanent guitarist, Berlin hoped to break out of the synth-pop category.

"Actually, we weren't even a band when we got the synthesizer tag," Nunn explained. "When we made that first EP, Berlin was just John Crawford, David Diamond and me, with other people helping out. Now we're a six-piece, and Berlin is a real group, not a project."

But the band's focal point remained Nunn, a sexy, diminutive blonde whose sensual vocals provided the perfect vehicle for Diamond's provocative lyrics. Nunn credited her parents for her ability to entertain.

"My father was a philosopher and my mother was an astrologer, and together it made for a pretty liberal household," she revealed. "But their philosophies never clashed, and they opened me up to a lot of things."

Nunn was called a leading practitioner of "bimbo rock," but a tour revealed her to be an energetic, hard-working performer instead of a little tease.

"Planning a concert production doesn't just entail money. It's also a lot of time and imagination—devising ways to present your songs. It's certainly the most fun of the things we've done," she enthused. "I believe in having confidence. Everybody should have a dream. For me, it was music, but there's that passion in every person. It's different from ego, which stems from insecurity. Confidence is all it takes to get something done, and Berlin's career has been a perfect example of that." ■

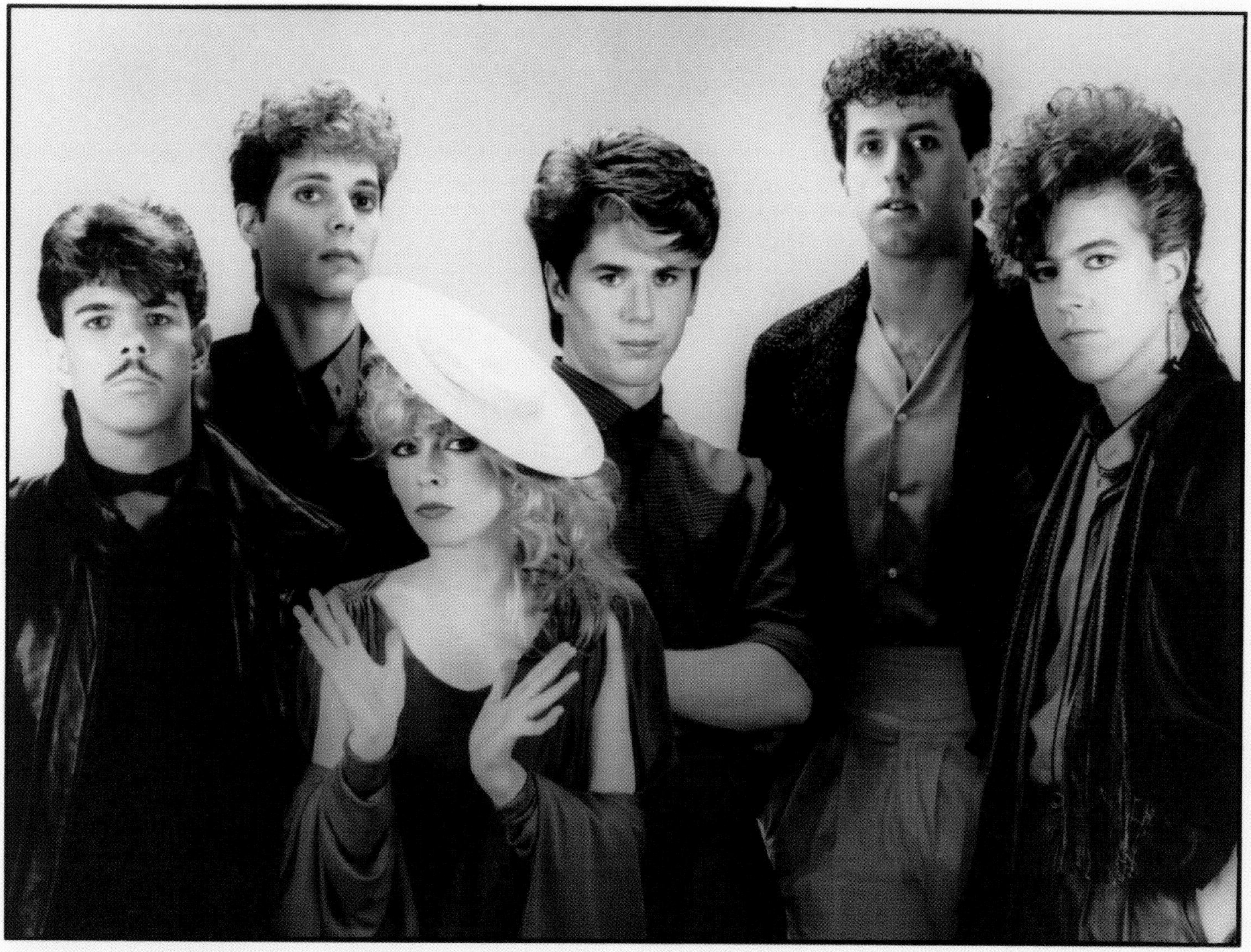

PHOTO CREDIT: DOUGLAS BRYANT 1984

DAVID DIAMOND ROB BRILL TERRI NUNN JOHN CRAWFORD MATT REID RIC OLSEN

BERLIN

GEFFEN RECORDS

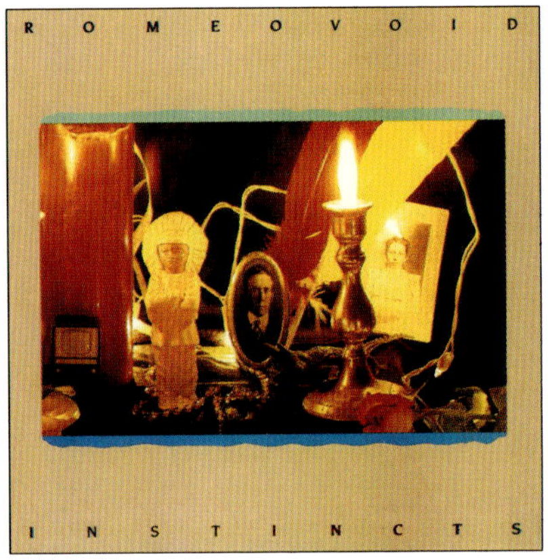

With the coy "A Girl in Trouble (Is a Temporary Thing)," Romeo Void attained some post-punk success.

Billboard 200: *Instincts* (#68)
Billboard Hot 100: "A Girl in Trouble (Is a Temporary Thing)" (#35)

ROMEO VOID was in danger of being remembered only for the careening dance-club hit "Never Say Never," an underground classic marked by the provocative line, "I might like you better if we slept together…" But "A Girl in Trouble (Is a Temporary Thing)" excited people, which excited the San Francisco-based group.

"We wanted to write a happy song," lyricist/vocalist Debora Iyall enthused. "Sometimes people misunderstand—criticizing something helps make it better or different or points out a direction. Everyone always said, 'Romeo Void is a real negative band,' and we thought, 'Wait a minute, we really care.'"

Hence "A Girl in Trouble," a song about relationships which Iyall called "my pep talk to women. It's got little axioms in it, like the line 'There's a way to walk, so stay away.' People who know how not to be victims know that, but it might as well be part of pop culture for everyone to know it. So we put it in a song, and we feel real positive about it."

Iyall wasn't kin to fashionable bimbo-rock practitioners à la Berlin or Missing Persons. Her ample appearance fueled her perceptions concerning romance, and her untraditional background shaped her strong self-image. After leaving an Indian reservation in Washington, her mother raised her in Fresno, California. "But I'm not sure I could say I'm a California kid," Iyall laughed. "I'm not blond, I don't surf, I'm not a vegetarian, I've never taken Transcendental Meditation and I don't have a peacock feather in my house."

After quitting high school at 16, Iyall began sitting in on poetry and conceptual art classes at Fresno State. At 23, she moved to the Eureka area and worked at the Indian Action Pre-School and received a grant from the Bureau of Indian Affairs to attend San Francisco Art Institute, where she met her future bandmates. "I'd been going to punk clubs in San Francisco, and I thought, 'If these guys can do it, I can definitely do it. And I have a lot to say as a writer.' My thing was always more personal than political. I don't think I have to address timely current events to be contributing."

The success of "A Girl in Trouble" had Iyall happy, and the challenge to wed art with popular music had Romeo Void equally enthused. "I haven't had to get a straight job yet," she concluded. "When I moved to San Francisco, I decided, 'Art is my state, don't debate.' And we all consider what we do with Romeo Void part of our art." ■

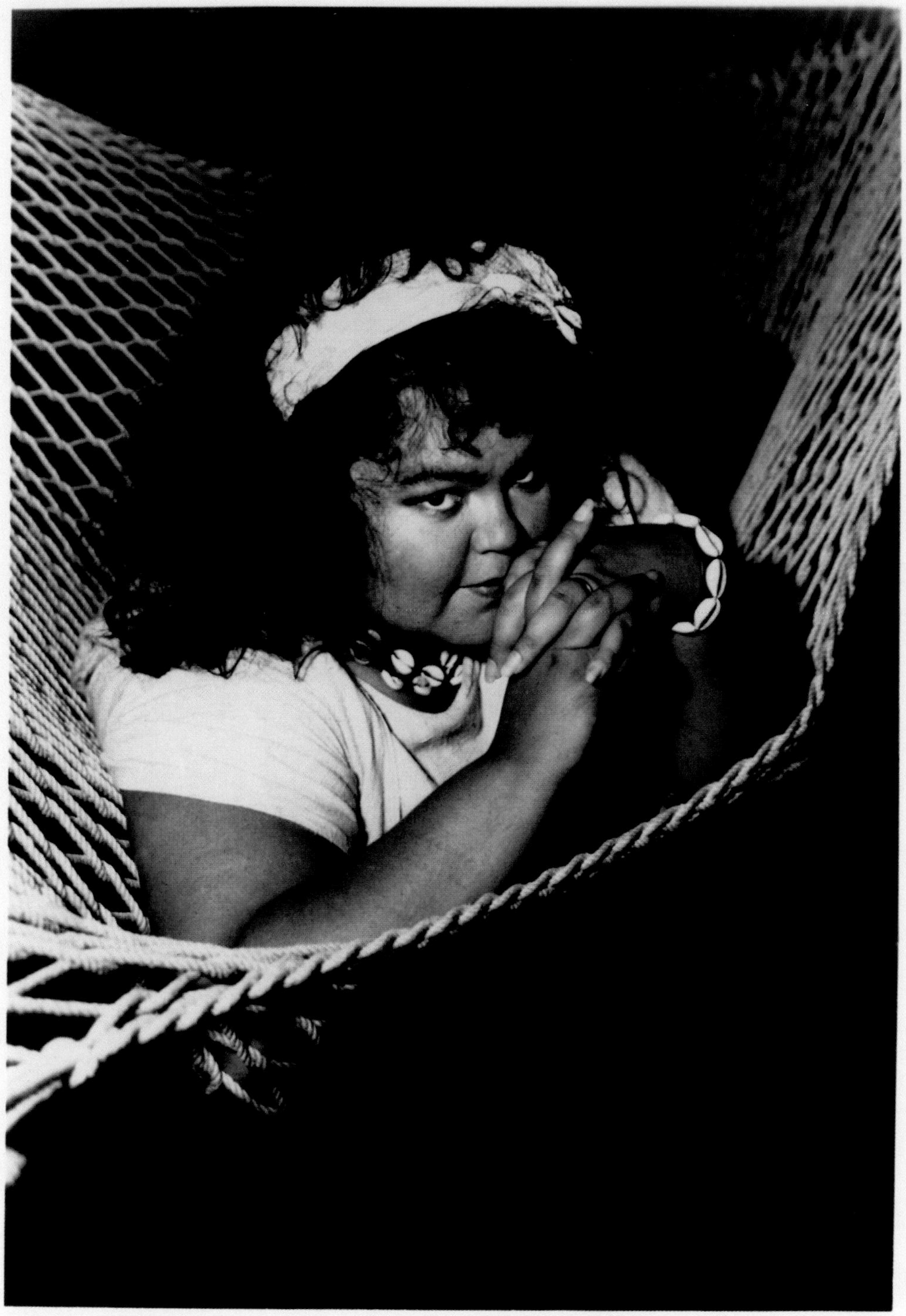

PHOTOGRAPH: H. BUFF HERR

Lead singer Debora Iyall

on 415/Columbia.

ROMEO VOID

Columbia 8408

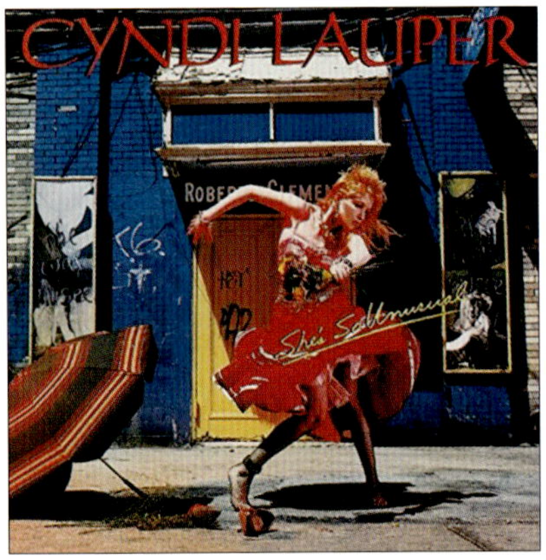

Billboard 200: *She's So Unusual* (#4)
Billboard Hot 100: "Girls Just Want to Have Fun" (#2); "Time After Time" (No. 1); "She Bop" (#3); "All Through the Night" (#5); "Money Changes Everything" (#27)

With *She's So Unusual*, her first solo record, Cyndi Lauper was singled out for once-in-a-lifetime success.

***SHE'S SO** Unusual* made Cyndi Lauper a household name. The mega-platinum album sold more than 3 million copies and spun off four consecutive Top 5 singles, a first for a female singer. She won a Grammy for Best New Artist, a solo vocal spot in the all-star "We Are the World" project—and even the chance to manage Wendi Richter in the World Wrestling Federation's inaugural WrestleMania event.

With her remarkably big voice, quirky visual style and zany exuberance, Lauper smashed the stereotype for female vocalists and won countless hearts. She was a multifaceted talent—the loony lady with the thrift-shop-elegant clothes and multicolor hair behind "Girls Just Want to Have Fun," and an artist with the sensitivity and professionalism to write a song such as "Time After Time." *She's So Unusual* accurately reflected the traits she'd worked on for years to develop.

"I'd always sung just for myself before I was a professional—I'd sing to make myself feel better, or I'd sing while I was taking a walk," Lauper recalled in her exaggerated New Yawk speaking voice. "But when I got my chance, I pushed myself into situations where something new could occur, where I could try to find a place where there's magic."

From the very beginning of her career, Lauper dedicated herself to communicating the intricacies of her voice in a recording studio—how her singing translated from microphone to tape, how machines would alter and treat it.

"If it wasn't right, I wanted to know how to fix it," she said. "I asked a lot of questions and did a lot of research so I wouldn't be miserable, because I did this to be happy. And when I recorded *She's So Unusual*, it was a situation of being handed the ball and not dropping it."

With her instant fame and status as one of rock's premier vocalists, Lauper was determined to maintain her popularity.

"It's hard to be happy in this world, but if you are, that's success. I've scrubbed floors, and if that made me happy, I'd still be doing that. But what made me truly happy was to sing; it made me feel free. It don't matter how much money you make—money don't buy pride." ■

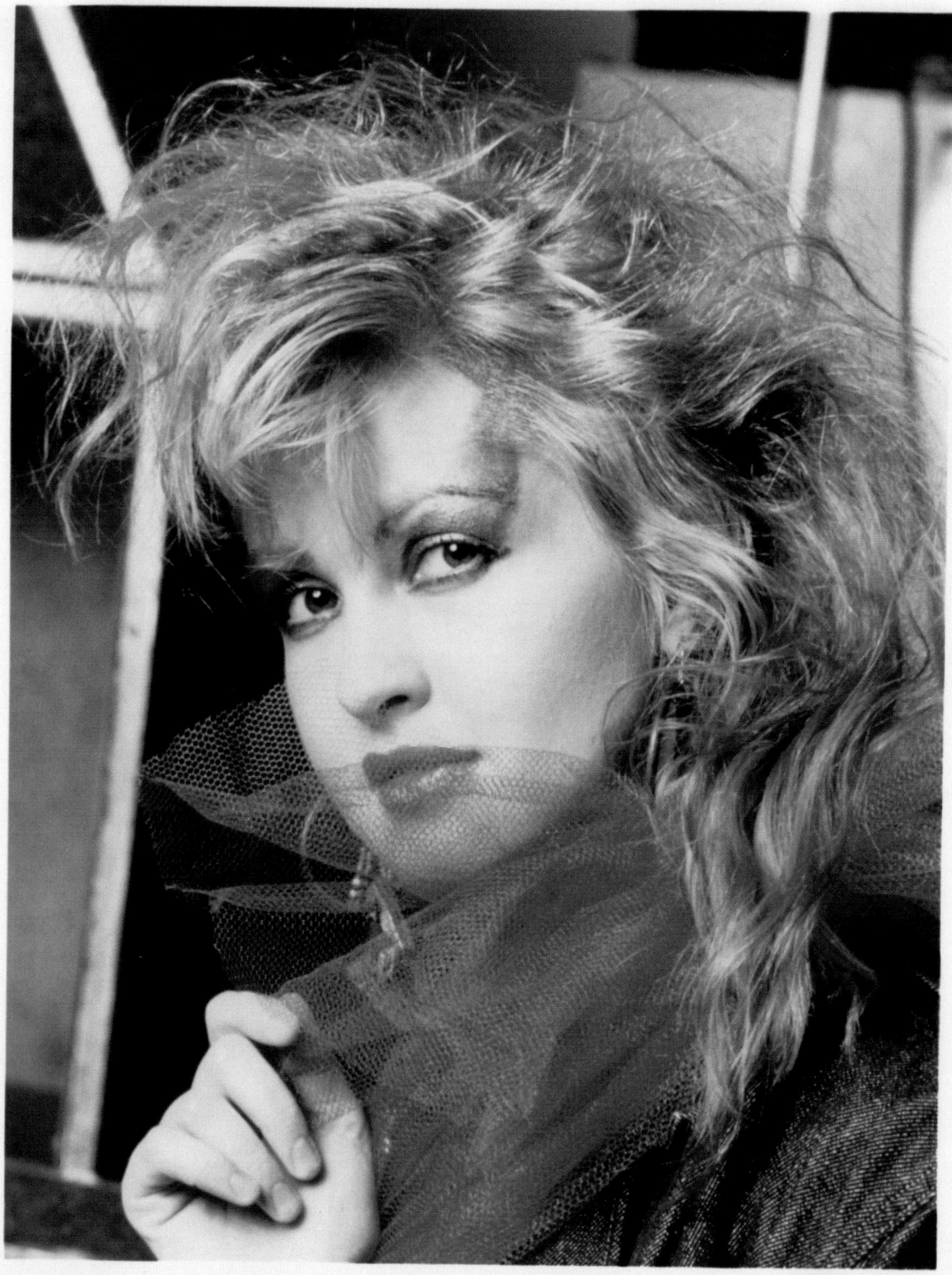

Photo: John Bellissimo

Management:
Dave Wolff
(212) 977-9340

CYNDI LAUPER

Portrait

8405

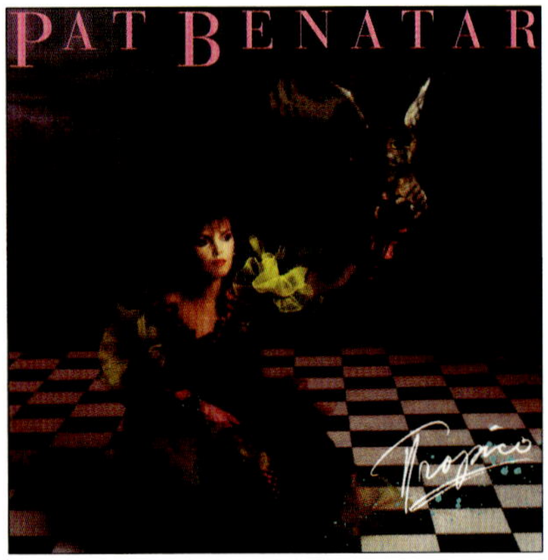

Shifting musical gears, Pat Benatar maintained her spot atop the charts with the soaring "We Belong."

Billboard 200: *Tropico* (#14)
Billboard Hot 100: "We Belong" (#5);
"Ooh Ooh Song" (#36)

PAT BENATAR had become the leading female rock vocalist of the early Eighties, with her multi-octave range translating into sales of more than 20 million records. She became accustomed to Top 20 hits ("Hit Me with Your Best Shot," "Shadows of the Night," "Love Is a Battlefield") and to playing the nation's biggest arenas.

But Benatar's music and image were transitioning from her tough-girl-in-Spandex pose to a more thoughtful, warmer stance. In doing so, she allowed herself to be challenged by other female vocalists.

"Everybody keeps asking me, 'Oh God, what about Madonna? What about Cyndi Lauper?' I say, what about them? They have their thing, and I have mine. I hope they're having a good time—man, it gave me some rest. They took over, and now I don't have to jump around in skin-tight clothes!"

The mellowing began with *Tropico*, her fifth studio album, designed by Benatar and her husband and producer Neil Giraldo after a short vacation from the business. The duo conceived another project around the same time—while planning a tour, the diminutive singer found out she was pregnant. She and Giraldo postponed the tour and hurriedly readied the videos for release.

"You see the fork in the road and you know there are two ways to go," Benatar explained. "You can keep going at a breakneck pace, killing yourself trying to be and stay No. 1. And if that's what makes you happy, you should do it. But it doesn't make me happy—it makes me crazy! I can't give it my undivided attention anymore—I have other things in my life now. Making music is one thing, but having to be a rock 'n' roll star is stupid."

The single "We Belong" became another Top 10 hit and earned Benatar a Grammy nomination for Best Female Pop Vocal Performance, and *Tropico* went platinum. But the album fell short of the sales of her other efforts, which Benatar ascribed to a failure of meeting her fans' expectations.

"Instead of making records that are expected of me, I'm making the records I want to make, which is the whole point," she said. "I think a lot of people are motivated by ambition. Ambition is poison for me. It makes me do stupid things I shouldn't do just to stay in chart positions, and that's wrong. When you have kids, it tends to make you really tune in on everything—your perspective is changed. Now my records are very reflective, and that's how they should be made." ■

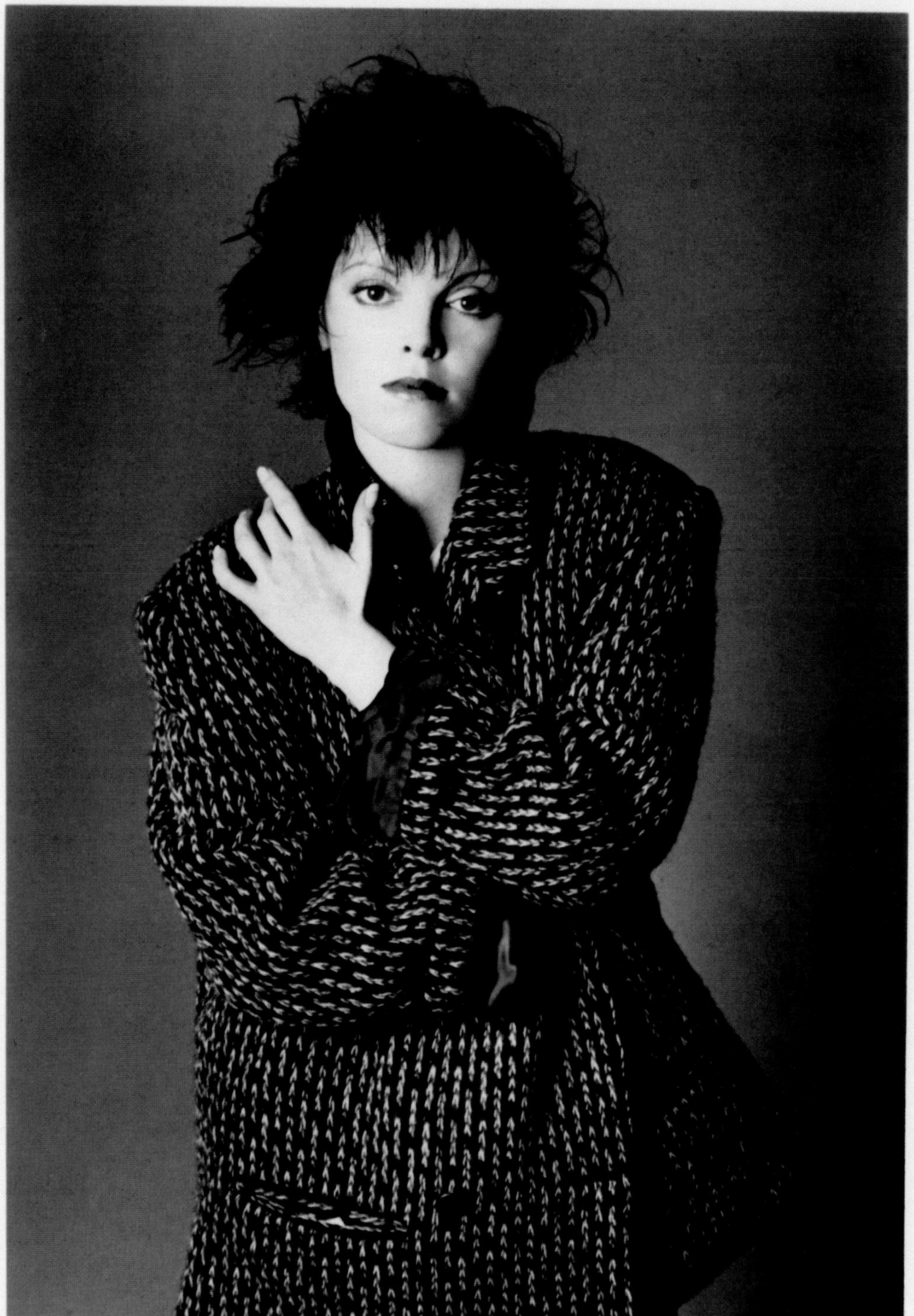

PAT BENATAR

Chrysalis™

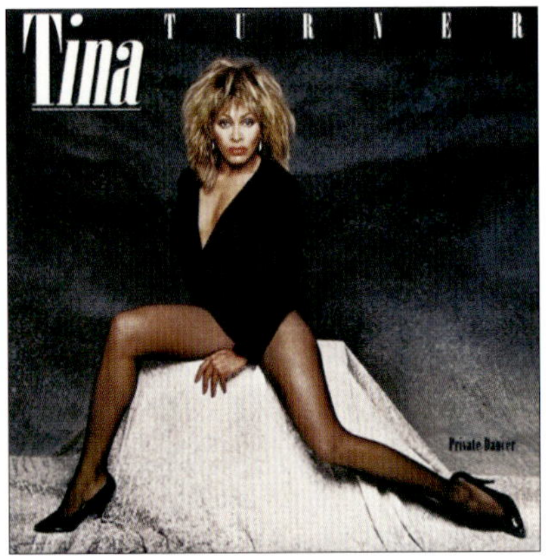

Tina Turner's expansive spirit emerged as she burst onto the rock scene with her album, *Private Dancer*.

Billboard 200: *Private Dancer* (#3)
Billboard Hot 100: "Let's Stay Together" (#26); "What's Love Got to Do with It" (No. 1); "Better Be Good to Me" (#5); "Private Dancer" (#7); "Show Some Respect" (#37)

TINA TURNER had made her own way in the world as a means of survival. After marrying Ike Turner in 1958, she got her start fronting his powerhouse R&B show. As the Ike & Tina Turner Revue, they strung together more than a decade of hits, including "A Fool in Love," "Come Together," the legendary "River Deep, Mountain High" and a Grammy-winning version of Creedence Clearwater Revival's "Proud Mary." Tina's give-it-all-you-got image—the resounding voice, the heartbreak face, the wild hair, the great legs—carried her through spectacular stage performances.

But her lifestyle as Ike's prisoner was hellish, defined by his increasing violence and dependence on drugs. "He kept control of me with fear," Turner said.

Her desperation and disappointment eventually led her to walk away from Ike and strike out on her own—with 36 cents in her pocket and her newfound Buddhist beliefs. A year after their split in 1975, she launched a solo career. And after a quarter of a century of performing, she finally became an overnight sensation, soaring to stardom with *Private Dancer* and the singles "Let's Stay Together," "Better Be Good to Me," the title track and "What's Love Got to Do with It," which went to No. 1 and won a Grammy Award for Record of the Year.

"'What's Love Got to Do with It' was something I wouldn't have taken on normally, but my manager's guidance told me that it could be one of those moves that ends up in something good," Turner said. "I've learned not to typecast myself."

The incessant touring that ensued included 70 European dates in 14 countries, a six-month 105-date US trek and sold-out tours of Australia and Japan. But her modest beginnings balanced out her emergence as one of the most admired entertainers in the world.

"I'm not supporting any causes," she said in reference to the abuse she suffered in her marriage to Ike. "I can't. It's too much responsibility, dealing with people who aren't able to handle those kinds of situations. Anything that anybody wants to look up to me for, fine, that's their need. But I don't try to live up to any image. I'm living the same life, I'm the same woman I was when I went out to get myself to where I am now. I was just a country girl who worked her way through life, and I'm still continuously doing that. And I'll keep going, because I don't want to get caught up in anything ever again." ■

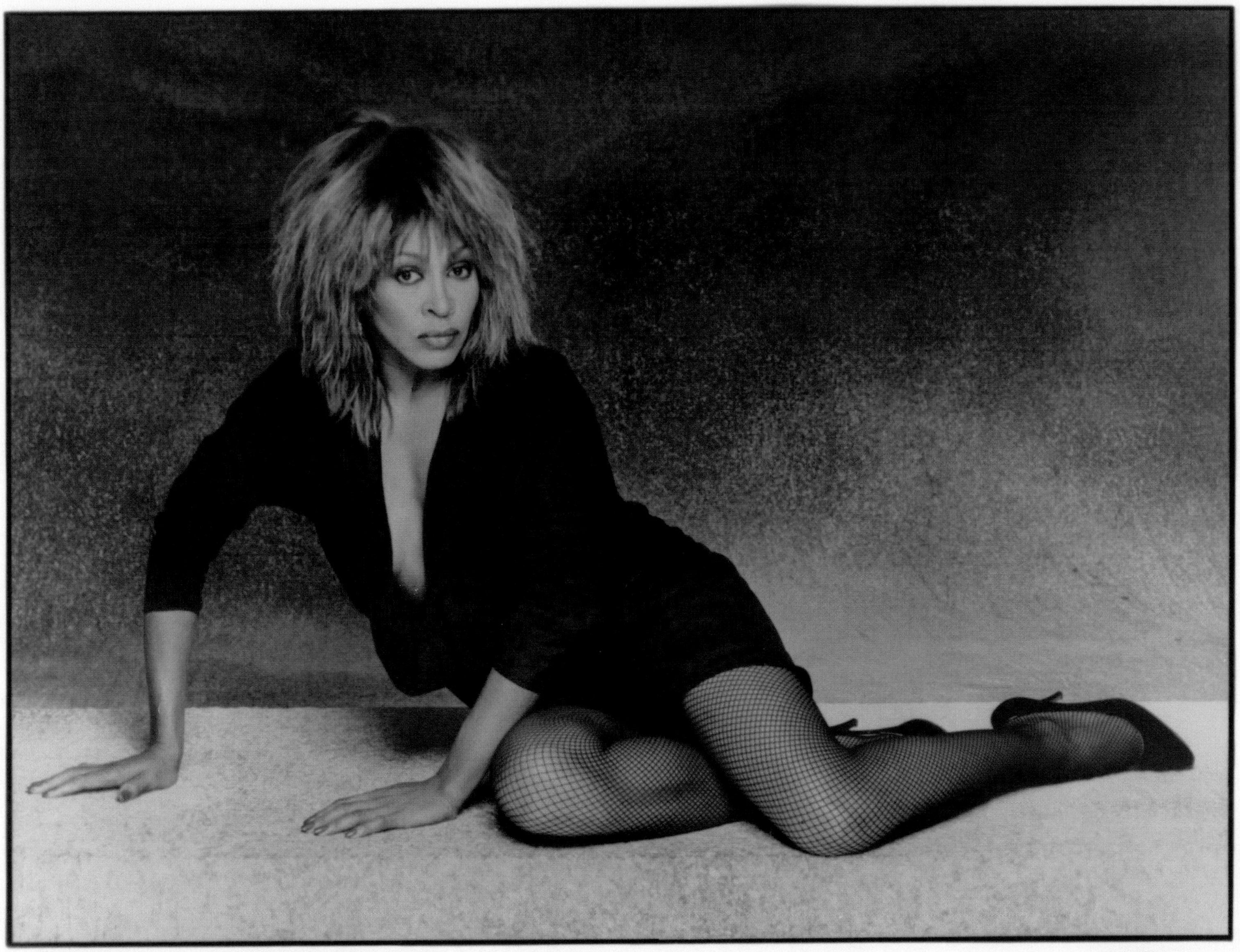

Photo: Brian Aris / 1984

TINA TURNER

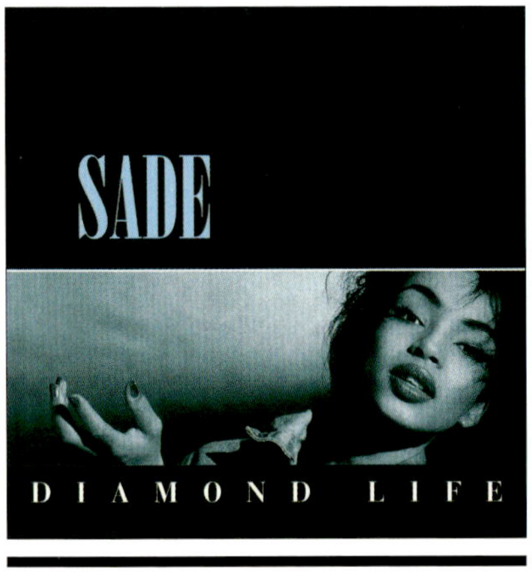

The Anglo-African chanteuse Sade reaped international acclaim with her notable debut, *Diamond Life.*

Billboard 200: *Diamond Life* (#5)
Billboard Hot 100: "Smooth Operator" (#5);
"Your Love Is King" (#54)

SADE'S COOL cocktail sound catapulted her to stardom, but the public imagined that the singer was a shy, reclusive prima donna. Sade said that image was a myth. She wasn't sultry or mysterious; she just didn't spend her time with journalists.

"I don't want people to have too much of me," the former model said. "I know it sounds like I resent giving it away—it's not like that—but I always feel I put a lot of myself there in the songs. That's how you get to know me."

Most people assumed Sade and her band of the same name came from a jazz or Latin music background. When "Smooth Operator" became the breakthrough single from her premiere album, *Diamond Life*, a few critics implied she should have covered the 1964 bossa nova hit "The Girl from Ipanema" by Stan Getz and Astrud Gilberto.

"They weren't used to hearing congas," Sade said. "There are a lot of people who are open to taking in different things if only they're made available. It isn't so amazing or incredible that people like what we do."

Diamond Life went on to become one of the top-selling debut recordings of the Eighties. The record company made a point of printing "Pronounced Shar-day" on the release. ■

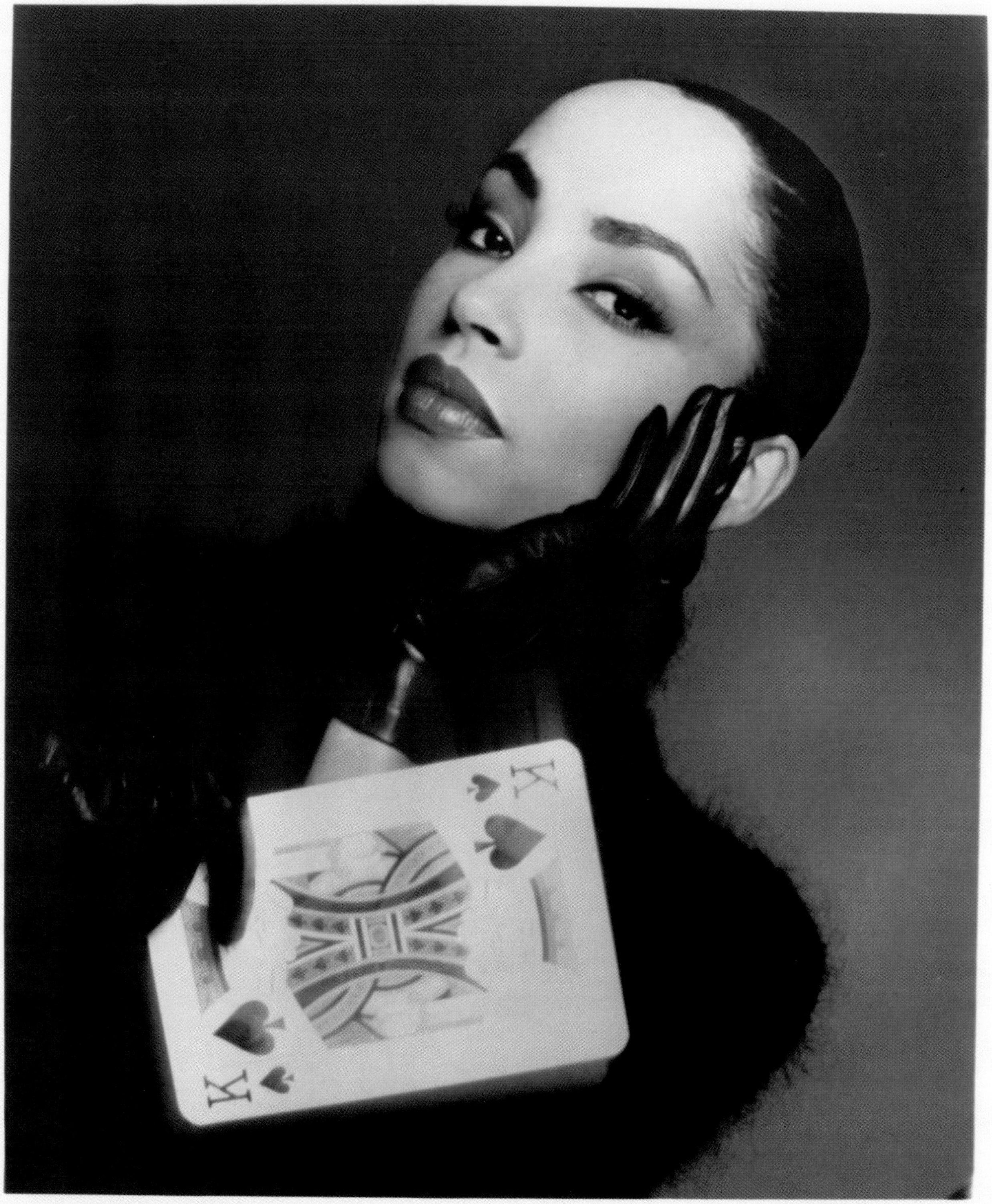

SADE

Epic
8410

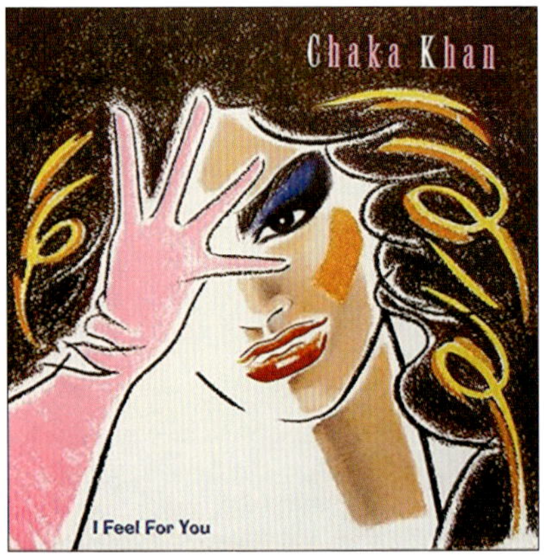

With her radical reworking of the title track, Chaka Khan earned a platinum album for *I Feel for You*.

Billboard 200: *I Feel for You* (#16)
Billboard Hot 100: "I Feel for You" (#3);
"This Is My Night" (#60); "Through the Fire" (#60)

THE LEAD vocalist and focal point of the funk band Rufus, Chaka Khan had balanced a solo career for at least five years before separating from Rufus for good in 1983.

"After ten years together, everyone wanted to get away and do something different musically," the sassy singer said. "I wanted to sing songs that the group didn't have to decide on democratically. They wanted to produce other acts."

For Khan, the decision to go it alone had proved to be the right one. Her impetuous style paid big dividends on "I Feel for You." With her smash single, she was the first R&B artist to have a crossover hit featuring a rapper, Grandmaster Melle Mel (of Grandmaster Flash & the Furious Five).

Khan had maintained longevity in a notoriously ephemeral business—not through her recordings, but her live performances.

"Absolutely, that's what I prefer," she said. "That's where I get to stretch and experiment, try new ideas out. It's necessary for me to be out there live to get that reciprocation from audiences that I don't get in the studio."

I Feel for You's title cut was a remake of a song originally written and recorded by Prince five years earlier.

"I've been so busy touring that I come home just in time to do an album, with no real time to write or concentrate," Khan said. "I'm tired of taking other people's stuff and remaking it. I want to write more and get totally involved. I play drums, so I usually collaborate with someone who plays guitar or piano, to show them the chords I want to use.

"I was uncomfortable on my own at first, but now I've grown into it. I wouldn't have it any other way. I'm probably better than I've ever been as a performer and a person. I wouldn't say that I'm calmer—I have the same energy level. I just have better outlets for it." ■

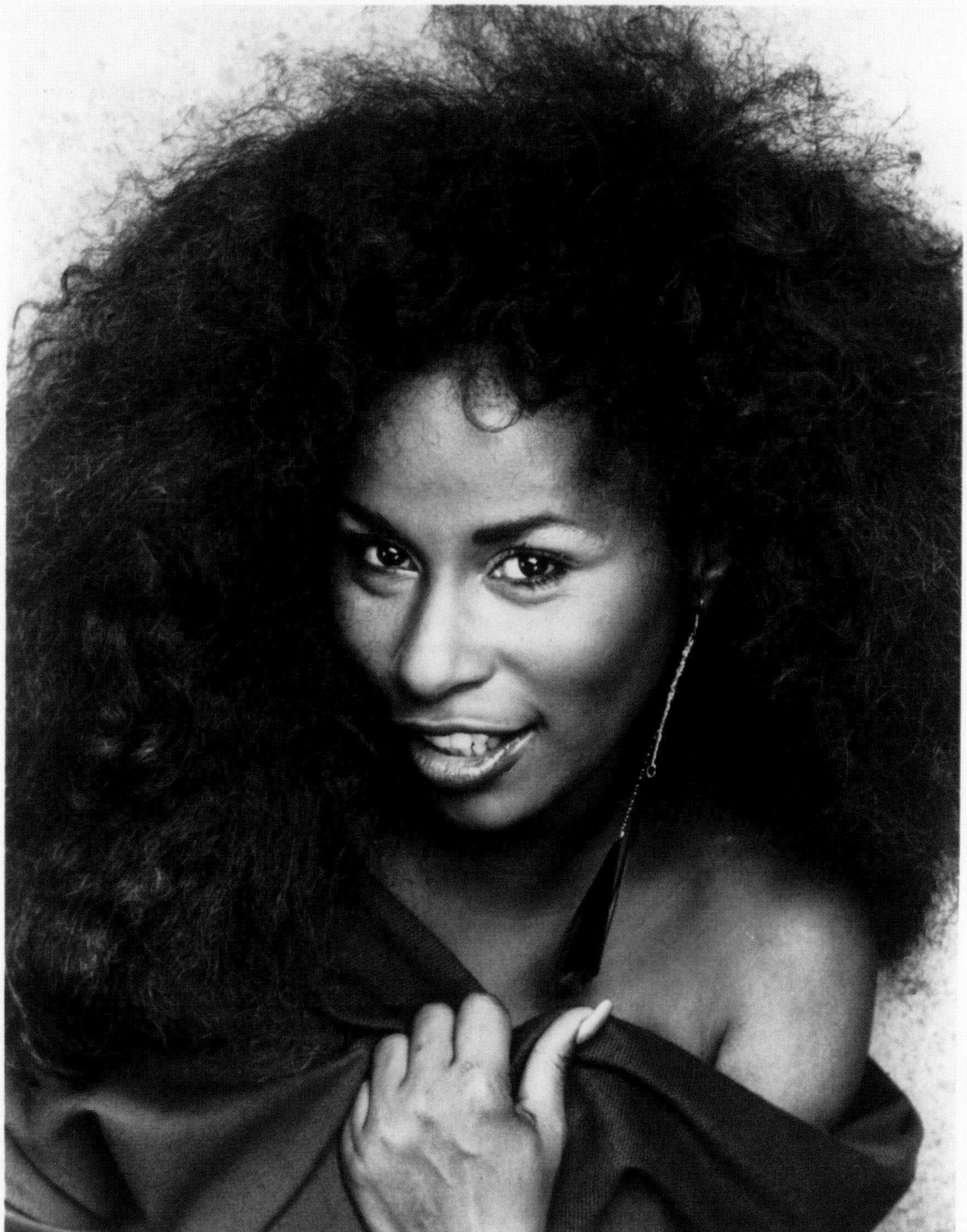

Photo Credit: Waring Abbott

CHAKA KHAN

DIRECTION
BURT ZELL MGMT

WARNER BROS.

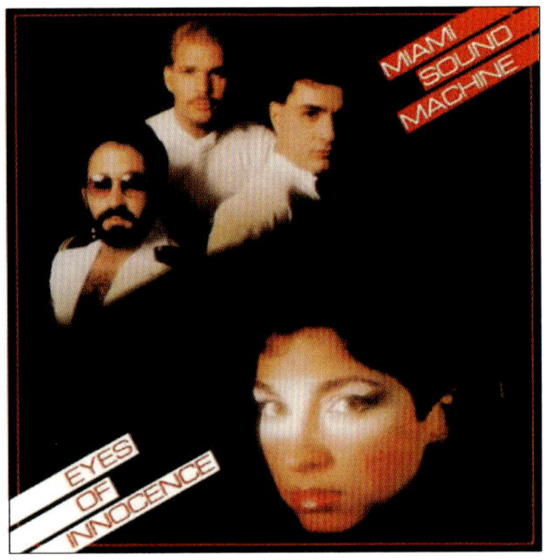

The Gloria Estefan-fronted Miami Sound Machine kicked off in America's dance clubs with "Dr. Beat."

THE DANCE track "Dr. Beat" introduced Miami Sound Machine in the United States, but the band hardly rated as the latest "overnight sensation." For years, the group had reigned as a best-selling act in Latin America.

"We started out recording half of our albums in English and half in Spanish," Gloria Estefan, MSM's comely lead singer, said. "But when we signed with a big international label, they felt it would be better from a marketing standpoint to sing in Spanish. So we pursued that for seven albums, and by 1984 we were playing 50,000-seat stadiums in Latin America."

The dance hit "Dr. Beat" not only topped all Latin American dance charts, it took continental Europe by storm, and it eventually reached No. 1 in the UK. At that point the group had the clout and confidence to take on the American pop market. *Eyes of Innocence*, the band's first English-language studio album, contained "Dr. Beat." The song broke through to a wider stateside audience, peaking at #17 on the *Billboard* Dance Club Play chart.

"We knew the time was right," Estefan said. "We didn't have that many Latin elements in our music anyway—it was pop music in Spanish."

In the amusing video, Dr. Beat, played by songwriter and drummer Enrique Garcia, saved a dance-maddened Estefan from a suicide jump, then rushed her to his clinic for some calming electro-shock therapy; in an emergency operation, he extracted a boombox from her belly, ending the entire scenario with a snip of the cord joining woman and machine. ■

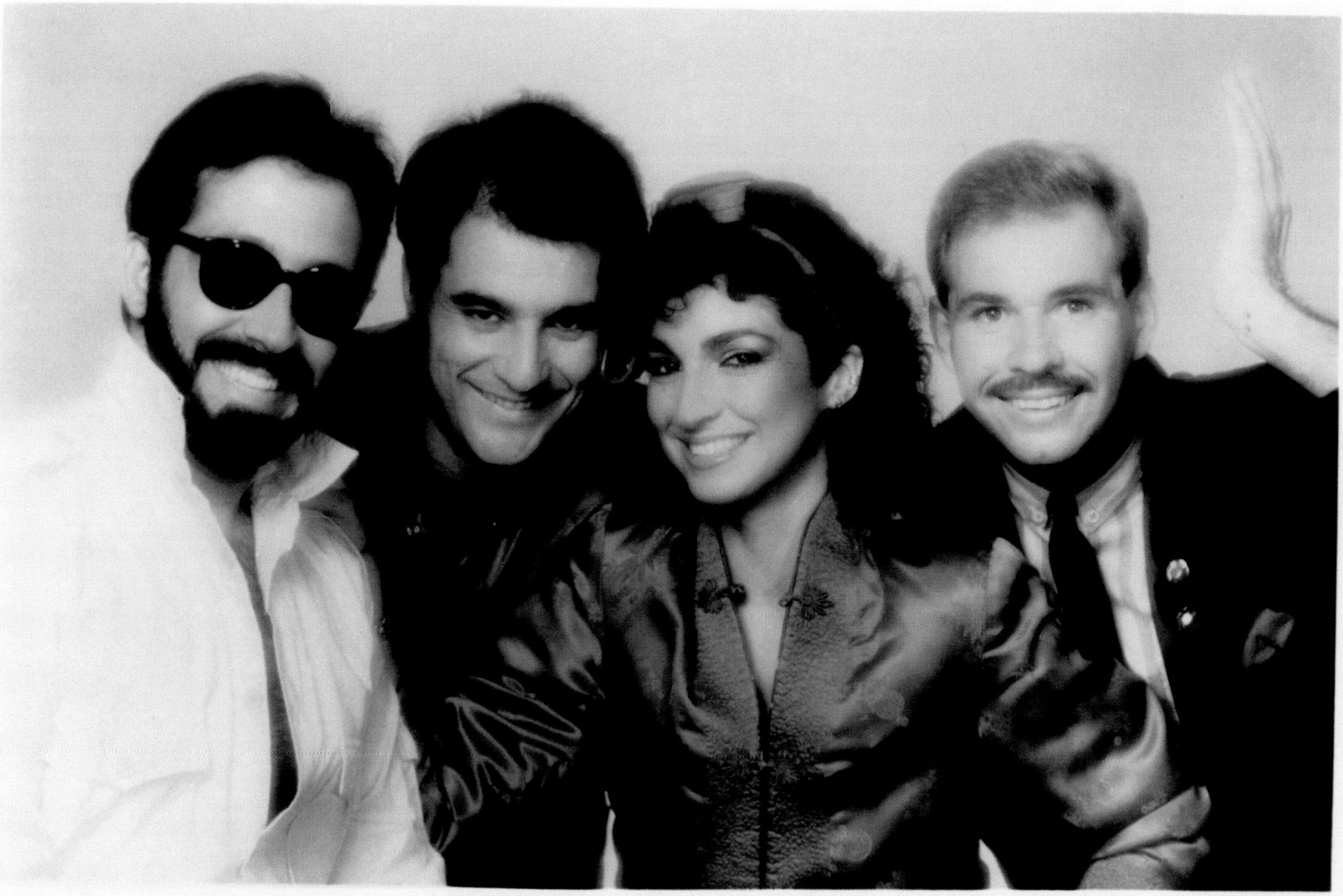

EMILIO ESTEFAN MARCOS AVILA GLORIA ESTEFAN KIKI GARCIA

MIAMI SOUND MACHINE

Epic

8409

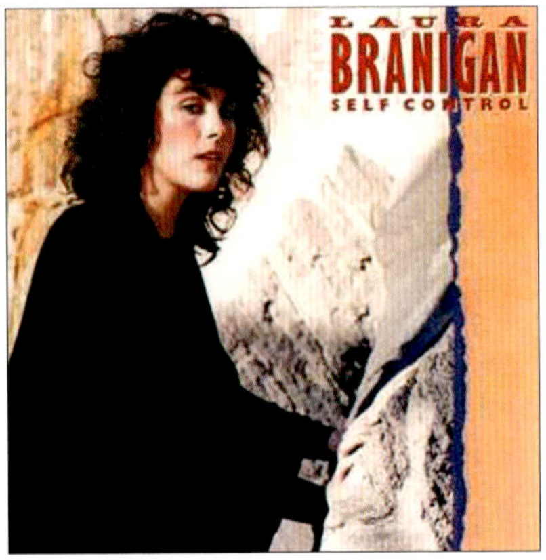

Laura Branigan's platinum-selling *Self Control* spawned pop, dance and adult contemporary smash hits.

Billboard 200: *Self Control* (#23)
Billboard Hot 100: "Self Control" (#4);
"The Lucky One" (#20); "Ti Amo" (#55)

THE SINGLES "Solitaire," "How Am I Supposed to Live Without You" and her signature smash "Gloria" had made Laura Branigan an international singing star. Taking advantage of the au courant European synth-pop sound, "Self Control" was her biggest commercial success, reaching massive proportions in the US and other parts of the world (No. 1 in Canada and West Germany).

The single was goosed along by the music video, as Branigan was one of the first acts in the MTV era to work with an Academy Award-winning film director. Crafted by William Friedkin (*The French Connection*, *The Exorcist*), the video, about finding sex in the sordid side of town, sparked some disputation over certain sadomasochistic elements and required minor edits before it aired.

"I do think you should treat controversial subjects...every few months," Branigan laughed by way of explanation.

Other hits from *Self Control* included "The Lucky One" (a US Top 20 hit which won her a Tokyo Music Festival prize) and the theatrical ballad "Ti Amo."

Branigan also devoted some time to her other passion—acting. Her credits included a dramatic guest role on the television police series *CHiPS*.

"I started out hitting the streets of New York after high school, knocking on doors looking for acting work," Branigan explained. "But then my voice took over! I suppose I'll always be on the lookout for an appealing role, but I will never, ever, ever give up singing." ■

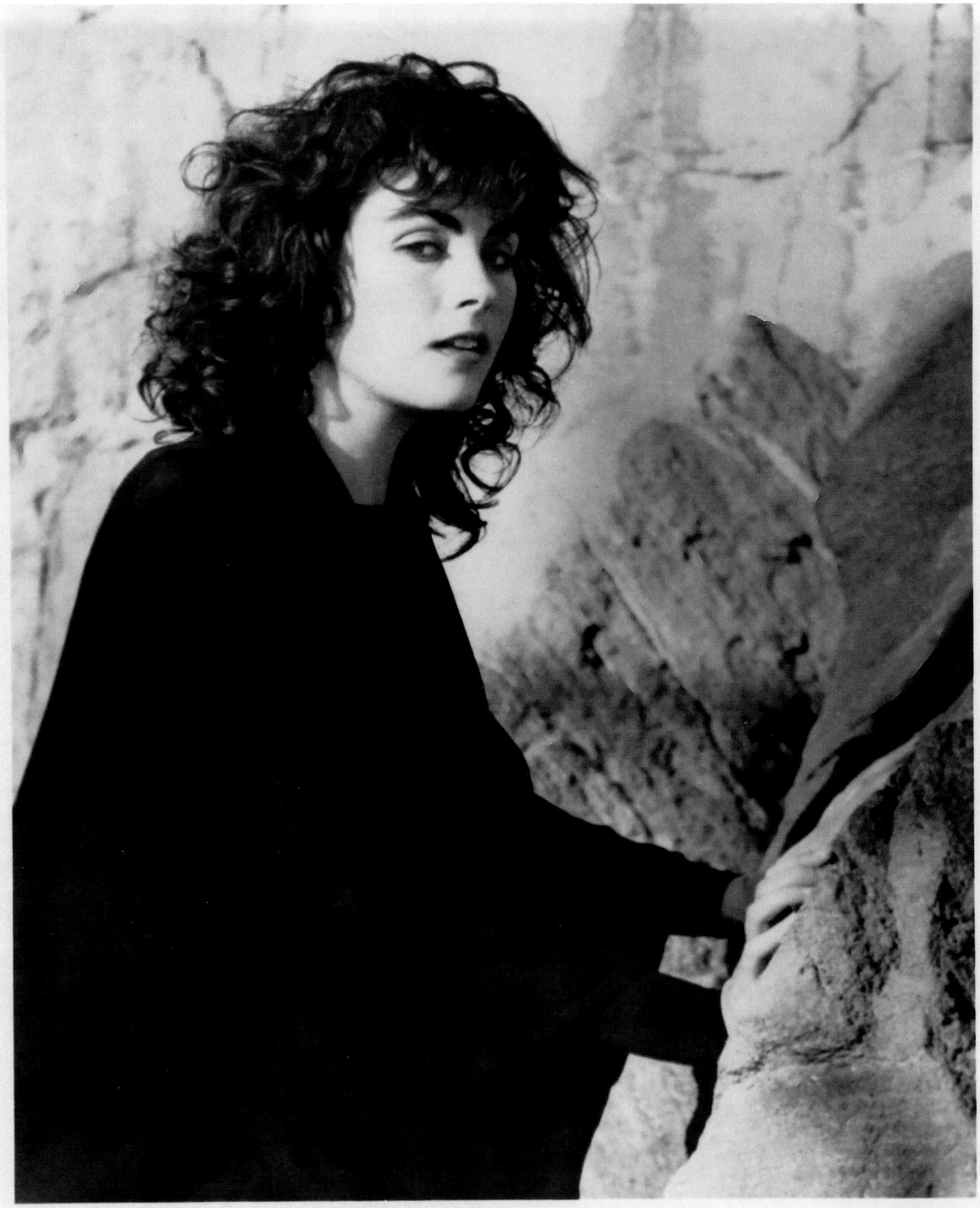

LAURA BRANIGAN

ATLANTIC

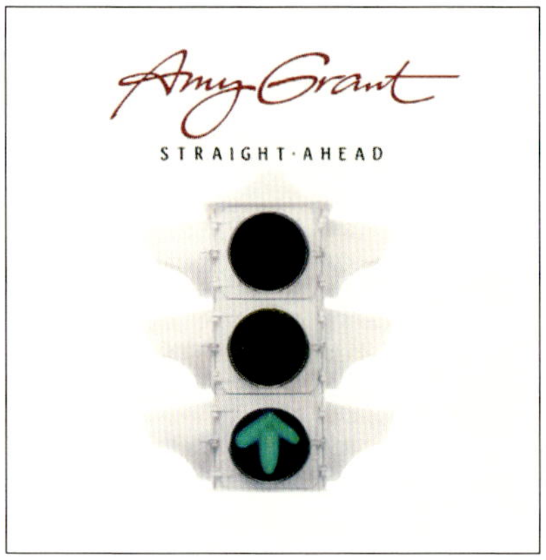

Amy Grant's *Straight Ahead*, the first Christian album to break into the pop charts, signaled her crossover.

Billboard 200: *Straight Ahead* (#133)

IN HER field of contemporary Christian music, Amy Grant was the undisputed champion. *Age to Age* had been No. 1 on the charts for a full year and won a Grammy Award, becoming the first certified-gold Christian album by a solo artist. But Grant was caught between two camps of ignorance: the "secular" audience that assumed the singer was another Jesus-saved-me performer, and the traditional gospel camp itself that refused to believe rock 'n' roll could carry the same message.

This lack of acceptance frustrated Grant, whose music was no more controversial than any other found on adult contemporary radio. She had the same attractive voice and appearance that had catapulted others to super-stardom, but she wasn't sure what more she could do to reach a wider audience.

"When I first heard the term 'contemporary Christian music,' I thought, 'What a mouthful! What a terrible name to slap on such wonderful music,'" Grant recalled. "But then I realized that they were trying to differentiate pop-sounding music with Christian lyrics from gospel. The only common denominator is the thrust of the lyric—the music runs the gamut from hard rock to jazzy stuff to four fat guys and a tenor slapped up onstage. I didn't grow up with any gospel influence—I never went to a Christian concert. I didn't feel the pressure of 'I'm a deviant.' I'm just singing."

Grant realized her role as contemporary Christian music's chance at pop stardom during a concert in Omaha. Playing to 1,500 people in a hall adjacent to an arena where the rock group Styx was playing to 15,000, she "could hear the echoes coming through the wall. So during a break I went and looked at all of the smoke bombs and risers and lighting systems. I thought, 'Whew! If I want to get the attention of the kids today, it is not going to happen the way I'm doing it now.' People said I didn't need a larger lighting system—'It's too flashy.' I say kids are being manipulated by *something* these days—why not let it be the Lord?"

So Grant embarked on her own crusade. She wouldn't be satisfied until she cracked the popular music mainstream, where she felt she belonged. Within the year, *Straight Ahead* was picked up for distribution by A&M Records, which re-issued the record as Grant appeared on the Grammy Awards singing "Angels," which won for Best Gospel Performance, Female.

"We can't hold back and try to win the approval of everybody," she conceded. "I'm not trying to sound disrespectful—I know I'll only sing to a handful of people in my life in the scheme of things—but it's my calling." ■

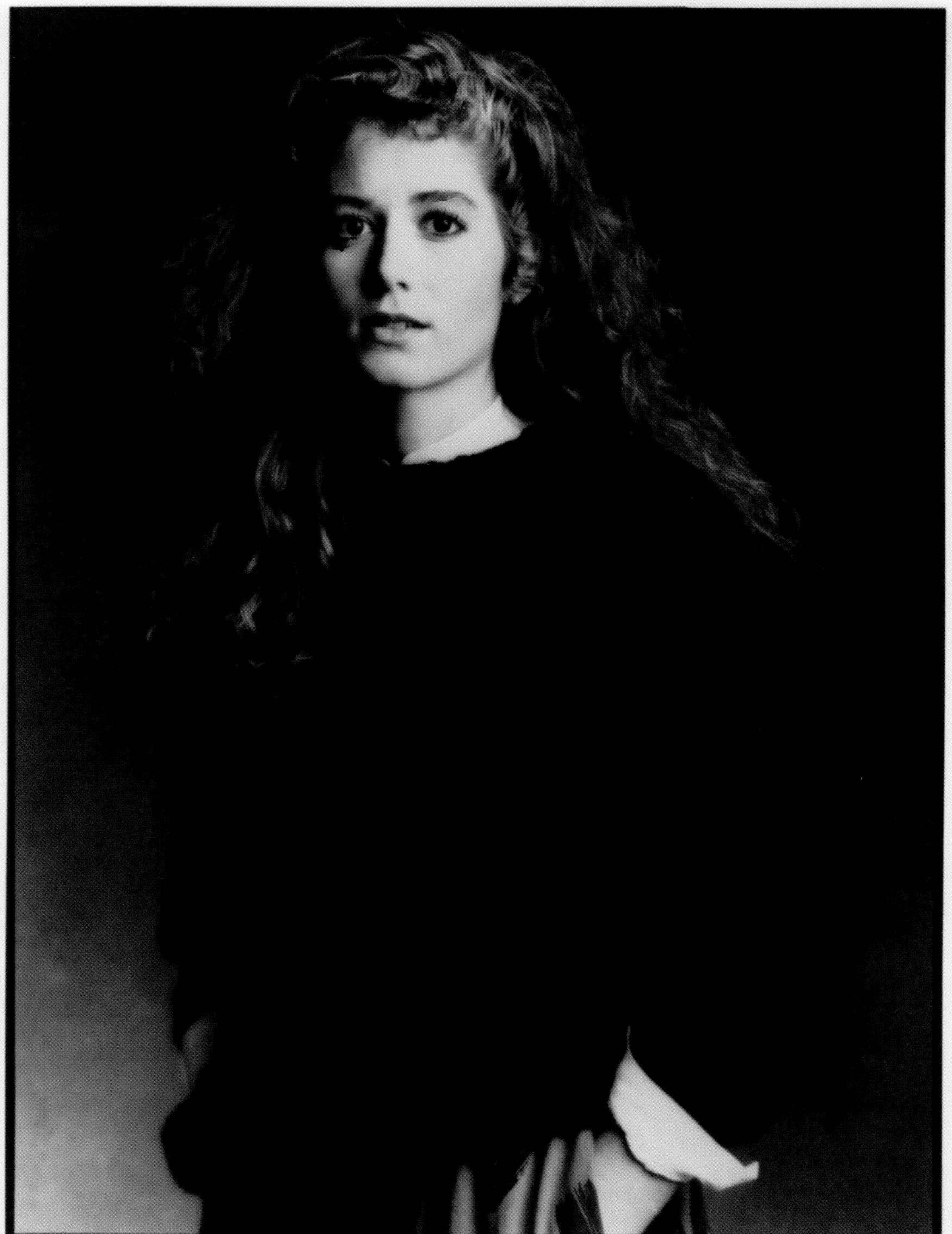

AMY GRANT

Exclusive management:
Blanton/Harrell Productions
(615) 329-2611

A&M RECORDS
Printed in U.S.A.

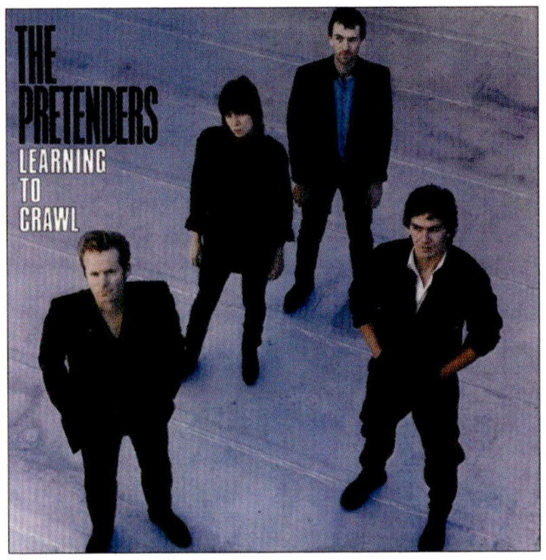

The Pretenders issued *Learning to Crawl* after a hiatus and the departures of two original bandmates.

Billboard 200: *Learning to Crawl* (#5)
Billboard Hot 100: "Back on the Chain Gang" (#5); "Middle of the Road" (#19); "Show Me" (#28); "Thin Line Between Love and Hate" (#83)

THE DEMANDS on a rock musician's time were challenging enough without the added pressures of parenthood, but Chrissie Hynde, the lead singer for the Pretenders, took her little Natalie on tour, breast-feeding by day and playing concerts by night. "It's not that big of a deal, really," she noted during a rare moment of peace. "I'm just determined not to let my career shove around my life."

Ironically, life had been shoving around Hynde's career for the past year. When the Pretenders made their splash on the rock scene in 1979, it was obvious that the band had more staying power than any of its contemporaries. Hynde's intelligent approach to her craft, her explicit lyrics and the slashing interplay of drummer Martin Chambers, bassist Pete Farndon and guitarist James Honeyman-Scott yielded a hit single ("Brass in Pocket") and two outstanding albums.

But in June 1982, the group nearly disintegrated. Farndon quit because of a personality conflict, and one week later, Honeyman-Scott died from a cocaine overdose at the age of 25.

"It was, needless to say, a very tough time," Chambers reflected. "Pete had changed into a different person since the band had started, and it was tough to see him go (Farndon attempted to start another band but died from drug abuse in April 1983). And James was my best friend in the world—forget how important he was to the band."

The sudden and traumatic depletion of the group's ranks tempted Hynde and Chambers to call it quits, but by summer's end they decided to persevere. The group had been rehearsing a song called "Back on the Chain Gang" before the upheaval, and a hit version was recorded using some friends (including guitarist Billy Bremner from Rockpile). When it came time to record an album, however, they had to assemble a permanent unit.

"James actually pulled us out of that one before he died," Chambers recalled. "At one point in time, we had considered adding another guitarist to the band—that would have allowed James to play some keyboards onstage and flesh out the sound. He recommended a friend, Robbie McIntosh. We never ended up adding him back then, but when James passed on, Robbie seemed like the logical replacement."

MacIntosh suggested another acquaintance, Malcolm Foster, to join as bassist. The reconstituted lineup went into the studio with producer Chris Thomas to work on *Learning to Crawl.*

"Chrissie is handling everything really well—it just seems like she's realloted her time," Chambers mused. "We used to go into rehearsal for five hours. Now we play for two hours and she disappears for a while to tend to the kid. But we seem to have pulled out of our rut. I didn't think we were capable of that, but there seems to be something special going on here." ■

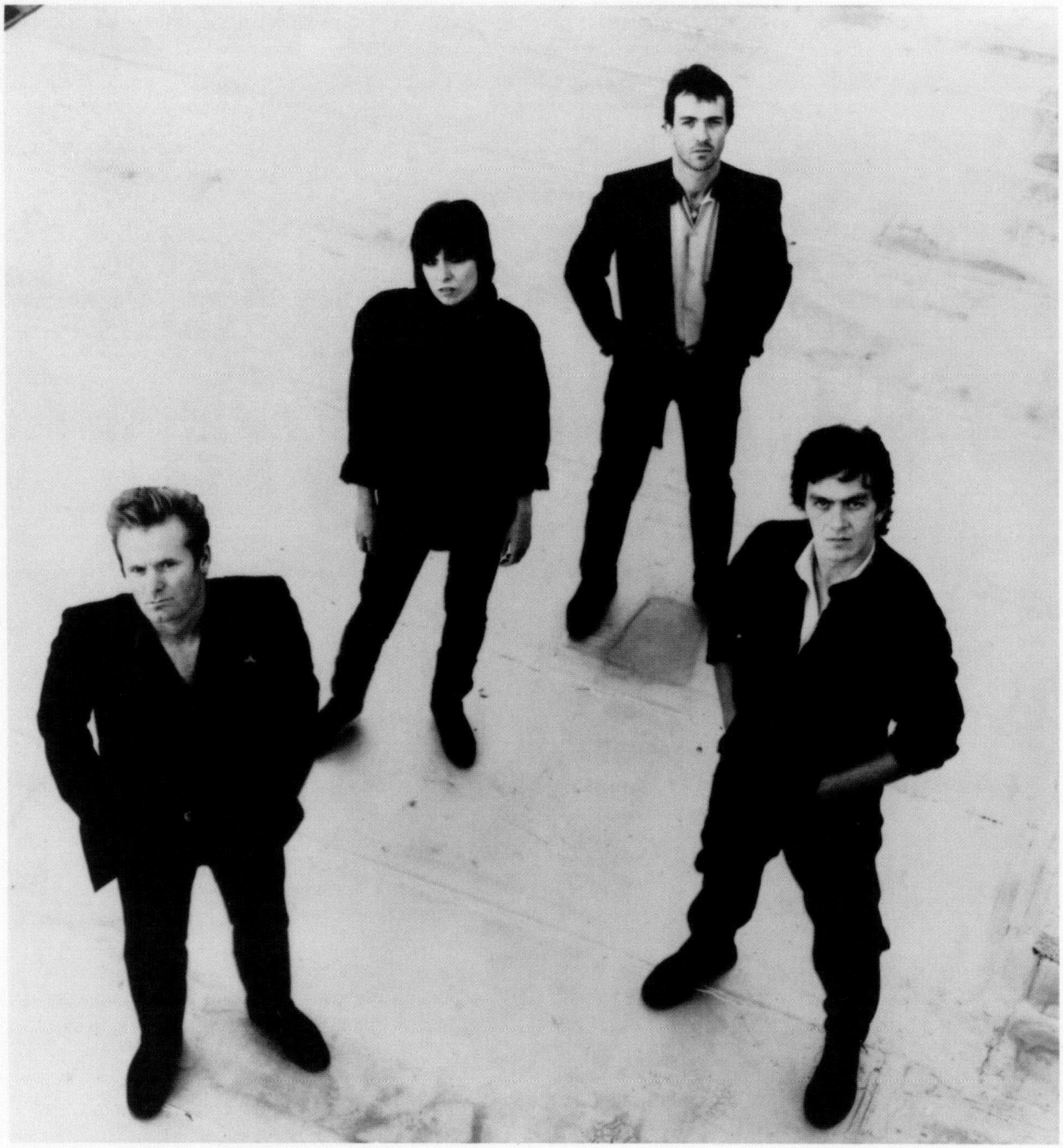

January, 1984

MARTIN CHAMBERS CHRISSIE HYNDE ROB MACINTOSH MALCOLM FOSTER

PRETENDERS

SIRE™

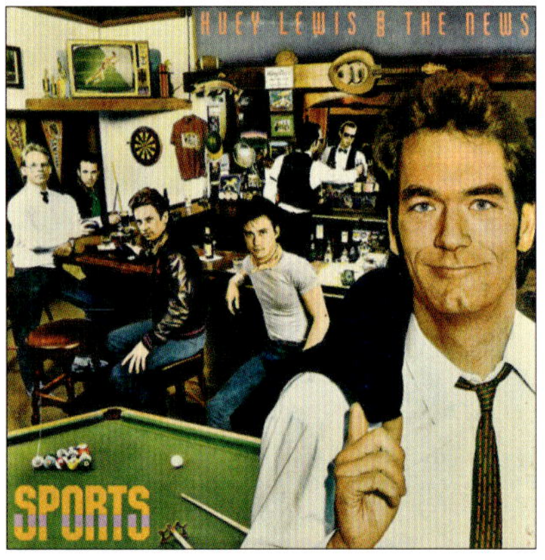

Billboard 200: *Sports* (No. 1)
Billboard Hot 100: "Heart and Soul" (#8); "I Want a New Drug" (#6); "The Heart of Rock & Roll" (#6); "If This Is It" (#6); "Walking on a Thin Line" (#18)

Huey Lewis & the News were propelled to international prominence by five smash singles from *Sports*.

HUEY LEWIS paid his musical dues in the Seventies, when he nurtured his chops with the veteran San Francisco band Clover. The group traveled to England to gig with Elvis Costello and other burgeoning new wavers, but the punk explosion made it impossible for outfits carrying the pub-rock label to continue, and Clover disbanded.

"Our records were too low-budget, and the timing was wrong—it's a luck thing," Lewis noted. "But I learned a lot from the English guys. Here were people who didn't have shag haircuts and high tenor voices, but they were getting over. I thought, 'Wow, I can do it like that!' They surrounded themselves with friends and did it on their own terms rather than chasing the proverbial rock 'n' roll duck."

The singer organized his troops, and Huey Lewis & the News made a lasting impression on the public. Having built a strong following by touring heavily, Lewis watched everything his band released get gobbled up with *Sports*—five singles became radio staples, and Lewis' down-to-earth image played well on MTV (an irony, considering he was the son of a jazz-buff father and hippie-artist mother). The group managed to be a self-contained unit, producing its own records.

"We fight a lot, but our band is like a team—we're tight like that," Lewis laughed. "The buck stops with me, but we all pitch in. There's not a San Francisco sound anymore, but there is a San Francisco feel or attitude. We're in that tradition—before we were in a band, we were all friends, and I think that's important in what sets us apart."

It was apparent from the title of the smash album that Lewis and his band of affable guys harbored an interest in athletics.

"Everyone thinks we're such big sports fans, but a couple of guys in the group can't even tell you how many outs there are in a baseball inning," the singer joked. "We try to cover all the bases—we're like a commercial Grateful Dead. I know the rap—how can our tunes be any good when we're not creeps? I guess that's just our tough luck, being regular guys. But that's okay. I'll get an attitude going one of these days." ■

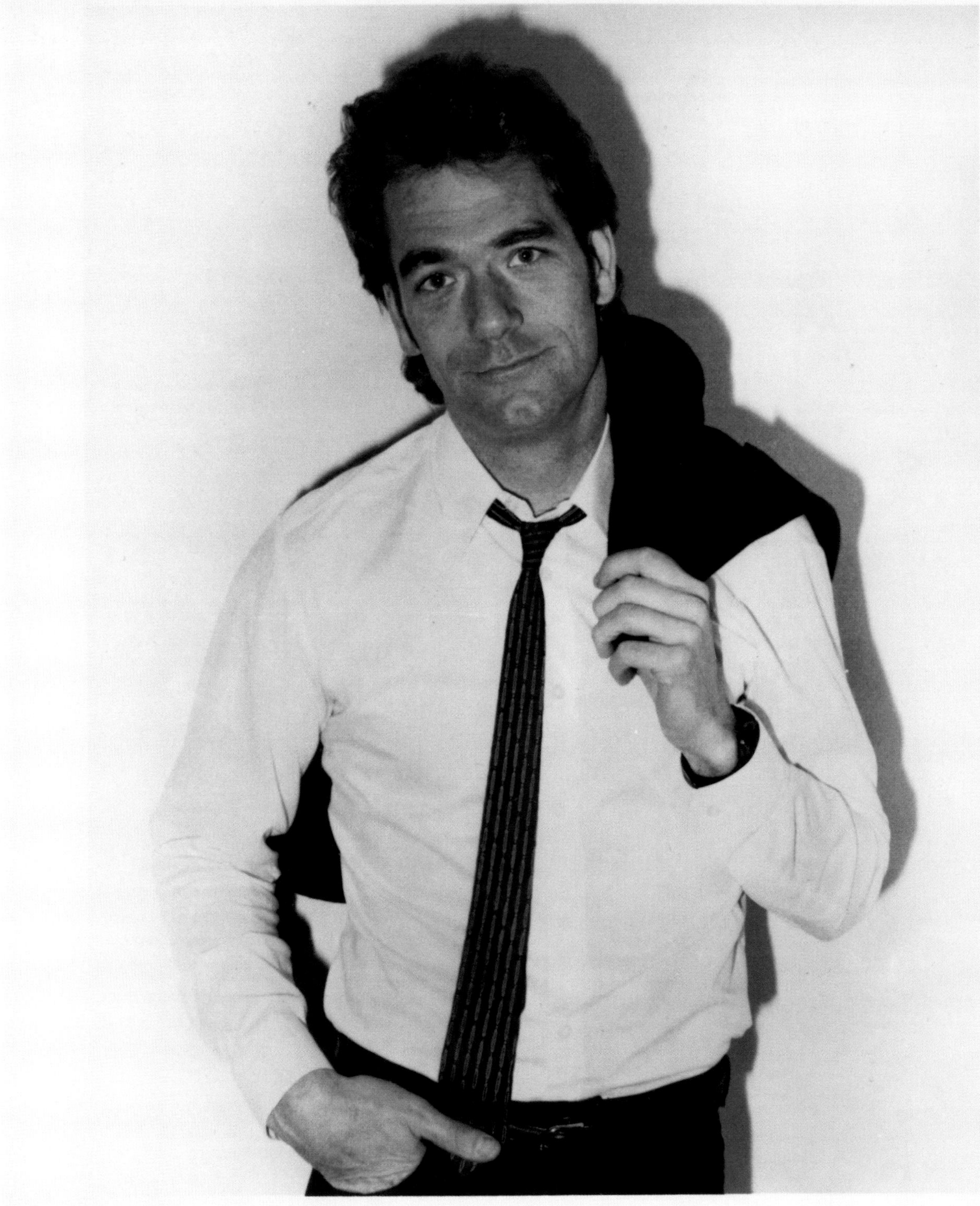

HUEY LEWIS

Chrysalis™

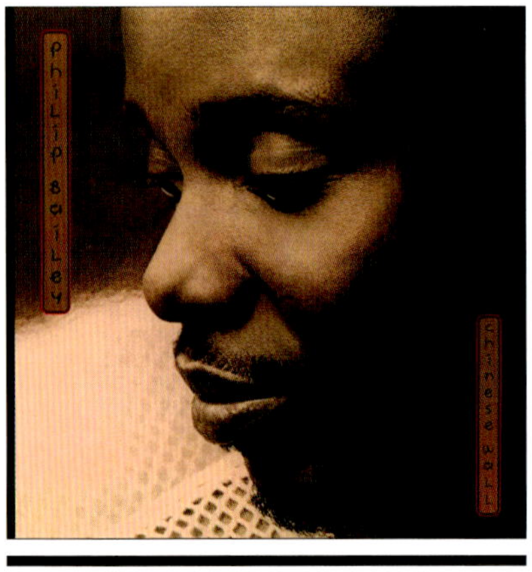

Billboard 200: *Chinese Wall* (#22)
Billboard Hot 100: "Easy Lover" (#2);
"Walking on the Chinese Wall" (#46)

"Easy Lover," a catchy duet with Phil Collins, helped Philip Bailey's *Chinese Wall* scale the charts.

A DOZEN years of work with Earth, Wind & Fire had gained Philip Bailey global recognition. He was the co-lead singer for the famed pop/R&B band, the soaring falsetto that dominated the hits. While Earth, Wind & Fire was working steadily, Bailey suppressed his solo urges, even though his role in the band was shrinking as leader and founder Maurice White sang more leads.

"The responsibility in the Fire has changed. Maurice uses the band as his solo project," Bailey said. "I'm a role player, and that has necessitated my solo projects, because there's so much more I want to say."

Bailey achieved success with the hit single "Easy Lover," a duet he co-wrote and sang with superstar producer and musician Phil Collins. When Collins attended an Earth, Wind & Fire concert in 1981, he was impressed and subsequently used the group's Phoenix Horns for several sessions. Bailey was similarly taken with Collins' talent upon seeing him at a Los Angeles performance in 1983. The recording of *Chinese Wall* finally allowed the two to join forces.

"There was a lot of music brewing inside of me that I wanted to share on record," Bailey said. "It's a pleasure to work with Phil—after so much success, he is still as much in love with his art now as when he first began to sing and write. That's been inspirational to me."

Bailey had a dual identity as a vocalist. While he recorded best-selling pop records, he was also a contemporary Christian artist. *The Wonders of His Love*, his first gospel album, peaked at #17 on the gospel chart.

"The Christian audience is a lot different than the secular audience," Bailey explained. "They're not as dependent on the hit record. It's just too bad that being on a gospel label has certain promotional restrictions. These messages need to be heard by everybody at large. It's not that my other work isn't meaningful, but a record can be a hit and not have much substance to it." ■

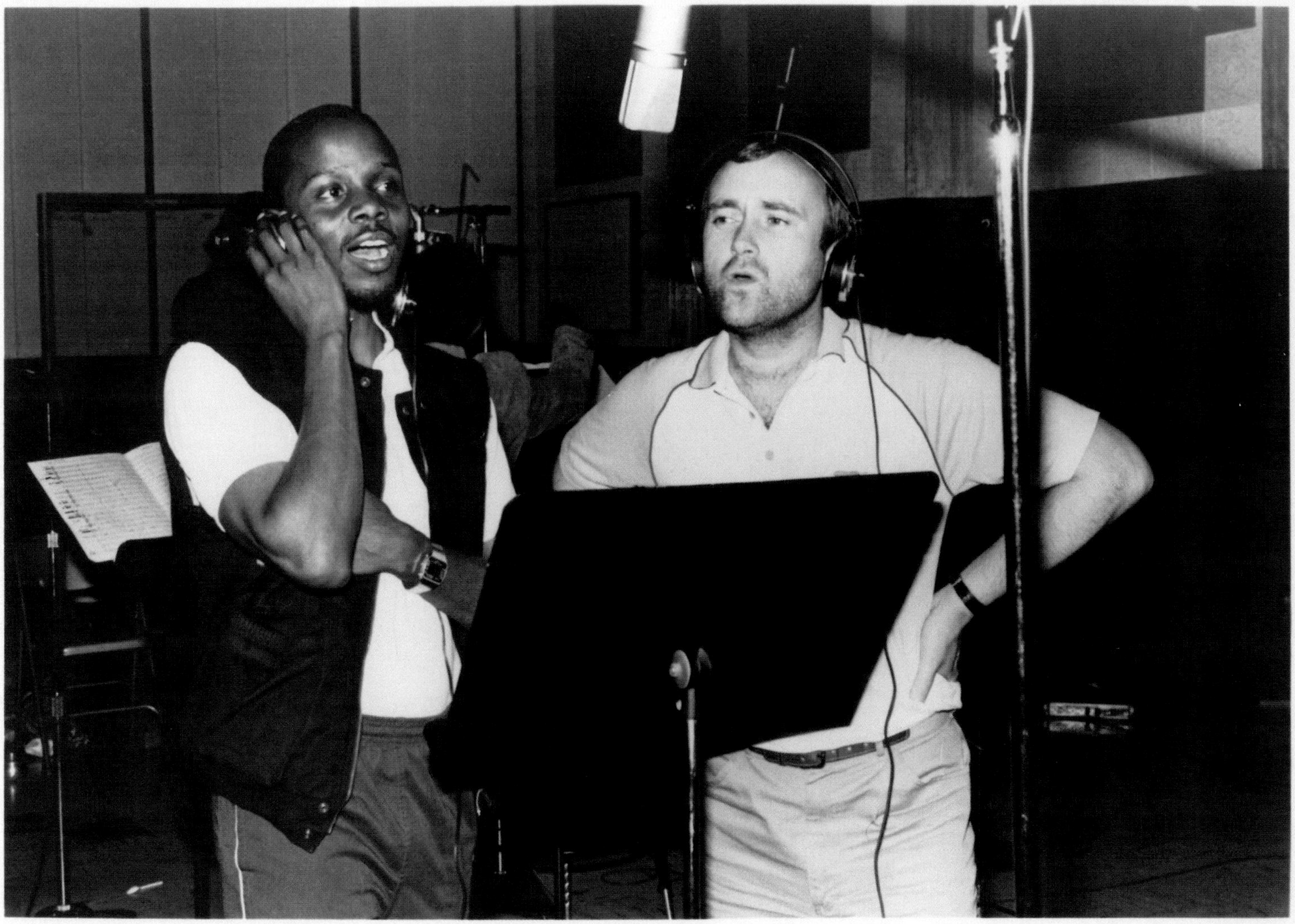

PHOTOGRAPH: LESTER COHEN

In the studio PHILIP BAILEY (left) and PHIL COLLINS (right).

PHILIP BAILEY

Columbia 8407

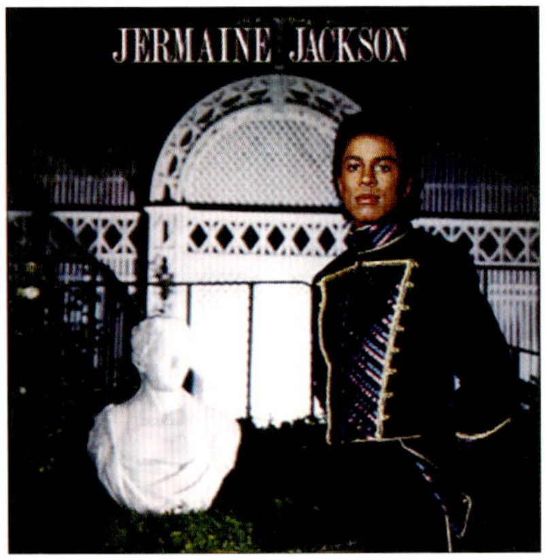

Jermaine Jackson scored a couple of big hits from his first album after shunning his Motown family.

Billboard 200: *Jermaine Jackson* (#19)
Billboard Hot 100: "Dynamite" (#15);
"Do What You Do" (#13)

BACK IN the early Seventies, Jermaine Jackson, the fourth of the Jackson family's nine children, faced a situation similar to what his brother Michael would encounter—that is, he was marketed as the first black teen sex symbol. He sang about love and heartbreak. He posed shirtless for every fan magazine in existence. He drove the young girls gaga. And then he got married.

"It happens to a lot of teen idols, even Elvis Presley and Mick Jagger," Jackson said. "You get married, and some girls see that as a reason to stop screaming. Those were wild times. I was 16 when the Jackson 5 was hot, and Michael was too young to get the girls' attention—so they all looked at me."

Jackson felt the wrath of his fans in 1975 when he refused to leave Motown Records with his brothers, who jumped ship to Epic Records. But Jackson survived the backlash—in 1984, *Jermaine Jackson*, recorded for a new label, Arista Records, became the No. 1 R&B album, featuring "Do What You Do" and the dance number "Dynamite."

"I sat down with my father-in-law (Berry Gordy Jr., president of Motown) and discussed my leaving," Jackson explained. "I wanted to see what it's like to be myself, to be independent enough to hold responsibility. If it wasn't for him, I wouldn't be on Arista—I had 45 years left on my contract at Motown. But they planted the seed—the Jackson 5. That seed grew into a beautiful tree with many branches—Michael, myself, the Jacksons, LaToya, Janet (his sisters)."

Subsequently, he rejoined the Jacksons in time for their "Victory" tour. He was allowed to showcase "Tell Me I'm Not Dreamin' (Too Good to Be True)" from his album, a duet with Michael. Jackson was angered that the corporate powers-that-be refused permission to release the song as an official single, although it received a lot of airplay.

"The world wanted to hear me and Michael singing again, and for two record company presidents to decide that two brothers can't sing together was disappointing. But I swallowed it. That's my whole attitude—you get knocked down, you get back up..." ■

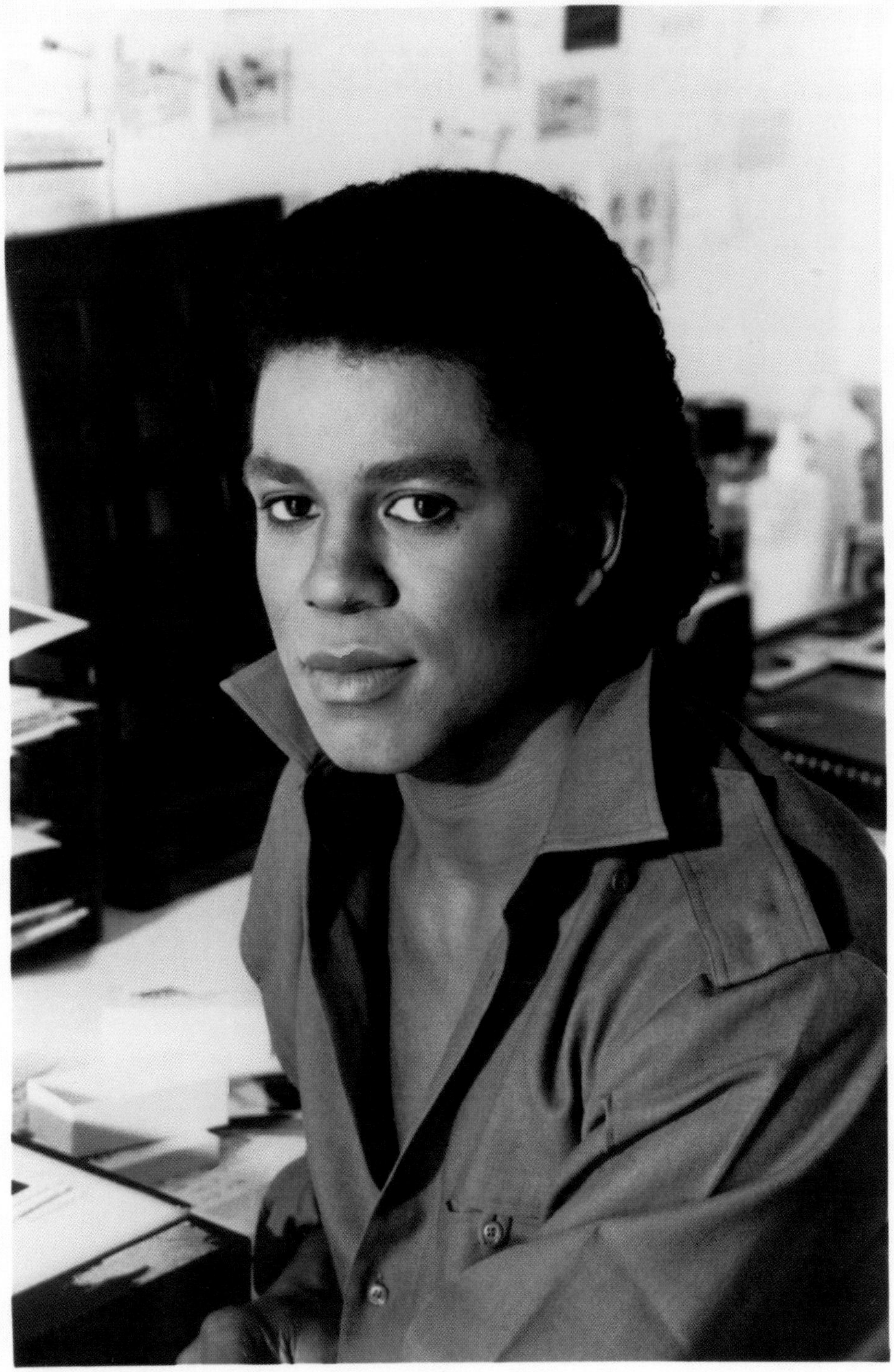

JERMAINE JACKSON

ARISTA

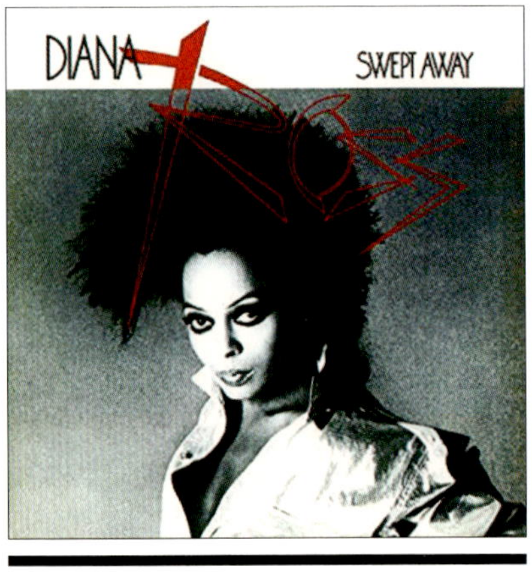

Billboard 200: *Swept Away* (#26)
Billboard Hot 100: "All of You" (#19); "Swept Away" (#19); "Missing You" (#10)

Diana Ross' *Swept Away* featured the hit "Missing You," dedicated to the late, legendary Marvin Gaye.

SINGER, ACTRESS, performer, businesswoman—over the course of her 25-year professional career, Diana Ross had established that her talents couldn't be restricted to one medium. But for all of her worldliness, Ross was still learning.

"I started off in this career being very sheltered," the former lead singer of the Supremes recalled. "I'm just now learning to interact with people, on a one-to-one. That's a whole new stage in my life. Most people don't understand that performers are protected so much sometimes that they don't get a chance to live their lives. People ask me, 'How do you walk around without security? How could you do this without somebody with you?' And it's my pleasure to finally not have the fear. I mean, I'm out there with the kids and people—and I never got a chance to do that. So this is a good time for me."

Much of Ross' enthusiasm stemmed from *Swept Away*, a solid set of hits. "All of You" was a duet with Julio Iglesias. The title track was written and produced by Daryl Hall. And the ballad "Missing You," produced and written by Lionel Richie, paid tribute to Marvin Gaye, who had been murdered by his father earlier that year.

Given her business ventures and her performance and recording activities, Ross' energy appeared to be endless, but she admitted to a darker side of the entire scene.

"I'm not all balanced as I would like to be as far as pleasure and my work. I should go out dancing more often, but I work a lot. I don't want to say I'm a workaholic, but it's work in my career which is also a pleasure, in a sense. But I don't have a lot of vacations and that. I'd like to have more fun." ■

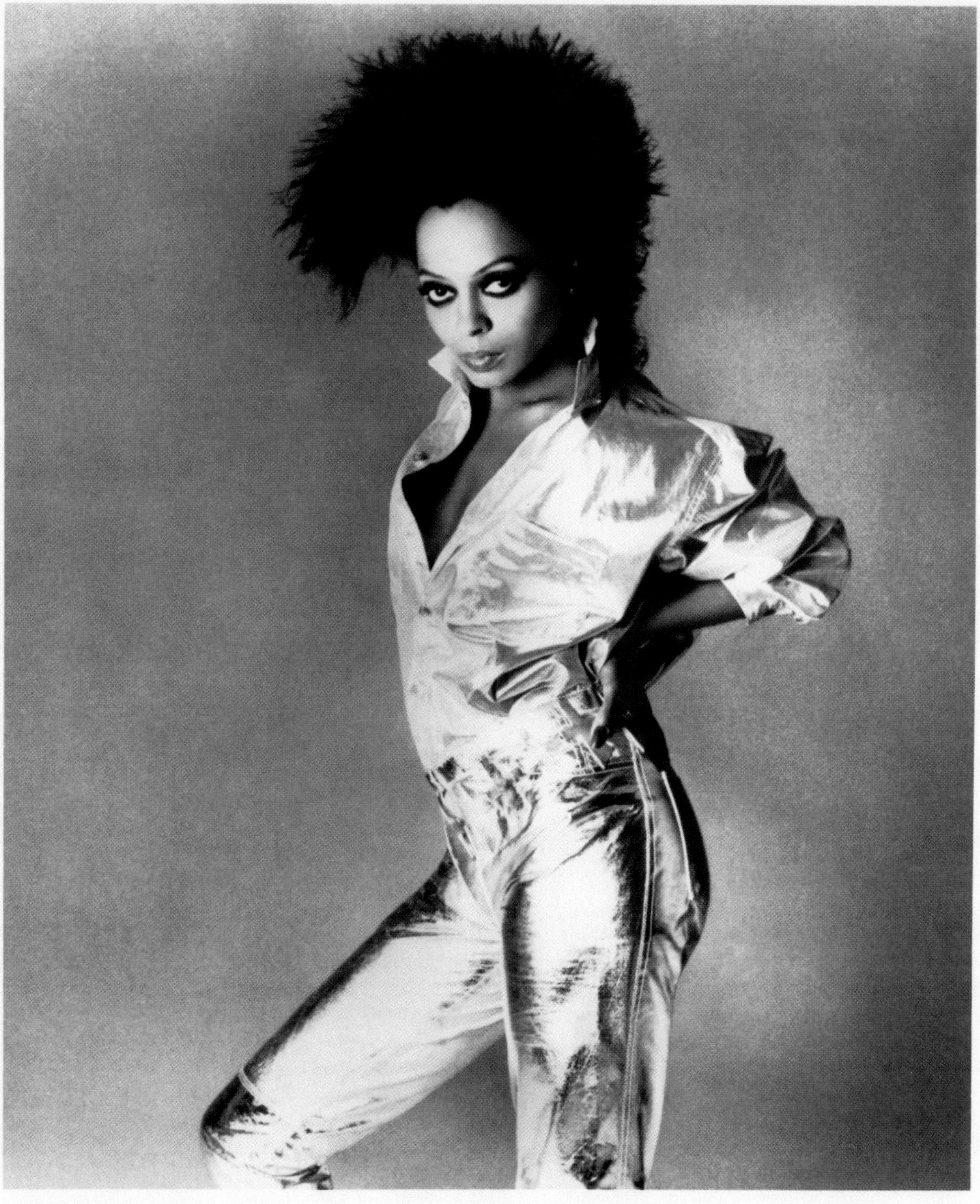

DIANA ROSS

RCA Records and Cassettes

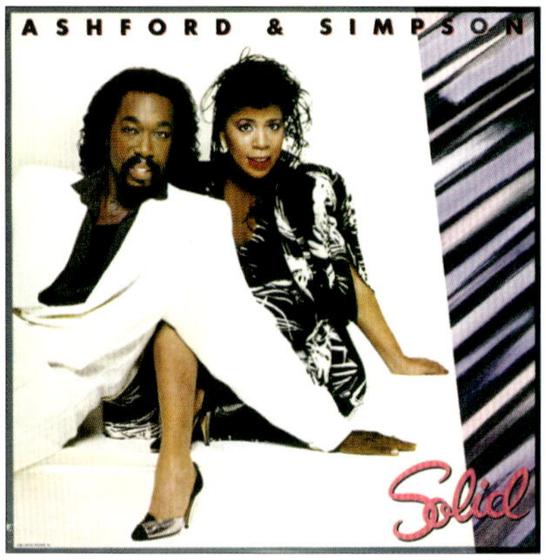

The songwriting alliance of Ashford & Simpson enjoyed its greatest success as performers with "Solid."

Billboard 200: *Solid* (#29)
Billboard Hot 100: "Solid" (#12)

NICK ASHFORD and Valerie Simpson's approach to R&B music was both sophisticated and progressive, with sleek production values enhanced by the natural chemistry between the two singers. The trademark combination of warmth and energy had marked the various phases of the husband-and-wife team's long career.

In the early Sixties, they made their mark as songwriting collaborators, penning such classics as "Let's Go Get Stoned" and "I Don't Need No Doctor" for Ray Charles and hits for the pairing of Marvin Gaye & Tammi Terrell.

In the Seventies, Ashford & Simpson made the transition from staff songwriters to recording artists, notching such hits as "Don't Cost You Nothing," "It Seems to Hang On" and "Found a Cure" under their own name. They also continued to work with other artists, achieving successes with Diana Ross, Chaka Khan and Gladys Knight & the Pips.

Their recording career enjoyed a resurgence with "Solid," their best-known duet. A chart-topping soul hit, it also made the pop chart.

"The pop audience is going to have to gravitate to our music—we're not going to change the music we love," Ashford said.

"Solid" was marked by some high harmonizing and Simpson's synthesizer work, with the lyrics representing the joys of wedded bliss.

"The idea for the title came from the streets, hanging out," Simpson explained. "Everybody uses that slang, and I thought I might as well apply it to the kind of relationship we have. We just hit people with dazzle and glitter and a lotta love." ■

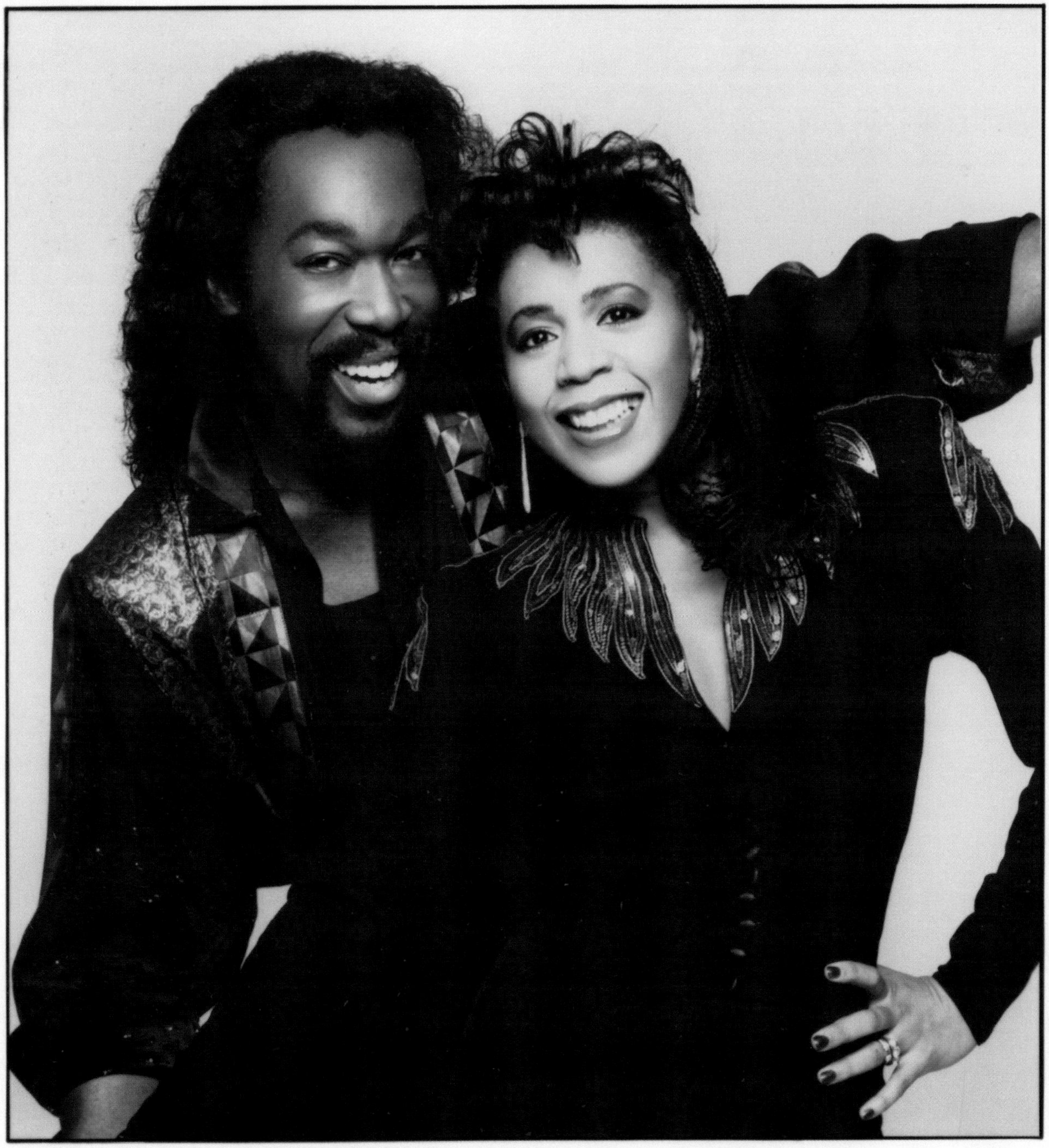

Photo: Bret Lopez / 1984

ASHFORD & SIMPSON

Capitol Records

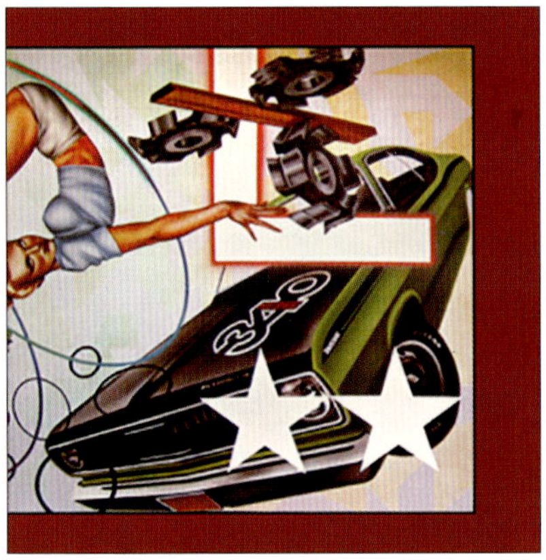

The Cars reconvened for *Heartbeat City*, featuring the Top 10 classics "Drive" and "You Might Think."

Billboard 200: *Heartbeat City* (#3)
Billboard Hot 100: "You Might Think" (#7); "Magic" (#12); "Drive" (#3); "Hello Again" (#20); "Why Can't I Have You" (#33)

AFTER 1981's *Shake It Up*, Ric Ocasek took a sabbatical from the Cars to commence work on his first solo album. The lanky lead Car had expressed the opinion that he and the other members—Greg Hawkes, Elliot Easton, Ben Orr and David Robinson—would self-produce their next record after utilizing Roy Thomas Baker for four albums.

"But when it came time to do it, I had just finished doing three records—my own, a Bad Brains record and an Iggy Pop record. I was starting to get tired of making all the decisions, so at the last minute we looked around for other producers."

They chose Robert John "Mutt" Lange, best known for his work with such decibel-busters as Def Leppard, AC/DC and Foreigner.

"I thought it would be an interesting combination, because we're not the type of band he'd normally do. He's used to doing guitar bands, and I know those are hard things to do, to get great records out of screaming guitars. I really respect Mutt for his capabilities as a sound technician. He's quite a perfectionist. I expected it to take eight weeks to make *Heartbeat City*, and it took six months, because he would try every conceivable way to get the perfect sound on tape."

The teaming of the two styles resulted in the band's fifth platinum album. "You Might Think," "Magic" and "Drive" all made big showings on the singles charts. The Cars hadn't ventured much into music video territory on past releases, but they gained ground with a vengeance, as Ocasek oversaw the production of five videos from the album.

"When we first thought about it, we were just going to do one, maybe two videos at the most," Ocasek enthused. "But then the record company got behind us. We had this idea that we would use directors that hadn't made any videos at all, so we kept making videos of songs that we weren't even sure would be singles." Andy Warhol directed the pop-art "Hello Again," while actor Timothy Hutton directed "Drive." "He's an old Cars fan," Ocasek confided. "We know him from hanging out backstage."

Ocasek estimated the price tag for "You Might Think," with its state-of-the-art technology, at a whopping quarter-million dollars, although he said the effects studio had absorbed the majority of the cost. The Cars won Video of the Year at the first MTV Video Music Awards.

Given the new emphasis on visuals, the Cars' tour featured the band's most exciting stage design yet, though rumors of internal squabbling persisted.

"There's some truism to it, but the real story is that the band has to have someone to oversee everything, and it just so happens that I usually do it," the notoriously stoic Ocasek chuckled. "I've always done it anyway, so it's nothing new." ■

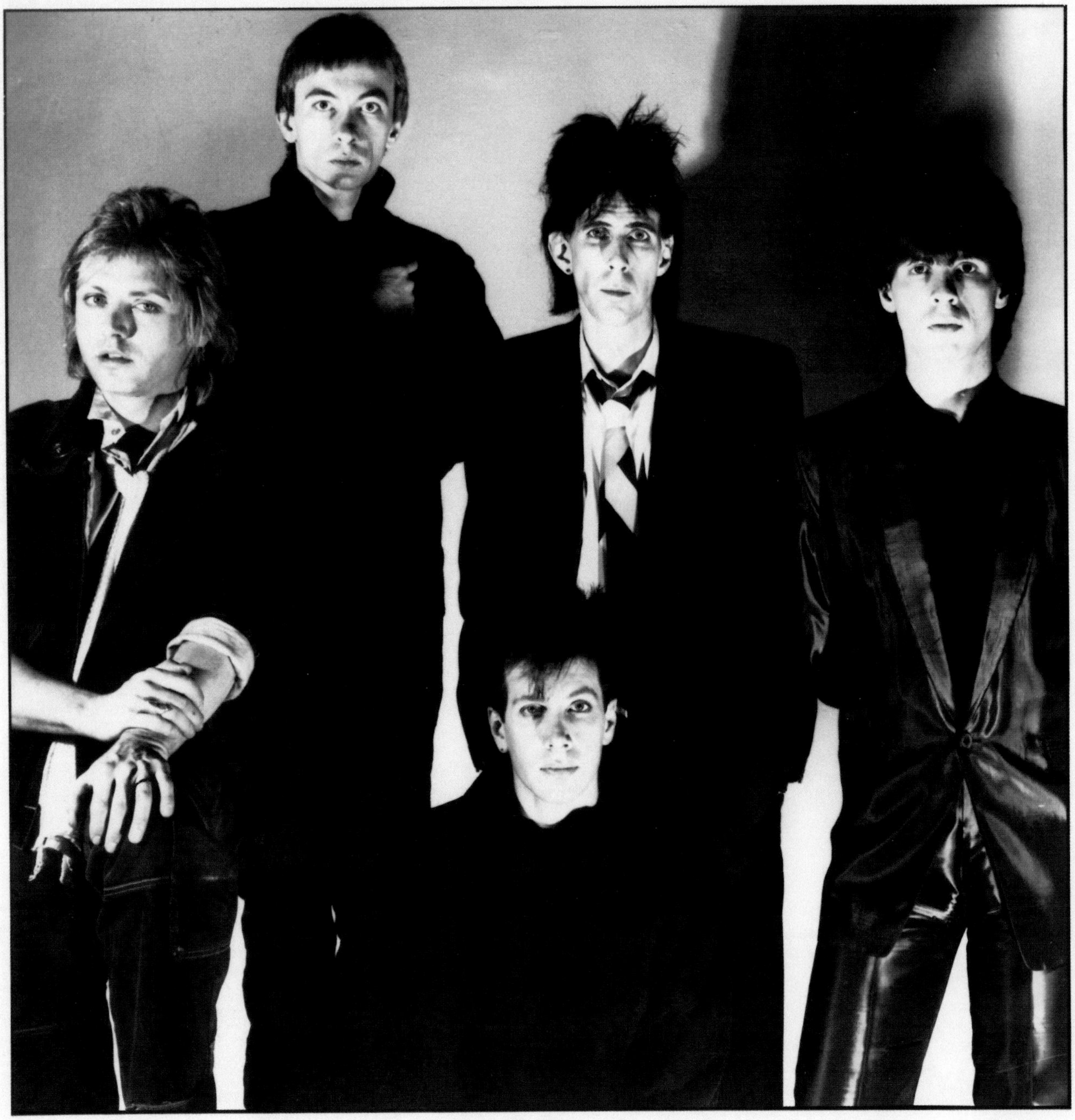

PHOTO CREDIT: GEORGE HOLZ /1984

BEN ORR GREG HAWKES DAVID ROBINSON RIC OCASEK ELLIOT EASTON

THE CARS

ELEKTRA

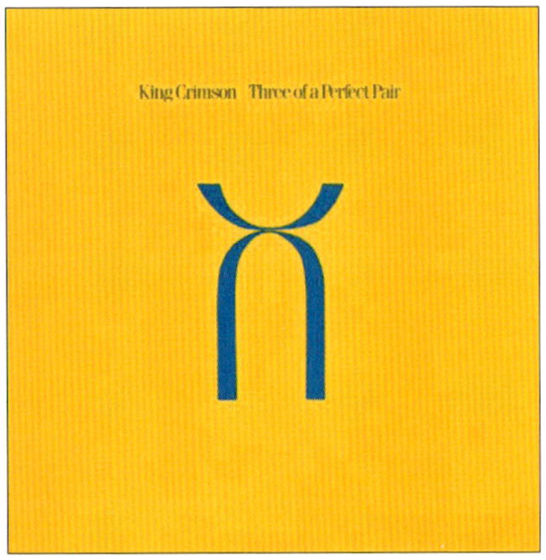

Billboard 200: *Three of a Perfect Pair* (#58)

King Crimson and founding member Robert Fripp were recognized as British progressive-rock royalty.

KING CRIMSON was a different but interesting guitar-hero band, best remembered for the sci-fi heavy-metal fury of "21st Century Schizoid Man" in 1969. Other songs found the band operating in a style one critic called "organized anarchy," but fans saw past the art-rock pretentions and respected the virtuosic musicianship. Led by Robert Fripp and ultimately reduced to a daring, focused power-trio concept, King Crimson released *Red* in 1974.

But Fripp broke up King Crimson rather than allowing it to get stale. He worked with Peter Gabriel, Daryl Hall, Brian Eno and David Bowie, and he had a hand in the development of the New York avant-garde music scene. In 1981, Fripp became interested in leading his own band again, reincarnating King Crimson in three consecutive albums with the same personnel: Fripp, drummer Bill Bruford, guitar wizard Adrian Belew and bassist Tony Levin. They gained respect for ferocious technique—their workouts on the *Disciple* and *Beat* albums were rhythmically knotty and harmonically exacting. By the time of *Three of a Perfect Pair*'s release, Fripp—despite his reputation as a less-than-democratic band leader—recognized that Crimson's identity in rock's experimental arena resulted more from collaboration than direction.

"The album presents the two distinct sides of the band's personality, which has caused at least as much confusion for the group as it has the public and the industry," Fripp said. "The left side is accessible, the right side excessive."

The song "Sleepless" verged on a commercial breakthrough, but King Crimson always remained vulnerable to Fripp's whims. The group splintered soon after.

"I went to sleep and King Crimson was not there at breakfast the following morning," Bruford admitted.

"The way I found out we broke up was through a fan," Levin added. "During an intermission, he said, 'Hey, I heard King Crimson is breaking up—they said so on MTV.' I said, 'It must be true.'" ■

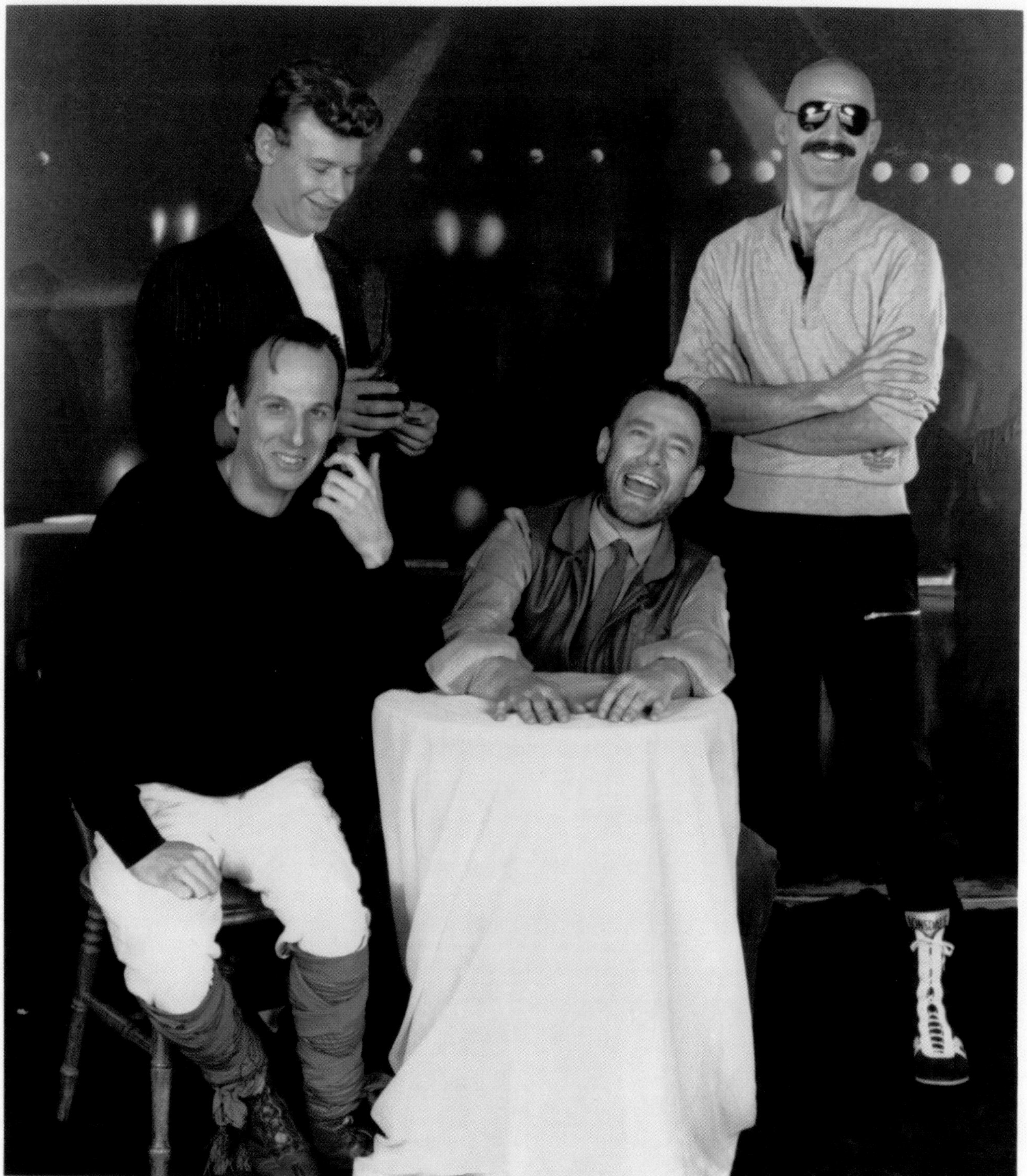

KING CRIMSON

eg

WARNER BROS.

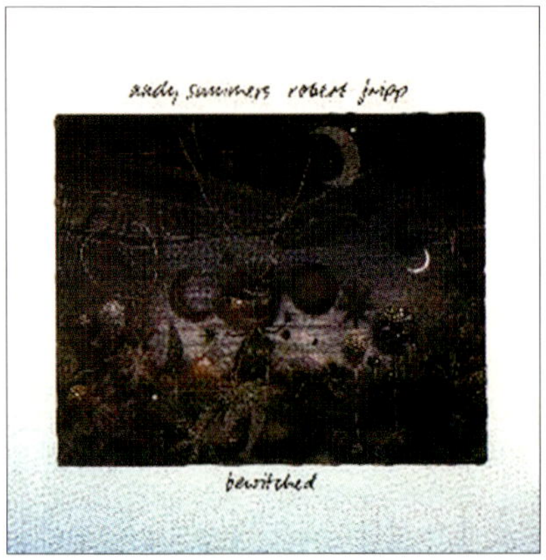

Guitarists **Andy Summers** and **Robert Fripp** paired up on *Bewitched*, the second of their two recordings.

THE POLICE, whose *Synchronicity* album was one of 1983's biggest successes, were dealing with the solo syndrome. Guitarist Andy Summers, the eldest member of the band, anticipated the division of interests, since he had sewn the seeds for a solo career over the years. *I Advance Masked*, a 1982 album recorded with King Crimson mastermind Robert Fripp, sold over 100,000 units in America, a respectable figure for a collection of progressive guitar textures.

So Summers expanded on that base, releasing a second Summers/Fripp collaboration, *Bewitched*.

"I would say it's a tad more accessible than the last one, sort of by design," Summers noted. "The first record was a moody, esoteric thing, so we came up with a 'dance' side on this album, with shorter, 'up' guitar instrumentals."

Despite Summers' disclaimer, however, *Bewitched* didn't adhere to verse-chorus-verse progressions. The album's centerpiece, the 11-minute "What Kind of Man Reads Playboy?," linked several non-vocal improvised sections together with extended abstract solos. The only single from the album, "Parade," failed to chart. But Summers wasn't concerned with commercial pressures—"Obviously, we're trying to express a different kind of music than I'm doing with the Police."

It became apparent that the three Police men were working their own beats.

"We don't need to stay together for the money anymore," Summers admitted with a shrug. "The reason to stay together now has to be really worthwhile musically. We have no plans to stay together, but we have no plans to break up. It's an open book—we'll see what gets written." ■

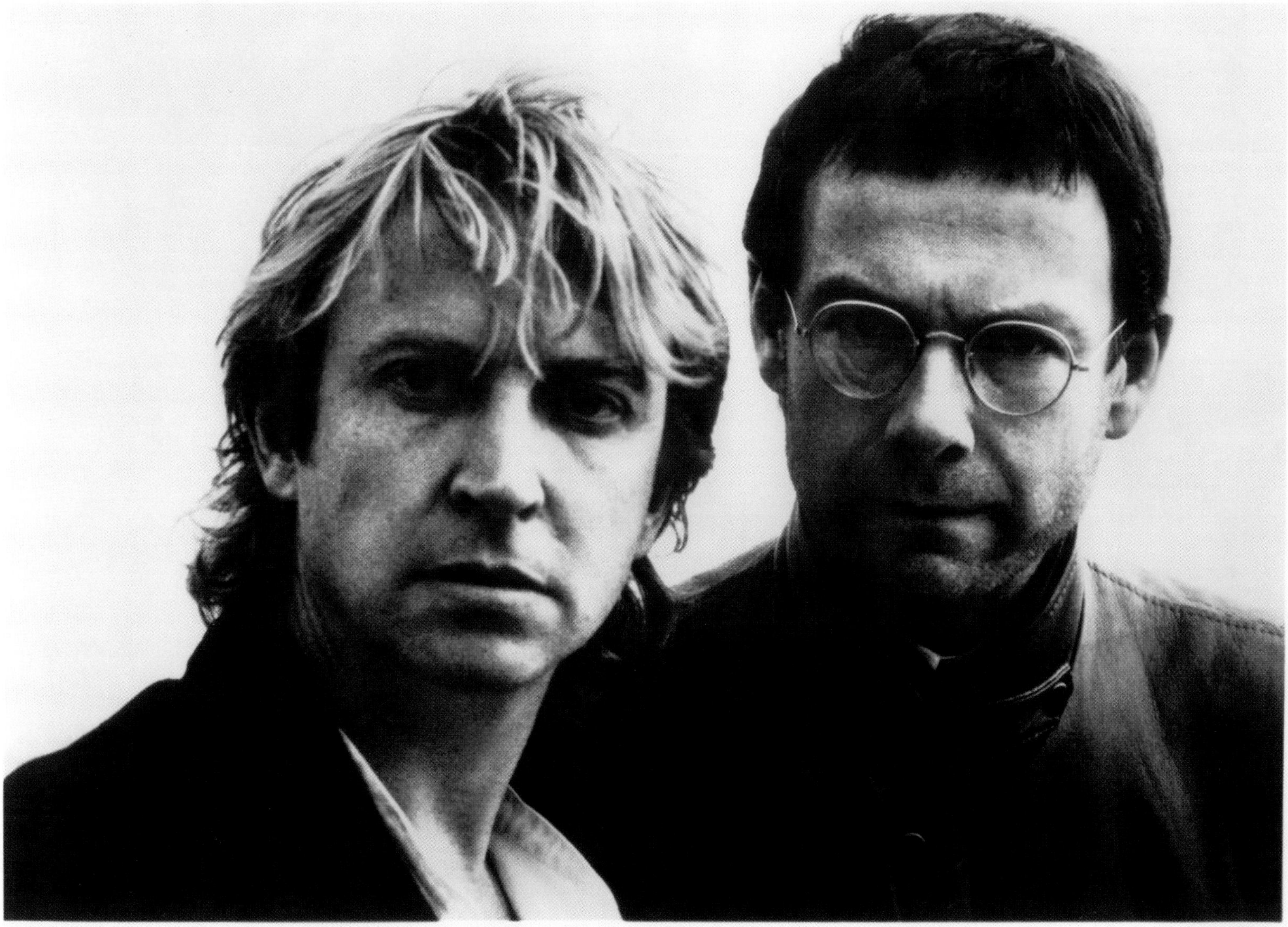

Andy Summers   Robert Fripp

Andy Summers & Robert Fripp

A&M RECORDS

Printed in U.S.A.

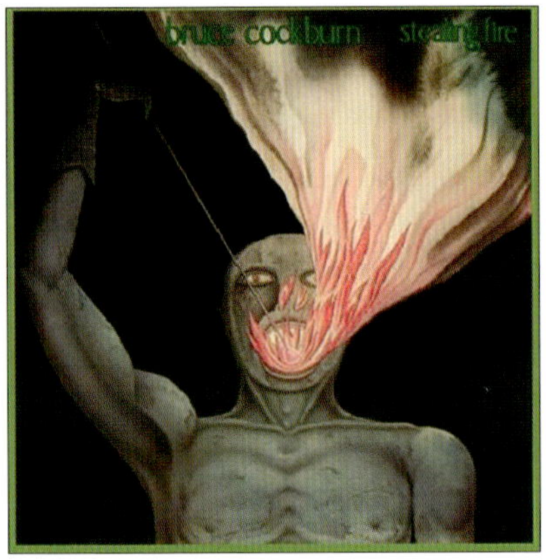

Politics and peace consumed Bruce Cockburn's *Stealing Fire* and the song "If I Had a Rocket Launcher."

Billboard 200: *Stealing Fire* (#74)
Billboard Hot 100: "If I Had a Rocket Launcher" (#88)

IN HIS 15-year recording career, Bruce Cockburn had shied away from celebrity trappings to produce consistently intriguing observations about human frailty. The soft-spoken musician fostered a journalist's knack for observation and a poet's skill for expression, which cemented his status as one of Canada's most important artists. In America, Cockburn had just one major hit, 1981's "Wondering Where the Lions Are."

But with *Stealing Fire,* he once again found his way onto US airwaves. The breakthrough coincided with the singer-songwriter's world crusade for human rights, and the single "If I Had a Rocket Launcher" was his finest merging of personal and political feelings. The venom in his voice was unprecedented, but the sentiments weren't to be construed as a call to arms; it was Cockburn's attempt to impart the frustrations he witnessed during a two-week tour through Nicaragua in 1983.

"They are feelings I never knew I had—feelings I'm not very proud of," he admitted. "I've been in some poor places, but that was the first time I'd been in a Third World country. I went through Oxfam (Oxford Famine Relief), which is a non-governmental aid agency. They asked me, hoping that my relative visibility in Canada would enable me to get the ear of enough people to spread the word of what is going on down there, in contrast to what is being reported."

Cockburn wrote "If I Had a Rocket Launcher" to "show how revolting the thought of killing is. I've tended to be apolitical like most Canadians because there's really nothing at stake. Now I've seen a new potential for involvement."

The record and tour were primarily a vehicle for Cockburn to spread the message about the problems in Central America.

"A lot of people don't know, which surprises me. Seeing a country at war and then seeing the difference from the one-sided images presented by the media here made me feel helpless and full of anger. But an artist's job is to make things emotionally accessible to people, to offer perspectives that somebody maybe didn't think about before. I can do that just by offering my own perspective." ■

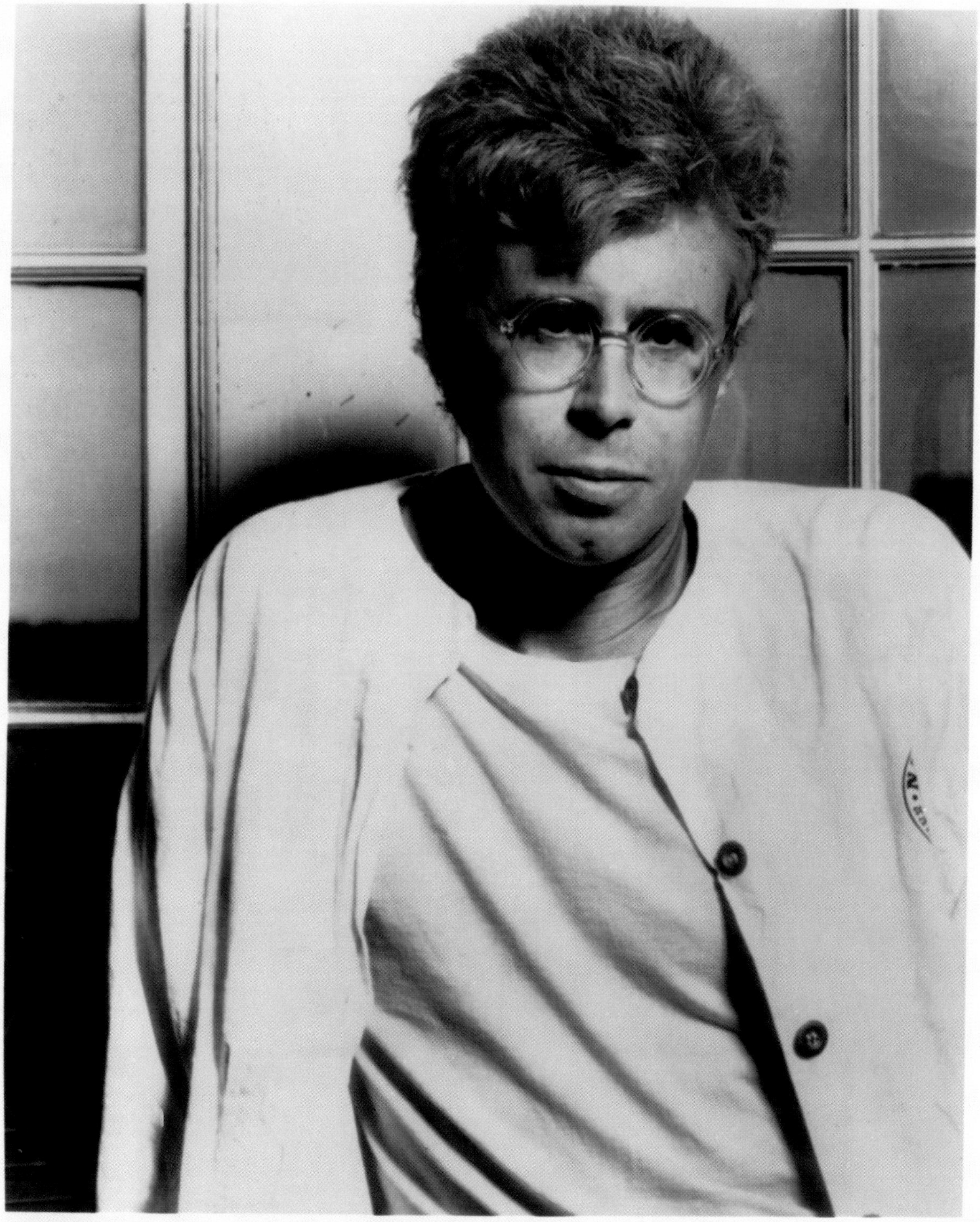

BRUCE COCKBURN

Gold Mountain®

MANAGEMENT:
Bernie Finkelstein
The Finkelstein Management Company Ltd.
(416) 364-6040

A&M RECORDS

Printed in U.S.A.

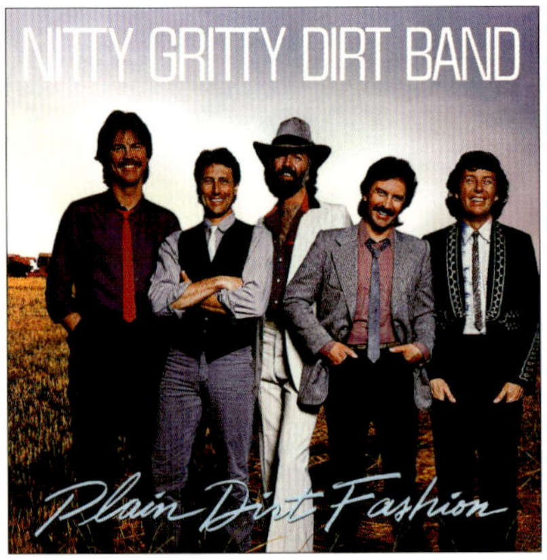

The Nitty Gritty Dirt Band's *Plain Dirt Fashion* spawned three country hits, reflecting the group's roots.

PLAYING ROCK, pop, country and other styles of songs, the Nitty Gritty Dirt Band had displayed an admirable penchant for musical eclecticism in its 17-year history. But by 1982, the band had reached a commercial nadir, foundering with no real direction. No one cared much about a group that sounded like the little-Eagles-that-could.

"I think our diversity has gotten in the way throughout our career," singer Jeff Hanna reflected. "I don't think the fact that we're unusual is good or bad, but playing everything from bluegrass to rock 'n' roll has dealt us our share of ups and downs over the years."

It was time for some changes. First, original members Hanna, John McEuen and Jimmie Fadden coerced Jimmy Ibbotson back into the fold, ending his six-year hiatus.

New management steered the musicians toward a country audience, and the group reverted to its original name after seven years as the Dirt Band. *Let's Go*, a 1983 release that returned the band to an identifiable rock-based country sound, landed the single "Dance Little Jean" on the Hot Country Songs Top 10.

"But even with a good-sized country hit, the record company couldn't sell any albums," Hanna said. "The Dirt Band was excess baggage—the president's chair kept switching around like it was some South American country, and since the newest regime hadn't signed us, they didn't care. In their defense, I don't blame them—how excited are they gonna get about us when they just signed David Bowie?"

The band began working with producers Marshall Morgan and Paul Worley, and midway through the ensuing album, the group switched to the Warner Brothers label. *Plain Dirt Fashion*, the resulting release, was straight country in its appeal, and audiences responded accordingly. "Long Hard Road (The Sharecropper's Dream)" was the Nitty Gritty Dirt Band's first country No. 1.

"It was the first song we recorded for the record, and we knew it was a centerpiece—we wanted to build the album around it. But we thought it was too outside to be a hit—it doesn't have a chorus that repeats itself, it's just a great little movie from top to bottom. Those type of songs aren't always hits, but this is wonderful—everything is coming together, important aspects of our career that go beyond the music. We should have dealt with them before now, but *c'est la vie*—now *there's* a couple of country words for ya!" ■

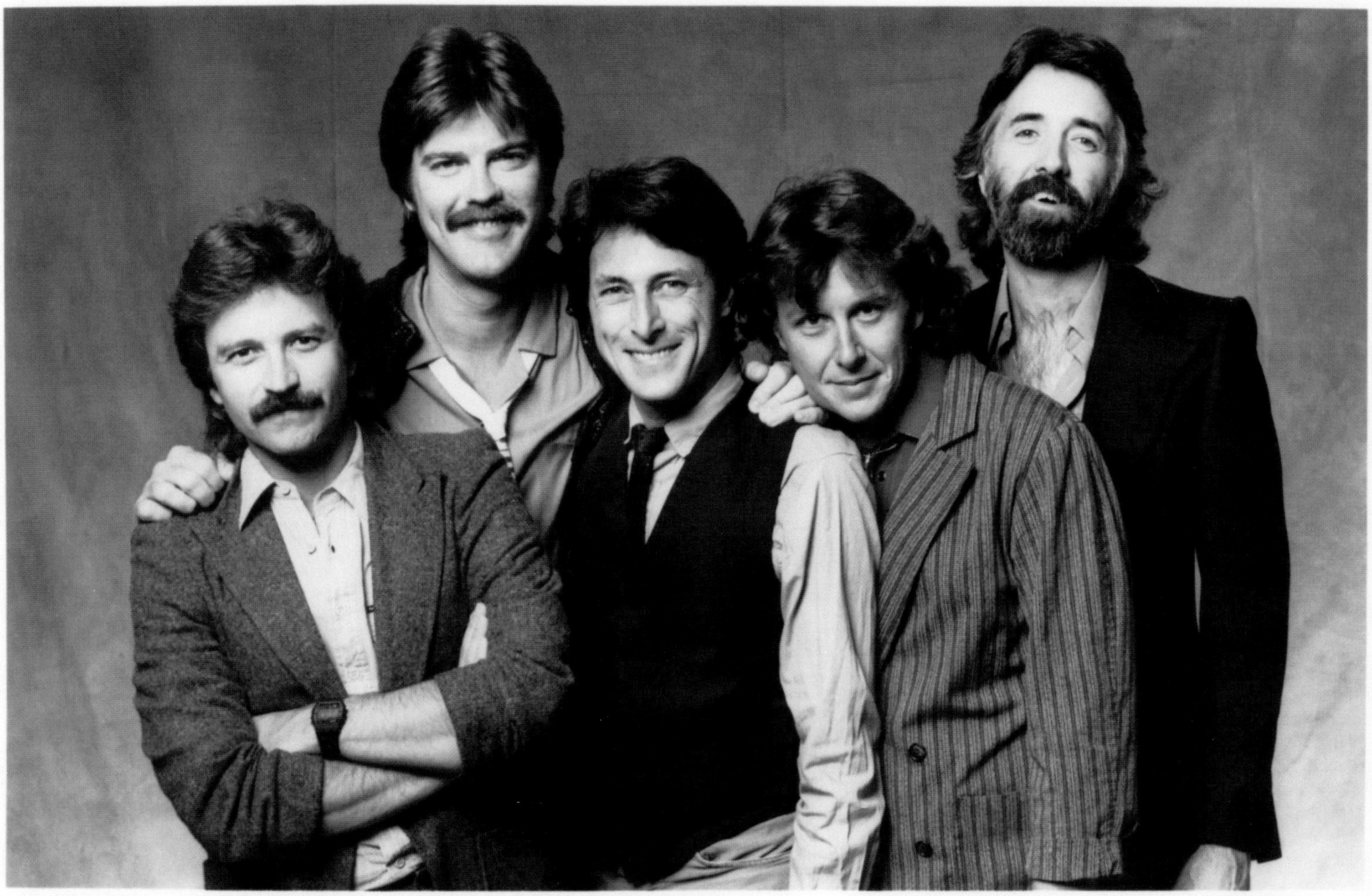

photo credit: Alan Messer 1984

The Nitty Gritty Dirt Band

WARNER BROS.

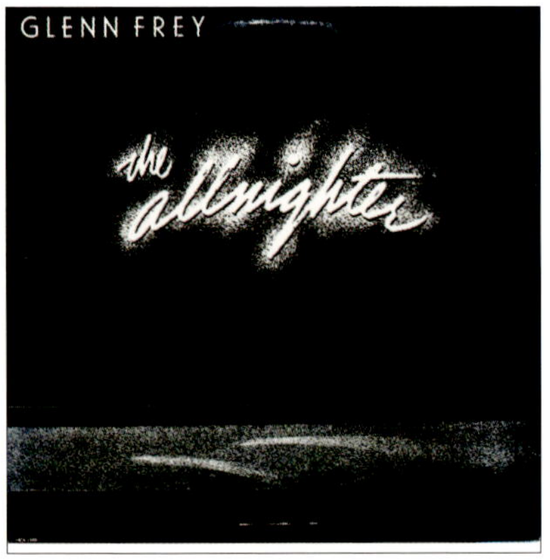

Billboard 200: *The Allnighter* (#37)
Billboard Hot 100: "Sexy Girl" (#20); "The Allnighter" (#54); "Smuggler's Blues" (#12)

Ex-Eagle Glenn Frey's solo single "Smuggler's Blues" led to an unexpected acting role on TV's *Miami Vice*.

WHEN THE Eagles disbanded around the turn of the decade, Glenn Frey realized that he had no career guarantees. The mystique surrounding the band's chart-topping popularity had been based on its members' relative anonymity.

"Nobody really knew what I looked like or who I was—or who anybody was in the Eagles, for that matter," the co-founding member of the group said.

But the phenomenon of the television series *Miami Vice* catapulted Frey into the solo spotlight. The hit "Smuggler's Blues," from *The Allnighter*, his second solo album, outlined the dangers of a drug smuggler's life and the pervasiveness of the drug trade. The song subsequently inspired an early episode of *Miami Vice* on which Frey guest-starred as a laid-back pilot.

"I just happened to be in the right place at the right time," he explained. "I was the first rock 'n' roller that (producer) Michael Mann asked to be on that show—to be followed by several hundred. But I got a great script based on 'Smuggler's Blues.' Not only did I get a role, but the tune became a hit and they aired the episode three times, which is unheard of."

With its stinging slide guitar, the bluesy, rocking feel of "Smuggler's Blues" outlined Frey's part of pop culture fabric.

"I'm no longer an underdog in my early 20s wearing blue jeans. I'm not selling angst anymore—that's just not me," Frey insisted. "Hey, I left a successful band—I'm not looking for underground recognition. I'm spoiled—I like everyone diggin' it. Once you know more about making music and records, you can't accept as much of the out-of-tune BS. I mean, it's not like your anger is quelled, it's like your ability to express yourself takes on a subtlety." ■

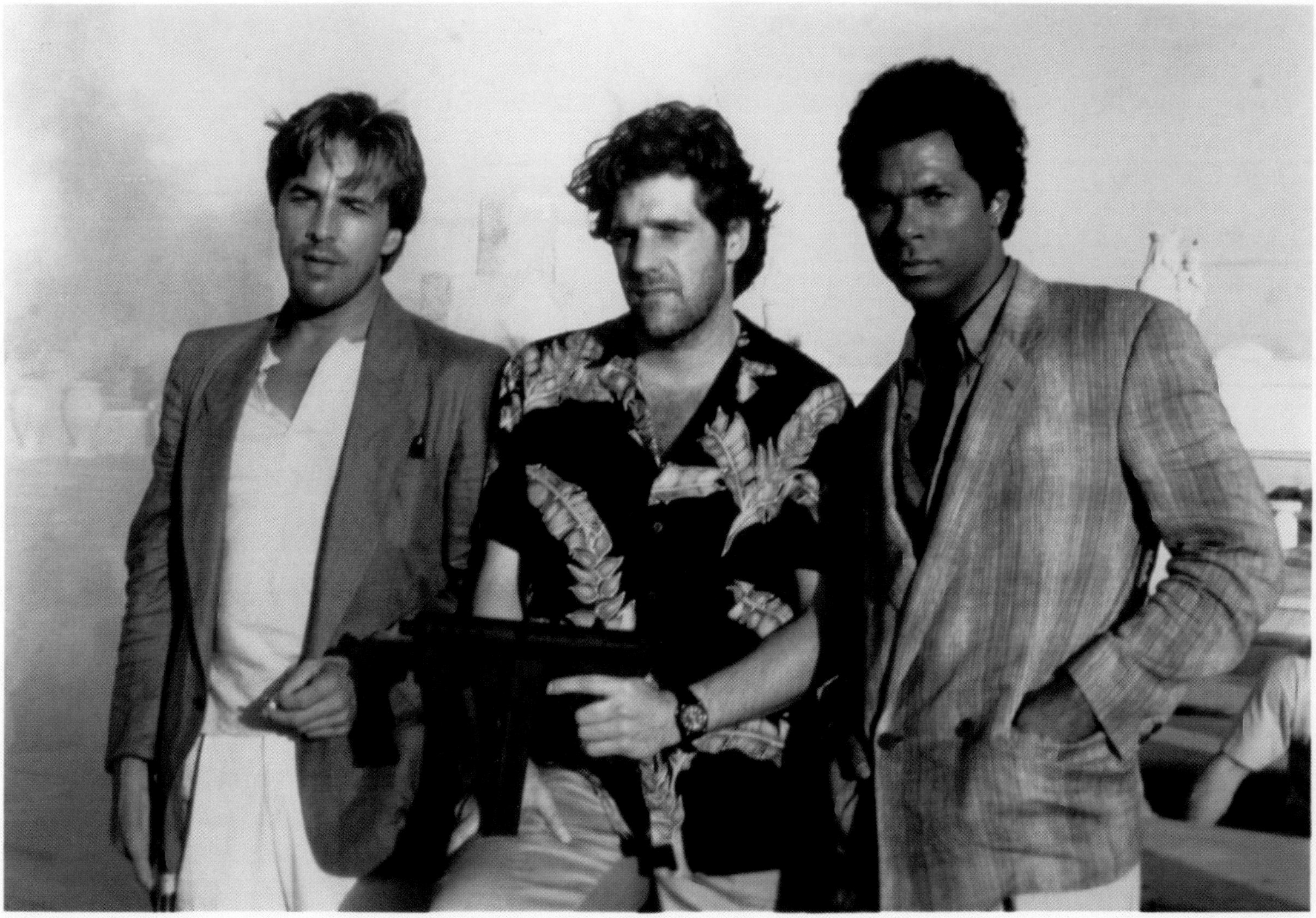

GLENN FREY (CENTER) ON "MIAMI VICE" WITH STARS DON JOHNSON (LEFT) AND PHILLIP MICHAEL-THOMAS (RIGHT)

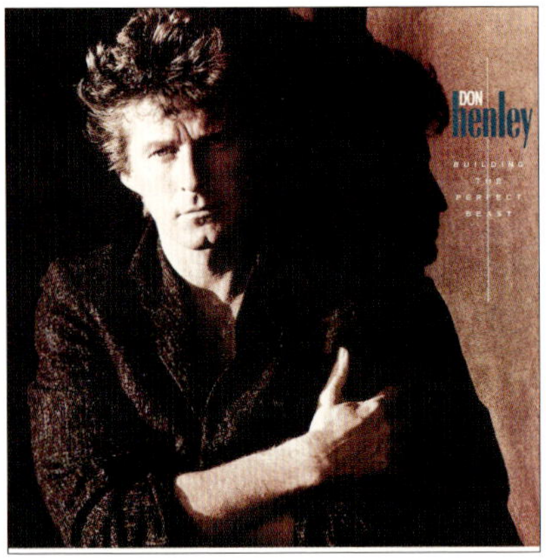

Building the Perfect Beast, Don Henley's second album, generated a plethora of radio-perfect singles.

Billboard 200: *Building the Perfect Beast* (#13)
Billboard Hot 100: "The Boys of Summer" (#5); "All She Wants to Do Is Dance" (#9); "Not Enough Love in the World" (#34); "Sunset Grill" (#22)

AS A member of the Eagles, Don Henley established himself as the driving force behind the top American band of the Seventies. In the Eighties, the vocalist-drummer had engineered an equally vital solo career. Since the Eagles' acrimonious breakup—attributed by band members to the arduous recording process of the album *The Long Run*—Henley said the differences between the ex-Eagles had been patched up.

"People don't understand what a band goes through. We stayed together longer and had more success than most groups, but a lot of our creative energy started going toward keeping the band together."

Four singles issued from Henley's blockbuster *Building the Perfect Beast* reached the Top 40, including "The Boys of Summer"; the music video for the song won MTV's Video of the Year award. Henley had found a potent new collaborator in Danny Kortchmar.

"Danny's originally from New York," Henley explained. "He's always played with people that are kind of mellow—James Taylor, Carole King, Jackson Browne—but he's a rock 'n' roll animal, so he welcomed this opportunity to break out. He's a bright guy—he keeps up with all of the new music and technology much better than I do. I'm more of a concept man—he tells me to go home and put on the cape with the big 'C' on it."

Henley's songs on the second side of the LP—"All She Wants to Do Is Dance," "Sunset Grill"—contained political references without being overt. "All of that stems from my feelings concerning environmentalism," he said. "If you're going to save or clean up something, you have to do it through the political process. It starts at a grass-roots level and multiplies. I have no solutions about changing the world, but if I can make a little ripple or dent, that's nice."

In support of his album, Henley embarked on his first solo tour. "It's been just like the old days—they come, they stand, they light their cigarette lighters," he laughed. "The best thing is that I can see the audience now—before, I was trapped behind my drums.

"Touring, by and large, has become a lot more complex than in 1980, when the Eagles broke up. We have a computerized lighting system, and a complicated keyboard setup. And Levi's jeans is sponsoring the tour. I don't know if I'd have been able to do it otherwise, it's gotten so expensive. I think Levi's is a good sponsor. I thought about it for a long time. I don't think there's anything negative that can be said about Levi's jeans—there aren't too many pairs of them that run off the road and kill somebody." ■

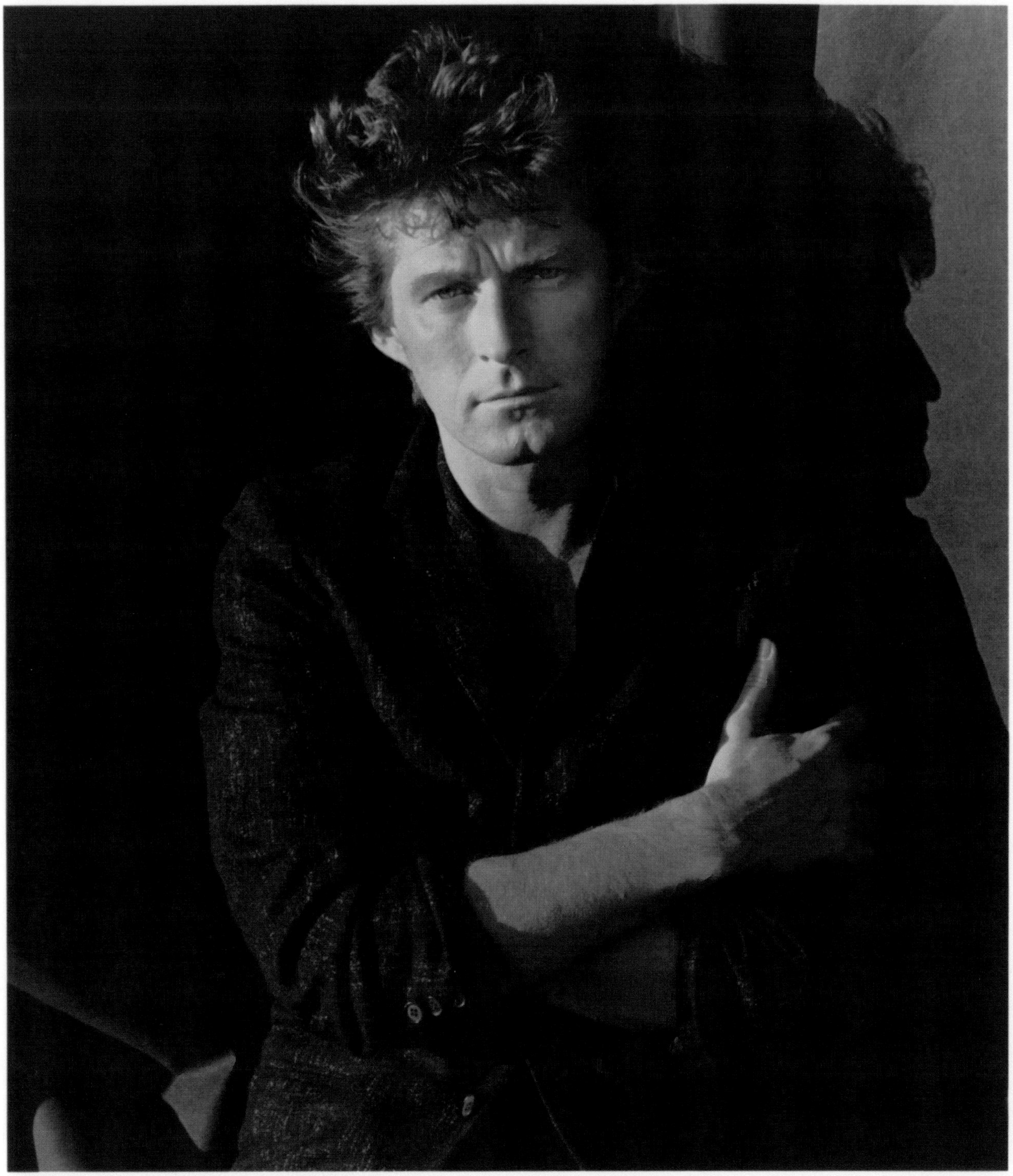

Photo Credit: Herb Ritts

DON HENLEY

GEFFEN RECORDS

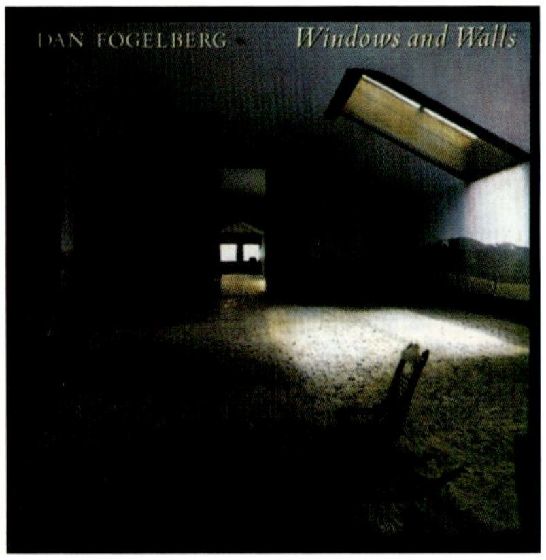

Dan Fogelberg released *Windows and Walls*, containing the single and video "The Language of Love."

Billboard 200: *Windows and Walls* (#15)
Billboard Hot 100: "The Language of Love" (#13); "Believe in Me" (#48)

THE INNOCENT *Age* was Dan Fogelberg's critical and commercial peak; the double album included four of his biggest hits—"Same Old Lang Syne," "Hard to Say," "Leader of the Band" and "Run for the Roses." Three years would pass before his next release, 1984's *Windows and Walls*, demonstrating that the Colorado-based bard was more eager to follow his muse than to abide by the external standards of the music world by churning out more pop hits.

"*The Innocent Age* was so personal that I didn't want to deal with that anymore," he explained. "I dug real deep on that one, so I wanted to see what other types of songwriting I could do."

Reclusive by nature, Fogelberg led a quiet life in Colorado's San Juan Mountains.

"It's a pretty calm existence here. I'm not a very social person," he said. "I cherish my privacy, and I don't want to give anything away. My private life is separate from my musical life. I'm an avid skier during the winter, and I prowl around the state. Summertime, I enjoy the solitude of hiking and mountain biking. The mountains have always been a very healing place for me. You go through a lot of changes in life, but these mountains will always be here."

In the years between *The Innocent Age* and *Windows and Walls*, music videos had become essential to getting exposure. A visualization of "The Language of Love," the album's first single, was Fogelberg's first foray into the video world, simply him and his three-piece band in white garments performing on white instruments on a white set. Despite radio programmers' interest in the newer sounds of new wave and dance pop, "Believe in Me" became a No. 1 adult contemporary hit. The public perceived Fogelberg as an ace balladeer rooted in Seventies rock, and he owned up to the lyrical leanings that earned him that tag.

"I've always been in touch with something that I write," he allowed. "I feel experiences deeply, and I have an outlet, a place where I can translate those feelings. A lot of people go to psychoanalysts. I write songs. It really isn't a reflection of my total being, though. I mean, I don't like being called an 'aching heartbreak kid' because I'm just not that way. I've written some sad stuff in my life, but I've written some uplifting songs." ■

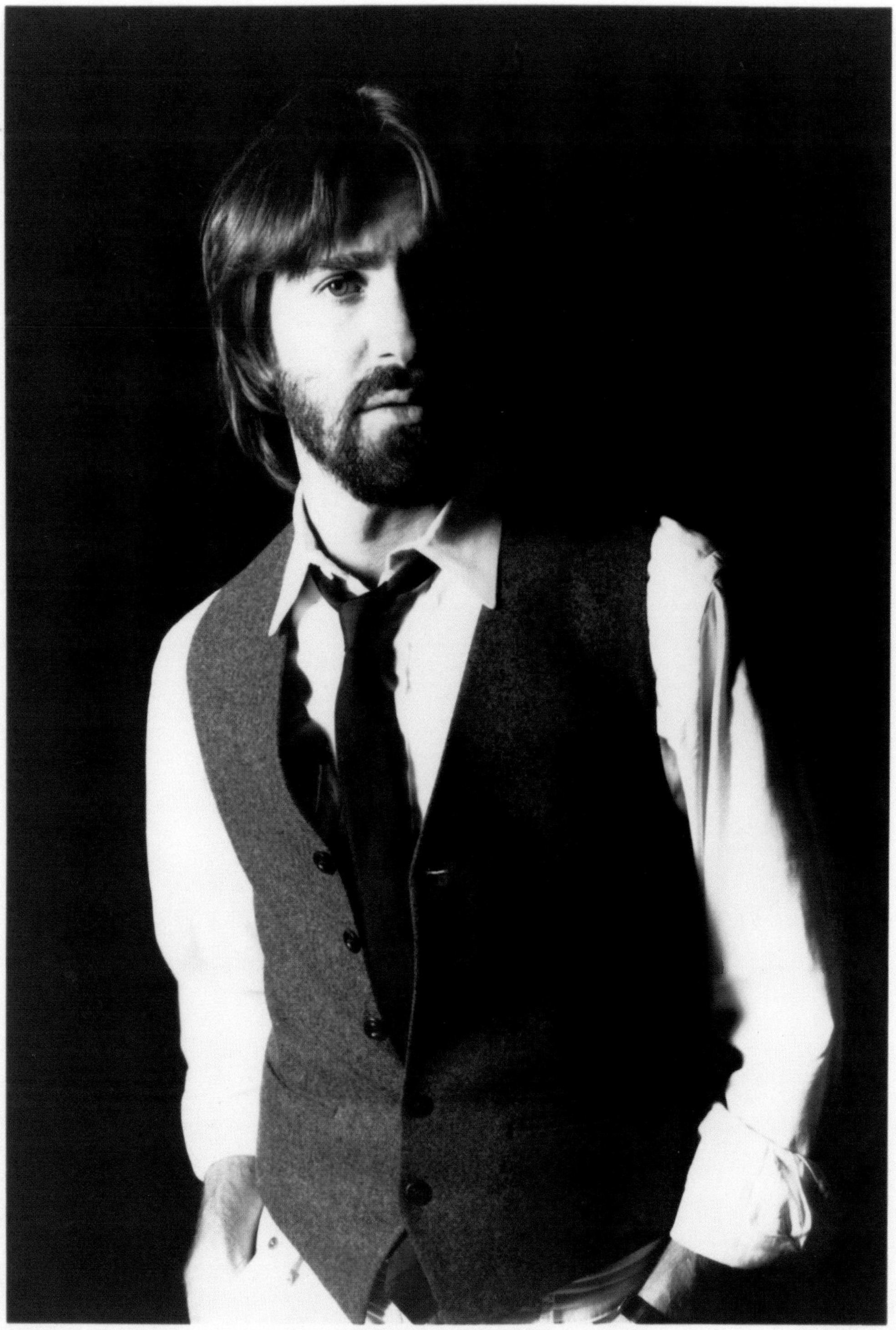

Photo Credit: Andy Kats

DAN FOGELBERG

Full Moon

Epic

8402

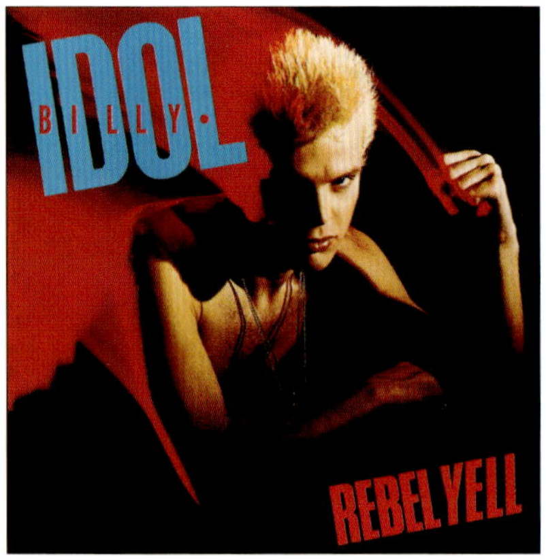

Billy Idol's *Rebel Yell* featured the MTV-driven classics "Eyes Without a Face" and the rowdy title track.

Billboard 200: *Rebel Yell* (#6)
Billboard Hot 100: "Rebel Yell" (#46); "Eyes Without a Face" (#4); "Flesh for Fantasy" (#29); "Catch My Fall" (#50)

BILLY IDOL reigned as the consummate radical rock star. His qualifications were obvious. He was an angry, aggressive, good-looking kid who had formerly fronted punk's Generation X. Idol's detractors longed to dismiss him as an uncouth poseur—something to do with the spiked hair, the penchant for black leather and studs, and especially his trademark sneer.

But with his best-selling *Rebel Yell* album, the former William Broad unveiled a superb understanding of mainstream rock idioms. He teamed with guitarist Steve Stevens, who added strength and flash to the melodic arrangements.

"I call Steve 'the supersonic godfather of the electric guitar,' because he's like a spaceship taking off," Idol said.

Idol himself emerged as a surprisingly intelligent entertainer—cocky yet self-effacing, menacing yet clever.

"I remember I worked at the post office one Christmas and I was singing to myself, and there was this guy who turned around to me and said, 'Never try to earn a living by singing, because you haven't got a voice.' And I thought, 'Right, I'm gonna do it,' even though I wasn't sure of myself for a long time. It's like the old joke, you know, 'There's nothing like a good singer, and I'm nothing like a good singer.' I have that kind of sense of humor. I don't need to take myself seriously to do what I do." ■

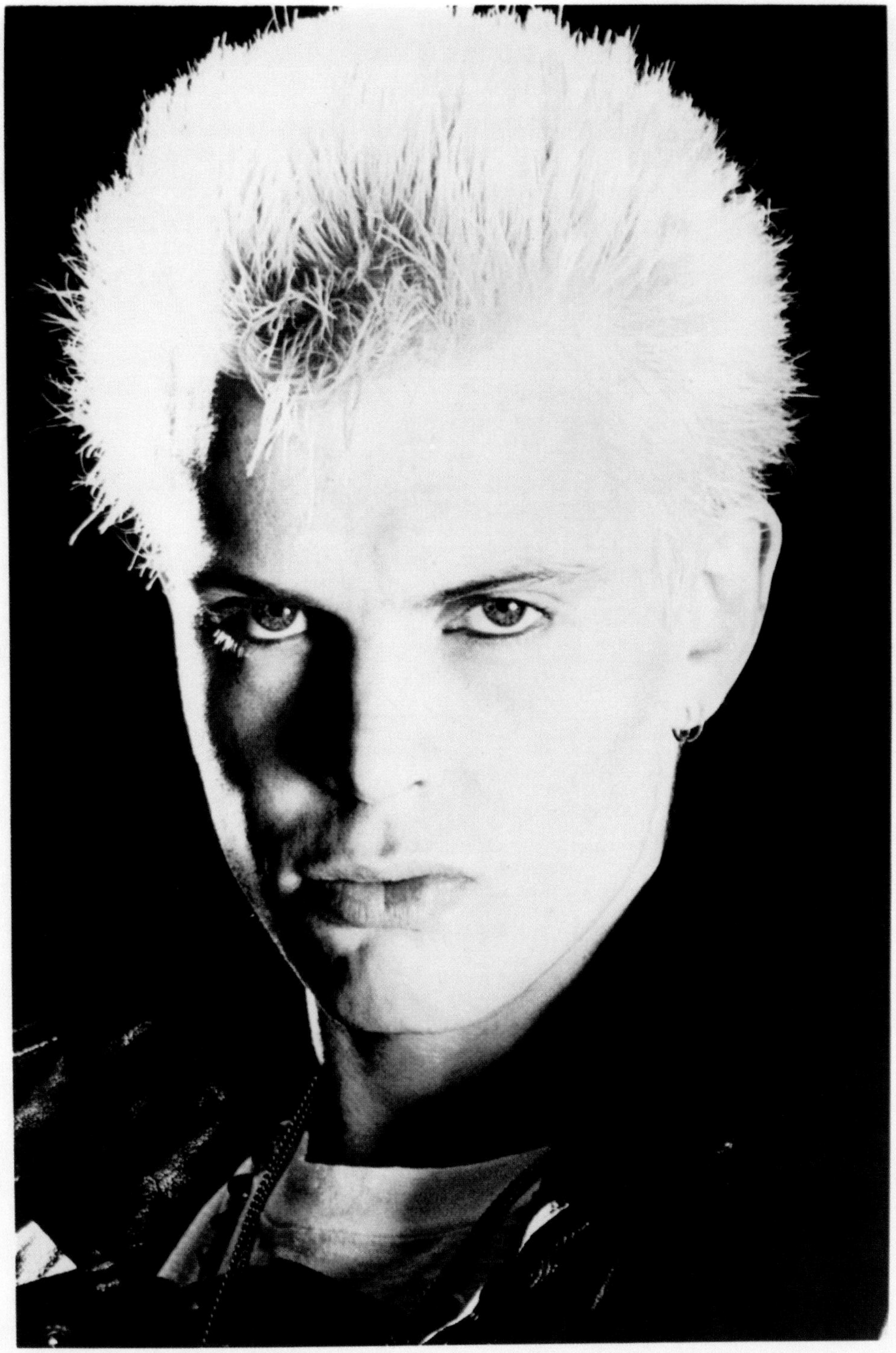

Photo credit: GEOFFREY THOMAS

BILLY IDOL

Direction/Management: AUCOIN MANAGEMENT INC

Chrysalis

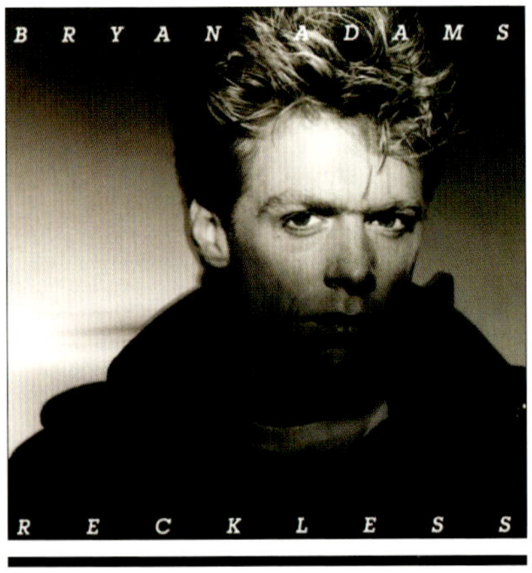

Billboard 200: *Reckless* (No. 1)
Billboard Hot 100: "Run to You" (#6); "Somebody" (#11); "Heaven" (No. 1); "Summer of '69" (#5); "One Night Love Affair" (#13); "It's Only Love" (#15)

Reckless, the fourth album by Bryan Adams, turned the Canadian rocker into a worldwide superstar.

AS A teenager, Bryan Adams had his songs (co-written with collaborator Jim Vallance) covered by the likes of Prism and Bachman-Turner Overdrive. He took the final step toward his own headlining status with 1983's *Cuts Like a Knife*, which chewed up the radio airwaves. Adams came off with cockiness borne out of confidence, a wiry little guy in the T-shirt-jeans-and-sneakers tradition who just happened to have a knack for penning memorable rock riffs.

"I've been playing in bands since I was 15—obviously this isn't the kind of thing that happens overnight," he explained. "It's a process of winning friends and fans, I guess. I've always been a bit of a workhorse, and I've tried to get out and pump my music as much as possible. I believe you've gotta go for it—that's all you've got. No one else is gonna believe in you if you don't. I've always followed my heart and instincts, and that's the best advice I could give anyone."

With *Reckless*, Adams had what music industry types termed a "career album." Six singles made the Top 20 on the *Billboard* Hot 100—"Run to You," "Summer of '69," the No. 1 "Heaven," "One Night Love Affair," "Somebody" and the Tina Turner duet "It's Only Love." Yet the Canadian performer somehow managed to keep a subdued public profile.

"I've never been one to capitalize on my image, even now when it would be very easy for me to do that," he said. "It's funny, people were saying I was married, and the next thing you know I was dating such-and-such a star. I don't disclose my personal life at all, and whether I do or not is my business. People have always touted me as being an MTV star, which is absolute rubbish. The exposure helps, but the biggest reason for my success is my extensive touring."

Adams got a kick out of the response to "Summer of '69"; a few critics pointed out that Adams was only 9 years old at that time, hardly capable of going through the career rigors outlined in the song.

"There's two sides of the story, Jim's and mine," he explained. "And 69 is a suggestive number. That's my position..." ■

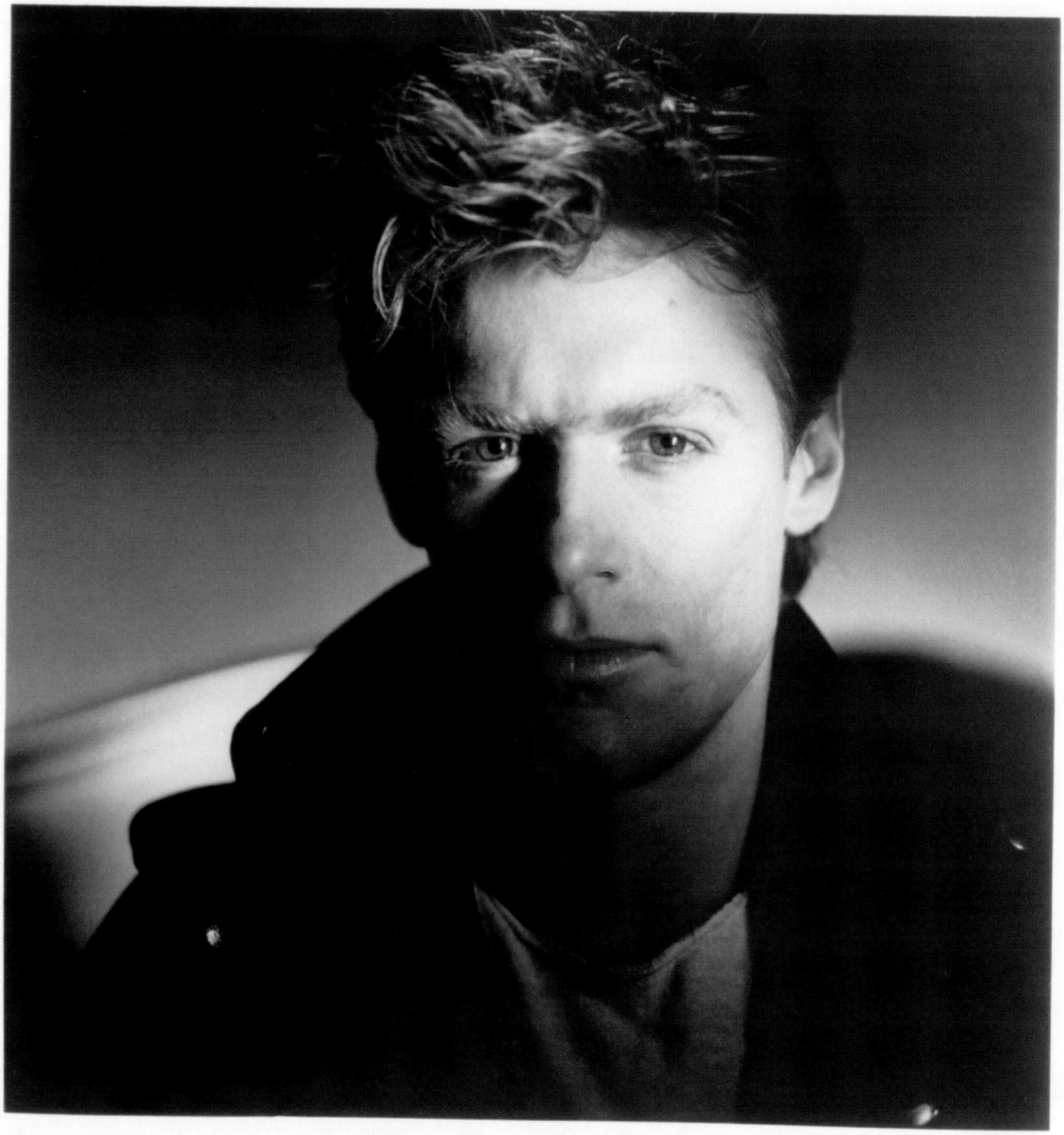

BRYAN ADAMS

Management:
Bruce Allen

A&M RECORDS
Printed in U.S.A.

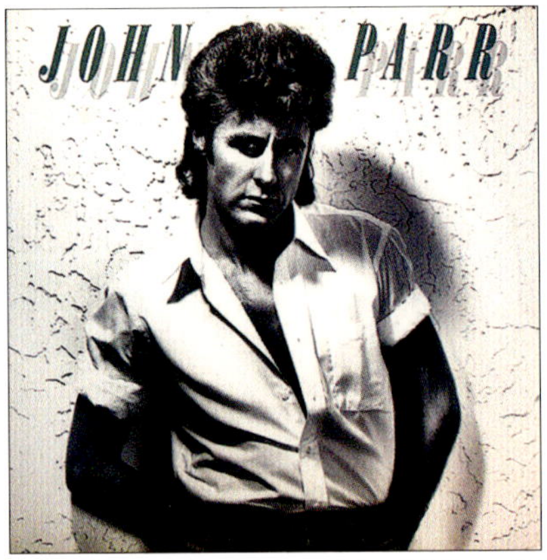

Billboard 200: *Naughty Naughty* (#48)
Billboard Hot 100: "Naughty Naughty" (#23); "Magical" (#73); "Love Grammar" (#89)

John Parr's debut album spawned "Naughty Naughty," a mainstream pop-rock strip-club anthem.

ANOTHER NEW recording artist trying to establish himself, John Parr managed to garner attention for the marginally raunchy video he made for "Naughty Naughty" and for a suspicious story about being discovered by former Who associate John Wolff. Allegedly, Wolff found Parr wandering the English countryside carrying nothing but a cassette. Wolff signed him, and the rest was supposed to be history.

Parr could then afford to laugh at such overblown publicity measures. "It was kind of embarrassing," the affable singer admitted. "I was in a crowd at a concert and got hit on the head. I did have amnesia for a few days, and John helped care for me. It was no big deal, but the record company made a huge, spectacular story out of it."

No matter how Wolff found Parr, what he got was a musician who had been "nearly finished off by the punk thing. I tried to survive it, but it beat me in England—I thought it was the final nail," Parr recalled. "I'd been gigging as a musician for 15 years, and I had assembled a band of musicians from northern England and gone into debt for one last-ditch attempt at getting a record deal. We were in the Bad Company/Foreigner style, and then punk came along and everyone was signing those bands—we couldn't even get a gig for free. So we quit, sold the equipment and I decided to concentrate on songwriting."

Parr's first break as a writer came when Meat Loaf solicited some songs for inclusion on his *Bad Attitude* album. Roger Daltrey, the Who's vocalist, contributed a duet to Loaf's album and became similarly enamored of Parr's material. On *Under a Raging Moon*, Daltrey's solo album, Parr furnished several tunes, including the title track.

"Naughty Naughty," the single from *John Parr*, was his first US hit record. "There's a climate around radio programmers that is seeing the back of the new wave revolution and saying hello once more to Foreigner, Chicago and their ilk," Parr concluded. "And that's where I belong." ■

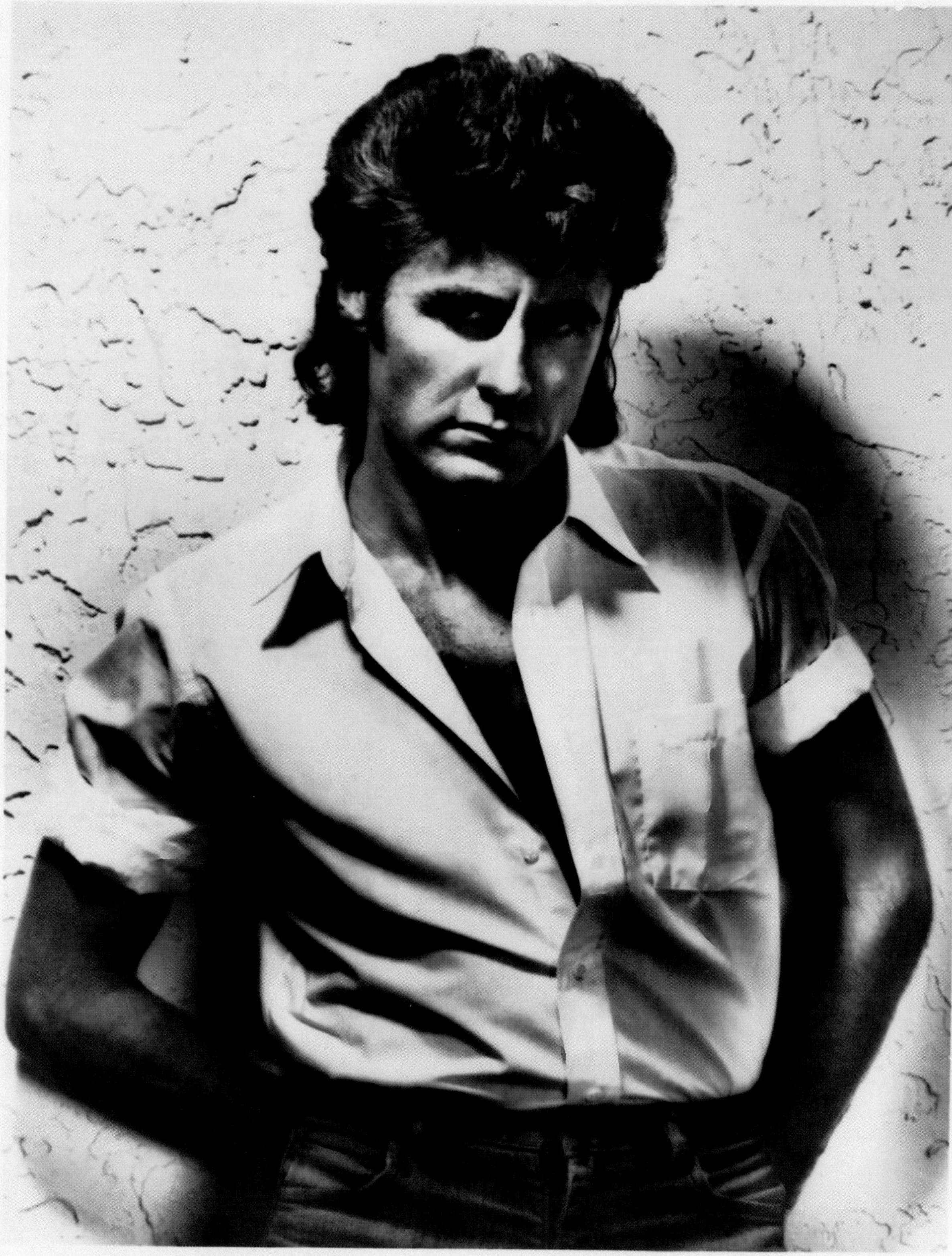

JOHN PARR

ATLANTIC

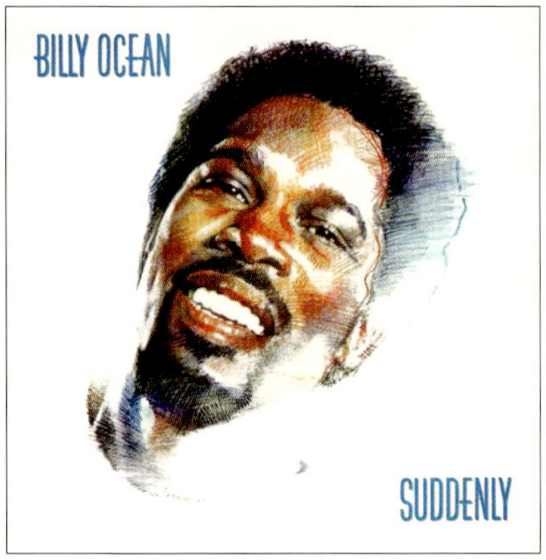

Billy Ocean joined the ranks of platinum-selling artists with his album *Suddenly* and three Top 5 hits.

Billboard 200: *Suddenly* (#9)
Billboard Hot 100: "Caribbean Queen (No More Love on the Run)" (No. 1); "Loverboy" (#2); "Suddenly" (#4); "Mystery Lady" (#24)

AFTER LABORING early in his career as a tailor and an auto assembly-line worker, Billy Ocean finally gained entry to the recording industry and soon faced major disappointment. Although his efforts culminated in 1982 with a Top 5 R&B hit "Nights (Feel Like Getting Down)"—a track immortalized on Jane Fonda's workout album—he wound up losing his record deal.

But the 34-year-old singer bounced back in a big way. Uptempo dance tracks marked the album *Suddenly*, but the material wouldn't have worked without the benefit of Ocean's powerful, expressive and soulful voice.

"I've been singing since I was three—you can either sing or you can't," he mused. "When I was in my early 20s, I did go to a teacher to check out what 'voice training' was all about. I did learn some things about breathing technique, but I left after a few lessons. They were expecting classical tones from me, but I'm not a classical singer. When a pop singer goes out and has to belt it out at night in a smoky room smelling of alcohol, all that technique doesn't do you any good!"

"Caribbean Queen (No More Love on the Run)" climbed to No. 1 on both the pop and black singles chart, and won Ocean the Grammy Award for Best Male R&B Vocal Performance. "Loverboy," "Mystery Lady" and the title track also became hits. Such commercial success couldn't have happened to a more gentlemanly artist. Born in Trinidad, Ocean had lived in England since age 9—and despite his American success (and relative lack of it in Britain), that's where he stayed.

"All of my family is in England, and my two kids are in school," he explained. "So moving wouldn't be fair—it's too late for me to make such a drastic change. I have good people taking care of the business side of my career, and my wife takes good care of my home life. That leaves me free to write songs, make records—and sing. So wouldn't it be wrong of me to be anything but sensible about it?" ■

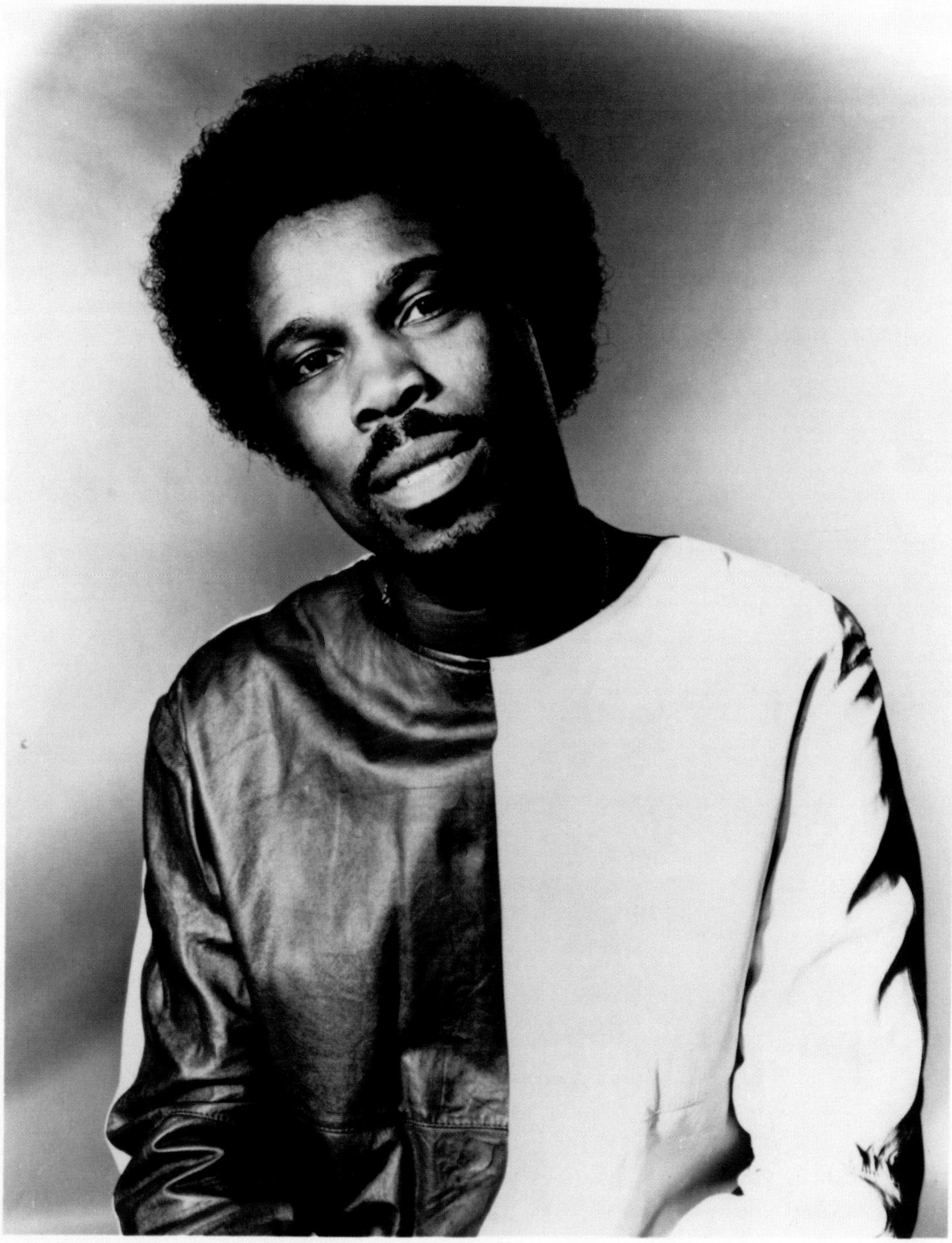

Billy Ocean

ARISTA

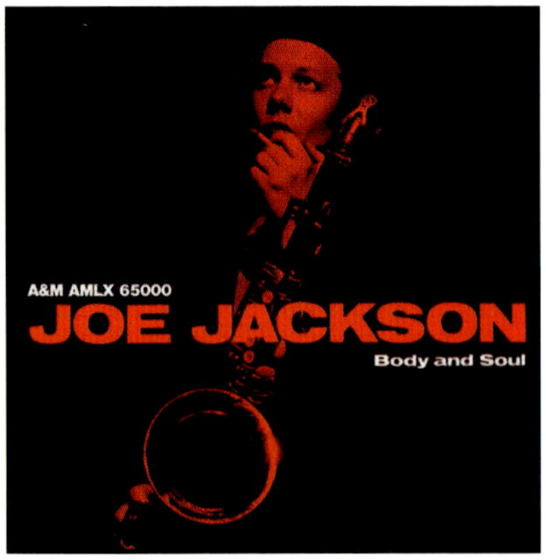

With *Body and Soul*, Joe Jackson expanded on the musical vision he first established with *Night and Day*.

Billboard 200: *Body and Soul* (#20)
Billboard Hot 100: "You Can't Get What You Want (Till You Know What You Want)" (#15); "Happy Ending" (#57)

JOE JACKSON had moved to New York City, where he recorded the jazz-inflected sound of *Body and Soul*. The cover photograph imitated the style of the classic Blue Note records of the Fifties.

"I really wanted to get back to an old-fashioned way of recording where everyone played all together and there were as few microphones as possible," he explained. "We looked for a place you could just set up and play and it would sound good. We settled on this old stone hall, where we built our own recording console—you have to fight a battle with the technology because nothing is set up the old way anymore. But we got a very live sound, something you couldn't get in a studio."

"You Can't Get What You Want (Till You Know What You Want)" was a hit, and Jackson established his individuality as a composer and his maverick outlook toward music-business methods.

"The art of arranging is pretty much dead. Most people can't read music, but they go in the studio and bash away and experiment, and the producer is given the job of making order of the chaos. I believe a lot of that order should already be imposed by the musician. When you go in the studio, everyone should know what they're playing.

"Now, I like the way some people in the band play, enough to say, 'Just do a solo along the lines of such-and-such,' so I'm not dictating every note. But I have to remain in control of it. I find it strange that people find that unusual. They say, 'God, what a dictator he is! He doesn't even let his band rock out!' But it's not the kind of band that gets together because everyone likes to jam. It's a band I handpicked to play my music." ■

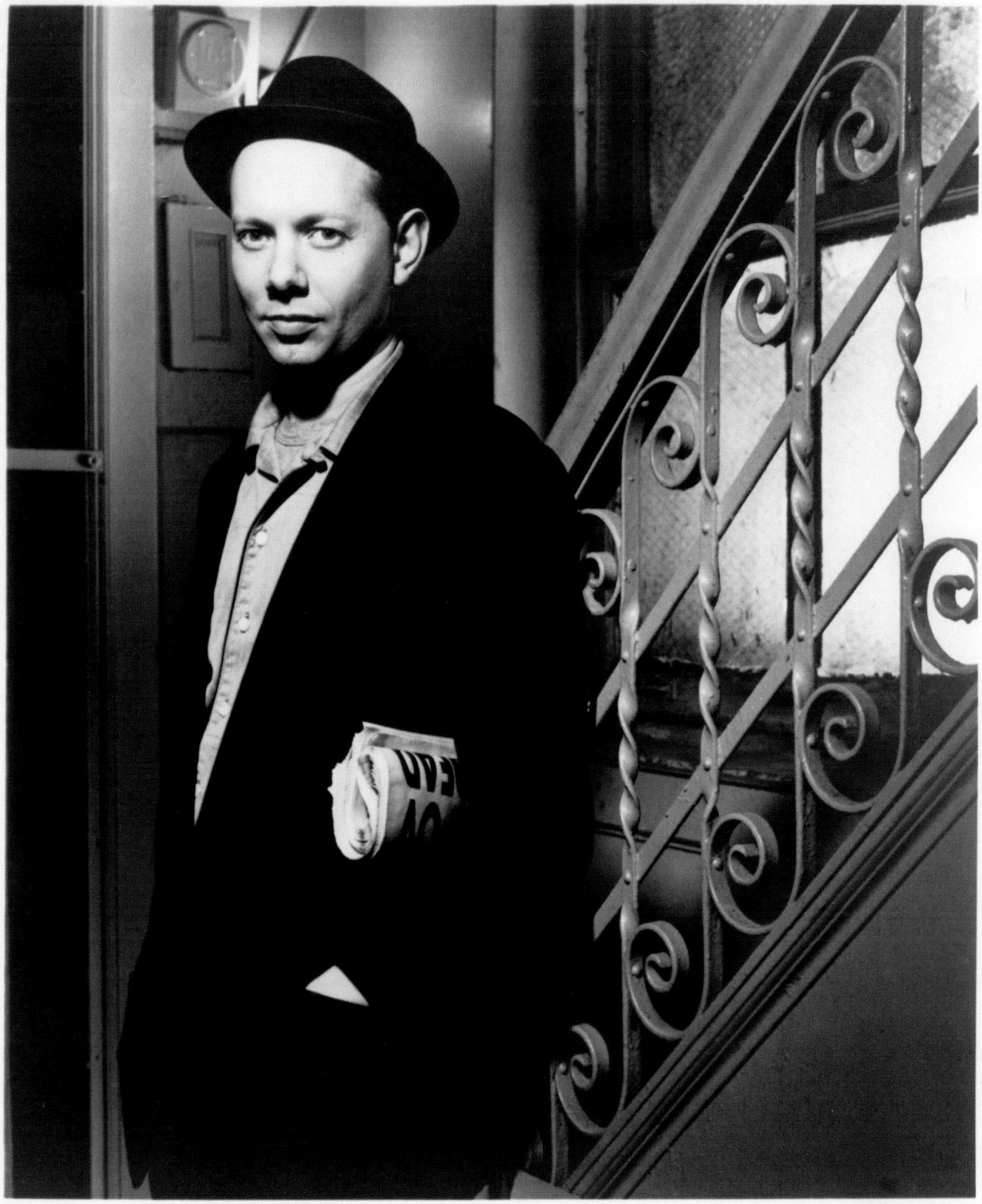

JOE JACKSON

A&M RECORDS

Printed in U.S.A.

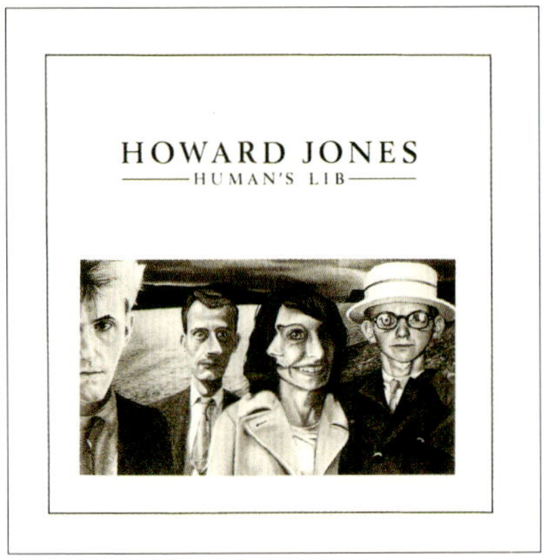

Billboard 200: *Human's Lib* (#59)
Billboard Hot 100: "New Song" (#27); "What Is Love?" (#33)

Howard Jones intended *Human's Lib* to serve as the starting point for his unique brand of synth pop.

GIVEN HIS overt reliance on synthesizers, Howard Jones could have been categorized as just another techno-merchant from hype-crazy England. But that wouldn't have given the musician credit for the two catchy hit singles on his debut album, *Human's Lib*. The lyrics to "New Song" and "What Is Love?" served as a forum for his ebullient outlook on life.

"I've always tried not to react to negative things, because you become a slave of them if you do," Jones noted. "The thing that gives people the most energy is being positive. It's just a more practical approach to life."

That approach had catapulted Jones out of his hometown area of High Wycombe, where he had enrolled in a music college at age 19. He gave up on his dream of a songwriting career when his ideas didn't jibe with the staff's, but then he discovered synthesizers.

"I had been trained on piano up to that point of my life," Jones recalled. "But synthesizers are now so organic-sounding that there is no need to play on acoustic keyboards anymore. I love those flute-y, reedy, natural sounds, but I found that I can get them on synths."

Jones began penning material that didn't resemble the doomy atmospherics of other synthesizer bands—he concentrated on writing bright, hooky melodies that he could couple with his optimistic lyrics. He also set about developing a unique stage presentation—using synthesizers to create a show he could pull off all by himself.

"I travel with nine technicians and a mime friend, Jed Hoile. Jed used to come to the pub gigs in the early days and dance in the audience. Everyone enjoyed what he was doing so much that I thought I'd get him onstage to create characters to the music. I don't use any tapes at all—the whole show is run live, so it's very flexible. The drum patterns are pre-programmed, but there are areas where I can do what I like—leave the keyboard, do a solo." ■

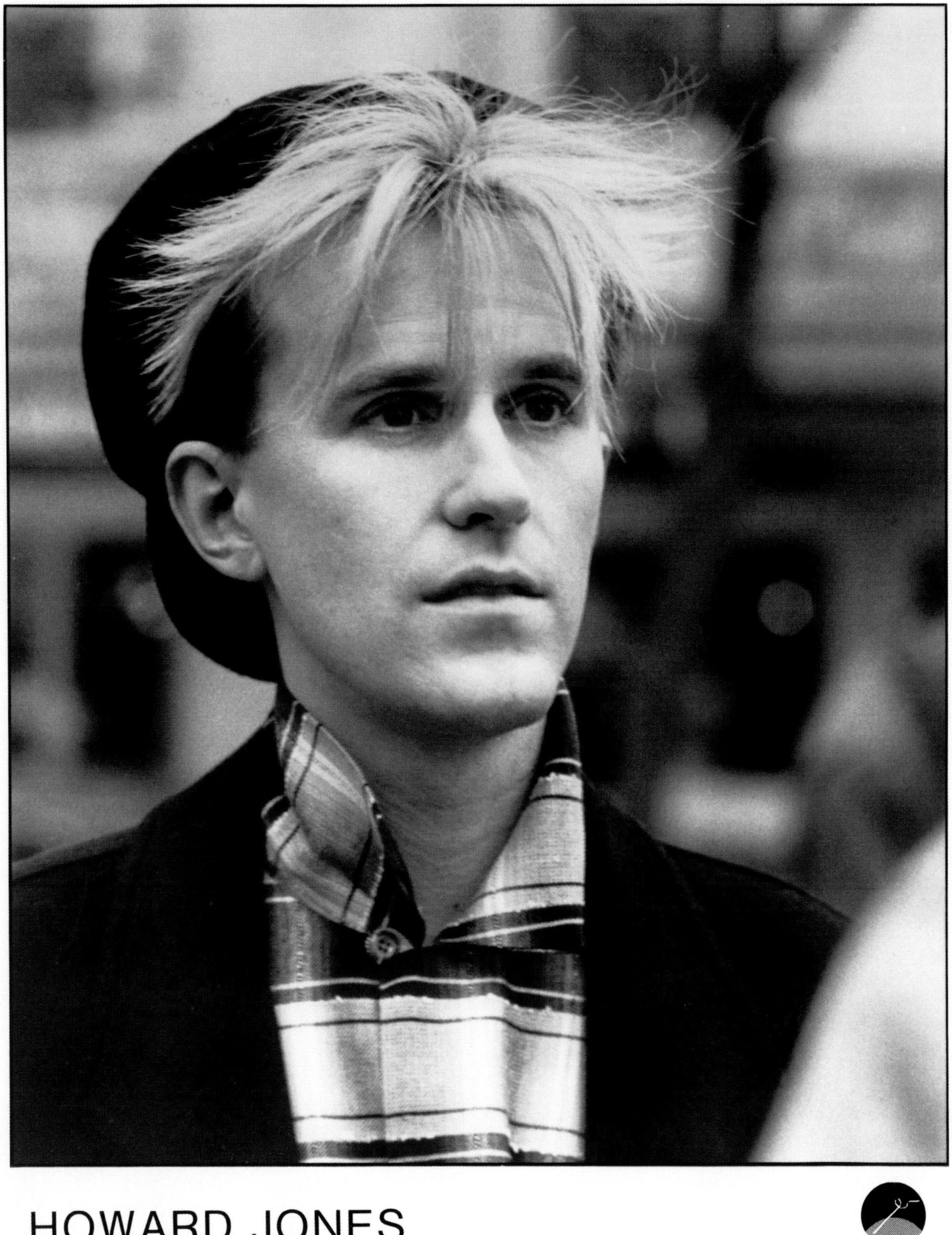

PHOTO CREDIT: CLAUDE GASSIAN/1984

HOWARD JONES

ELEKTRA

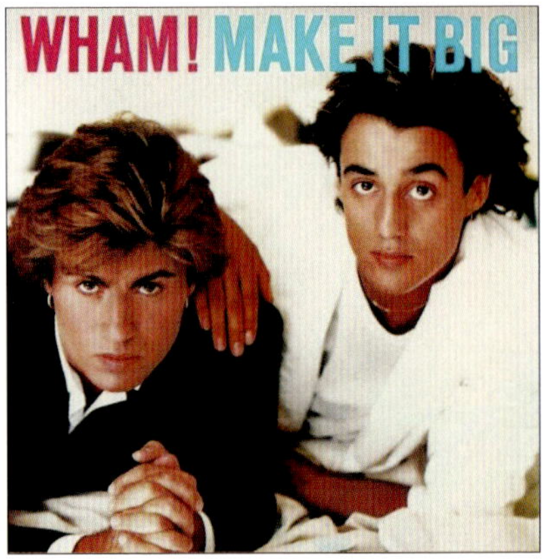

Billboard 200: *Make It Big* (No. 1)
Billboard Hot 100: "Wake Me Up Before You Go-Go" (No. 1); "Careless Whisper" (No. 1); "Everything She Wants" (No. 1); "Freedom" (#3)

Wham!, the UK pop duo of George Michael and Andrew Ridgeley, scored four bouncy hits off *Make It Big*.

GEORGE MICHAEL and Andrew Ridgeley had known each other since their childhood in the northwest London suburb of Watford.

"One of the main reasons we became friends was music," Ridgeley remembered. "George had a tape recorder at his house and we used to go over there and thrash things out on his drum kit and an old acoustic guitar."

Michael and Ridgeley joined the ska movement as members of a short-lived group called the Executive. They formed Wham! in 1981 and rushed into a recording contract with an independent label.

"I've known since I was about seven that I wanted to be a pop star, but I never really thought about how I was going to do it," Michael said. "We were both convinced that once our songs were heard by the right people we were going to make it."

After struggling out of the gate, the pair needed a fresh approach. Wham! moved to a recording contract with Epic, and *Make It Big* marked the emergence of an updated pop image. Michael was credited as the sole producer, beginning with the No. 1 hit "Wake Me Up Before You Go-Go," accompanied by a video in which the pair cavorted in a line of casual sportswear. *Make It Big* also included "Everything She Wants," "Freedom" and Michael's solo single "Careless Whisper."

Wham!'s hordes of devotees—mostly screaming teenage girls—resulted in some hard-to-shake stigmas. Many perceived Michael as a bubblegum glamour boy, all teeth and earrings.

"I believe 'Wake Me Up Before You Go-Go' will be a classic ten years from now," he stated. "Yet one can't rest on past laurels." ■

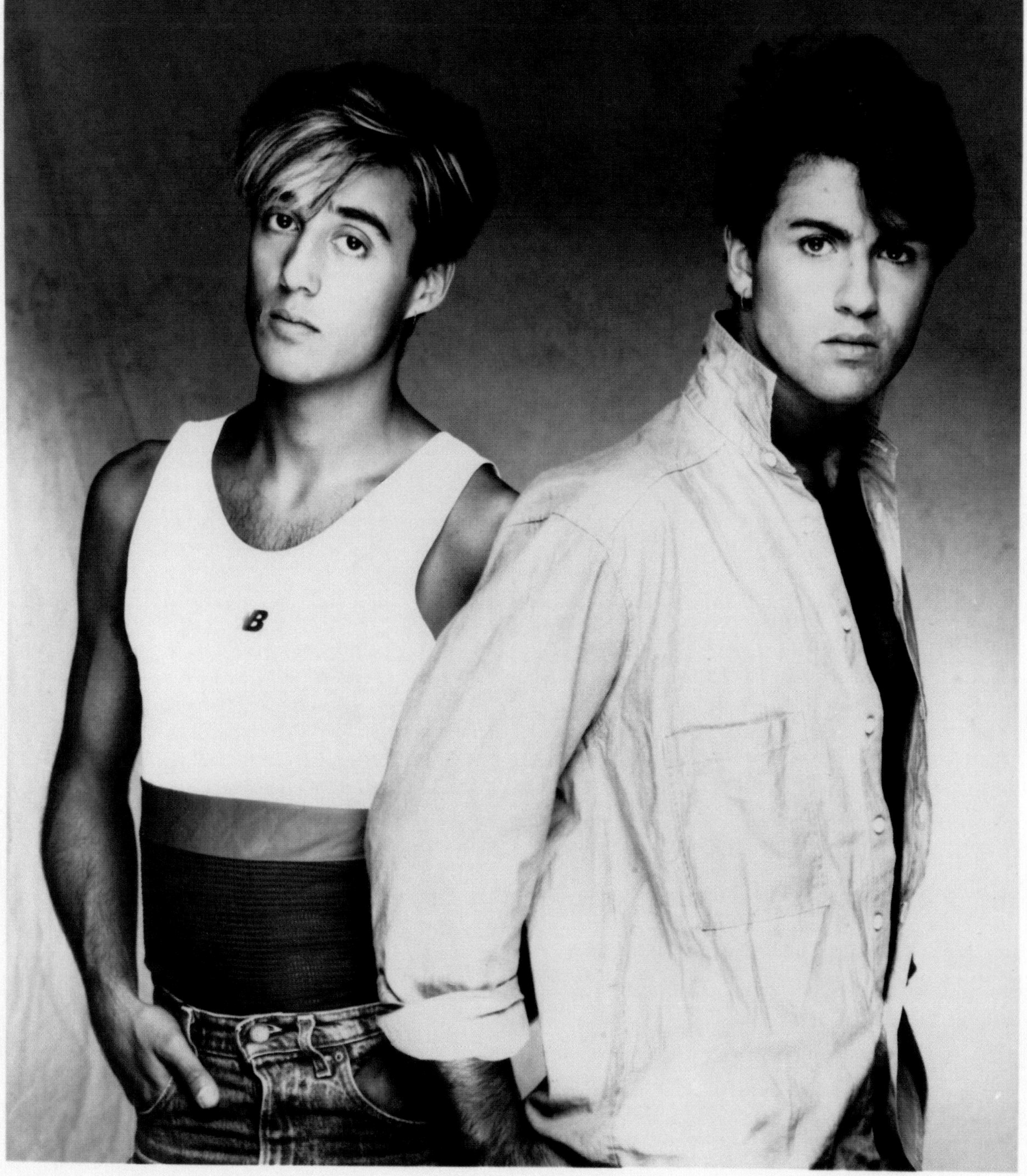

PHOTOGRAPH: BRIAN ARIS © D.P.A.

ANDREW RIDGELEY (left) and GEORGE MICHAEL (right)

WHAM!

Columbia

8410

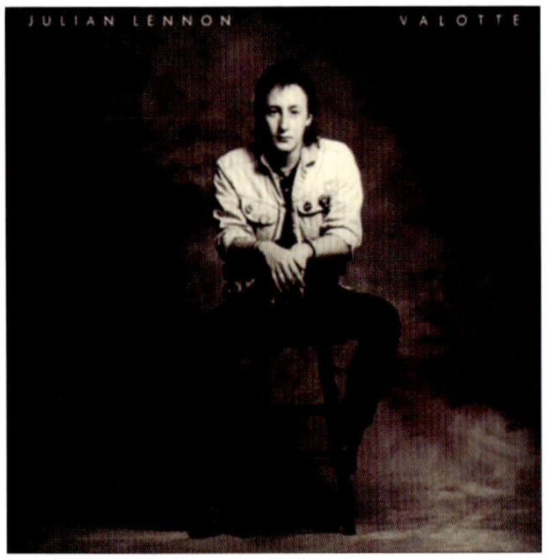

After his father's murder in 1980, Julian Lennon followed in his footsteps and began a singing career.

Billboard 200: *Valotte* (#17)
Billboard Hot 100: "Valotte" (#9); "Too Late for Goodbyes" (#5); "Say You're Wrong" (#21); "Jesse" (#54)

WHEN JULIAN Lennon spoke, the resemblance to his father, the late John Lennon, was uncanny. John's fans prized the vocal similarity, but cynics suggested that Julian's status as the son of a former Beatle accounted for the chart position that *Valotte*, his 1984 debut, attained. The album generated a pair of hits (the title track and "Too Late for Goodbyes") and earned him a Grammy nomination for Best New Artist.

Lennon displayed a maturity and sophistication that belied his youth, although the shy demeanor projected in his two performance videos was no ruse. Lennon, who lived in London, had been affected by media workings since his birth in 1963, an event that was something of a public-relations embarrassment to the people surrounding parents John and his first wife, Cynthia. It wasn't good for the Beatles' image for John to admit to having a wife, much less a child. But as the private lives of the Beatles became increasingly public, Julian was eventually accepted and occasionally paraded.

In November 1968, John and Cynthia were divorced. Julian lived in England with his mother, went to school and was starting to jam with other musicians when the news that shook the world arrived on Jan. 8, 1980—John Lennon had been murdered outside his New York apartment building.

The ensuing months brought Julian press attention, but this time as a "young socialite" who went clubbing and lived it up. He soon finished sowing his wild oats and sought refuge in music. *Valotte* was named in honor of the remote Manoir de Valotte, a French château that inspired the music. To record the album, Lennon recruited Phil Ramone, the producer who had shaped Billy Joel's repertoire, particularly his personal tribute to the Beatles, *The Nylon Curtain.*

"I've grown up with music," he noted, lighting the first of many cigarettes. "I'm just glad I still have the opportunity. I got caught up in some nasty deals before I entered into a serious contract with a record company, but I worked my way out of that. I'm just lucky to still be able to get out and do it."

Growing up in public had its distressing moments. Lennon handled the never-ending mentions of his father's legacy. "I knew from day one that people were really going to look at comparisons. Obviously, there are a few which I notice myself. I'm not trying to hide them; I don't want to. Why should I? That's just part of me. Sure, our voices are similar, so I'm proud of it. But I pick my nose and they say it's the same way as my dad. It gets to be too much after a while."

But Lennon thought his father would understand his decision to be a musician. "I'm pretty sure he'd say, 'Do it—but don't blame me!'" ■

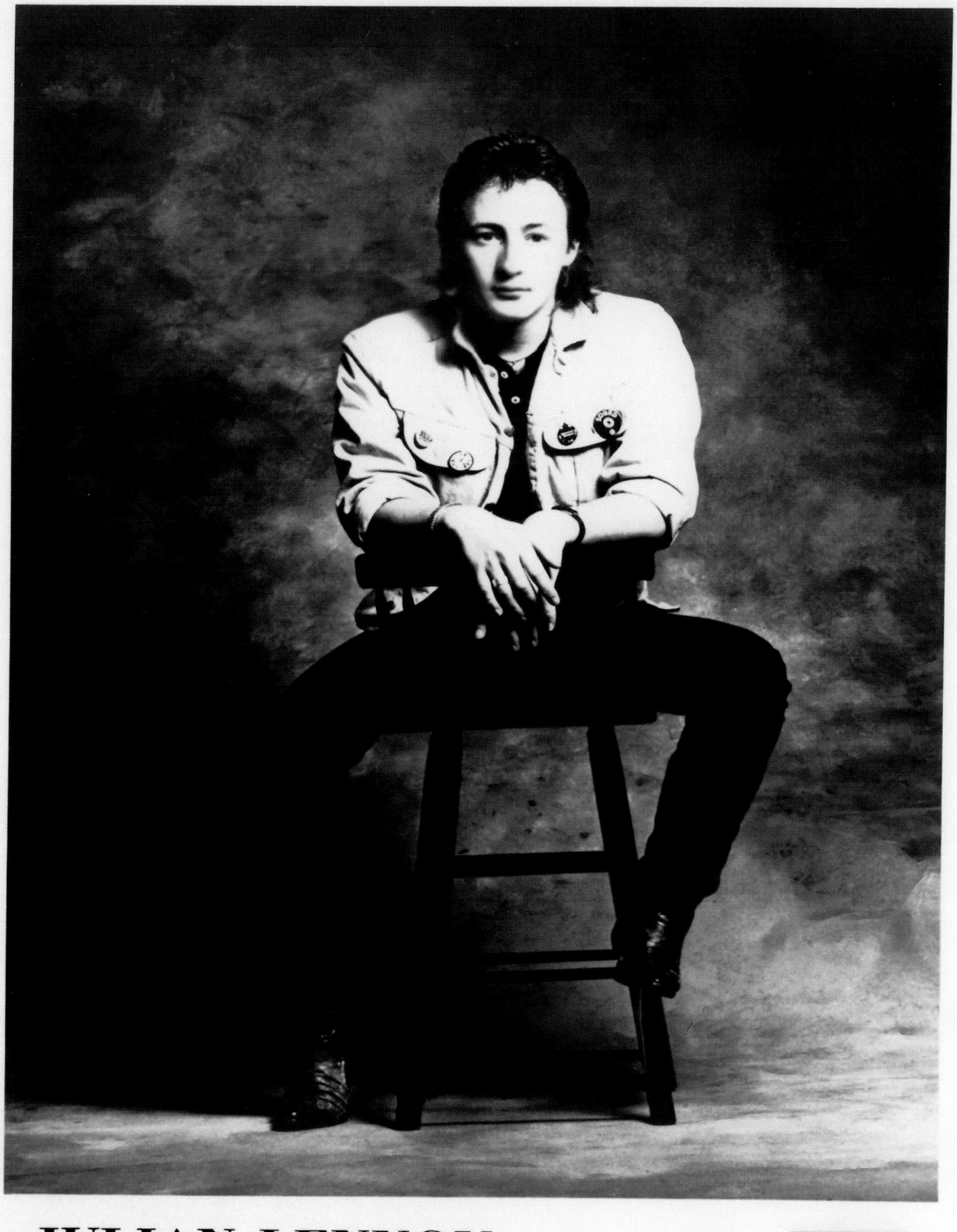

JULIAN LENNON

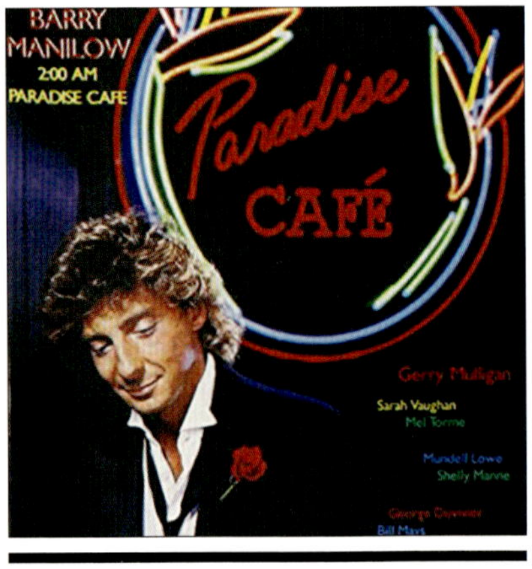

Billboard 200: *2:00 AM Paradise Cafe* (#28)

Pop entertainer Barry Manilow changed direction, making *2:00 AM Paradise Cafe* with several jazz greats.

WITH A string of 25 Top 40 hits ranging from 1974's "Mandy" to 1983's "Read 'Em and Weep," Barry Manilow had firmly established himself as an international superstar.

But during that chart-busting stretch, much of the public perceived him as sickly sweet, and critics ridiculed his songs as "processed cheese." His old-fashioned, grandiose, sentimental songs were ignored by the rock and jazz worlds.

Yet Manilow managed to redefine his musical image. In 1984, he walked away from middle-of-the-road pop, deciding to engage in other creative forms. His *2:00 AM Paradise Cafe* album found him making swinging, smoky jazz tunes recorded live in one take in the studio with a small all-star combo including Sarah Vaughan, Mel Tormé and Gerry Mulligan. The scope of the material put the hard-working Manilow in a different light, and he received excellent notices.

"Reviews that I never dared to dream about," he said. "It's never fun to be beaten up. Yet I stood behind my music, and the public loved me no matter what the critics said, so I tried not to pay attention to their put-downs. But after so many years of being told how lousy I was, and the public being told that what they liked wasn't any good, I began to doubt myself. I admit it, I sat down and said, 'You know, maybe I stink.'

"So I needed to do something, and the *Paradise Cafe* album was a way of proving to myself that I am as good as I think I am, and to give my fans something to be proud of. I thank the critics for pushing me to take that risk, because it was the most rewarding thing I've ever done. I wish they hadn't been so cruel, but I did get something out of it. Now they seem to respect me. And I didn't go after their respect, I went after my own." ■

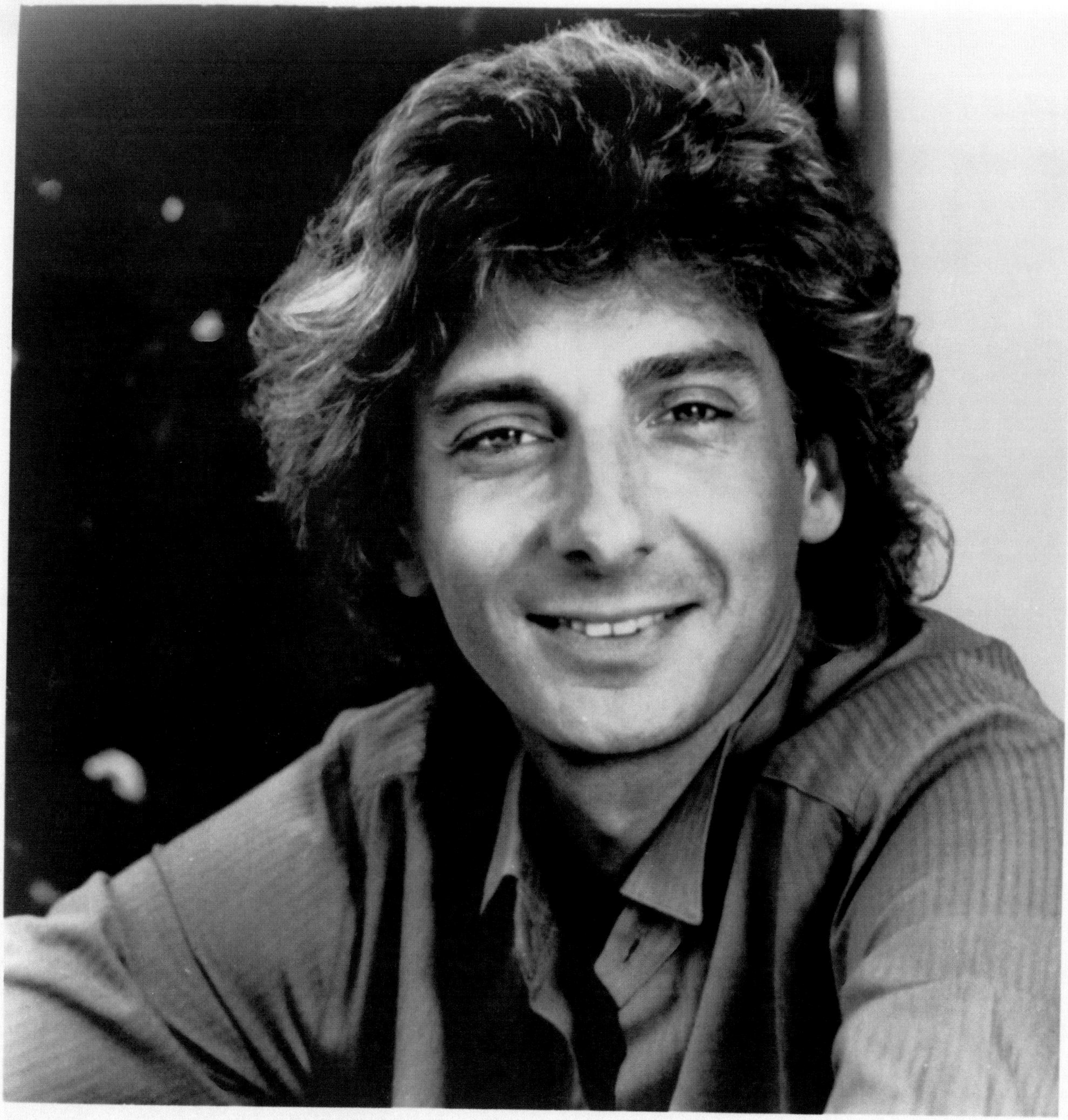

BARRY MANILOW

ARISTA

Public Relations:

ROGERS AND COWAN

9665 Wilshire Boulevard
Beverly Hills, CA 90212
(213) 275-4581

122 East 42nd Street
New York, NY 10168
(212) 490-8200

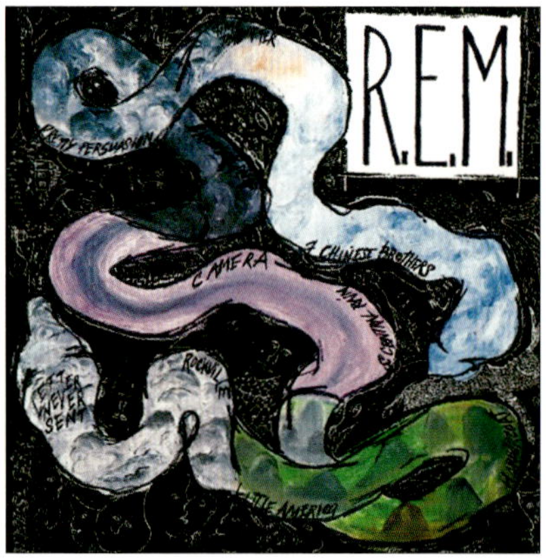

The album *Reckoning* continued R.E.M.'s influence as the standard-bearers of the rock underground.

Billboard 200: *Reckoning* (#27)
Billboard Hot 100: "So. Central Rain (I'm Sorry)" (#85)

FEW OTHER new American bands had experienced the lavish praise heaped upon R.E.M., a quartet from Athens, Georgia. The rock press fell over itself to hail *Murmur*, the group's 1983 album; it was voted Album of the Year by the *Rolling Stone* and *Record* magazine critics polls, and #2 Album of the Year by the *Village Voice*'s Pazz and Jop poll. Those credentials were prominently displayed on a sticker adorning the cover of the follow-up, *Reckoning*.

"Our only consideration was that we didn't want to make it sound like *Murmur*," bassist Mike Mills explained. "There are still all sorts of little sounds on the record that you can pick up at a later date, but mostly we wanted a cleaner, straight-ahead sound, more of a stripped-down rock 'n' roll feel. We haven't worried so far about what other people think of it."

R.E.M.'s original ensemble sound had stoked the fervor surrounding the band. The two biggest factors were the group's instrumental prowess (guitarist Peter Buck's folksy strumming and Mills' inventive bass work, in particular) and vocalist Michael Stipe's gloomy baritone, which often functioned as another instrument in the mix. Recorded with producer Mitch Easter and his partner Don Dixon, *Reckoning* added to the band's burgeoning reputation with such songs as "So. Central Rain (I'm Sorry)" and "Pretty Persuasion."

"Usually we have bits and pieces of material when we all meet to practice, then we gradually evolve it into a song," Mills explained. "Michael will listen as we do it, and he'll either use words he's already got or make up something—it's a real two-way street."

The camaraderie among band members stemmed from their early days, when R.E.M. was formed as "sort of an antidote to boredom. Bill (Berry, drummer) and I had known each other for years—we were messing around at school (the University of Georgia), playing in the dorm room with friends, but we weren't looking real hard for something to do. We met Peter and Michael in a record store and we decided to play together. As it turns out, there was a big party coming up, a very informal setting, so we went ahead and did that. It was just to kill time instead of doing homework!"

With *Reckoning* ensconced on the charts, R.E.M.'s approach had proven inspirational to any number of bands who wanted to pursue creative success. "We never thought about being a model for other groups until it was pointed out to us. If anything, though, I'm as proud of that as anything we've done," Mills concluded. "We've shown that you can make it on your own without doing all of the usual music biz tricks that people make you think you have to do. I think it's real healthy—it's good for the state of rock 'n' roll in general." ■

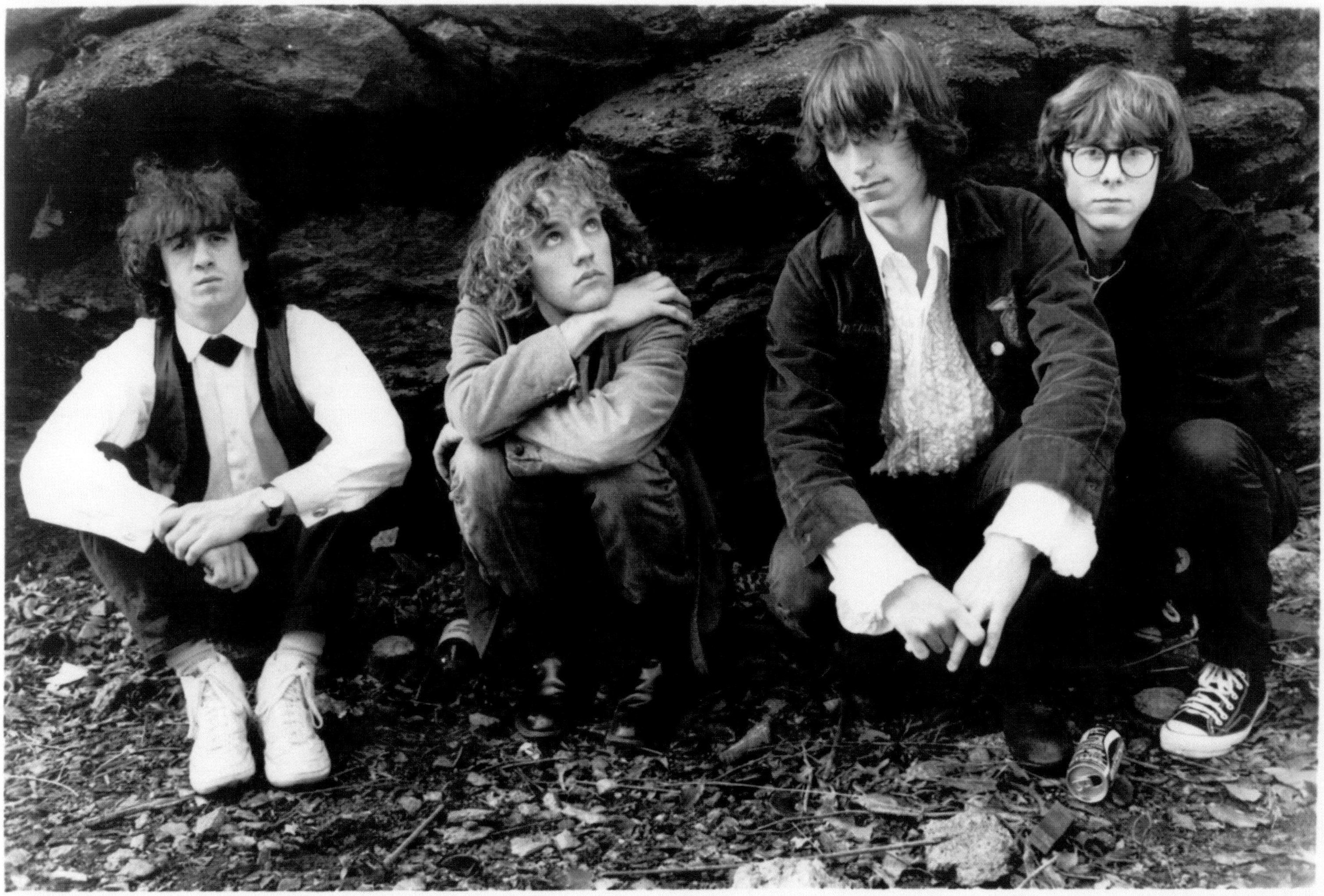

PHOTO: LAURA LEVINE

R.E.M. BILL BERRY MICHAEL STIPE PETER BUCK MIKE MILLS

I.R.S.

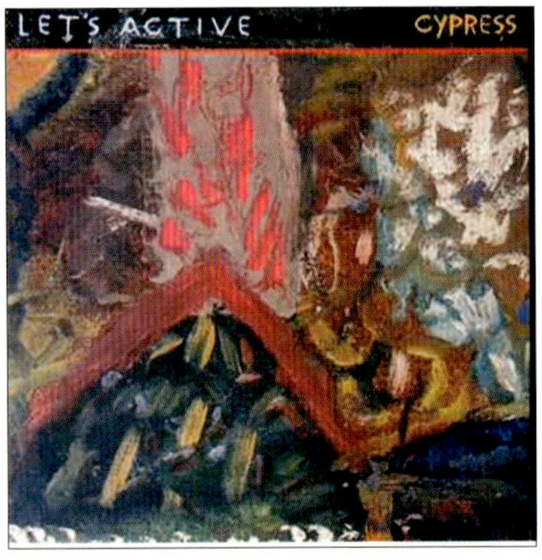

Billboard 200: *Cypress* (#138)

The producer of R.E.M.'s early albums, the guitarist and songwriter Mitch Easter also fronted Let's Active.

MITCH EASTER knew plenty about making records. His work producing R.E.M.'s first two discs at his Drive-In Studio at his parents' house in North Carolina had quickly earned him a reputation as the go-to engineer for Southern guitar-pop bands. But Easter's labor of love was Let's Active, a band he formed in 1980.

"I started playing at age 12, but it was hard being from the South," the multi-instrumentalist said. "There was no music industry, so you couldn't get discovered or figure out what to do with yourself. I wanted a studio just so I could use it, but I made it a commercial proposition so I could have a job, too. And it filled a gap and took off. I got my name on a lot of records real fast. But I've always been in bands, trying to get something going."

Most Southern bands, including Let's Active, were lumped together by their address.

"The fame we get is that we're revivalist and precious, which is something you get sick of really fast," Easter said. "We're like a box of candy instead of a three-course meal."

Cypress, Let's Active's first album, illustrated Easter's moody, ringing vision of "jangle pop."

"Most of what I've done has been with tiny budgets. With good musicians or the right chemistry, you can make a really hot record," he noted. "I enjoy that fast-cheap-and-efficient ethic." ■

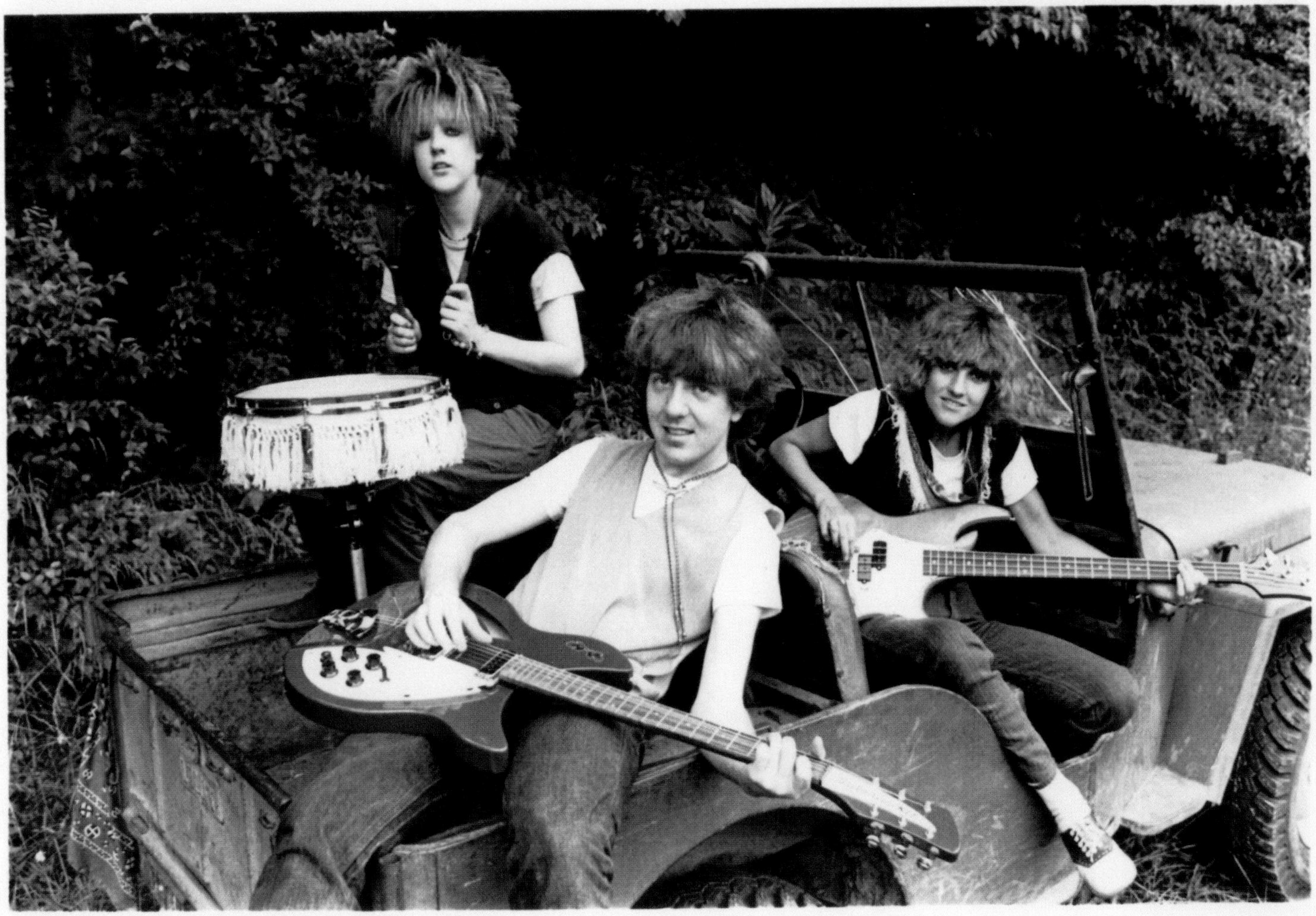

Photo: Laura Levine

LET'S ACTIVE   Sara Romweber   Mitch Easter   Faye Hunter

I.R.S.

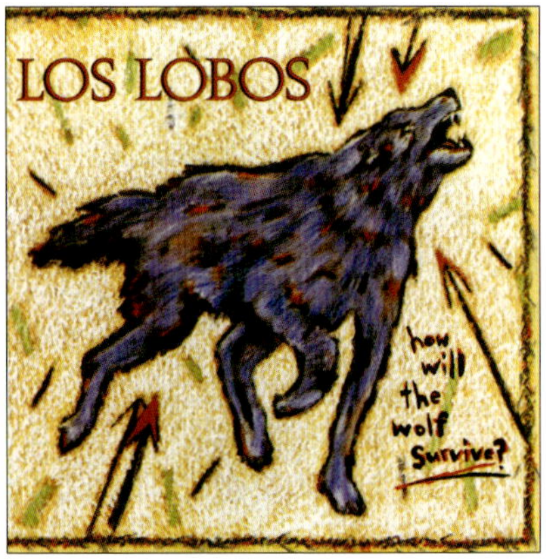

Los Lobos signed a recording contract and produced the exceptional album, *How Will the Wolf Survive?*

Billboard 200: *How Will the Wolf Survive?* (#47)
Billboard Hot 100: "Will the Wolf Survive?" (#78)

THE MEMBERS of Los Lobos were late artistic bloomers. In the late Seventies, the Hispanic quintet from East Los Angeles had survived by performing acoustic Mexican folk music and covering Top 40 standards at every party, bar, restaurant, dance or wedding reception that would have it. Shifting to rock after getting caught up in the Hollywood club scene, Los Lobos started drawing attention outside its home base.

But then the band embarked on a systematic exploration of American and Mexican folkloric music. *How Will the Wolf Survive?* combined an astounding number of genres, from rock 'n' roll to R&B to country to traditional Mexican norteño.

"Once we formed Los Lobos, we reached a point where we were disenchanted with contemporary music," drummer Louie Pérez said. "We didn't want to be a jukebox playing other people's songs, so we stopped being a garage band and concentrated on our roots. Music is becoming multi-ethnic, and that's something we try to explore. That's why we include traditional songs on our records and in our concerts."

But Los Lobos didn't settle for being a "roots" band, simply dredging up old material for audiences who'd never heard it before and calling it their own. The group built on those cultural origins and constructed music that delivered more than the sum of its influences. Purchasing a van, the band toured the country for the first time.

"Some people think our songs are about being disenchanted with the American Dream, about going unfulfilled," Pérez said. "But they're really about hope and faith and resilience, getting up in the morning and doing what you have to do. It would be easy for us people who grew up in a Mexican community to write songs that pigeonhole everything. But by touring, we see some common denominators about growing up in America. It's real stuff that we sing about." ■

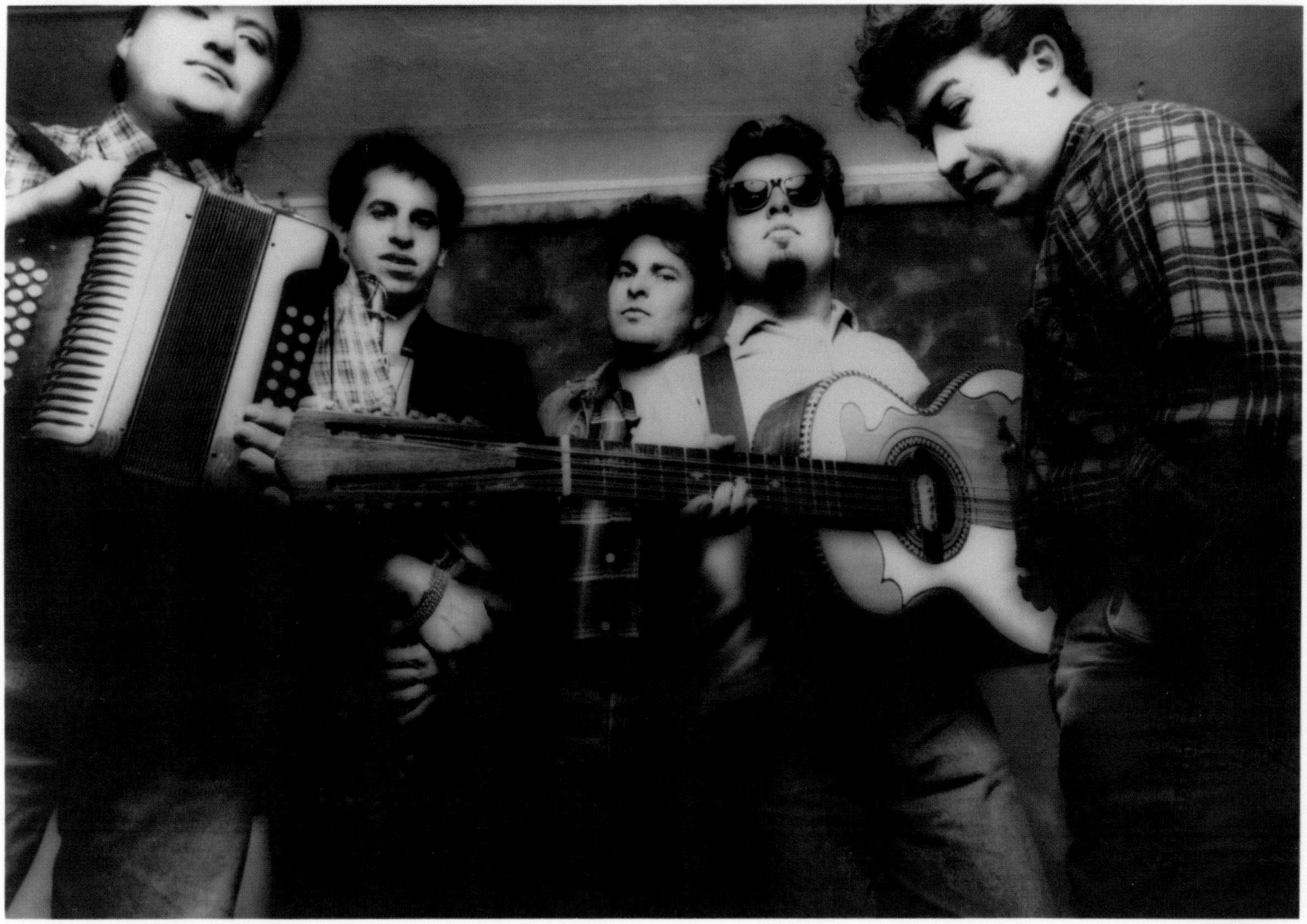

Photo Credit: Caroline Greyshock

LOS LOBOS

WARNER BROS.

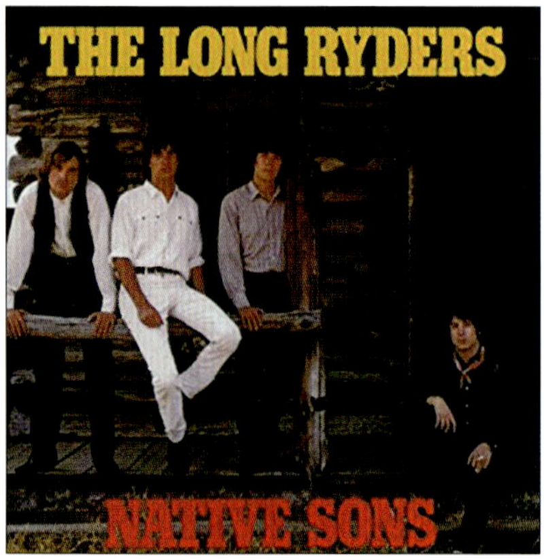

The Long Ryders' musical obsessions were captured on *Native Sons*, bolstering their "cowpunk" cred.

THE LONG Ryders' beginnings could be traced to guitarist Stephen McCarthy's move to Los Angeles from his native Virginia to expand on his country music roots.

"Some ridiculous things were going on in L.A. at the time," McCarthy recalled. "There was still *Urban Cowboy* stuff, which I hated. I loved country music, but I had to get into something that was more rock 'n' roll."

McCarthy answered a newspaper ad for a "Creedence-meets-the-Clash" band and met guitarist Sid Griffin, a Kentucky native who had also made his way out west. With drummer Greg Sowders and bassist Tom Stevens, they formed the Long Ryders to parade their influences—they named themselves after a Walter Hill western, with a "y" spelling in tribute to the Byrds. The band forged a reputation in the competitive Southern California music scene, but not as mere revivalists—the sound was country-influenced but infused with classic-rock energy, "meaning everyone from Chuck Berry to the Sex Pistols," according to McCarthy.

The independent record release *Native Sons*, featuring guest vocals from former Byrd Gene Clark, clicked with critics, but they placed too much emphasis on the band's country pertinence.

"Sure, it's overplayed," McCarthy shrugged. "I grew up with country music, so the band might be playing a really fast song and I'll put country-esque licks around it. But we're definitely more of a rock band. A lot of people think we're trying to be the heirs to the throne of Gram Parsons or the Flying Burrito Brothers—and we love that music a lot—but we really don't sound that much like them at all. They've influenced us, but our rhythm section has been influenced by the Ramones even more. We're somewhere between the two." ■

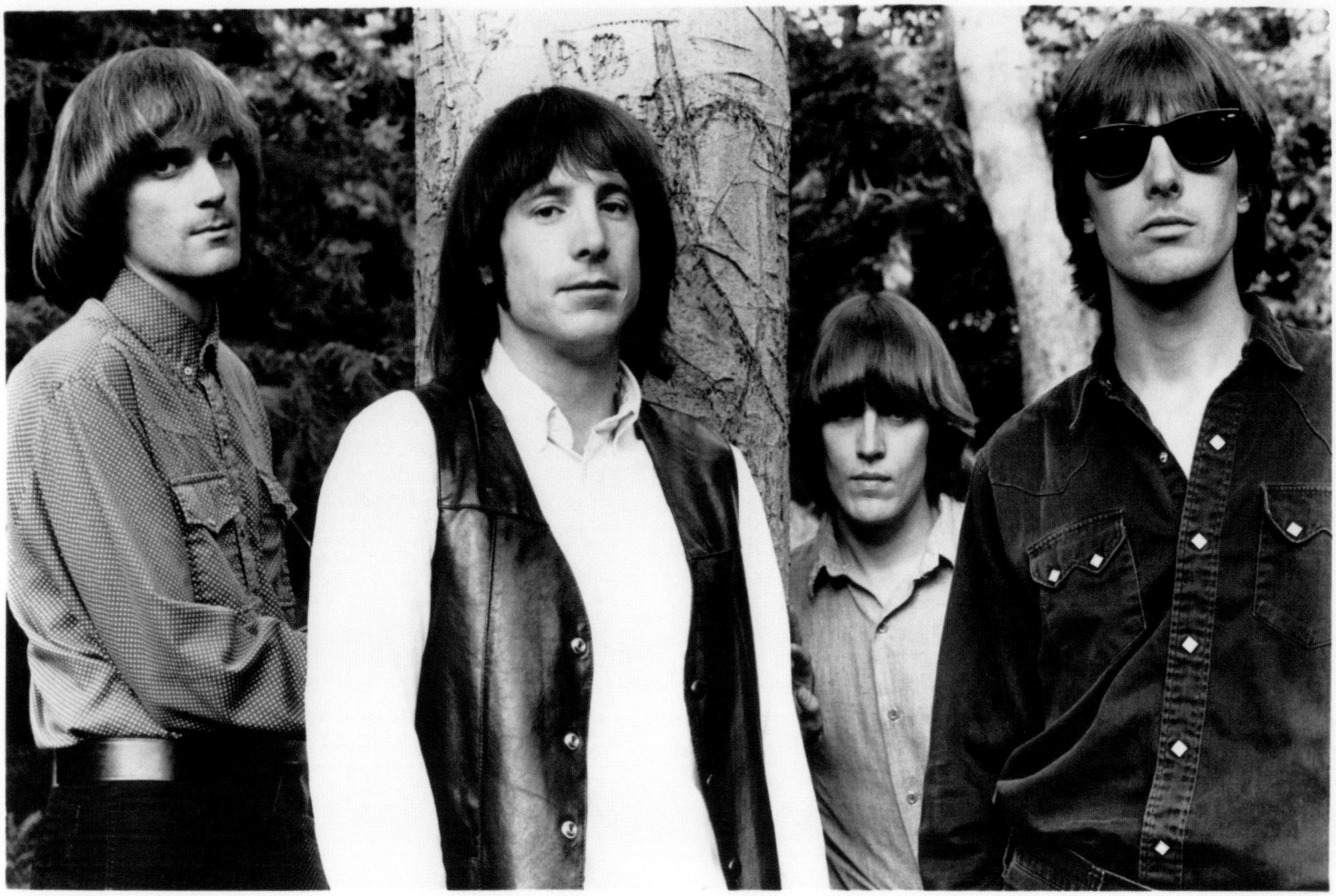

photo:Ed Colver

SID GRIFFIN GREG SOWDERS TOM STEVENS STEPHEN MCCARTHY

THE LONG RYDERS

FRONTIER
BOX 22, SUN VALLEY
CALIFORNIA 91352

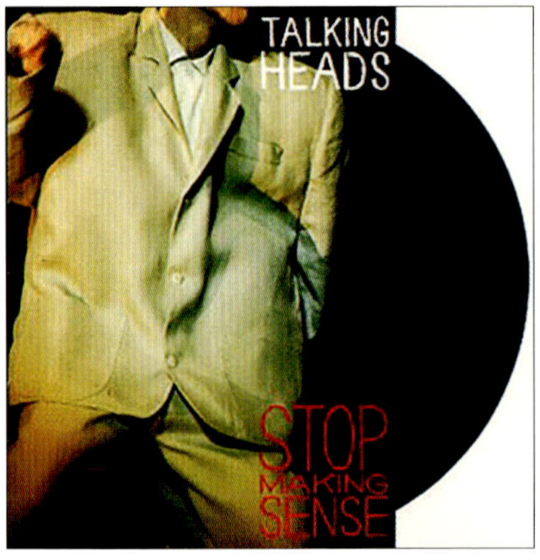

Talking Heads became the subject of *Stop Making Sense*, director Jonathan Demme's lauded concert film.

Billboard 200: *Stop Making Sense* (#41)
Billboard Hot 100: "Once in a Lifetime" (#91)

BY 1983, Talking Heads had emerged as America's premier thinking-man's rock outfit, thanks in large part to the commercial success of the album *Speaking in Tongues* and its Top 10 hit "Burning Down the House." The tour that followed provided the material for director Jonathan Demme's movie *Stop Making Sense* and generated a live album of the same name.

Forgoing interview segments and documentary filler, the concert footage captured everything spectacular about the show, designed by the band to fit a beginning-middle-end format. Well-suited to the film medium, the tour was not only musically superior—Talking Heads represented a seamless melding of rock, funk and techno influences—but visually triumphant as well. Through the use of inventive lighting and stage design, the band managed to create a different look for each song.

In particular, the intimate look at leader David Byrne's unique herky-jerky stage presence was worth celebrating. While other kids were standing in front of their bedroom mirrors pretending to dance like Mick Jagger, who knew where the young Byrne was? His animated, Gumby-esque stage moves were ultimately hilarious and unsettling, and his nonstop performance could have been edited down into a substantial aerobics workout tape. And he wore a white "big suit"—a businessman's uniform that gradually increased in size as the concert progressed.

"I had no reaction to seeing myself on screen," the gangly singer said quietly. "I think the other members of the band were more surprised, seeing themselves in that detail, whether their shirts were ironed or not. I had seen myself on video and knew what to expect. I grew into the role when I realized I was becoming a focal point on stage. But it was more of an attitude change than a physical change."

That kind of progressive thinking had already marked Talking Heads' musical career.

"I've noticed that it works in our favor," Byrne admitted. "I'll buy a record if it's got some really great songs on it, but I might not buy the next one by the same artist if it doesn't have the hits on it. Whereas with us, I think some people buy us sight unseen. It's kind of a 'let's see what they're up to' attitude.

"But I've always been afraid that we'd get stuck in that rut of recording an album and then touring. Now that *Stop Making Sense* is out, I feel that there's no need to go out and tour next time we release an album. We've captured that on film—not just the performance, but the whole stage show makes some kind of statement. To make the statement again seems bizarre." ■

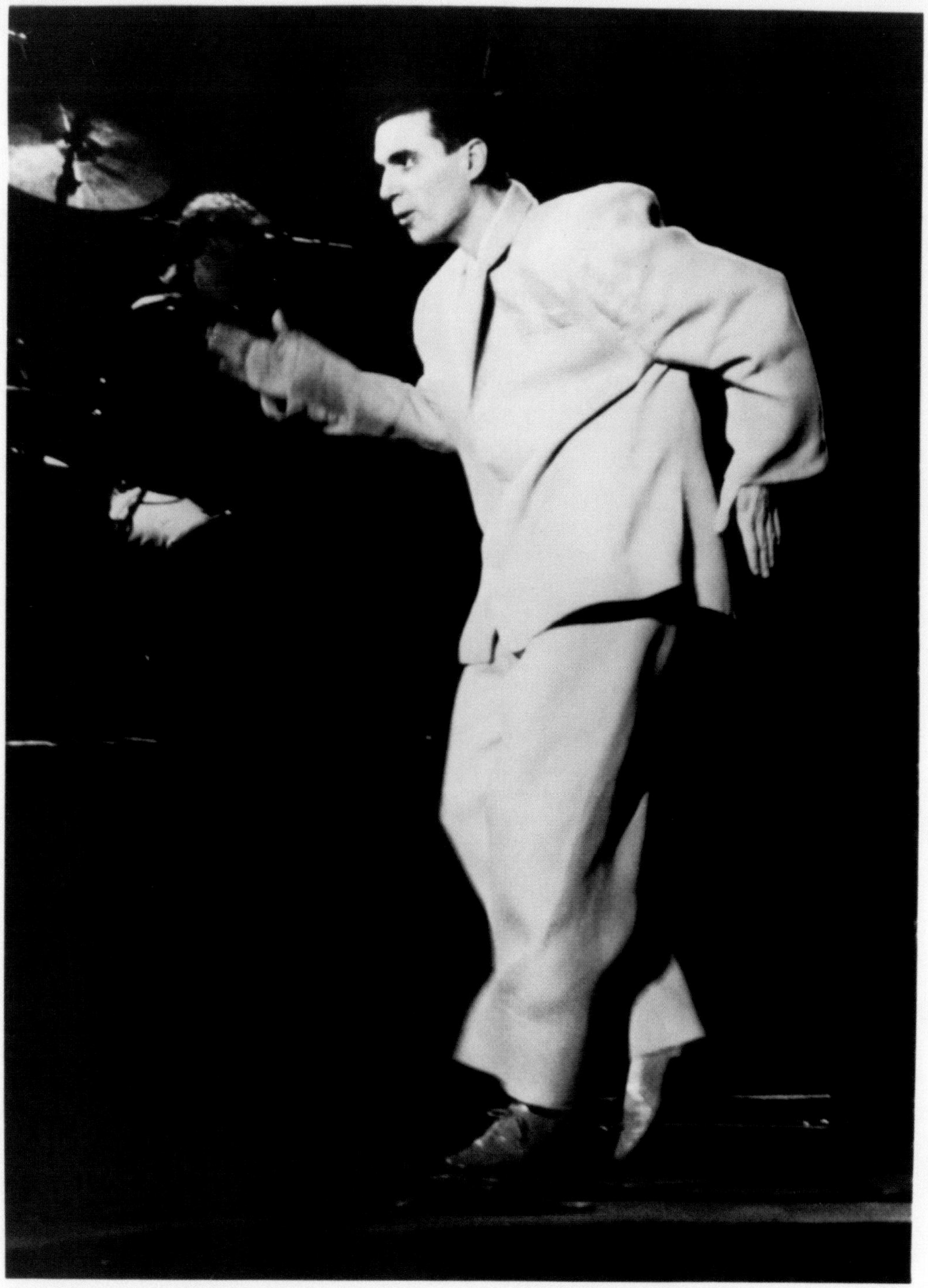

Photo Credit: Hugh Brown

TALKING HEADS FILMS PRESENTS STOP MAKING SENSE

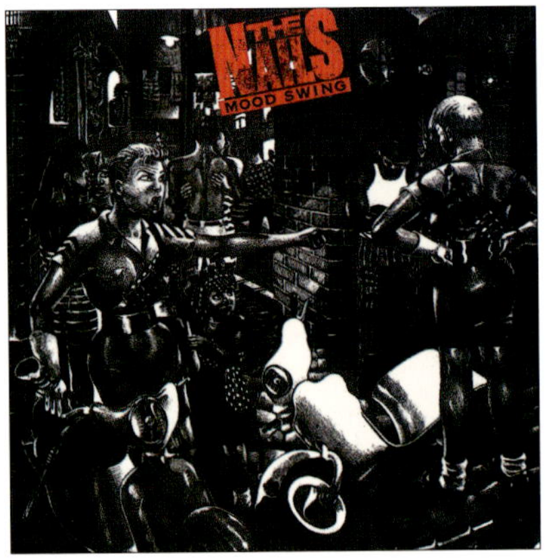

The Nails re-recorded "88 Lines About 44 Women" for *Mood Swing*, the band's first major-label album.

IN 1976, Patti Smith look-alike Marc Campbell arrived in Boulder, Colorado, from San Francisco, where he'd been turning out 16mm films and performing "sexually explicit" songs in small clubs in a duo called the Pits of Passion. While reading the University of Colorado bulletin board one day, he noticed a card posted by student David Kaufman, who sought to form a reggae band.

They formed the nucleus of the Ravers, a five-piece band that soon set the Rocky Mountain music scene on its edge. The New York/London punk explosion hadn't penetrated Colorado, where numerous country bars still ruled the area.

The Ravers recorded "Cops Are Punks," and the single received national attention from the magazine *Trouser Press*. One fateful day, the police raided the band's basement rehearsal hall, mistakenly thinking it was a bomb factory. Shortly thereafter, Campbell and Kaufman moved the entire group to New York City. Years of steady gigging in Manhattan clubs followed.

Once transplanted, the group slowly began its transition to the Nails, mining the rich "American poetic tradition" also worked by Lou Reed, the Doors and Bruce Springsteen. Campbell explained that the Nails' music emanated from "a mystical and sexual area. I write in a cinematic way, trying to create through language and sound, texture and atmosphere, a specific mood. Each of the songs—little fictions, I call them—tells a story to explore those moods."

Originally recorded for the 1981 EP *Hotel tor Women*, "88 Lines About 44 Women" was re-recorded and distributed nationally on RCA Records in 1984. Many members of the male species knew at least a few of the archetypal females in the lyrics, and a lot of women recognized themselves in the tightly compacted two-line life stories. The Nails had constructed a sardonic song that took an unflinching look at real life in the New York tradition of Lou Reed's "Walk on the Wild Side," the New York Dolls' "Personality Crisis" and Jim Carroll's "People Who Died."

Los Angeles progressive radio giant KROQ-FM put "88 Lines About 44 Women" in heavy rotation, and the song zoomed up the dance floor charts. The Nails subsequently played their first US tour, concentrating on southern California and Colorado. ■

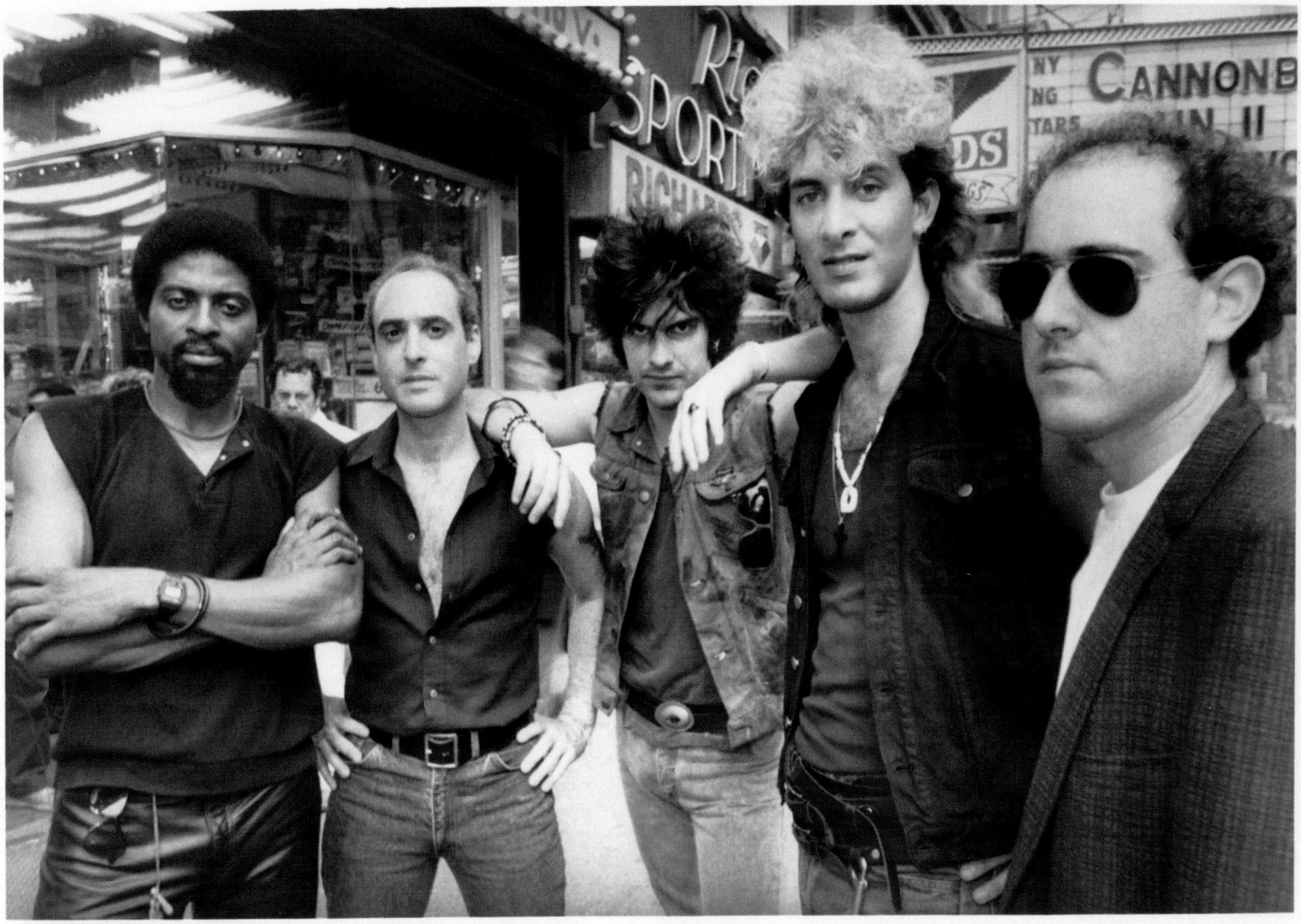

THE NAILS

Terry Dunne Management
125 East 15th Street, New York, N.Y. 10003
(212) 254-2956

RCA
Records and Cassettes

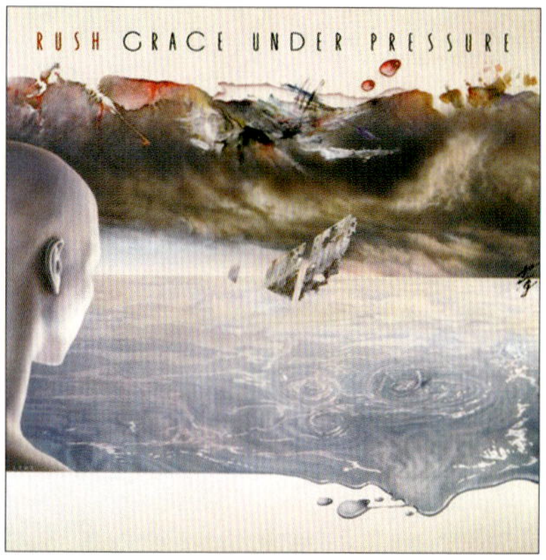

Billboard 200: *Grace Under Pressure* (#10)

Grace Under Pressure marked yet another development in the evolution of Rush's synth-driven sound.

OLD OPINIONS die hard, as Rush could testify. Few people besides the Canadian band's fans realized that the members—bassist Geddy Lee, guitarist Alex Lifeson and drummer Neil Peart—had evolved over the years from a pedestrian heavy-metal outfit into one of rock's most musically articulate acts. Peart professed an understanding of the group's reputation.

"I have a comprehension of the music scene at a certain time, but never how we fit into it," he professed. "No one can listen to or like all the music in the world, and I'm guilty of it, too. I hear of a group spoken of in a certain context, and until proven differently I don't take them seriously. So people have convenient labels and preconceptions—some still call us a heavy-metal band, but anyone who knows our music and the changes we've been through realizes that's absurd."

The band's continued experimentation with new sound textures on synthesizers and sequencers, as well as varying musical styles, came into play on *Grace Under Pressure*.

"Sound checks became an important part of our 'research and development,'" Peart explained. "A lot of valuable spontaneity goes on during those afternoons on tour—we arrive at the hall in a variety of moods, and they're expressed very directly in the way we start playing. Sometimes very interesting things are investigated under those circumstances, so we started recording them for reference."

To name the album, Peart borrowed an Ernest Hemingway phrase to describe the long, arduous search for a different person to manage the recording after making the decision to leave long-time producer Terry Brown. Current events found in the Toronto-based newspaper *The Globe & Mail* inspired much of the album's lyrical content.

"I found myself reading it over breakfast every day, before I would start working on lyrics," Peart revealed. "The topics of the day, especially as expressed in the editorials and letters to the editor, were necessarily on my mind. This was the time of the Korean 747 shoot-down, the ongoing cruise-missile controversies, acid rain threatening health and wars raging everywhere. Songs like 'Distant Early Warning' and 'Between the Wheels' were definitely interwoven with these thoughts and feelings." ■

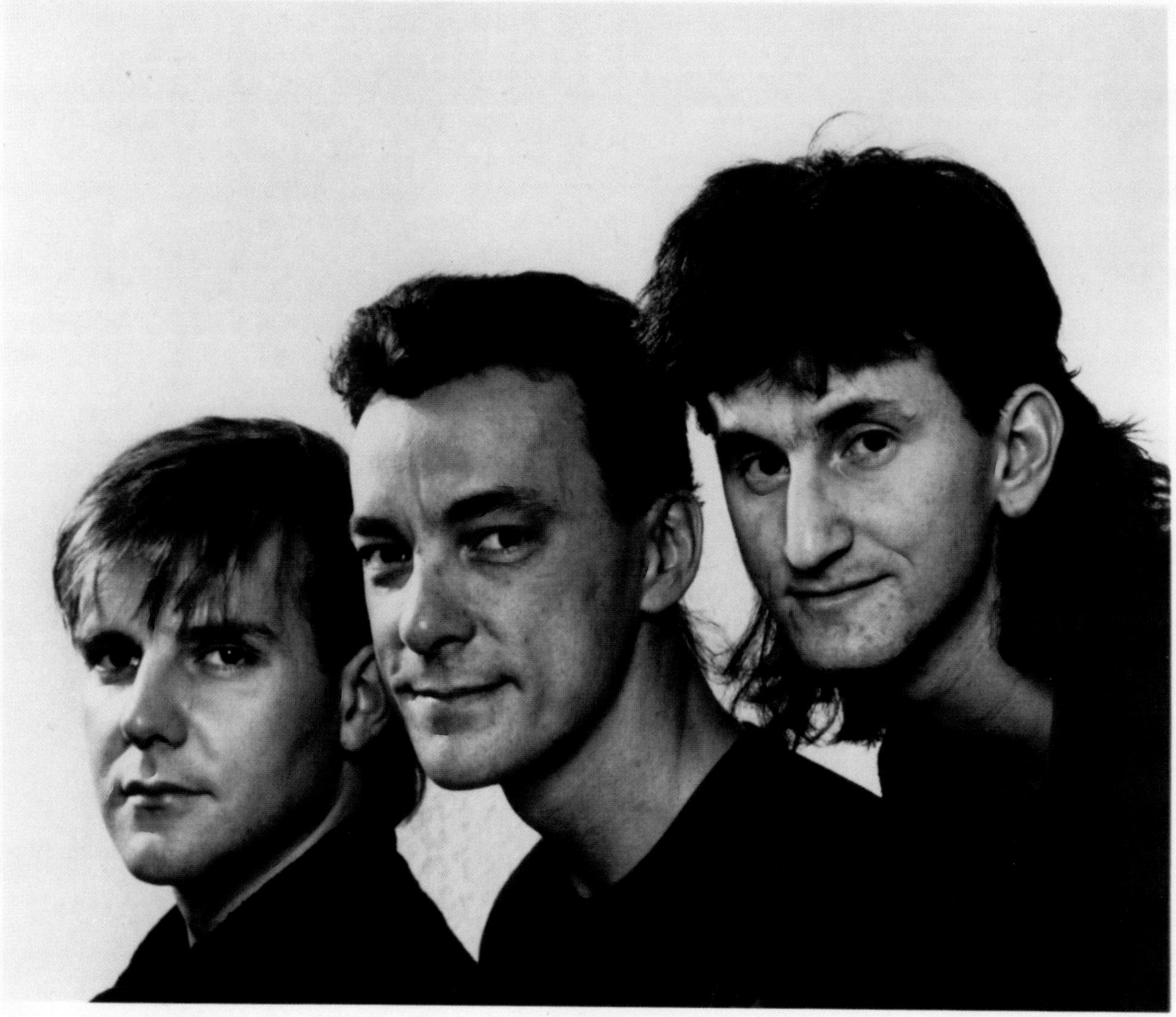

Alex Lifeson Neil Peart Geddy Lee

R U S H

Mercury

PolyGram Records

SRO MANAGEMENT

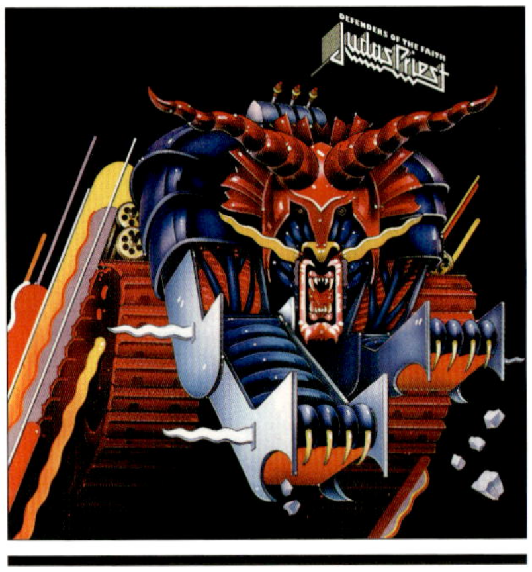

Judas Priest continued its influence as elder statemen of heavy metaldom with *Defenders of the Faith*.

Billboard 200: *Defenders of the Faith* (#18)

JUDAS PRIEST cranked out ear-splitting sound. Lead singer Rob Halford's ability to screech over an impressive multi-octave range competed ferociously with the double lead guitar din of K.K. Downing and Glenn Tipton. But the English band wasn't your average gaggle of heavy-metal bashers. In concert, Halford rode onstage in full leather-chains-and-chrome regalia on a half-ton Harley-Davidson Low Rider motorcycle. He gleefully cracked whips throughout the show, and ended by firing machine gun blanks into the crowd.

"Then studs and leather became the rockers' uniform," Halford said. "I got the idea for wearing them from, um, a shop I was looking around in."

For *Defenders of the Faith*, graphic artist Doug Johnson designed another formidible beast character—Metallian, a catlike animal that jumped from the cover of the album.

"Our onstage act is kind of 'heavy-metal assault,'" the surprisingly soft-spoken Halford admitted. "Heavy-metal music was slighted for a while—a lot of the bands of our ilk were labeled as 'dinosaur rock' when other styles of music were fashionable. But it comes full circle, and the heavy-metal audiences are among the most faithful."

Judas Priest's leather-and-chains appeal was scrutinized by the Parents Music Resource Center for "Eat Me Alive." Although Halford wouldn't deny that the group's early output was heavy on demonic, doom-laden imagery, he dismissed the criticism, maintaining that the song was intended as a spoof of sex-and-music relationships.

"These battles between parents and their children have been going on since day one—'Get back in the cave by six o'clock,' you know?" he insisted. "Maybe someday more parents will simply get behind what we're doing." ■

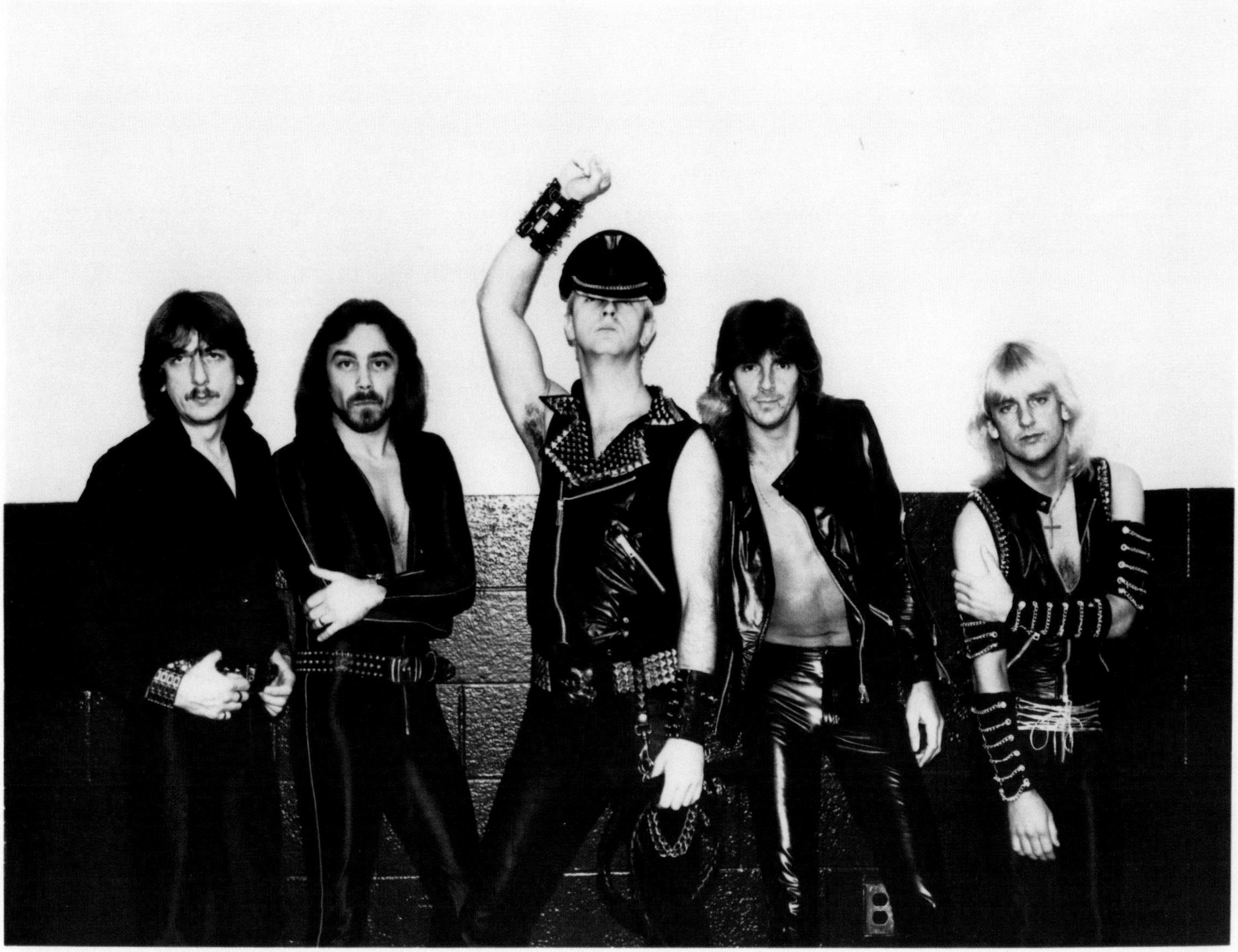

PHOTOGRAPH: ROSS MARINO

JUDAS PRIEST

Columbia
8401

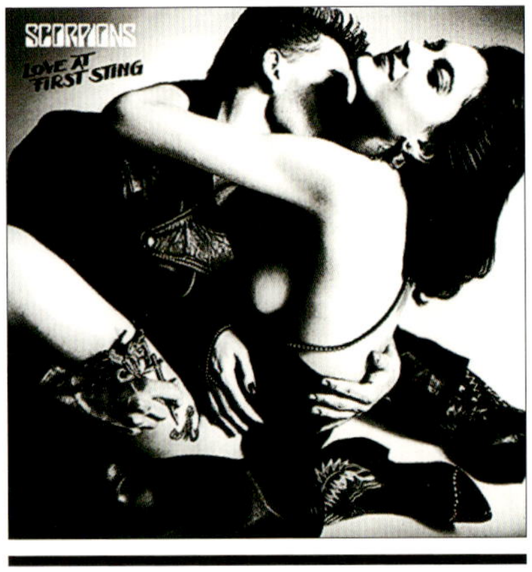

Billboard 200: *Love at First Sting* (#6)
Billboard Hot 100: "Rock You Like a Hurricane" (#25); "Still Loving You" (#64)

Scorpions' *Love at First Sting* and the anthemic "Rock You Like a Hurricane" made the German rockers stars.

IN THE world of heavy metal, bands reaped what they sowed—and for Scorpions, it was harvest time. After an exhaustive, 77-concert tour of the United States and Canada to support its 1982 *Blackout* album, the Teutonic band saw *Love at First Sting* get enthusiastic response from American radio programmers.

"We're not the people who do eight hours work and then go home to family," founder/guitarist Rudolf Schenker said. "If you want to do something extreme, you always have to cut something else. If you want to have everything, you can't have everything, *verstand*? Rock 'n' roll is still our first love, and that's how we live. We're happiest with the opportunity to tour around the world."

All of which sat well with drummer Herman Rarebell. "We made a lot of fans last year," he said. "Scorpions is a live act, and that's what helped *Blackout* go platinum. We won't have to tour as hard anymore—we'll be out on the road just as long, but we won't be hitting the same places twice. That's the point."

Scorpions were proud of their reputation as hard-rock crazies in concert. "Well, yes, we really freak out," singer Klaus Meine said in his clipped German accent. "But that's what people have come to expect. We've been building up for success in America step by step."

Rarebell was happy to be out with his bandmates at all—following the last tour, he suffered a case of exhaustion and delayed the recording of *Love at First Sting* for two months. "I don't have any idea how many dates we did on that tour," he allowed, "but I was out of it. Once I got well, though, everything went smoothly. We didn't have anything happen this time to rival what happened to Klaus during *Blackout* when he had throat surgery."

Love at First Sting solidified Scorpions' burgeoning reputation as a premier metal band—the anthem "Rock You Like a Hurricane," "Big City Nights" and the power ballad "Still Loving You" dominated MTV and FM radio. "But we never plan for the radio when we make records," Rarebell insisted. "If a song is commercial and people play it, we don't mind, but that is not what we're trying to do."

On the extensive worldwide tour of arenas, Scorpions played to 2.2 million spectators and logged more than 45,000 miles with 48 tons of equipment and a crew of 54. Schenker described life on the road for Scorpions, related to backstage parties, as "one of the last adventures, where new stories happen every night." ■

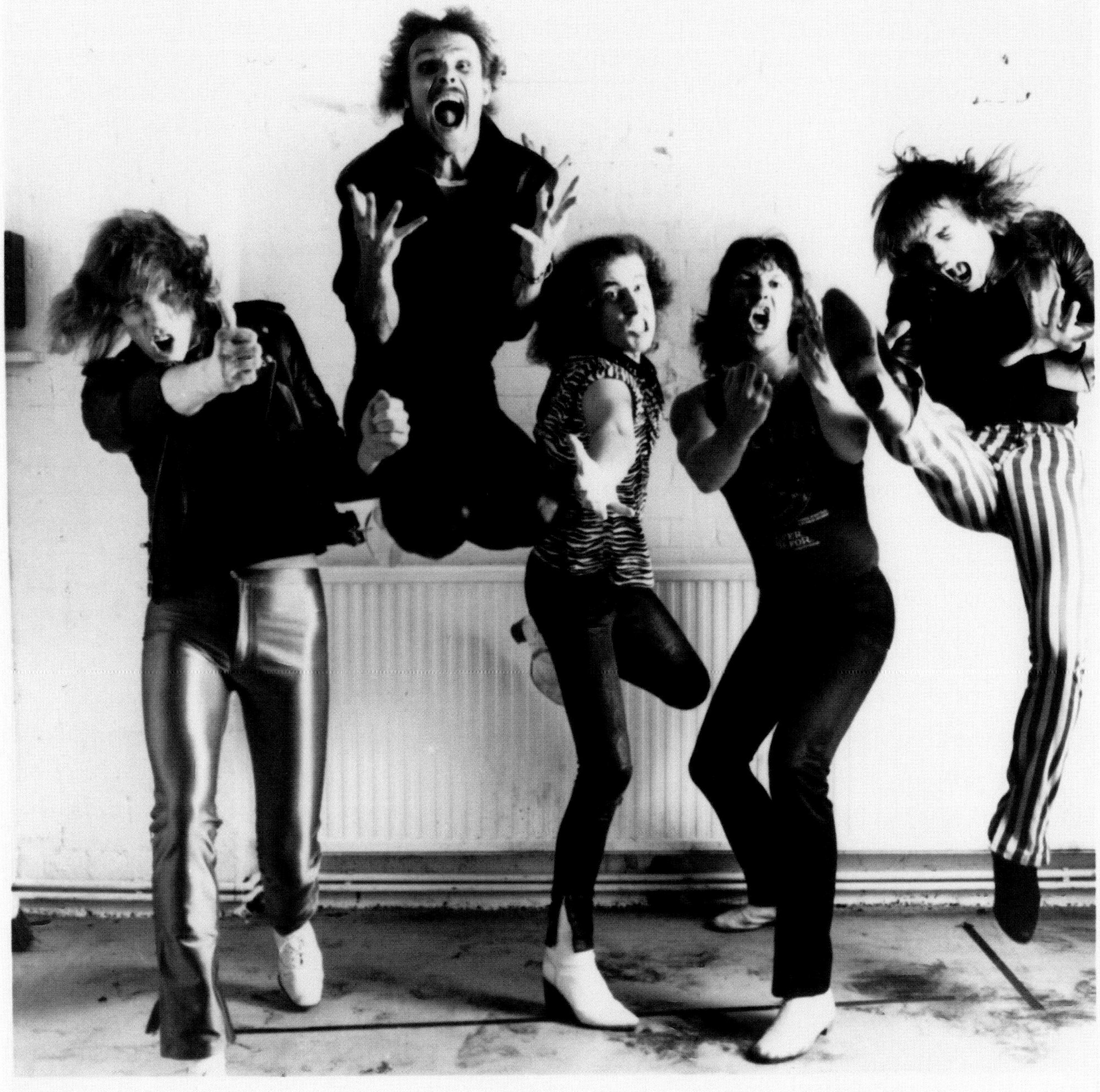

PolyGram Records

SCORPIONS

Management:
Contemporary Communications Corp.
65 W. 55th St.
New York, N Y 10019
Phone: 212/765-2600

mercury

Billboard 200: *This Is Spinal Tap* (#121)

The soundtrack to the "mockumentary" *This Is Spinal Tap* parodied the ephemera of the heavy-metal scene.

INTRODUCING A gracelessly aging British band, *This Is Spinal Tap* was the funniest movie ever made about rock 'n' roll, a fictional and admirably accurate spoof of heavy-metal stereotypes and the music business. Penned by actors Christopher Guest, Harry Shearer, Michael McKean and director Rob Reiner, the film chronicled the group's history of constant personality clashes and musical differences, and captured the wicked mishaps on the disastrous "Smell the Glove" tour.

Guitarist Nigel Tufnel (Guest) explained why the settings on his amplifier numbered up to 11, because "When you're on 10, all the way up, where can you go? Eleven. One louder." He composed at his piano and spoke earnestly about his foray into classical music ("I'm influenced by Mozart and Bach, and it's sort of in-between those—it's like a Mach piece, really") and then revealed the piece was called "Lick My Love Pump." And he came close to a meltdown over the backstage catering when the cold cuts were big and the bread was small.

Tufnel claimed the movie was "a gross distortion."

"It was a double-edged gun—it made us infamous, but it made us look pathetic," Tufnel said. "The director, Marty DeBergi (Reiner), chose to show us not finding the stage. But you saw us performing—we must have found the stage on those occasions."

The songs on the accompanying soundtrack—notably "Sex Farm," "Big Bottom," "Hell Hole" and "Tonight I'm Gonna Rock You Tonight," all co-written by the cast members—blended into heavy-metal culture. Yet many of the genre's adherents didn't get it—they thought that Spinal Tap was a real group. The people laughing hardest were the very folks the band lampooned—musicians like Ozzy Osbourne and Aerosmith's Stephen Tyler claimed to be the inspiration for *This Is Spinal Tap*.

Meanwhile, Tufnel explained his latest invention.

"Guitarists are always saying, 'Could you make the tone a little warmer?' I've designed something—it's made of wool and goes over the knobs of the guitar. It's a tone cozy." ■

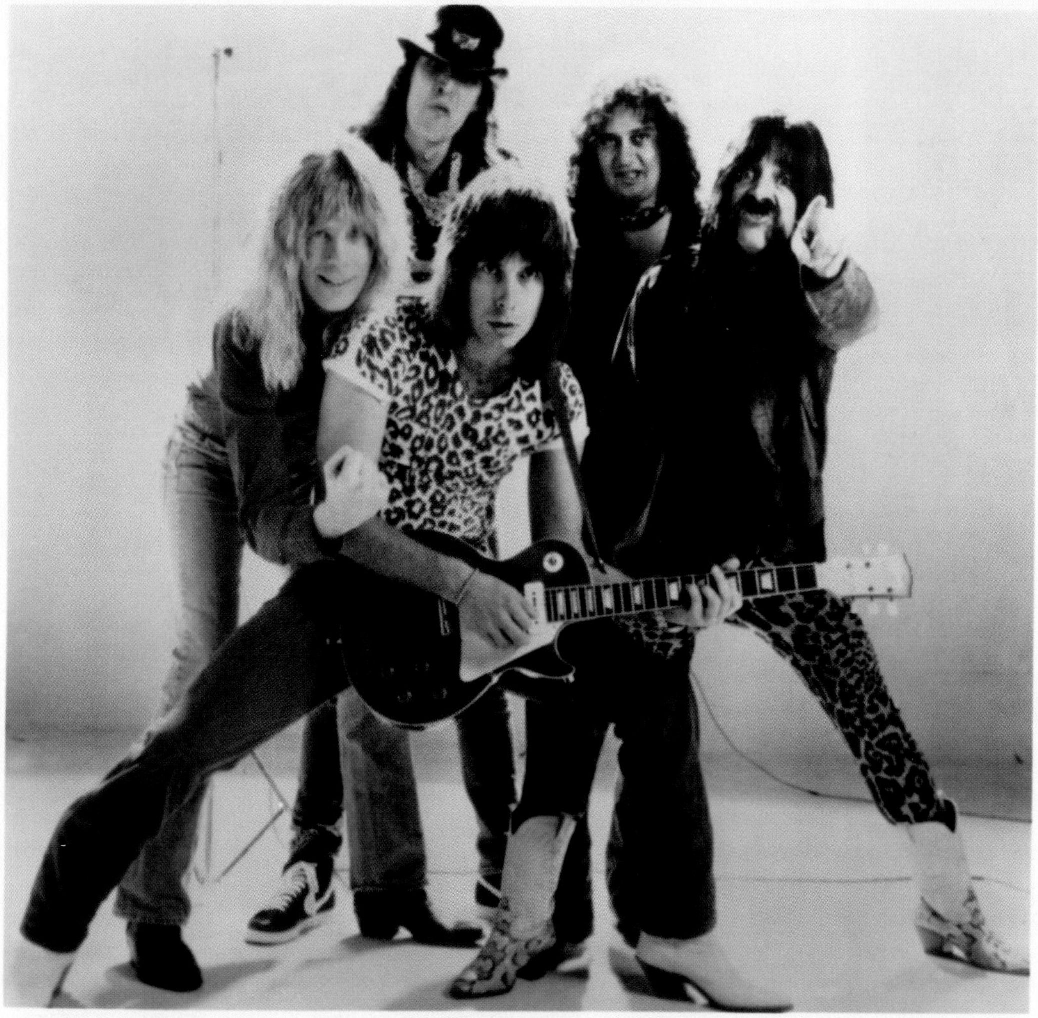

EMBASSY PICTURES

Spinal Tap™

polydor

POLYMER

PolyGram Records

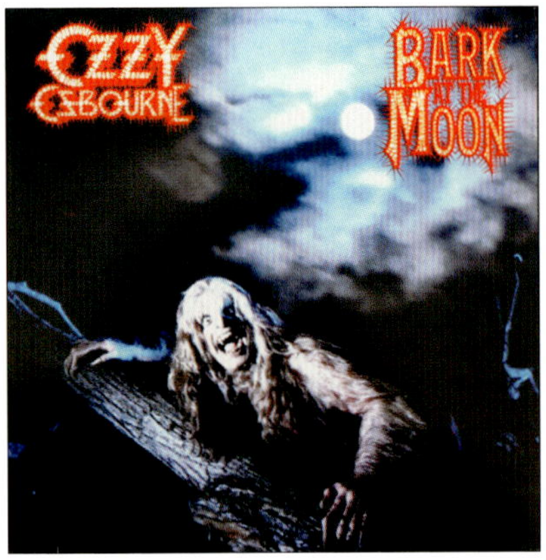

Reeling from boycotted shows and guitarist Randy Rhoads' death, **Ozzy Osbourne** released *Bark at the Moon*.

Billboard 200: *Bark at the Moon* (#19)

OZZY OSBOURNE didn't mind being famous. He just didn't care for how he became that way—as if biting the head off a dove at a big corporate meeting or a bat onstage was something to reconsider. When he embarked on his campaign of outrageous stunts, he only did it to get out from under the shadow of Black Sabbath, his former band. The expected backlash came to a boil during a tour of the Midwest—several conservative officials campaigned to have the Oz's concerts banned.

"I've done my publicity-craving all too well," he insisted. "I'm not a monster like people think."

The controversy had settled down a bit, though—and so had Osbourne. *Bark at the Moon* followed in the wake of such nice-guy gestures as a donation to the SPCA, another ploy to erode his I-snack-on-puppies image. Osbourne in reality was extremely polite, although he had a distracted air about him, as if he were listening to voices no one else could hear. He also had a domestic side—it seemed as if his wife Sharon was perpetually pregnant. "I've got to find out what's causing it!" the singer quipped.

A year after guitarist Randy Rhoads had died in a plane crash, Jake E. Lee joined Osbourne to record *Bark at the Moon*. Osbourne intentionally endeavored to come off with his tongue planted firmly in his cheek—he envisioned himself as sort of a Vincent Price of the heavy-metal set—and he had a ball doing what he was doing. *Bark at the Moon* contained the title track, a fan favorite. The music video, featuring Osbourne transforming into a werewolf, became popular on MTV.

"Stephen King writes horror books. John Carpenter makes horror movies. I sing some horror songs—and that's all it is, a different angle on entertainment. If everybody wrote Pat Boone songs, it would be a pretty boring industry, wouldn't it?"

That November, Osbourne admitted himself to the Betty Ford Center for rehab of drug and alcohol addiction. ■

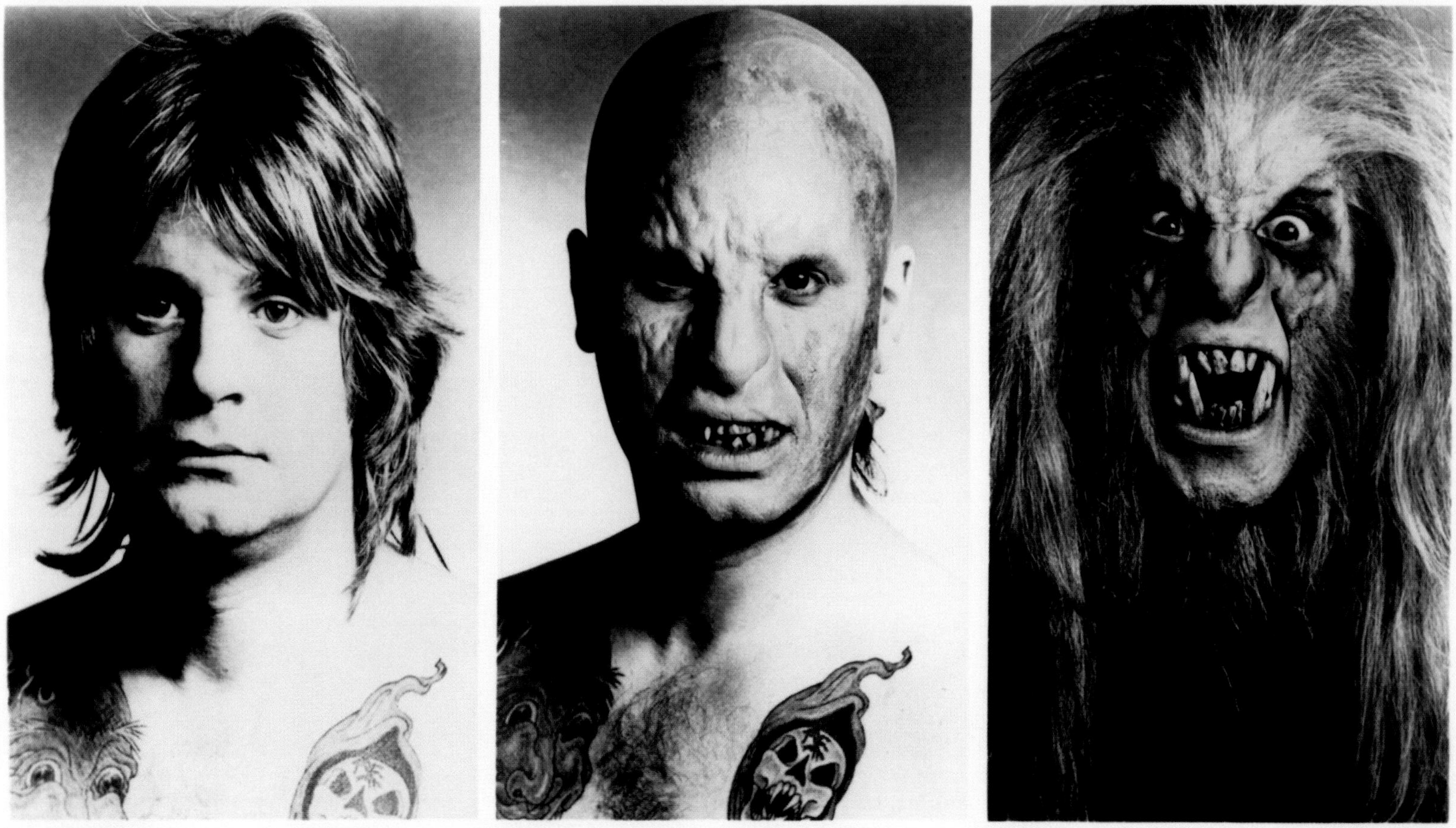

JENSEN
COMMUNICATIONS
PUBLIC RELATIONS
(213) 841-3343

OZZY OSBOURNE

Epic

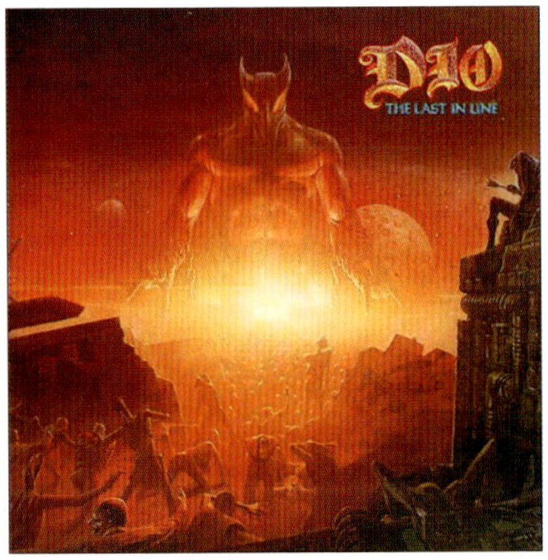

Billboard 200: *The Last in Line* (#23)

Ronnie James Dio got his due as a heavy-metal force with his group Dio's second album, *The Last in Line*.

RONNIE JAMES Dio had been the frontman of Ritchie Blackmore's Rainbow, and he had replaced Ozzy Osbourne in Black Sabbath for three albums. He then formed a self-named band because he believed it had commercial value.

"I don't consider this a solo career," he insisted. "It's a band, a band called Dio. It's my name out in front, but let's face it, it makes more sense. Who the hell knows who the other members are, generally speaking? It is my band—I control it, I spend all my money on it—so why not call it Dio? I think it was the intelligent thing to do."

The Last in Line, the band's sophomore effort, became the biggest hit of Dio's career; the title track hit the Top 10 of *Billboard*'s Album Rock Tracks chart. Not that the diminutive vocalist had any doubts. His ego was substantial, but he claimed he was merely confident of his abilities, and the group became an arena headliner. He felt he'd finally solved the personality clashes he'd endured in past bands.

"I knew we were going to do well because we deserve to," the outspoken Dio noted. "We're a good band, we work hard, we believe in our fans, they believe in us. That's really all you need. I don't think you need MTV and *Circus* (a heavy-metal periodical) or the other things that break an artist. If I thought my career would soar or fall on what people in the media have said about me, I'd have to get the hell out. Because I haven't been treated very kindly in the past."

Although Dio was a New England native and a San Fernando Valley resident, he was often assumed to be British because of his association with English performers—many of whom had propagated his reputation as a prima donna.

"The media admires certain people. And those media people might think it's my fault that those bands failed or something. I think they ought to put the blame where it lies, with the bands themselves. I couldn't care less about what people say about me. I know what I am. I know how well I sleep every night. And I know what I've done with my life and what other people haven't done with theirs." ■

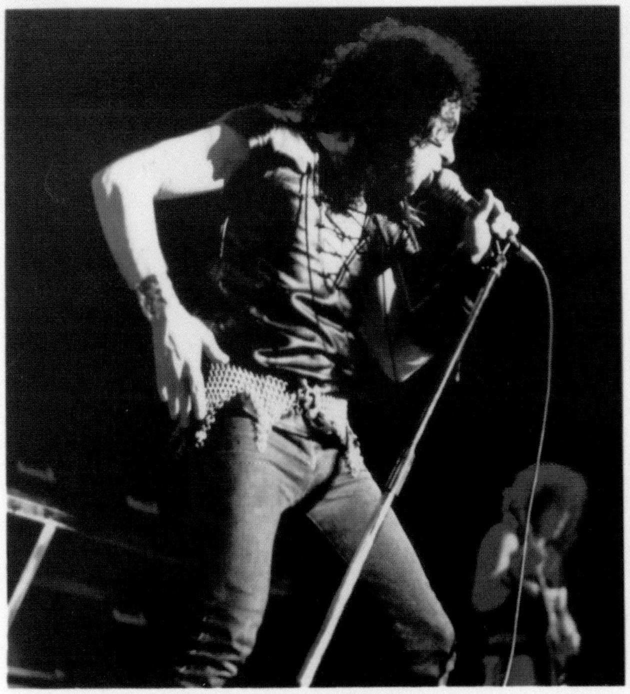

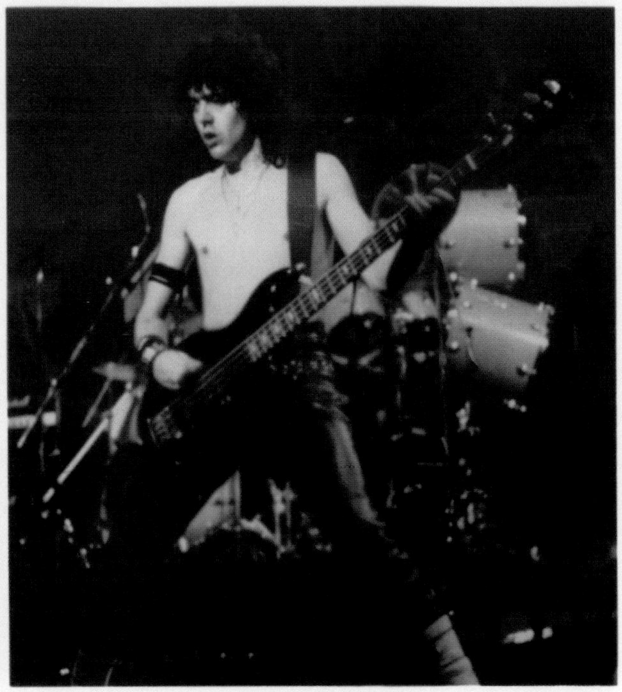

Ronnie James Dio

Jimmy Bain

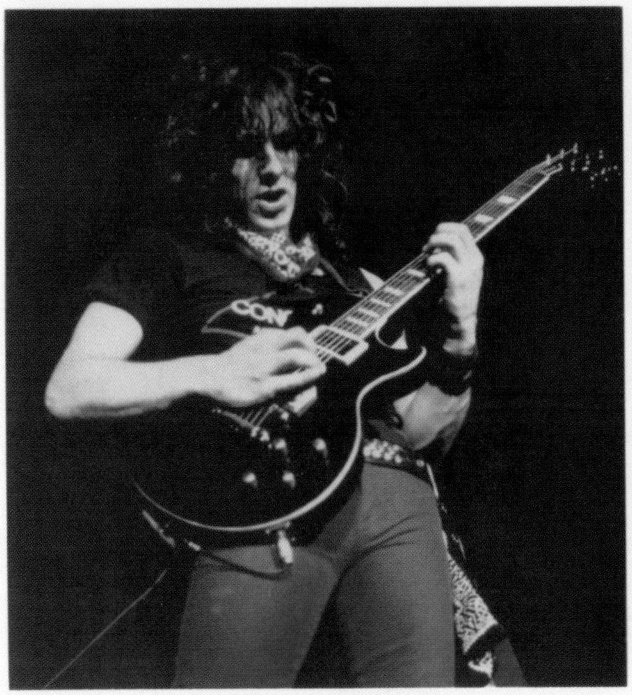

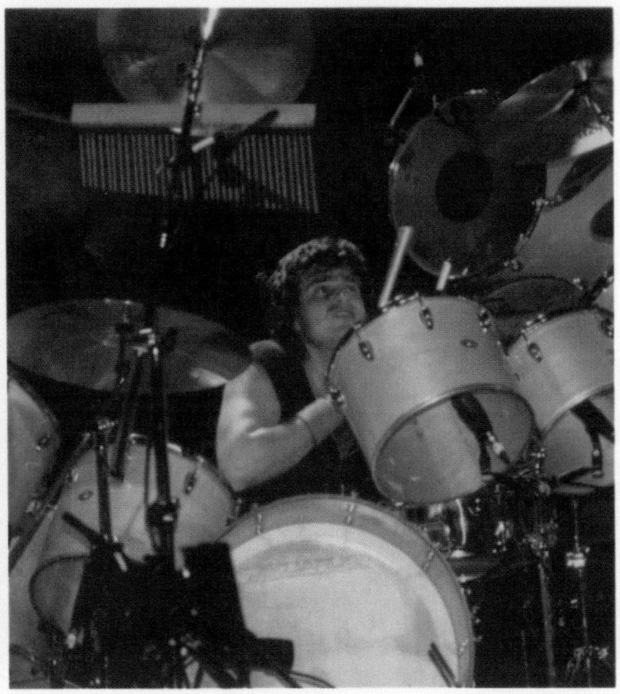

Photo Credit: Richard Kirkland

Vivian Campbell

Vinny Appice

DIO

WARNER BROS.

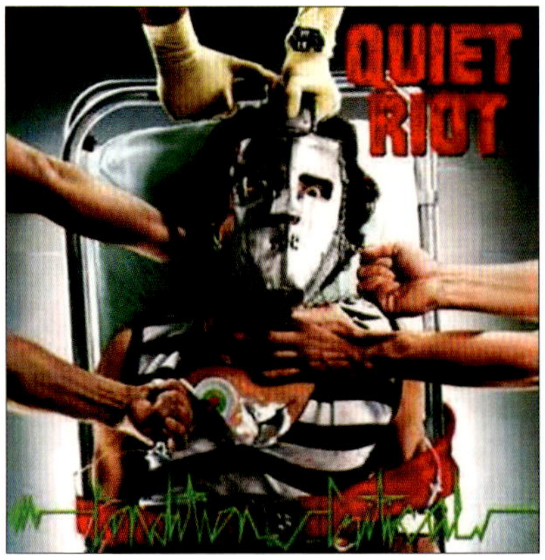

Despite its platinum status, Quiet Riot's *Condition Critical* wasn't nearly the smash its predecessor was.

Billboard 200: *Condition Critical* (#15)
Billboard Hot 100: "Mama Weer All Crazee Now" (#51)

FOR QUIET Riot, 1983 was a heady year—or, more accurately, a bang-your-heady year. After nearly a decade of gigging on the Los Angeles club circuit, the band scored with *Metal Health*, the first heavy-metal debut album in history to reach No. 1 on the charts.

But 1984 was a sobering time for the group—as sober as a group that penned such anthems as "Party All Night" could be. Quiet Riot adjusted to the fact that every album couldn't sell 5 million copies.

"We knew it from the day that *Metal Health* went No. 1," lead singer Kevin DuBrow noted. "That day, as ecstatic and happy as we all were, I said, 'This is something that isn't going to happen every album. We're gonna have to live this down.'"

The process started with *Condition Critical*. Like *Metal Health*, it featured a Slade cover song, "Mama Weer All Crazee Now," but the album quickly slid off the charts after selling 1 million units.

"And it only took eight weeks. It took eight months for *Metal Health* to build to that point," DuBrow said. "That's very nice by me. But anything less than 5 million records, and people are going to say we're going downhill. That's the way the industry is—they build you up, they tear you down."

As Quiet Riot's presence began to fade, the band intended to consolidate its following by touring incessantly, but DuBrow realized he and the boys had to scale back their surfeit of equipment, the size of which prevented them from doing sound checks.

"We had a lot more stuff on the road—a full laser show, elevators for us to come onstage—but we left it at home," he explained. "It took six semis to take it around, and it took all day for the crew to set that shit up. The lasers looked nice when they worked—which was two out of five shows.

"Ah, we never expected to get so big so fast, so we think we've done pretty well for ourselves." ■

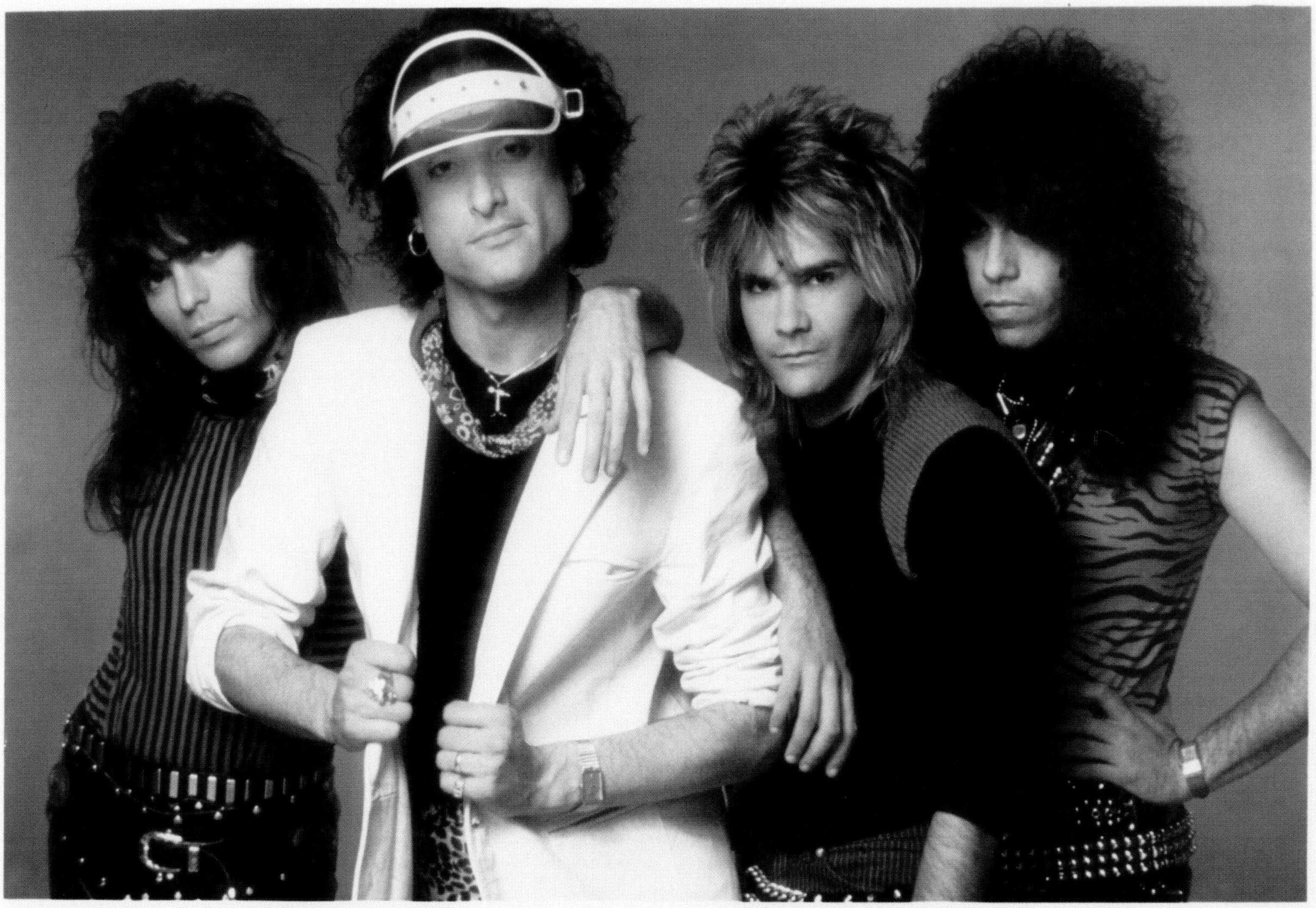

L-R: Rudy Sarzo; Kevin DuBrow; Carlos Cavazo; Frankie Banali

PASHA

QUIET RIOT

EPA
EPIC PORTRAIT ASSOCIATED
8306

WARREN ENTNER MGT.
(213) 655-3942

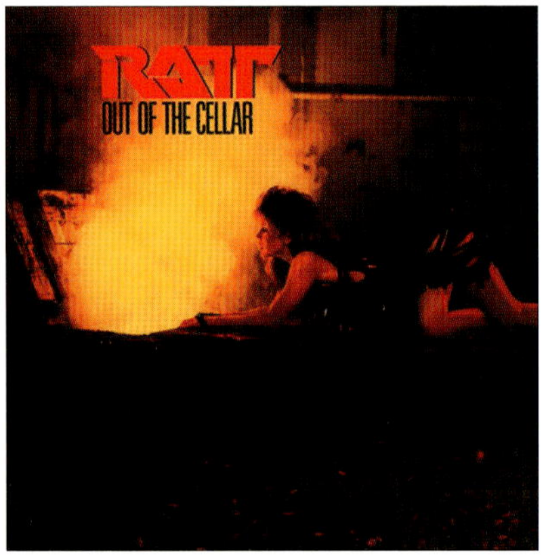

Ratt broke onto the scene with "Round and Round," a song endowed with one of pop metal's sharpest hooks.

Billboard 200: *Out of the Cellar* (#7)
Billboard Hot 100: "Round and Round" (#12); "Wanted Man" (#87)

WHENEVER MUSIC industry executives spotted a musical fad, a "feeding frenzy" followed—major labels rushed out to sign any acts that resembled the trendsetting artist. In the wake of Quiet Riot's successful heavy-metal launch, every satin-and-leather-clad group from Southern California—bands such as Black and Blue, Great White and Ratt—got a record deal.

Ratt's entry in the debut album sweepstakes, *Out of the Cellar*, took off on the strength of the song "Round and Round," a definitive classic with its Aerosmith-like feel and slightly phased vocal on the chorus.

Guitarist Warren DeMartini wasn't convinced about the extent of Quiet Riot's influence. "I think those guys deserve a lot of credit, but they're not totally responsible for the resurgence of heavy metal," he insisted. "If any band got the companies interested in signing bands like us, it was Def Leppard—they got the corporate types to thinking about the salability of rock 'n' roll again. And last year's US '83 Festival was another turning point—the hard-rock day drew more than the other two days put together."

Despite the glut of L.A. metal groups receiving attention, DeMartini sensed a bit of camaraderie between bands rather than any intense rivalry. "We're friendly with them all. Heck, Mötley Crüe kidnapped (Ratt guitarist Warren) Crosby and took him to Boise in their tour bus as a gag. The bands are kinda like tennis pros—they're all intense and are there to get better, but they all came from somewhere."

In Ratt's case, the Whiskey in L.A. was its major stomping ground before Marshall Berle took the quintet under his management wing. Berle was the son of comedian Milton Berle, the legendary entertainer known as "Mr. Television." Milton took an interest in Ratt's career by appearing in the band's "Round and Round" video dressed in drag as his Uncle Miltie character.

It took more than that to put Ratt above the competition, though; DeMartini credited producer Beau Hill. "Atlantic wanted to expose him, and we were a brand-new act, so they suggested that we work together. He's not a real heavy-metal fan, so it made the album controversial—he was conservative and wanted to make it a bit lighter. As it turned out, he helped make the record for a wider audience. This has been in our hearts for a long time. I just turned 21, and I can't remember a time when I wasn't listening to the Who or Jimi Hendrix. We're not about to slack off now—we want to make America Ratt-infested."

In 1984, Ratt played over 200 concerts in front of what an exuberant trade ad called "1,537,534 screaming rodents." ■

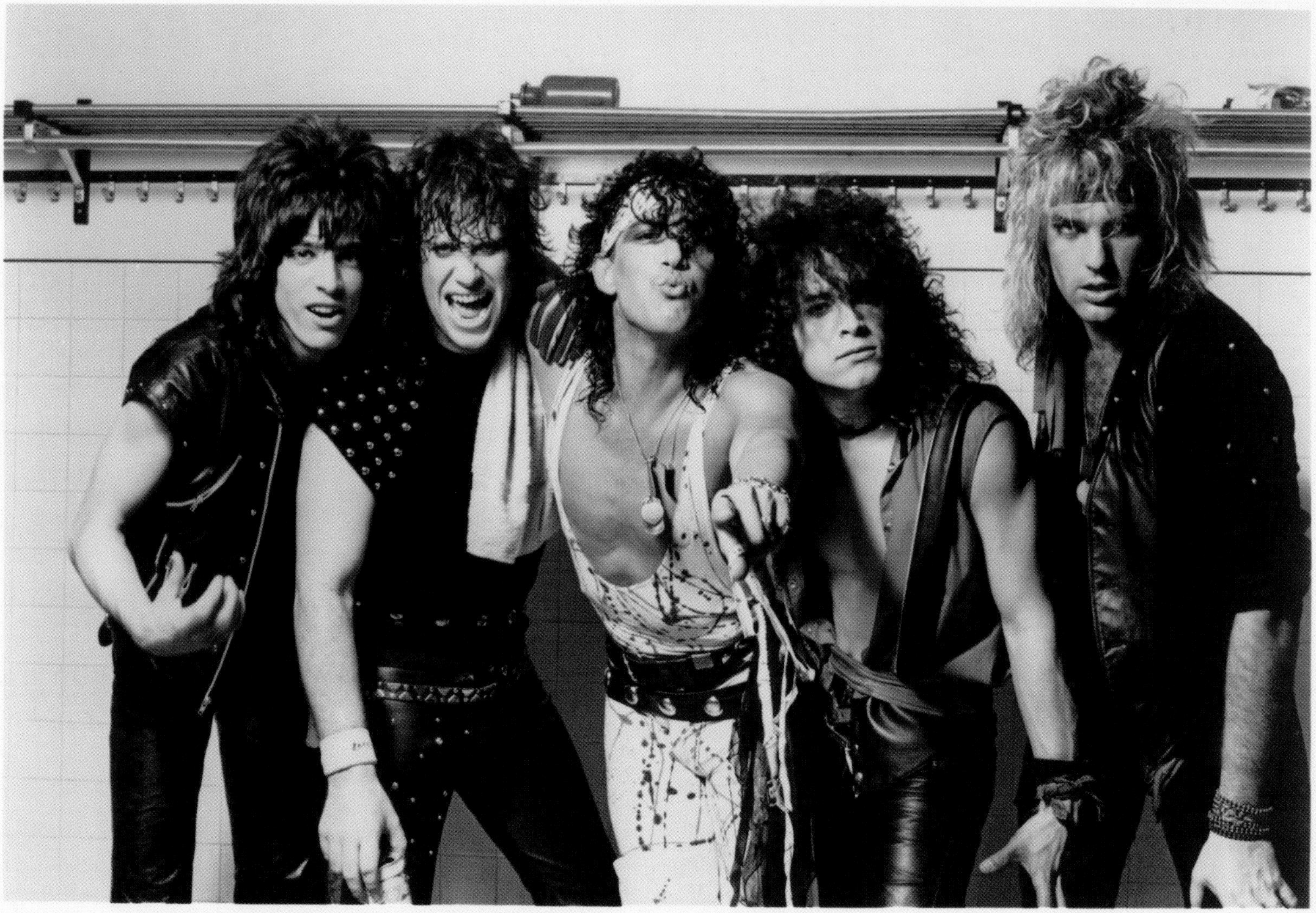

Warren DeMartini Bobby Blotzer Stephen Pearcy Juan Croucier Robbin Crosby

RATT

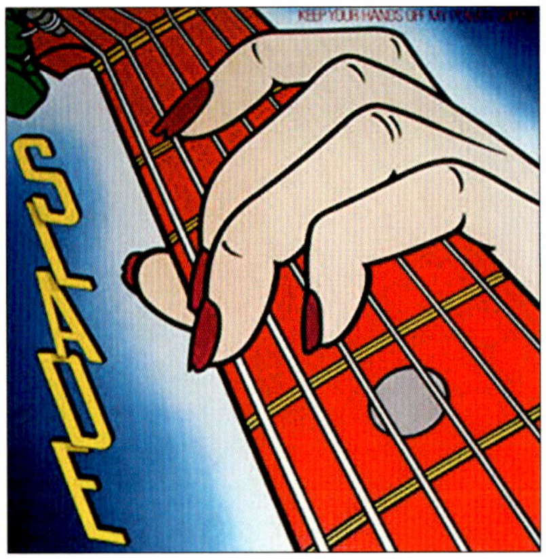

The American success of "Run Runaway" and "My Oh My" indicated new interest in the British group Slade.

Billboard 200: *Keep Your Hands Off My Power Supply* (#33)
Billboard Hot 100: "Run Runaway" (#20);
"My Oh My" (#37)

IN THE early Seventies, Slade was England's most popular group in years. The band had a staggering string of raucous working-class anthems whose misspelled titles belied their brilliant pop structures—among them "Gudbuy T' Jane," "Mama Weer All Crazee Now" and, of course, "Cum On Feel the Noize." The colorful, tight group featured the leather-lunged voice of frontman Noddy Holder, and more than a few people expected them to duplicate their UK success in America.

But despite some notice in a few progressive markets such as St. Louis, Chicago and Detroit, the band never came close to making an impact in the US. *Sladest*, a wonderful greatest-hits compilation of the band's singles, languished in cut-out bins shortly after its 1973 release. Slade ceased touring in the States in 1978, but the group continued to work, and the original foursome—Holder, bassist Jim Lea, guitarist Dave Hill and drummer Don Powell—got a second big chance at the stubborn American market when Quiet Riot hit the top of the charts with a cover version of "Cum On Feel the Noize." Although Slade had hung together for 19 years, there was no resentment.

"We're just happy that there's been a lot of new interest," Holder insisted. "We just weren't here at the right time the first time. Radio didn't want to play us—they said we were 'too rowdy.' And I guess we did stick out like a sore thumb. We were really pleased when Quiet Riot hit the charts. I mean, we never had a hit ourselves, so why not? It was quite lucrative for us on a publishing level alone—Quiet Riot sold close to 5 million copies, and that's a lot of records!"

Slade finally broke into the American market with *Keep Your Hands Off My Power Supply*. The band still cranked out catchy, inventive power pop, and they'd even learned how to spell. Both "Run Runaway" and the power ballad "My Oh My," polished by outside producer John Punter, enjoyed Top 40 success. "My Oh My" was a nice drinking song, with some choir-like vocals that suggested the camaraderie of the group. The band had toned down its image since the days when Holder would appear at their carnival-like stage shows wearing huge platform boots and a glittered top hat.

"But we still look pretty colorful onstage," he declared. "We play because we like to play—that hasn't changed about us. If America decides to latch on this time around, we'll be appreciative." ■

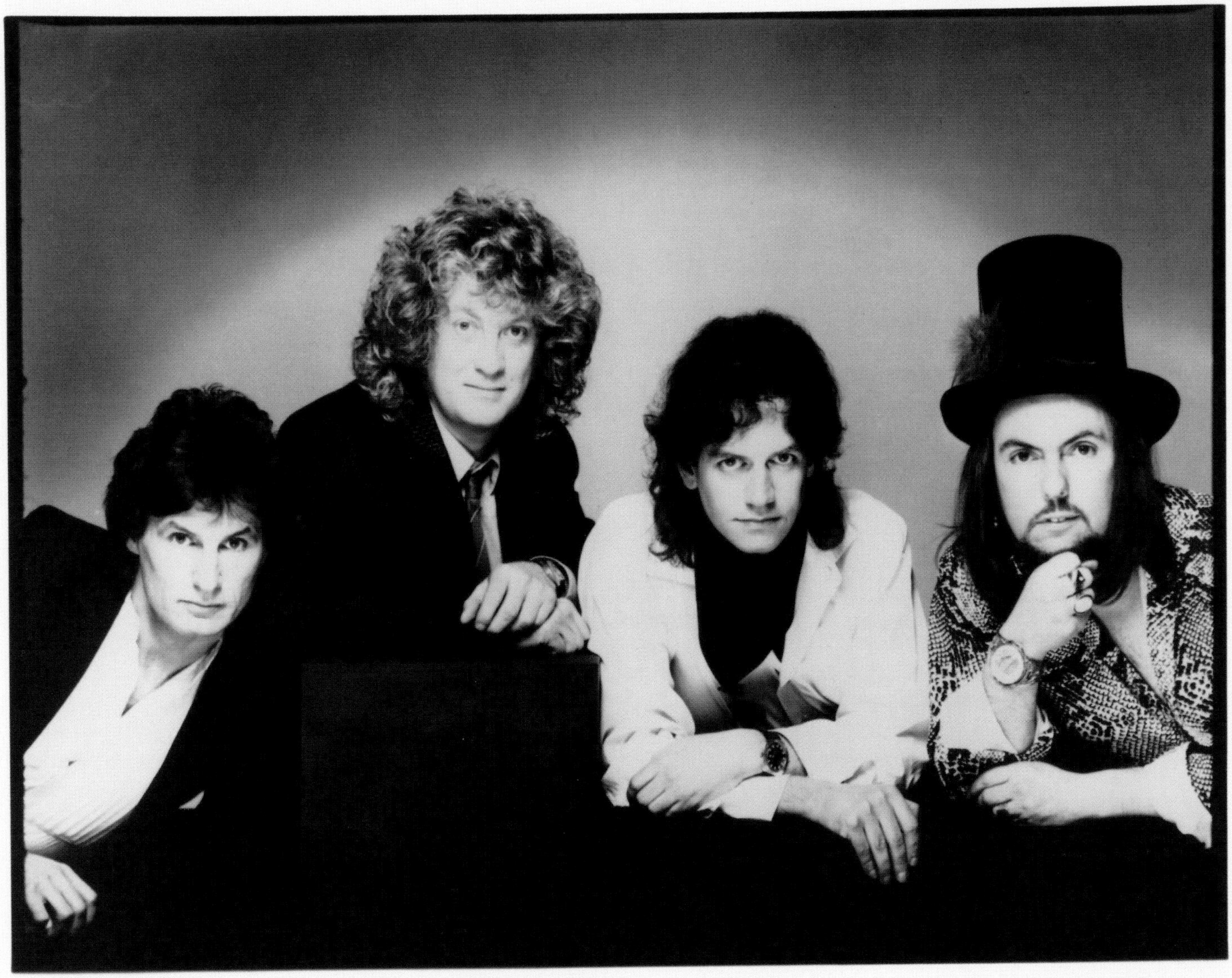

Photo: Simon Fowler

Don Powell   Noddy Holder   Jim Lea   Dave Hill

SLADE

CBS
ASSOCIATED RECORDS

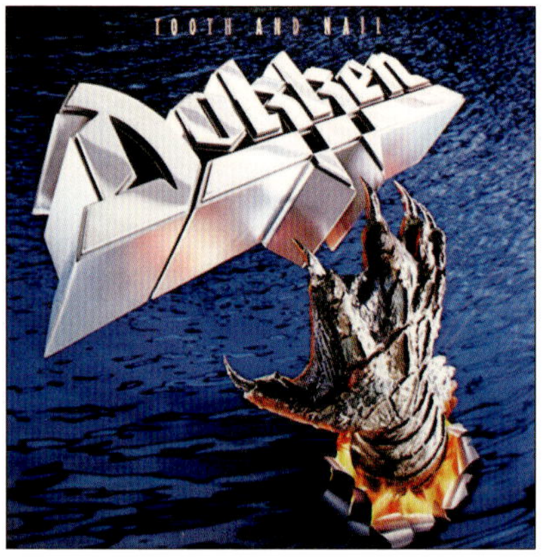

After an unsuccessful debut release, the hard-rock band Dokken hit the sweet spot with *Tooth and Nail*.

Billboard 200: *Tooth and Nail* (#49)
Billboard Hot 100: "Alone Again" (#64)

THE DOKKEN story wasn't the conventional play-the-clubs-and-get-discovered saga. Don Dokken, the band's leader, had risen to the top of the L.A. club scene in 1979, but never parlayed that success into a recording contract.

"There was a real good reason—new wave came in," he recalled. "We couldn't get a gig anymore as a rock band. Nobody would book us—they said we were dinosaurs. The Knack was blazing, and I didn't have a skinny tie. Everybody was going new wave, cutting their hair off and buying Fender Twin Reverbs."

Dokken's recourse was to go to Europe, where he quickly learned the nuances of the metal trade on the concert circuit.

"European heavy metal is a lot different, that's for sure. It's more riff-oriented and less hook, because you don't make it over there on radio—there's only two stations! You make it by touring."

Dokken made his own album in 1981, around the same time he met Scorpions producer Dieter Dierks. The German band was entering the studio, and singer Klaus Meine was suffering from throat problems, so Dierks recruited Dokken to sing some of the high background tracks and provide guide vocals. Armed with those credentials, Dokken returned to Los Angeles and signed a deal following a few showcase gigs. *Breaking the Chains* was the same album as the 1981 release, remixed for American consumption.

"When I got back to L.A., people were talking about this new thing—and here's Mötley Crüe in their black leather and studs. I said, 'You've gotta be kidding. I'm in Europe for three years and now bands are coming out of the woodwork calling themselves heavy metal!' At that point I decided to get rid of my leathers—everybody looked the same, like one huge band."

The singer hooked up with a lineup featuring star guitarist George Lynch; despite a notoriously strained relationship between the two, Dokken formulated a sweeping, anthemic sound on the album *Tooth and Nail*, and the power ballad "Alone Again" provided the breakthrough hit.

"I'm not a screamer," Dokken said. "We're not trying to compete with the Judas Priest/Quiet Riot crew—that's hardcore metal. We like to sing, like Def Leppard." ■

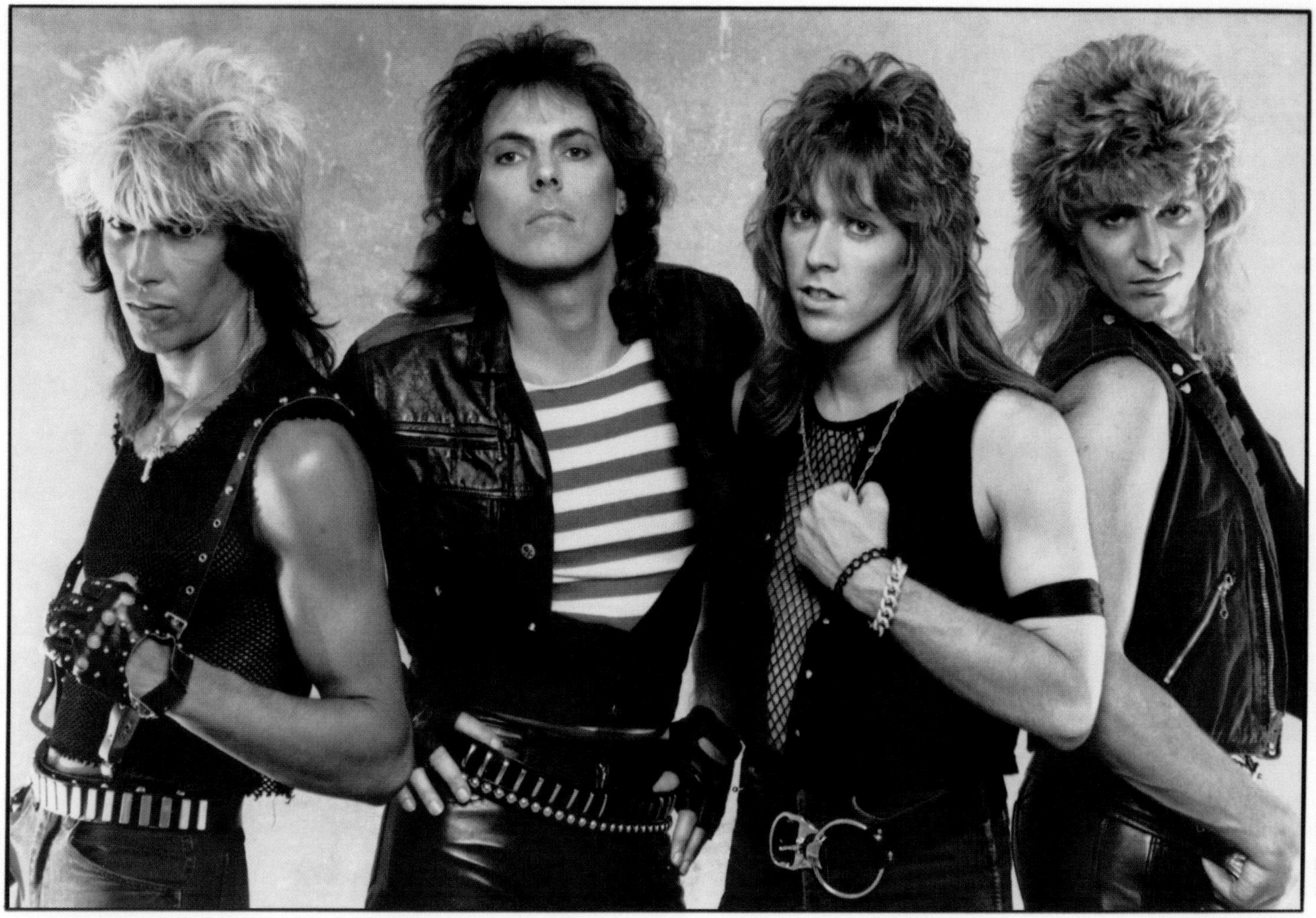

PHOTO CREDIT: MARK WEISS/1984

GEORGE LYNCH DON DOKKEN JEFF PILSON MICK BROWN

Dokken

ELEKTRA

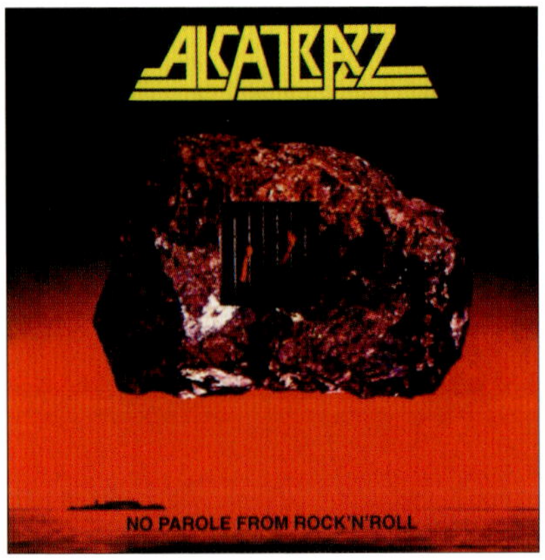

"Island in the Sun," a hard-edged anthem by Alcatrazz, became a riveting clip on the rock-video circuit.

Billboard 200: *No Parole from Rock 'n' Roll* (#128)

ALCATRAZZ WAS new to the spotlight, one of a slew of "heavy-pop" groups primed to ride the radio airwaves. Some industry insiders were projecting Swedish guitarist Yngwie Malmsteen to become the next Eddie Van Halen, and singer Graham Bonnet—who eschewed the look of a typical rocker in favor of short-cropped hair and a suit and tie—had achieved notoriety by briefly replacing Ronnie James Dio in Rainbow and Gary Barden in the Michael Schenker Group.

"It was time to change that, to build my own group," Bonnet explained. "It's too early to see if the chemistry in this band will turn into something truly special, but we've all been pleased so far."

The band recruited bassist Gary Shea and keyboardist Jimmy Waldo from New England, a one-hit wonder group in 1979 with "Don't Ever Wanna Lose You." When New England's success stalled, the demoralized musicians regrouped.

"When we first considered starting from square one again with Alcatrazz, we balked," Waldo admitted. "New England was nothing but ego problems, record company problems, the works. With Alcatrazz, what you hear is what we want to play, not what we've figured out to be commercially acceptable."

MTV gave "Island in the Sun" decent support—Malmsteen took a sizzling solo and Bonnet sang hard—but the song received minor radio play. Even so, the album *No Parole from Rock 'n' Roll* spent 18 weeks on the *Billboard* charts, and a second video for "Hiroshima Mon Amour" became big in Japan. ■

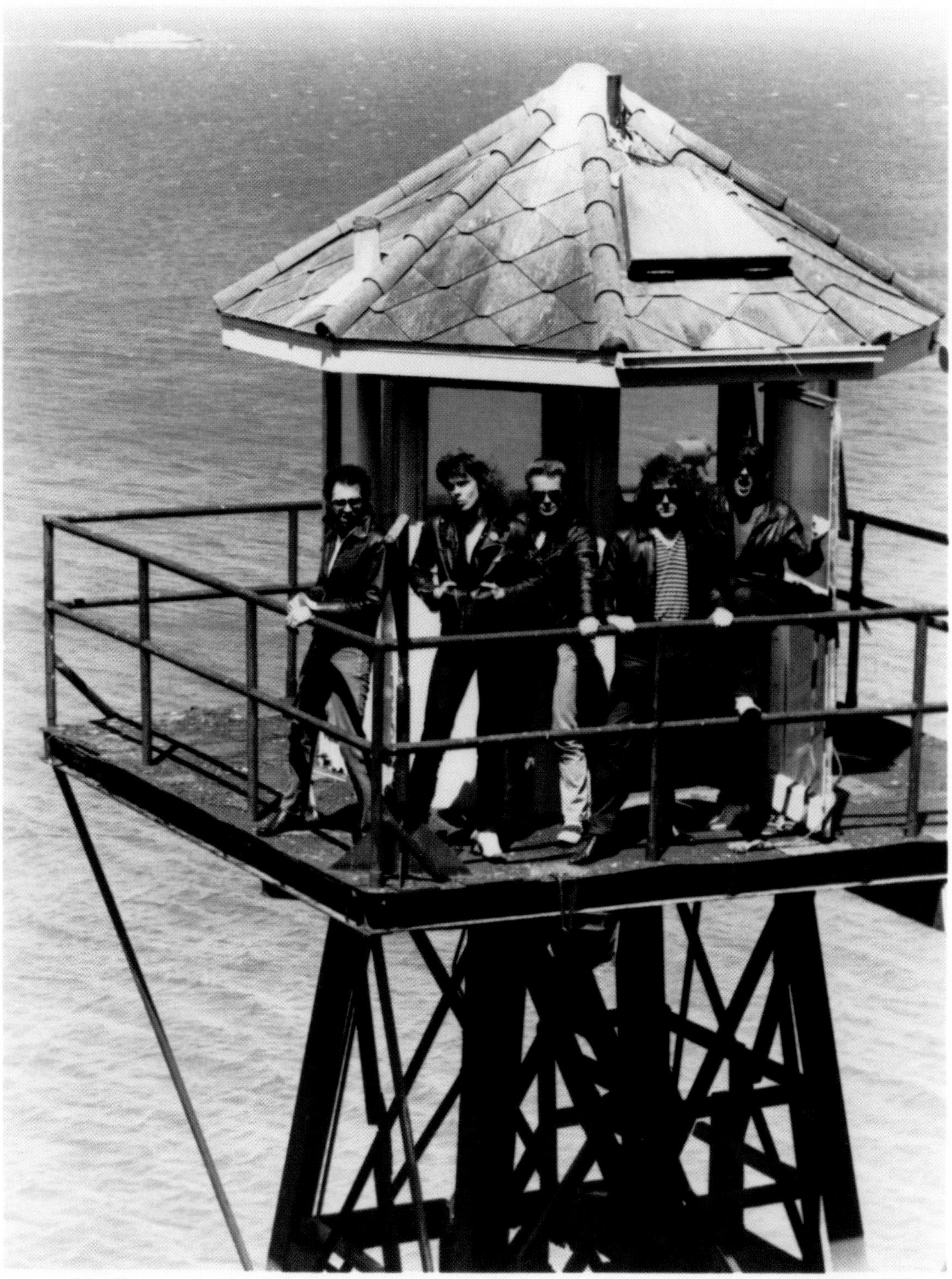

DE NOVO ARTISTS
ANDREW TRUEMAN

ALCATRAZZ

ROCSHIRE RECORDS ™

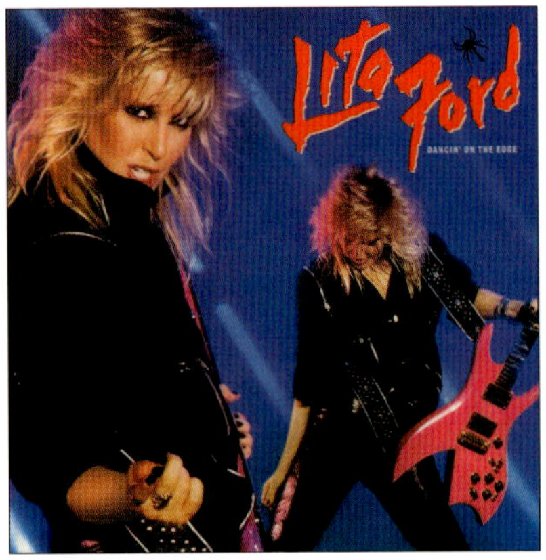

Billboard 200: *Dancin' on the Edge* (#66)

Sporting good looks and a new band, Lita Ford designed *Dancin' on the Edge* to promote her new image.

COMPRISED OF five teenaged girls from Los Angeles, the Runaways held more appeal as jailbait than as musicians. Yet the band managed to perform at a passable professional level, thanks largely to lead guitarist Lita Ford, whose aggressive playing anchored the pop-punk group's otherwise ratty-around-the-edges performances.

The Runaways split up in 1979, and three years later, the 24-year-old was still looking for her due as a musician.

"After being in the Runaways for five years, I took some time off to clear my head out," Ford explained. "I didn't know if I wanted to play with girls or guys, if I wanted to sing, if I wanted to front a group. I finally just made up my mind that I wanted my own band."

The hype-filled Runaways days left Ford with some insight into music-industry workings. "We had one problem—we weren't commercial at all. We were singing about things that no labels wanted to sign, so we had to clean up our act a little bit."

Image problems persisted on Ford's first album, *Out for Blood*. The cover art showed her scantily clad against a spider's web backdrop, brandishing a broken guitar with blood-and-guts inner workings ("The most repulsive cover you can imagine," a label executive noted in retrospect).

"It stopped the album from being displayed in quite a few stores," Ford allowed. "I'm not a bad girl, you know, so I don't need to portray that image. It was just the wrong thing to do."

1984's *Dancin' on the Edge* performed better, with "Gotta Let Go" topping *Billboard*'s Mainstream Rock chart. The album resulted in a Grammy nomination for Best Female Rock Vocal.

"I want to do something that's never been done before, or at least push hard for it, and that's to become a top female guitarist and singer. I was 11 when I started playing, and even if I had known girls weren't supposed to play rock guitar, it wouldn't have stopped me—because I never did what I was supposed to do, anyway. I want to break the world open for more females. So many of them start and then they just stop before anything really happens. If you can play it, go for it." ■

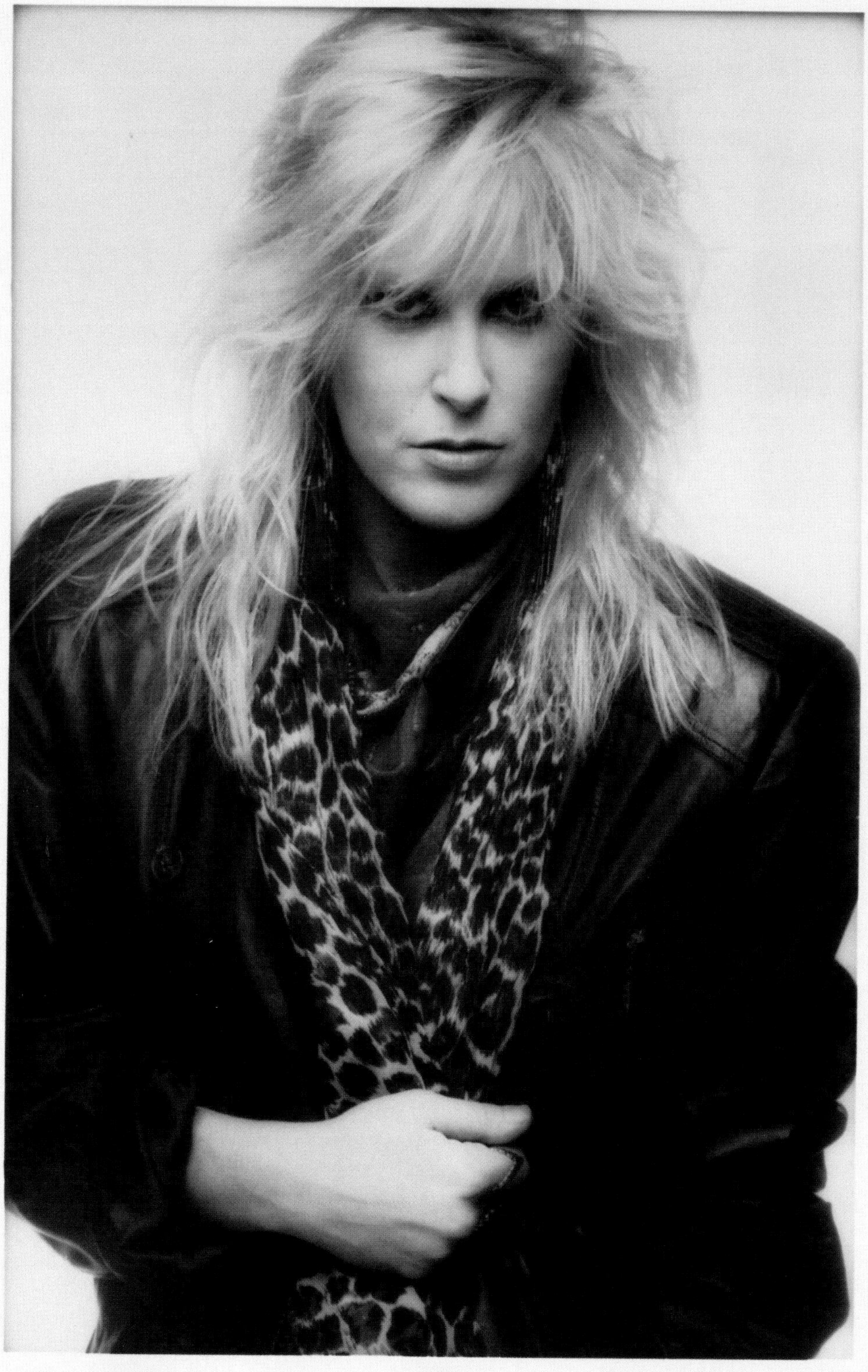

LITA FORD

Mercury

PolyGram Records

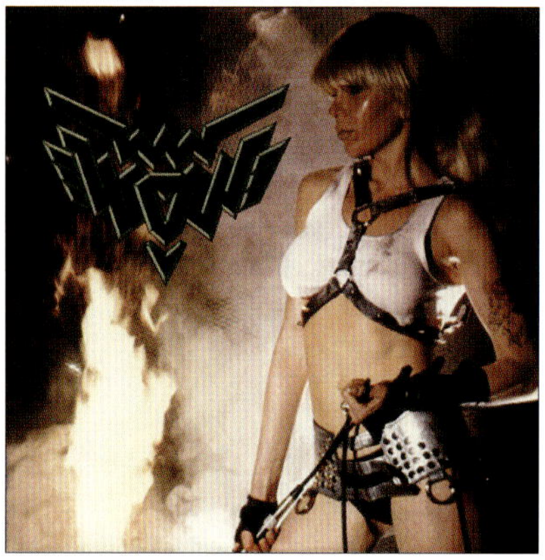

After coming to prominence as the Plasmatics' lead singer, **Wendy O. Williams** embarked on a solo career.

THE PLASMATICS rode their media whoring and garbage-disposal sound to the tune of four albums. Singer Wendy O. Williams' much-publicized shenanigans—chainsawing guitars in half, barely concealing her Barbie-doll bosom in whipped cream, eliciting obscenity charges in several cities—had made her the female face of punk rock.

Putting the Plasmatics on hold in her latest ploy to grab some ink, Williams announced a new solo release—"It's kinda like when Diana Ross left the Supremes, y'know?"

Williams found a patron in Gene Simmons, the bass player for Kiss, and her album *W.O.W.* featured several members of the band. Accordingly, the single "It's My Life" was a nearly palatable pop-metal anthem—her voice could still serve as a soundtrack substitute for cattle mutilations, but at least there was an audible hook.

Williams worked on out-machoing the competition and being a musical Evel Knievel. Some of the notable stunts she performed with the Plasmatics included driving a school bus through a wall of TV sets and jumping out of a Cadillac as it crashed into an exploding stage. In the video for "It's My Life," Williams exited a speeding open-top car via a rope ladder dangling from an airplane, moments before the car nose-dived off a cliff and blew up in mid-air.

"I love having people put up the money so I can do the things I really want to do," Williams explained. "I have no problem topping my last stunts—I have lists of things that would get my adrenaline going and get other people's adrenaline flowing, too. I like to get that rush every day. I have to do these things to mellow me out and make me a civilized human being for short periods of time."

Is that why "the queen of shock rock" shed her signature Mohawk for a ponytail? "Nah, I'm just as radical as ever, no closer to the middle of the road," she insisted. "I'm the only performer in history to be on the cover of *Vegetarian Times* and *Kerrang* (a heavy-metal magazine). That's a combination of who I am. I'm just an extreme and excessive person—in all areas. I'm lucky I have sane people around me."

Williams still couldn't get the mainstream to listen to her music, but she earned a Grammy nomination in the Best Female Rock Vocal Performance category for the album. ■

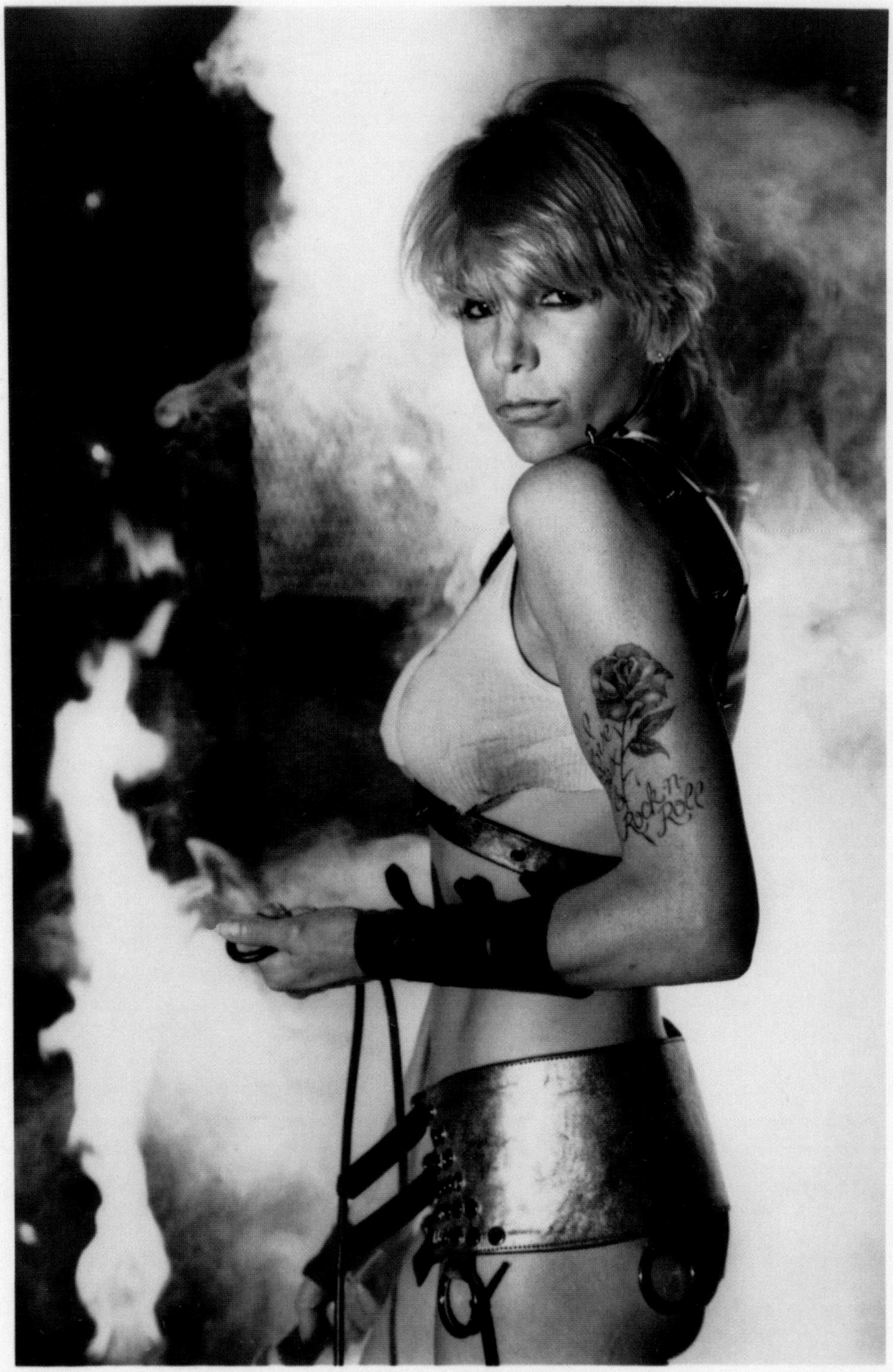

Photo : Butch Star

WENDY O. WILLIAMS

Marketed by Jem Records Inc., South Plainfield, NJ 07080

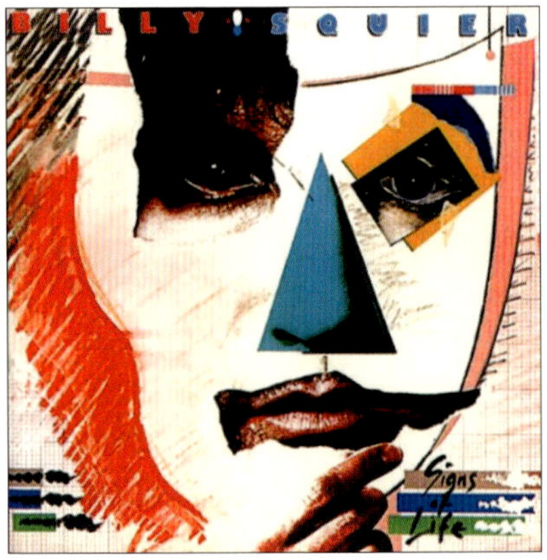

Billboard 200: *Signs of Life* (#11)
Billboard Hot 100: "Rock Me Tonite" (#15); "All Night Long" (#75); "Eye on You" (#71)

Riding the single "Rock Me Tonite," *Signs of Life* became Billy Squier's third consecutive smash recording.

BILLY SQUIER had racked up millions of record sales since emerging as an arena-rock hero in 1980. But the strong-willed musician, who had languished for several years in critically acclaimed but commercially ignored groups, stayed up at night fretting about his career.

"I try to maintain control over every facet," he explained. "I guess things aren't as comfortable as they may be perceived. I'm going through a restructuring of my organization, trying to shore up what I consider weak links. I'm at the point where I want to make a leap, and I need people around me who can reflect that."

Signs of Life was a departure, however unplanned. Reinhold Mack (professionally credited simply as "Mack"), the producer of every previous Squier release, wasn't considered to work on the album.

"I love the guy, and he had a tremendous influence on me. But after the last album (*Emotions in Motion*), we had a parting of the ways," Squier admitted. "We mixed it, and it wasn't right. It wasn't his fault, since we were co-conspirators. But more work had to be done, which he didn't agree with. I remixed the record, and he'll tell you that I ruined it and that it's a piece of trash. At that point there was no way to work with him again."

Squier opted for Jim Steinman, who wrote and produced Meat Loaf's bombastic *Bat Out of Hell*. But Steinman's sublimated his penchant for musical overkill.

"Jim was just a different consultant on the project," Squier shrugged. "It was not done to make me more acceptable to a pop audience, or to get a Steinman sound, or anything like that. I wouldn't allow it."

"Rock Me Tonite" was Squier's biggest hit, but the video of the track seemingly hurt his career. The premise: In a ripped pink T-shirt, Squier spasmed on his bedroom floor like a worm with palsy, then got up and skipped to the bed where he wriggled around a little more. Some plot. Squier's concert ticket sales immediately suffered.

"It was a very miscommunicated concept in a situation where I ultimately put myself in the hands of a director who said, 'This will be great.' I didn't think it would be, and I paid the price for it." ■

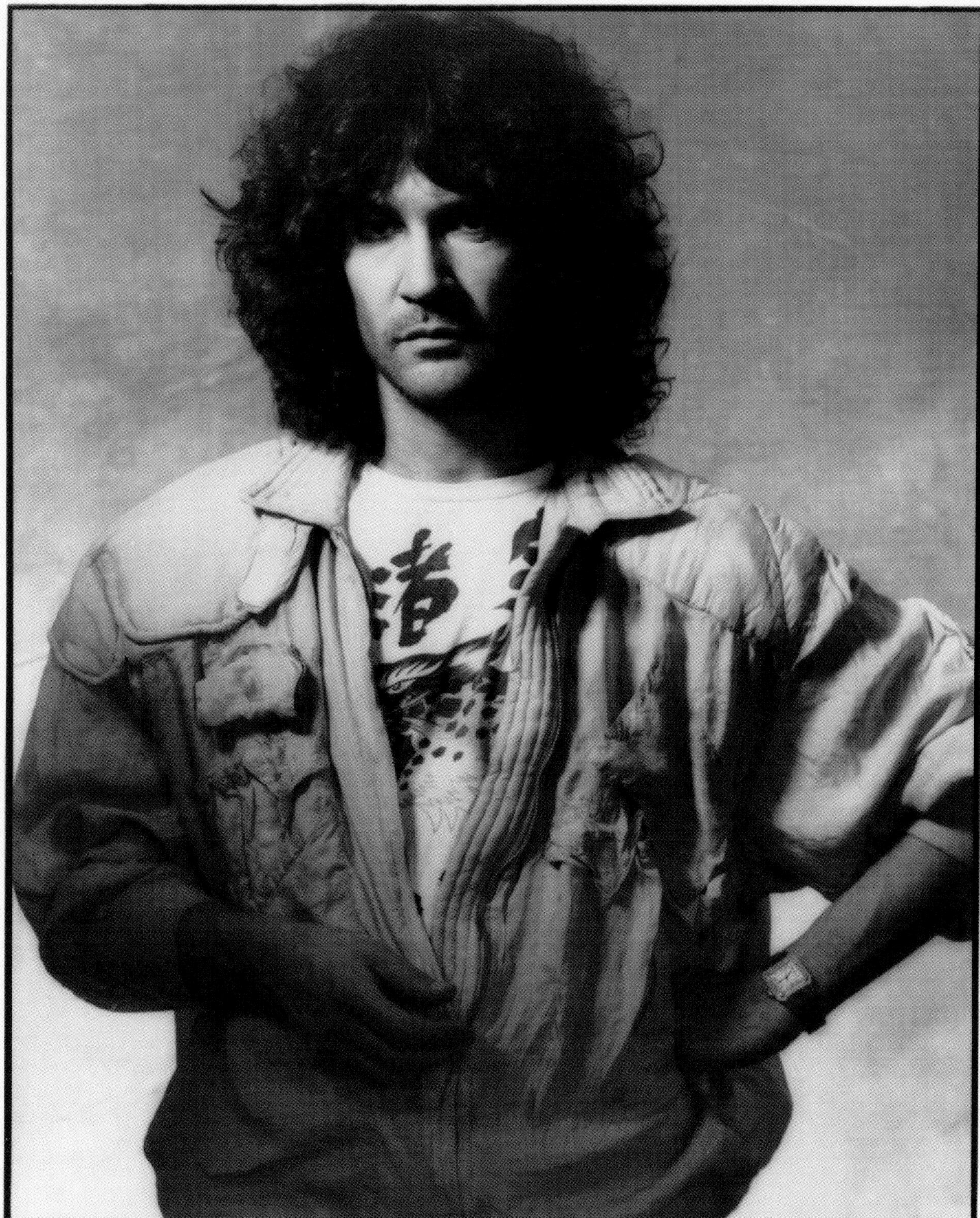

Photo: Norman Seeff / 1984

BILLY SQUIER

Capitol Records

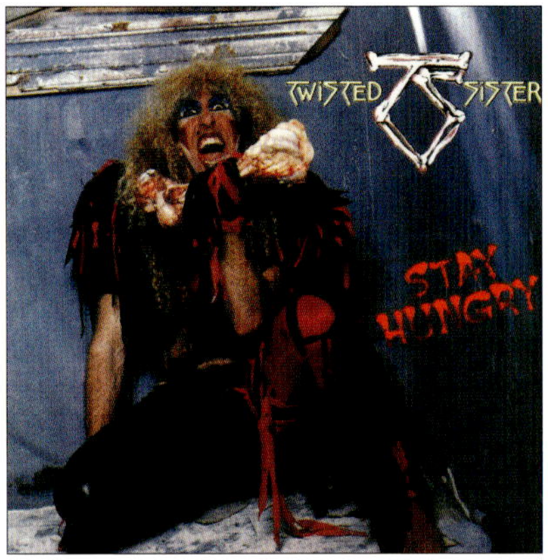

Twisted Sister unleashed the album *Stay Hungry* and a pair of megahits that saturated radio and MTV.

Billboard 200: *Stay Hungry* (#15)
Billboard Hot 100: "We're Not Gonna Take It" (#21); "I Wanna Rock" (#68)

DEE SNIDER, who hailed from Long Island, formed his first band when he was seven. "We used to mime to Beatles records, using tennis rackets as guitars, and charge our friends to come in and see us," he recalled. "I had business sense even in those days."

In 1976, Snider linked up with guitarists Jay Jay French and Eddie Ojeda in Twisted Sister, setting out to shock New York City's glam-rock scene.

"At our first gig, we were playing to something like 25 people," Snider said. "We went onstage wearing dresses, lingerie, anything to get a reaction. After the first number, 20 of them walked out, and five tough-looking bikers stayed behind. They said, 'You guys have got real guts to come out here dressed like that.'"

The quintet paid its dues in clubs for years, morphing into hard-rock heroes in the tri-state area of New York/New Jersey/Connecticut. Rejected multiple times by every record company in the land, the band finally inked a contract in 1982.

Stay Hungry, Twisted Sister's second major-label album, launched the band into the pop-culture stratosphere. The stirring anthems "We're Not Gonna Take It" and "I Wanna Rock" were made into comedic videos featuring tongue-in cheek violence against teachers and parents, which placed the group squarely in the crosshairs of conservative groups.

"Basically, we're just a bunch of dirtbags," Snider defiantly admitted. "We despise those who sit on the fence. Either dig it or get out. It's all or nothing. People either love us or they hate us. There is no one in-between." ■

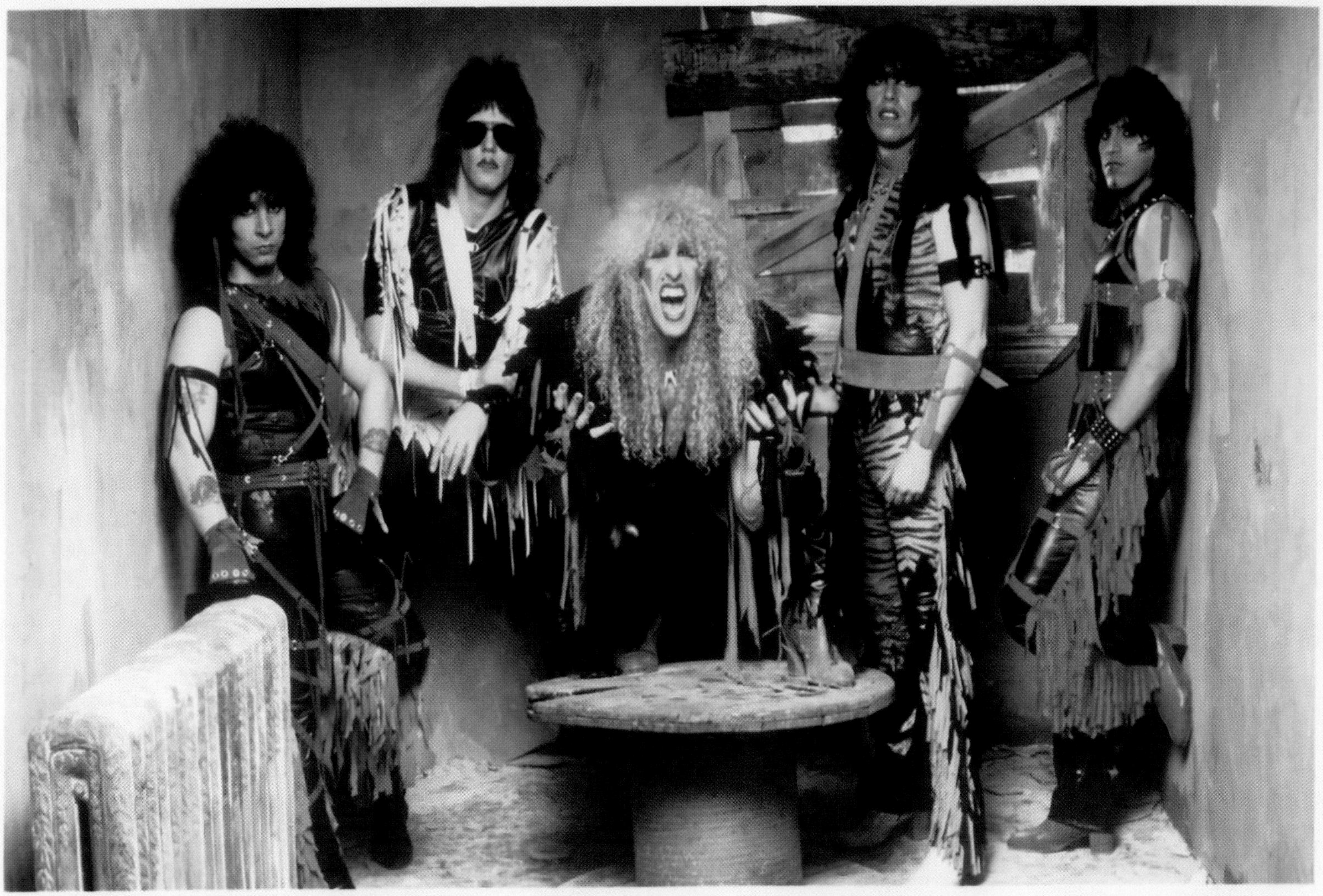

A. J. PERO JAY JAY FRENCH DEE SNIDER MARK MENDOZA EDDIE OJEDA

TWISTED SISTER

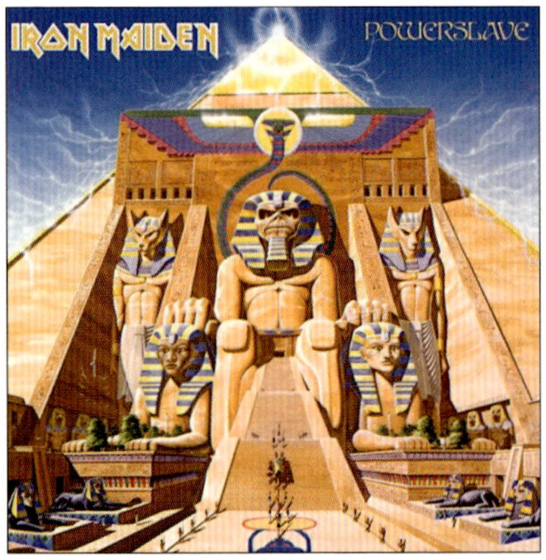

Iron Maiden's *Powerslave* adapted a Coleridge poem into the 13-minute "Rime of the Ancient Mariner."

Billboard 200: *Powerslave* (#21)

THREE WORLD tours had made the British metal band Iron Maiden international headliners, with gold and platinum records from 15 different countries and Top 10 chart status in others. It added up to almost 300 performances in 28 nations over a 13-month period.

"If somebody says, 'Hey, you want to play here? I've never heard of it,' we go, 'Yeah, sure!'" lead singer Bruce Dickenson laughed.

The *Powerslave* excursion took Iron Maiden behind the Iron Curtain for eight shows. "It was all fairly simple, cut and dried," Dickenson noted. "We just said, 'Hey, we're turning up, this is how much we get paid, this is what we're bringing—see you on Wednesday!' Bands have played there before, but they've done it on the cheap, because you don't get paid a lot of money. But we thought we'd take the whole lot"—meaning Iron Maiden's full arsenal of senses-searing lights and stage effects.

The band's work ethic had its drawbacks—"I think I have a home," Dickenson paused, "and I get to see it two or three days a year"—but it also propelled Iron Maiden into a powerful and unique commercial niche in the progressive-metal market.

"You've got all the pop-metal crossover bands, and in a year, the careers of 50 percent of those acts are finished. And I suspect that the record companies are too stupid to be aware of it. It's like punk all over again. There were some really good new wave bands, and some really awful new wave bands, and there were some bands that weren't new wave at all—they were just cashing in on the whole thing. And they all got signed. At the end of the day, the only ones who came out were the ones who actually had some songs. That's why we're pleased—we've established a fairly distinct identity without the support of the media."

By support, Dickenson meant radio airplay—in America, the band had never had a charting single.

"But if radio says your kind of band is no longer hot, what are you gonna do? The only reason kids come to your shows is because they've heard you on the radio—there's been no word-of-mouth generated. Whereas with us, it's the other way around. We don't want to be a part of a trend—that was always the intention. We prefer to ride out trends and make our own way." ■

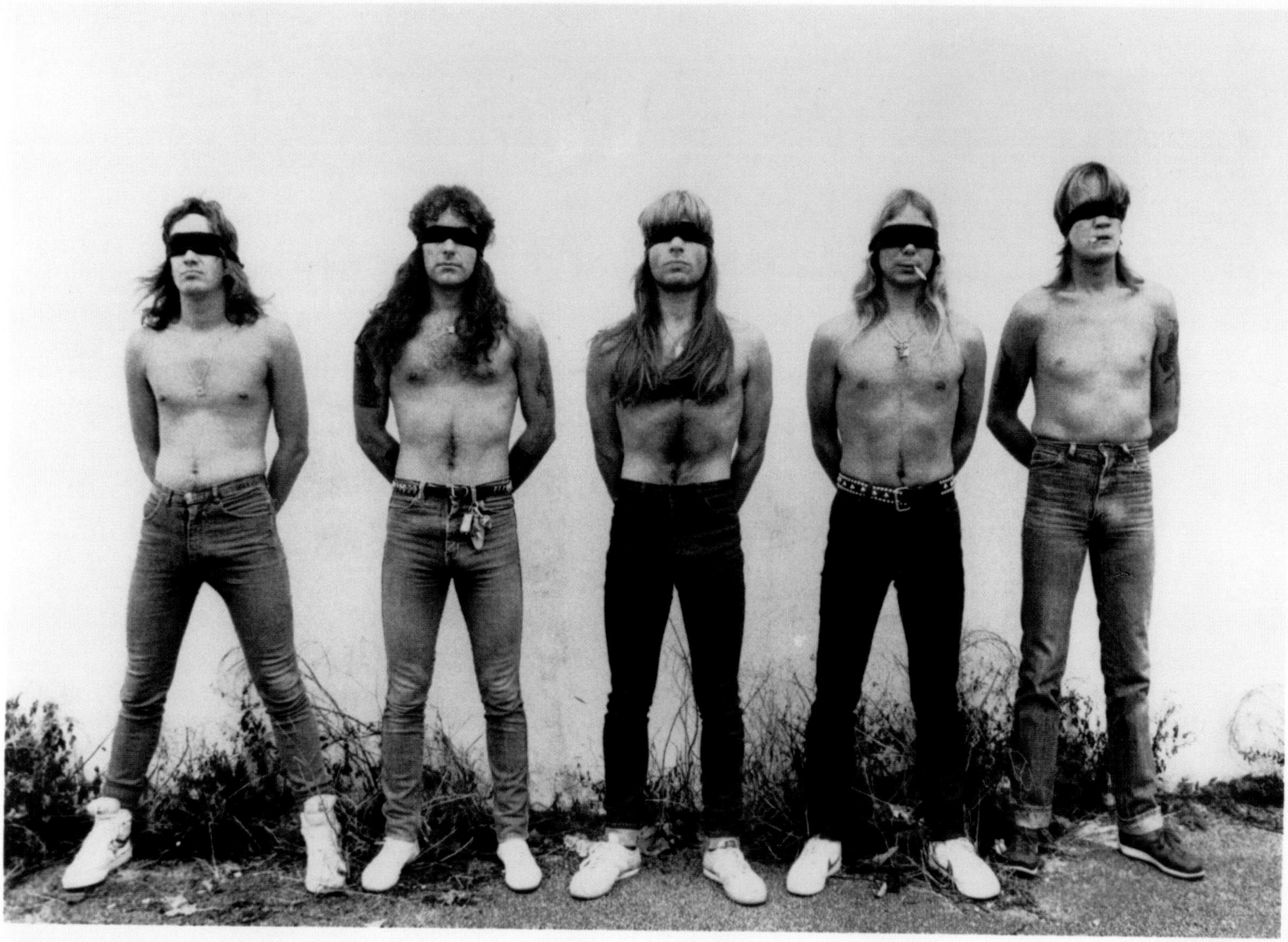

IRON MAIDEN

Capitol RECORDS

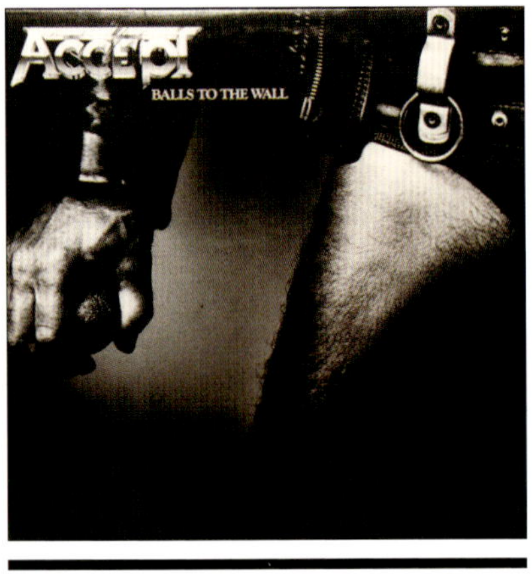

Billboard 200: *Balls to the Wall* (#74)

Riding a punishing riff, Accept's anthemic "Balls to the Wall" became the German group's signature.

COLORFUL LEAD singer Udo Dirkschneider formed Accept in 1977 with guitarist Wolf Hoffmann and bassist Peter Baltes, following the German heavy-metal trend set by Scorpions. The uncompromising title track to the *Balls to the Wall* album nailed the band's no-nonsense approach, with Dirkschneider's unusual throaty growl and Hoffman's crunching barre chords.

"Some people call our music 'dinosaur' heavy metal," Baltes said. "We had the same questions asked when punk came out—'Is your music outdated?' I say if you kick ass onstage, it doesn't matter."

The "Balls to the Wall" video received American airplay on MTV. It consisted of scenes filmed in the rubble of a demolition site just outside of London's Heathrow Airport. For the crashing finale, Dirkschneider, "the little general," jumped on top of a huge demolition ball. The airport police tried to break things up, as the video lights were interfering with the field's landing lights.

"At first they thought we were somehow associated with the airport," Hoffmann said. "It took a lot of convincing to get them to allow us to continue." ■

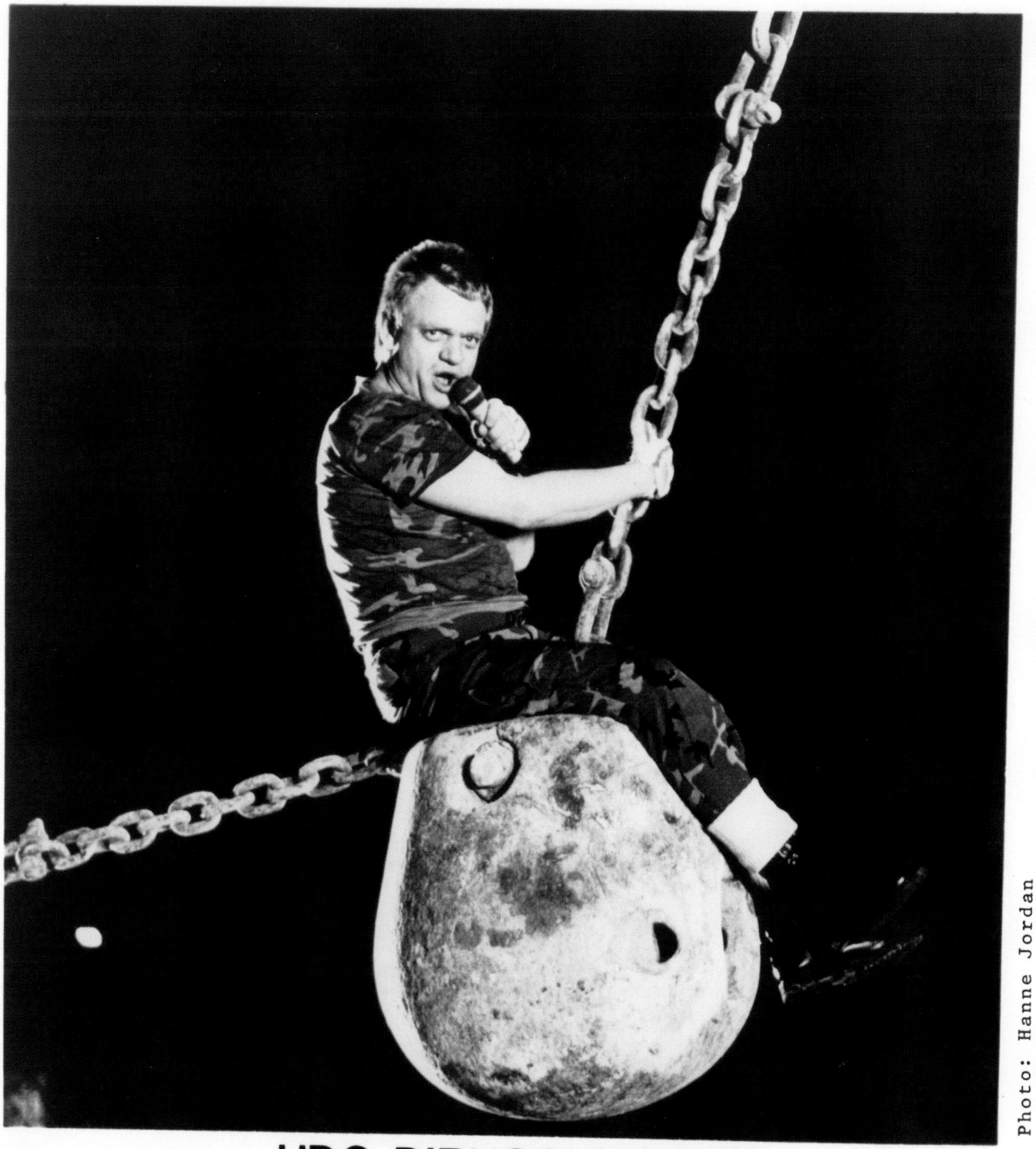

Photo: Hanne Jordan

UDO DIRKSCHNEIDER

of

ACCEPT

Portrait

8404

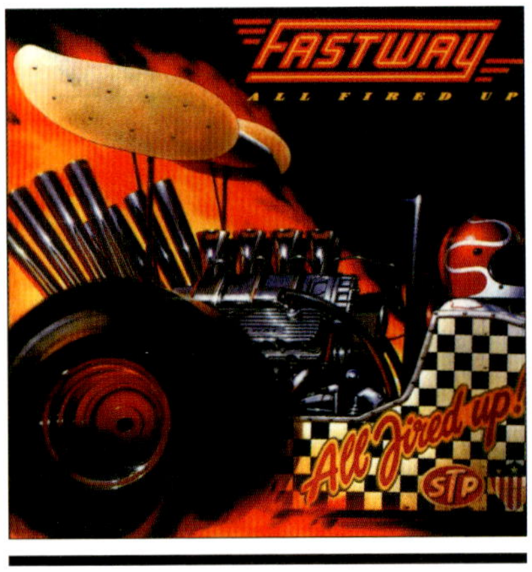

Billboard 200: *All Fired Up* (#59)

Fastway, a newcomer to the heavy-metal pack, gave things a go in America with the promising *All Fired Up*.

FASTWAY HAD its roots in Motörhead, a Hell's-Angels-meets-the-Ramones power trio that created a big sensation in its native Britain but remained unknown in the US. "Fast" Eddie Clarke was the guitarist for the faster-and-louder outfit.

"Motörhead started off with a bang, but the quality deteriorated over the last couple of albums," Clarke recalled. "I figured, hey, we're not going to happen in America now, because we're getting worse. The last straw was when it was decided that Motörhead would do a single with Wendy O. Williams of the Plasmatics. That put me over the edge, and I left. I had to put together a whole new band, even though I didn't have any plans for one. I just happened to run into Pete Way."

Way was the ex-bassist for UFO, another British heavy-metal act, and by combining surnames with nicknames, he and Clarke created the moniker Fastway. Both musicians shared a love for Humble Pie's *Rockin' the Fillmore* live album, and they recruited drummer Jerry Shirley (who'd played with Humble Pie in 1981) after a mutual friend introduced them to round out the new trio. The group was awarded instant supergroup status, but prior to entering the studio to record Fastway's debut album, Way resigned to join up with Ozzy Osbourne's band.

"We ended up having to use a session guy on the record," Clarke explained. "But I was intent on going ahead with the whole thing. I'm a bit impatient that way."

An advertisement in a British music paper brought about the discovery of youthful singer Dave King. In England, the public reaction to Fastway wasn't as enthusiastic as Clarke had hoped.

"We stiffed," he confessed. "The audiences were divided by their loyalties to Motörhead and their limited understanding of my new direction."

So Fastway came to America. *All Fired Up*, Clarke and company's second album of blues-based rock 'n' roll, made it onto the *Billboard* chart, but it failed to break the band worldwide. Shirley and bassist Charlie McCracken left soon after. ■

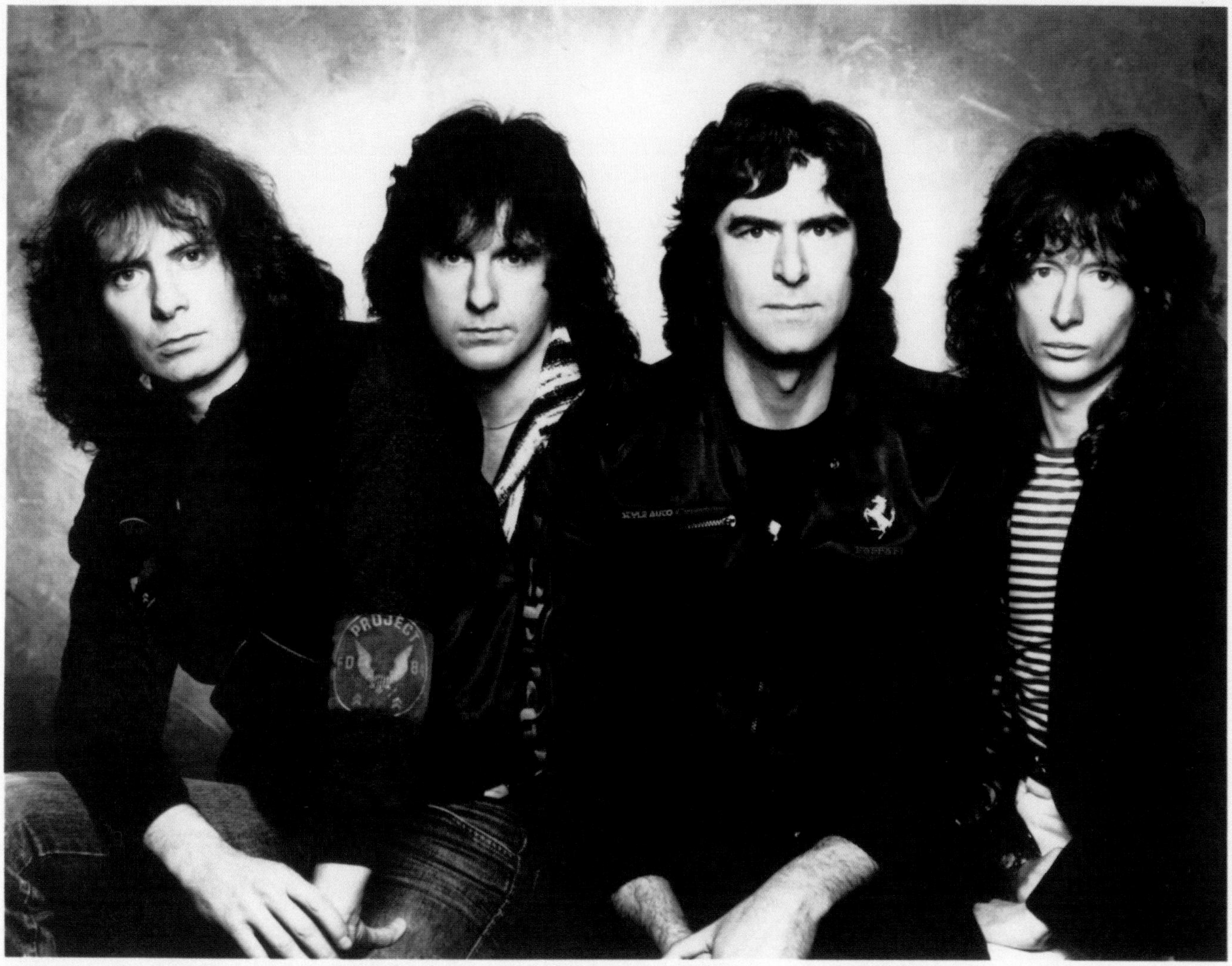

FASTWAY from left): Fast Eddie Clarke, Jerry Shirley, Charlie McCracken, David King

Columbia
8405

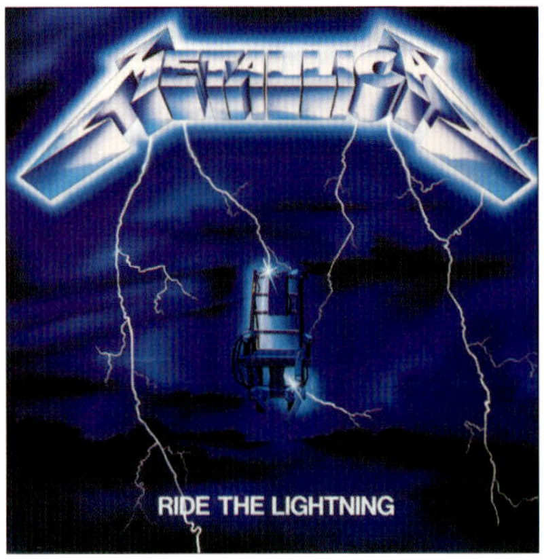

Despite never making a video or receiving radio airplay, Metallica thrived thanks to fan word of mouth.

Billboard 200: *Ride the Lightning* (#100)

METALLICA OPERATED outside the rock industry mainstream. For the San Francisco-based quartet, it was simply a matter of relating to their youthful audience.

"We're pretty young ourselves, so we think we know what they're into, like great packaging and stuff," 21-year-old drummer Lars Ulrich noted. "Disenfranchised heavy-metal fans have been looking for an alternative to the usual crap, and we're it."

Ulrich formed Metallica with guitarist James Hetfield. "I stole the name from a friend," Ulrich admitted. "He showed me a list of possible names for his band, and I told him to use any one but that horrible one! When we first started playing, we'd go down to Los Angeles and find that the clubs were into Mötley Crüe and Ratt clones, the usual metal stuff. They wouldn't accept us for ourselves."

Without any kind of industry exposure, the band's first album, *Kill 'Em All*, sold 150,000 copies worldwide, making it one of the best-selling independent records in history. Ulrich attributed that early success to "luck as much as planning—we just got together to play what we liked."

Ride the Lightning was released in July 1984 by the independent label Megaforce Records. Two months later, Elektra Records signed the band to a multiyear deal and reissued the album. The members of Metallica had filled a void with an intriguing new brand of brutal, thrashing speed metal. The high-decibel music intentionally sounded reckless and skittish rather than calculated. The lyrics, written by Hetfield, pondered messages that seemed serious compared to the usual sexist twaddle, kill-your-parents cheerleading and half-baked sci-fi escapism indigenous to the metal genre.

Kids also liked Metallica because the band members looked and acted like them instead of glamming up. Dressed in torn jeans and T-shirts, the group gave the impression it traveled to gigs in old Camaros instead of limousines.

"The underground was happening," Hetfield said. "We got all kinds of fans—skinheads, punks, headbangers. We weren't relying on the radio, and video wasn't our thing. We got most of our following playing live everywhere."

"We got to this point by ourselves—no interference from a record company, no help from anyone else—and that's very satisfying," Ulrich said. ■

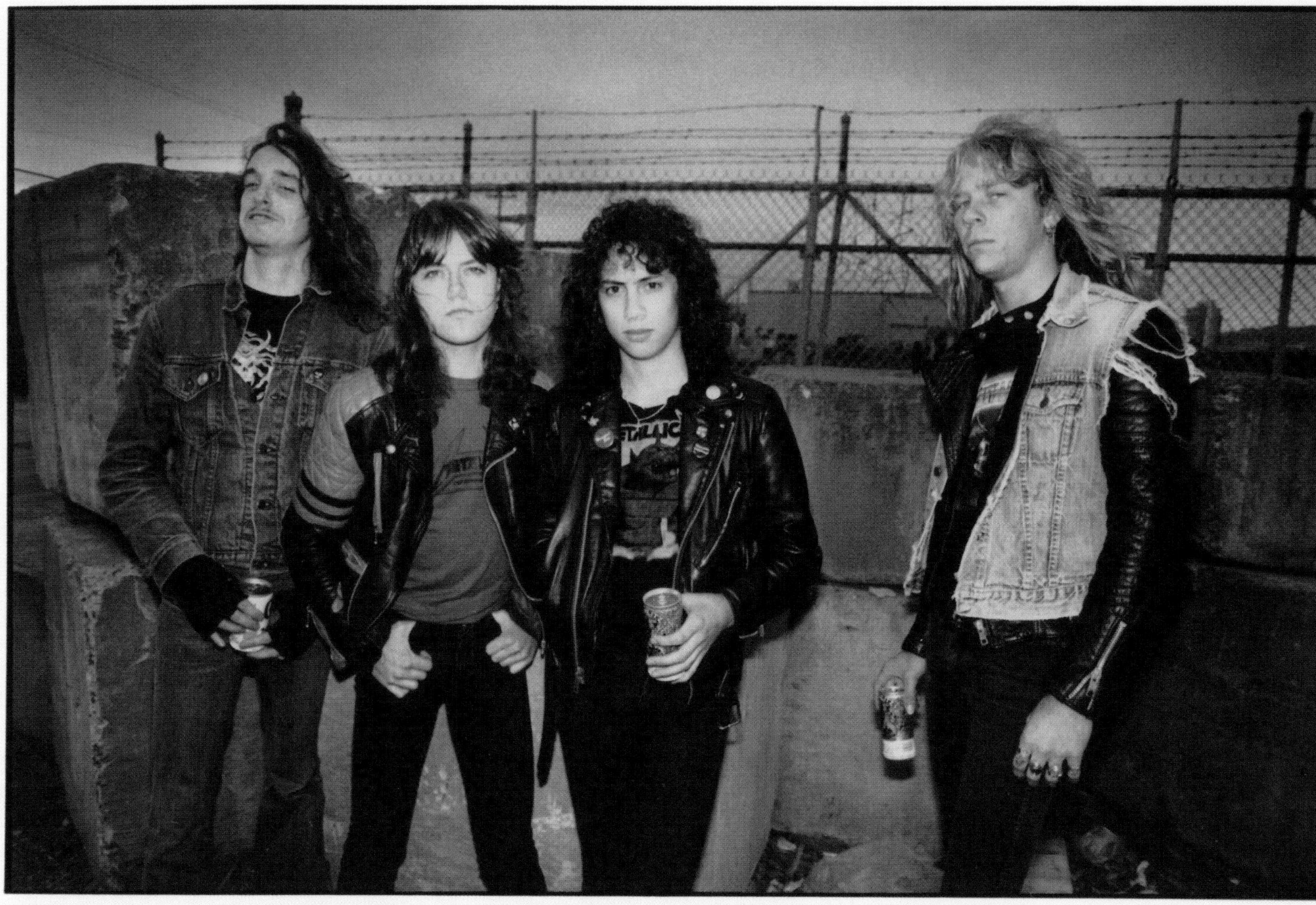

PHOTO CREDIT: ROSS HALFIN/1984

CLIFF BURTON LARS URLICH KIRK HAMMETT JAMES HETFIELD

METALLICA

ELEKTRA

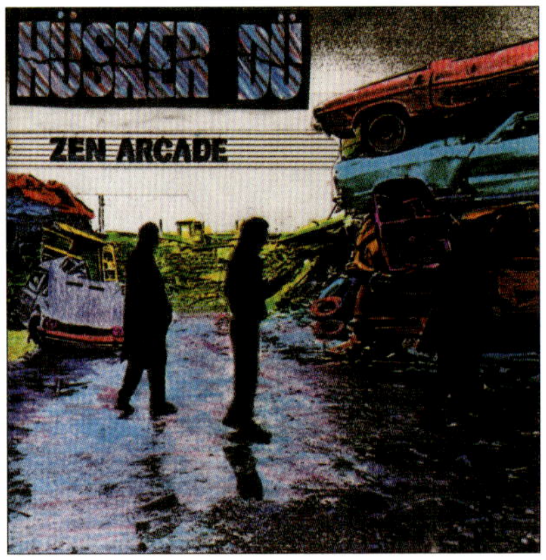

Hüsker Dü's *Zen Arcade* transcended the trappings that undermined other American hardcore outfits.

HÜSKER DÜ hailed from Minneapolis, the starting point for Prince and such acclaimed new music groups as the Replacements and the Suburbs. But Hüsker Dü (the name, from a Danish board game, meant "Do you remember?") was the only band in the hardcore category to develop beyond the genre's harder-faster-louder limitations. Maintaining the unstoppable energy that was part of the punk continuum, the trio—guitarist and vocalist Bob Mould, bassist Greg Norton and drummer Grant Hart—offered intelligence and melody as well.

"People get this image that we'll have Mohawk haircuts," group leader Mould said. "When they see us setting up, they think we're the road crew. Then we plug in and blow them away. We just wear everyday clothes and sing songs about everyday stories. We don't have any of those pretentions."

With Mould and Hart coming into their own as songwriters, Hüsker Dü enjoyed a major breakthrough with the sprawling *Zen Arcade*, a double-LP that mixed crash-and-burn screamers, blistering hard-rock workouts, psychedelic jamming and folk-rock introspection. The record generated so much critical and commercial enthusiasm that the independent SST Records couldn't keep up with demand, prompting the major record labels to come courting.

The influence of the album stretched beyond the underground music province. Mould was surprised by the reaction to *Zen Arcade* "in terms of across-the-board acceptance," he said. "I mean, it was written up in *Time* and *USA Today* and other places that you've never seen hardcore mentioned. But no, I knew it was head and shoulders above most of the albums in the hardcore/punk genre we've been thrown into." ■

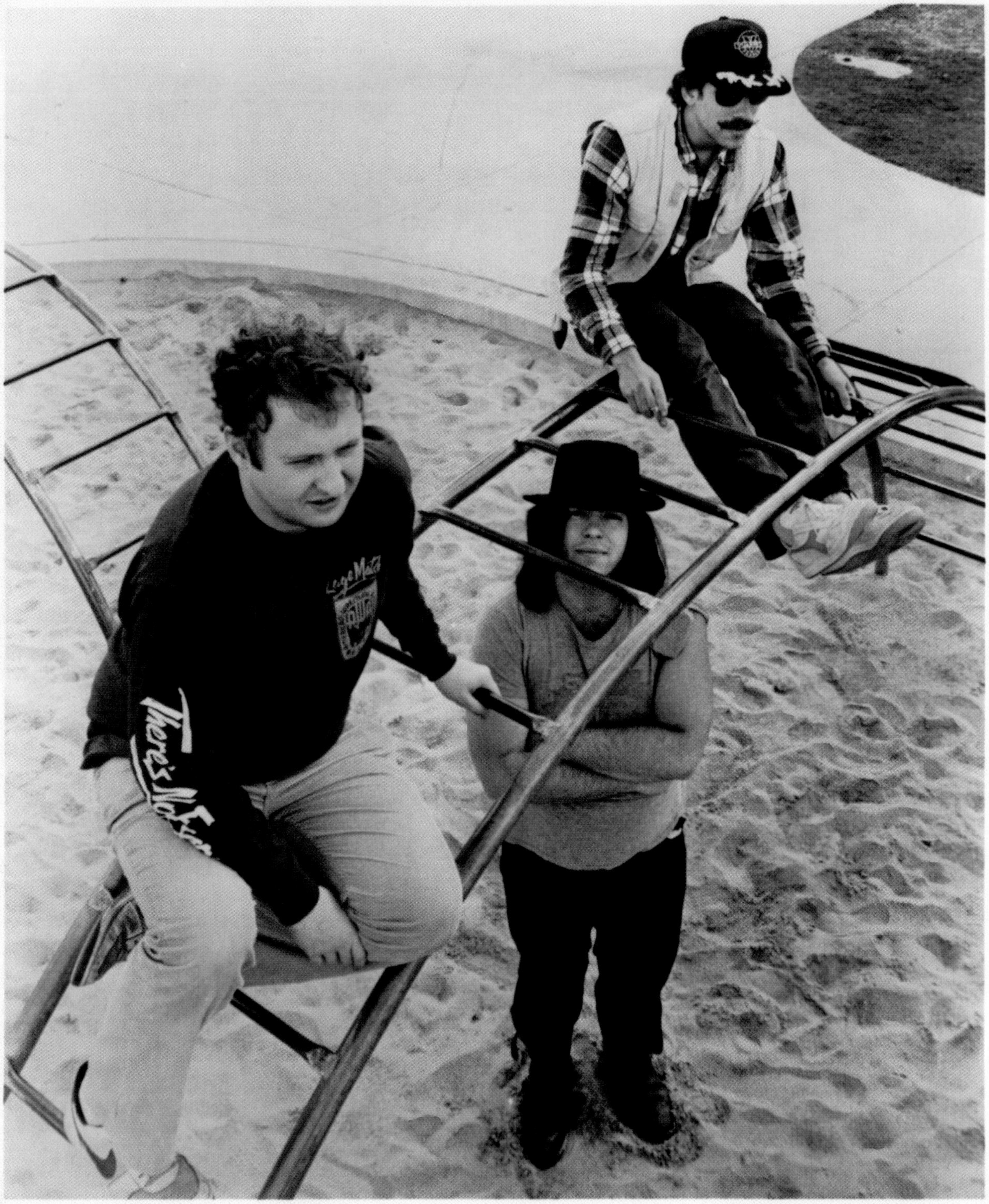

HÜSKER DÜ

photo: Naomi Petersen

P.O. BOX 1 LAWNDALE CA 90260
OFFICE: (213) 376-7213

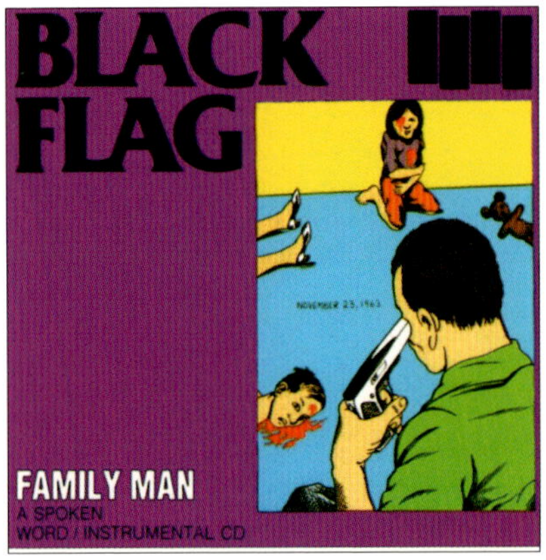

After losing time to a legal battle, Black Flag became impossibly prolific, cutting a triad of albums.

INNOVATORS IN the first wave of Los Angeles hardcore punk, Black Flag steadily compiled a recorded catalog through multiple personnel changes. The Black Flag sound was tenacious, but not in the framework of most hardcore material; the group was equally enamored of thickly textured, agonized drones. Guitarist Greg Ginn, the recognized leader who wrote the majority of the songs and lyrics, purposed SST Records to release material by Black Flag and spearhead the nationwide network of underground bands.

"We've built our reputation on moving things around," Ginn admitted.

After a rancorous legal dispute prevented the band from releasing any new material for three years, Black Flag released three studio albums in 1984—*My War*, *Family Man* and *Slip It In*—and toured constantly.

"We jam a lot when we're at home, usually five or six hours a day," Ginn noted. "So there's a lot of different stuff that we want to get out."

Despite the fecundity, Black Flag retained an anti-authoritarian and nonconformist ethic, unrestrained by commercial boundaries or the criteria of the hardcore punk genre. Ginn ceded much of the spotlight to Henry Rollins, who evolved into a vocalist with considerable impact, leading some people to compare him to the Doors' doomsday frontman Jim Morrison. Ginn and the rhythm section incorporated influences from Jimi Hendrix to Black Sabbath to the Sex Pistols in a single song. *Family Man* wasn't typical Black Flag fare—one side of the record featured Rollins' unaccompanied spoken-word material, while the other reprised some moody instrumentals borne out of previous recording sessions.

"We don't try to categorize our audience, because we don't want them to do that to us," Ginn concluded. "I think a lot of Journey-type bands try to calculate who they're playing to, and that's why a lot of music sounds the same. We'll play for anybody at any time, but we play for ourselves first. When other people like it, that's cool, but we don't want to stagnate. We like staying off-balance." ■

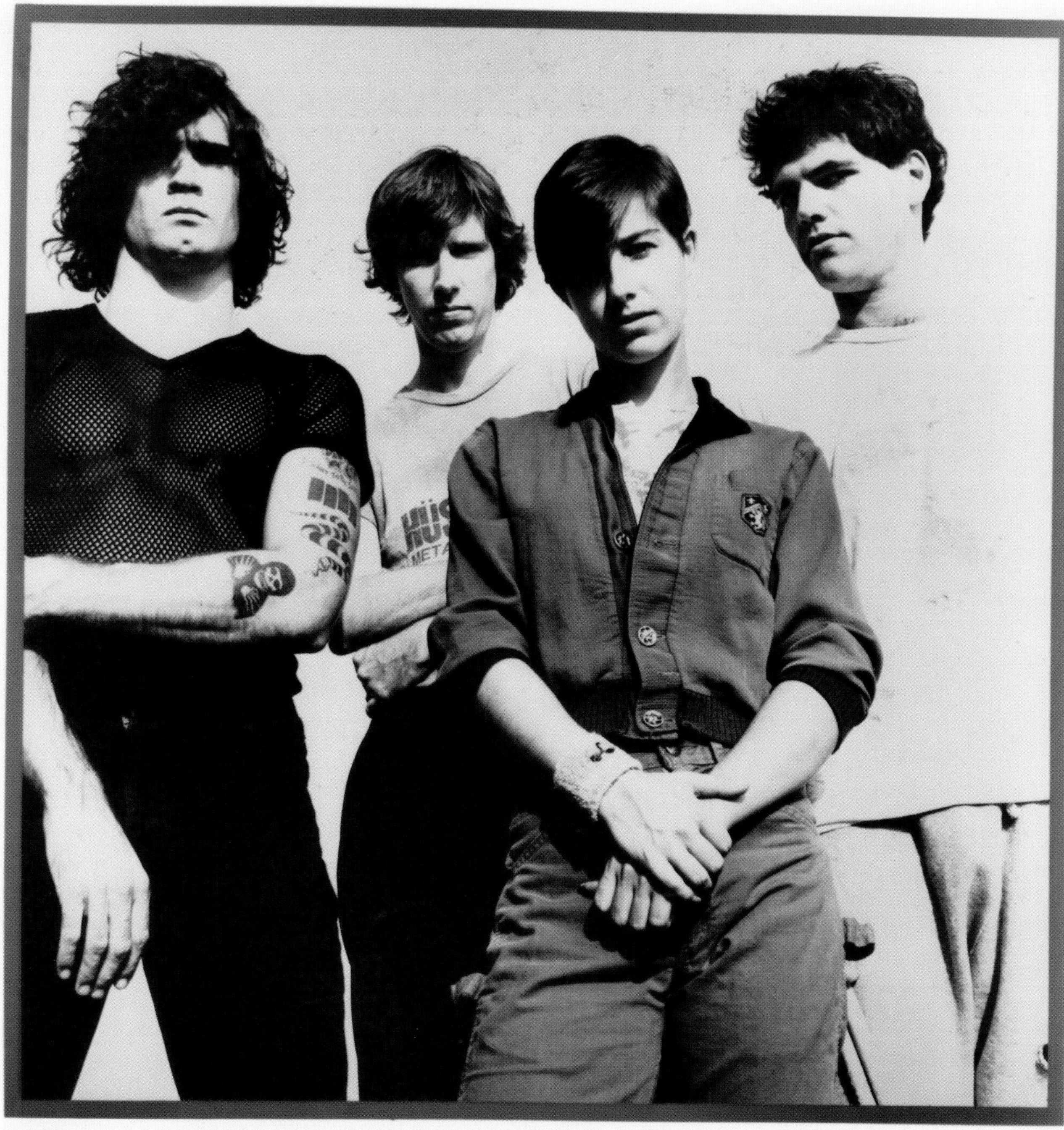

PHOTO: ED COLVER

BLACK FLAG

P.O. Box 1, Lawndale CA 90260 OFFICE (213) 376-7213 BOOKING (213) 372-5536

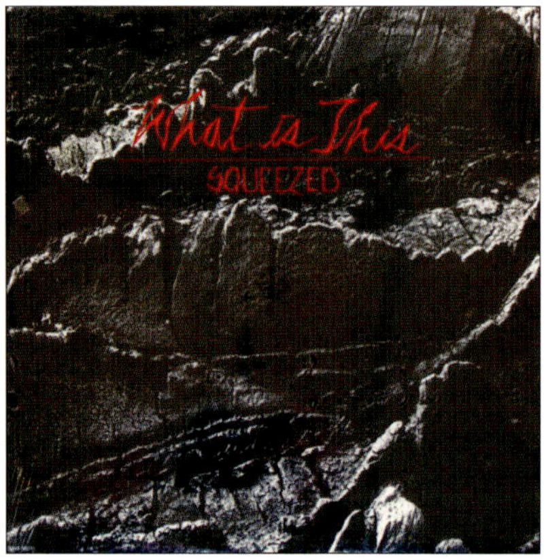

Hillel Slovak and Jack Irons made Red Hot Chili Peppers a sideline to their "proper" group, What Is This.

***SQUEEZED*, A** debut five-song EP, showcased What Is This' inventive yet sophisticated sound, which critics compared to Cream's. The similarity didn't bother Alain Johannes, the group's singer-guitarist.

"If you're going to describe something for people, the easiest way is to compare it to other things," he reasoned. "People have picked up on the rawness and the blues aspect of what we do, but people really hear Cream, and I don't know why. When the press said my voice sounds like Jack Bruce's, I went out that day and got the first Cream record I'd ever listened to in my life—although I remember hearing 'Sunshine of Your Love' on the radio a couple of times."

Yet What Is This—Johannes, guitarist Hillel Slovak, drummer Jack Irons and bassist Chris Hutchinson—had managed to forge its own identity, because "a lot of things are trendy in Los Angeles, whatever the latest is—the funky stuff, the rap stuff, the techno-pop stuff. But we've still got a good audience here. I moved to L.A. ten years ago, and you get all the input from the world here. I lived in Mexico City for eight years and nothing was happening. I was playing flamenco guitar and that was it. I wish I was older when I did it—I'm 22 now, and I don't remember some of the great things that happened to me!"

Slovak and Irons played with Anthony Kiedis and Flea in the Red Hot Chili Peppers, but they stayed with What Is This when the project received a deal with MCA Records. The band played its first shows outside of California.

"We're driving around in a cargo van and a Lincoln Continental, hey!" the Chilean-born Johannes enthused. "But it's rugged to go out on the road and build a band's consciousness a little. When we're in L.A. we can't play that often, because people get sick of you four times a month. And we can't rehearse too much, because we like to keep things fresh. So we're excited. What Is This isn't a question, it's a statement." ■

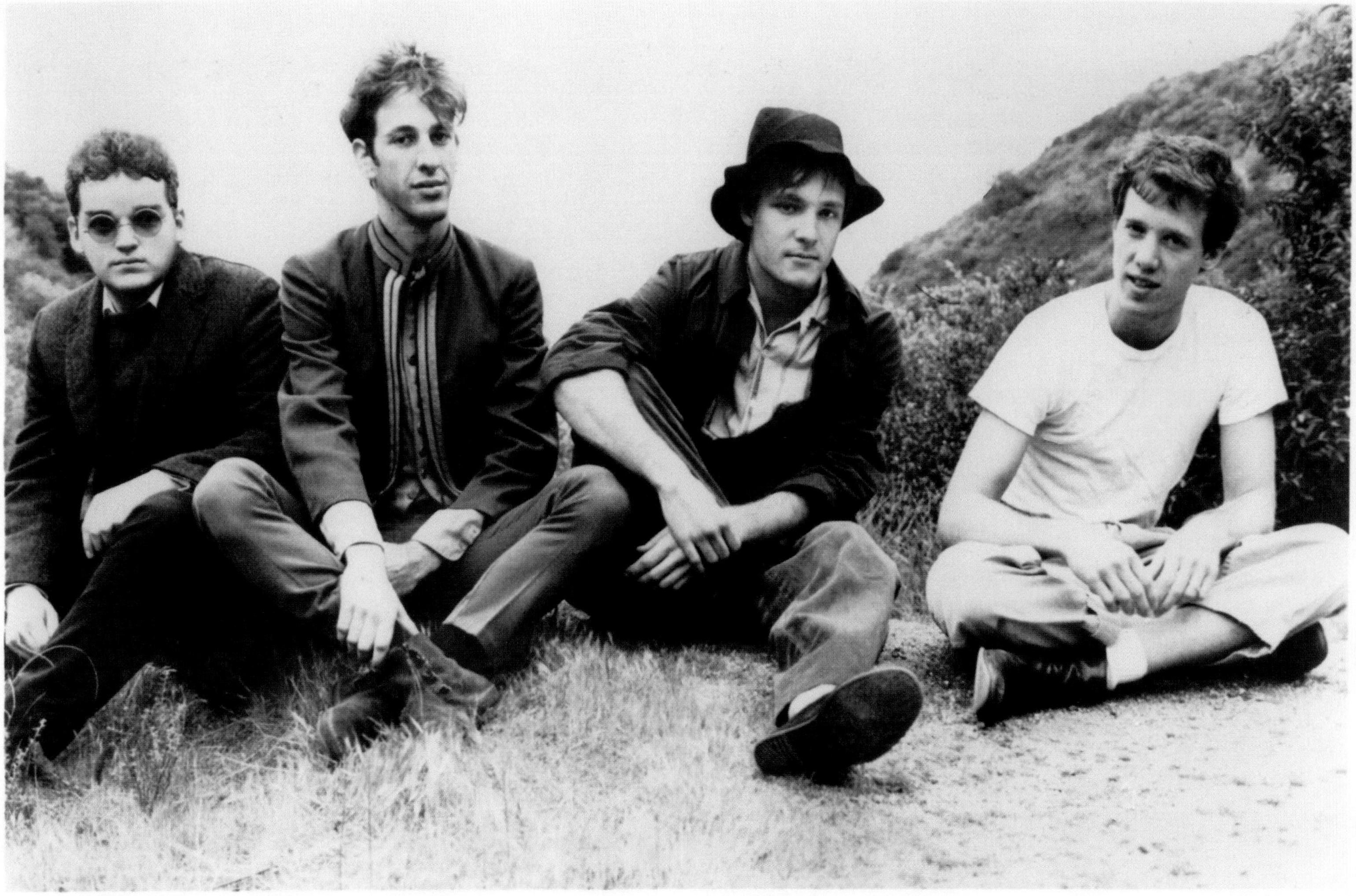

4/84

ALAIN JOHANNES HILLEL SLOVAK CHRIS HUTCHINSON JACK IRONS

What is This

MCA RECORDS

SAN ANDREAS RECORDS ™

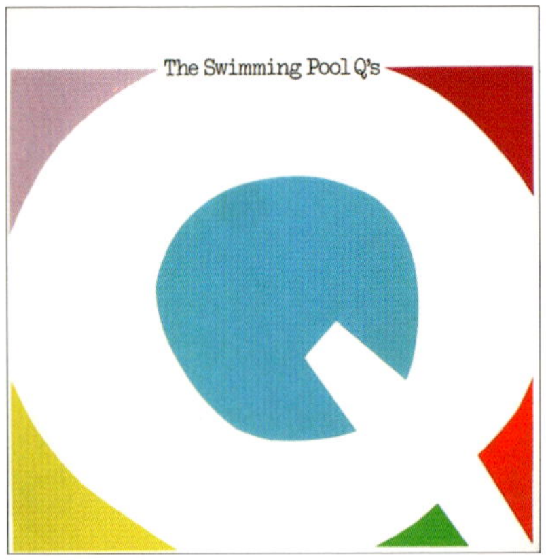

The Swimming Pool Q's garnered the acclaim usually reserved for the likes of R.E.M. and the B-52's.

AS FAR as Jeff Calder of the Swimming Pool Q's was concerned, there was a right way to attain rock stardom, and a write way. Before he got the itch to form the Q's, he suffered through a stint as a rock journalist.

"After I got out of college, I wanted to be a writer," Calder explained. "I didn't know about anything but music, so that seemed like the best thing to write about. I thought I was so smart, too, but I didn't know shit. I may not be any smarter now, but at least I've got something to write about."

Calder's career as a Florida-based writer included contributions to *Rolling Stone* as well as various screenplays and short stories "that I can assure you never went anywhere. I decided to do the other thing I always wanted to do, which was be in a band. I met Bob Elsey, our guitar player, and we hit it off pretty well. We still do, and the rest is..." In keeping with his journalism training, Calder edited his cliché before its completion.

Elsey brought Calder to his native Atlanta, where the Swimming Pool Q's headquartered for nearly seven years. Although the local Southern-boogie scene fostered in the Seventies by Lynyrd Skynyrd had died out, Calder noted that Atlanta and nearby Athens were breeding "some of the best new pop music in America right now."

But the Q's "were always the one band from the South that never got any attention," Calder noted. "We were kind of unusual among the other bands—we really liked to play live, instead of fooling around making tapes and just talking about performing. So we had to struggle around the South finding places to play."

The band signed to A&M Records and released *The Swimming Pool Q's*, its first major label album, and the single "The Bells Ring." The group also got a high-profile slot as support act on Lou Reed's *New Sensations* tour. But Calder's background as a rock critic didn't translate to much help in the music business.

"For the most part, writers have a kind of hostility toward the biz. I was the same way, and I had to drag myself kicking and screaming into it. Now I don't feel uncomfortable or weird with disc jockeys, record company executives or anybody."

And Calder's writing craft had undergone a similar transformation in his new line of work. "I certainly didn't read any books about songwriting," Calder laughed in explaining the Q's eclectic pop stylings. "It's like anything else—you have to learn from the experience of trying to do it. I think most successful songwriters have one thing in common—they stuck with it. And that's my bottom line—hanging in there and trying to keep doing it." ■

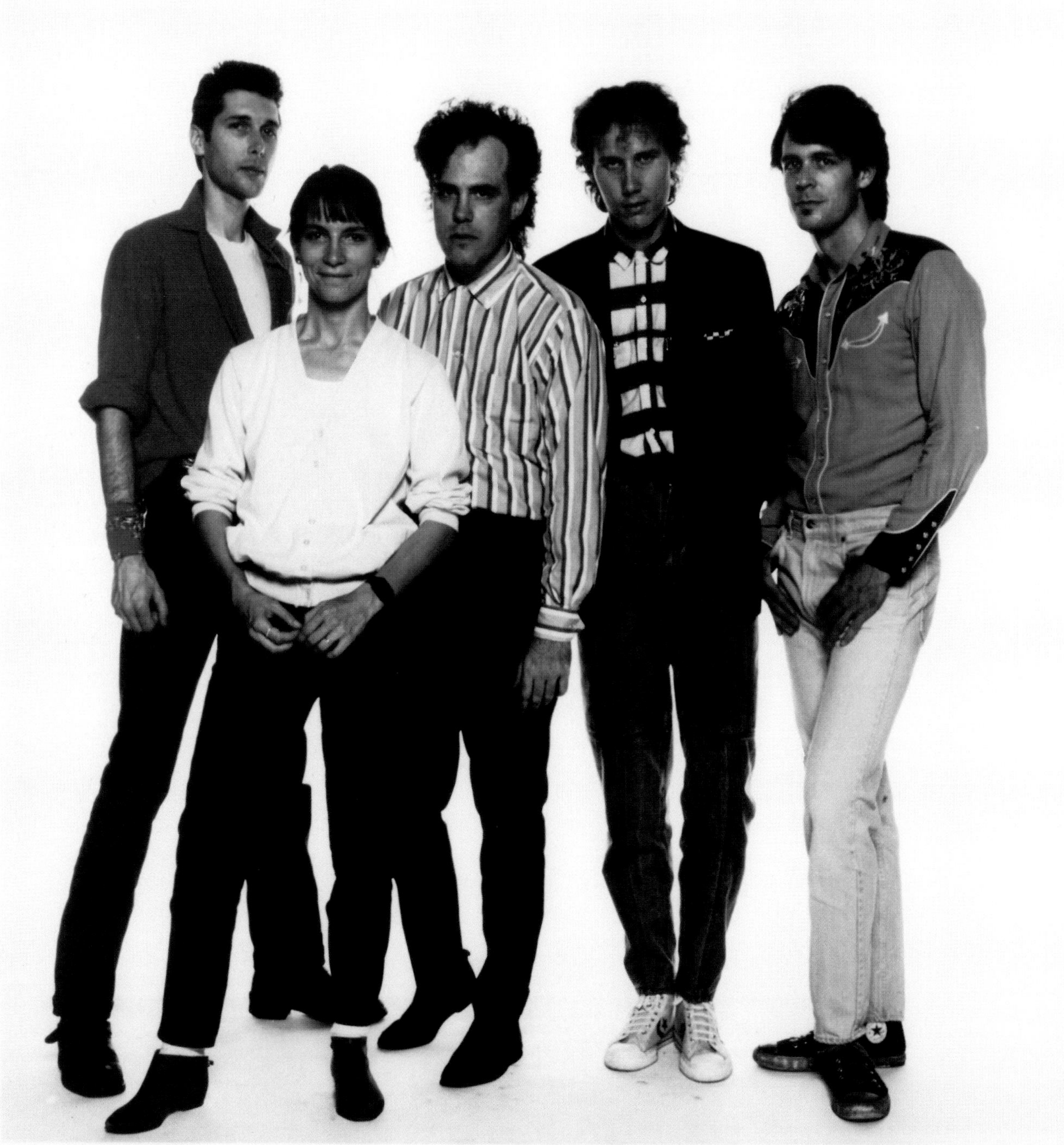

J.E. Garnett Anne Richmond Boston Jeff Calder Billy Burton Bob Elsey

THE SWIMMING POOL Q'S

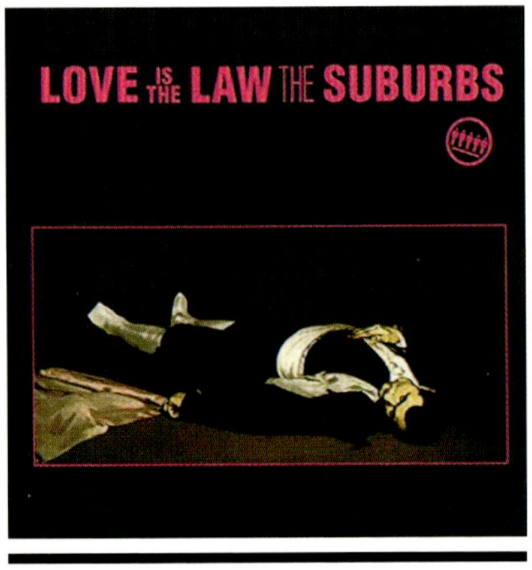

The Suburbs, one of the Twin Cities' most influential bands, got feet moving in clubs with "Love Is the Law."

THANKS TO the success of the Replacements and Prince and his various protégés, a hotbed of new musical activity had emerged—the "Minneapolis scene."

But the Suburbs laid claim to being the first Minnesota band of that vintage to headline the most influential music clubs by performing its own compositions.

"We were making records in 1977 before any of the other stuff started happening," keyboardist Chan Poling explained. "But things were changing all over the world back then. I remember Talking Heads and Blondie and the B-52's coming through town around the same time. Minneapolis has always tried to keep up that way."

If the Suburbs had yet to meet with the same commercial success as their peers, it was because the group's material—which included smatterings of jazz and country as well as rock—wasn't easily categorized. Poling attributed the band's wild musical vision to his childhood friendship with guitarist Beej Chaney.

"We hung out in high school and developed our own sense of humor," Poling noted. "I was a straight jazz guy until Beej turned me on to Ornette Coleman and the Rolling Stones. The first rock record I really liked was (David Bowie's) *Young Americans*, which isn't real traditional."

The duo moved to California in 1975, but after a period of starvation they moved back to the heartland with a bunch of songs and found band members.

"We spent a month drinking…er, hanging out and talking about what we wanted to do," Poling said. "Pretty soon we realized we all had the same ideals—keep it original, wild and complex."

After releasing an array of independently distributed material, the Suburbs finally latched onto a major label. Tracks such as "Hell A" and "Perfect Communist" on the *Love Is the Law* album reflected the group's quest for "an emotional kick." But the band's major exposure came from dance clubs; the title track was produced by Steven Greenberg, the mastermind behind Lipps Inc.'s "Funkytown" and countless rap records.

"I'd much rather get on the radio," Poling admitted. "But there's only so much you can do without compromising your ass off." ■

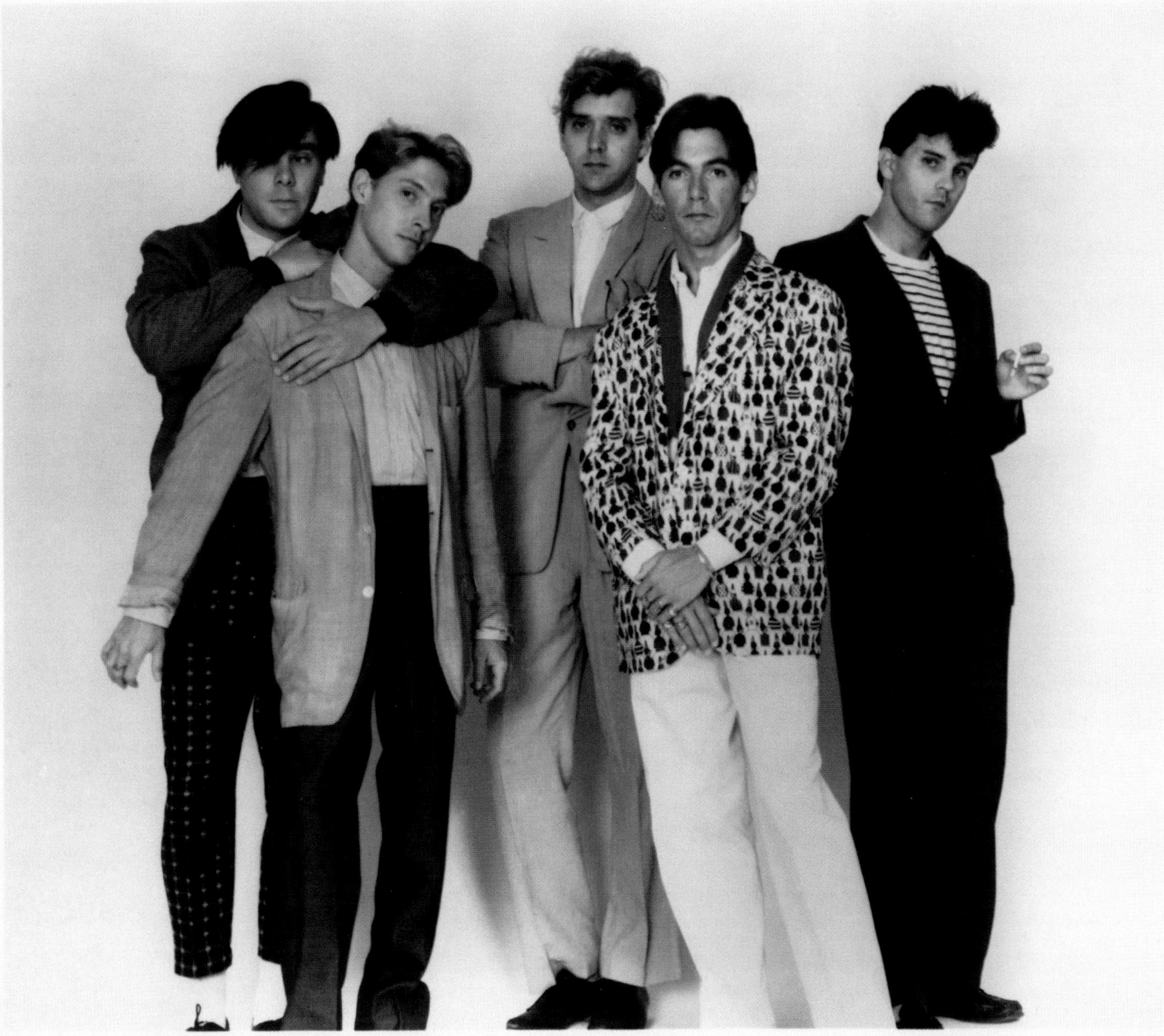

THE SUBURBS

PolyGram Records

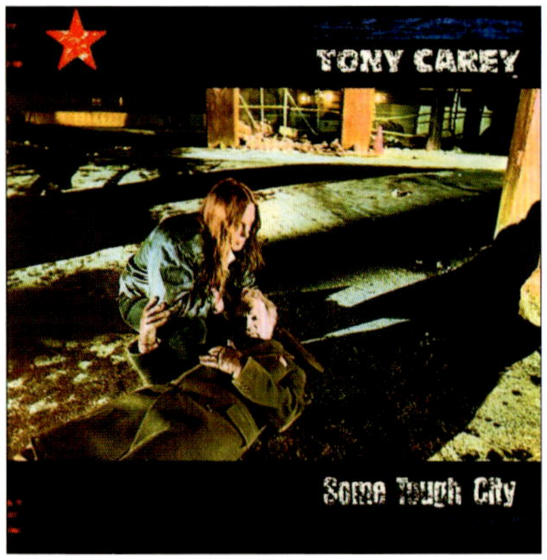

Tony Carey had success with *Some Tough City* and the hits "A Fine Fine Day" and "The First Day of Summer."

Billboard 200: *Some Tough City* (#60)
Billboard Hot 100: "A Fine Fine Day" (#22); "The First Day of Summer" (#33)

THE SONGS on Tony Carey's *Some Tough City* album were those of a no-gimmicks rocker, a city animal who chronicled the underbelly of American life. No one figured that Carey lived in Frankfurt, Germany, churning out an assortment of musical styles besides his urban pose.

In the mid-Seventies, Carey played keyboards for guitarist Ritchie Blackmore in the first edition of Rainbow. "I was one of the first guys he hired—and fired, and hired, and fired!" Carey recalled. The stint with the notoriously volatile Blackmore gave him the impetus to do more than play in someone else's band. Then, during a two-week recording session in Frankfurt in 1978, the California native's career was turned upside-down.

"It was all accidental, just as the best things that have ever happened to me have been," Carey recalled. "I went over to do the session, and I met my wife, my producer, my soundman, my future home—all in those first two weeks. I didn't have anything going on that I cared about, so I was willing to cut loose and not go home."

In Germany, Carey worked with producer Peter Hauke, learning how to engineer and perform in the recording studio. Working on a number of projects—writing the lyrics and music, singing all vocals and playing most of the instruments—he saw a couple stick in 1983. The first—a single from his first American release, "I Won't Be Home Tonight"—made its way onto FM playlists. The second reflected Carey's chameleonic nature—calling himself Planet P, he released an album of cosmic gadgetry that resulted in the hit "Why Me?" The music was a far cry from the gritty rock that he released under his own name.

In 1984, Carey rode the crest of *Some Tough City* and the smash single "A Fine Fine Day." The album cover and video for the single concerned Uncle Sonny, an underground-type character. Carey even thanked Uncle Sonny in the album's liner notes, but there was no such person.

"In spirit he dictated what songs I'd keep on the rest of the album—the sleazebag tunes, the street-corner love songs. There aren't many expatriates in rock 'n' roll, but since I'm living in Germany now, that's what I am. My hero is John Steinbeck because he wrote about the less fortunate, and that's what I want in my songs." ■

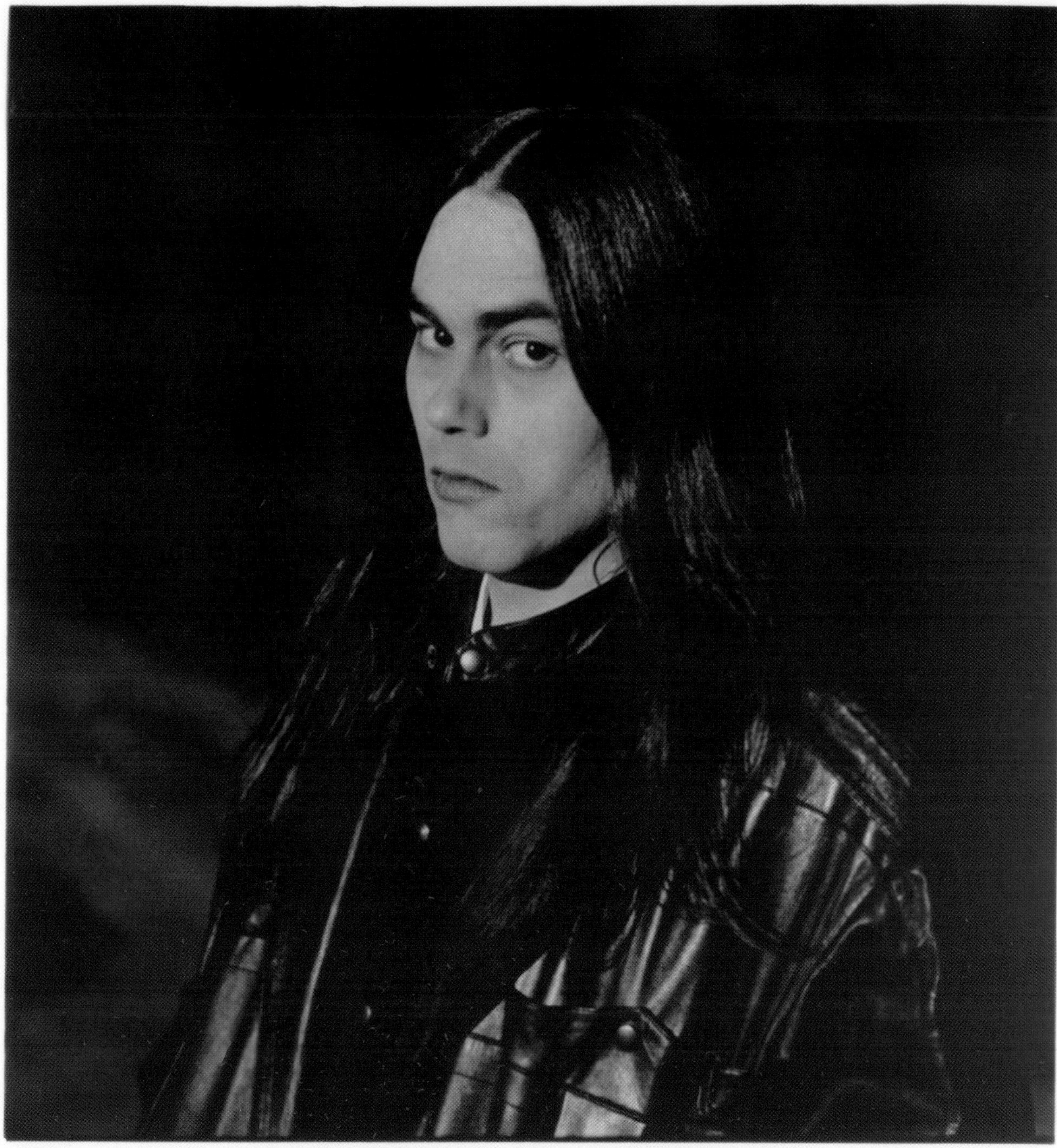

2/84

TONY CAREY

MCA RECORDS

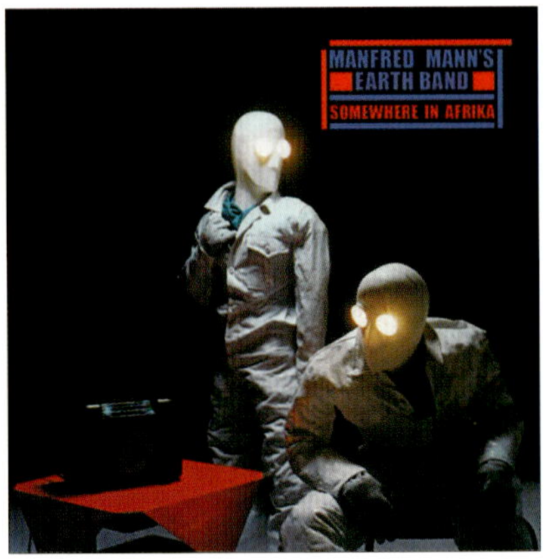

"Runner" by Manfred Mann's Earth Band accompanied ABC's broadcast of the 1984 Summer Olympics.

Billboard 200: *Somewhere in Afrika* (#40)
Billboard Hot 100: "Runner" (#22)

FITTINGLY, IN an Olympic year, the airwaves were saturated with "Runner," a stirring anthem to feet-beaters across the world. And the person behind "Runner" was a marathoner in a musical sense—Manfred Mann.

Mann had offered such memorable pop ditties as "Do Wah Diddy Diddy" and "Pretty Flamingo" back during 1964-65's British Invasion. A decade later, he topped the charts by covering a song called "Blinded by the Light" by a then-unknown songwriter named Bruce Springsteen.

"I don't think anyone says, 'I want to be a success for a year,'" the keyboardist allowed. "If there's a secret to my longevity, that's it. I think it's the goal of any musician to transcend one period of time, but perhaps other people have had more glory in mind for themselves than I ever had."

Yet despite a five-year reign on the charts in the Sixties and the presence of such talents as Jack Bruce, Klaus Voorman, Paul Jones and Mike D'Abo in the band, Mann became disenchanted.

"I started off as a jazz musician," he allowed. "After five years of 'Do Wah Diddy Diddy,' I felt very limited by the parameters of pop—it became a quest for more hit singles, nothing else. And the madness of that time—everyone was making up the rules as they went along."

Mann returned to the jazz form by creating the experimental Chapter Three, which only lasted two years, but it served "to make me whole, in a way. I got it out of my system." Mann then formed the Earth Band. Even with "Blinded by the Light" and the distinctive vocal talent of singer Chris Thompson, the outfit hadn't made the same splash that Mann had two decades earlier. "Runner" changed that.

"I'm always looking for the obscure song that people might have missed," he explained. "'Runner' was suggested by my record company—I got it in the mail and I just thought it was a song we could do well. I'm simply in the habit of listening. If there's a record playing in the next room, I'll go find out who it is."

Somewhere in Afrika, the parent album of "Runner," continued in the Mann tradition of offering distinctive interpretations of others' songs. The record included Sting's "Demolition Man," Al Stewart's "Eyes of Nostradamus" and Bob Marley's "Redemption Song"—as well as the South African-born Mann's powerful feelings about his home country's apartheid policies. ■

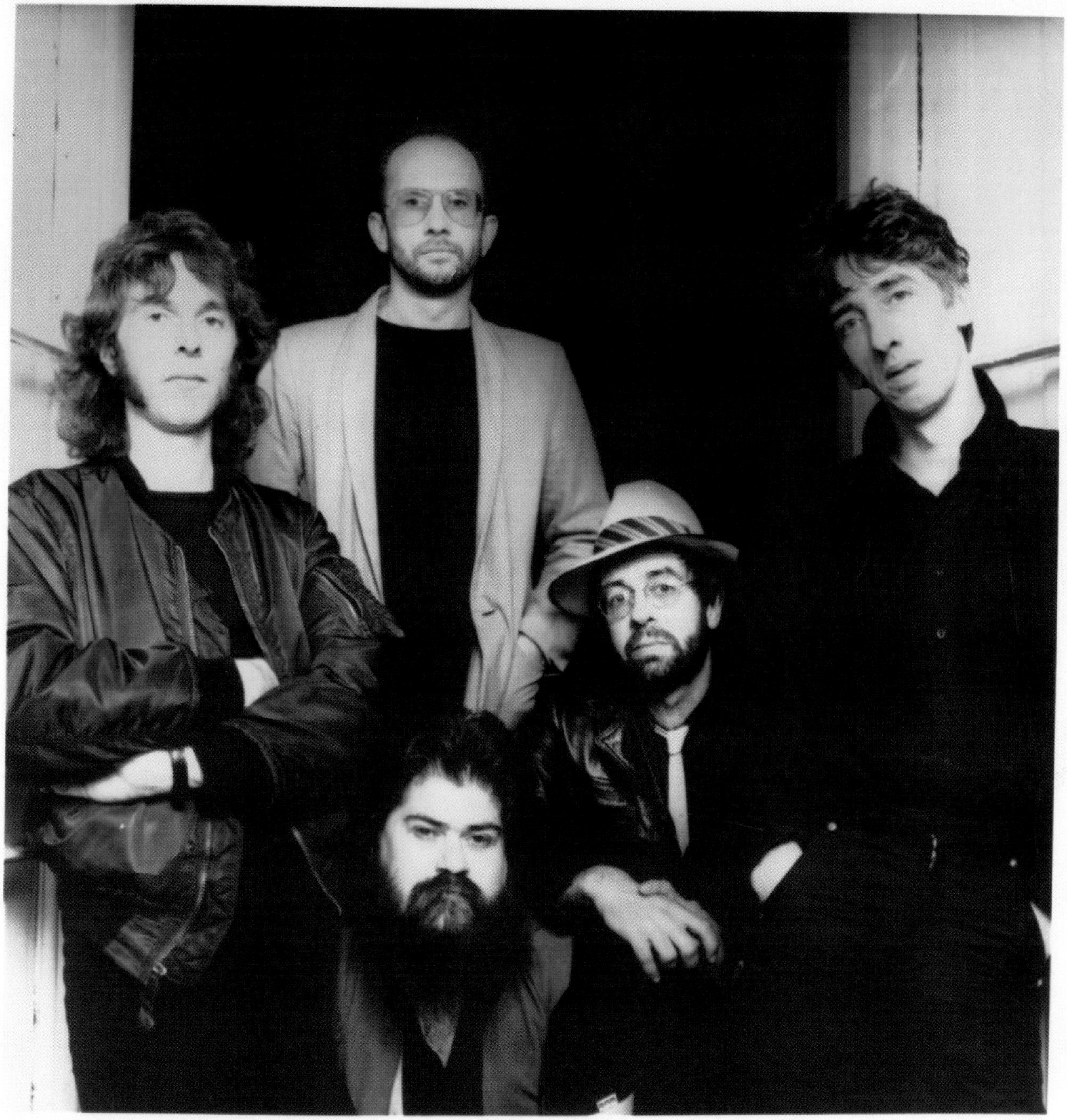

MANFRED MANN´S
EARTH BAND

ARISTA

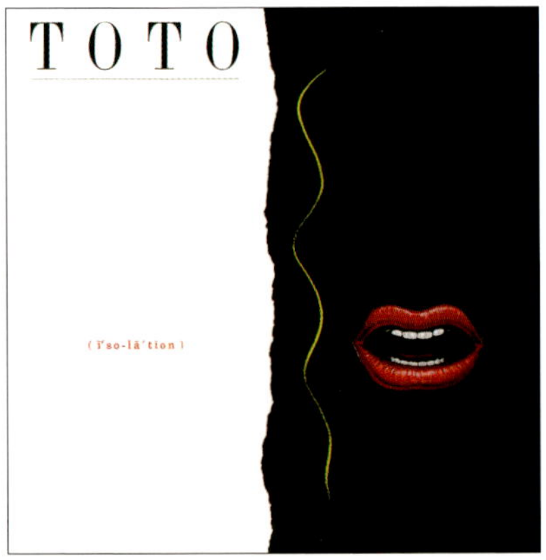

Billboard 200: *Isolation* (#42)
Billboard Hot 100: "Stranger in Town" (#7); "Holyanna" (#71)

Isolation by Toto achieved gold-record status, largely on the strength of the single "Stranger in Town."

THE MEMBERS of Toto enjoyed a reputation as some of the best session players in the business, having played with everyone from Boz Scaggs to George Benson to the Tubes. Wanting to create something of their own, they racked up a string of smash hits such as "Hold the Line," "Africa" and "Rosanna." When it came down to sheer musical ability, there should have been no stopping Toto.

But despite the track record of impressive singles, Toto had never imparted a perceptible image or totally committed to making the proper career moves. On their infrequent tours, the pale, studio-tanned band members didn't make any concessions to arena-rock looks or sensibilities, and singer Bobby Kimball—a pudgy good ol' boy from Louisiana—had zero stage presence.

So Toto cut back on outside projects and replaced Kimball with Fergie Frederiksen, a frontman who displayed a larger—albeit unoriginal—repertoire of crowd-pleasing stage moves.

"We all welcomed the change in direction," keyboardist Steve Porcaro noted. "Unfortunately, he joined when we were two-thirds of the way through recording *Isolation* and things were kind of disjointed—we were also in the middle of doing the soundtrack for the *Dune* movie, and maybe we bit off more than we could chew."

Isolation, Toto's fifth album, did not achieve the acclaim of its predecessors, but "Stranger in Town"—recorded while Kimball was still a member of the group—cracked the charts.

"To be frank, I haven't agreed with the selection of singles from *Isolation*," Porcaro admitted. "I want people to hear our new lead singer, and we haven't released a single that he sings lead on."

At the close of the tour in support of *Isolation,* the band moved on and fired Frederiksen. ■

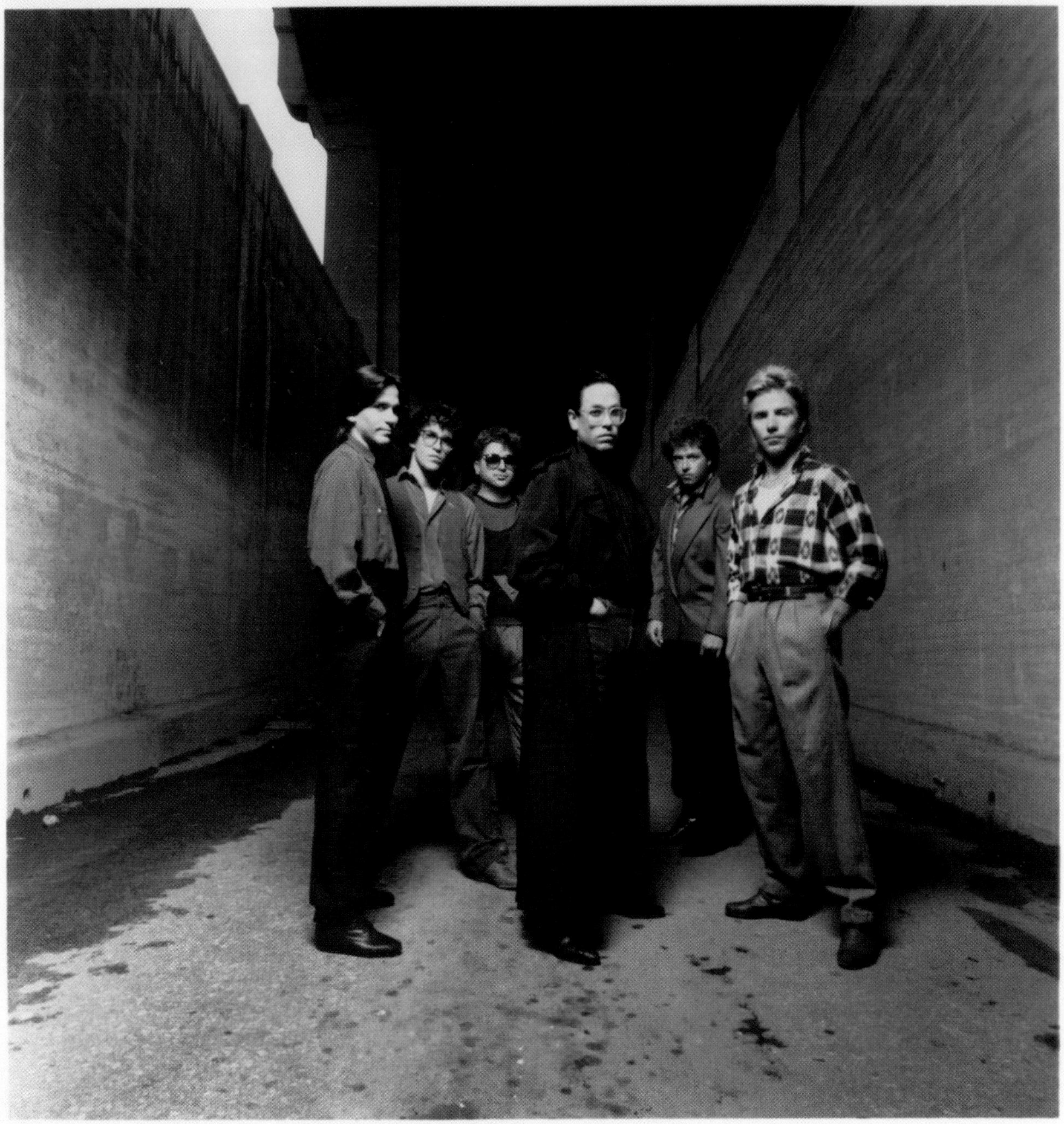

Photo Credit: Jim Shea

David Paich
Steve Lukather
Steve Porcaro
Michael Porcaro
Jeff Porcaro
Fergie Frederiksen

The Fitzgerald Hartley Co
7250 Beverly Boulevard Los Angeles California 90036
(213) 934-8002

TOTO

Columbia

8410

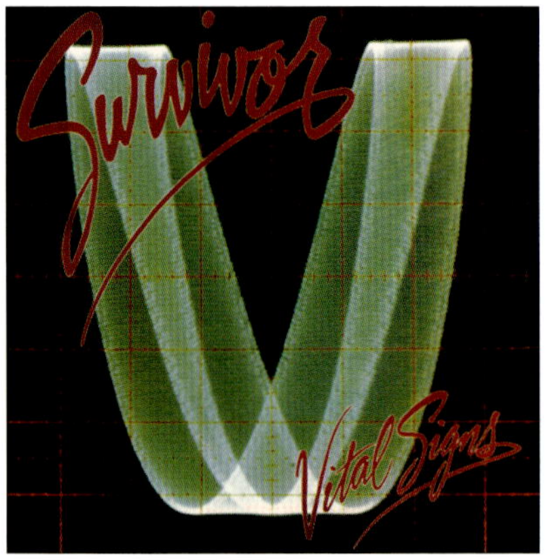

Welcoming vocalist Jimi Jamison into the ranks paid off for Survivor, giving the group two Top 10 hits.

Billboard 200: *Vital Signs* (#30)
Billboard Hot 100: "I Can't Hold Back" (#13); "High on You" (#8); "The Search Is Over" (#4); "First Night" (#53)

SURVIVOR'S TWO founding members, keyboardist Jim Peterik and guitarist Frankie Sullivan, refused to be satisfied. The Chicago-based duo joined forces in the late Seventies (Peterik had formed the Ides of March at age 14 and later penned its 1970 smash "Vehicle"), but their first hit collaboration was a composition that didn't make it onto the first Survivor album circa 1980. Instead, 38 Special recorded "Rockin' Into the Night" and scored a commercial breakthrough. From that point on, Survivor became the most important priority for Peterik and Sullivan.

"It took a couple of years to realize that there's only so much you can do with outside projects," Sullivan said. "In the long run, unless you're Phil Collins with Genesis, it really takes away from what you're trying to accomplish as a band."

Survivor's big break came when actor Sylvester Stallone commissioned the group to provide the theme song for his film *Rocky III*—"Eye of the Tiger" became one of the biggest-selling singles of 1982. But that success, Sullivan said, "was a double-edged sword. It certainly was wonderful having the No. 1 song for six weeks, but there's always a downside to anything that becomes that big. People didn't know who we were, and all of a sudden we had the top record in the country. It was associated with Stallone's film, and a lot of people heard that Survivor wasn't really a band, just guys that wrote the song for the movie—a lot of things that couldn't be further from the truth."

The band followed that success with a major personnel move, as it replaced lead singer David Bickler with Jimi Jamison in an effort to gain a strong frontman (drummer Marc Droubay and bassist Stephan Ellis rounded out the group). *Vital Signs*, Survivor's first album with Jamison, provided a kick-start. The smash singles "I Can't Hold Back" and "High on You" ensued, both written by Peterik and Sullivan.

Yet Survivor faced another challenge, intent on translating their hits into an identifiable entity. "We have a way to go with our image," Sullivan admitted. "We've always been perceived by a lot of people as being different than what we really are." ■

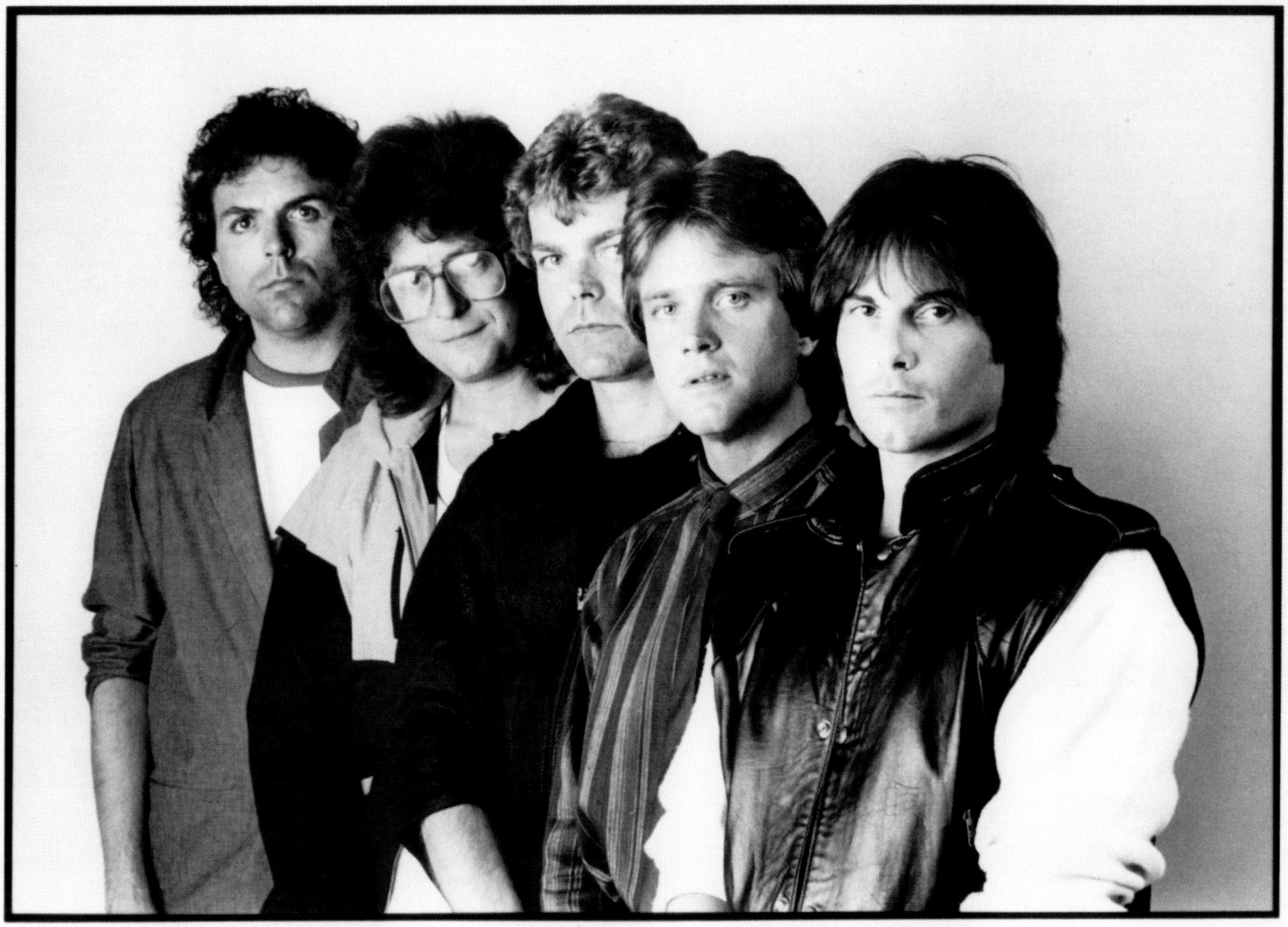

Photo Credit: Jim Marshall

Marc Droubay | Jim Peterik | Stephan Ellis | Frankie Sullivan | Jimi Jamison

SURVIVOR

JOHN BARUCK MANAGEMENT COMPANY INC

Scotti Brothers™

EPA EPIC PORTRAIT ASSOCIATED

8410

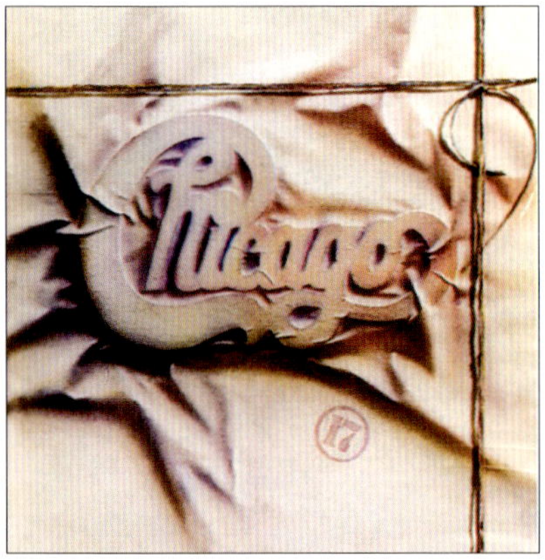

Chicago 17 became the best-selling album in Chicago's history and received a troika of Grammy Awards.

Billboard 200: *Chicago 17* (#4)
Billboard Hot 100: "Stay the Night" (#16); "Hard Habit to Break" (#3); "You're the Inspiration" (#3); "Along Comes a Woman" (#14)

EIGHTEEN YEARS after forming the nucleus of Chicago, the seven-piece unit found itself in the midst of a major comeback with *Chicago 17*, thanks to four Top 20 hits—"Stay the Night," "Hard Habit to Break," "You're the Inspiration" and "Along Comes a Woman."

"Only Michael Jackson can sneeze at that," woodwind player Walt Parazaider said.

Parazaider cited two factors as the key to the jazz-rock veterans' continued success: the production skills of David Foster and the recruitment of singer-keyboardist Bill Champlin. Foster, whose prior credits as a producer included work with Hall & Oates and Earth, Wind & Fire, had been solicited for 1982's *Chicago 16* album.

"We're real proud that we've been a viable act through the late Sixties and Seventies, and now the Eighties," Parazaider noted. "And David Foster has been a big part of that. He sat us down and said, 'Look, I've been a fan of you guys for years—I learned the trombone as a teenager just so I could play 'Make Me Smile.' I might be stepping on toes a lot of times, but when the final decision comes down—even though it's a democratic band—it's gotta rest with me, because I really feel I know where you guys have to go."

Foster's expertise resulted in the streamlined, crisply produced hit "Hard to Say I'm Sorry" and worldwide sales of 2 million for *Chicago 16*, and *Chicago 17* expanded on that breakthrough. Champlin, described by Parazaider as "our first-round draft choice," also made his way into the group's framework.

"The funny thing is, when we were putting Chicago together in the Sixties, Bill was putting together the Sons of Champlin," Parazaider recalled. "And we really liked their records—it's ironic how people with similar ideas eventually gravitate toward each other."

What was next for the corporate-minded musicians? "Chicago has always planned ahead," Parazaider said. "You've got to know what you're doing to stay on top."

The success, however, changed the long-established group dynamics. *Chicago 17* was the band's last album with founding bassist and vocalist Peter Cetera. ■

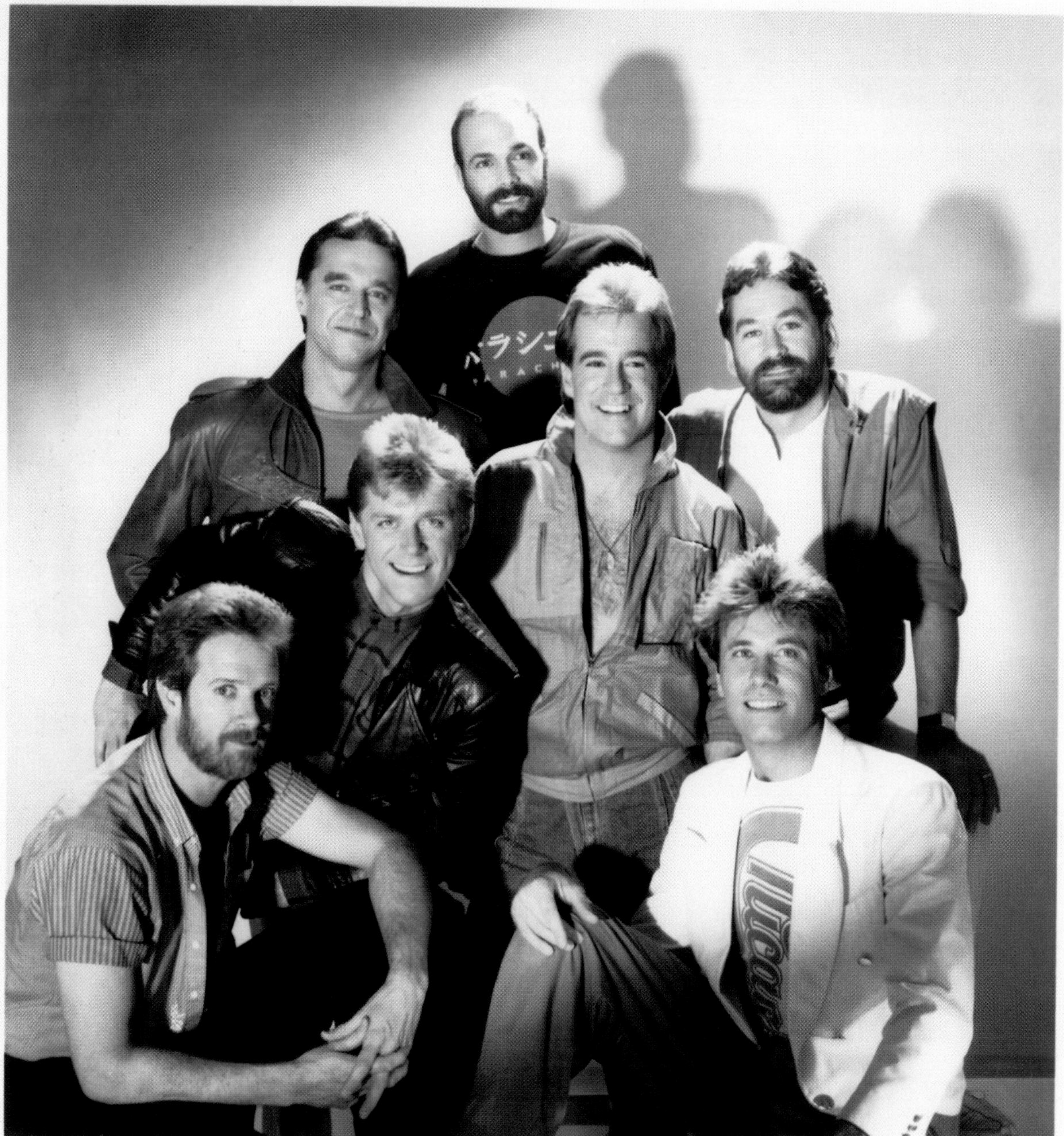

PHOTO CREDIT: HARRY LANGDON 1984

Danny Seraphine

Walt Parazaider James Pankow Bill Champlin

Lee Loughnane Peter Cetera Robert Lamm

Chicago

WARNER BROS.

Full Moon

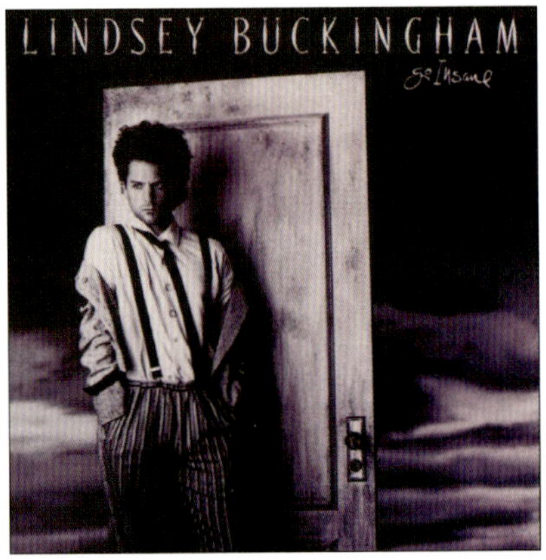

Go Insane, the second solo album from Lindsey Buckingham, demonstrated the guitarist's musical iconoclasm.

Billboard 200: *Go Insane* (#45)
Billboard Hot 100: "Go Insane" (#23)

FLEETWOOD MAC was America's most popular band in the late Seventies, and lead guitarist Lindsey Buckingham's penchant for challenging the rules and preconceptions of pop music emerged when he shaped the controversial and experimental *Tusk* album as a follow-up to the blockbuster *Rumours*.

With Fleetwood Mac on a hiatus between albums, Buckingham continued to be an ambitious studio wizard who would rather tinker with sounds and structures than crusade for Top 40 canonization. *Go Insane* extended his rich, layered production, arrangements and guitar playing outside of the band's framework.

"Recording on my own is a fairly insular process, and that's the way I like it," Buckingham reflected. "It's not a political process in the sense that doing a Fleetwood Mac album would be. It's not as much of a verbalizing process, it's more subconscious and intuitive. With the new record, I was able to punch my way out of the Fleetwood Mac microcosm and reaffirm my own abilities for the first time since I've been making records."

On *Go Insane*'s title track, Buckingham sharpened his Top 40 hit with massed choral sounds. But his heart was with such sophisticated yet accessible tracks as "Play in the Rain" (an experimental piece that ended Side One and continued on Side Two) and "D.W. Suite" (a three-part work of "musical cinema" composed in memory of Beach Boy Dennis Wilson) that he could only have accomplished through hours of obsessive work in a recording studio—which was precisely how Buckingham achieved his goals.

"I see the whole process as a painting," he allowed. "You can have an idea for a tune, but the work is going to develop a personality and will of its own. When you begin, you're enforcing your will on the canvas, and if you're sensitive, at some point the canvas may enforce its will on you and lead you to an ultimate conclusion.

"It's really your duty to pursue improvement. Talent doesn't mean a lot if you don't have passion and discipline—and gratitude for the situation you're in. I feel like I'm improving. If I were still doing juiced-up folk-rock like 'Go Your Own Way,' I should just hang it up." ■

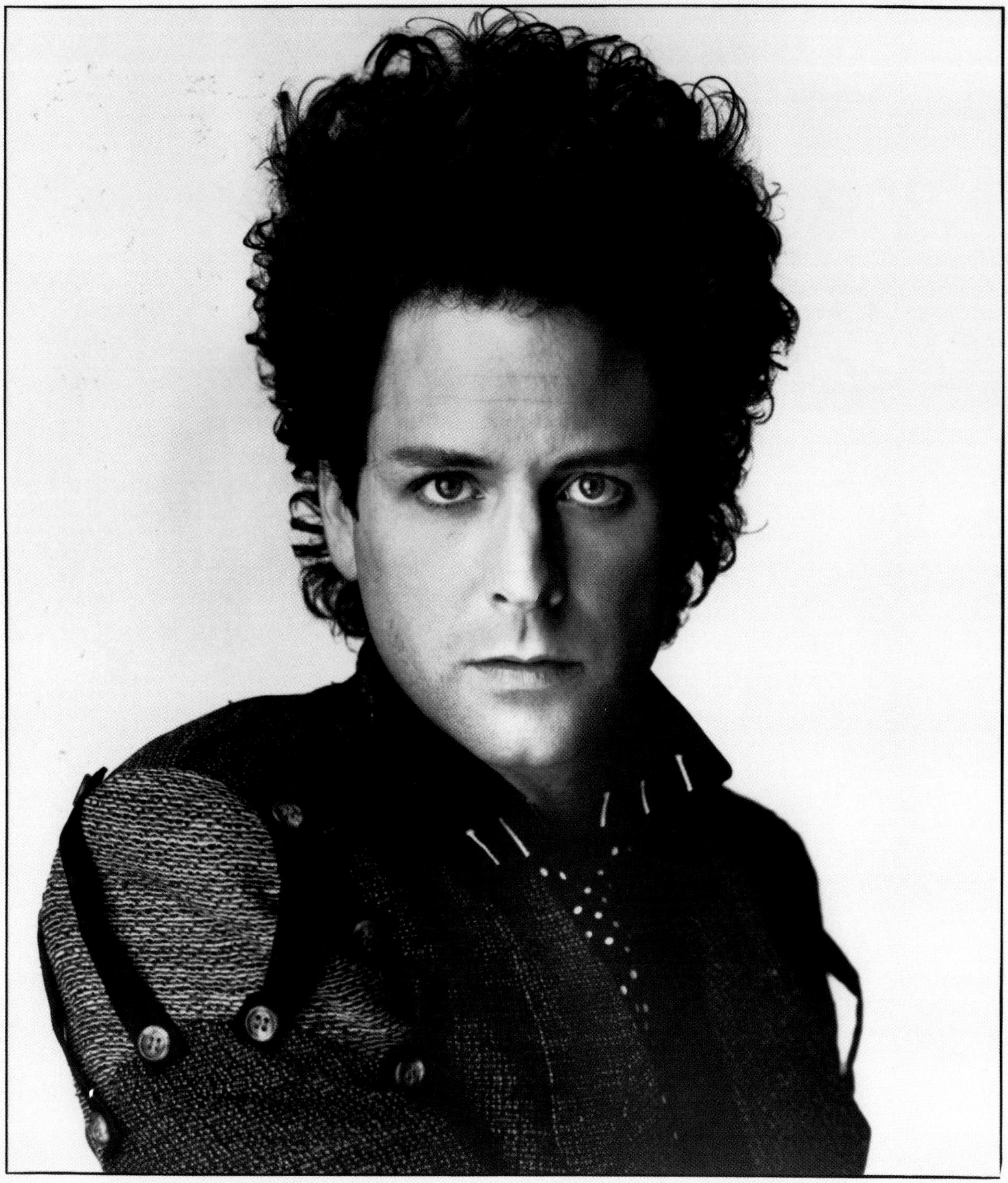

PHOTO CREDIT: MATTHEW ROLSTON /1984

LINDSEY BUCKINGHAM

ELEKTRA

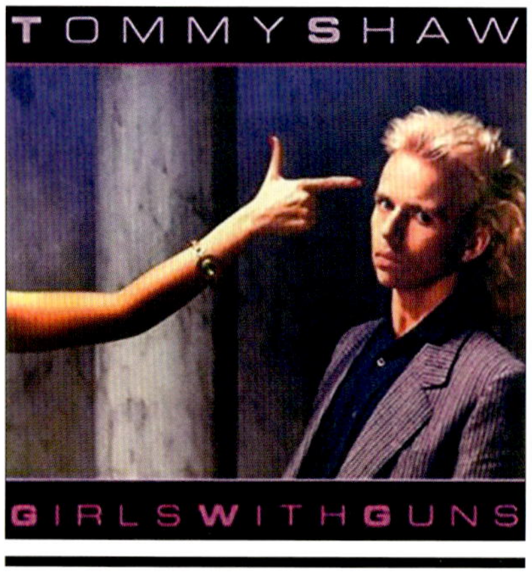

Tommy Shaw, lead guitarist of Styx, made a confident solo debut with the release of *Girls with Guns.*

Billboard 200: *Girls with Guns* (#50)
Billboard Hot 100: "Girls with Guns" (#33); "Lonely School" (#60)

TOMMY SHAW wrote the hits "Too Much Time on My Hands," "Blue Collar Man" and "Fooling Yourself" for Styx, one of America's most popular groups. But Shaw, a likable and candid sort, was crisscrossing the country with his own band, opening shows and enduring the indignities often accorded bottom-of-the-bill acts. He actually enjoyed the fact that he wasn't being allowed a sound check.

"This is fun, this is rock 'n' roll," he exclaimed. "I mean, I rode a tour bus between gigs for my very first time. With Styx, we flew to every gig."

Shaw's sentiments could have been dismissed as those of rock's answer to Richie Rich, a "poor little rich kid" from a wildly successful band. But the blond guitarist—he was known among Styx fans as "the cute one"—seemed sincere in his return to his musical roots. A good ol' boy from Alabama, Shaw had been specifically recruited into the Chicago-based group in 1976.

"When disco music came into play, I said the hell with it," he recalled. "I was in a band playing original music, and that was tough enough without a recording contract. So I moved back down to Alabama from Chicago in 1975 and started playing country rock—I even played steel guitar for three months. But I left my number registered in the Chicago phone directory—heck, it was the first time I had a phone. Styx called me through directory assistance after a mutual friend recommended me."

But by the early Eighties, Shaw had become openly critical of the direction Styx had taken. "It started when we did the *Paradise Theater* album (in 1981) and had all of this elaborate staging to go with the show," he mused. "We were set to perform at a theater in Chicago, and part of the stage set wasn't working—and we cancelled the show! We could have played—but we couldn't because the show wasn't working."

So Shaw was "just waiting" for a call to do the next Styx album, but he wasn't fazed—the excitement surrounding his solo album *Girls with Guns* had him busy. The project was surprisingly potent, rich in pop-rock values and appealingly produced by Mike Stone (of Journey fame). The synth-propelled title track, a clever ode to assertive women, reached #6 on the *Billboard* Mainstream Rock Tracks chart. ■

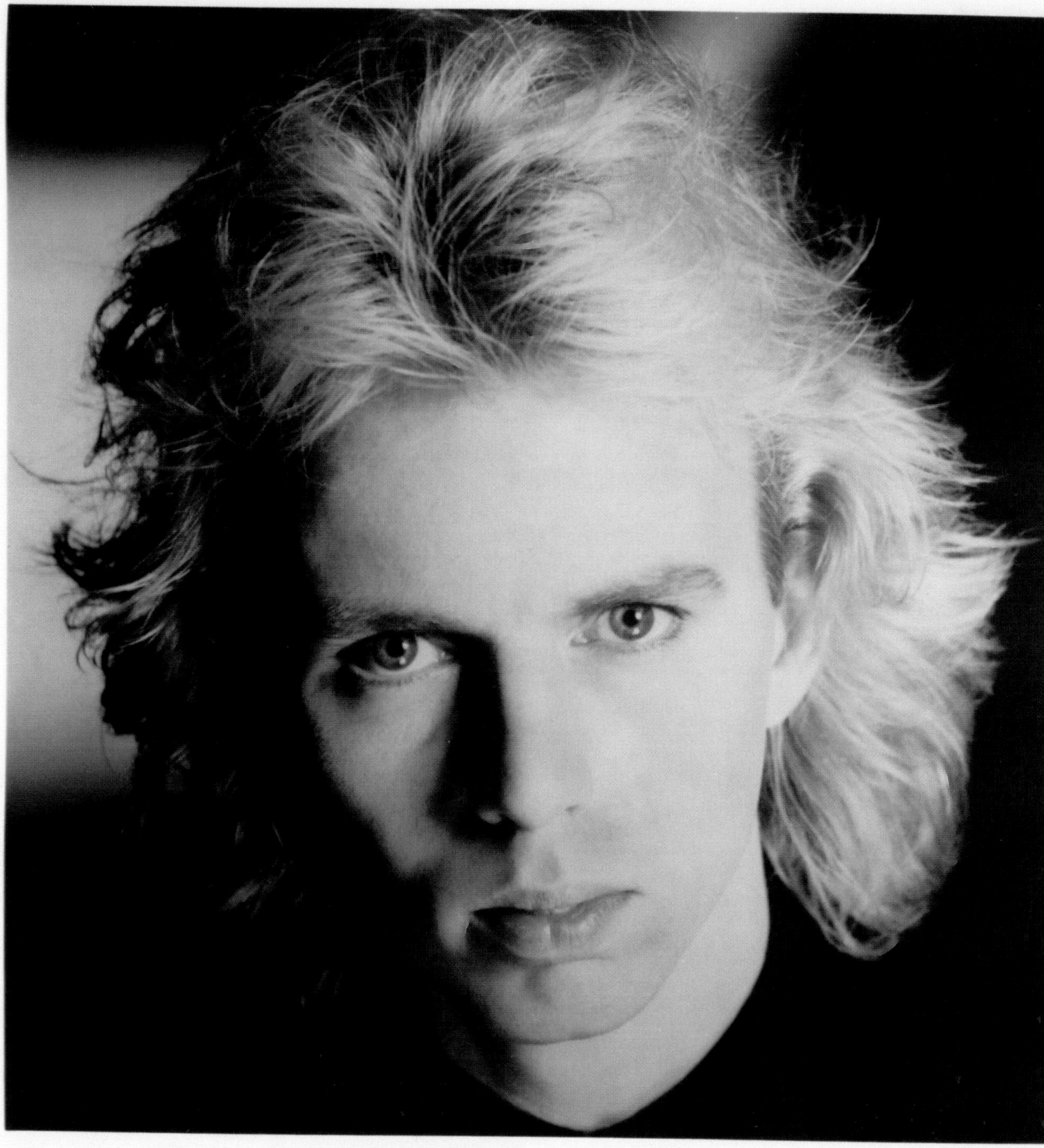

TOMMY SHAW

Direction:
Jerry Kramer
Mental Management, Inc.
(213) 462-2680

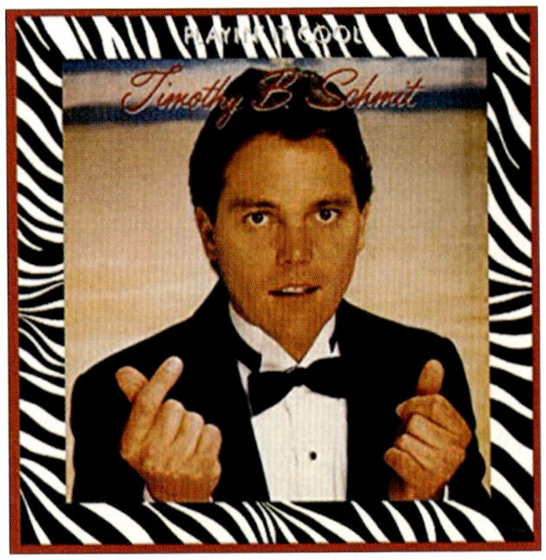

Billboard 200: *Playin' It Cool* (#160)

Vocalist and bass player for both the Eagles and Poco, Timothy B. Schmit flew solo on *Playin' It Cool*.

TIMOTHY B. Schmit's career had been predicated on right place/ right time axioms. He replaced Randy Meisner in Poco in 1969 and stayed on for eight years. And when Meisner left the Eagles in 1977, Schmit was again recruited as his substitute.

Schmit wrote and sang lead on the 1975 song "Keep On Tryin'," Poco's biggest hit single to that point, but the band never attained the major commercial breakthrough that many people predicted, a fact that Schmit understood with the benefit of hindsight.

"We didn't make hit singles," he shrugged. "We had a couple of songs that mid-charted, but it wasn't quite enough. I know that we tried like you can't believe, but we just did not make hit songs."

Schmit's four-year stint with the Eagles wasn't particularly prolific, given that band's drawn-out methods of working in the studio. He co-authored the hit "I Can't Tell You Why" for the album *The Long Run* before the group split in 1981.

"That album was the longest project I've ever been involved in, but I wouldn't say it was hard. The options were all there, to participate as much as you wanted to, to throw out your ideas or keep quiet. I think for a first appearance in the Eagles, it was probably right to do just one song—although I really didn't come up with much more, so that's another reason!"

That take-it-easy attitude carried over to Schmit's first solo effort, *Playin' It Cool*. The project allowed him to display his crystal-clear voice over the course of an entire album. Teaming with guitarist Josh Leo, he gathered the cream of his Southern California friends—Don Henley, Carl Wilson, Joe Walsh and J.D. Souther—to help.

"I had always wanted to do a solo project," Schmit admitted. "A couple of years after the Eagles' breakup, I was still doing nothing, so I decided to pursue this. If people hear echoes of the Eagles or Poco, that's because those bands are part of what I've done. I didn't want to go to left field, be pretentious and pretend I'm a new waver or something." ■

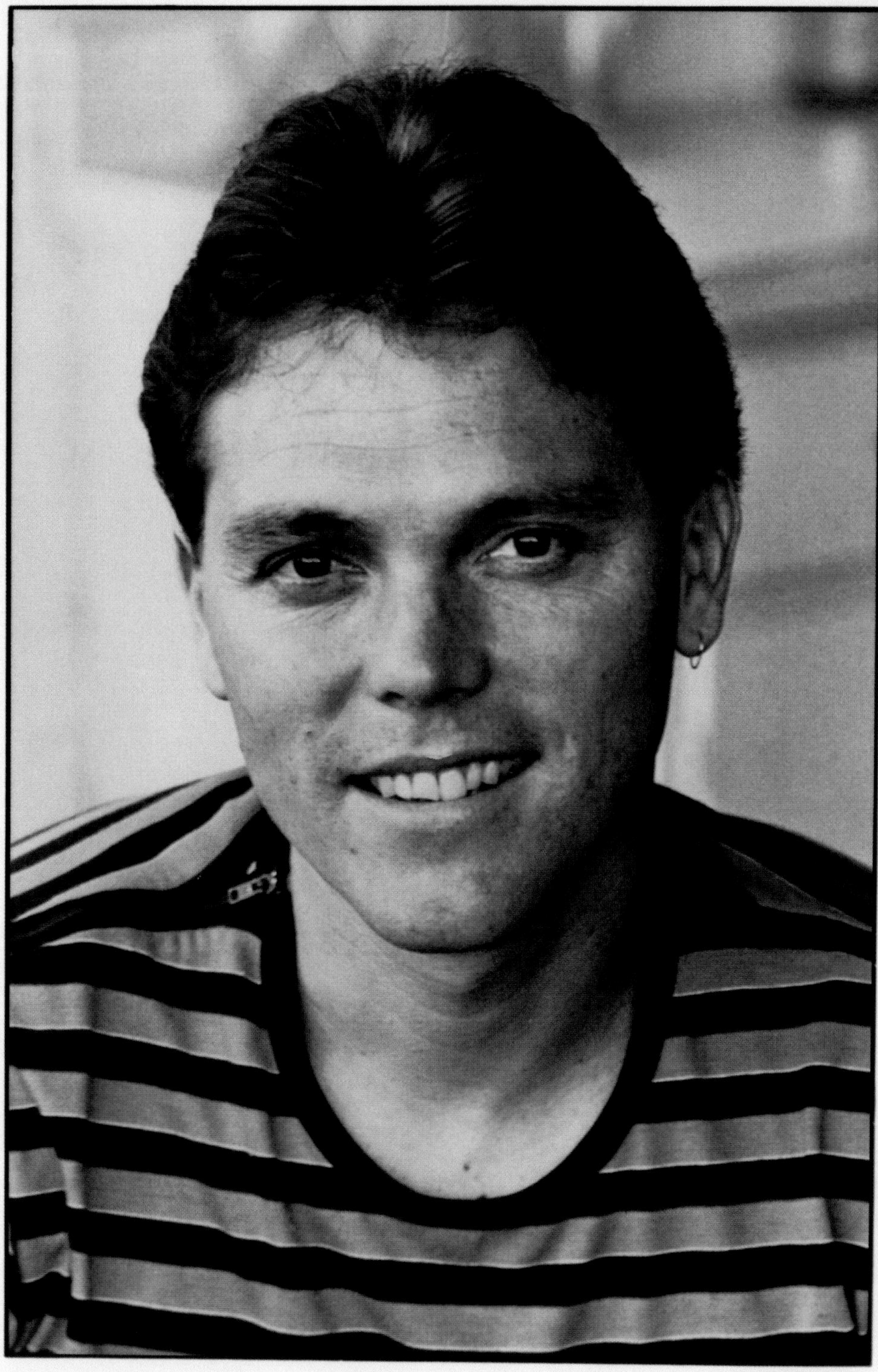

PHOTO CREDIT: HENRY DILTZ/1984

Timothy B. Schmit

ASYLUM

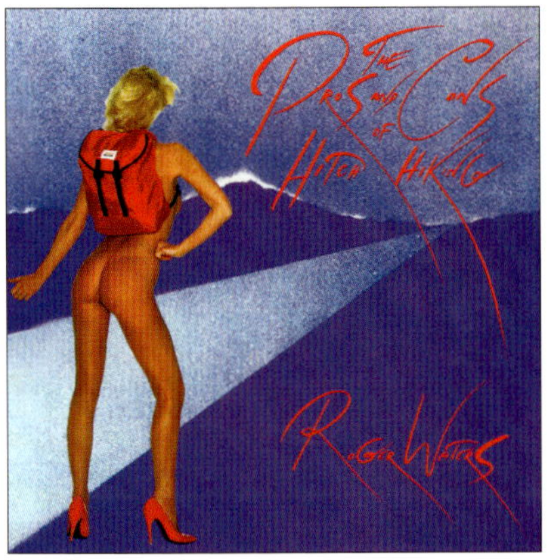

Billboard 200: *The Pros and Cons of Hitch Hiking* (#31)

Pink Floyd's Roger Waters embarked on a solo career, releasing *The Pros and Cons of Hitch Hiking*.

FOR 19 years, Roger Waters played bass with Pink Floyd, one of the most progressive and successful British bands in rock history. And from *Wish You Were Here* and *Animals* to *The Wall* and *The Final Cut*, he went from sole lyricist to co-producer to total mastermind of the group.

Waters finally embarked on a solo career with the release of *The Pros and Cons of Hitch Hiking*. Despite his track record, however, the album stalled at sales far below the platinum standards he set with Pink Floyd. But Waters, a notorious recluse, wasn't willing to turn back.

"I can't see us working together again," he admitted of Pink Floyd's status. "I'm being much less bashful about owning up to what my position was in Pink Floyd. It makes me slightly uncomfortable, but I just think there's no reason people shouldn't know stuff like that. It's not a great exposé, but I've realized that people out there who I know are really interested in the work I've done over the years don't know that I do it. When they see my name, they make no connection between that and Pink Floyd. That's all I'm trying to do, squeeze that gap together."

Ironically, Waters wrote *The Pros and Cons of Hitch Hiking* in 1979, at the same time he composed *The Wall*. "I made demo tapes of them both and presented them to the band," Waters revealed. "I said I was going to do one as a band album, and one as a solo piece for sure, because I'd been feeling it out to do something on my own for quite a while. They chose *The Wall* on the grounds that, if anything, it was less personal than this one was."

Waters' solo tour featured a multimedia presentation of *The Pros and Cons of Hitch Hiking*, a spectacle that matched up against past Floyd extravaganzas. He stepped out as a frontman—the phlegmatic demeanor was still intact, but he took charge of his touring band (Eric Clapton on lead guitar received obvious attention).

"I've completely overestimated the public's recognition of my name," the master of venomous lyrics admitted. "In Europe I had to pull shows out—I couldn't sell a ticket. There is not a large following for *me*. But I'm trying to change that. I'm planning on being prolific. Can I do anything else to give people a better idea of who I am?" ■

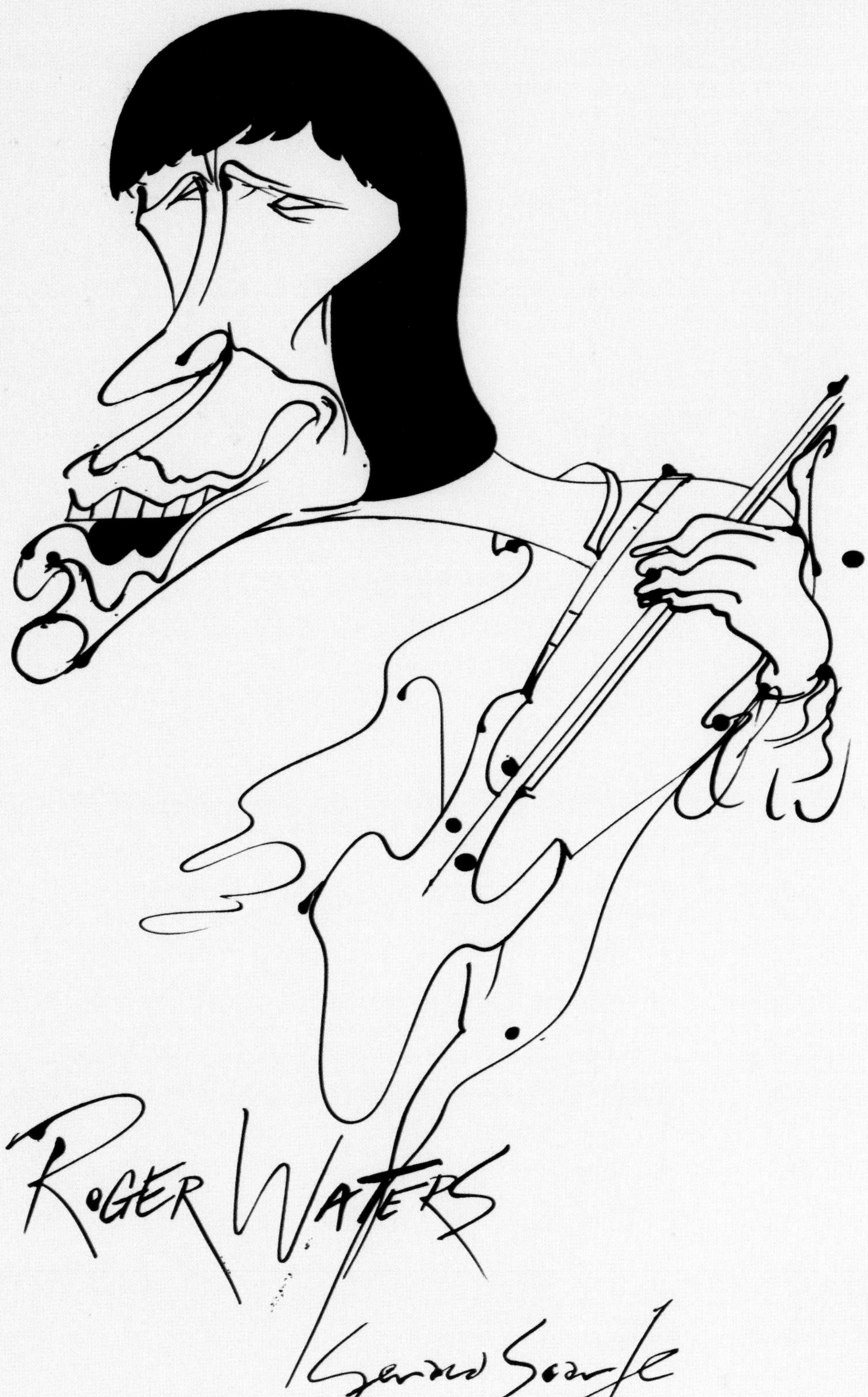

Columbia

8405

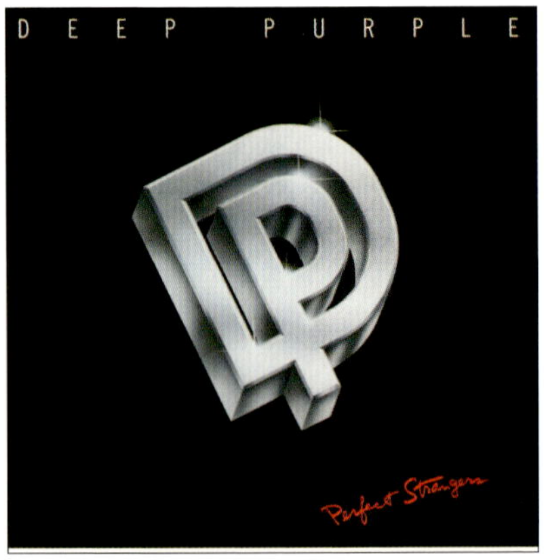

Deep Purple's reunion and the surprisingly potent *Perfect Strangers* met with an enthusiastic reception.

Billboard 200: *Perfect Strangers* (#17)
Billboard Hot 100: "Knocking at Your Back Door" (#61)

DEEP PURPLE was considered a pioneering heavy-metal and hard-rock band, and the return of the classic edition of the lineup—drummer Ian Paice, singer Ian Gillan, guitarist Ritchie Blackmore, bassist Roger Glover and keyboardist Jon Lord—turned out to be a viable vehicle for some old pros to update their considerable appeal.

"I think there came a point in everyone's lives of vague dissatisfaction," said Lord, a veteran of every previous Deep Purple lineup as well as various stints with non-Purple bands. "Perhaps we had more fun together than when we were apart. It took one guy to vocalize those feelings, and that was Ian (Gillan). He was like a cheerleader going around to everyone saying that people had talked about it, but we were the only ones that could do it."

The group convened in a Connecticut hotel room and immediately agreed to restart operations. The resulting album, *Perfect Strangers*, included the singles and concert staples "Knocking at Your Back Door" and the title track.

"The name Deep Purple must mean something special to a lot of people," Lord concluded. "We seem to have fit into modern Eighties rock without shouldering anybody out of the way—we don't look or sound out of place. And I don't play as well with anybody else. What I'm trying to say is that maybe we're not the best band in the world—but we're easily the best for each other."

In the band's early Seventies heyday, Deep Purple defined heavy metal with such seminal albums as *In Rock* and the best-selling *Machine Head*. Much of the appeal derived from the fact that the group was English and therefore more exotic to an American audience. But more important, Deep Purple's thundering style was not as blues-based as, say, Led Zeppelin's. Occasional classical influences crept in, particularly in Lord's rhythm playing, a prime example being his rumbling hook to the band's signature tune, "Highway Star."

"While I have breath and life, that art will not disappear," Lord proclaimed. "There is a way to make keyboards serve a role in this music that is not being pursued. It's the advent of the 'push-button monster,' as I call it. Push a button, hit a note and you sound like the London Symphony Orchestra. I'm glad it's here for younger musicians, because it gives them a chance to sound good. But I hope it doesn't destroy the search for technique or perfection, which a lot of older musicians went through." ■

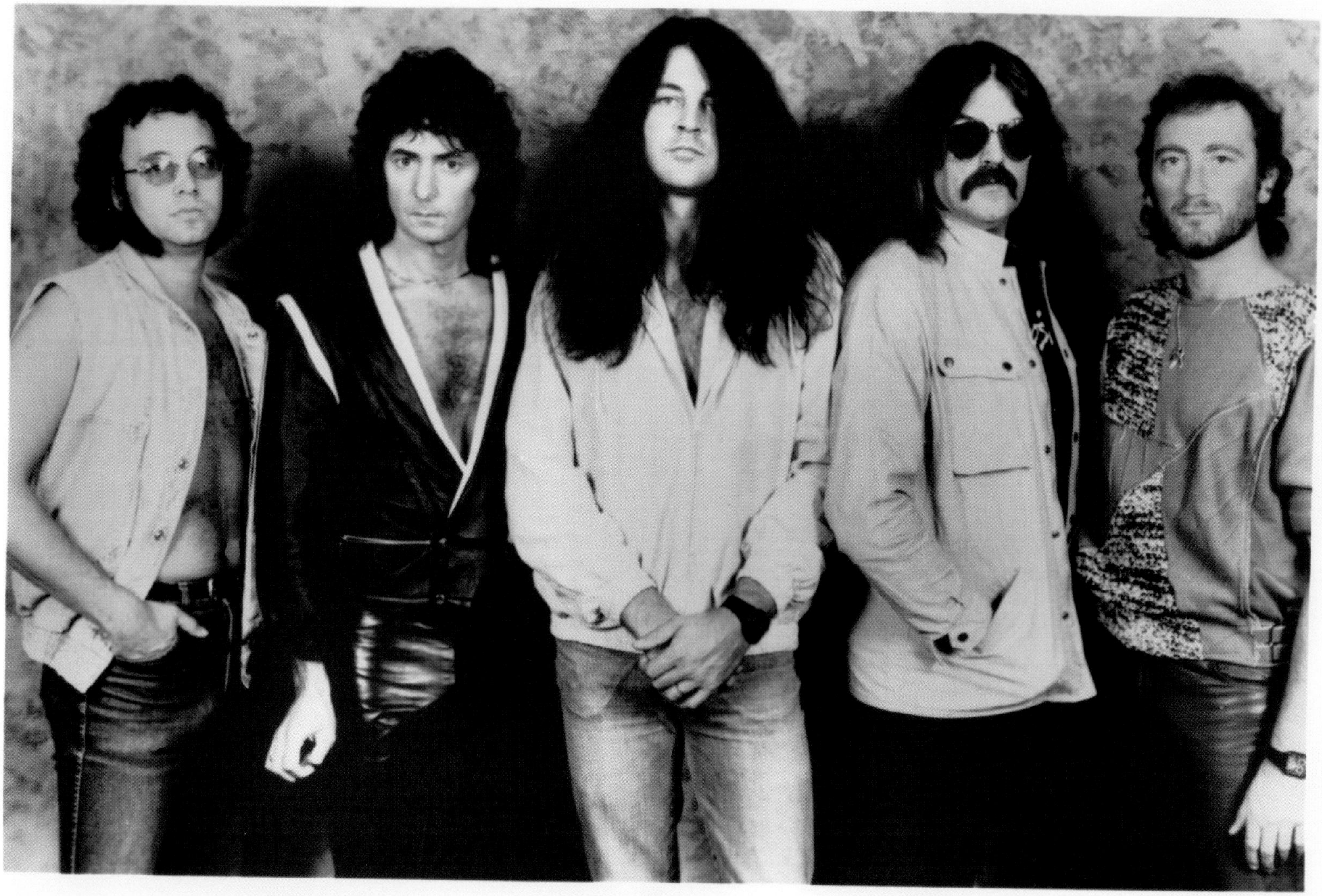

DEEP PURPLE

PolyGram Records™

mercury

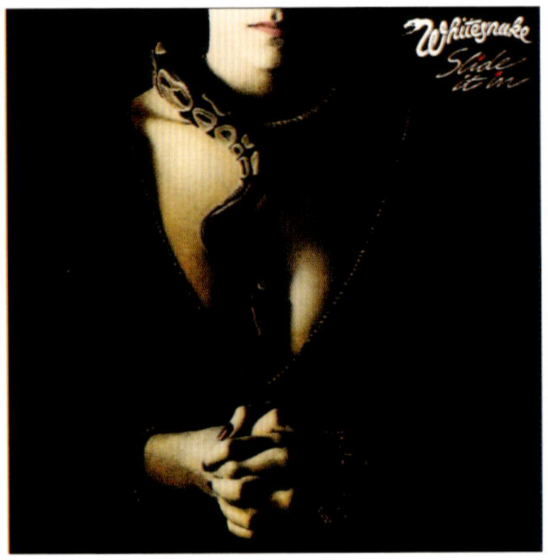

Whitesnake broke with *Slide It In*, the English hard-rock band's first album to make the American charts.

Billboard 200: *Slide It In* (#40)

DAVID COVERDALE had earned his shot at stardom. The British vocalist broke onto the music scene when he replaced Ian Gillan in Deep Purple in 1973. Following a pair of solo albums, Coverdale formed Whitesnake, eventually recruiting a pair of Purple alumni, keyboardist Jon Lord and drummer Ian Paice.

The early incarnation of Whitesnake was a potent if commercially underappreciated outfit with an exciting live act and some fine R&B-derived tunes ("Ain't No Love in the Heart of the City," "Fool for Your Loving," "Don't Break My Heart Again"). But unfortunately for the group, that brand of music was lost in the wake of UK punk and new wave during the late Seventies and early Eighties.

But Coverdale persevered with his classic approach to British hard rock, albeit with a revolving-door policy regarding his fellow musicians. Coverdale, Lord and Paice were the veterans, and *Slide It In* was remixed for its US release with new guitarist John Sykes' flashy soloing. The revised version spawned "Slow an' Easy" and "Love Ain't No Stranger," which gained rock radio airplay.

"I bust my bollocks for what I do," Coverdale remarked. "I get very well paid for it, but it's 24 hours a day, 52 weeks a year nonstop."

"I still get a thrill going onstage," Lord said of the teenaged hordes he faced on tour. "The battle is that little buzz of nervousness that I always get. I've never been terribly sure of what a rock audience wants, but a good portion comes to enjoy good music played by good musicians. Our experience adds to that appreciation." ■

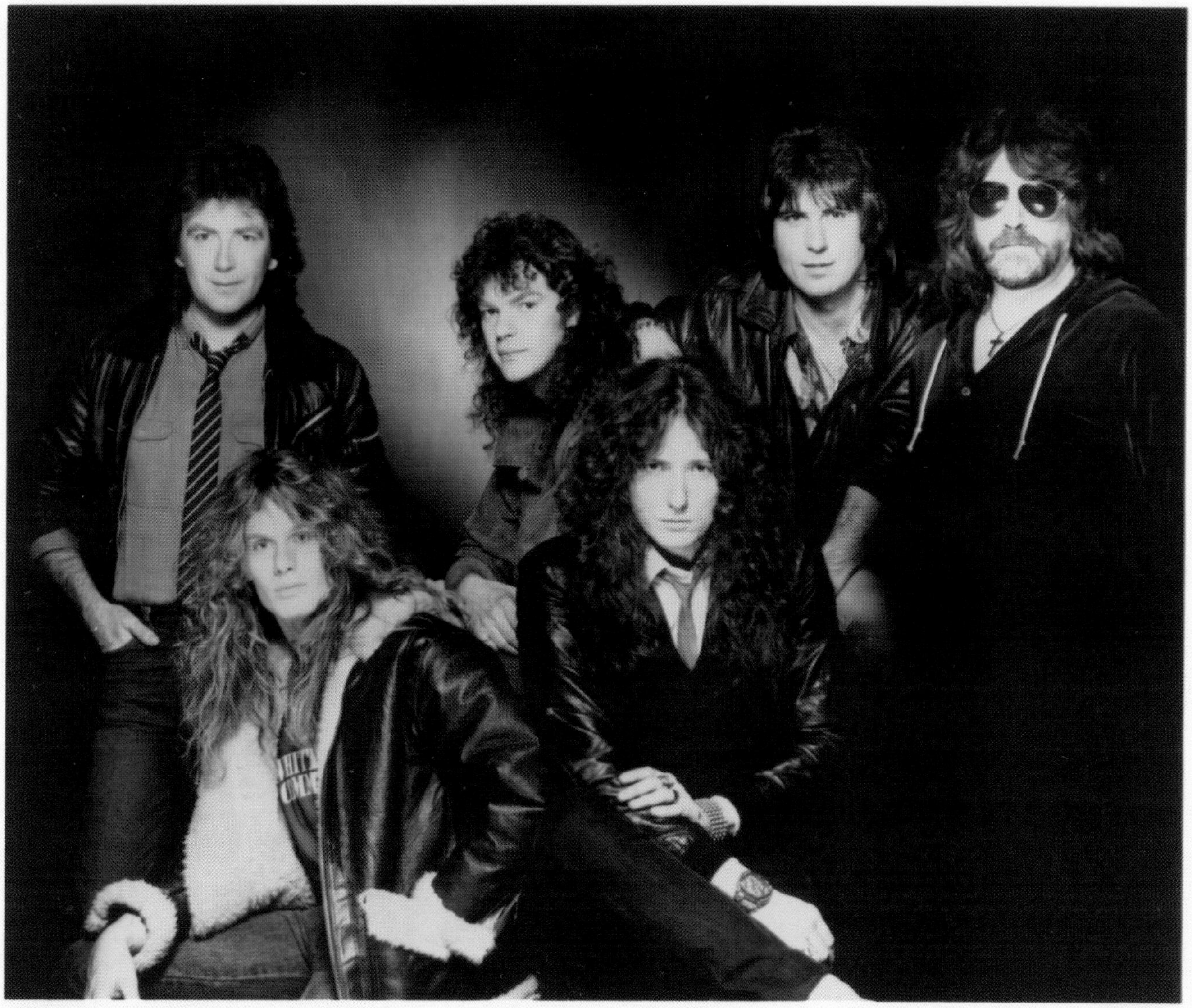

Photo Credit: Simon Fowler

Whitesnake

GEFFEN RECORDS

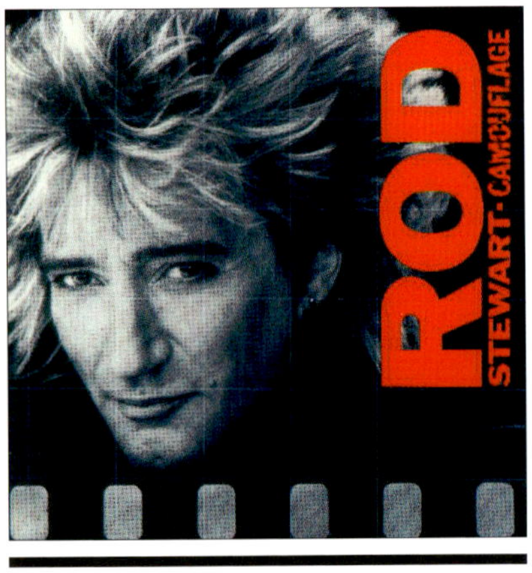

Rod Stewart had a Top 10 hit with "Infatuation," which reunited him with old friend Jeff Beck on guitar.

Billboard 200: *Camouflage* (#18)
Billboard Hot 100: "Infatuation" (#6); "Some Guys Have All the Luck" (#10); "All Right Now" (#72)

IT SEEMED that famous rock stars had their problems, too. After success arrived for Rod Stewart, so did musical lethargy—once the working-class-made-good artist removed himself from the streets, he found it hard to write hit songs about how the Rolls needed a tune-up. His 1983 album *Body Wishes* didn't come near the Top 10 like past efforts.

But Stewart was anxious to reestablish himself. He released *Camouflage*, and three pop singles came from the album—"Infatuation," "Some Guys Have All the Luck" and a cover of the Free hit "All Right Now." Stewart wrote "Infatuation," the biggest hit.

"Well, I'm not an excellent songwriter or lyricist—I'm pretty good in black and white," he said. "But writing is honesty. You can't write about yourself. I'm a great observer of people, so I just approach it like I was writing about a character in a book."

The album marked a reunion of sorts between Stewart and Jeff Beck, who played guitar on several tracks and made a cameo in the "Infatuation" video. The two had been members of the Jeff Beck Group, the short-lived but highly influential Sixties band. Stewart explained the mystique about British musicians.

"I just think we're still innovators of rock 'n' roll. There's the competition in England, just millions of bands. Of course, now you just put on your sunglasses and go ask the record company for $20,000. No one gave us any money when we started. We just asked our dads."

When Stewart ran into his old mates in England, he said, "There was a certain amount of envy. They all got drunk and came over to me house saying, 'We coulda done what you did, Stewie.' Me dad had to throw them out. If you buy them a round of drink, they think you're being flash, and if you don't, you're tight. You can't win..." ■

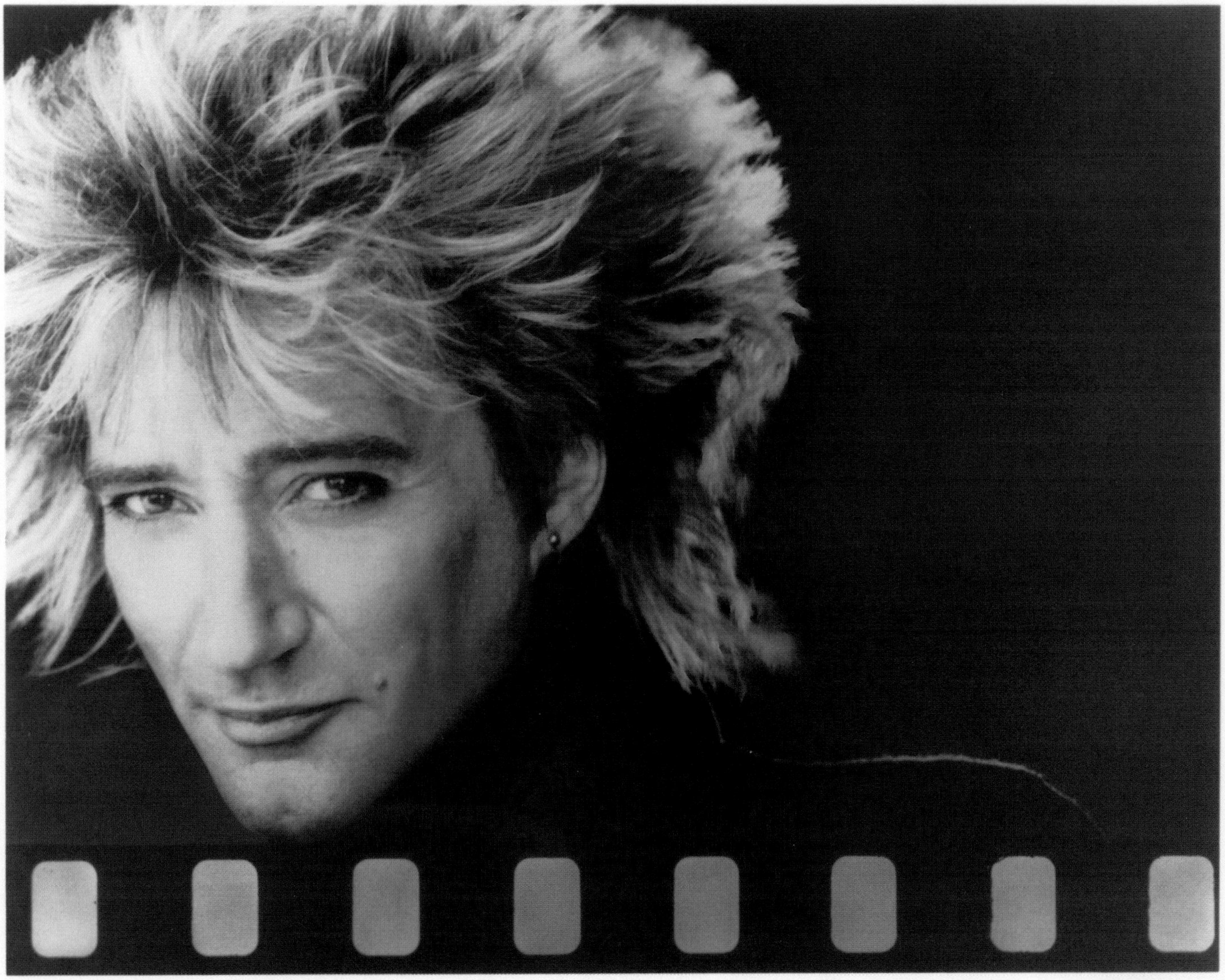

Photo Credit: Stephen Meisel

ROD STEWART

WARNER BROS.

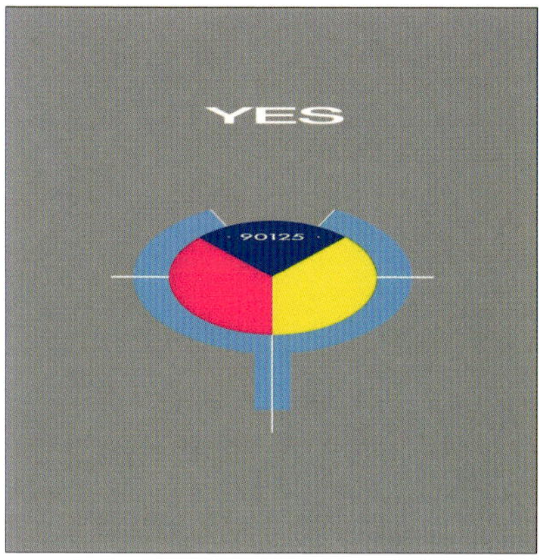

Featuring Trevor Rabin, a new-look Yes produced *90125* and the No. 1 single "Owner of a Lonely Heart."

Billboard 200: *90125* (#5)
Billboard Hot 100: "Owner of a Lonely Heart" (No. 1); "Leave It" (#24); "It Can Happen" (#51)

YES HAD always carried the reputation of being rock's leading progressive band of the Seventies, but by 1980 the veteran English group had seemingly run out of steam. Jon Anderson, whose high-pitched vocals were a Yes trademark, left the group. His replacements, Geoff Downes and Trevor Horn, hailed from a techno-rock group called the Buggles (known for "Video Killed the Radio Star").

"It appeared to be a chaotic time, and a lot of that was due to bad management," bassist Chris Squire admitted. "But we had every intention of continuing and recording another album with that lineup."

It was then that Downes and original guitarist Steve Howe left to form the commercial supergroup Asia. Squire was philosophical about the split. "I was upset at the time, but maybe they just wanted to try something simpler, you know?"

Squire and drummer Alan White then set about rebuilding a group. The duo's first recruit, South African guitarist Trevor Rabin, had been a session musician in London and Los Angeles. "I never considered holding an audition," Squire noted. "That's silly. You go out and get what you want."

Original Yes keyboardist Tony Kaye, whom Rick Wakeman had replaced in the early Seventies, returned. The foursome recorded an album's worth of material—ironically, with Trevor Horn producing—and completed everything but the vocals.

"It was always in the back of my mind to have Jon rejoin us to sing," Squire admitted. "As it happened, he was interested. He did two or three tracks, we all liked it, and we decided we were a group."

The return of the revamped Yes to the rock scene seemed especially dramatic—the band had a hit album, *90125*, and a smash single, "Owner of a Lonely Heart." There had been only one hitch with that scenario—Squire had dubbed the new group Cinema, but with the addition of Anderson's vocals, the resemblance to the classic Yes sound was apparent to all.

"That was Yes 're-formed,' although not in the typical sense," Squire acknowledged. "We never officially announced that we split up. It was simply an on-hold situation—although I suppose that when two-fifths of the band left in 1980, it must have seemed like a not-as-much-on-hold situation." ■

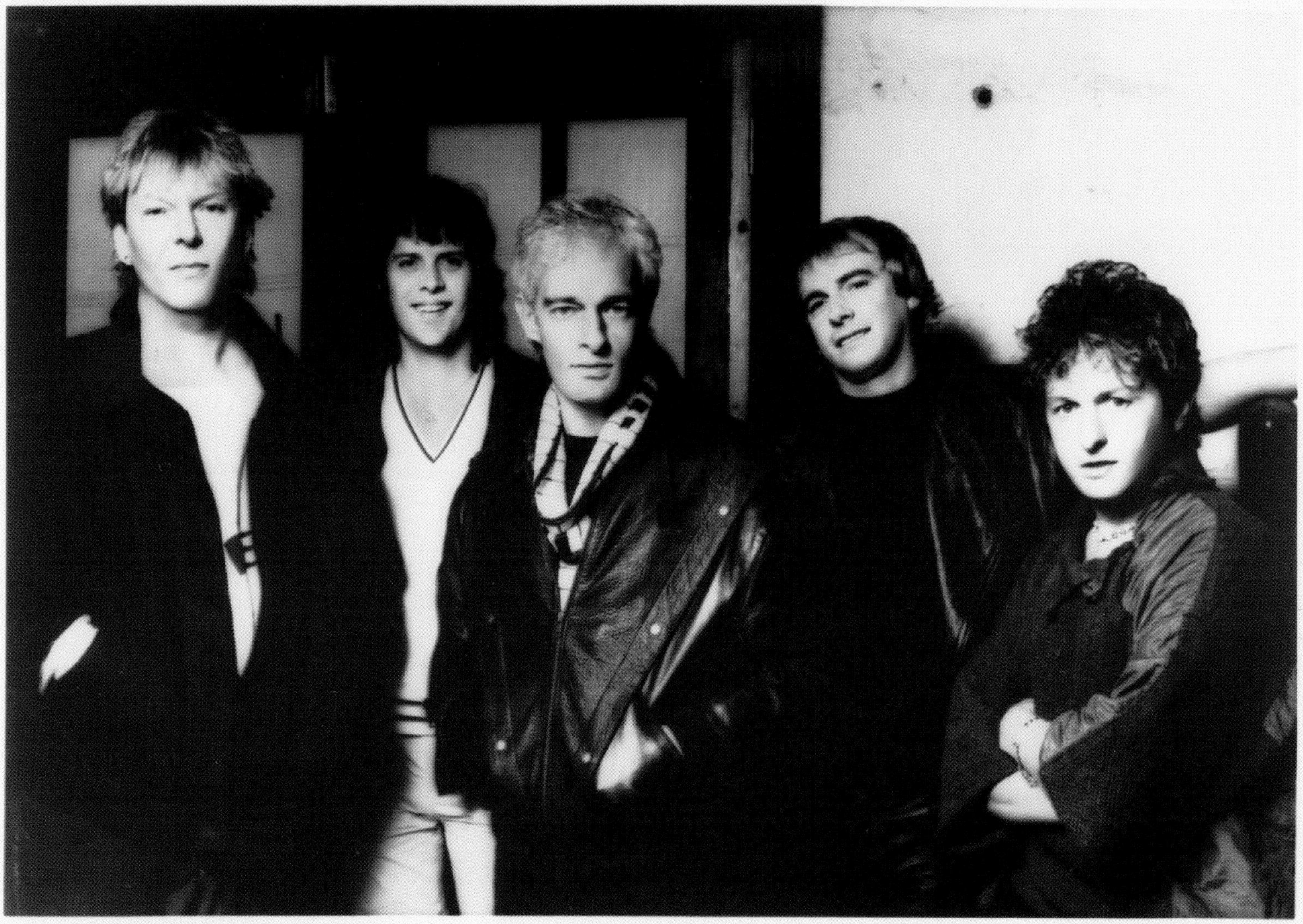

CHRIS SQUIRE TREVOR RABIN TONY KAYE ALAN WHITE JON ANDERSON

YES

AMERICAN TALENT INTERNATIONAL LTD
888 SEVENTH AVENUE (212) 977-2300
NEW YORK, N.Y. 10106

ATI

ATCO

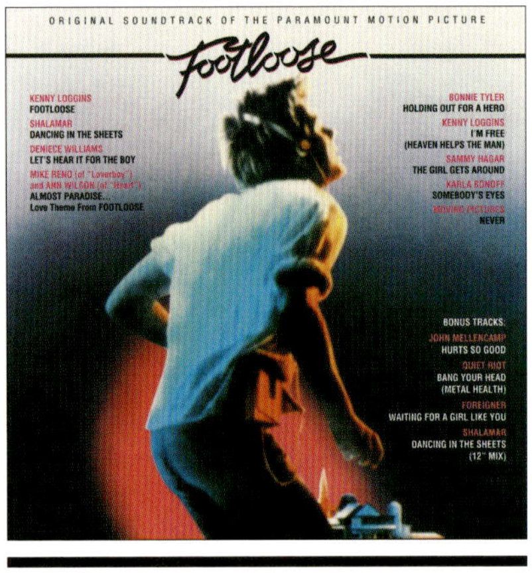

Billboard 200: *Footloose: Original Soundtrack of the Paramount Motion Picture* (No. 1)
Billboard Hot 100: "Footloose" (No. 1);
"I'm Free (Heaven Helps the Man)" (#22);
"Let's Hear It for the Boy" (No. 1);
"Holding Out for a Hero" (#34);
"Almost Paradise" (#7);
"Dancing in the Sheets" (#17)

"Footloose," from the movie of the same name, became another one of Kenny Loggins' signature tunes.

KENNY LOGGINS had enjoyed chart-topping success from his early days with Loggins & Messina ("Your Mama Don't Dance") through his late Seventies hits as a solo artist ("Whenever I Call You 'Friend,'" "This Is It"). But in the Eighties, he developed a parallel career as a consummate film music artist. It started with "I'm Alright," the theme from the 1980 comedy *Caddyshack*, and in 1984, he achieved spectacular exposure with the bouncy No. 1 title track from *Footloose*.

"A lot of people must think that somewhere along the line, I sold my soul to Hollywood to become a soundtrack writer," Loggins said. "But basically, it's all been one thing leading to another. It started when Barbra Streisand recorded a song of mine for *A Star Is Born*. Jon Peters (her boyfriend and the movie's producer) called me for *Caddyshack*, and I wrote 'I'm Alright.' And 'Footloose' was a favor for a friend who wrote the script."

In addition to writing the script, that friend, Dean Pitchford, composed the songs for the soundtrack. His credits included an Academy Award for the lyrics to "Fame" and two Top Ten hits, "Don't Fight It" by Loggins and Steve Perry (Journey) and Melissa Manchester's "You Should Hear How She Talks About You." To score *Footloose*, he composed songs after the film had been shot and edited in order to complement specific scenes—an approach influenced by the booming rock video market.

In addition to "Footloose," Loggins performed "I'm Free (Heaven Helps the Man)." Other hits on the soundtrack included Bonnie Tyler's "Holding Out for a Hero," Shalamar's "Dancing in the Sheets," Deniece Williams' "Let's Hear It for the Boy" and Ann Wilson (Heart) and Mike Reno (Loverboy) duetting on the ballad "Almost Paradise."

Loggins found himself answering cynics who minimized the importance of hit-making. "If anybody says I'm only doing hits, that's the most naïve thing I've ever heard," he fumed. "If I knew what a hit was, I'd do it more often, to be honest. I'm not embarrassed by the work I've done for soundtracks. The power of the soundtrack has kept me in the eye of the public as a current artist, and there's a lot to be said for that." ■

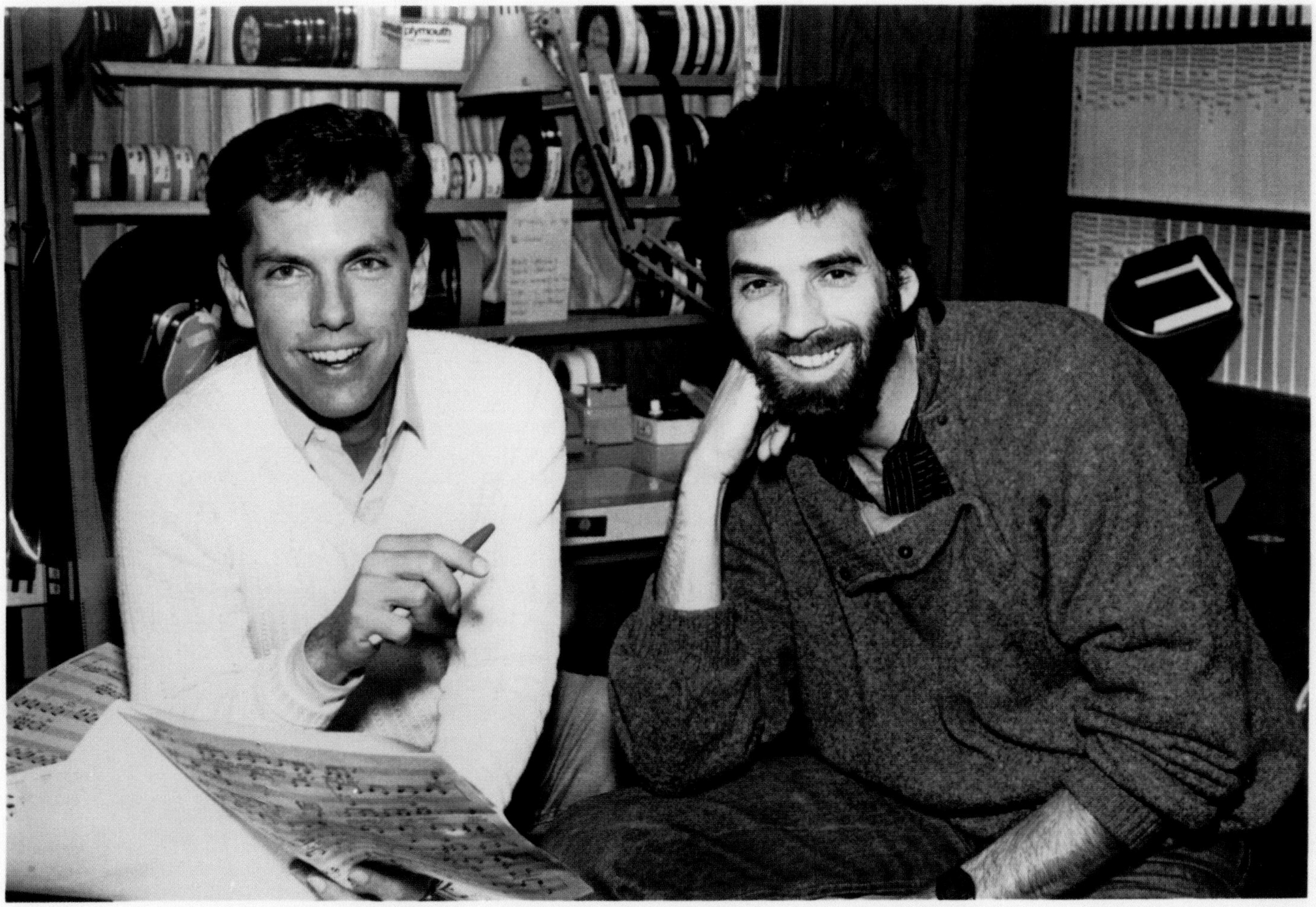

PHOTOGRAPH: SAM EMERSON

FOOTLOOSE screen-writer and songwriter Dean Pitchford left with Kenny Loggins right , performer and co-writer of the title single, "Footloose," and "I'm Free," both from the original soundtrack album on Columbia Records

Footloose

Columbia
8401

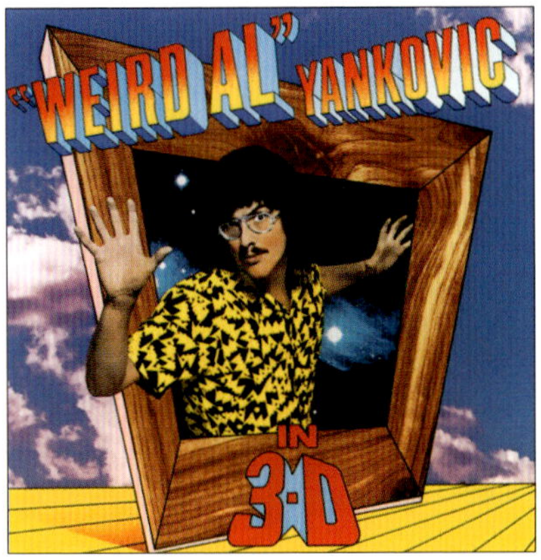

Billboard 200: *"Weird Al" Yankovic in 3-D* (#17)
Billboard Hot 100: "Eat It" (#12); "King of Suede" (#62); "I Lost on Jeopardy" (#81)

"Weird Al" Yankovic established his own brand of musical parody with "Eat It" and "I Lost on Jeopardy."

"WEIRD AL" Yankovic claimed his purpose in life was "to slam a stapler against the forehead of American pop culture." He had made considerable progress, managing to infiltrate the music business through parody, a genre that was dormant in pop music until Yankovic grabbed his "stapler." Everyone made up dumb lyrics to hit songs, but Yankovic actually recorded such silliness. First it was "My Bologna," spoofing the Knack's "My Sharona," then "Another One Rides the Bus" (Queen's "Another One Bites the Dust"), then "Ricky" (a Lucille Ball-inspired sendup of Toni Basil's "Mickey").

"Weird Al" Yankovic in 3-D, his second album, produced "King of Suede" (a spoof of "King of Pain") and "I Lost on Jeopardy" (a jab at the Greg Kihn Band's "Jeopardy," about a *Jeopardy!* contestant's reasons why he lost). But the parody that really put Yankovic over the top was "Eat It," his near-duplication of the omnipresent "Beat It" song and video that came right on the heels of Michael Jackson-mania. The single earned Yankovic a Grammy Award in the Best Comedy Recording category.

For the most part, composers lent their blessing to parodies—"Eat It" was endorsed by Jackson—but there had been times when Yankovic had problems getting the permissions he needed to do a parody. He was still frustrated by "a short, humorless guy that dresses in purple, but I can't mention any names."

Yankovic considered himself a comedian rather than a parodist, citing satirists and musicians Spike Jones, Stan Freberg, Tom Lehrer and Allan Sherman as influences. Yet he was facing a career crisis. "Having the videos be so popular is kind of a stigma, because people aren't sure what to expect when they come to a 'Weird Al' concert—'Is it just you and your videos or what?'"

But live performances weren't new to Yankovic. "In college I used to play coffeehouses. I didn't have a bona fide band back then, just a friend who played Jew's harp while I played the bongos. Then I went on the road with Dr. Demento (whose syndicated radio show featured the strangest music found anywhere) and played the accordion—I was kinda the Sting of my day. I finally put a band together in 1982."

That band provided the real key to Yankovic's success—it never failed to re-create faithfully the original music of whatever song he decided to parody. So a listener was usually suckered into thinking he was hearing the real item—and then along came Al. He knew that the day would arrive when people could spell his name.

"I've kept a diary of every misspelling," he concluded. "In grammar school, I thought everyone learned, '*i* before *e* except after *c* and in "Weird Al" Yankovic.' I'll always remember driving the tour bus into Seattle, and in letters larger than I'd ever seen my name before, there it was: 'Seattle welcomes Wired Al Jackovich!'" ■

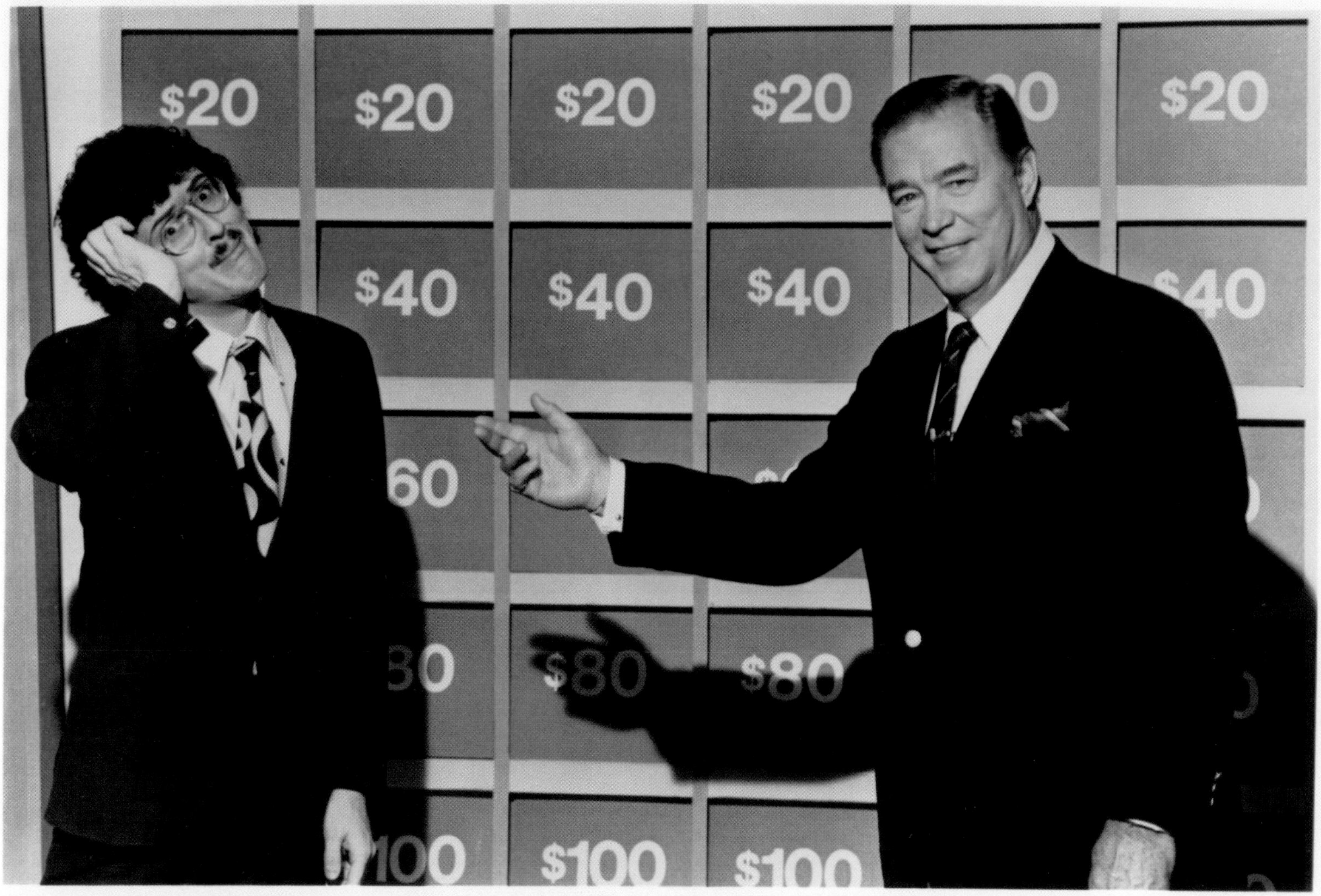

"Weird Al" Yankovic and Jeopardy host Art Fleming during the "I Lost on Jeopardy" video shoot.

ROCK'N'ROLL RECORDS

CBS
ASSOCIATED RECORDS

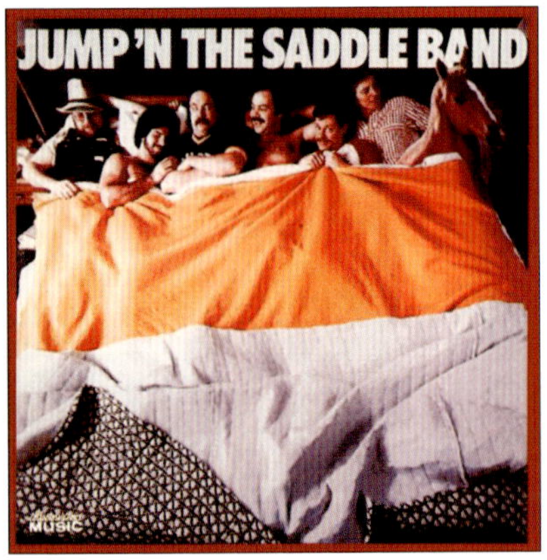

Jump 'N the Saddle Band started a national phenomenon with the smash novelty hit "The Curly Shuffle."

Billboard Hot 100: "The Curly Shuffle" (#15)

A SIX-PIECE outfit, Jump 'N the Saddle Band played for nearly a decade on the Chicago club circuit with the stated goal of "having fun onstage and mixing it with fine music." One night, in the middle of a typically boisterous set, singer Peter Quinn spontaneously broke into the backward-skipping dance that pop culture authorities associated with Curly from the Three Stooges. When a patron asked what he was doing, Quinn replied, "The Curly Shuffle, I guess."

Quinn, a Three Stooges fan ("but not fanatic") went home and wrote a tune called "The Curly Shuffle" in less than an hour. The result was a song that exploded into a major hit—"Nyuk-nyuk-nyuk" once again became a popular greeting between friends, and "Curly Shuffle" contests were held at discos across the country.

"It's really been something," guitarist T.C. Furlong admitted. "It kills me when we go to Disneyland and see little kids doing the song—singing 'Hey Moe, hey Moe' and shuffling around the place."

Furlong was particularly proud that the tune broke a novelty-record barrier that existed on the airwaves in the early Eighties. "Nobody had played 'character records' for a long time, but radio really opened up for us," he said. "The drive-time jocks got off on playing it as a goof, and then everyone picked up on it. I don't think 'Weird Al' Yankovic would be having as much success with 'Eat It' (his Michael Jackson parody) if we hadn't paved the way."

But Yankovic had a video and album ready to support his single, whereas Jump 'N the Saddle Band had rush-released its first LP, a collection that showcased a slew of bar band standards. "I wish we could have had more time to work on it," Furlong admitted. "The song was #40 when we were sent into the studio, and it was falling off the charts by the time we got the album done." ■

Tom "Shoes" Trinka   Rick Gorley   Vince Dee

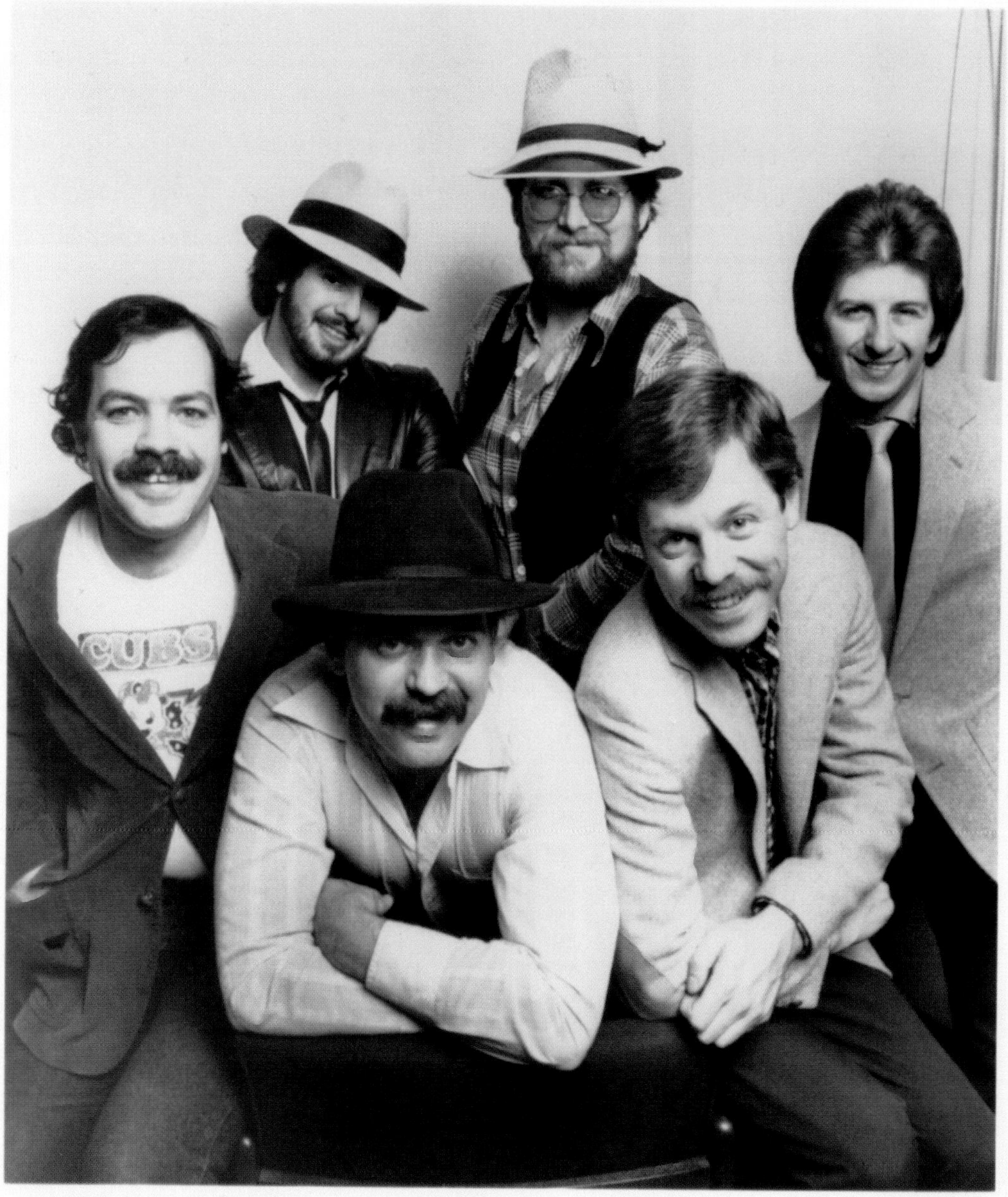

Barney Schwartz   Peter Quinn   T C. Furlong

JUMP'N THE SADDLE BAND

ATLANTIC

empire agency, inc.
P.O. BOX 514
MARIETTA, GEORGIA 30061
TELEPHONE (404) 427-1200

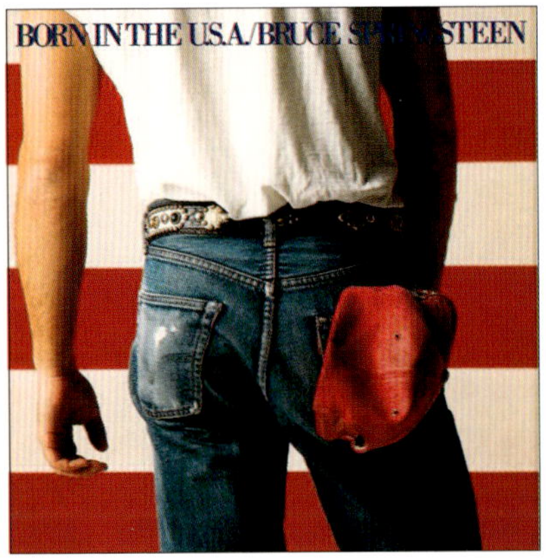

Bruce Springsteen reached his broadest audience when *Born in the U.S.A.* put seven hits in the Top 10, including the Grammy-winning "Dancing in the Dark."

Billboard 200: *Born in the U.S.A.* (No. 1)
Billboard Hot 100: "Dancing in the Dark" (#2); "Cover Me" (#7); "Born in the U.S.A." (#9); "I'm On Fire" (#6); "Glory Days" (#5); "I'm Goin' Down" (#9); "My Hometown" (#6)

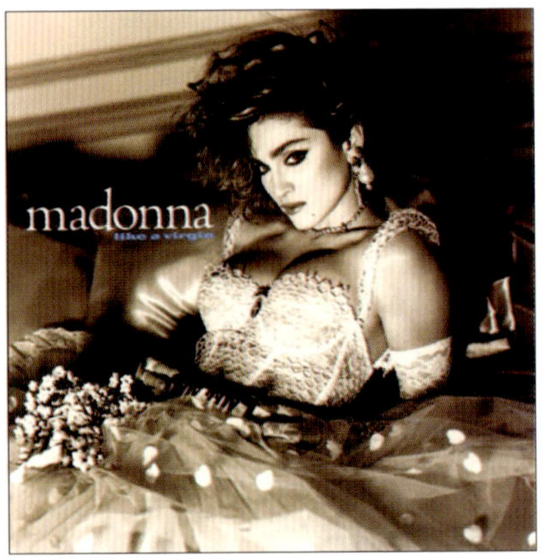

Madonna's *Like a Virgin* became a lightning rod for criticism by conservative groups and a source of imitation by teenage girls adopting her salacious image.

Billboard 200: *Like a Virgin* (No. 1)
Billboard Hot 100: "Like a Virgin" (No. 1); "Material Girl" (#2); "Angel" (#5); "Dress You Up" (#5)

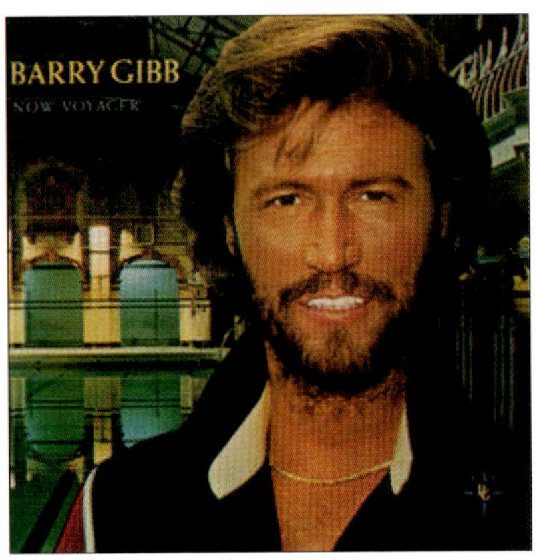

Now Voyager, Bee Gees lead singer **Barry Gibb**'s first solo record, featured the hit "Shine, Shine" and "Face to Face," a pairing with Olivia Newton-John.

Billboard 200: *Now Voyager* (#72)
Billboard Hot 100: "Shine, Shine" (#37)

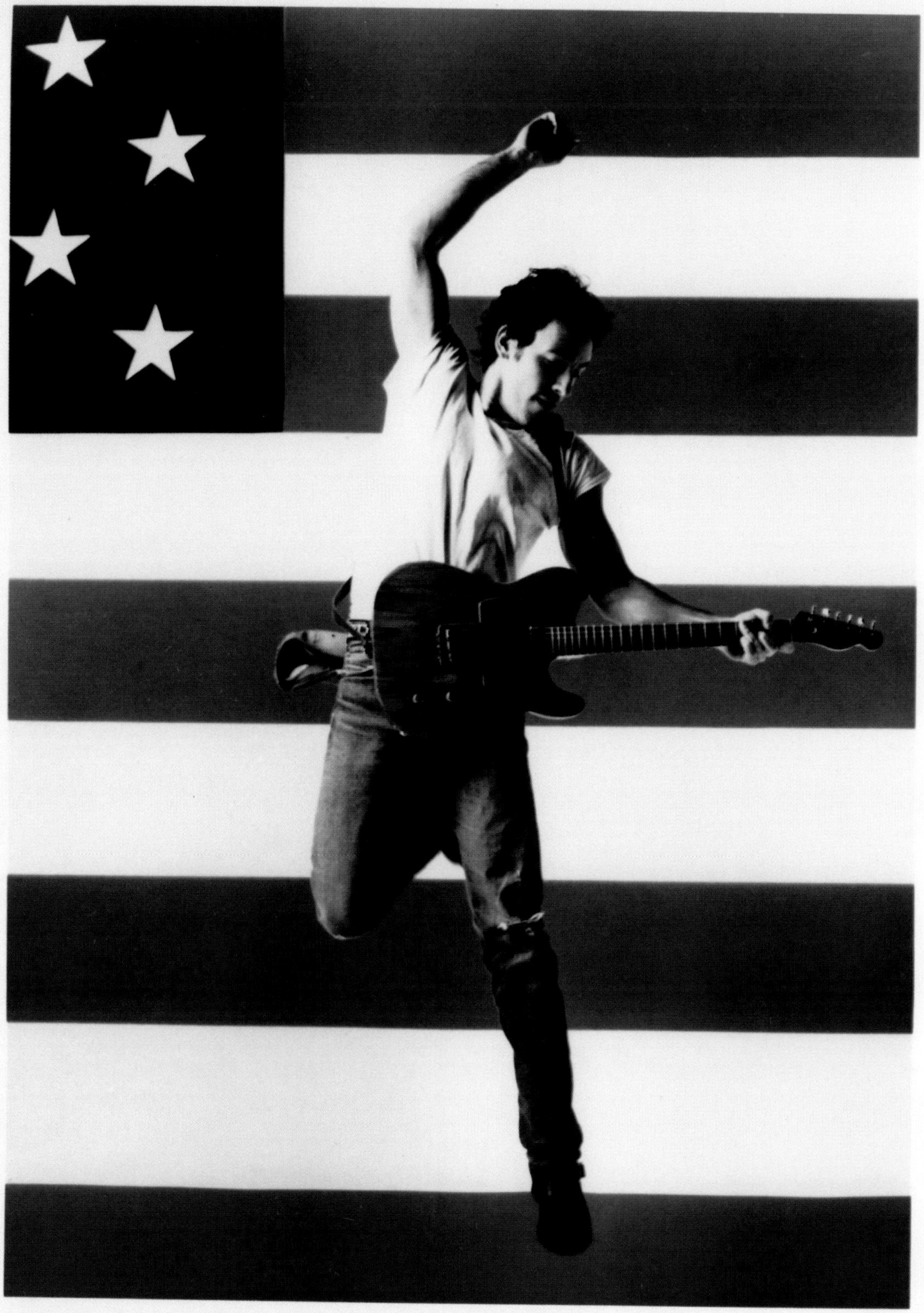

PHOTOGRAPH: ANNIE LEIBOVITZ LTD.

BRUCE SPRINGSTEEN

Columbia
8405

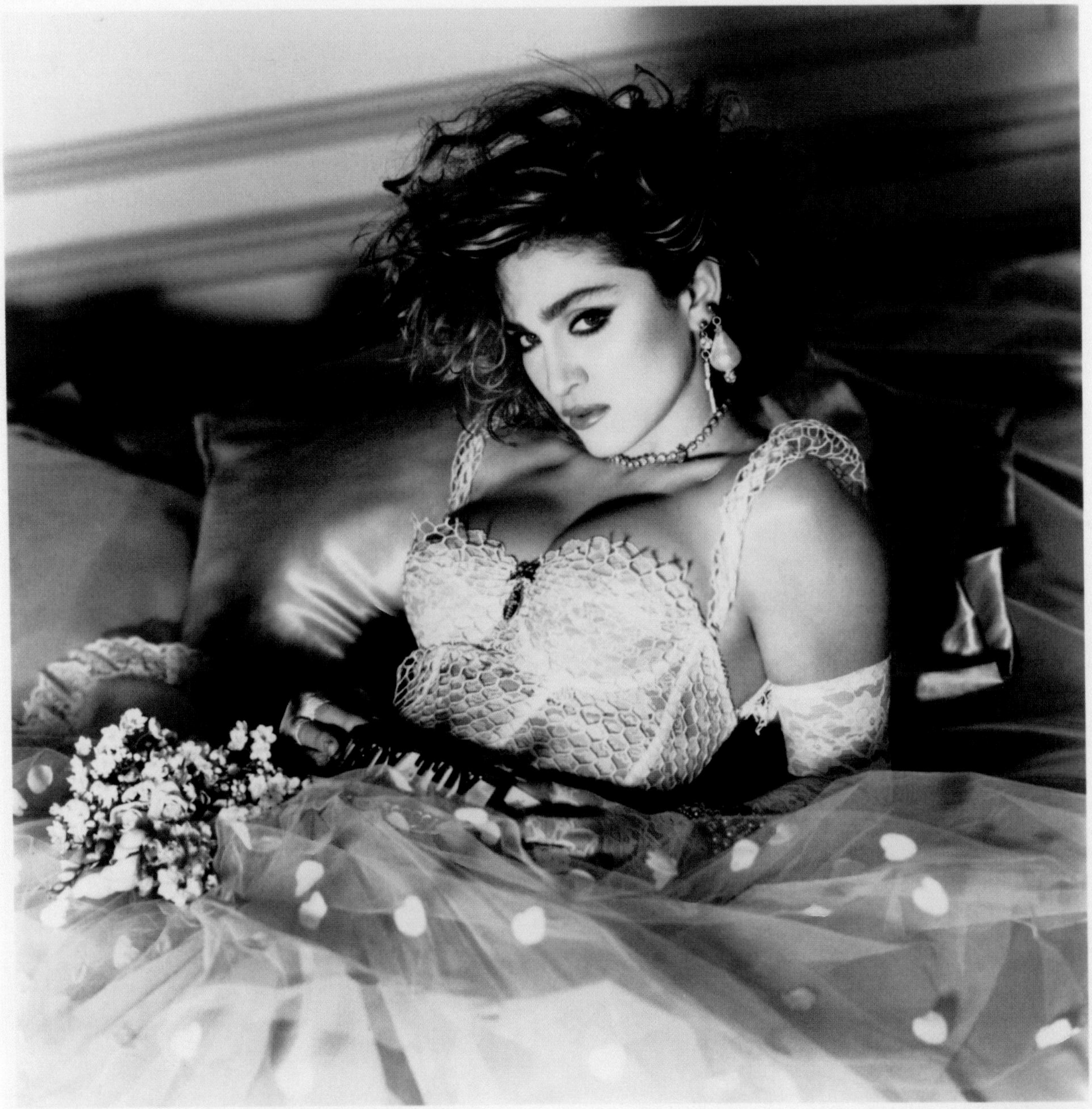

Photo Credit: Steven Meisel

MADONNA

SIRE™

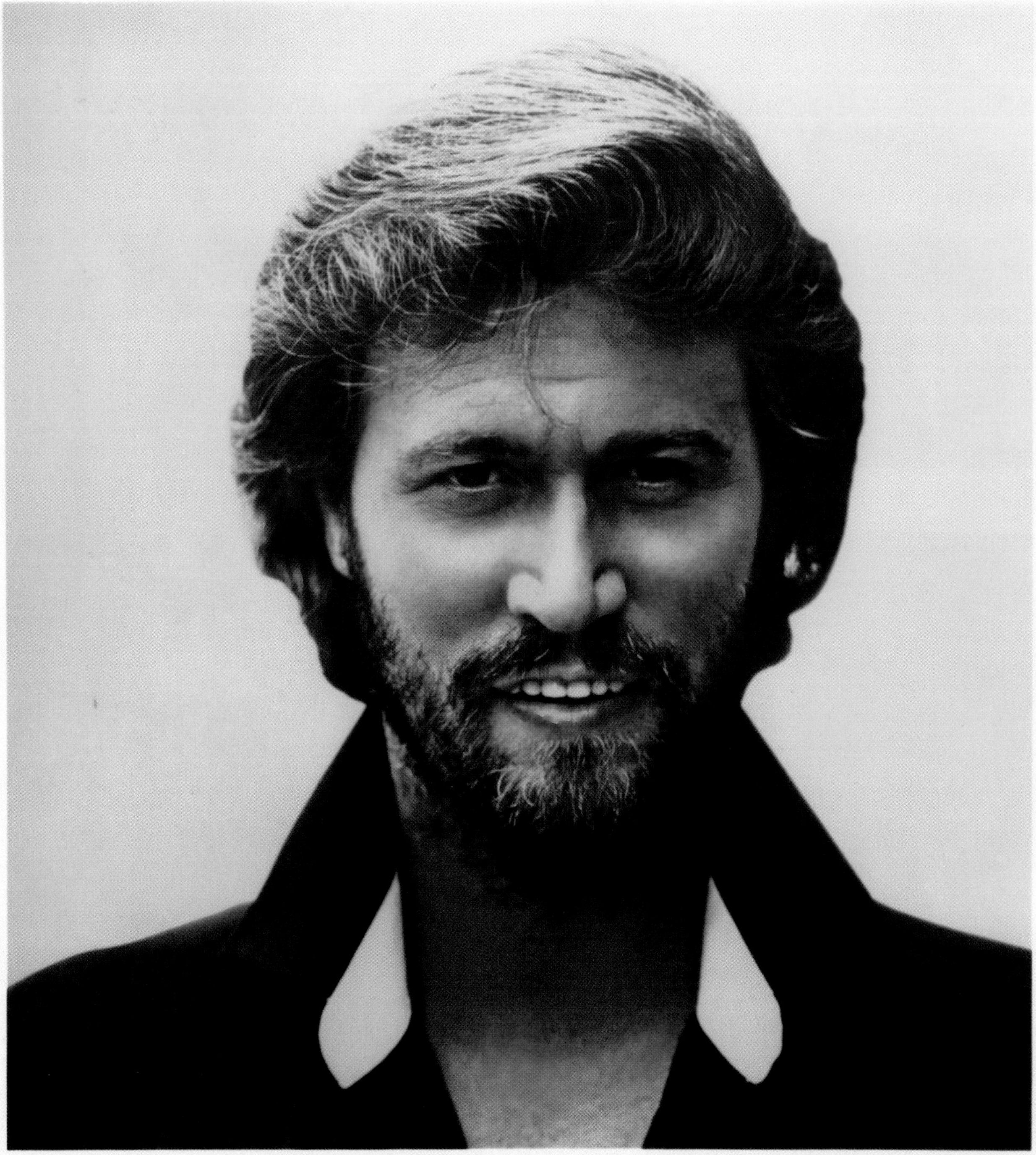

9/84

BARRY GIBB

MCA RECORDS

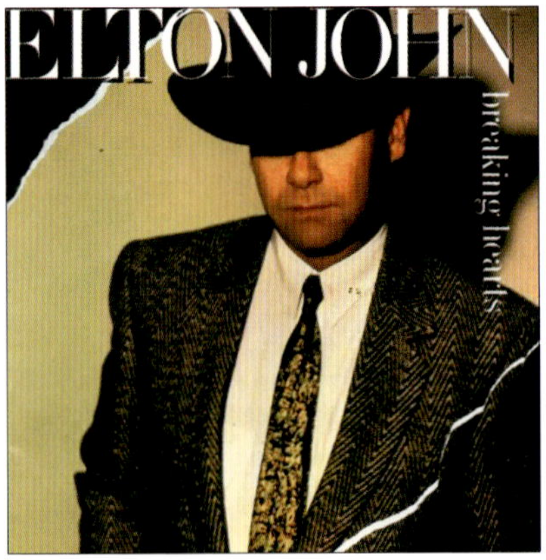

Breaking Hearts marked the last album to feature the core members of **Elton John**'s classic band lineup of Davey Johnstone, Dee Murray and Nigel Olsson.

Billboard 200: *Breaking Hearts* (#20)
Billboard Hot 100: "Sad Songs (Say So Much)" (#5); "Who Wears These Shoes?" (#16); "In Neon" (#38)

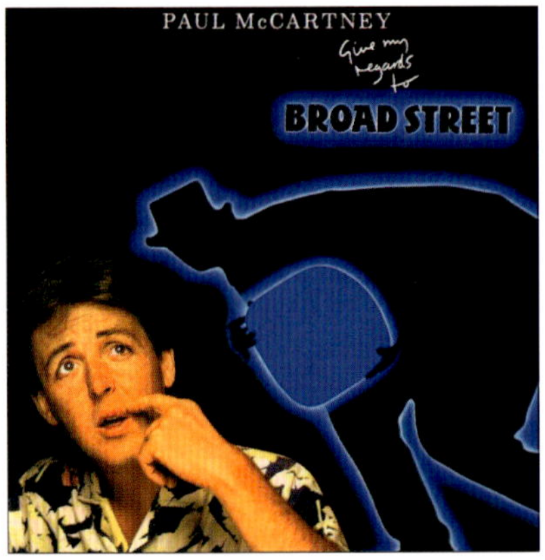

Paul McCartney's musical film, *Give My Regards to Broad Street* disappointed fans, but the soundtrack produced the hit single "No More Lonely Nights."

Billboard 200: *Give My Regards to Broad Street* (#21)
Billboard Hot 100: "No More Lonely Nights" (#6)

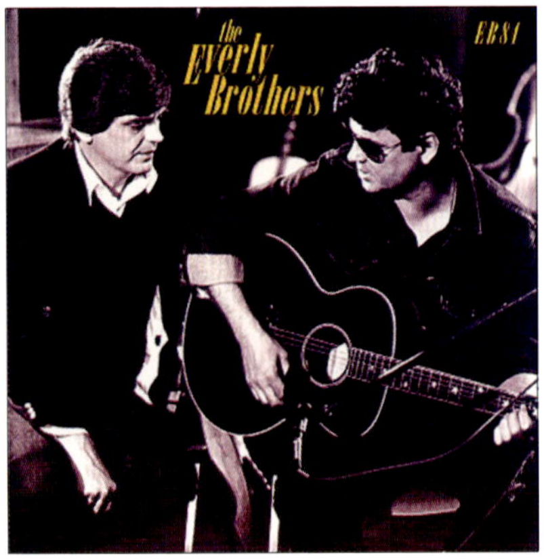

The Everly Brothers convened for *EB 84*, an album produced by Dave Edmunds and featuring the Paul McCartney-penned "On the Wings of a Nightingale."

Billboard 200: *EB 84* (#38)
Billboard Hot 100: "On the Wings of a Nightingale" (#50)

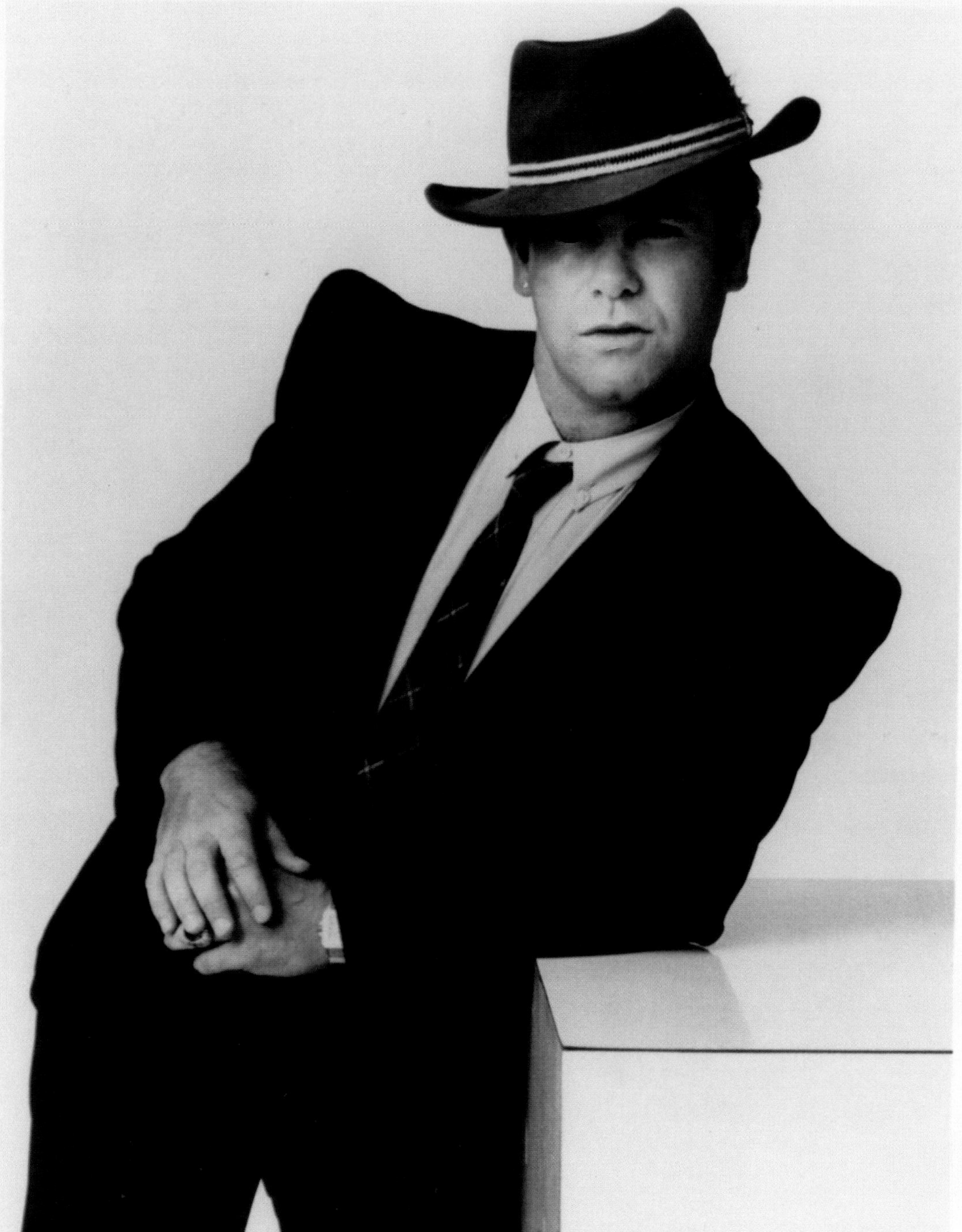

ELTON JOHN

GEFFEN
RECORDS

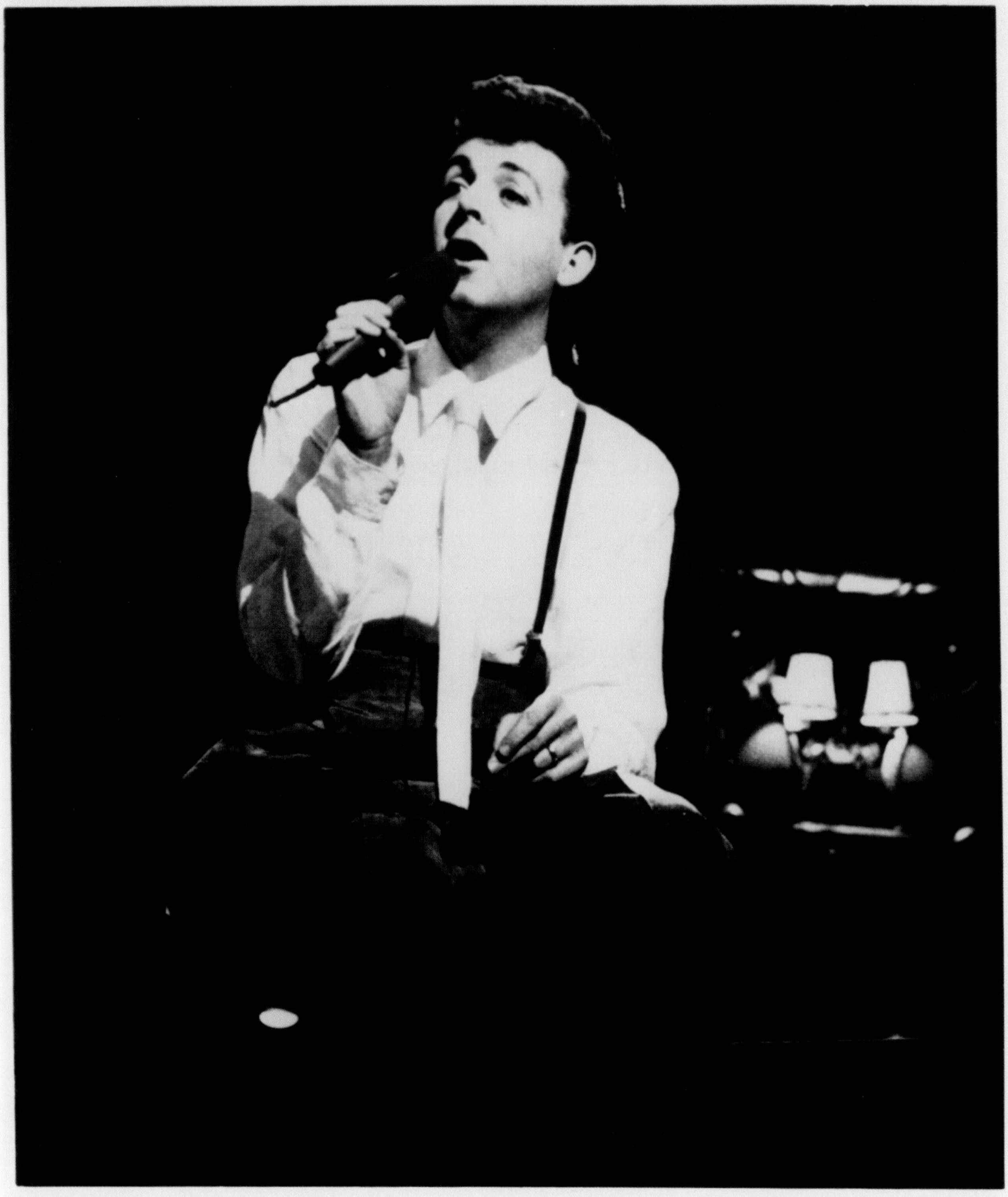

PAUL McCARTNEY

Give my regards to
BROAD STREET
A Twentieth Century Fox Release

Columbia
8410

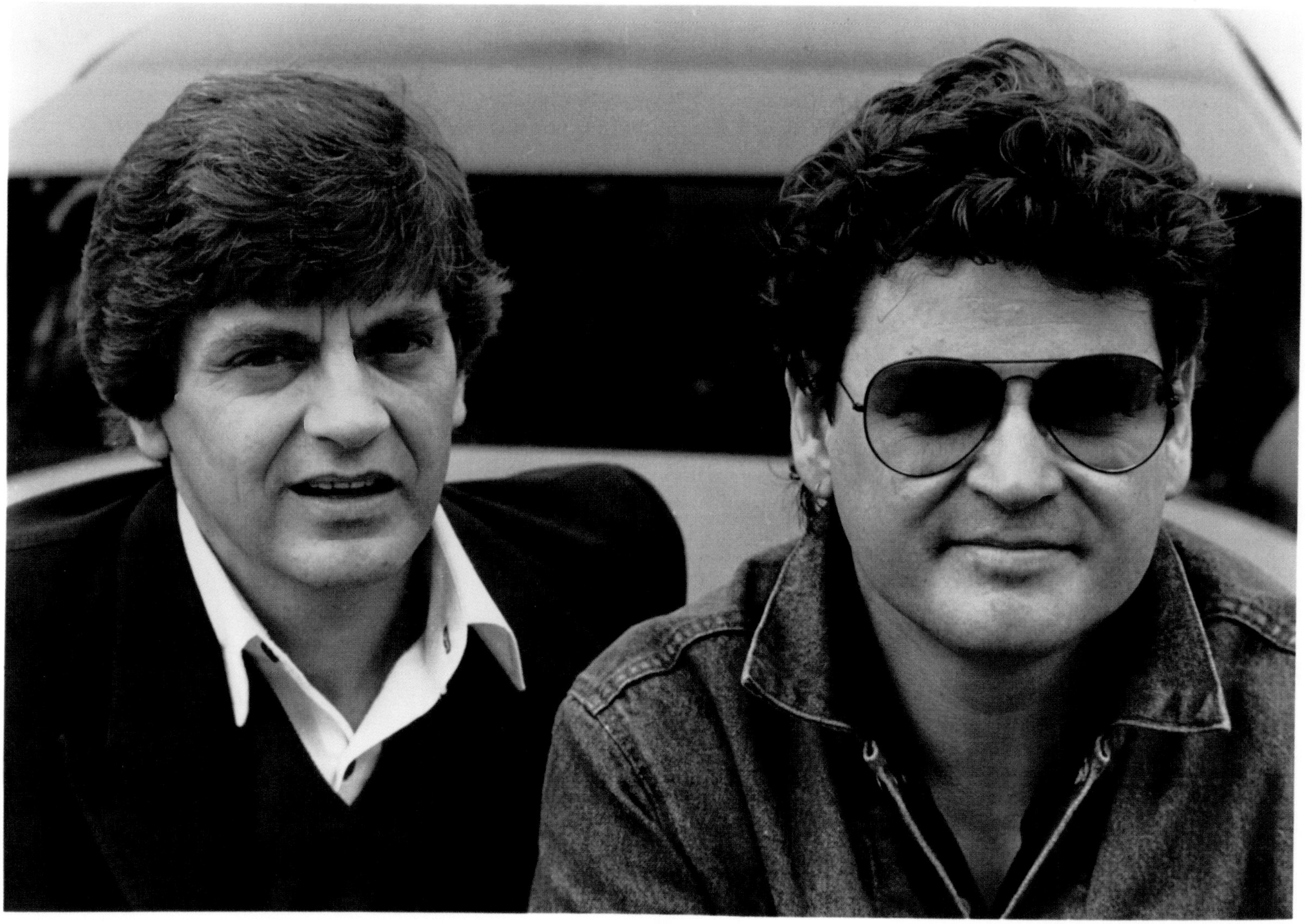

EVERLY BROTHERS

PolyGram Records

Photo Credit: Ed Caraeff

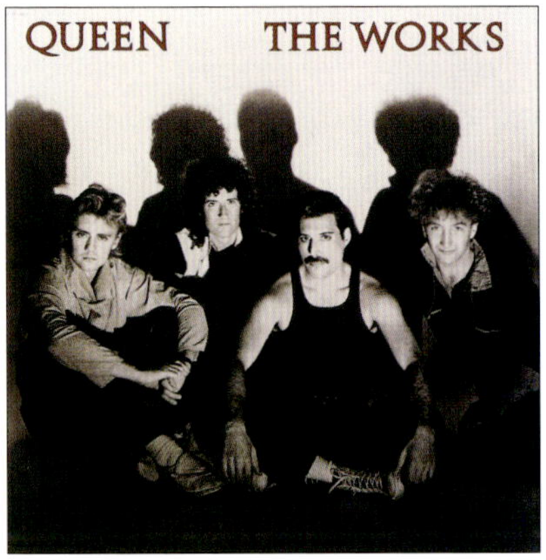

The Works retained **Queen**'s international popularity, with the single "Radio Ga Ga" at the top of the charts in numerous countries—except for America.

Billboard 200: *The Works* (#23)
Billboard Hot 100: "Radio Ga Ga" (#16); "I Want to Break Free" (#45); "It's a Hard Life" (#72)

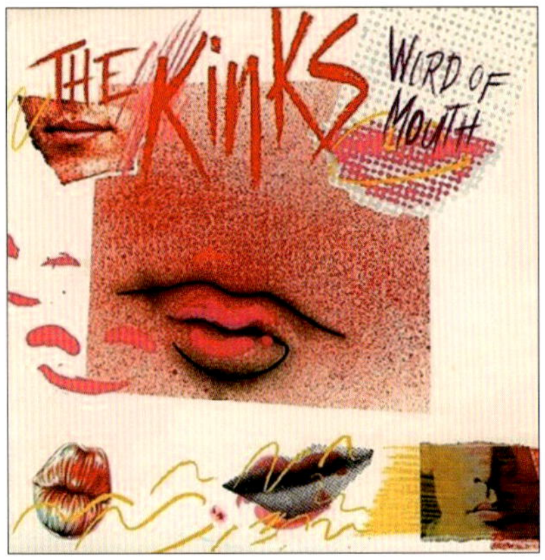

The Kinks' last album to crack the American charts, *Word of Mouth* featured "Do It Again" and the fan favorite "Living on a Thin Line" by Dave Davies.

Billboard 200: *Word of Mouth* (#57)
Billboard Hot 100: "Do It Again" (#41)

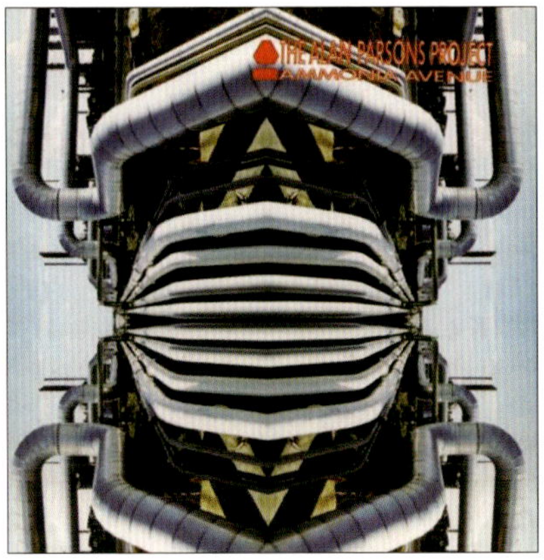

The Alan Parsons Project notched another Top 20 hit with the single "Don't Answer Me," a Phil Spector-influenced effort from the album *Ammonia Avenue*.

Billboard 200: *Ammonia Avenue* (#15)
Billboard Hot 100: "Don't Answer Me" (#15); "Prime Time" (#34)

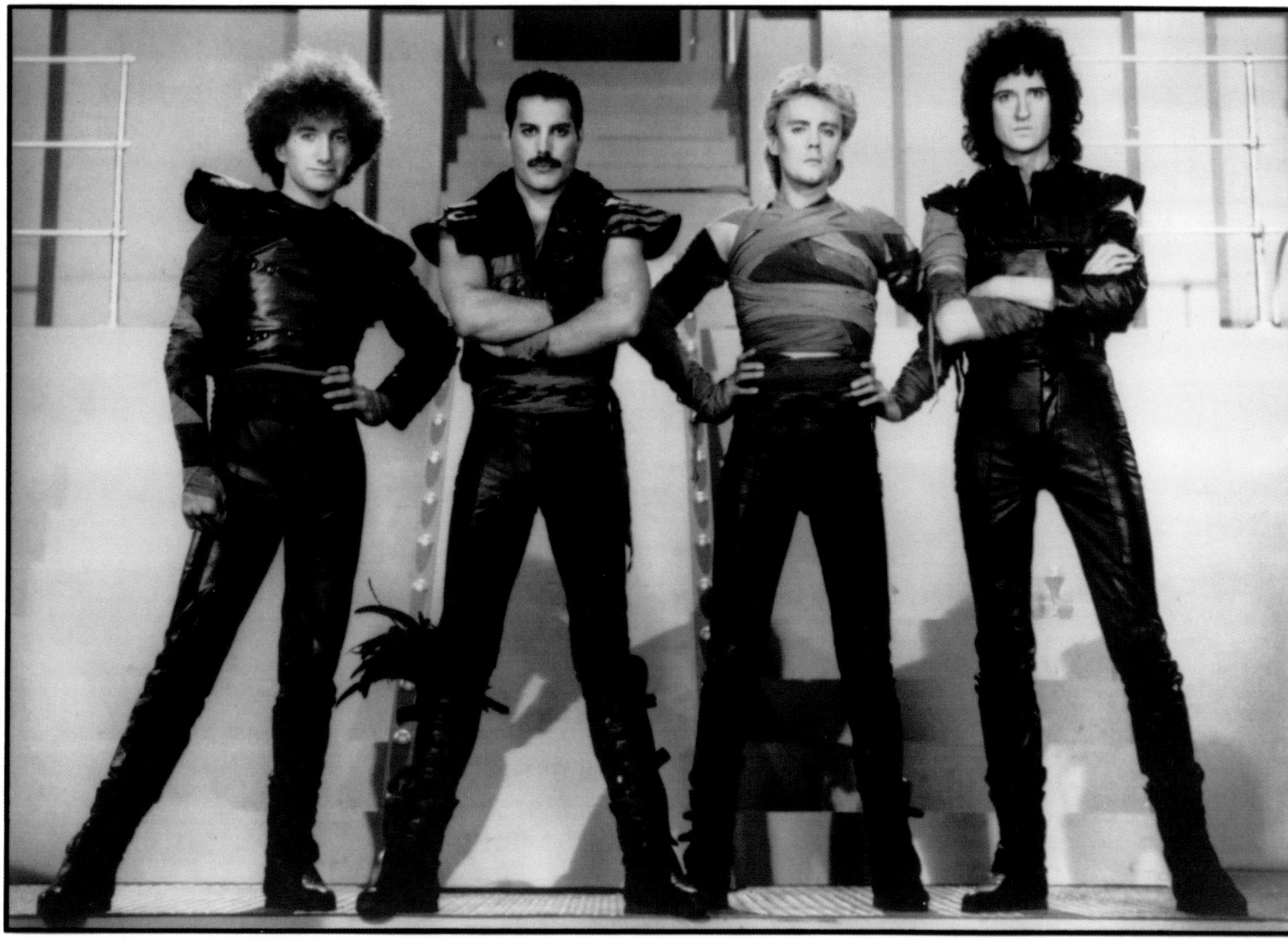

QUEEN

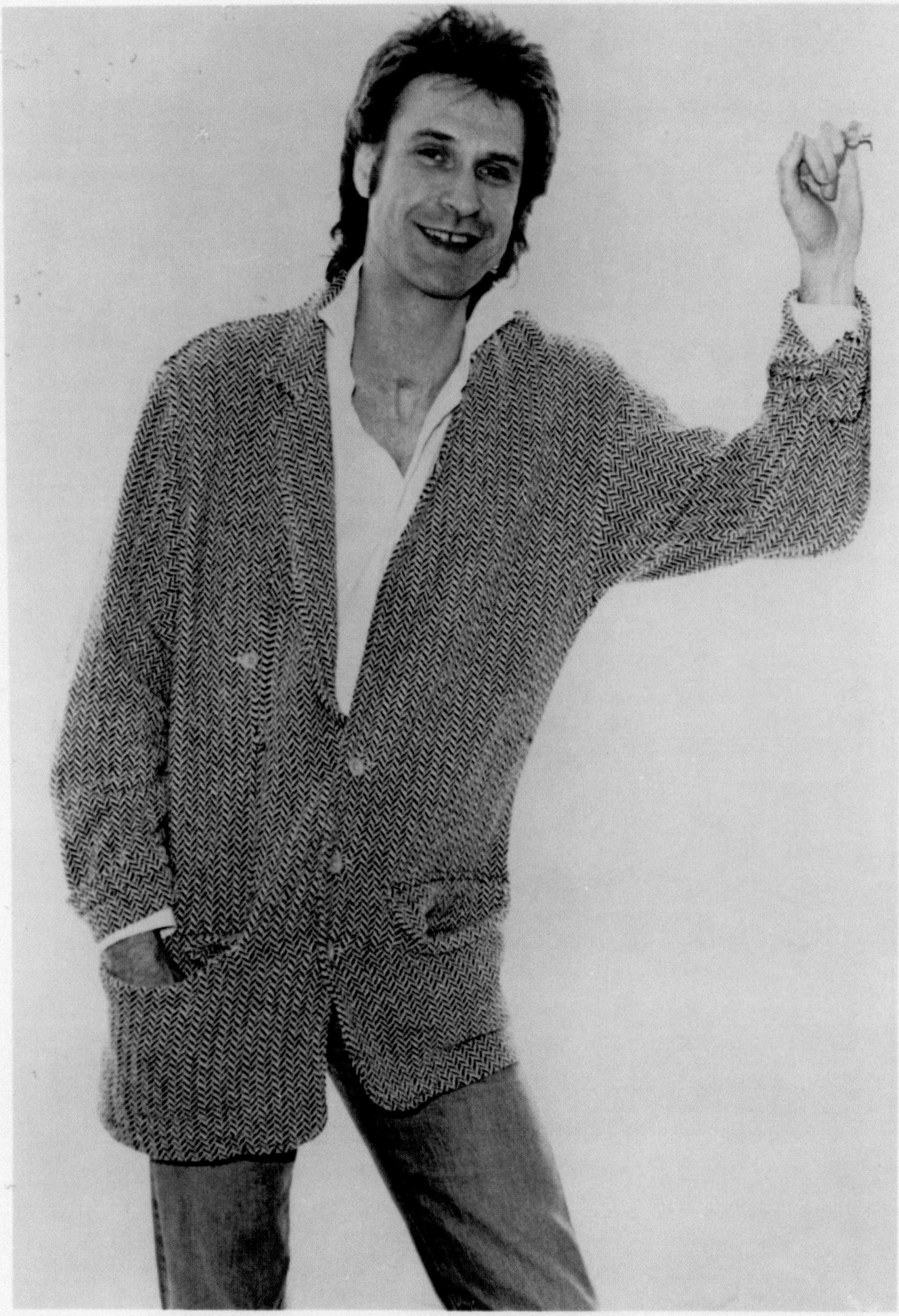

RAY DAVIES / THE KINKS

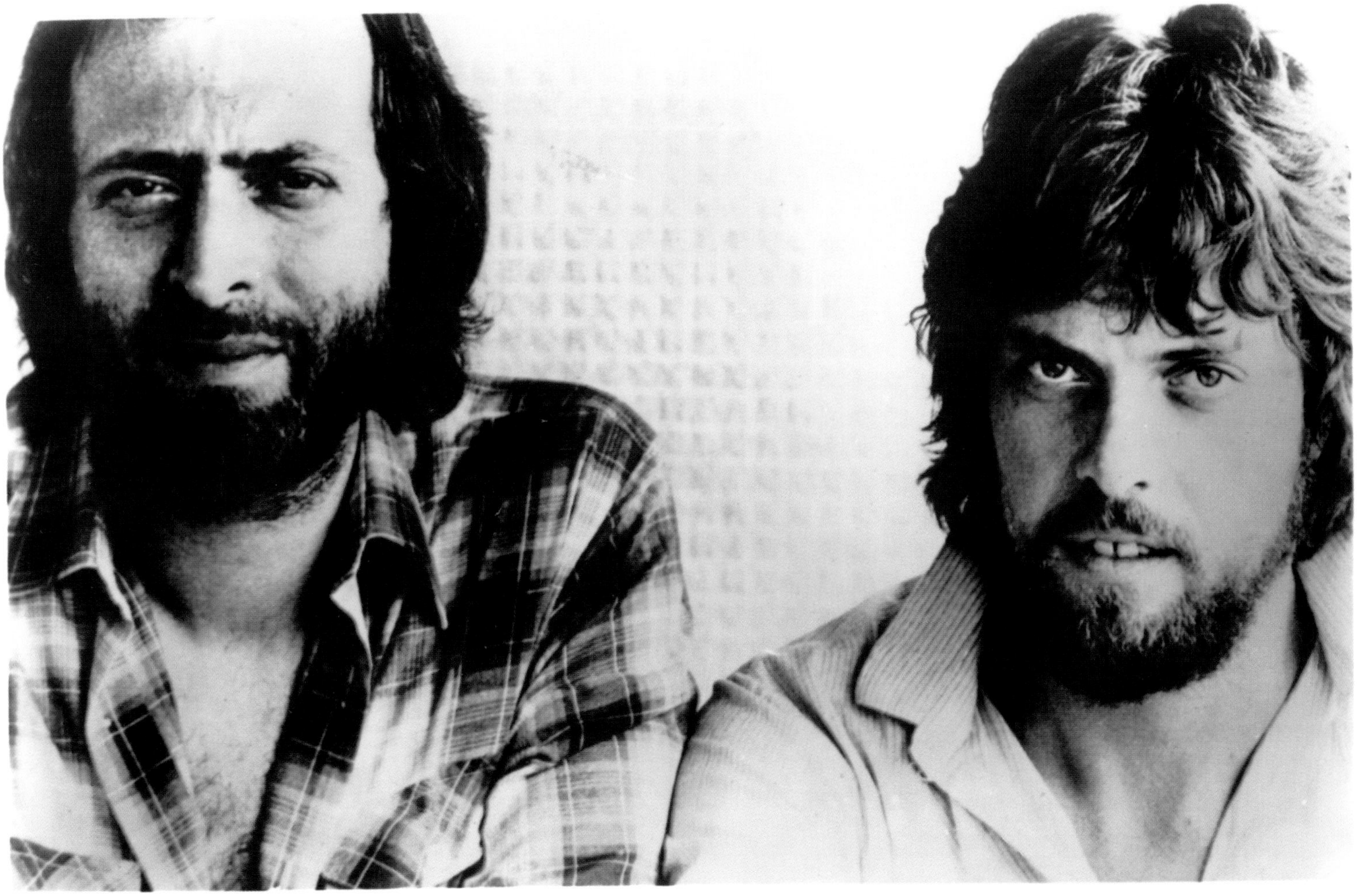

ERIC WOOLFSON

ALAN PARSONS

THE ALAN PARSONS PROJECT
AMMONIA AVENUE

ARISTA

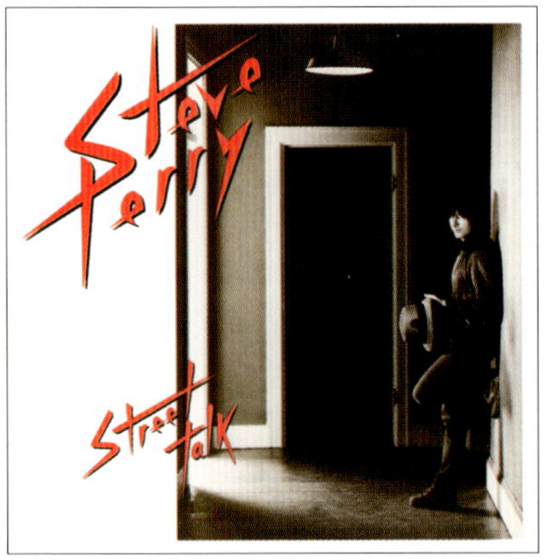

While Journey took a brief break from touring and recording, lead singer **Steve Perry** issued his first solo album, *Street Talk*, an homage to American R&B.

Billboard 200: *Street Talk* (#12)
Billboard Hot 100: "Oh Sherrie" (#3); "She's Mine" (#21); "Strung Out" (#40); "Foolish Heart" (#18)

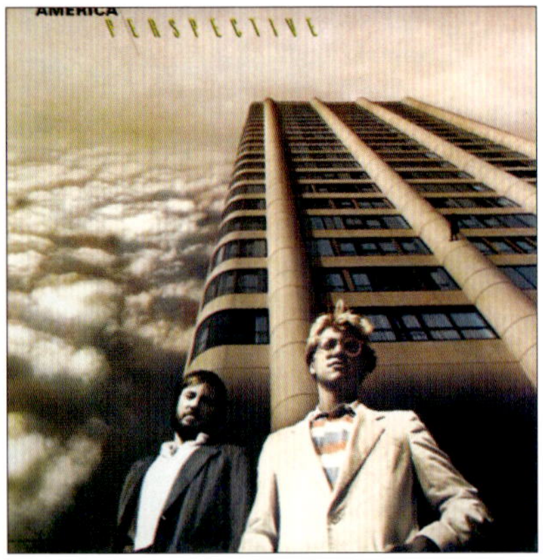

On *Perspective*, the folk-rock duo **America** opted for synthesizers and drum machines, resulting in a pair of secondary hits on the adult contemporary charts.

Billboard 200: *Perspective* (#185)

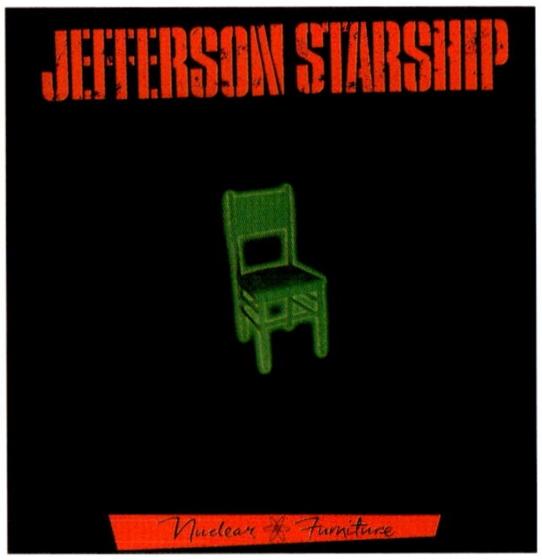

Upon the release of *Nuclear Furniture*, **Jefferson Starship** leader Paul Kantner left the band, with the remaining members renaming themselves Starship.

Billboard 200: *Nuclear Furniture* (#28)
Billboard Hot 100: "No Way Out" (#23); "Layin' It on the Line" (#66)

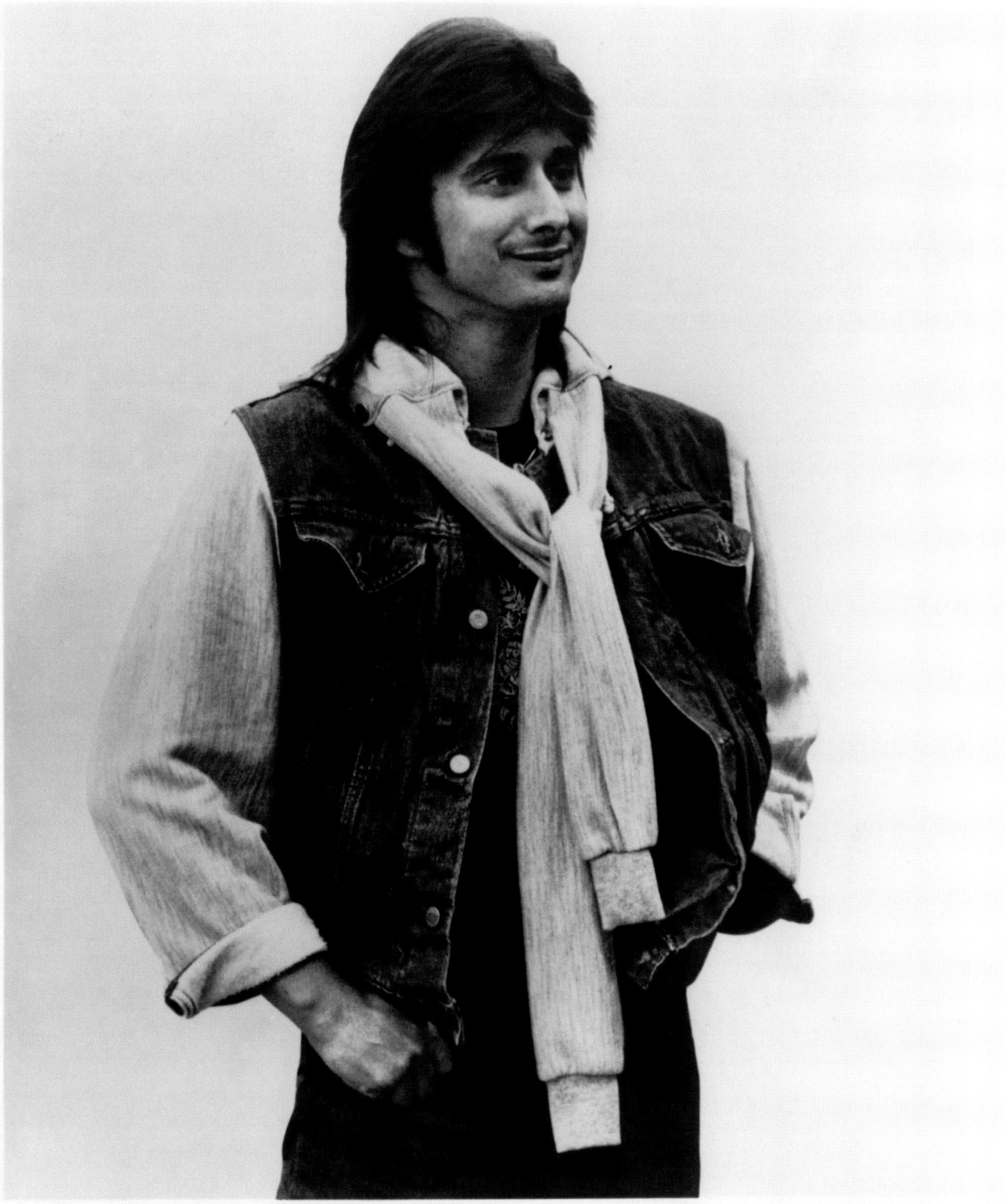

STEVE PERRY

Columbia

8403

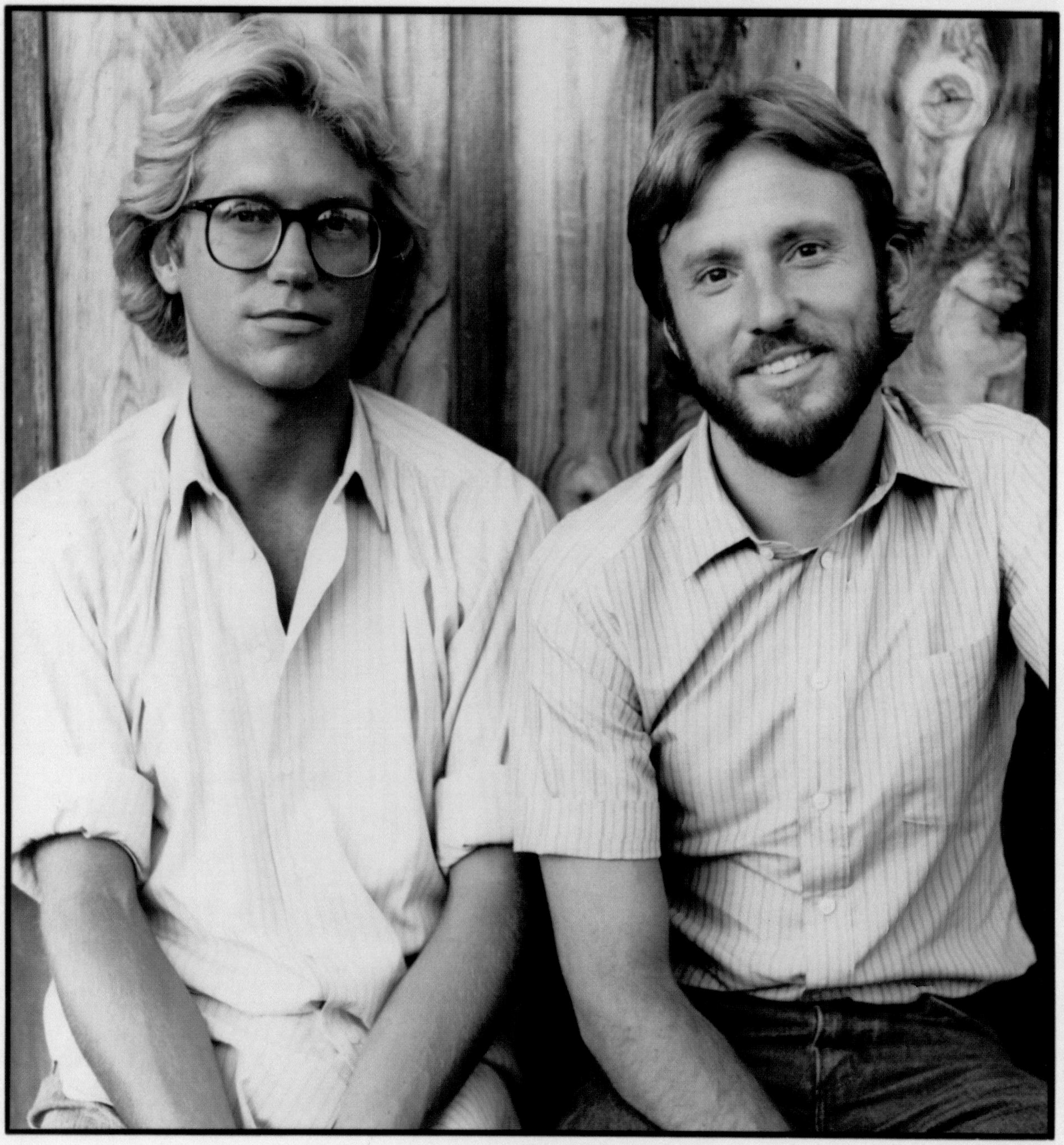

1984 / Photo: Henry Diltz

Personal Management:
KATZ-GALLIN-MOREY

AMERICA

Capitol Records

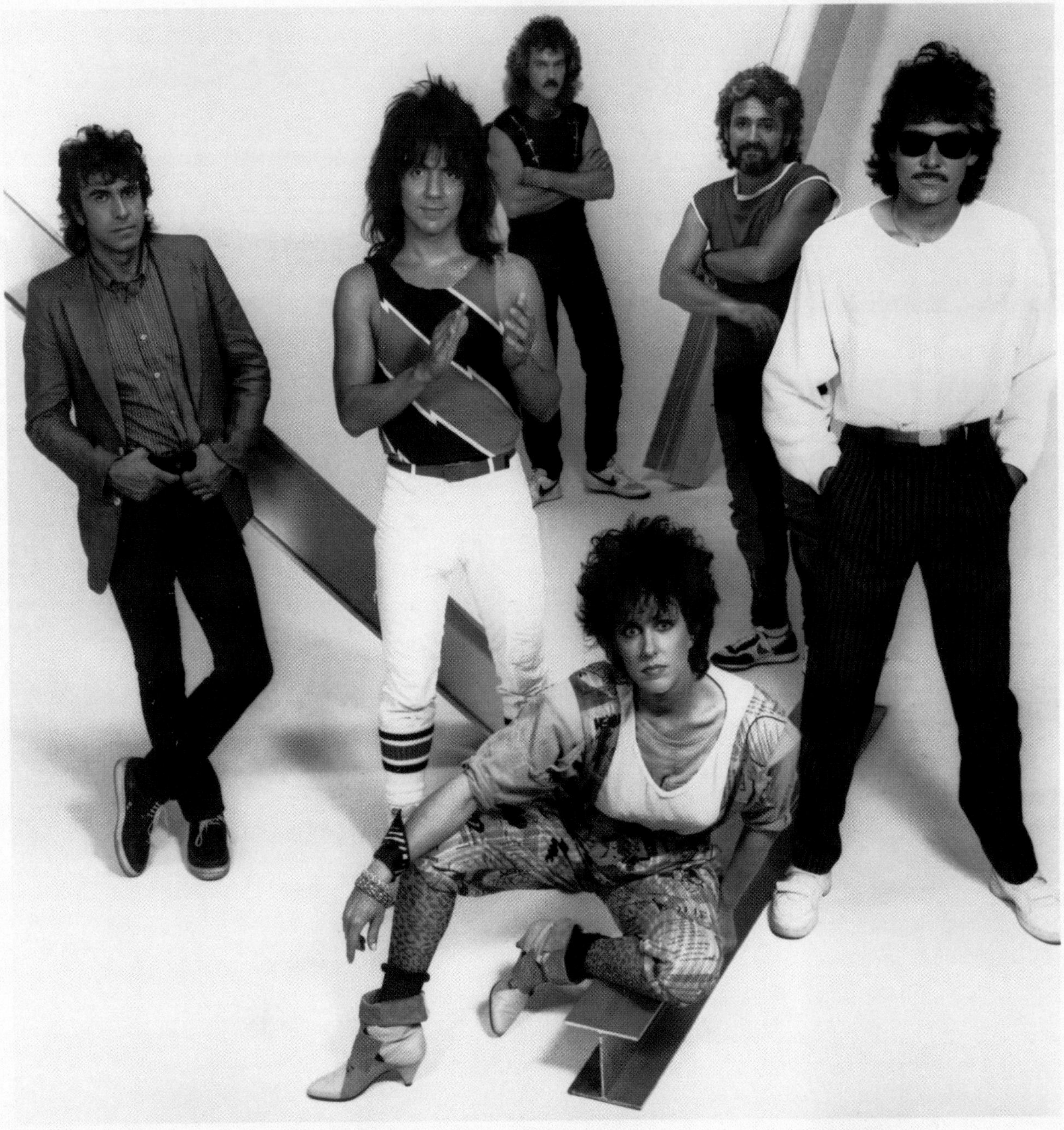

JEFFERSON STARSHIP

RECORDS

Manufactured and Distributed by RCA Records

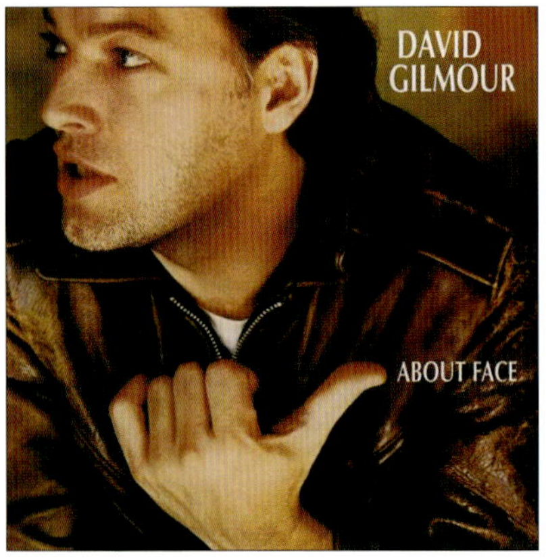

Following the acrimonious dissolution of the classic Pink Floyd lineup, guitarist and vocalist **David Gilmour** released *About Face*, his second solo album.

Billboard 200: *About Face* (#32)
Billboard Hot 100: "Blue Light" (#62)

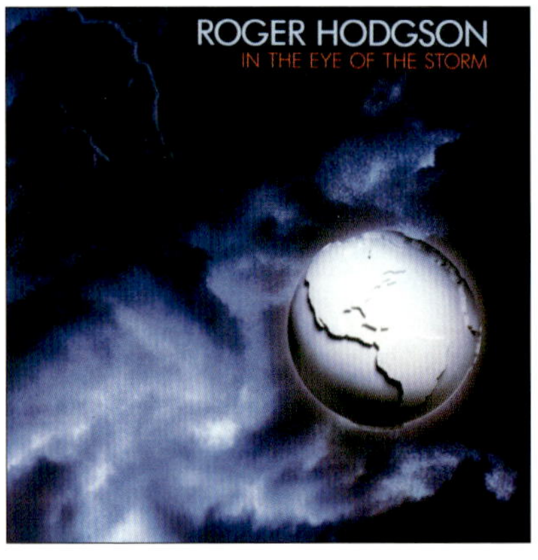

Roger Hodgson, having departed Supertramp, recorded *In the Eye of the Storm* at his UK home studio, playing the majority of the instruments himself.

Billboard 200: *In the Eye of the Storm* (#46)
Billboard Hot 100: "Had a Dream (Sleeping With the Enemy)" (#48)

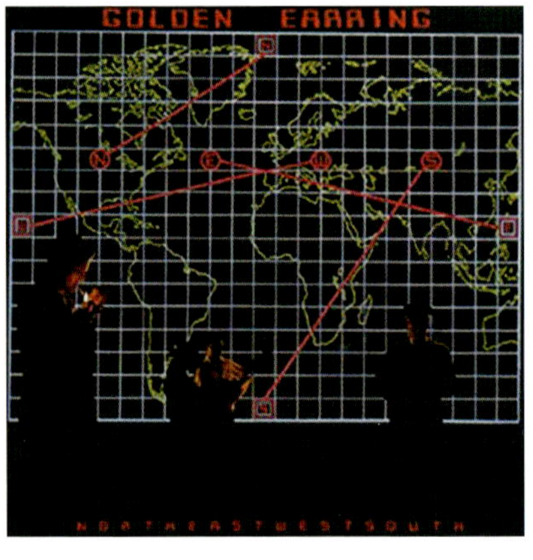

The most successful band from the Netherlands on the US charts, **Golden Earring** climbed to No. 1 in its native country with "When the Lady Smiles."

Billboard 200: *N.E.W.S.* (#107)
Billboard Hot 100: "When the Lady Smiles" (#76)

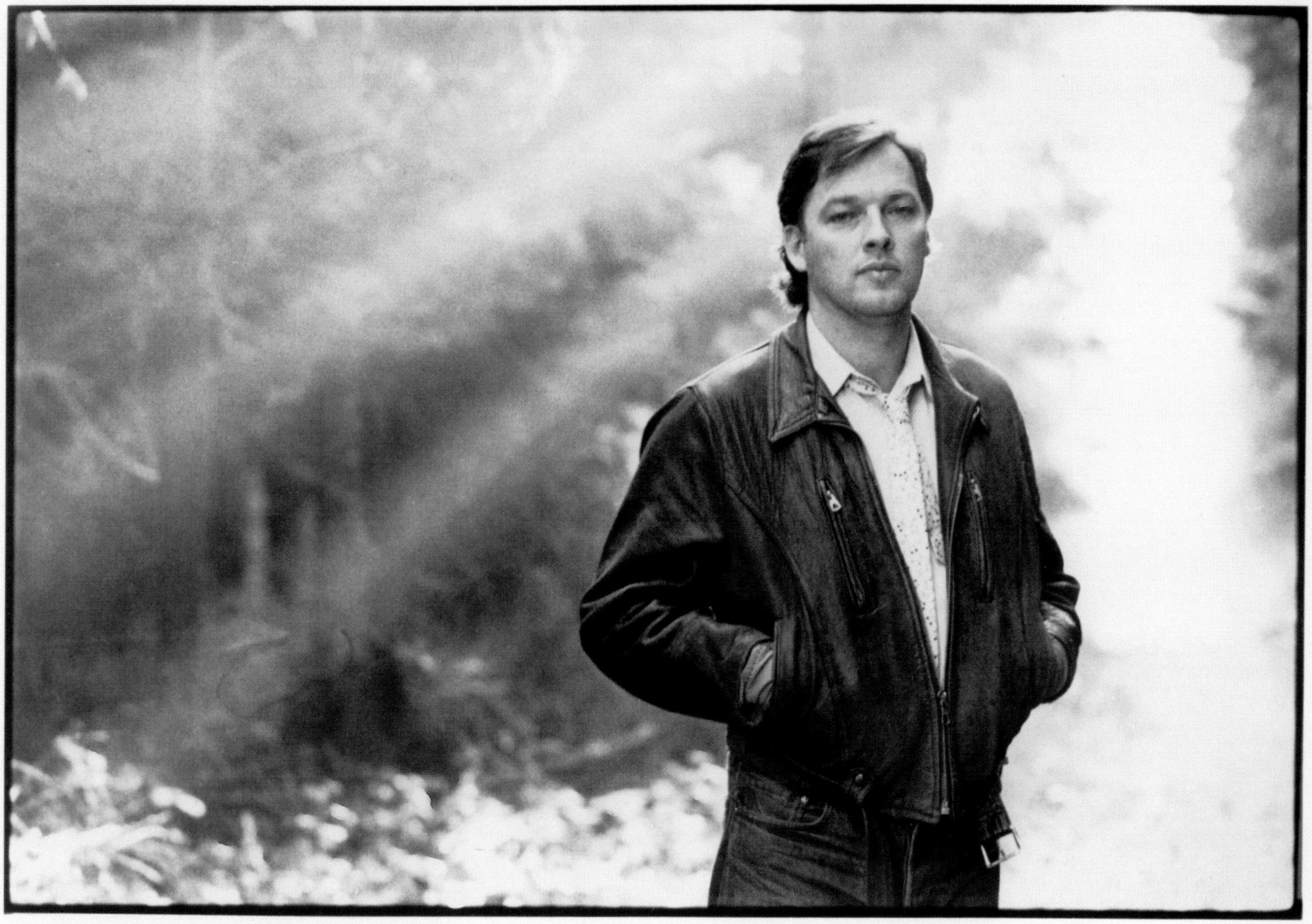

PHOTOGRAPH: JILL FURMANOVSKY

DAVID GILMOUR

Columbia
8402

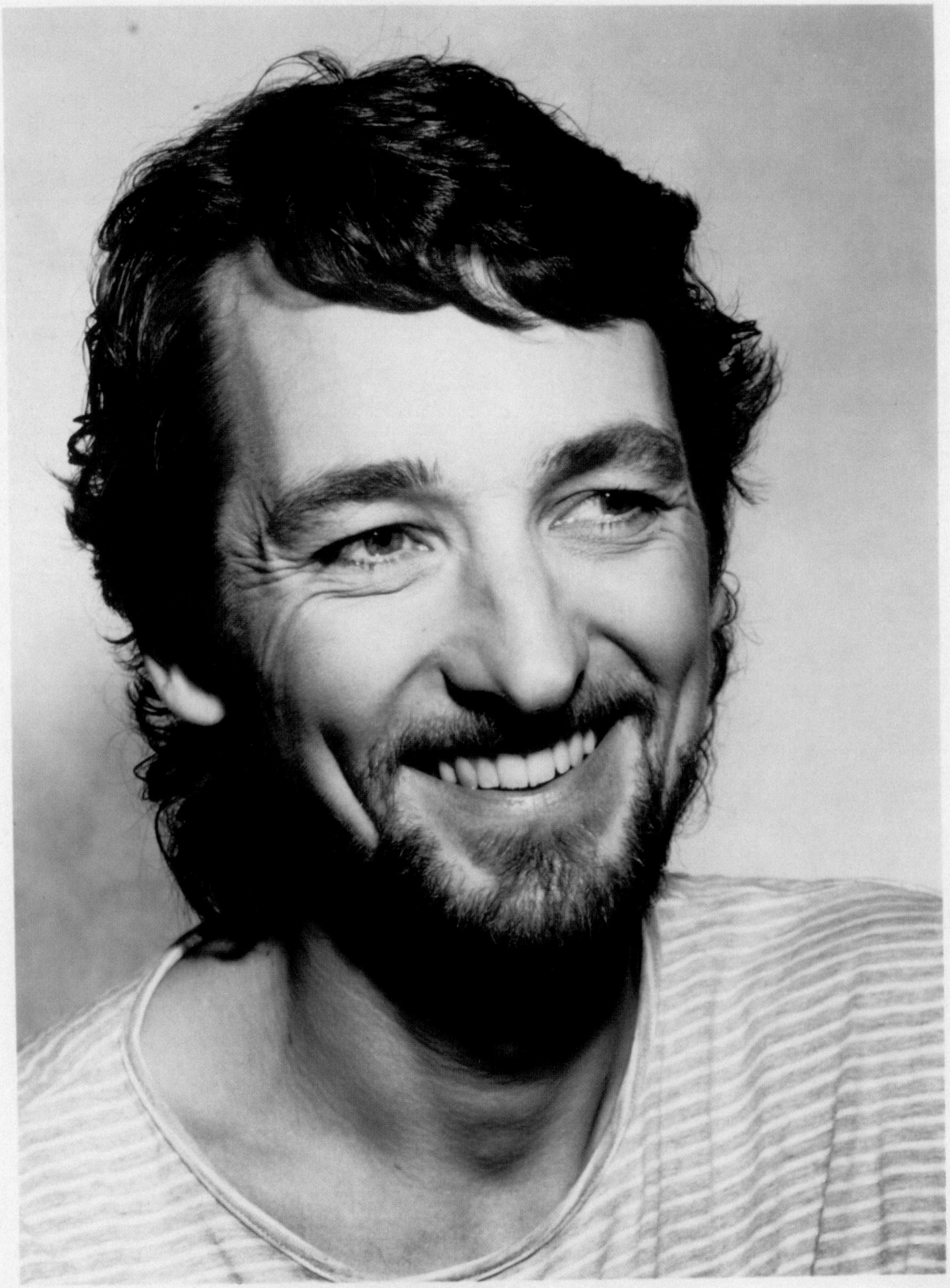

ROGER HODGSON

Representation:
Doug Pringle
(916) 265-8003

A&M RECORDS

Printed in U.S.A.

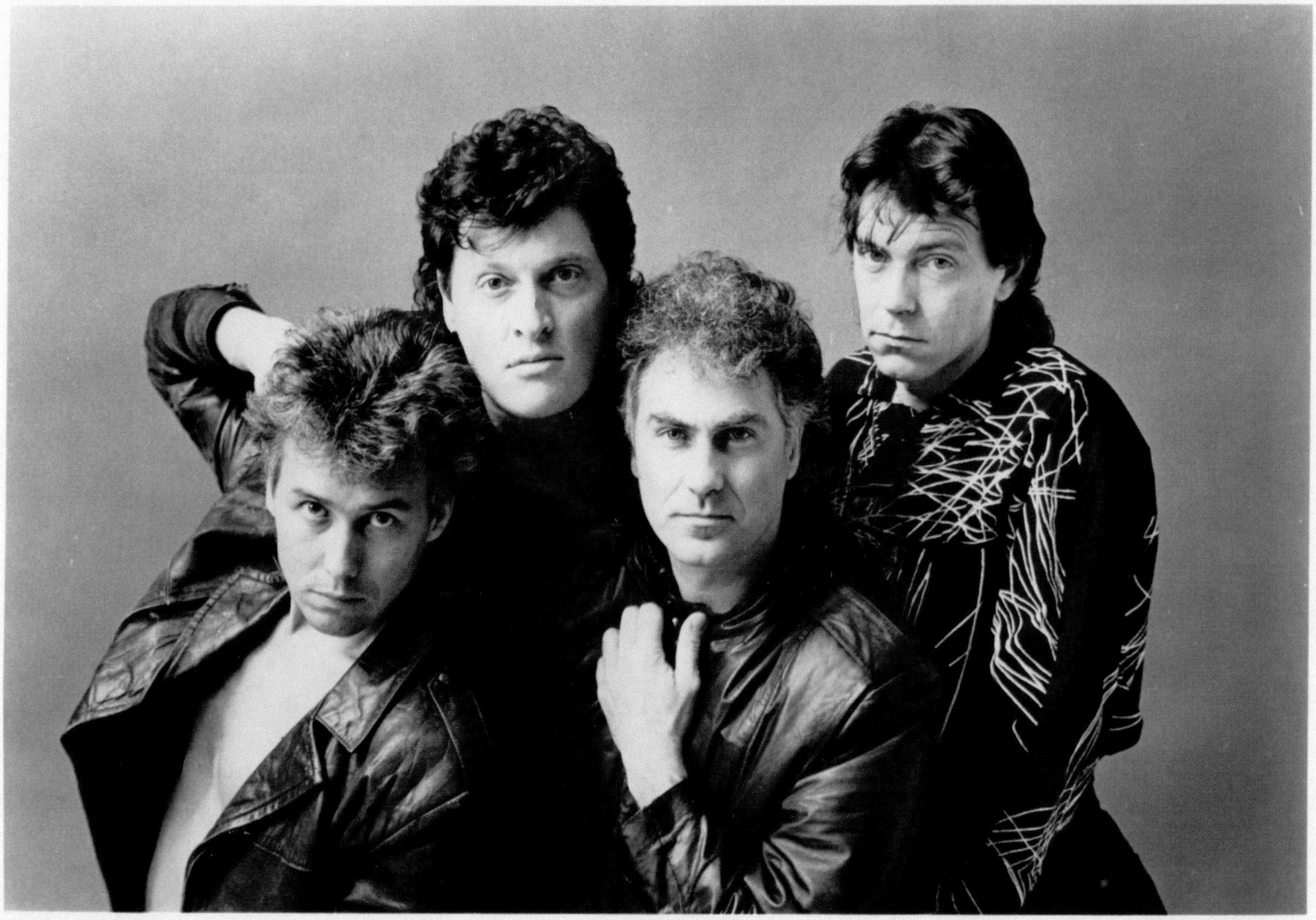

GOLDEN EARRING

PolyGram Records™

Photo Credit Mark Weiss

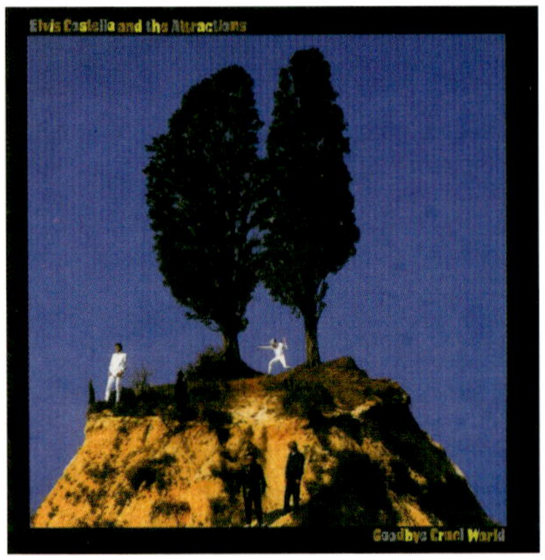

A troubled **Elvis Costello** declared his retirement and the breakup of the Attractions, his backing band, before making his ninth album, *Goodbye Cruel World*.

Billboard 200: *Goodbye Cruel World* (#35)
Billboard Hot 100: "The Only Flame in Town" (#56)

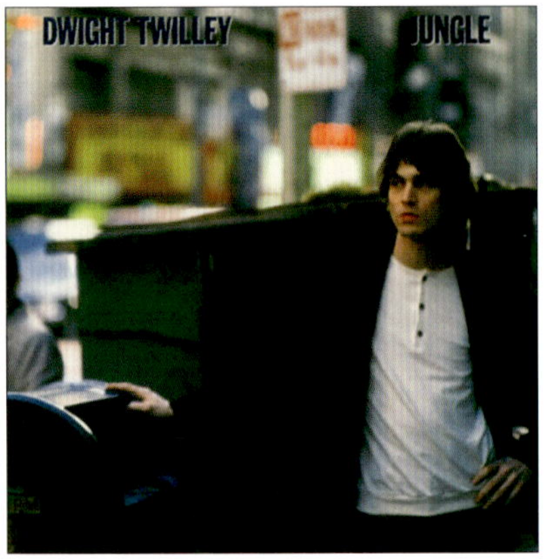

Power-pop hero **Dwight Twilley** made a return to the charts with "Girls," a hit single from his *Jungle* album featuring backing vocals by guest Tom Petty.

Billboard 200: *Jungle* (#39);
Billboard Hot 100:"Girls"(#16);
"Little Bit of Love" (#77)

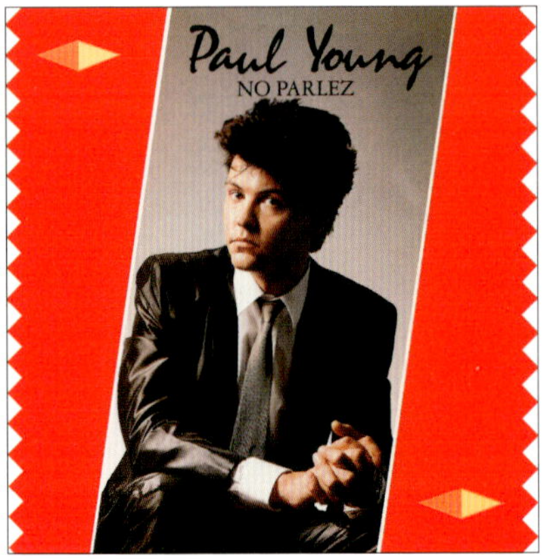

The debut *No Parlez*, a UK No. 1 album, gave English pop-soul singer **Paul Young** his first Top 40 single in America, the self-assured "Come Back and Stay."

Billboard 200: *No Parlez* (#79)
Billboard Hot 100: "Wherever I Lay My Hat (That's My Home)" (#70); "Come Back and Stay" (#22); "Love of the Common People" (#45)

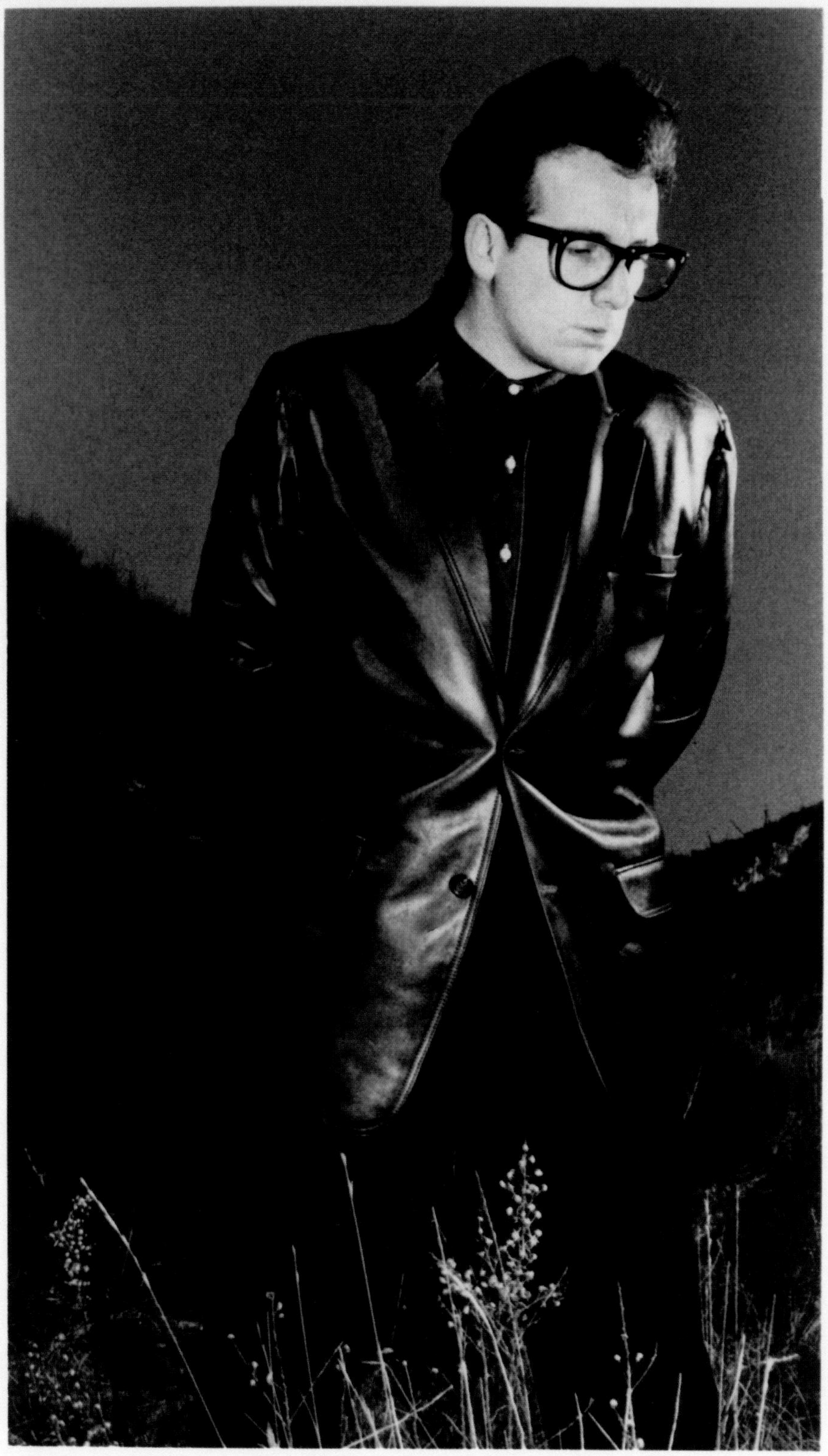

ELVIS COSTELLO

Columbia
8405

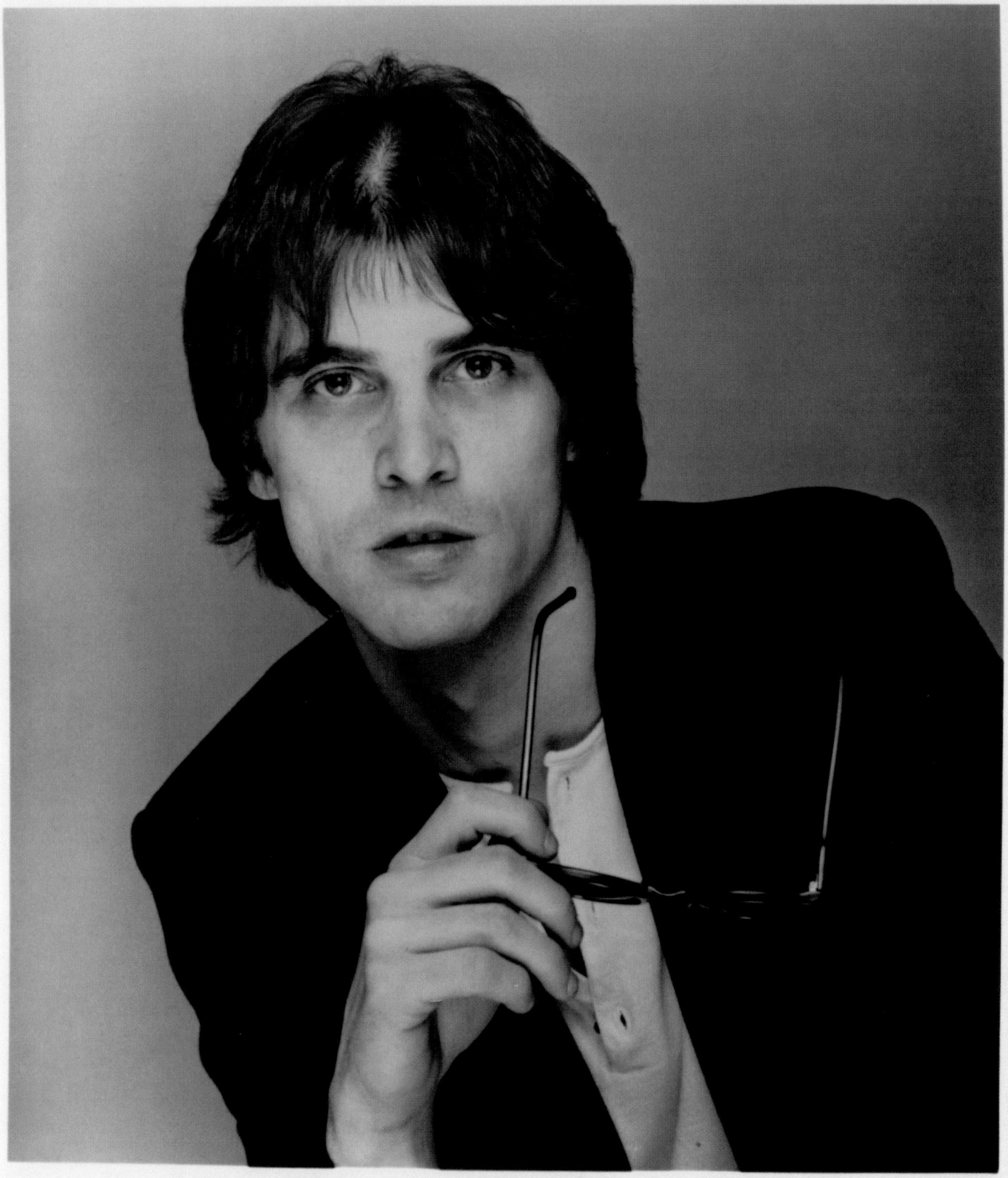

DWIGHT TWILLEY

EMI AMERICA

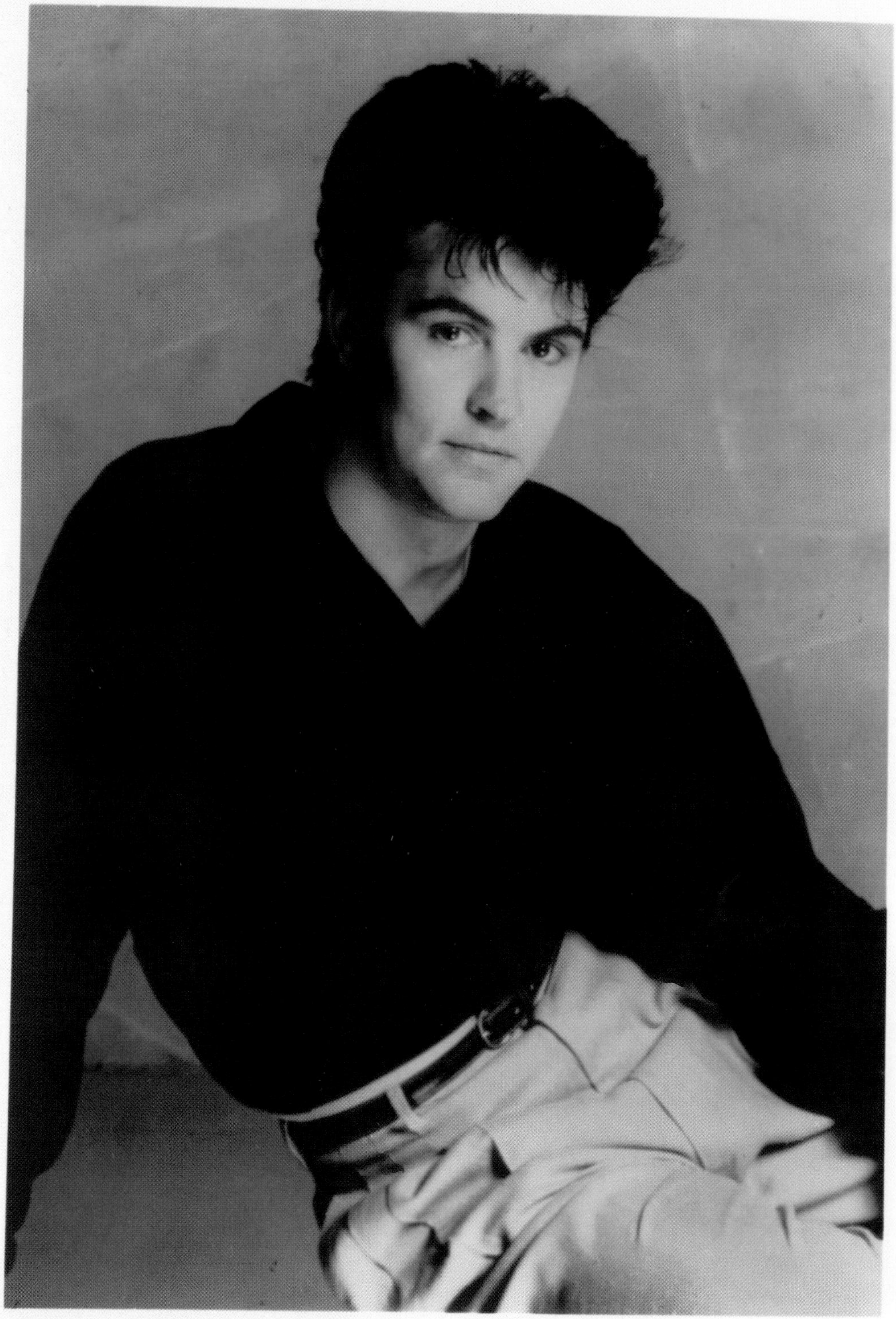

Paul Young

Columbia
8401

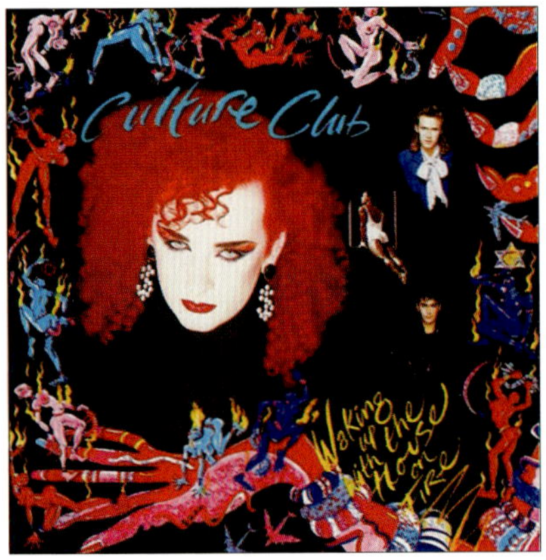

"The War Song" became a Top 20 hit in the US, but *Waking Up with the House on Fire* didn't enjoy the same success as **Culture Club**'s previous albums.

Billboard 200: *Waking Up with the House on Fire* (#26)
Billboard Hot 100: "The War Song" (#17);
"Mistake No. 3" (#33)

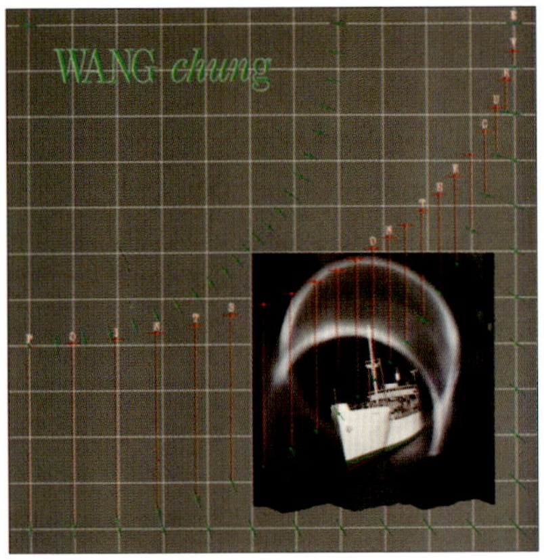

Wang Chung's "Dance Hall Days" gained the British group entry with an American pop audience, rising all the way to the No. 1 spot on the dance chart.

Billboard 200: *Points on the Curve* (#30)
Billboard Hot 100: "Dance Hall Days" (#16)

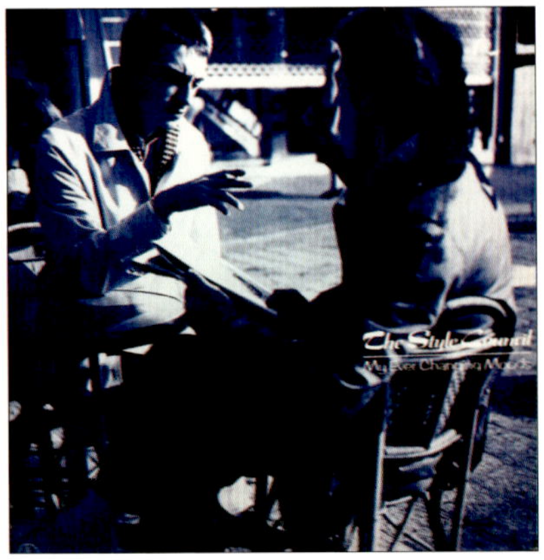

The Style Council, founded by ex-Jam frontman Paul Weller, pursued a more soulful musical direction and found success with "My Ever Changing Moods."

Billboard 200: *My Ever Changing Moods* (#56)
Billboard Hot 100: "My Ever Changing Moods" (#29);
"You're the Best Thing" (#76)

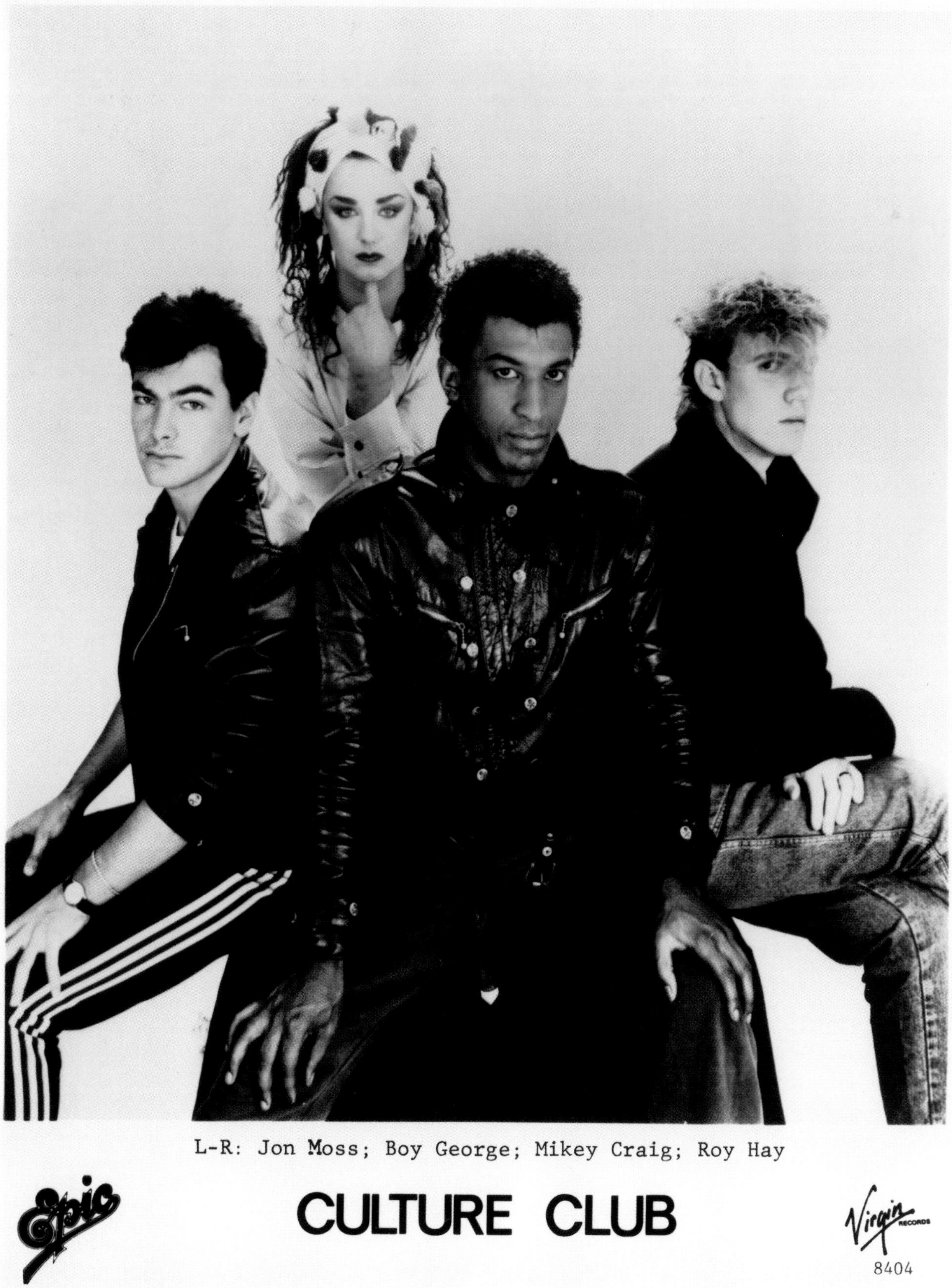

Photo: David Levine

L-R: Jon Moss; Boy George; Mikey Craig; Roy Hay

Epic

CULTURE CLUB

Virgin Records

8404

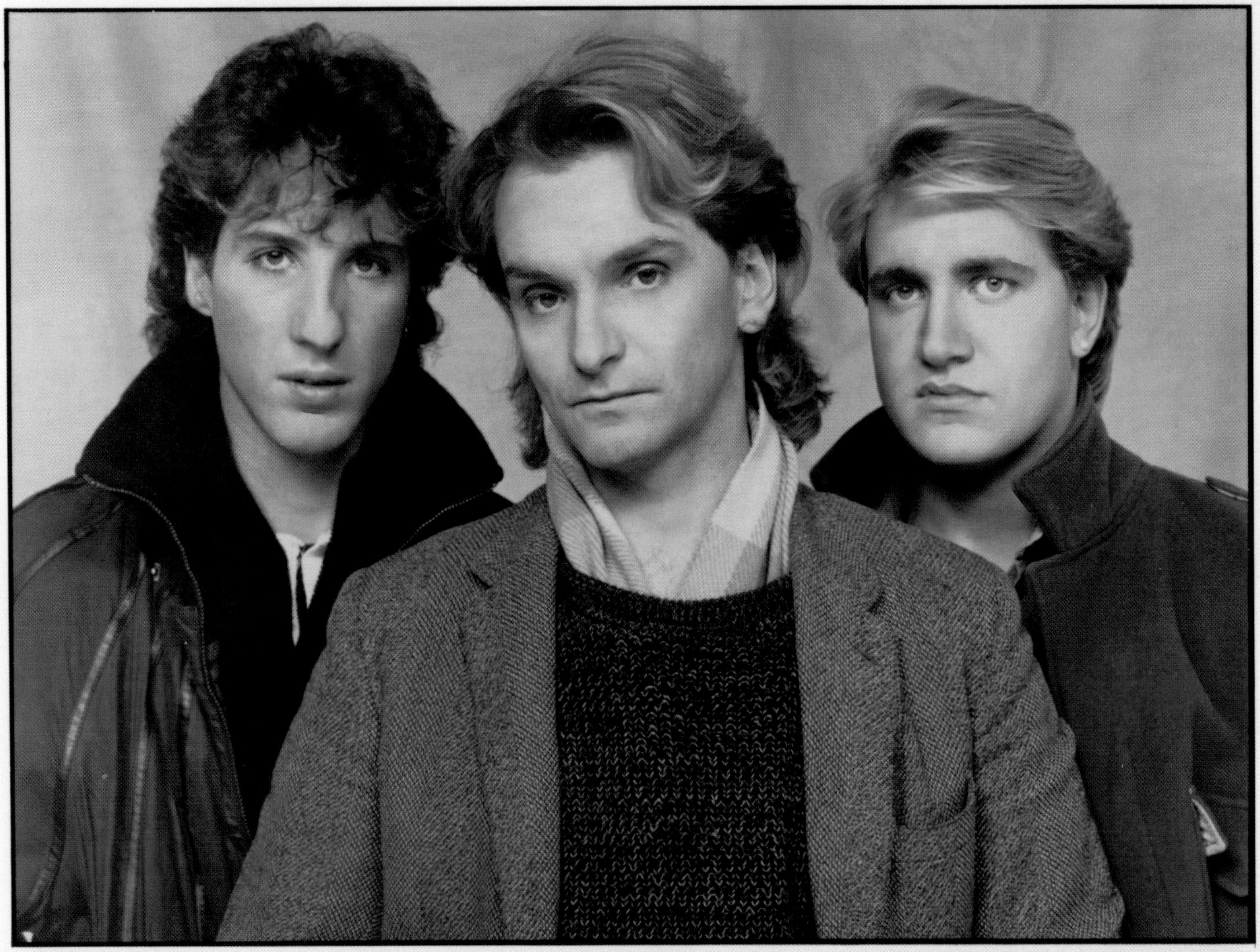

NICK FELDMAN JACK HUES DARREN COSTIN

GEFFEN RECORDS

Wang Chung

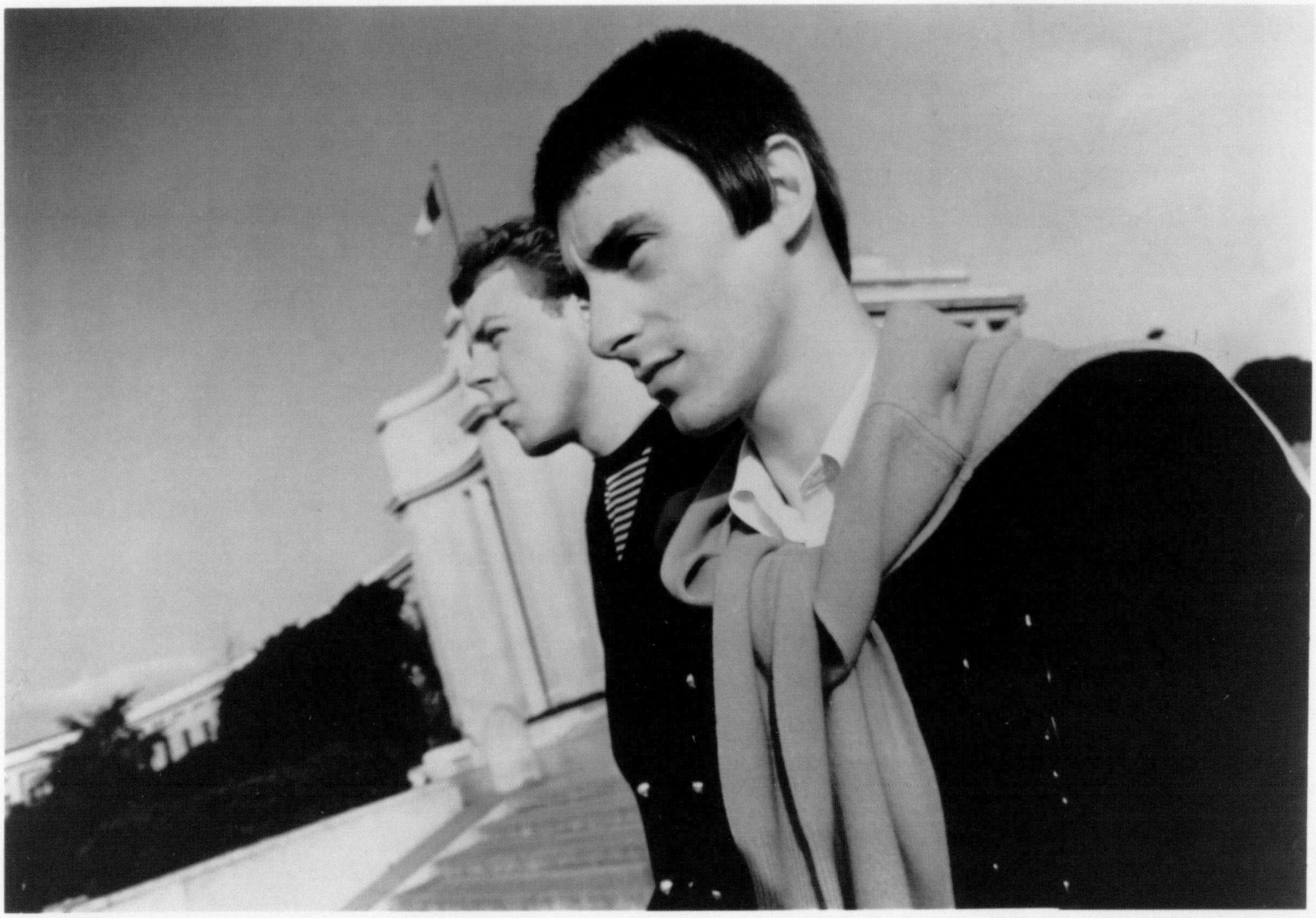

MICK TALBOT PAUL WELLER

The Style Council

GEFFEN RECORDS

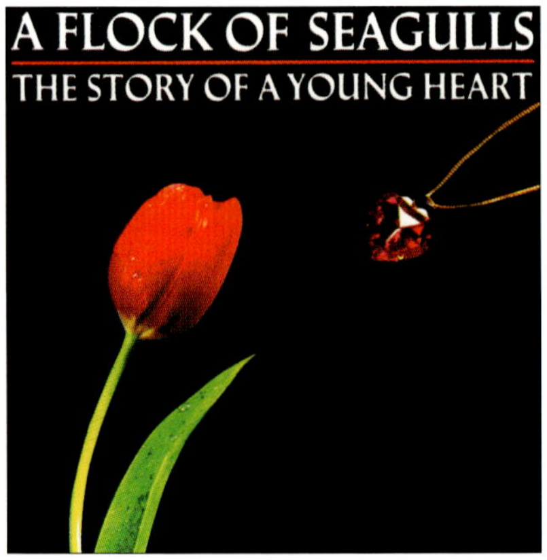

The Story of a Young Heart, **A Flock of Seagulls**' third album, yielded "The More You Live, the More You Love," the English synth-pop band's last hit single.

Billboard 200: *The Story of a Young Heart* (#67)
Billboard Hot 100: "The More You Live, the More You Love" (#56)

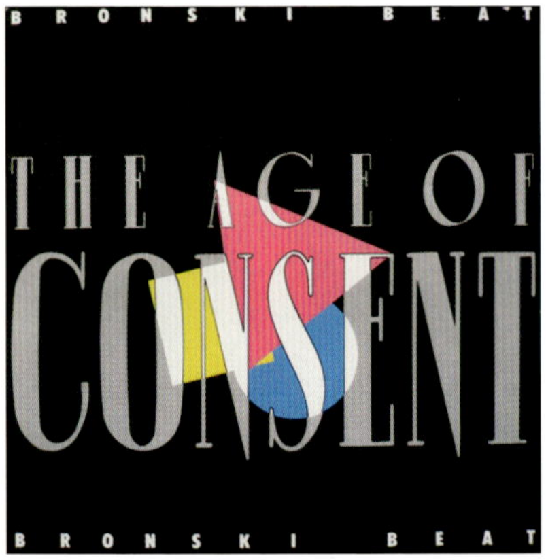

Bronski Beat hit the US chart with "Smalltown Boy," an emotional vignette centering around vocalist Jimmy Somerville's life experiences as a homosexual.

Billboard 200: *The Age of Consent* (#36)
Billboard Hot 100: "Smalltown Boy" (#48)

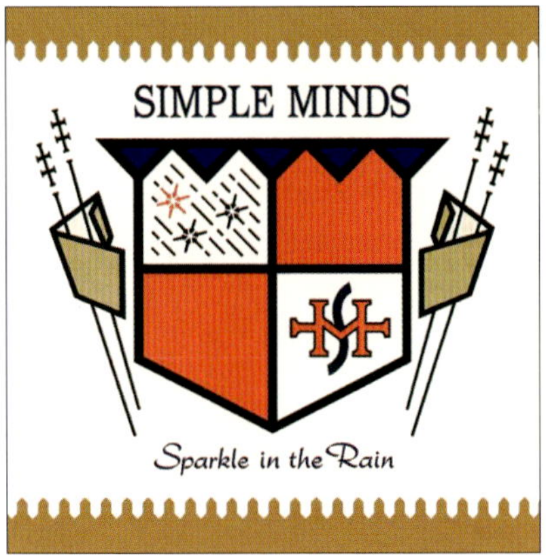

Simple Minds' *Sparkle in the Rain* topped the UK charts and earned the Scottish art rockers and lead singer Jim Kerr a positive critical response in the US.

Billboard 200: *Sparkle in the Rain* (#64)

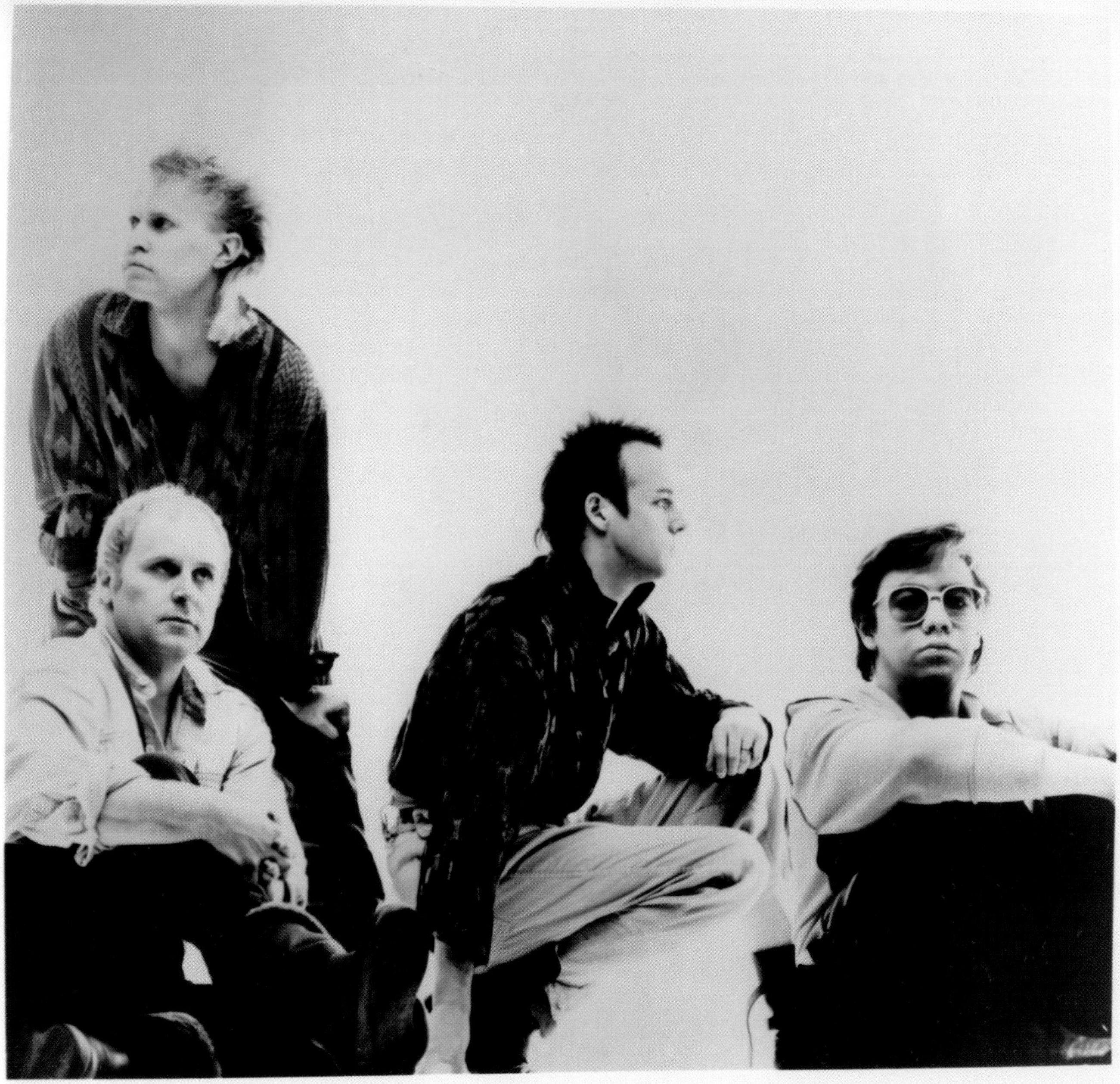

A FLOCK OF SEAGULLS

JIVE

ARISTA™

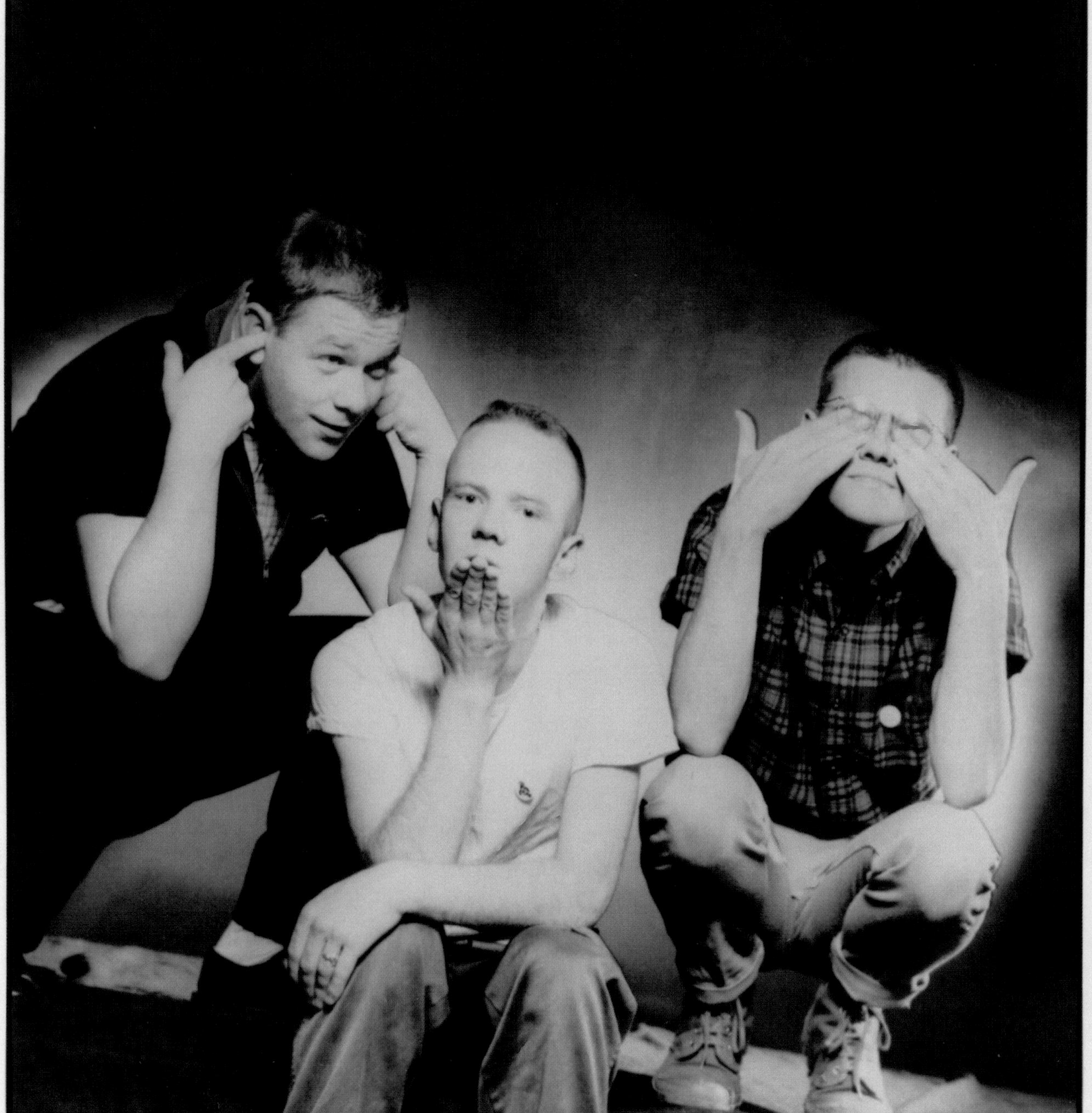

LONDON

BRONSKI BEAT

MCA RECORDS

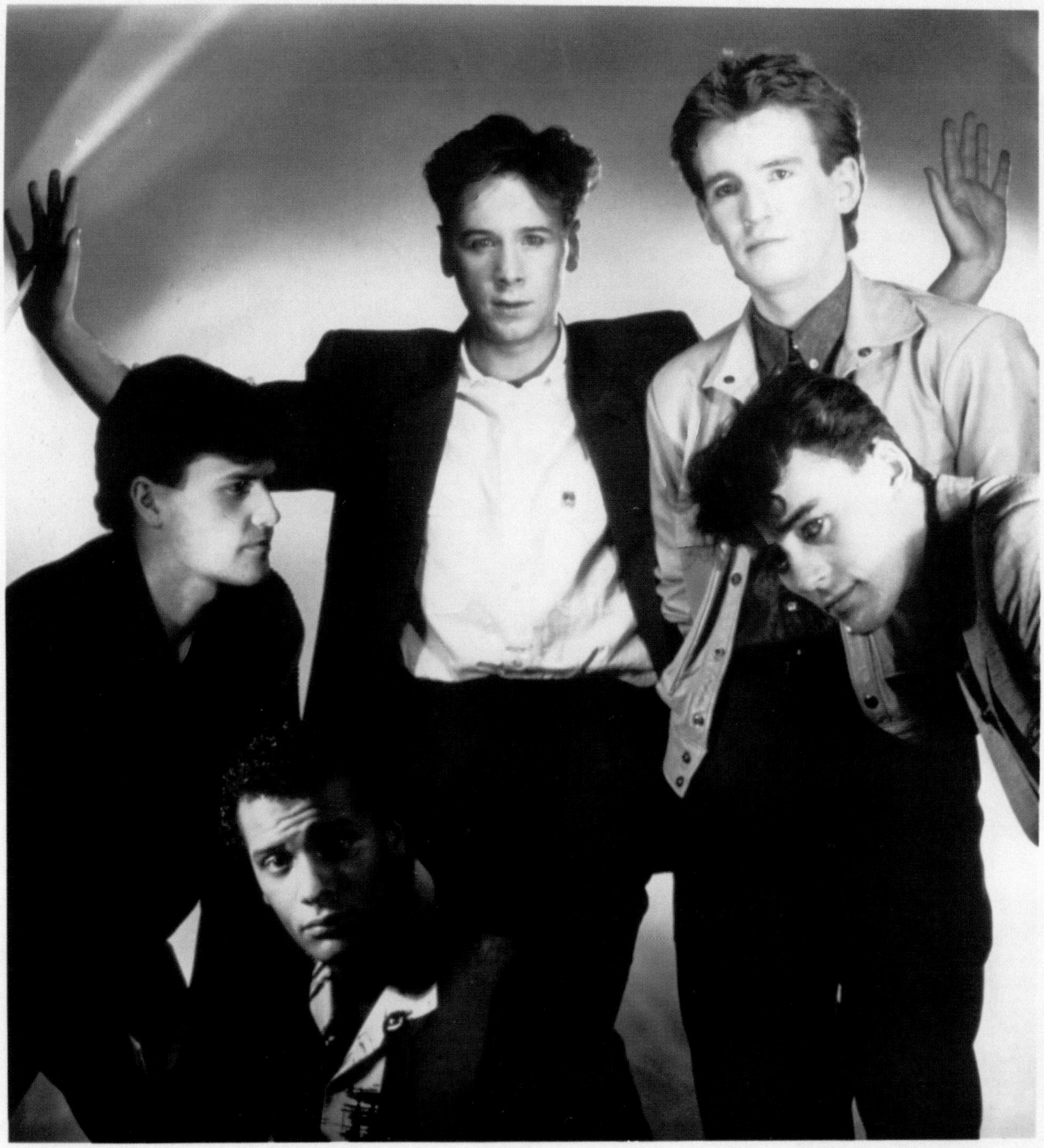

Charlie Burchill Mel Gaynor Jim Kerr Derek Forbes Mick MacNeil

SIMPLE MINDS

Printed in U.S.A.

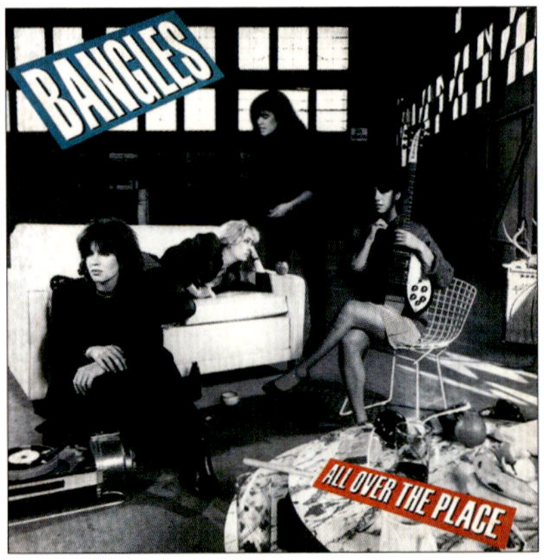

The Bangles, an all-female band, went into heavy rotation at college stations across the country with "Hero Takes a Fall" and "Goin' Down to Liverpool."

Billboard 200: *All Over the Place* (#80)

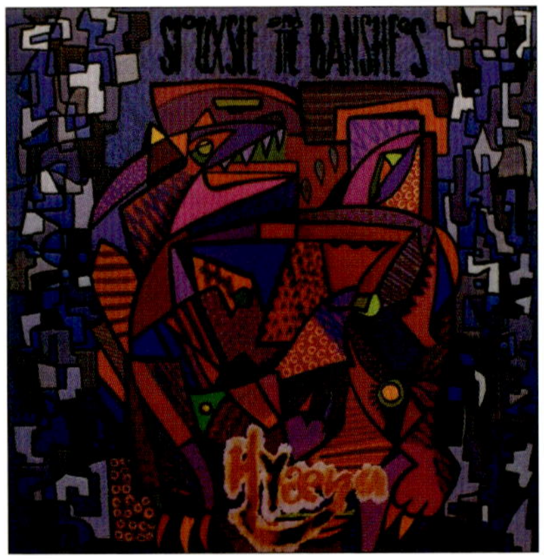

In the songwriting and recording of **Siouxsie & the Banshees**' *Hyæna*, Robert Smith of the Cure offered his talents to the British alternative-rock group.

Billboard 200: *Hyæna* (#157)

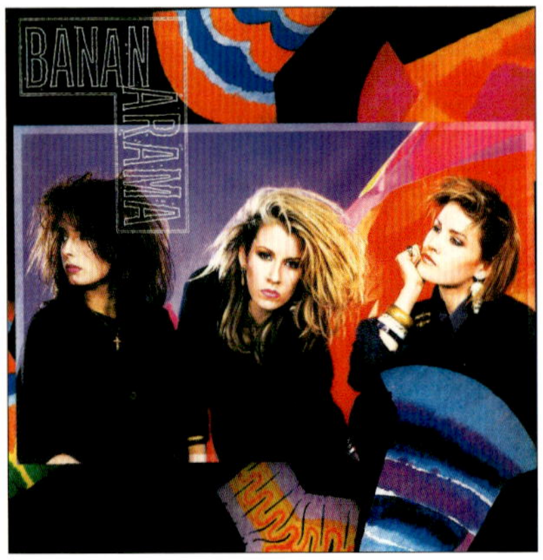

One of Britain's most successful girl groups, **Bananarama** scored its first American hit when "Cruel Summer" was showcased in the film *The Karate Kid*.

Billboard 200: *Bananarama* (#30)
Billboard Hot 100: "Robert DeNiro's Waiting" (#95); "Cruel Summer" (#9); "The Wild Life" (#70)

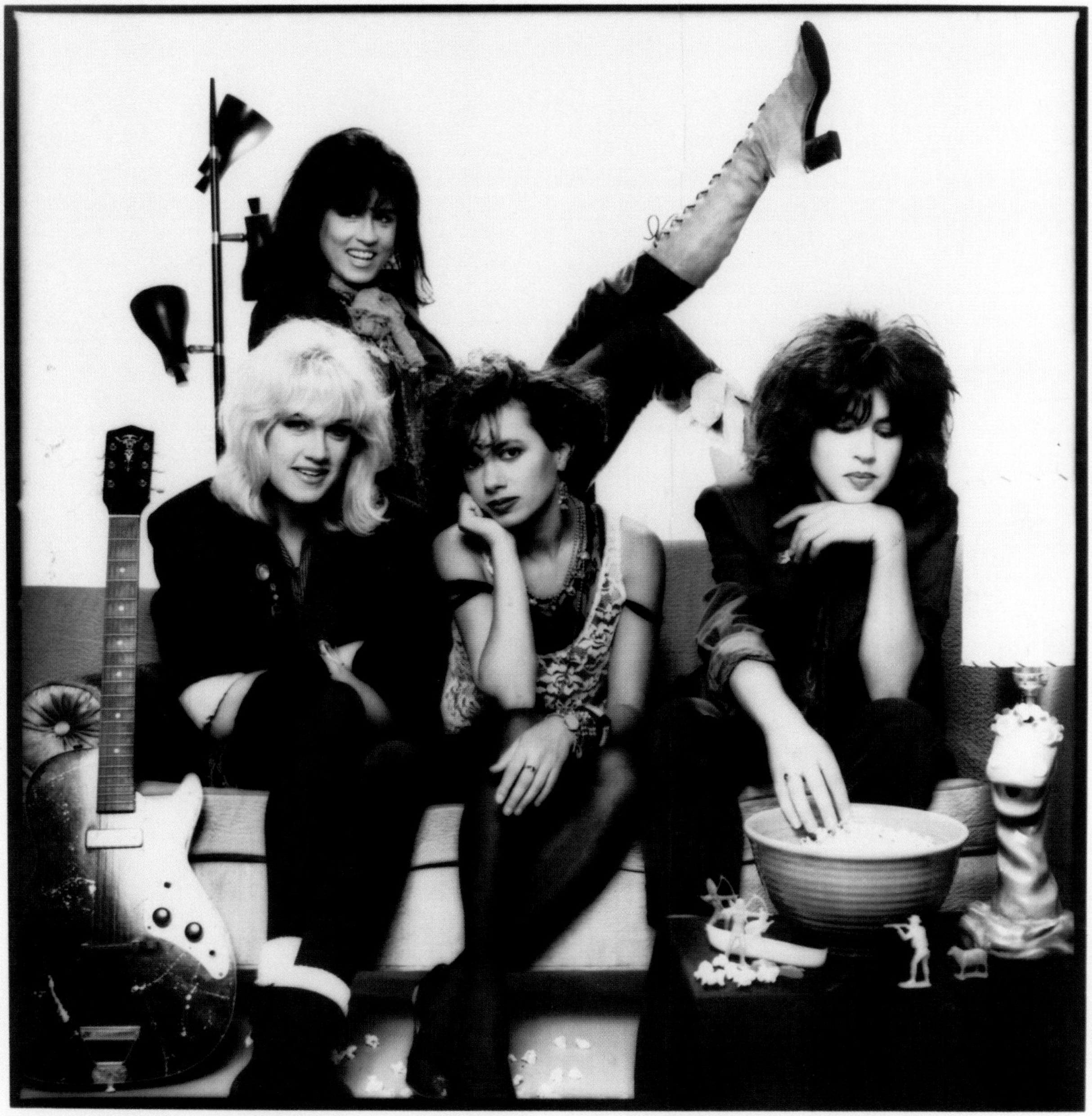

PHOTOGRAPH: DENNIS KEELEY

From left: (seated) Debbi Peterson, Susanna Hoffs, Michael Steele, and (top) Vicki Peterson

BANGLES

Columbia
8410

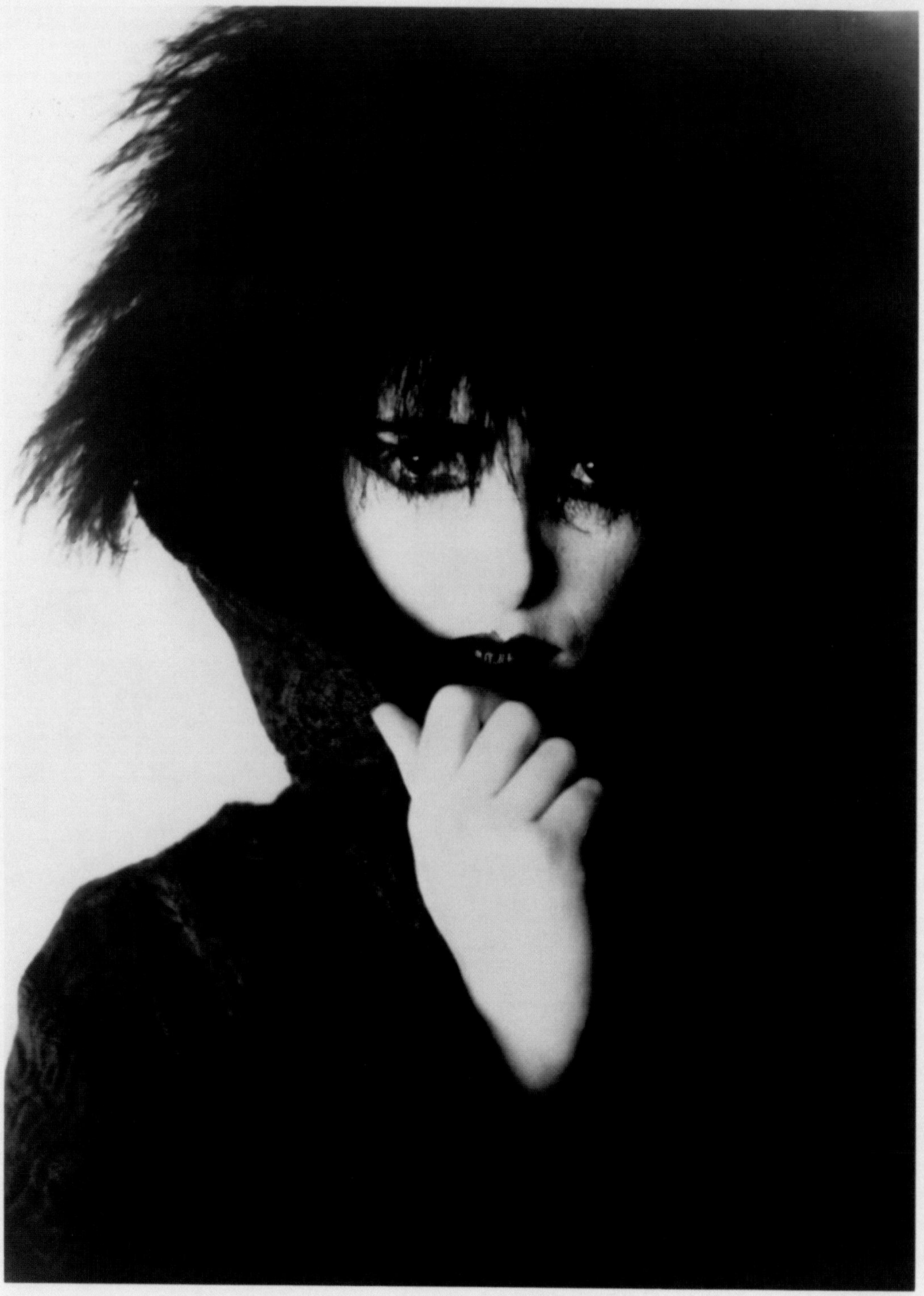

Siouxsie and the Banshees

GEFFEN RECORDS

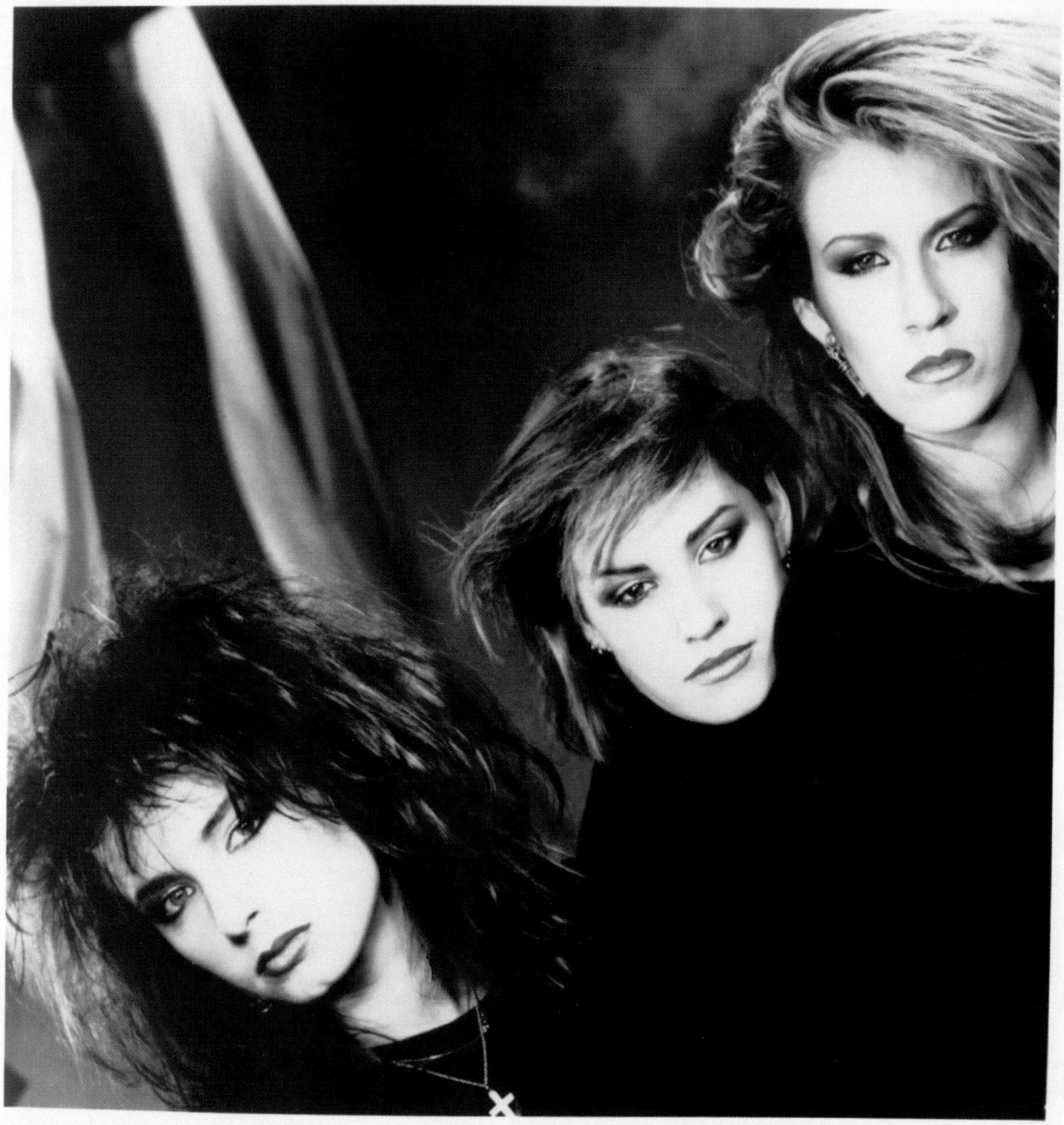

BANANARAMA

LONDON
RECORDINGS

PolyGram Records

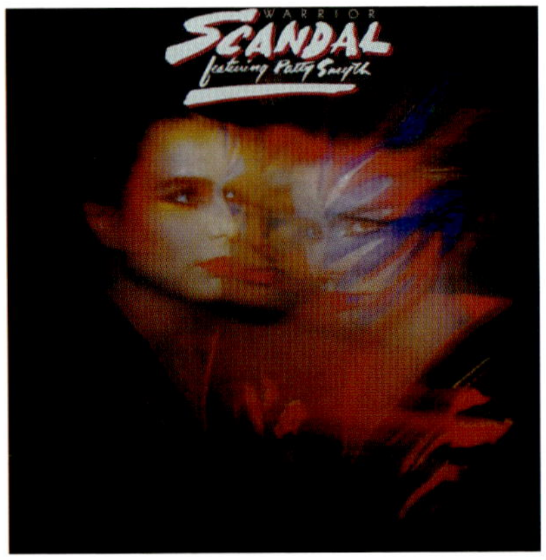

Formed by guitarist Zack Smith and fronted by vocalist Patty Smyth, the mainstream pop-rock group **Scandal** cracked *Billboard*'s Top 10 with "The Warrior."

Billboard 200: *Warrior* (#17)
Billboard Hot 100: "The Warrior" (#7); "Hands Tied" (#41); "Beat of a Heart" (#41)

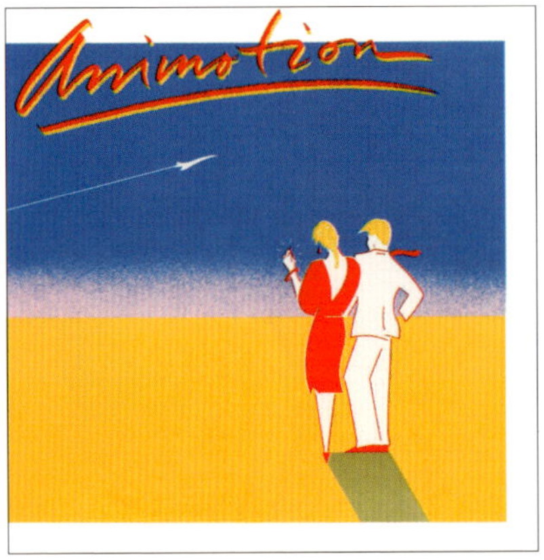

Catching the wave of MTV-compatible synth pop, the anthemic "Obsession" became an international success for the Los Angeles-based outfit **Animotion**.

Billboard 200: *Animotion* (#28)
Billboard Hot 100: "Obsession" (#6); "Let Him Go" (#39)

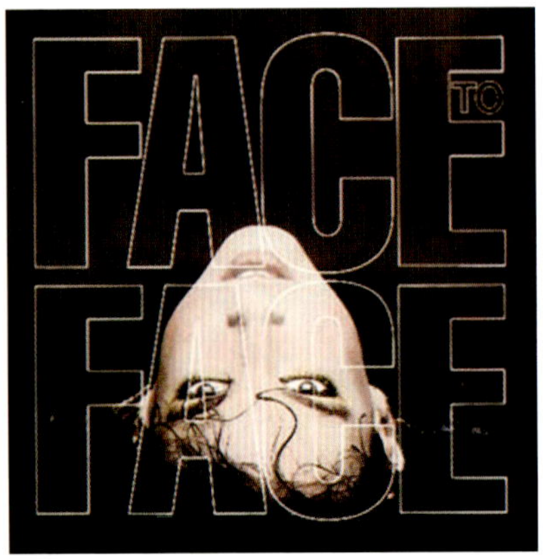

Face to Face got help from dance producer Arthur Baker, and "10-9-8" emerged as the hit track from the Boston-based new wave band's self-titled album.

Billboard 200: *Face to Face* (#126)
Billboard Hot 100: "10-9-8" (#38)

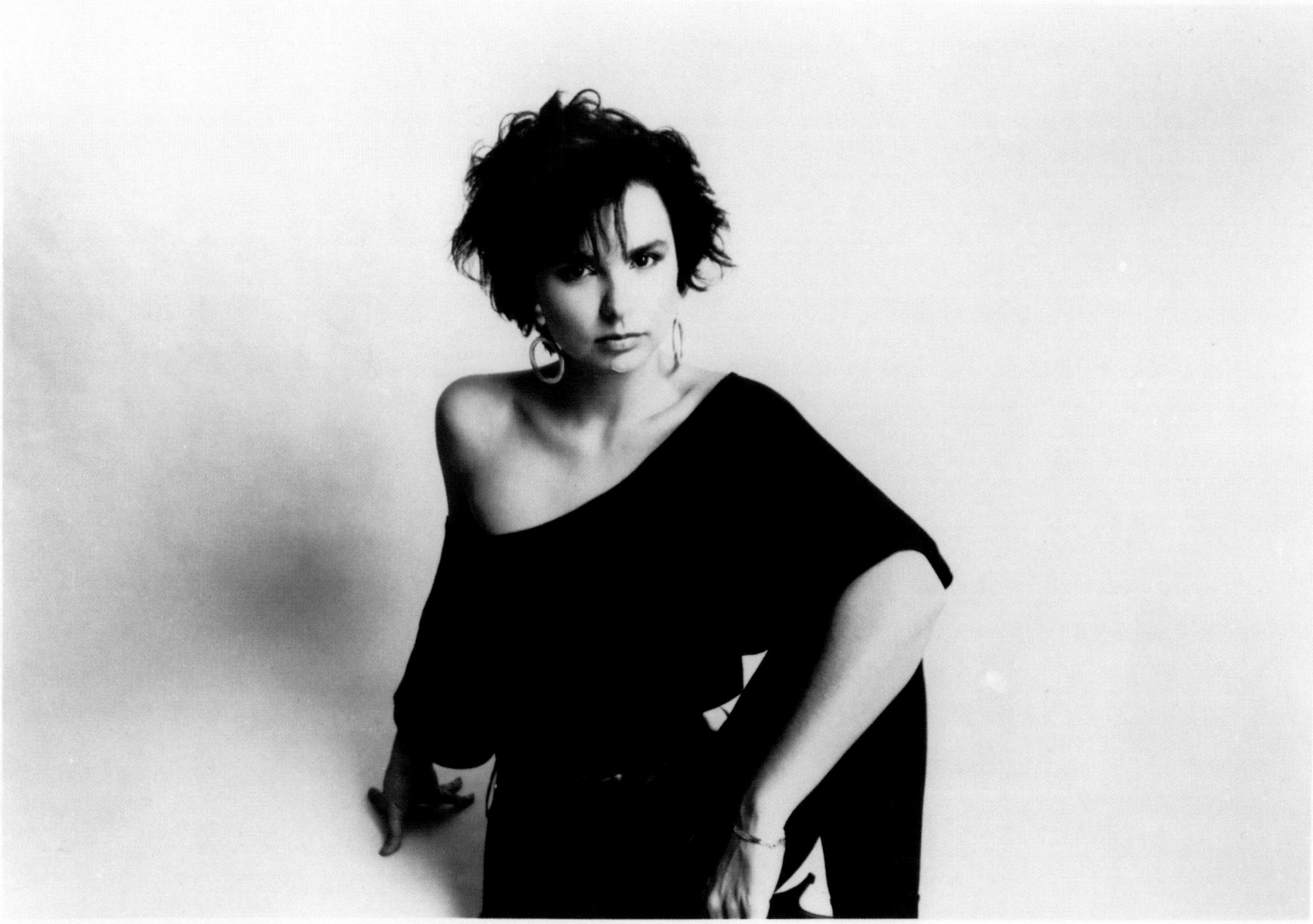

PHOTOGRAPH: BUFF HERR

SCANDAL
featuring Patty Smyth

Columbia
8407

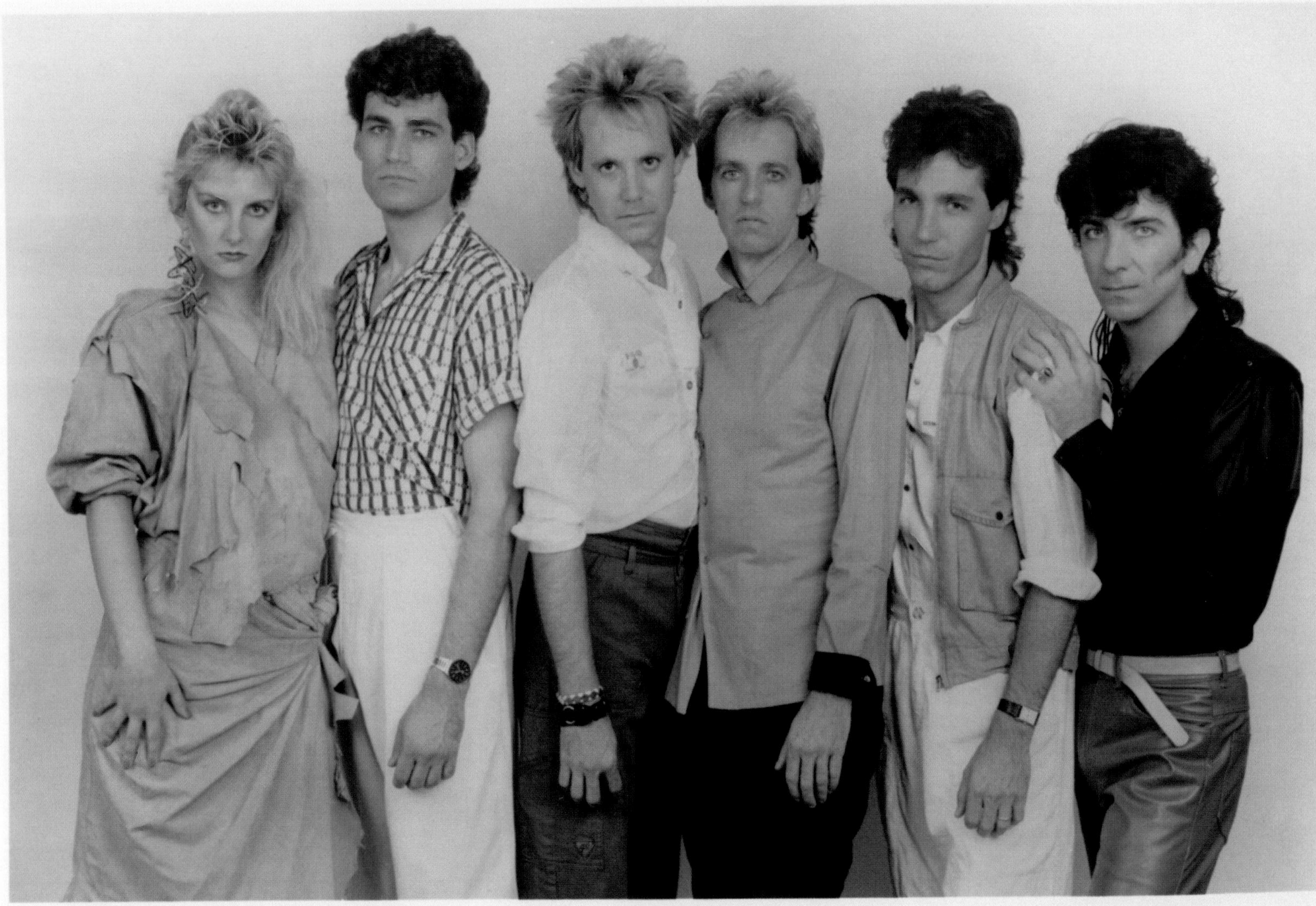

Animotion

mercury

PolyGram Records™

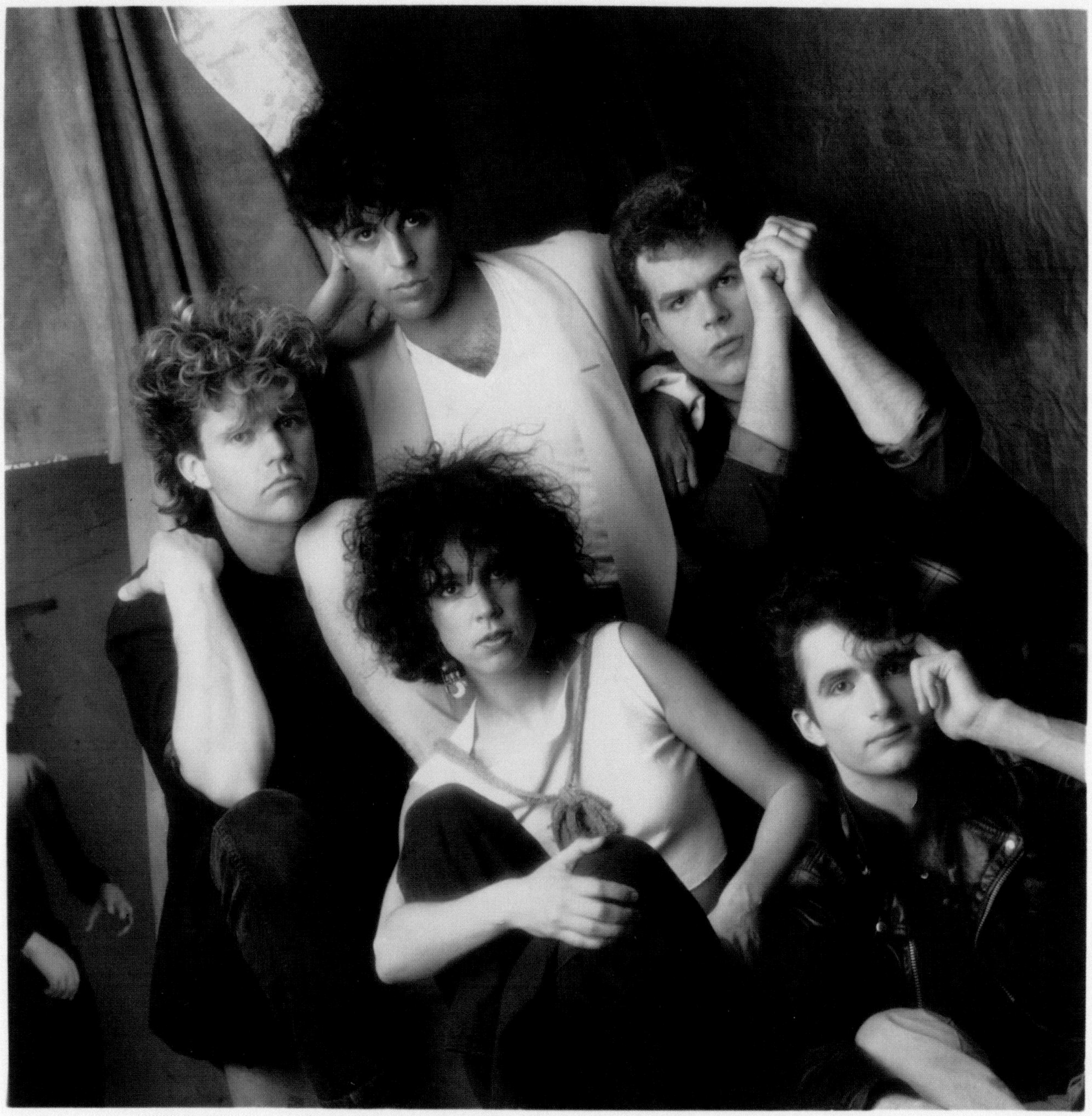

Top Row L-R: William Beard; Angelo; Stuart Kimball
Bottom Row- Laurie Sargent; John Ryder

FACE TO FACE

Epic 8406

Photo: Carrie Branovan

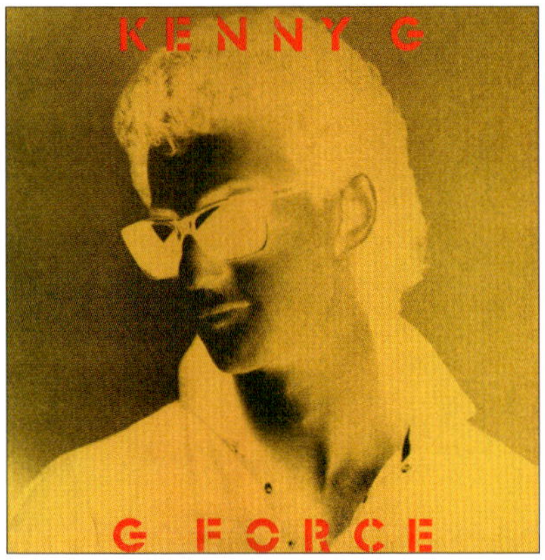

From saxophonist **Kenny G**'s second album, the platinum *G Force*, the R&B-oriented tune "Hi, How Ya Doin'?" featured uncredited vocals by Barry Johnson.

Billboard 200: *G Force* (#62)

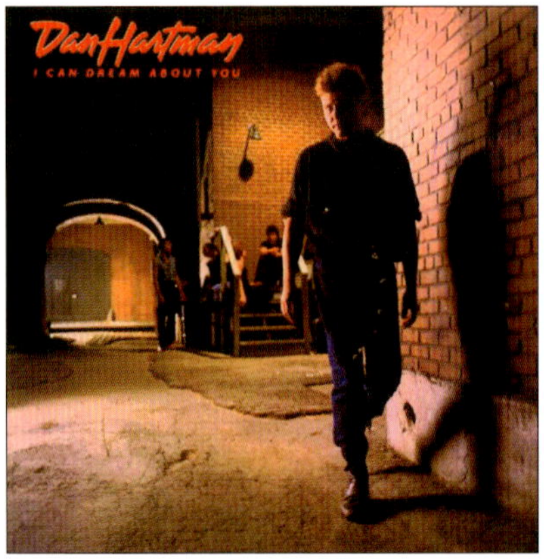

Dan Hartman wrote and recorded his biggest hit, "I Can Dream About You," a pop-soul song featured on the soundtrack album to the film *Streets of Fire*.

Billboard 200: *I Can Dream About You* (#55)
Billboard Hot 100: "I Can Dream About You" (#6); "We Are the Young" (#25); Second Nature" (#39)

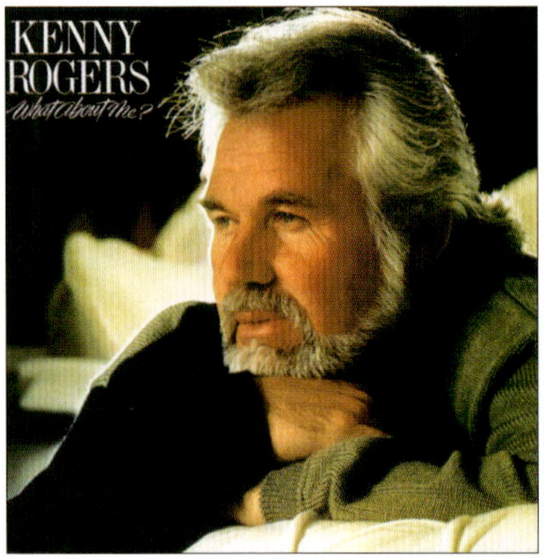

The title track of *What About Me?* by **Kenny Rogers**, sung as a trio with Kim Carnes and James Ingram, reached No. 1 on the adult contemporary charts.

Billboard 200: *What About Me?* (#31)
Billboard Hot 100: "What About Me?" (#15); "Crazy" (#79)

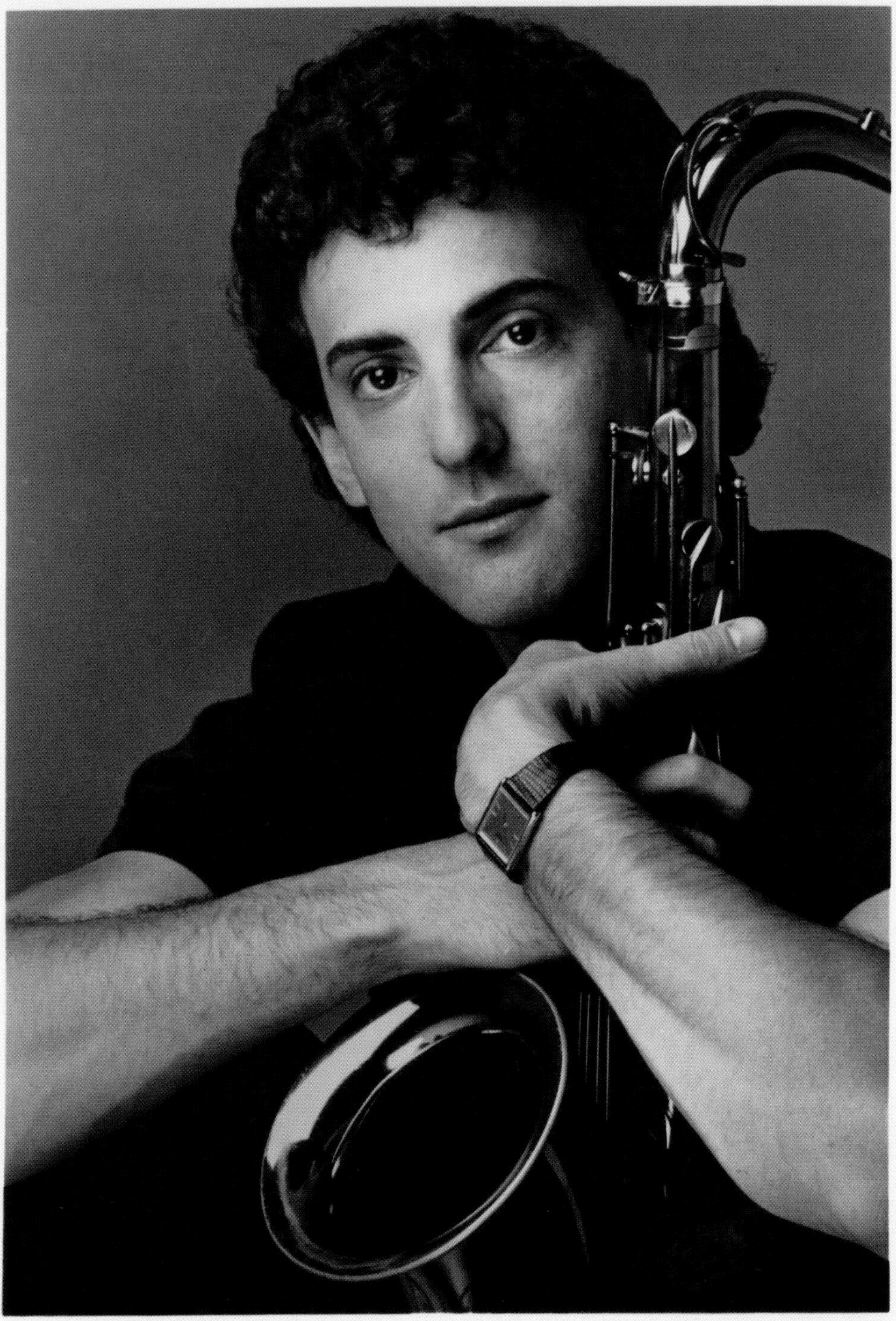

KENNY G

ARISTA

Jeffrey Ross Music

(206) 285-6838

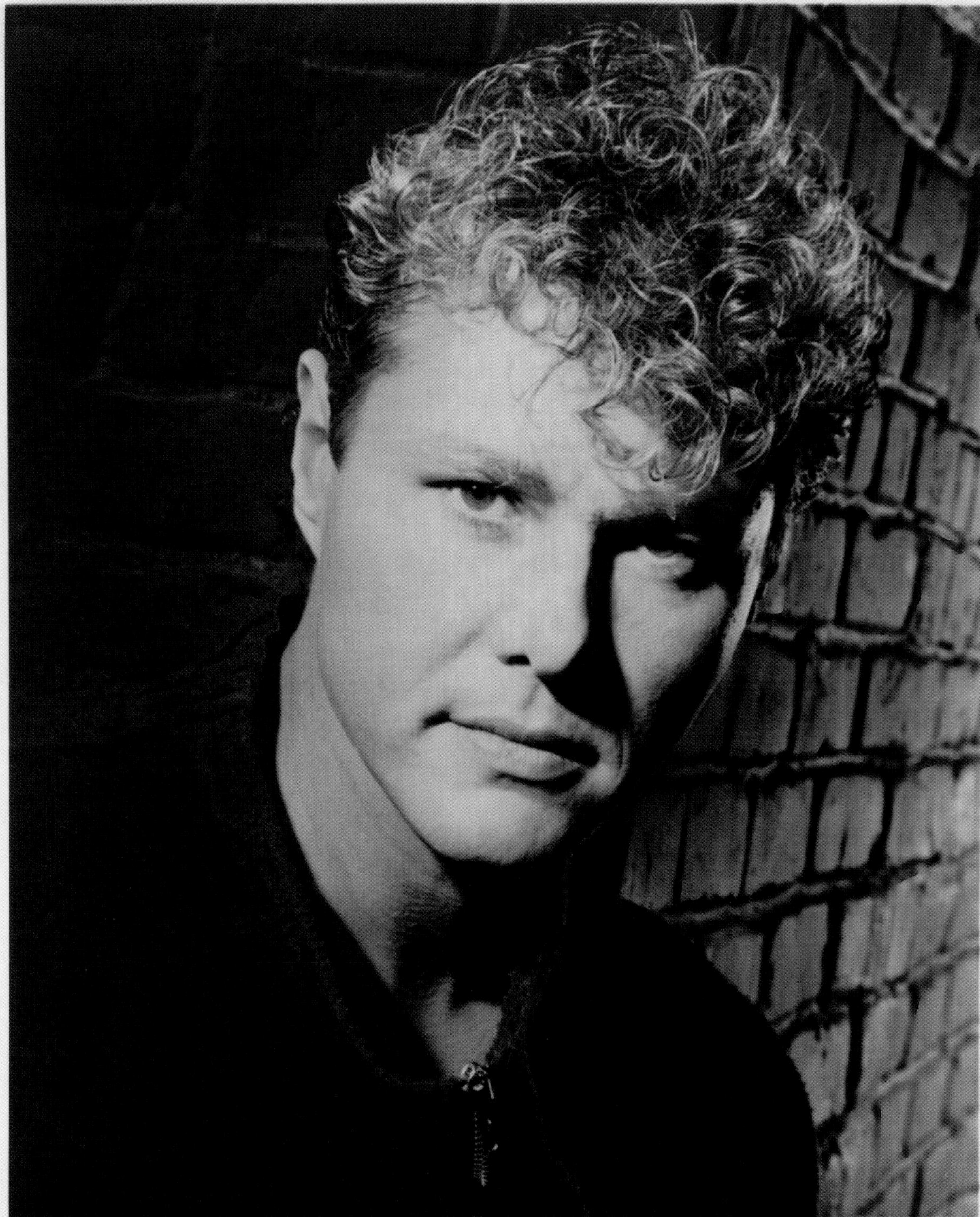

10/84

Dan Hartman

MCA RECORDS

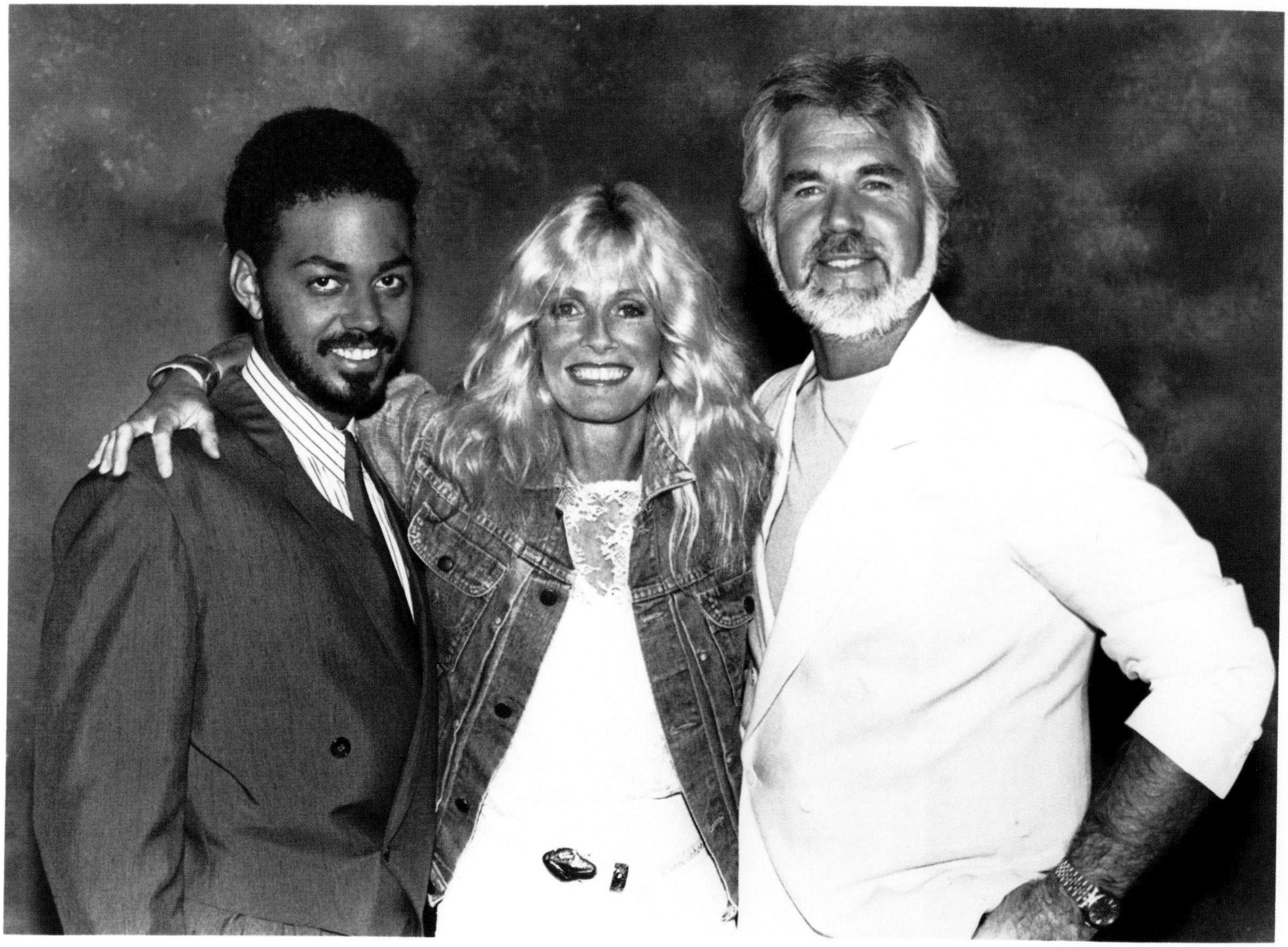

JAMES
INGRAM

KIM
CARNES

KENNY
ROGERS

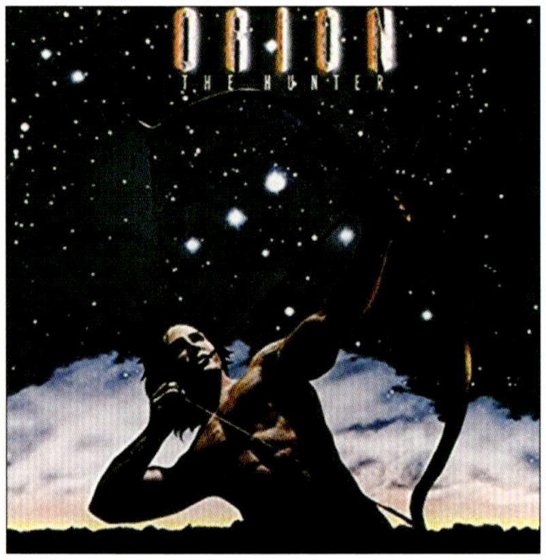

Featuring former Boston guitarist Barry Goudreau and future Boston vocalist Fran Cosmo, **Orion the Hunter** recorded "So You Ran," a minor chart entry.

Billboard 200: *Orion the Hunter* (#57)
Billboard Hot 100: "So You Ran" (#58)

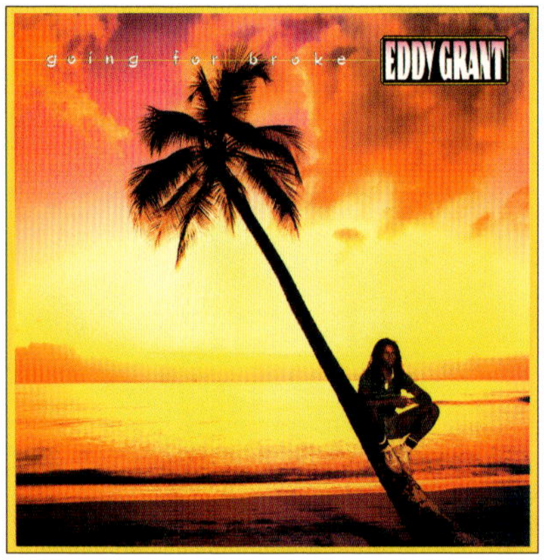

Scrapped as the theme for the feature film *Romancing the Stone*, **Eddy Grant**'s title song made the charts as a track from his own album, *Going for Broke*.

Billboard 200: *Going for Broke* (#64)
Billboard Hot 100: "Romancing the Stone" (#26)

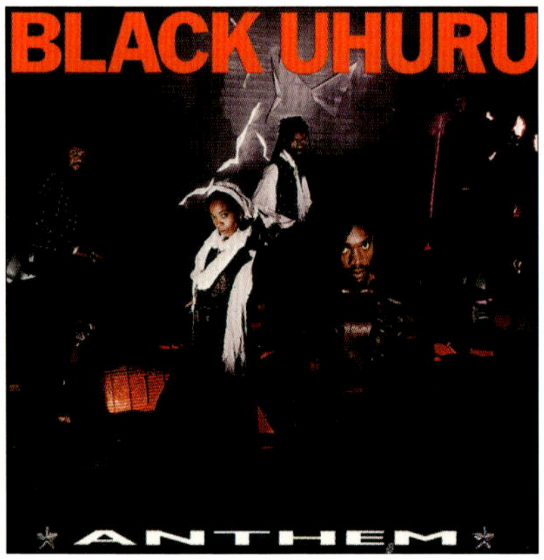

One of Jamaica's most venerable groups, **Black Uhuru** reached a peak with *Anthem*, which picked up the first-ever Grammy Award for Best Reggae Album.

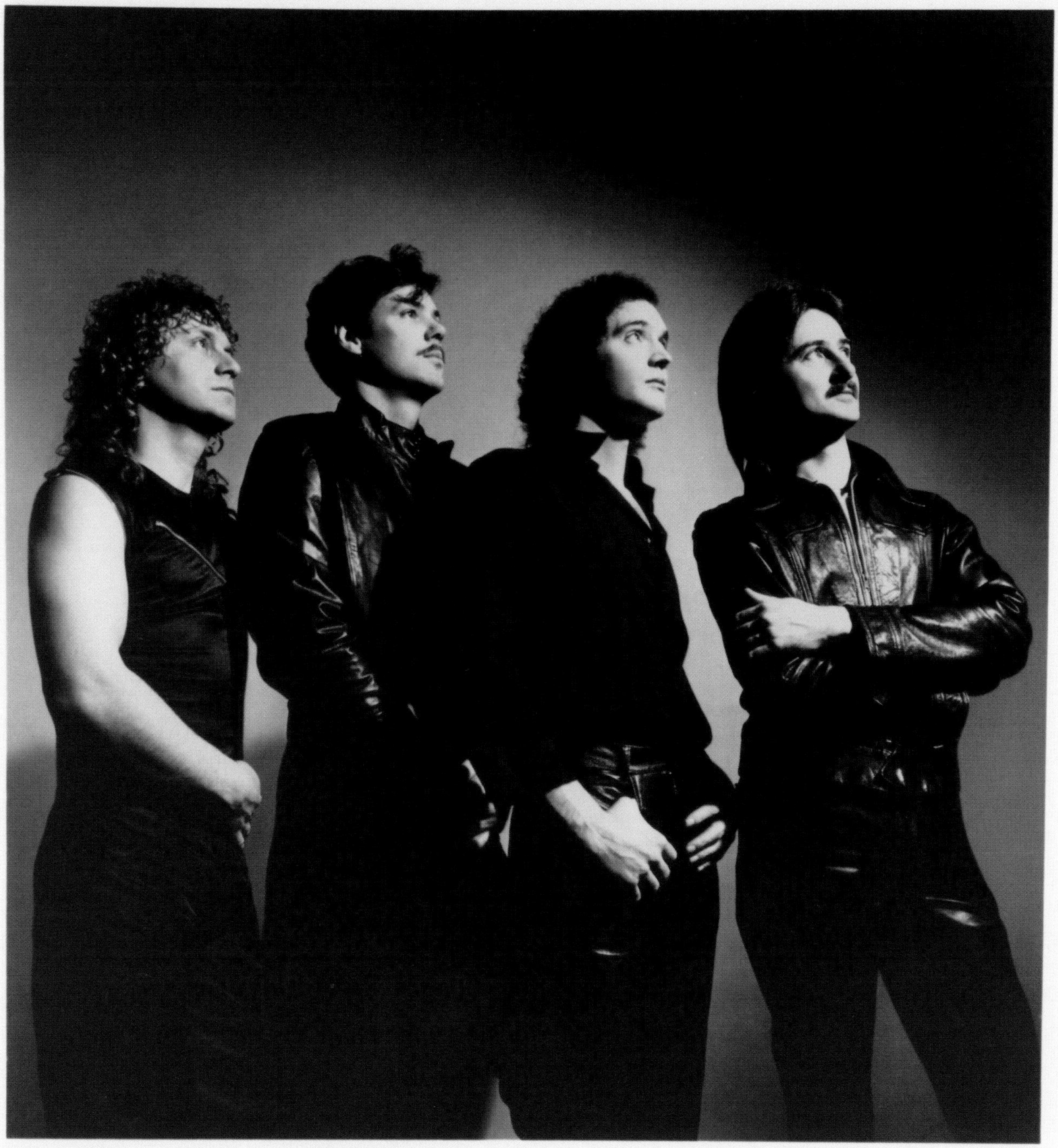

Photo: Allan Luftig

L to R: Bruce Smith; Michael DeRosier; Fran Cosmo; Barry Goudreau

ORION THE HUNTER

Portrait
8403

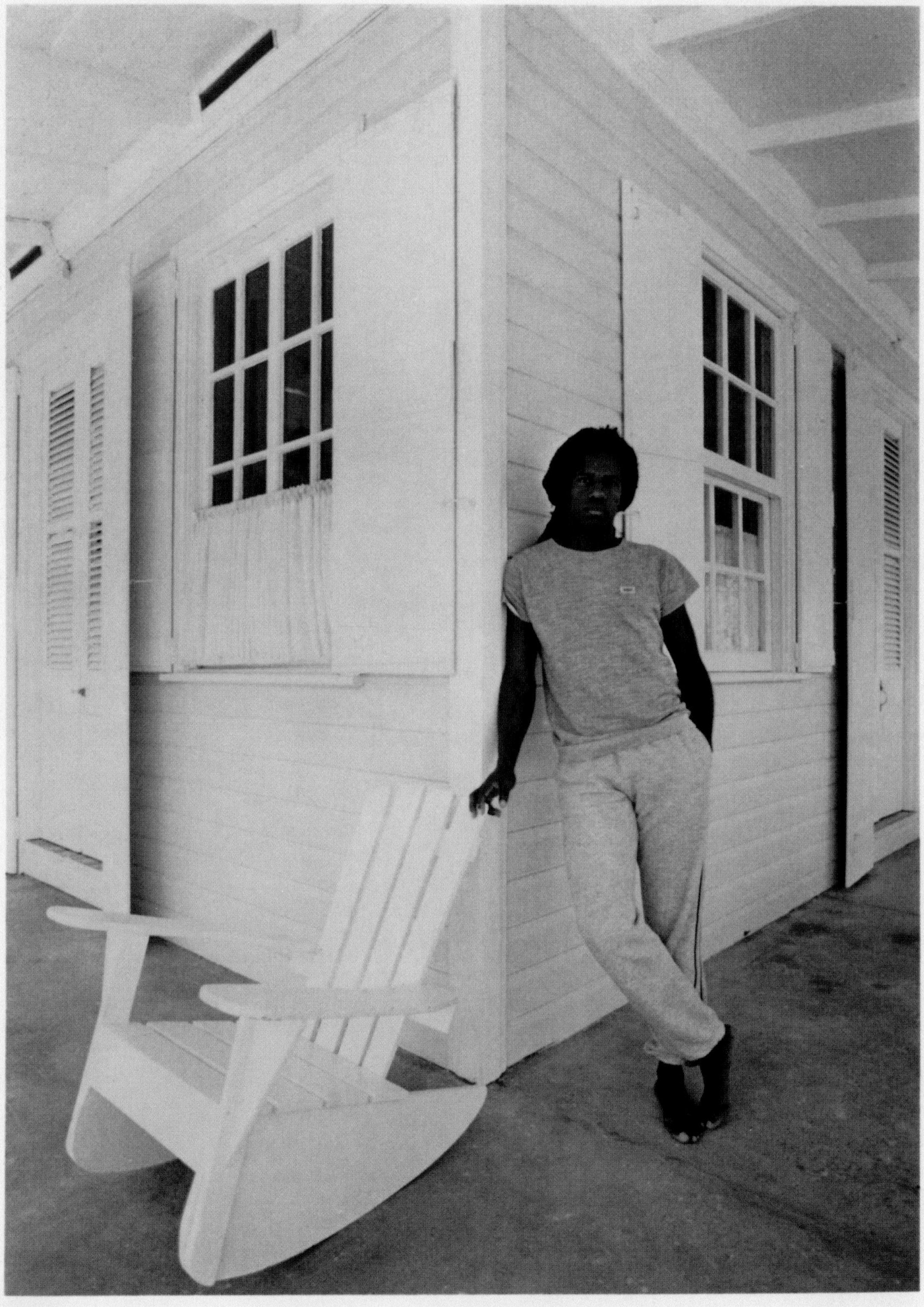

EPA

EDDY GRANT

Portrait
8405

BLACK UHURU

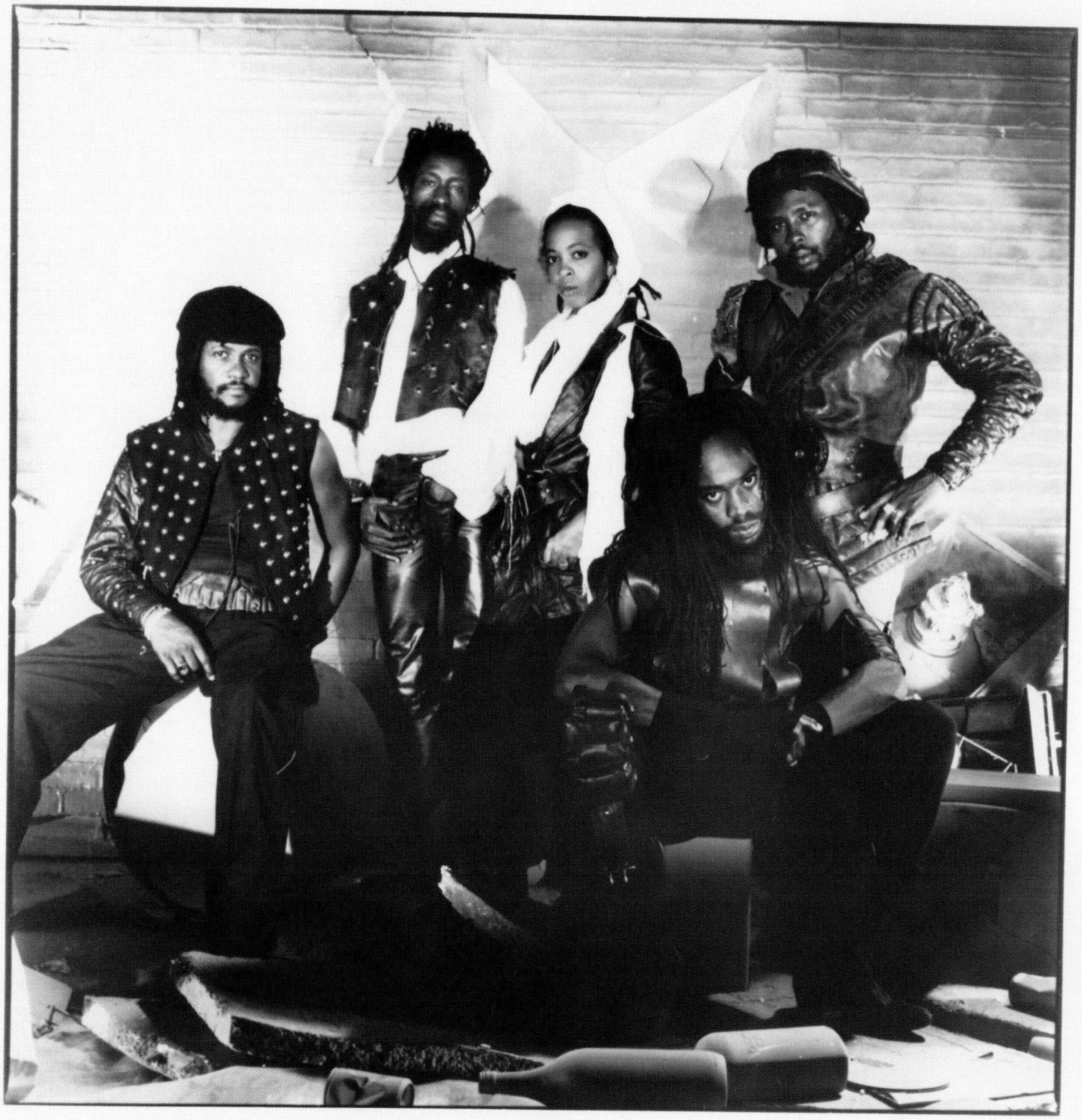

Photo Credit: MIKE PRIOR 1984

ISLAND

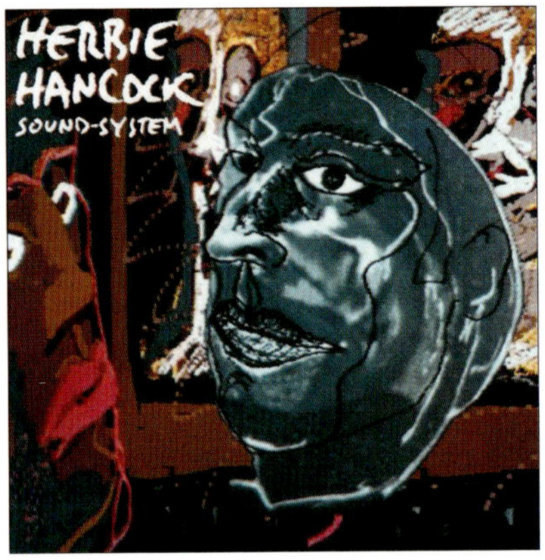

Continuing the experiments in electronic music that marked 1983's *Future Shock*, *Sound-System* was another triumph for keyboardist **Herbie Hancock**.

Billboard 200: *Sound-System* (#71)

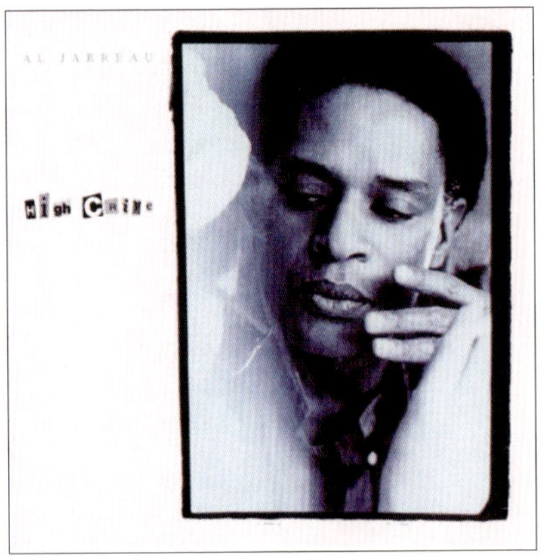

The smooth ballad "After All" fueled jazz vocalist **Al Jarreau**'s *High Crime*, crossing over to the *Billboard* pop charts and skyrocketing in the Phillipines.

Billboard 200: *High Crime* (#49)
Billboard Hot 100: "After All" (#69)

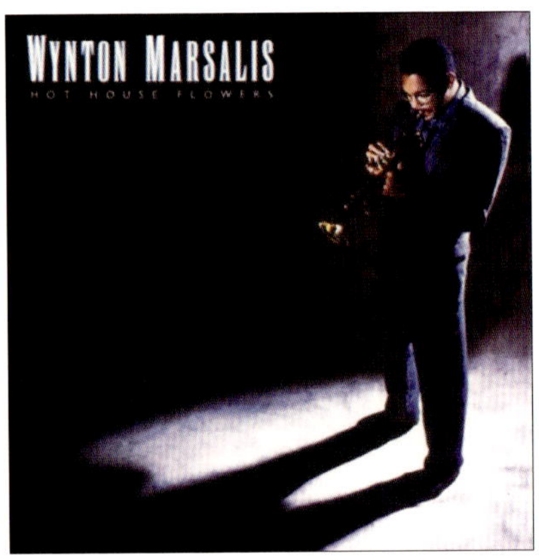

Hot House Flowers by trumpeter **Wynton Marsalis** reached No. 1 on the jazz album charts and won a Grammy for Best Jazz Instrumental Performance, Solo.

Billboard 200: *Hot House Flowers* (#90)

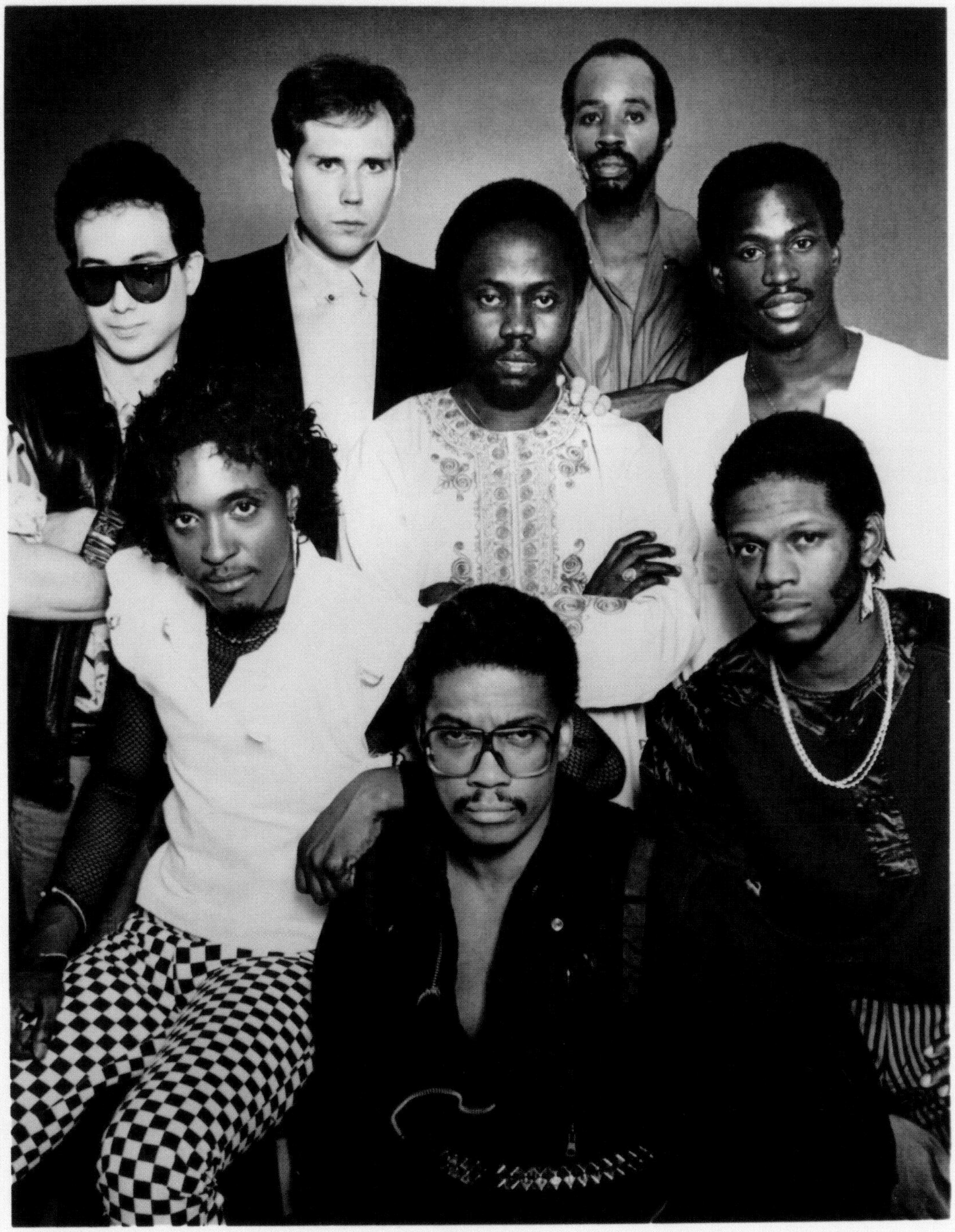

Photo Credit: Geoff Thomas

Jeff Bova
Anton Fier
Bernard Fowler
Foday Musa Suso
Herbie Hancock
J.T. Lewis
Wayne Brathwaite
D. St.

Adams Dad Management Company

827 Folsom Street San Francisco, California, 94107
(415) 777-2930

HERBIE HANCOCK
and the ROCKIT BAND

Columbia

8407

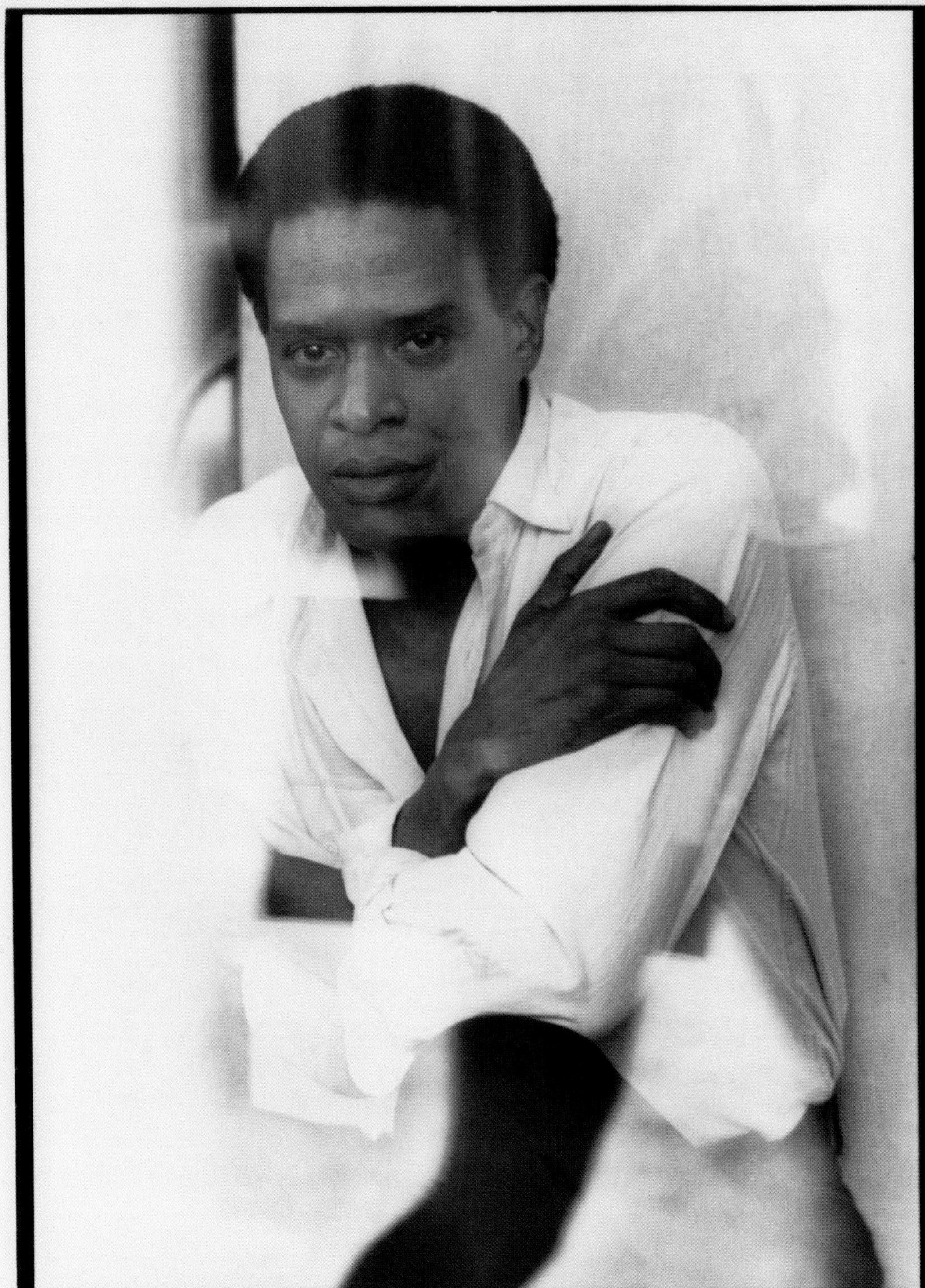

AL JARREAU

WARNER BROS.

Photo Credit: Just Loomis

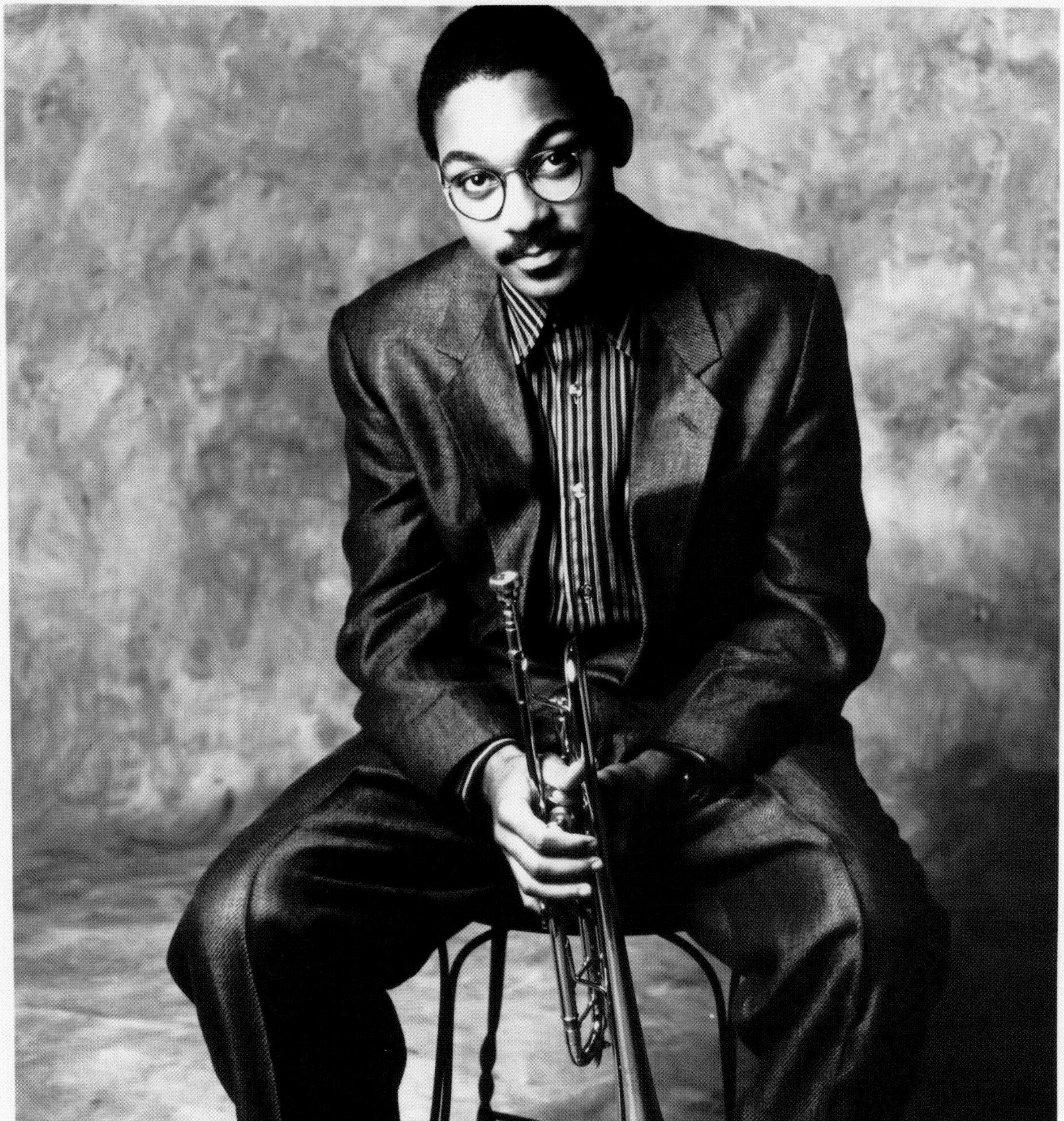

PHOTOGRAPH: CAROL FRIEDMAN

WYNTON MARSALIS

Columbia

8409

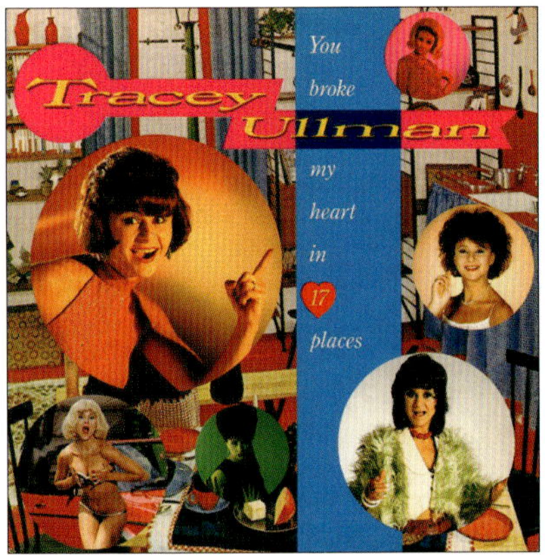

British actress-comedian **Tracey Ullman**'s Top 10 version of Kirsty MacColl's "They Don't Know" highlighted a cameo from Paul McCartney in the video.

Billboard 200: *You Broke My Heart in 17 Places* (#34);
Billboard Hot 100: "They Don't Know" (#8);
"Breakaway" (#70)

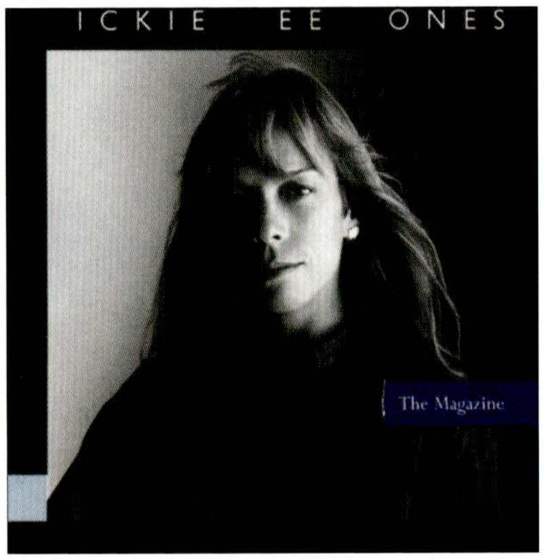

For her album *The Magazine*, **Rickie Lee Jones** wrote a batch of songs while residing in Paris, and "The Real End" made its way onto the *Billboard* pop charts.

Billboard 200: *The Magazine* (#44);
Billboard Hot 100: "The Real End" (#83)

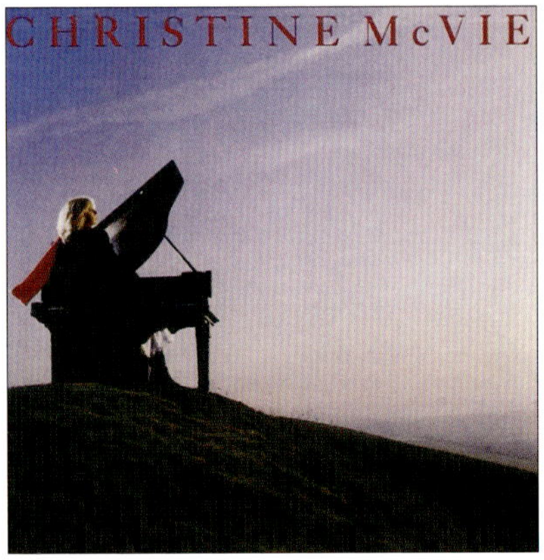

The keyboardist and singer with Fleetwood Mac since 1970, **Christine McVie** issued a second solo album and garnered a Top 10 hit, "Got a Hold on Me."

Billboard 200: *Christine McVie* (#26)
Billboard Hot 100: "Got a Hold on Me" (#10);
"Love Will Show Us How" (#30)

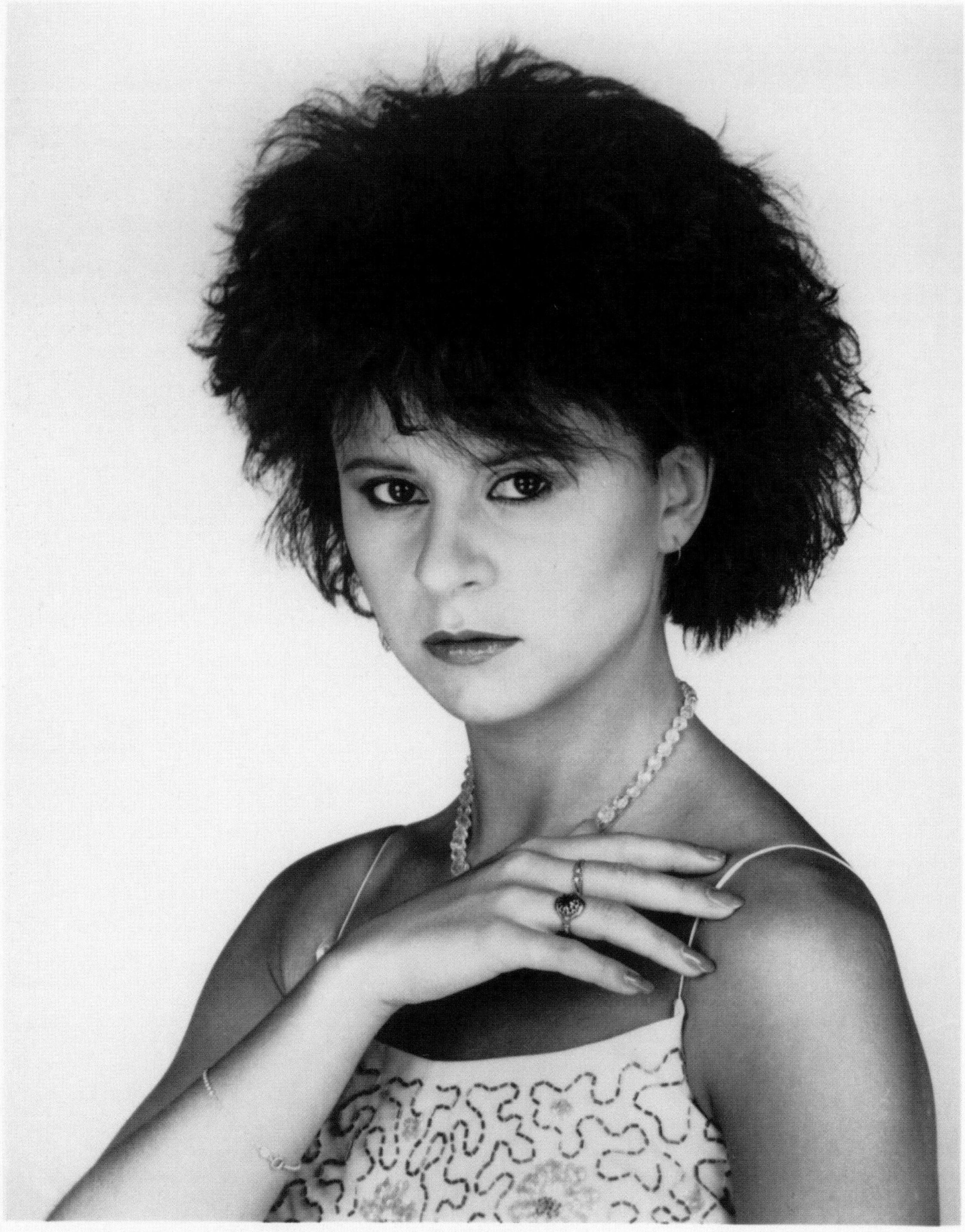

2/84

Tracey Ullman

STIFF records

MCA RECORDS

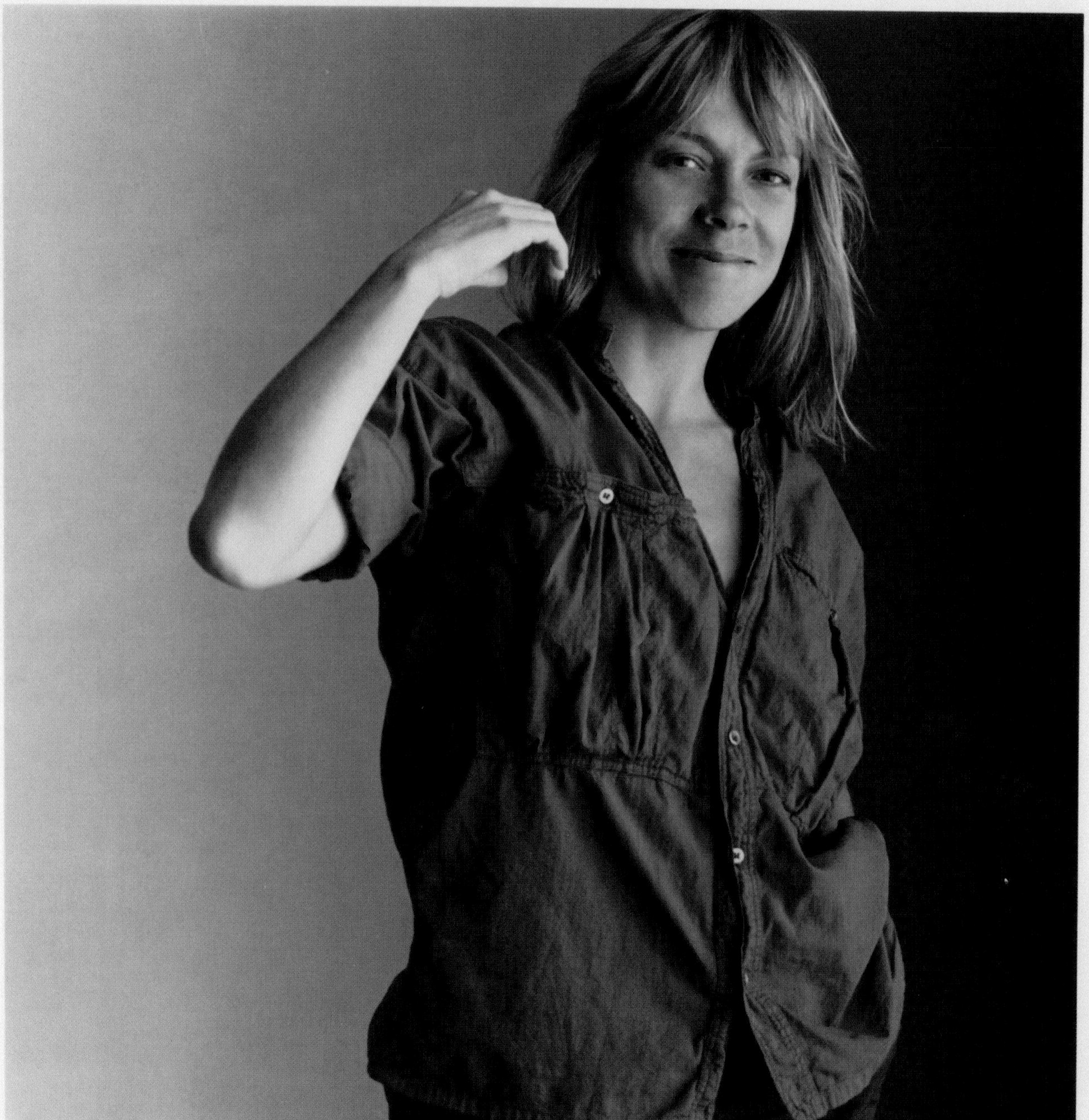

Photo Credit: Ethan Russell

RICKIE LEE JONES

WARNER BROS.

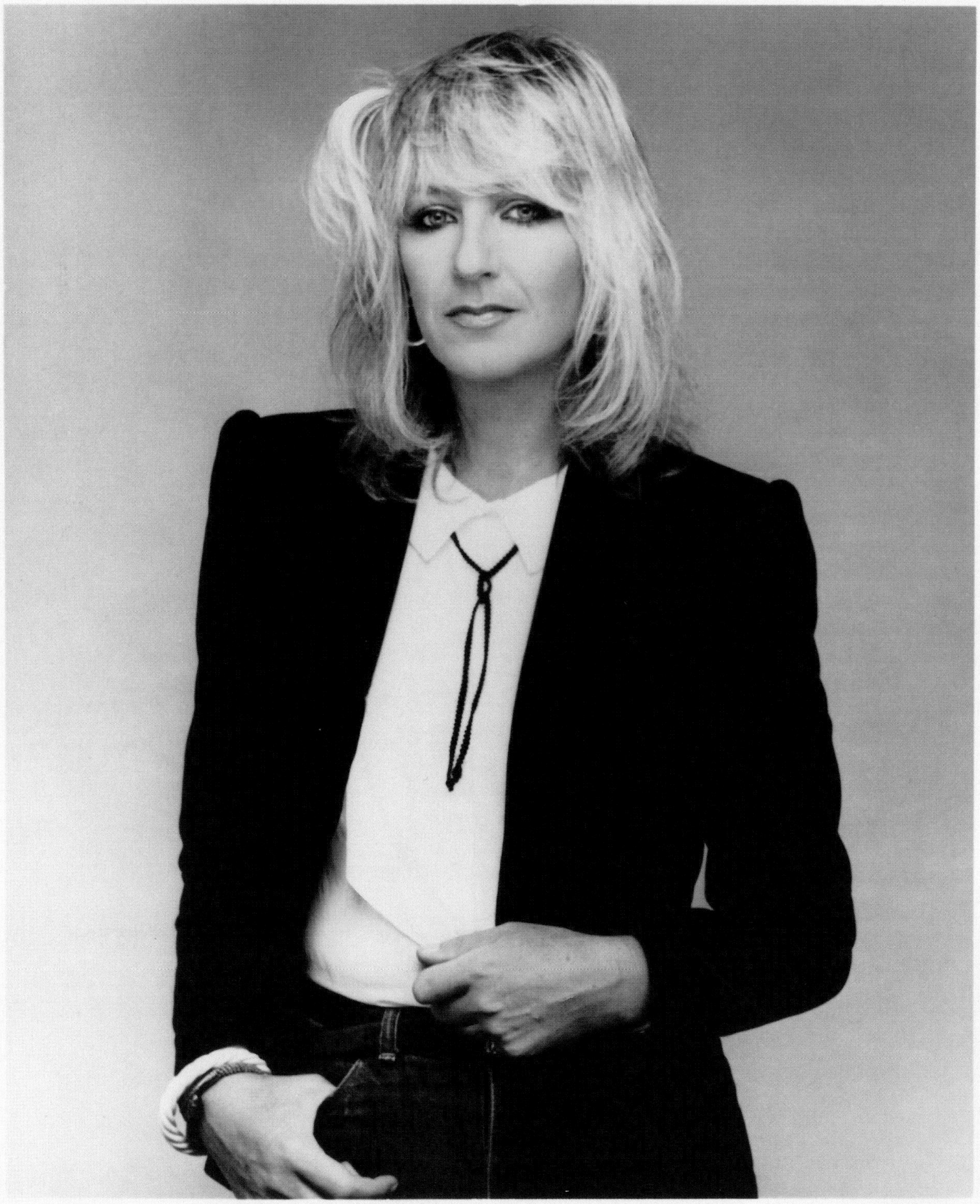

PHOTO CREDIT: SAM EMERSON

CHRISTINE McVIE

WARNER BROS.

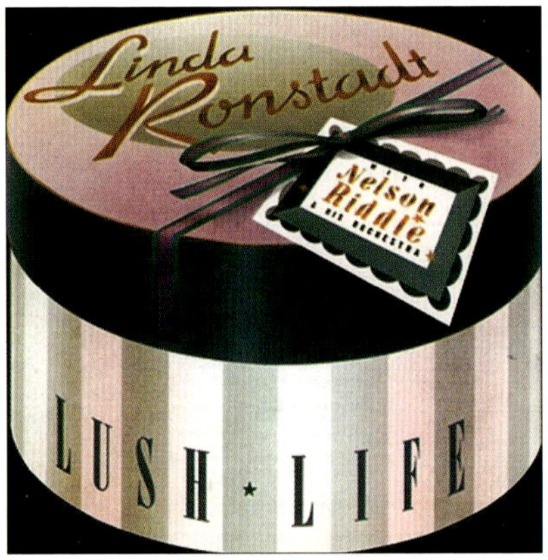

Linda Ronstadt's *Lush Life* was the second in a trio of albums featuring classic pop standards recorded in tandem with bandleader-arranger Nelson Riddle.

Billboard 200: *Lush Life* (#13)

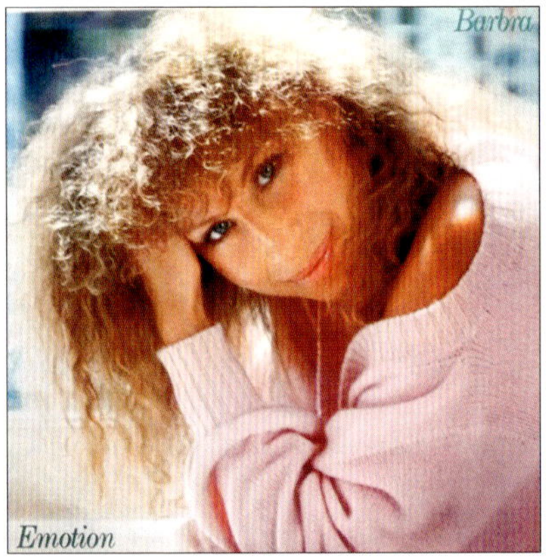

Recorded with an extensive team of producers and songwriters, Barbra Streisand's *Emotion* was her first album of contemporary material in four years.

Billboard 200: *Emotion* (#19)

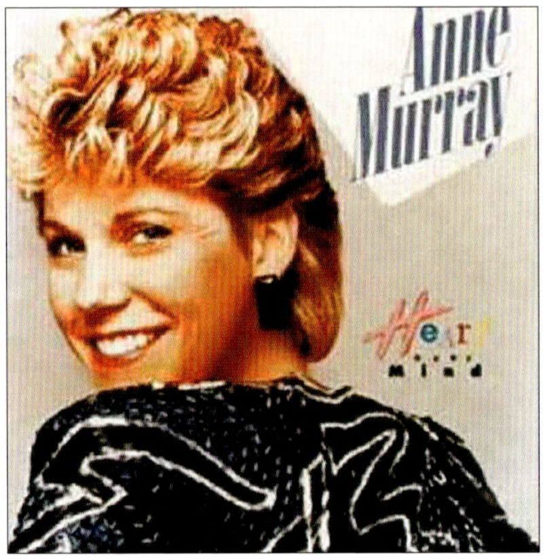

Canadian Anne Murray continued her string of No. 1 country singles with "Nobody Loves Me Like You Do," a pairing with singer-songwriter Dave Loggins.

Billboard 200: *Heart over Mind* (#92)

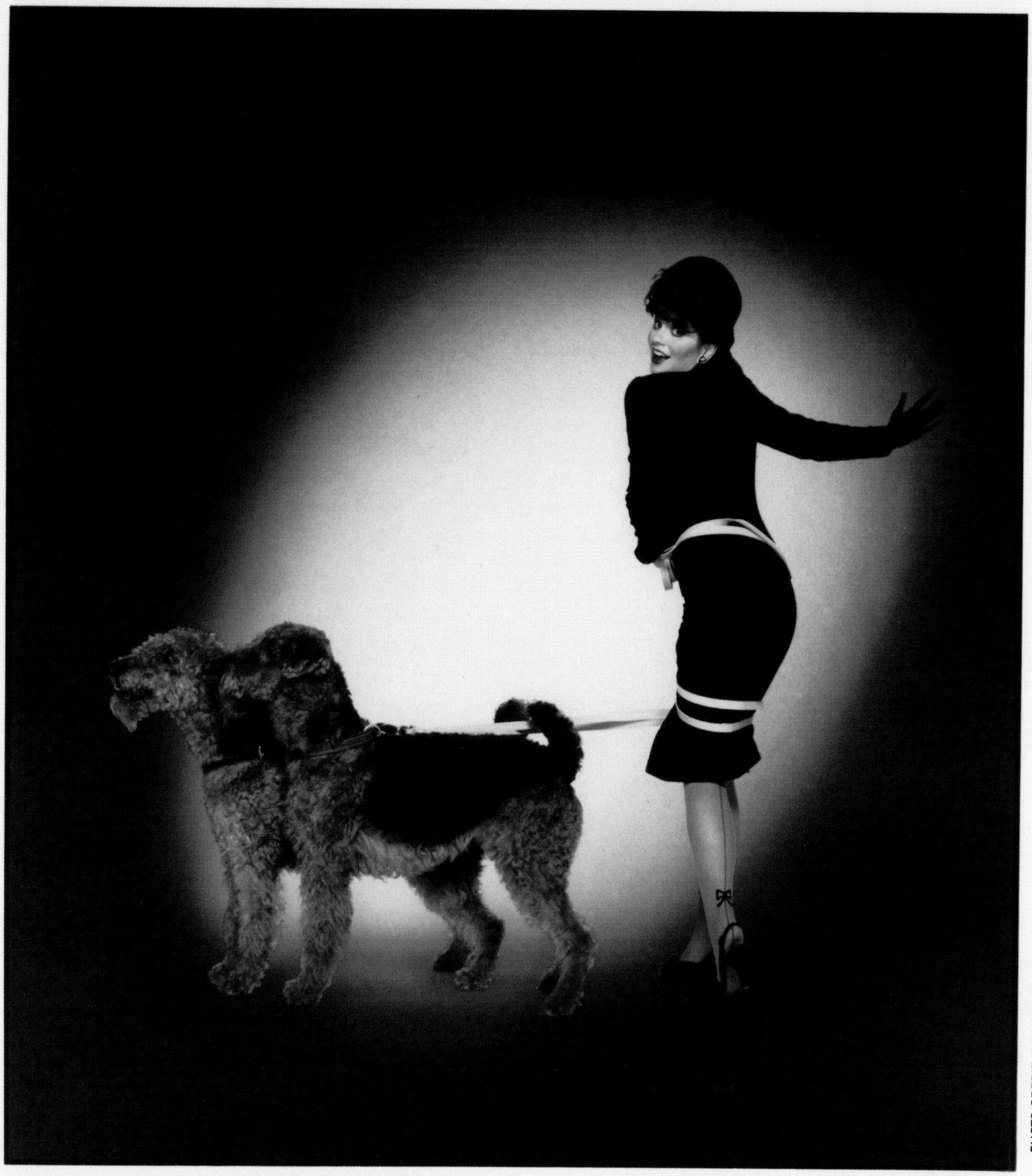

PHOTO CREDIT: BOB BLAKEMAN/1984

Linda Ronstadt

ASYLUM

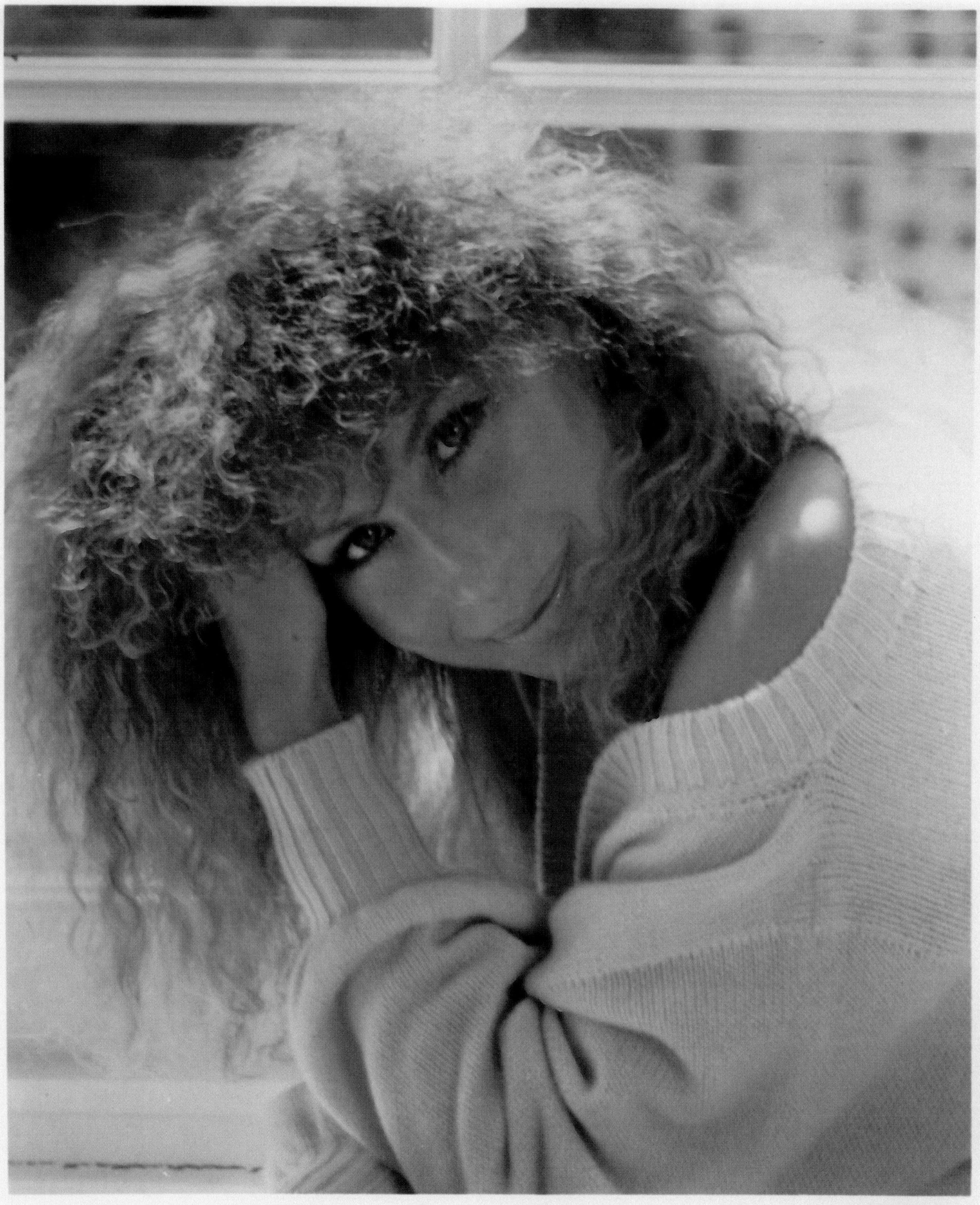

Photo Credit: Greg Gorman

BARBRA STREISAND

Columbia

8410

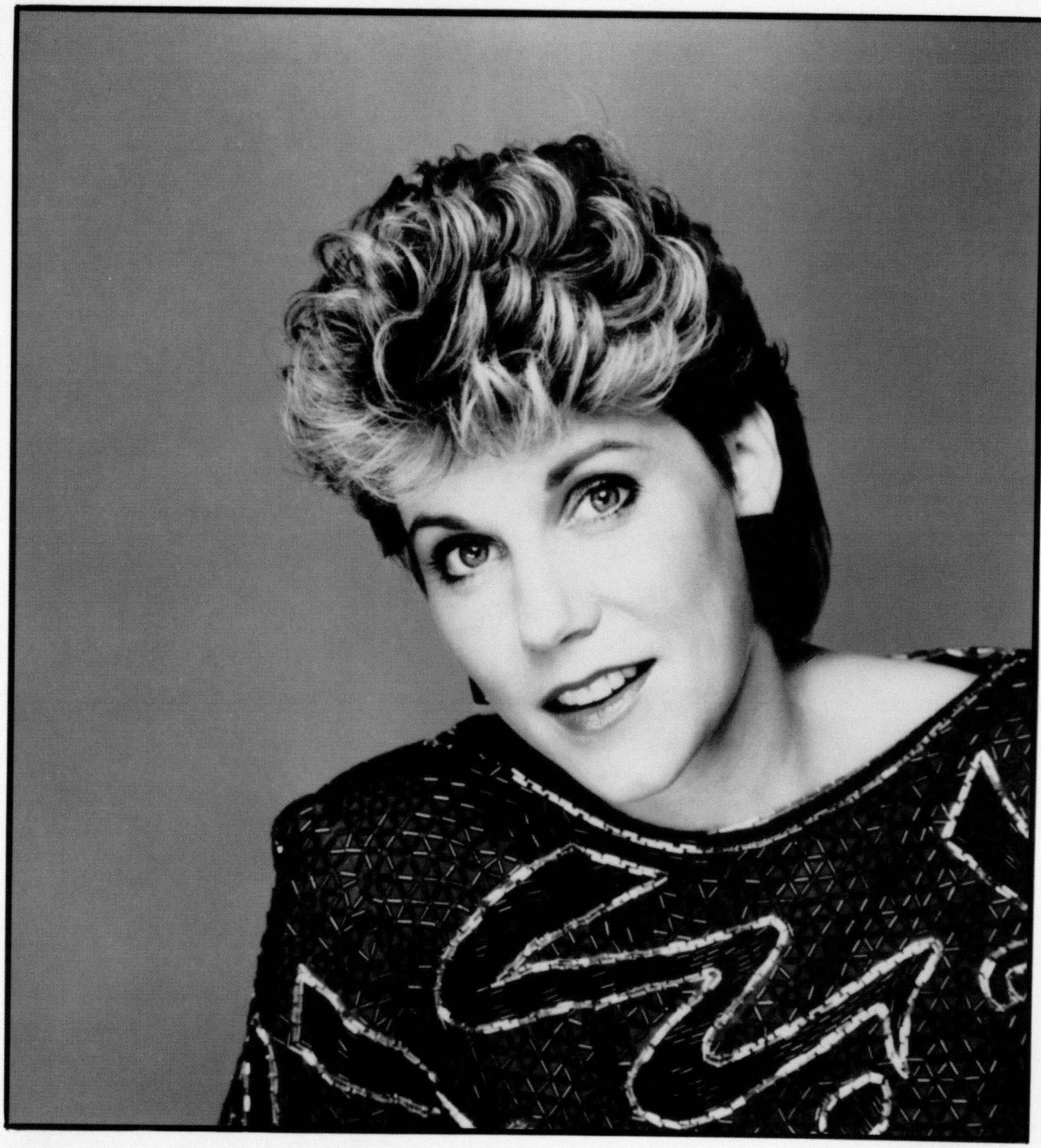

Photo: Bill King, New York / 1984

ANNE MURRAY

Capitol Records

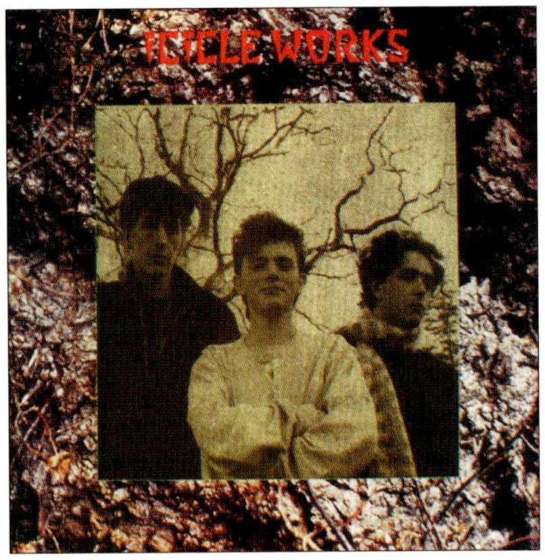

A Liverpool trio led by singer-songwriter Ian McNabb, **Icicle Works** scored its lone Top 40 hit on the US charts with "Whisper to a Scream (Birds Fly)."

Billboard 200: *Icicle Works* (#40)
Billboard Hot 100: "Whisper to a Scream (Birds Fly)" (#37)

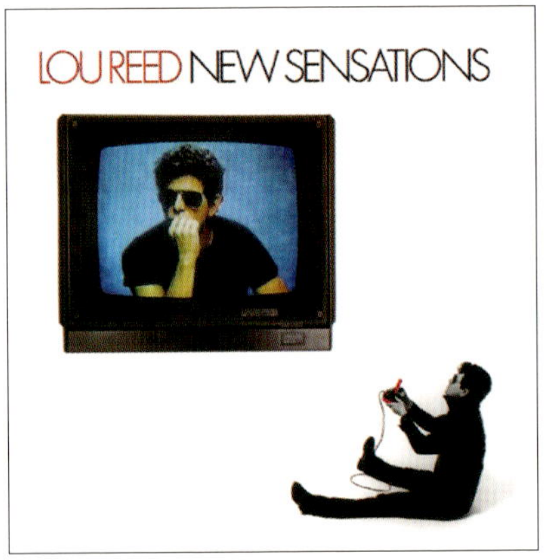

Lou Reed commenced his *New Sensations* album with the unexpectedly sanguine "I Love You, Suzanne," which was placed into heavy rotation on MTV.

Billboard 200: *New Sensations* (#56)

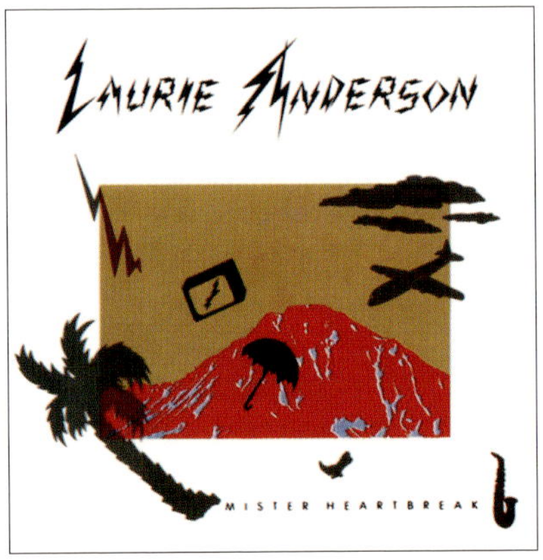

Arising as America's most recognized performance artist, **Laurie Anderson** intrigued and entertained with the accessible, pop-oriented *Mister Heartbreak*.

Billboard 200: *Mister Heartbreak* (#60)

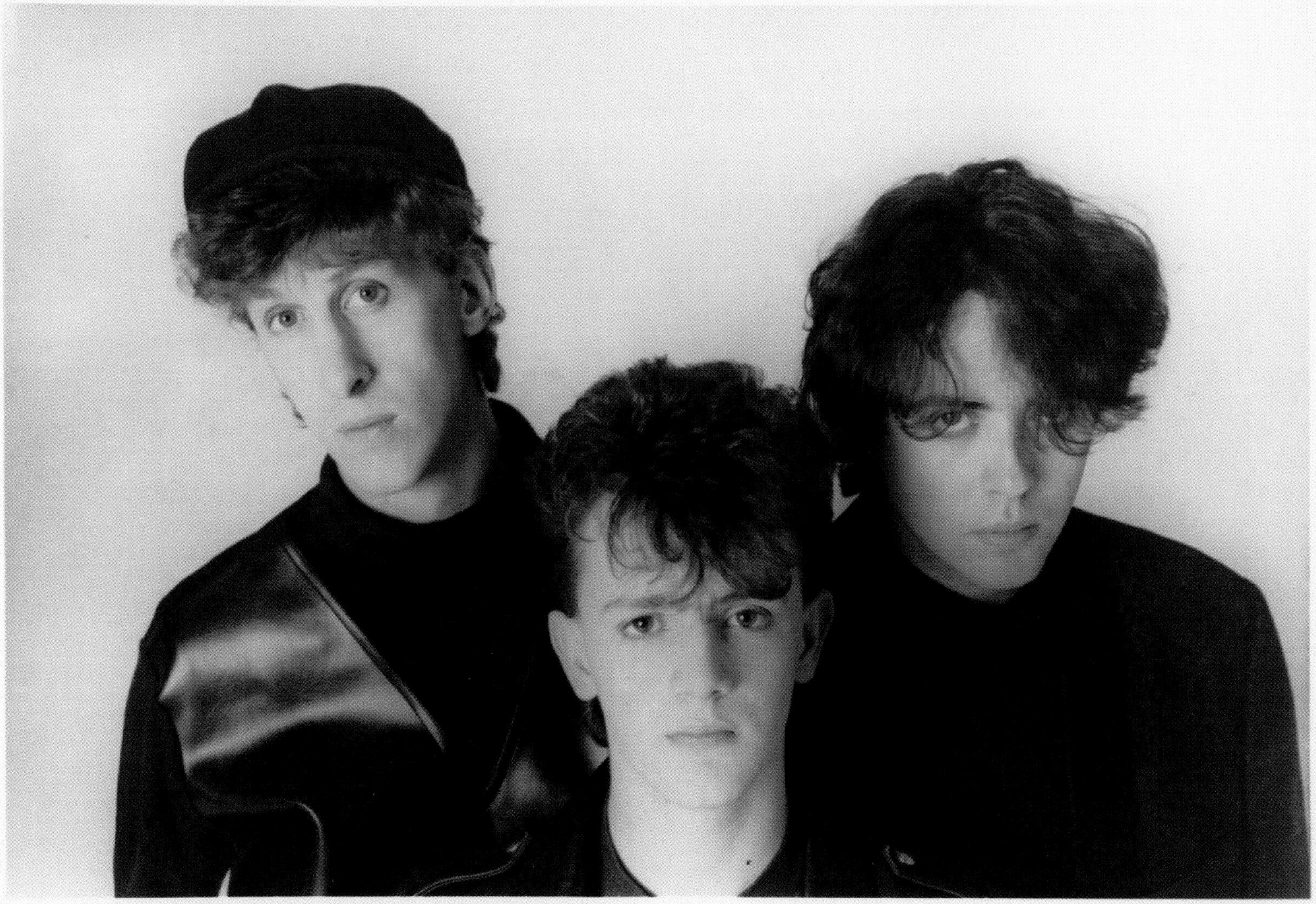

ICICLE WORKS

ARISTA

Beggars Banquet

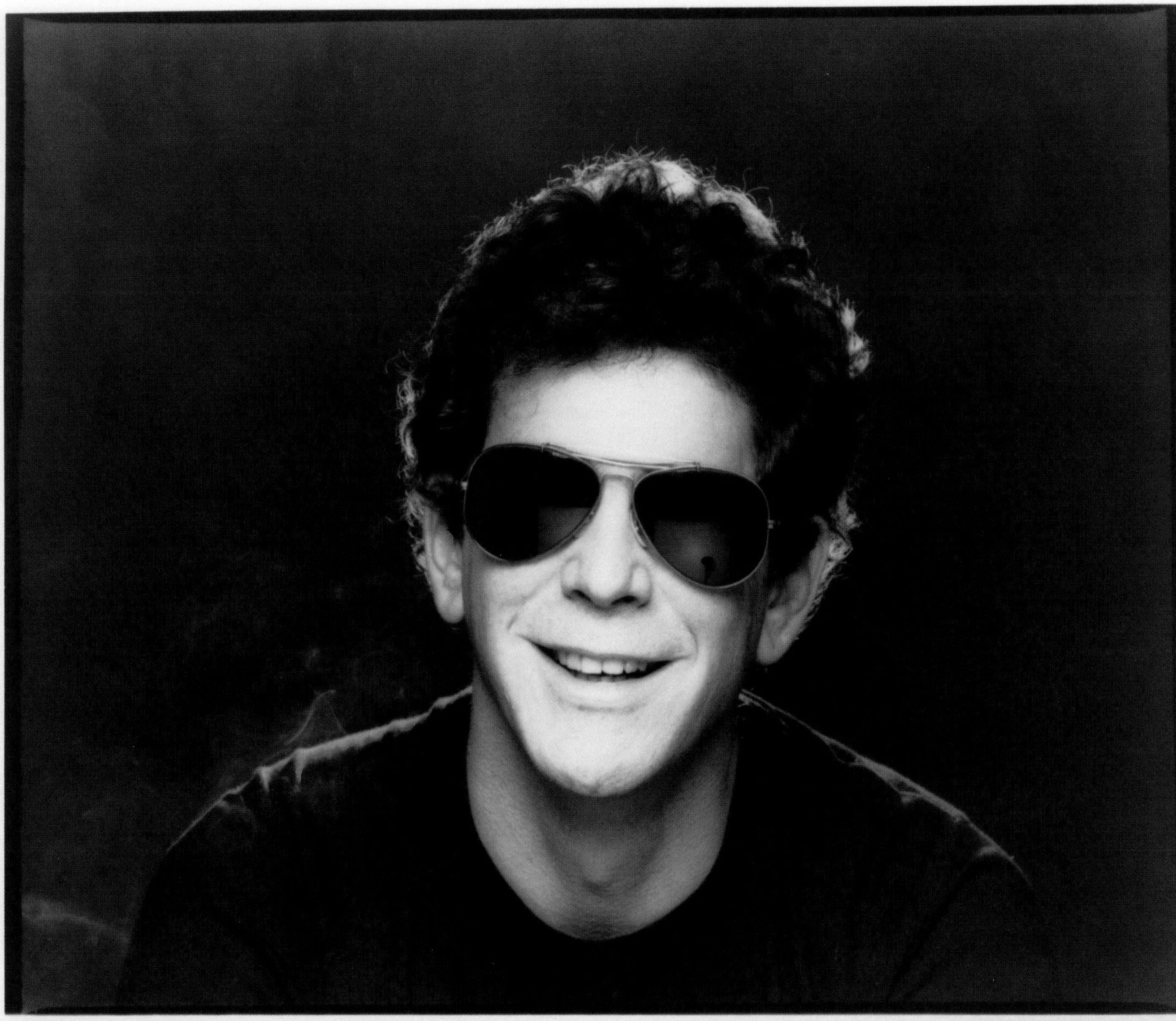

LOU REED

RCA Records and Cassettes

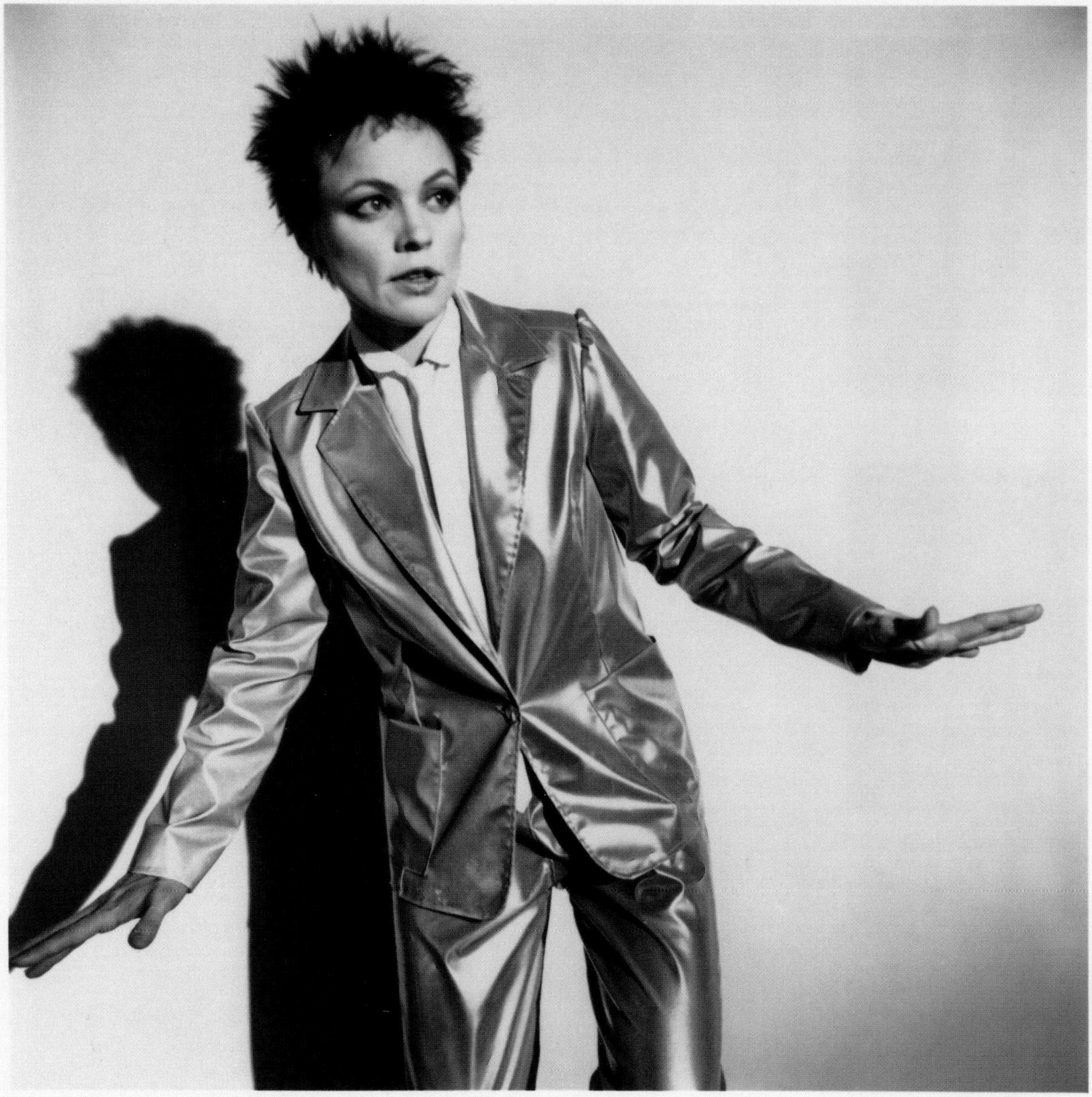

PHOTO CREDIT: GEORGE HOLZ

LAURIE ANDERSON

WARNER BROS.

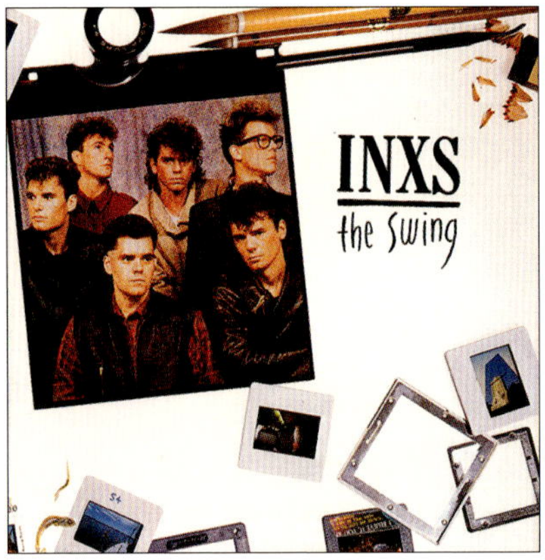

A product of Australia's pub scene, **INXS** amplified its profile around the world with *The Swing* and "Original Sin," a lead single recorded in New York City.

Billboard 200: *The Swing* (#52)
Billboard Hot 100: "Original Sin" (#58);
"I Send a Message" (#77)

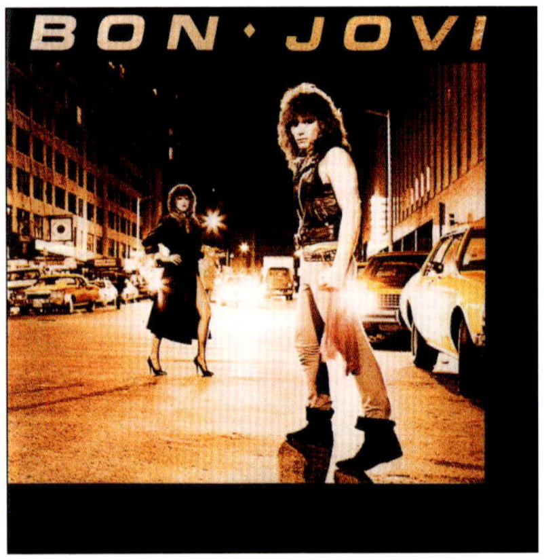

The original demo of "Runaway" led to the formation of **Bon Jovi**, the release of the New Jersey group's eponymous debut album and its first Top 40 hit.

Billboard 200: *Bon Jovi* (#43)
Billboard Hot 100: "Runaway" (#39);
"She Don't Know Me" (#48)

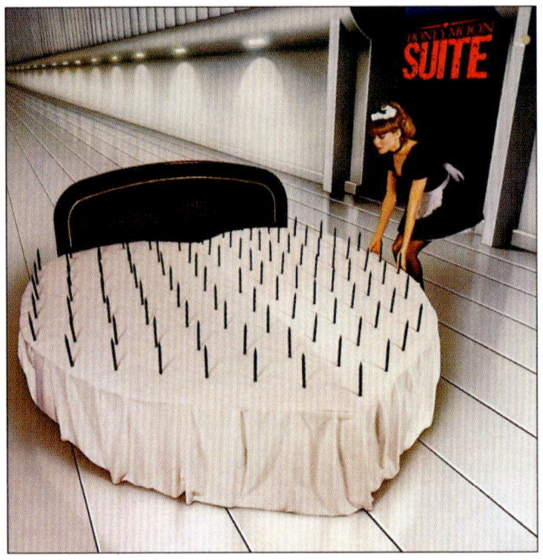

Honeymoon Suite's self-titled debut release generated a smash in "New Girl Now," earning the Canadian hard-rock band a significant following in the US.

Billboard 200: *Honeymoon Suite* (#60)
Billboard Hot 100: "New Girl Now" (#57)

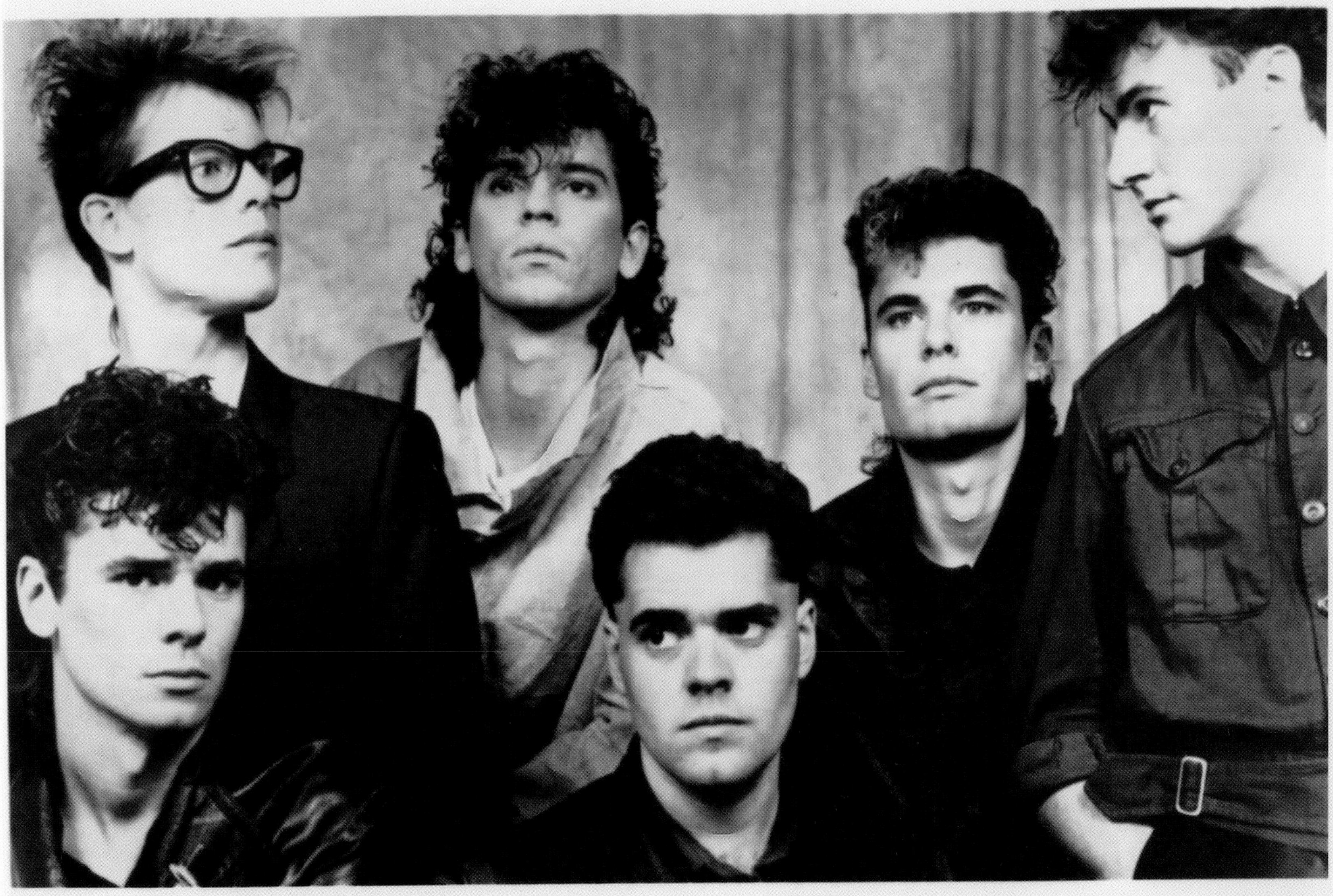

TIM FARRISS KIRK PENGILLY MICHAEL HUTCHENCE ANDREW FARRISS JON FARRISS GARRY GARY BEERS

INXS

ATCO

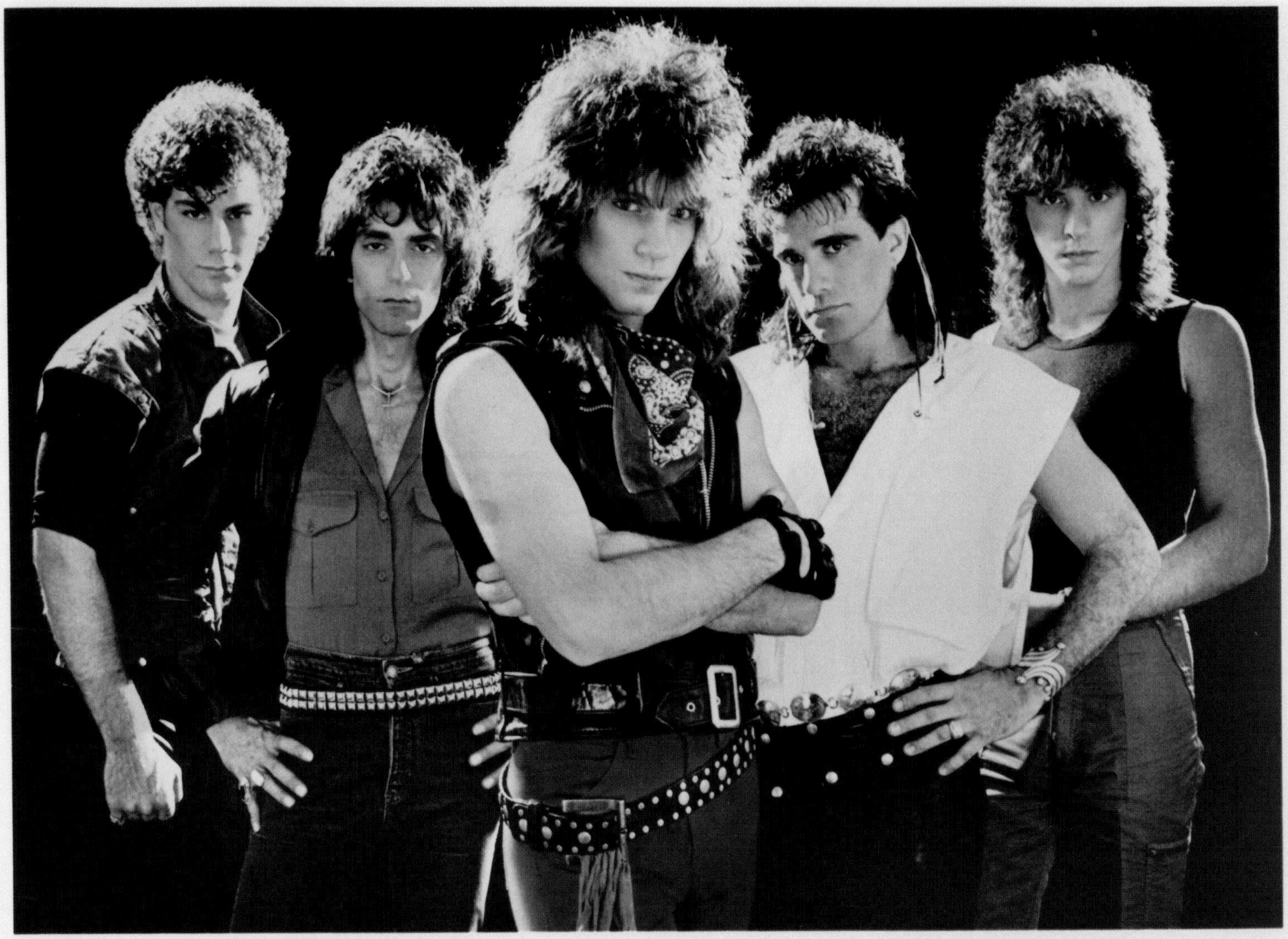

DAVID RASHBAUM
ALEC JOHN SUCH
JON BON JOVI
RICHIE SAMBORA
TICO TORRES

BON JOVI

Mercury

PolyGram Records

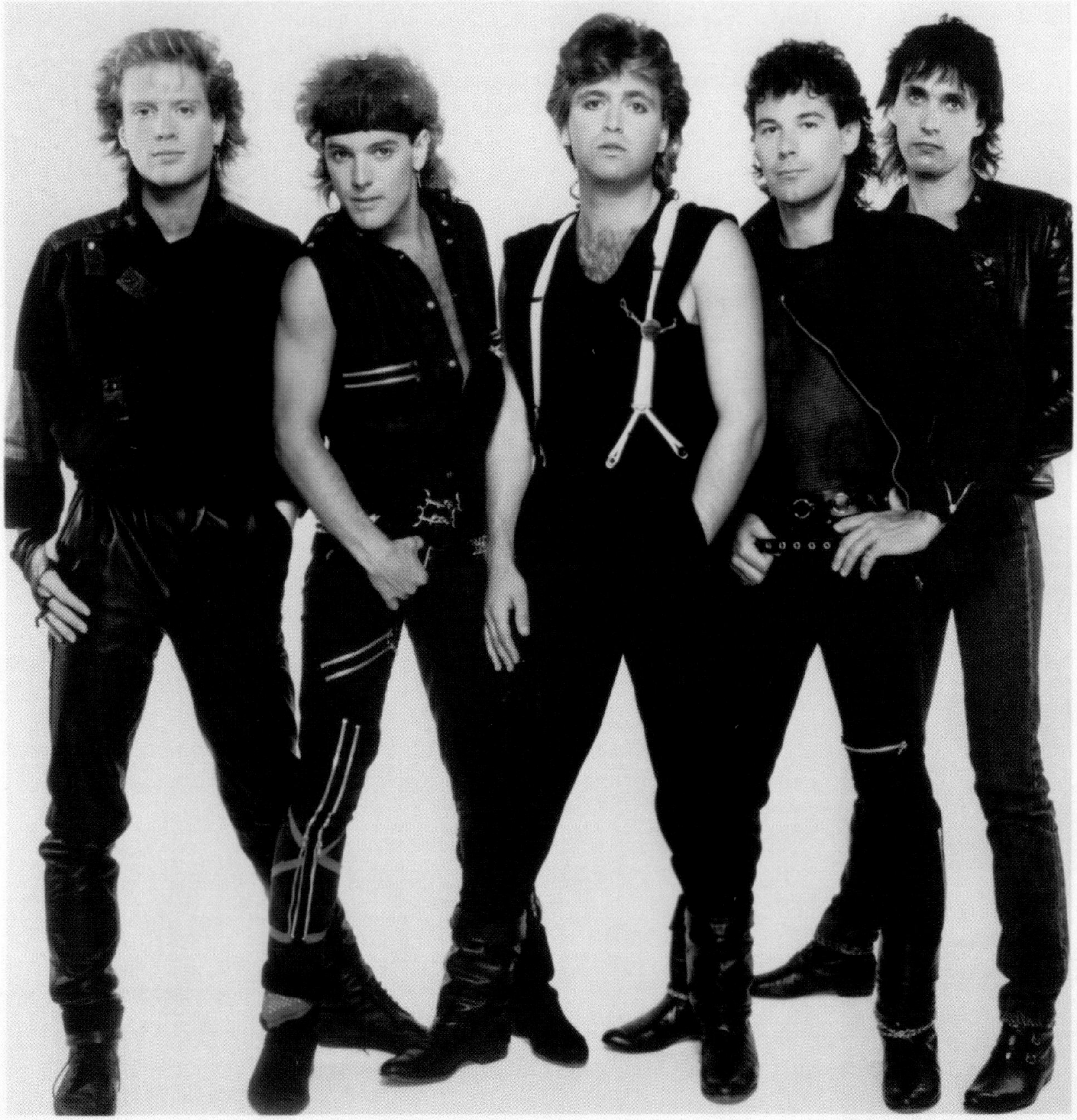

Photo by: Patrick Harbron

RAY COBURN DERRY GREHAN JOHNNY DEE GARY LALONDE DAVE BETTS

HONEYMOON SUITE

WARNER BROS.

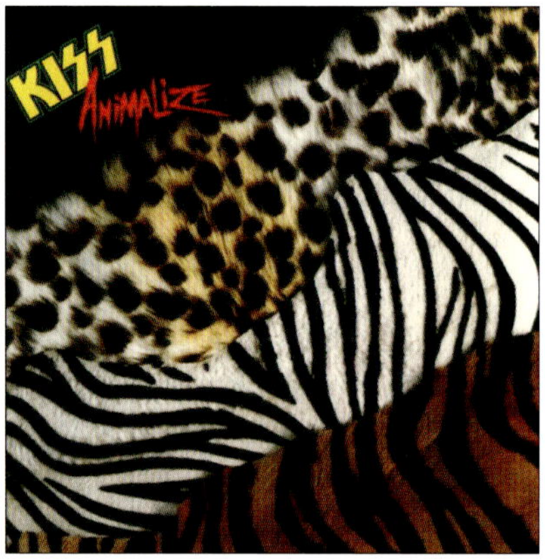

Featured on the *Animalize* album, Mark St. John fell ill with a form of inflammatory arthritis and became the third lead guitarist to exit **Kiss** in two years.

Billboard 200: *Animalize* (#19)
Billboard Hot 100: "Heaven's on Fire" (#49)

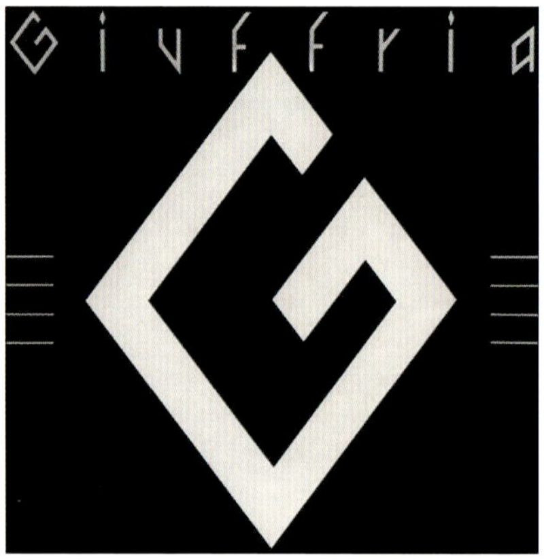

Giuffria, the outfit led by keyboard player Gregg Giuffria after his departure from Angel, managed a Top 20 triumph with the wistful "Call to the Heart."

Billboard 200: *Giuffria* (#26)
Billboard Hot 100: "Call to the Heart" (#15);
"Lonely in Love" (#57)

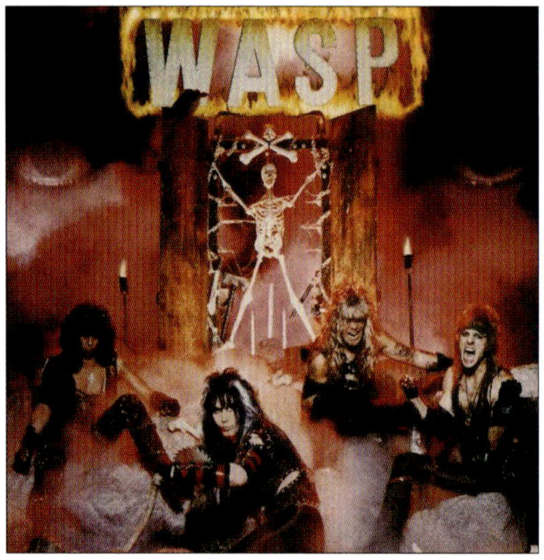

Capitol Records expunged **W.A.S.P.**'s debut single, the controversial "Animal (Fuck Like a Beast)," from the Los Angeles shock-rock quartet's first album.

Billboard 200: *W.A.S.P.* (#74)

KISS®

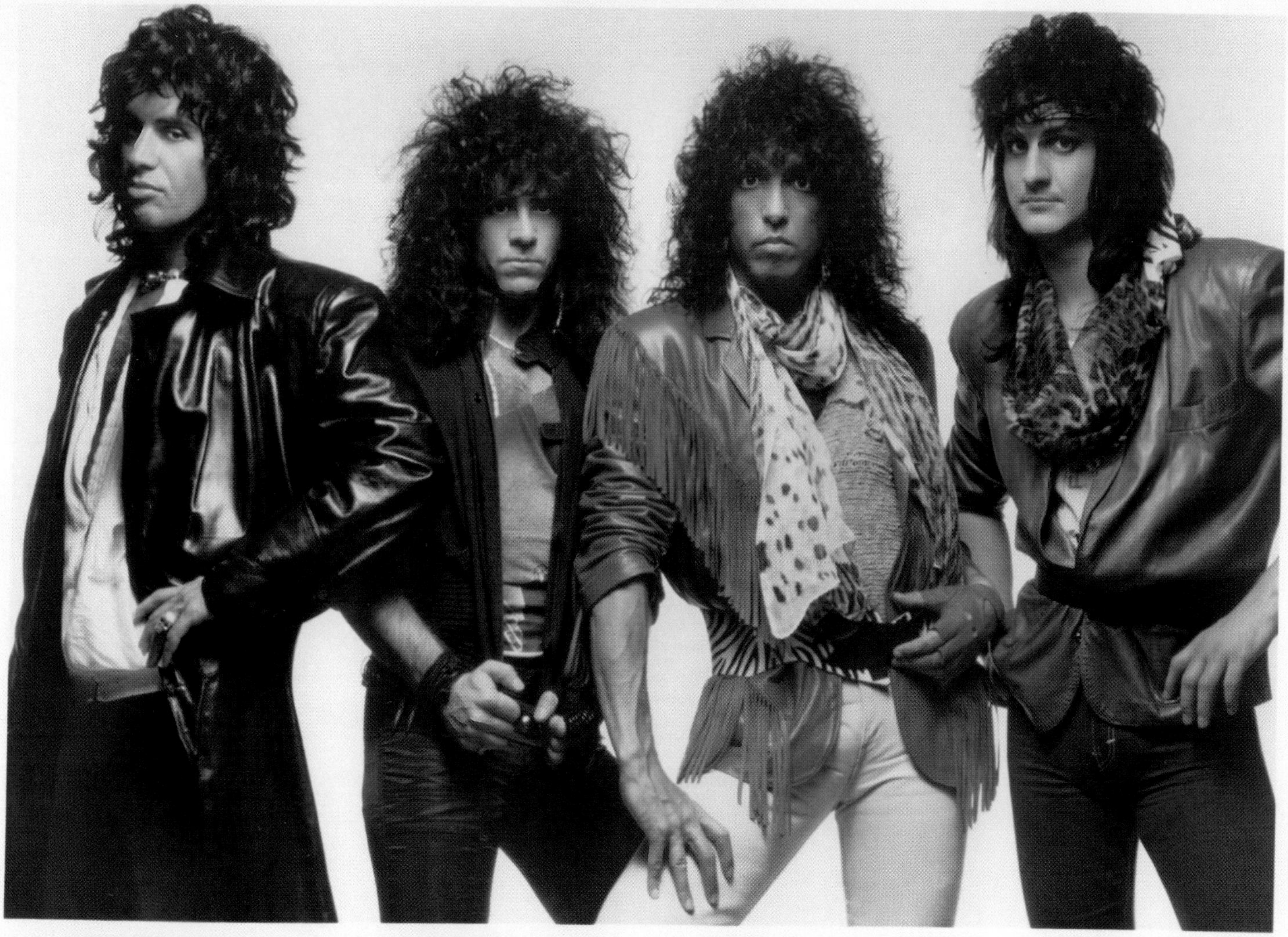

GENE SIMMONS ERIC CARR PAUL STANLEY MARK ST. JOHN

PolyGram Records

Mercury RECORDS
810 SEVENTH AVENUE NYC 10019

BOOKING AGENCY: AMERICAN TALENT INTERNATIONAL
888 SEVENTH AVENUE NYC 10019

GENERAL CONTACT: GLICKMAN/MARKS MANAGEMENT
655 MADISON AVENUE NYC 10021 (212) 752-7455

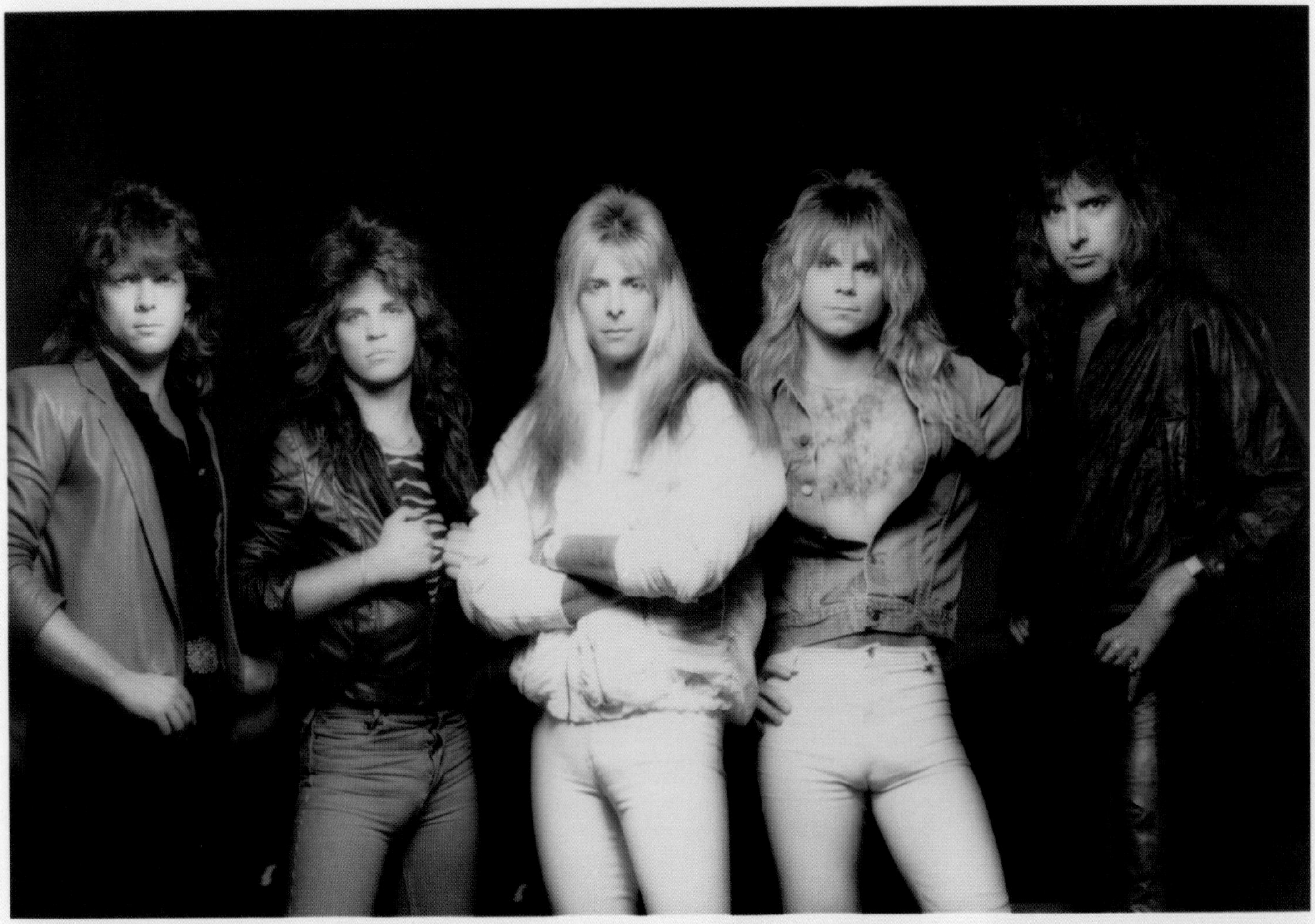

CHUCK WRIGHT CRAIG GOLDY GREGG GIUFFRIA DAVID GLEN EISLEY ALAN KRIGGER

GIUFFRIA

CAMEL RECORDS INC.

MCA RECORDS

BULLET MANAGEMENT
8255 SUNSET BLVD.
SUITE 103
LOS ANGELES, CA 90046
(213) 654-6661

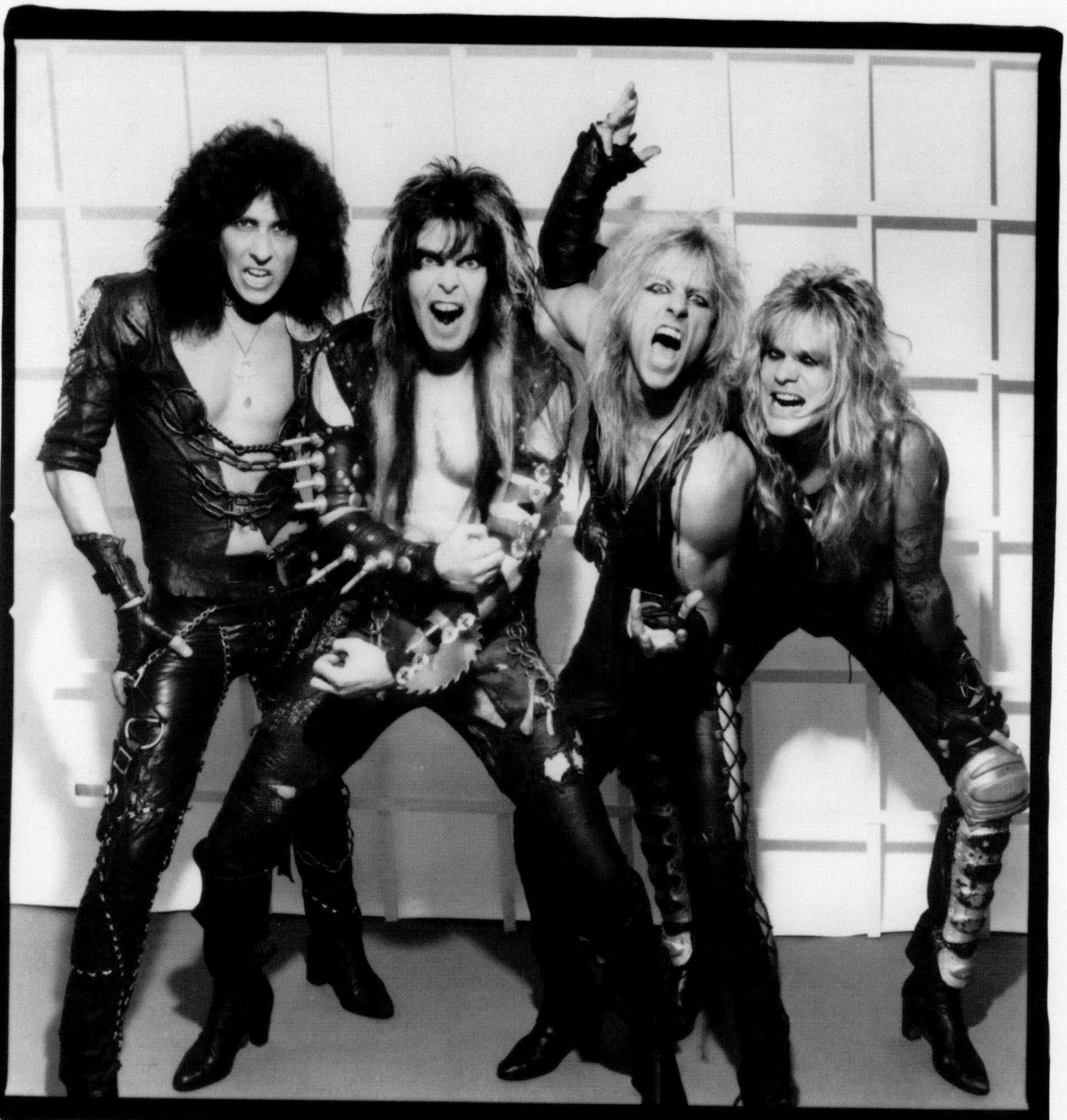

Photo: Moshe Brakha / 1984

W.A.S.P.

Capitol Records

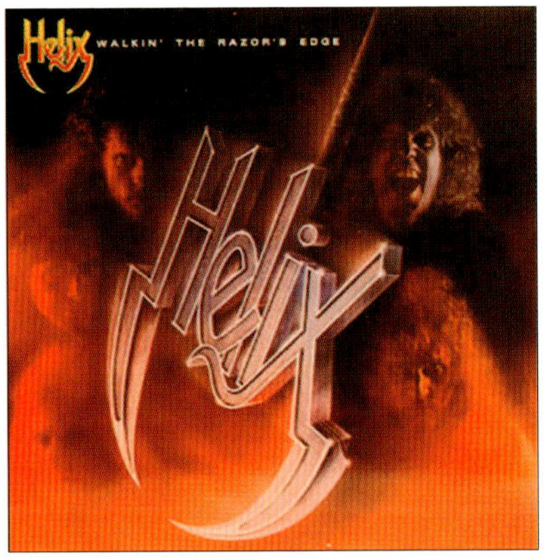

Boasting the hit "Rock You," *Walkin' the Razor's Edge* put the Canadian heavy-metal quintet **Helix** on the verge of a mainstream breakthrough in the US.

Billboard 200: *Walkin' the Razor's Edge* (#69)

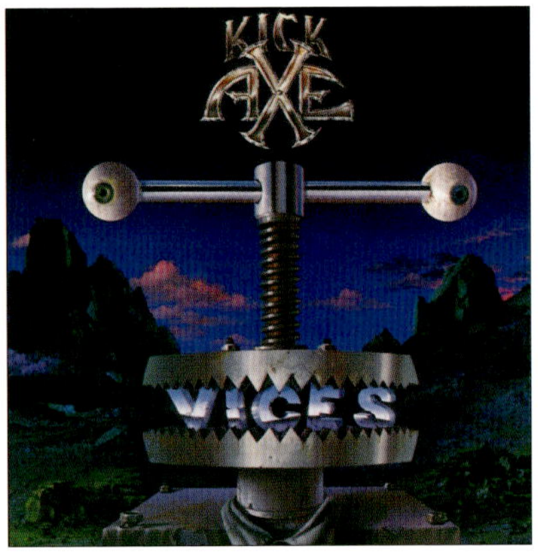

Kick Axe released a debut album, *Vices*, which produced "Heavy Metal Shuffle," a near-smash single for the rowdy rockers from Regina, Saskatchewan.

Billboard 200: *Vices* (#126)

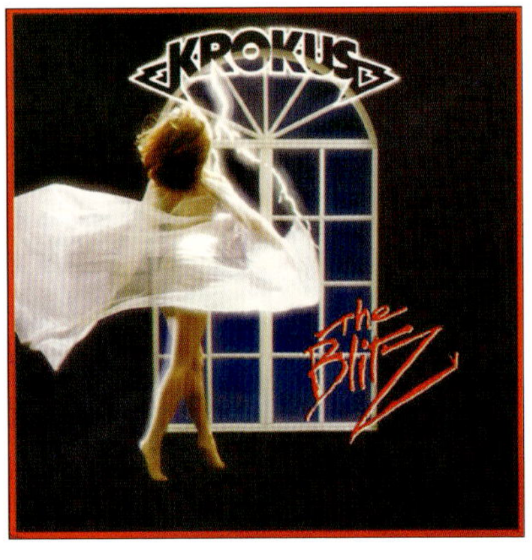

With the single "Midnite Maniac," the hard-rock band **Krokus** emerged as the first act to come out of Switzerland and enter the *Billboard* Hot 100 chart.

Billboard 200: *The Blitz* (#31)
Billboard Hot 100: "Midnite Maniac" (#71)

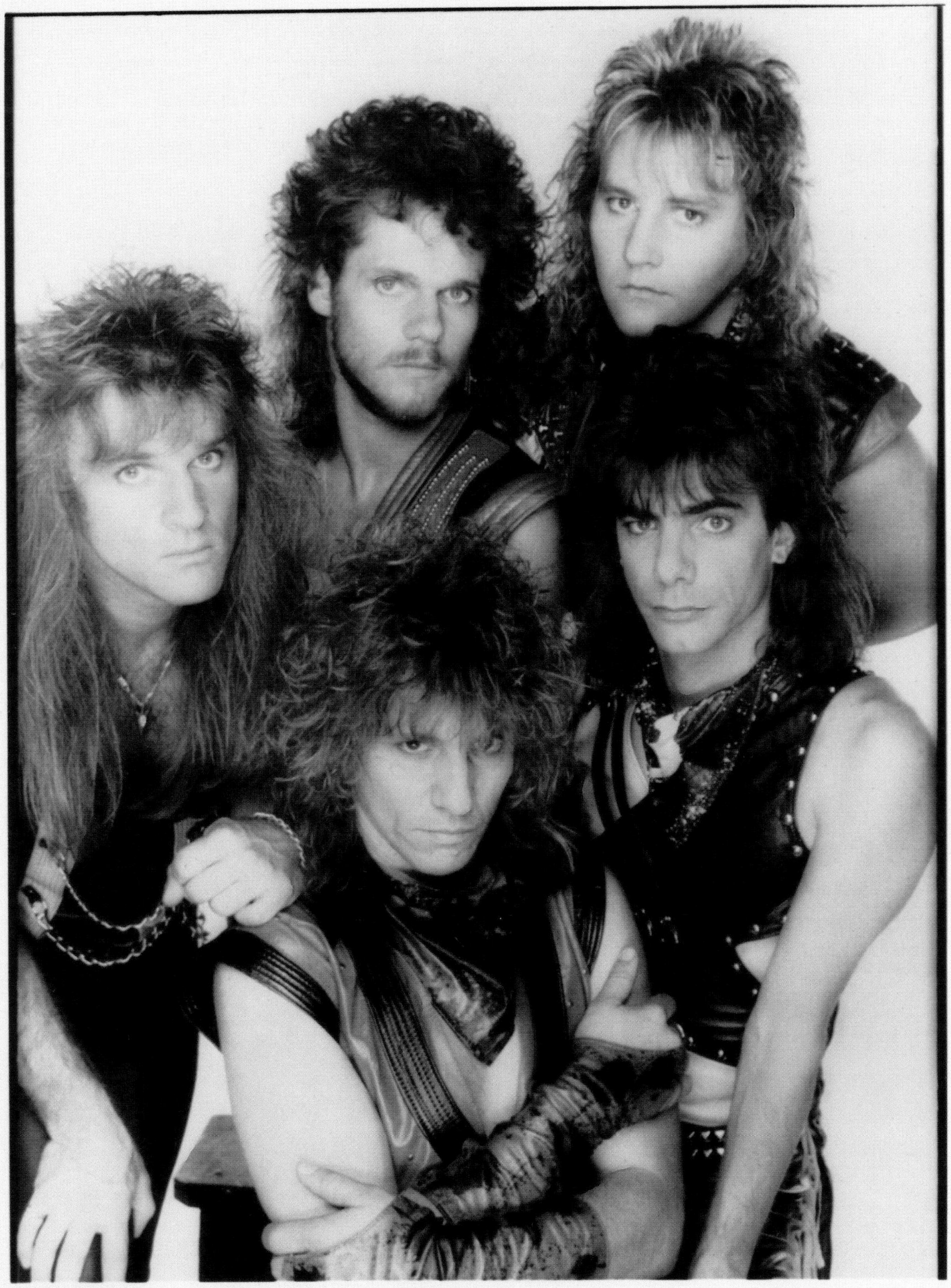

Helix

Capitol Records

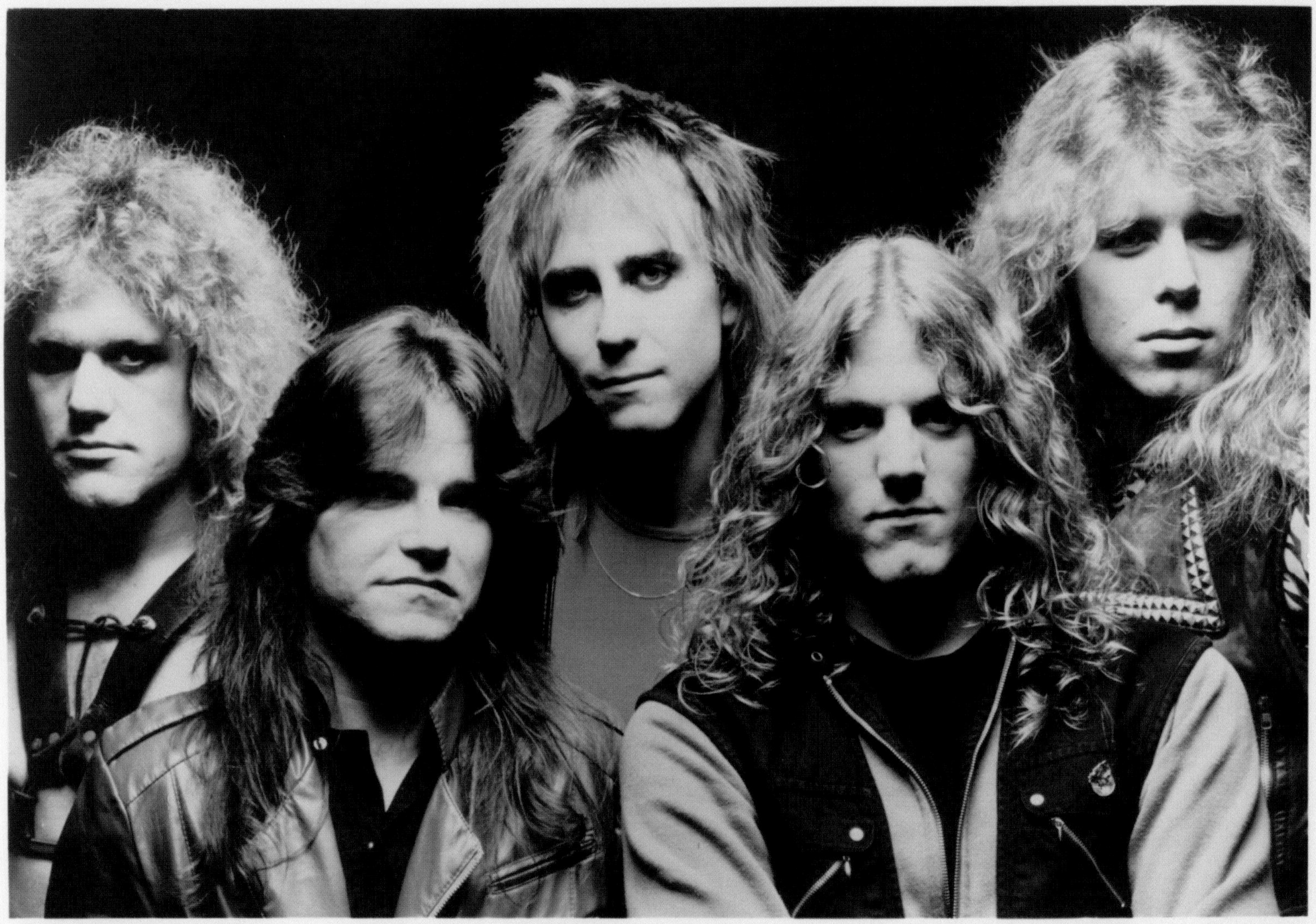

PASHA

KICK AXE

EPA
EPIC PORTRAIT ASSOCIATED
8405

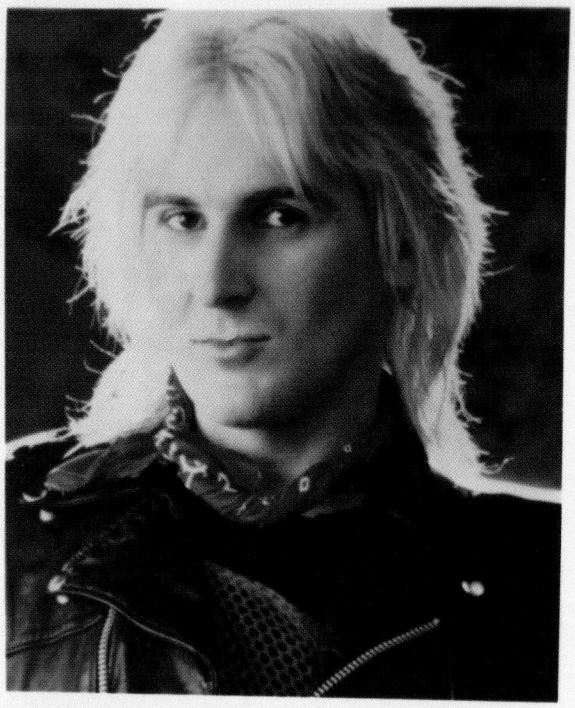 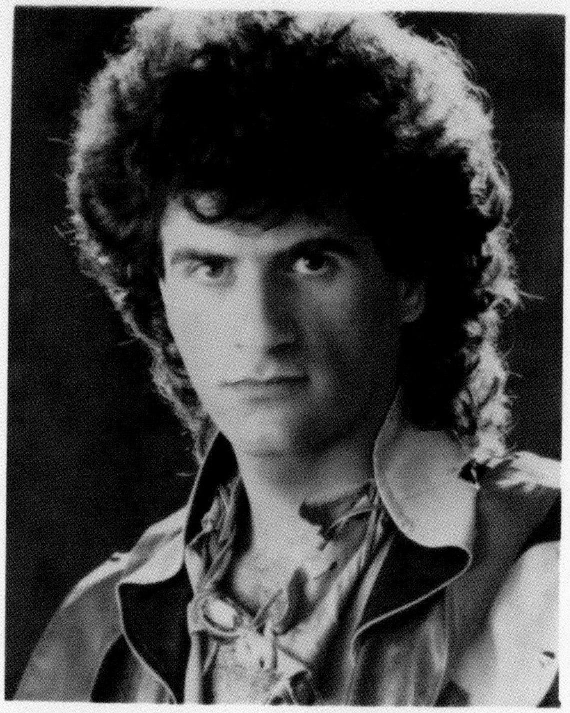

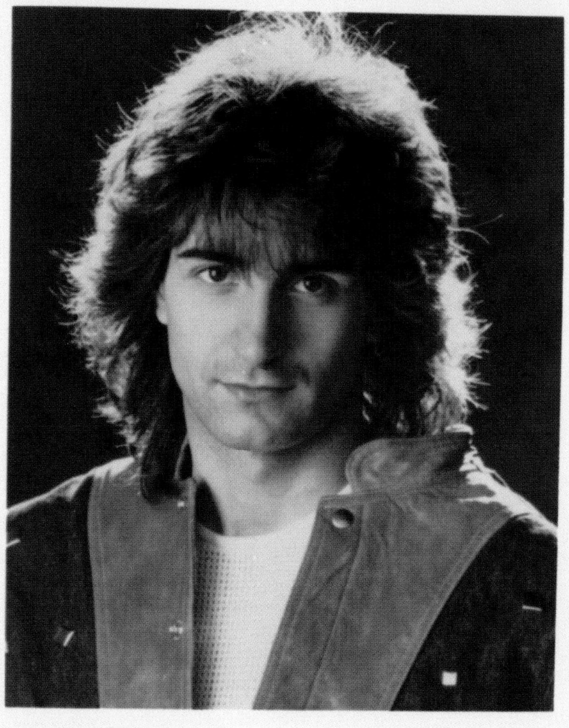 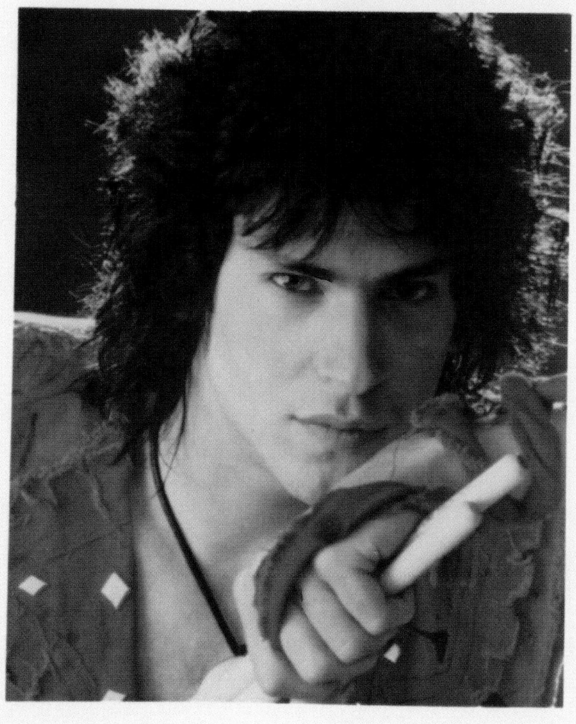

Career Direction:
BUTCH STONE ENTERPRISES
Route 8 Box 272
Mountain Home, AR 72653
(501) 481-5131

Booking: ATI
(212) 977-2300

KROKUS

ARISTA

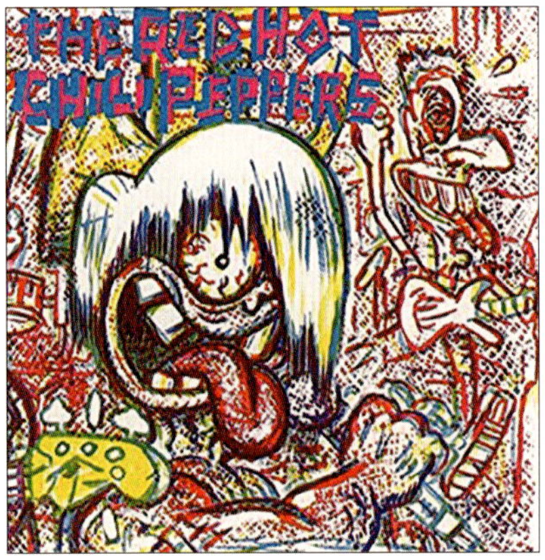

The Red Hot Chili Peppers' self-titled debut album reaped college radio airplay and MTV rotation, expanding a fan base for the band's funk-metal hybrid.

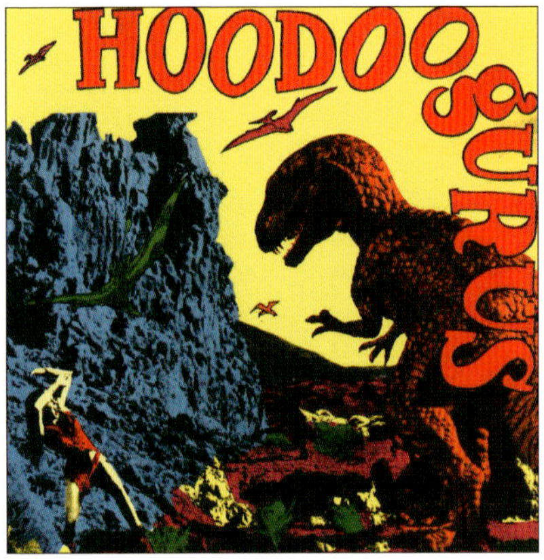

Stoneage Romeos, Hoodoo Gurus' first album, extended the Australian rock band's popularity, rising to No. 1 on the alternative and college network charts.

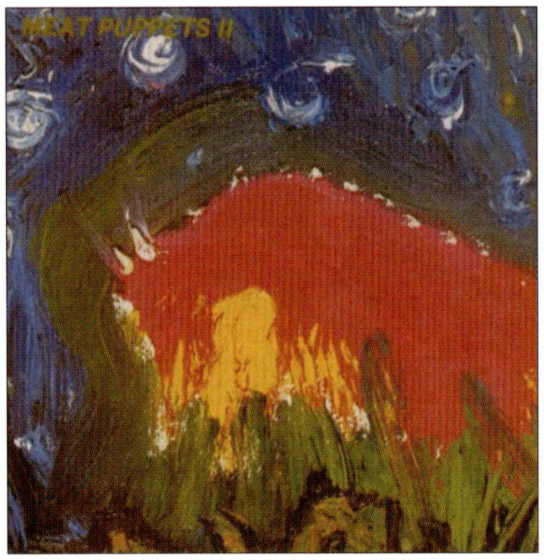

Experimenting with country and psychedelic rock, Meat Puppets developed a sound unlike anything else in the American underground on *Meat Puppets II*.

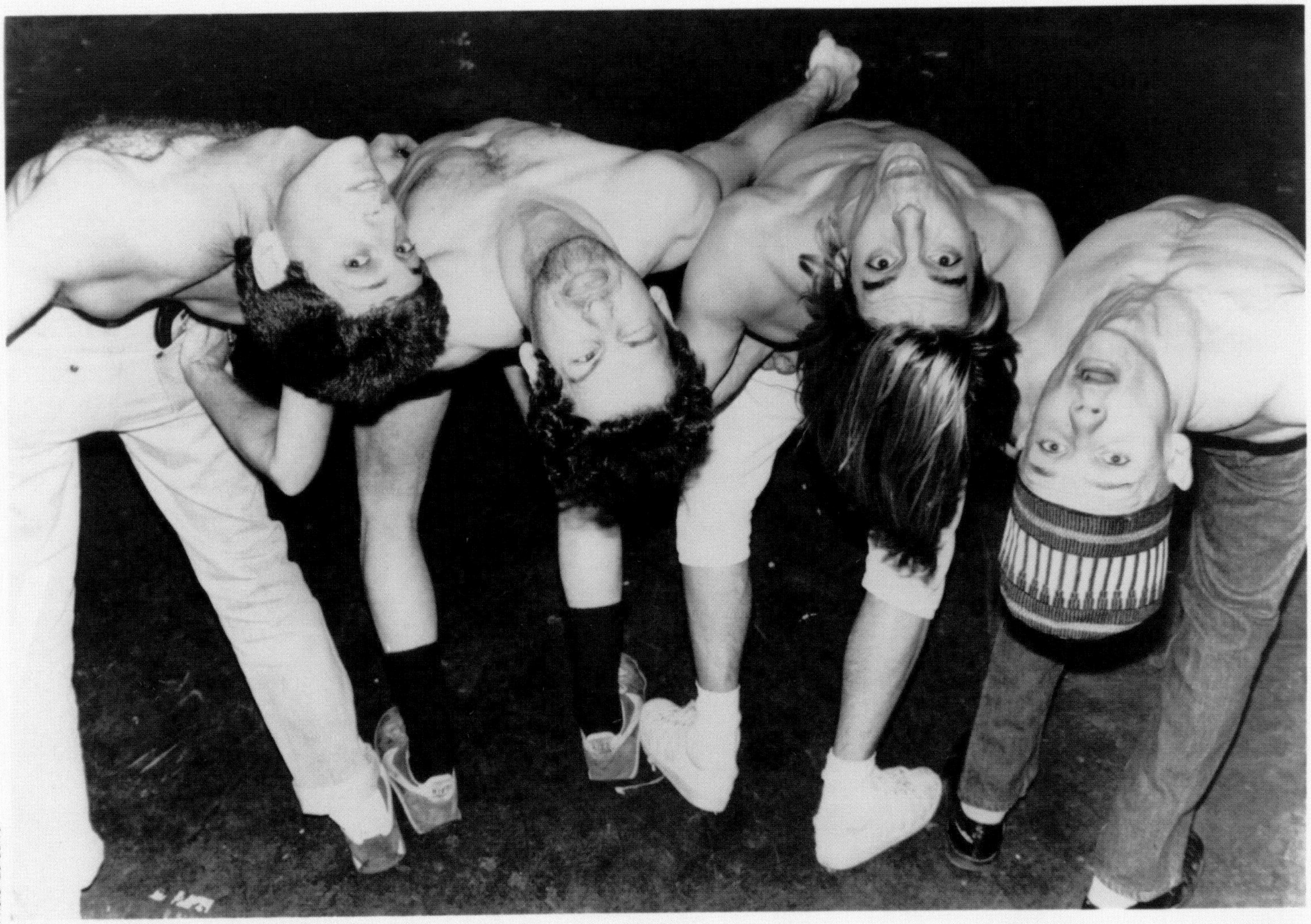

Photo: Ed Colver

THE RED HOT CHILI PEPPERS

ICM

Lindy Goetz Management
(213) 650-4722

ENIGMA

EMI AMERICA

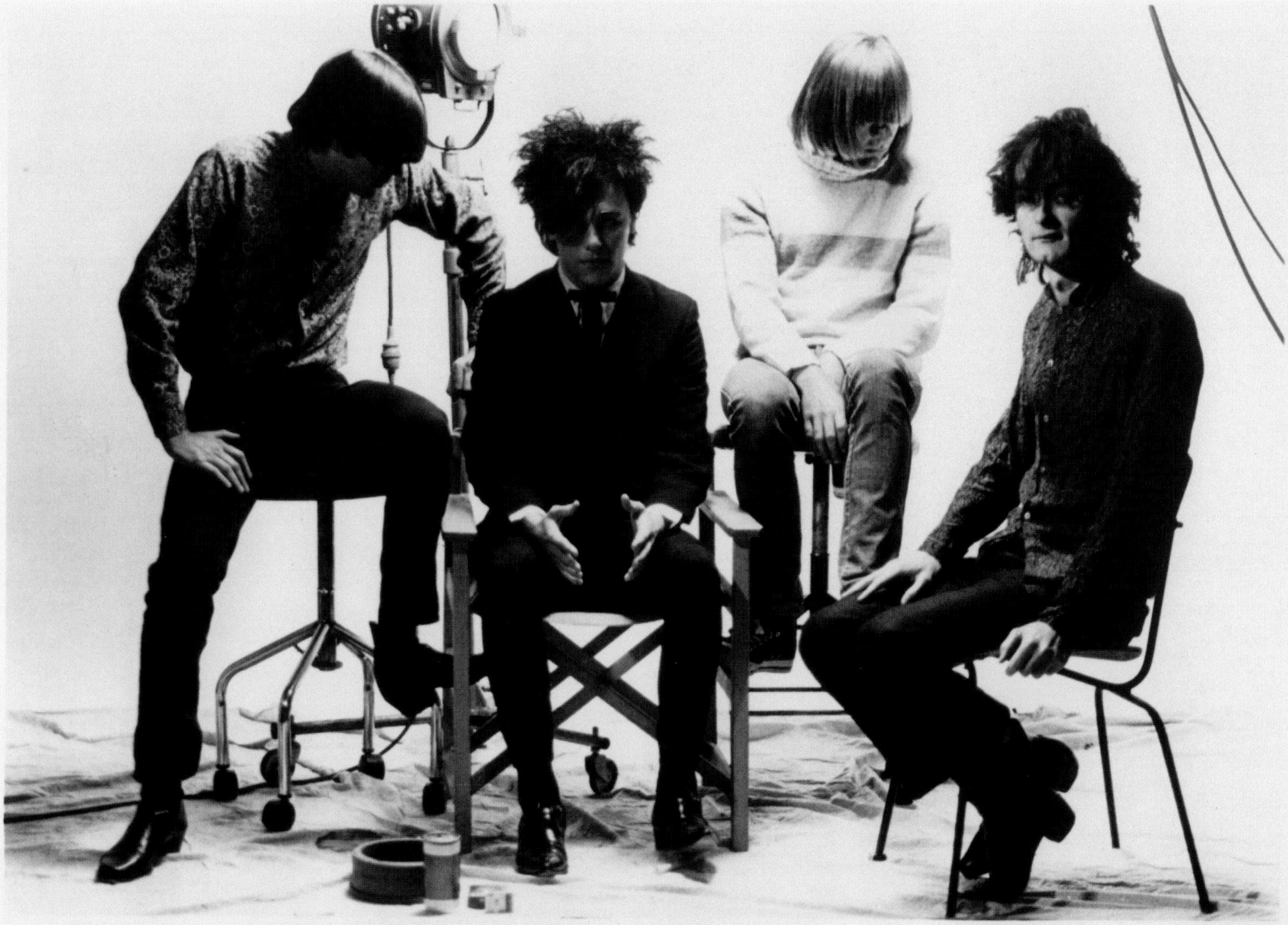

Clyde Bramley | Brad Sheperd | James Baker | Dave Faulkner

MANAGEMENT:

bigtime

(213) 274-8515

HOODOO GURUS

A&M RECORDS

Printed U.S.A.

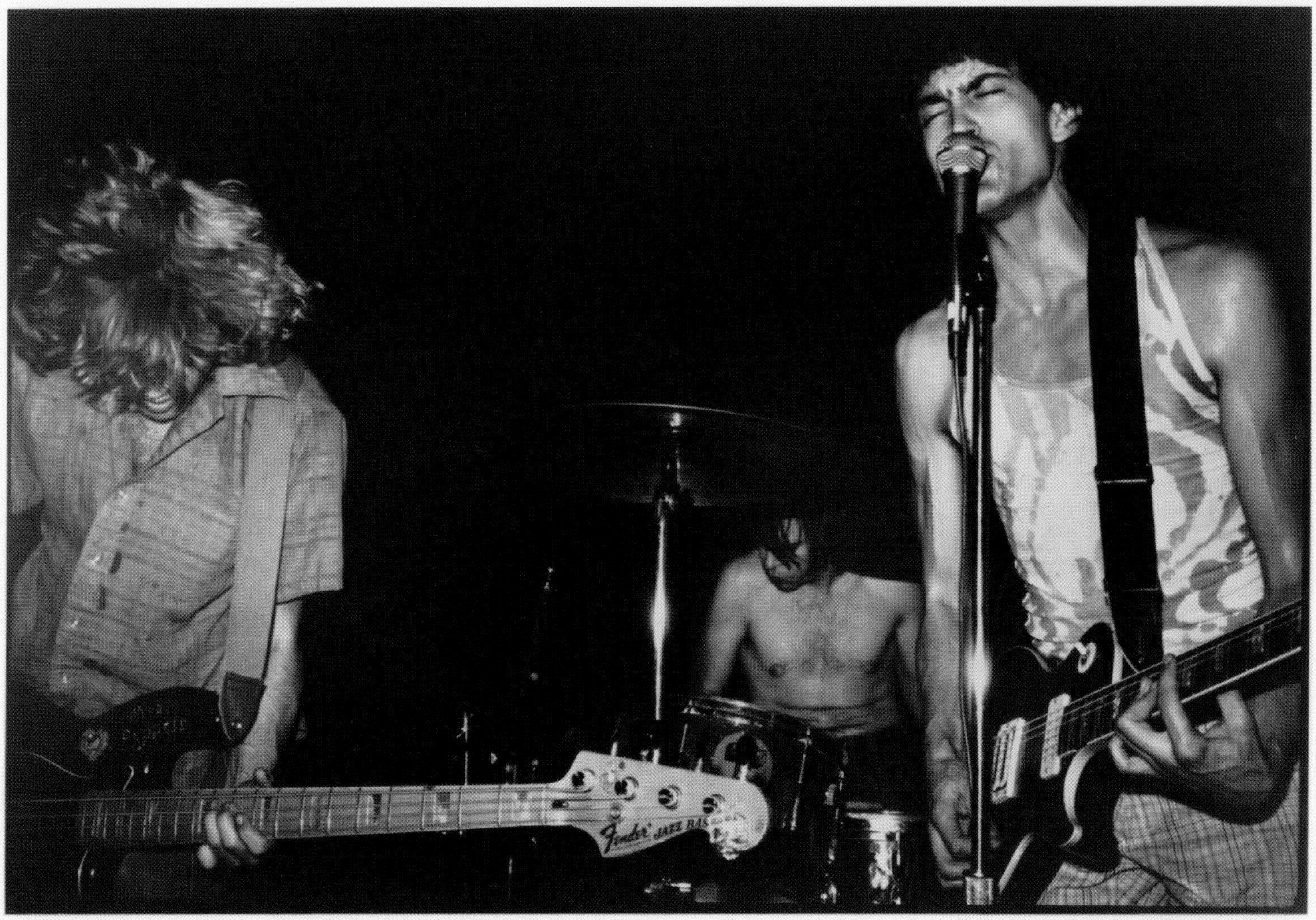

MEAT PUPPETS

P.O. BOX 1 LAWNDALE CA 90260
OFFICE: (213) 376-7213
BOOKING: (213) 372-5536

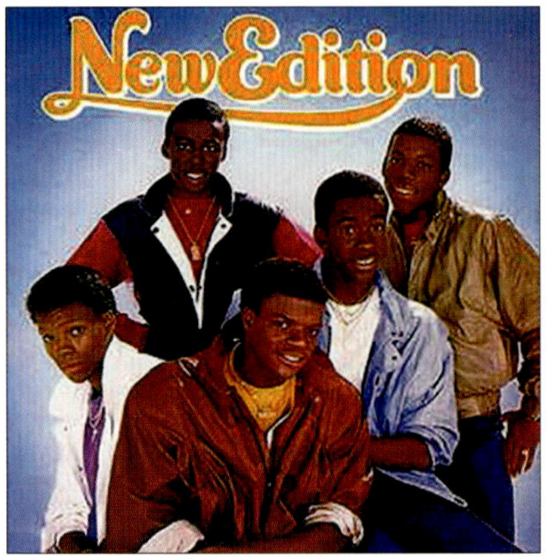

Promoting a clean-cut teen image, **New Edition**'s self-titled second album spun off a pair of Top 20 pop smashes, "Cool It Now" and "Mr. Telephone Man."

Billboard 200: *New Edition* (#6)
Billboard Hot 100: "Cool It Now" (#4); "Mr. Telephone Man" (#12); "Lost in Love" (#35)

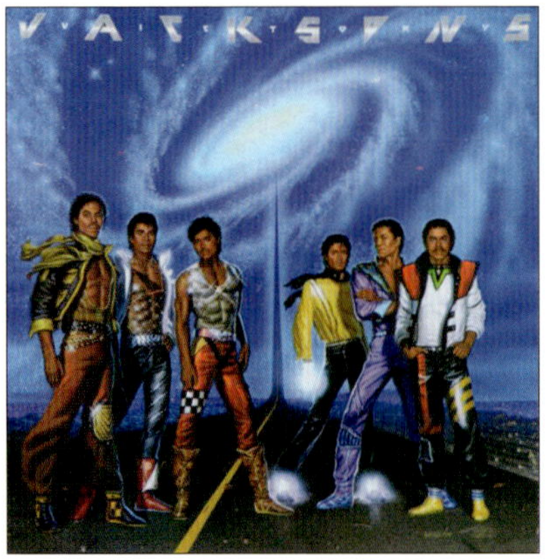

The Jacksons' *Victory*, featuring all six Jackson brothers, included "State of Shock," a duet pairing Michael Jackson with the Rolling Stones' Mick Jagger.

Billboard 200: *Victory* (#4)
Billboard Hot 100: "State of Shock" (#3); "Torture" (#17); "Body" (#47)

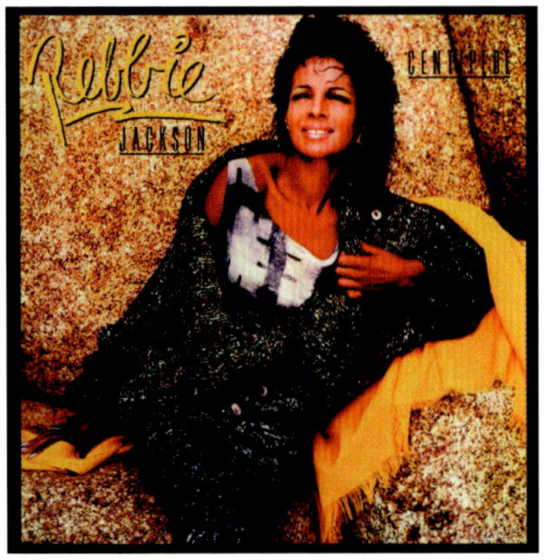

The eldest sibling of the famed musical family, **Rebbie Jackson** had her biggest hit when her brother Michael wrote and produced the track "Centipede."

Billboard 200: *Centipede* (#63)
Billboard Hot 100: "Centipede" (#24)

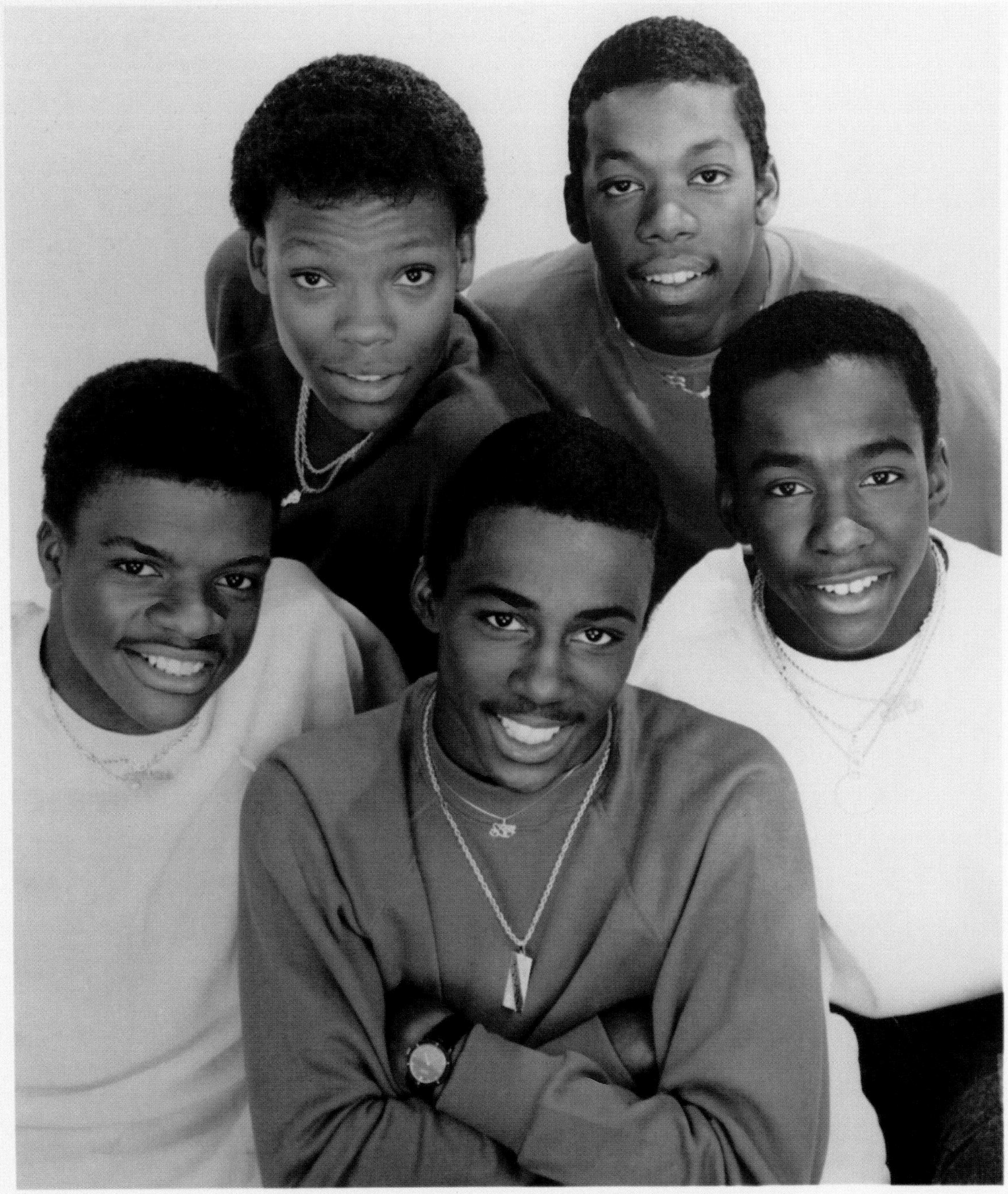

RONALD DE VOE
MICHAEL BIVINS
RICKY BELL
RALPH TRESVANT
BOBBY BROWN

New Edition

MCA RECORDS

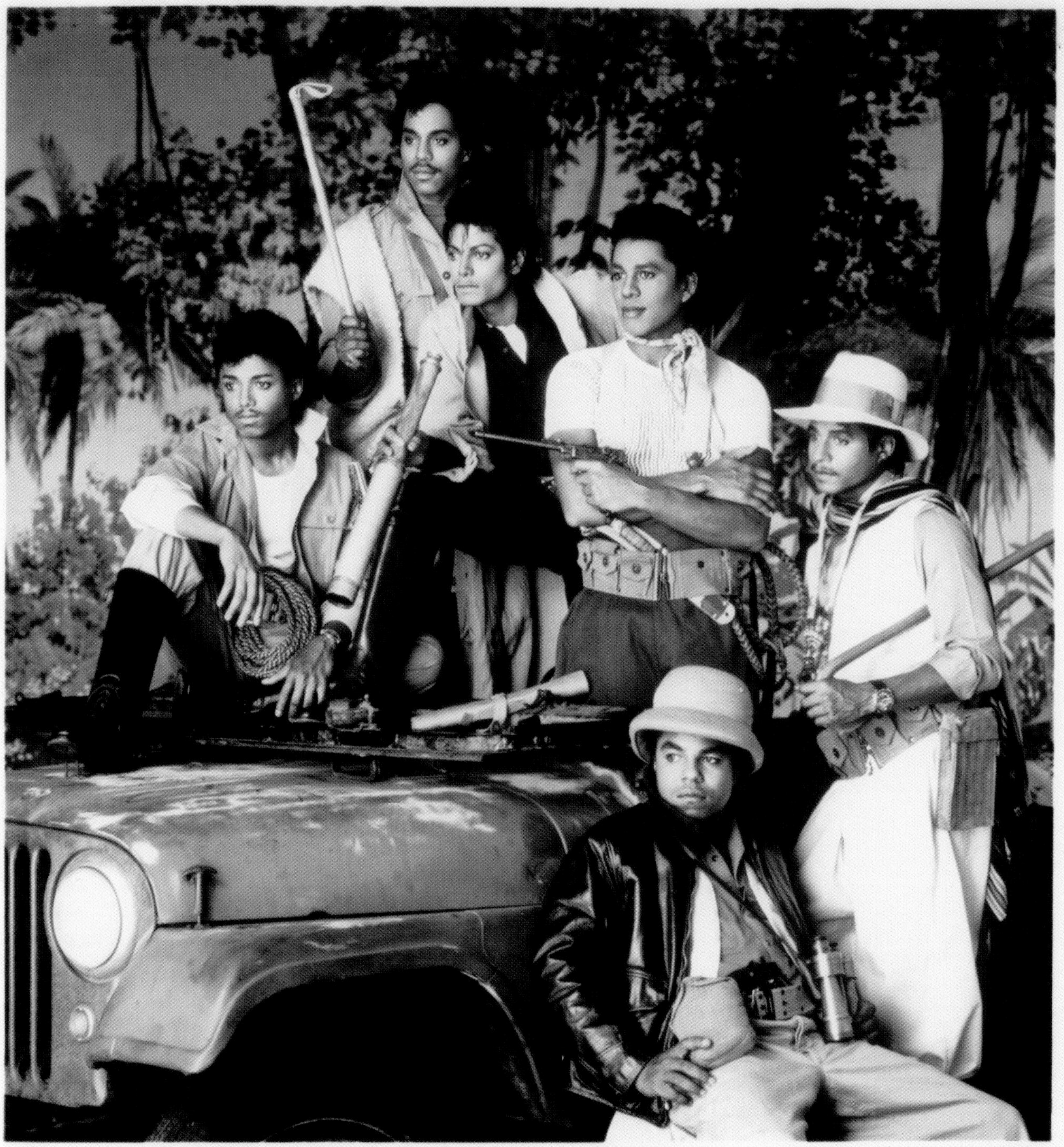

JACKSONS
VICTORY

Marlon

Randy Michael Jermaine Jackie

Tito

Epic
8405

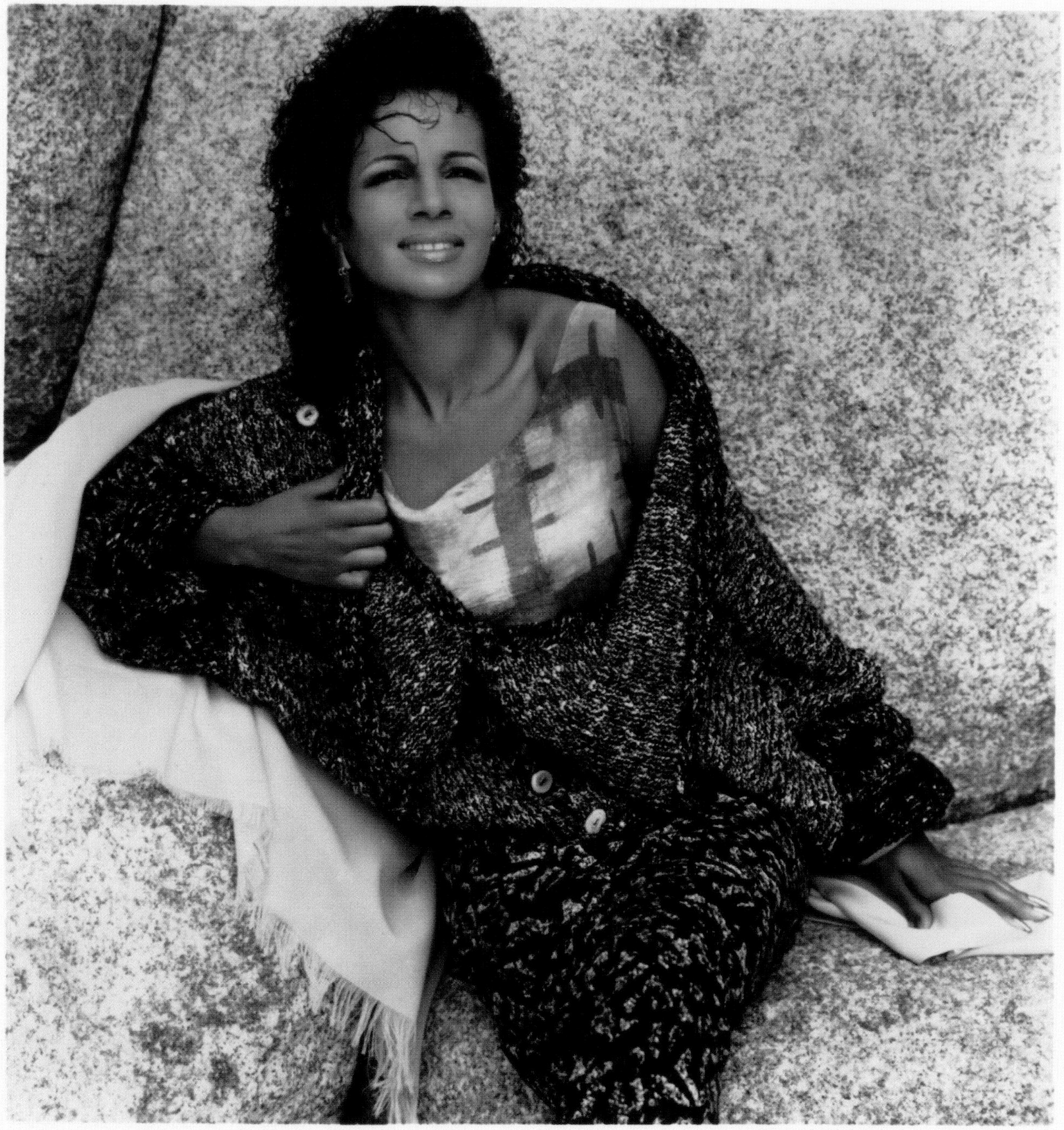

Photo Credit: Matthew Ralston

REBBIE JACKSON

Columbia

8405

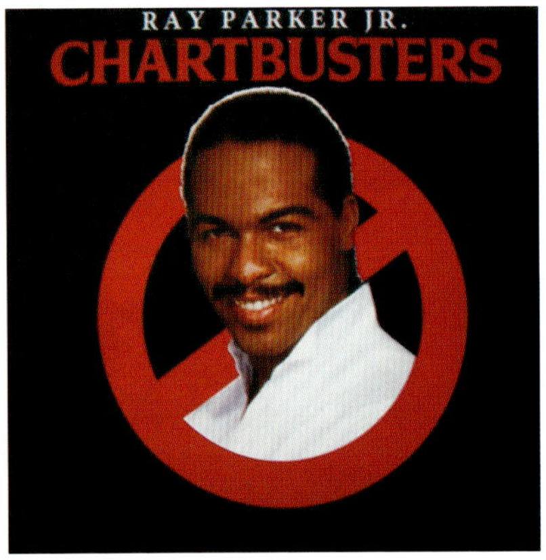

Although **Ray Parker Jr.**'s theme song to the film *Ghostbusters* held the No. 1 spot on the pop and R&B charts, he was sued for copyright infringement.

Billboard 200: *Chartbusters* (#60)
Billboard Hot 100: "Ghostbusters" (No. 1); "Jamie" (#14)

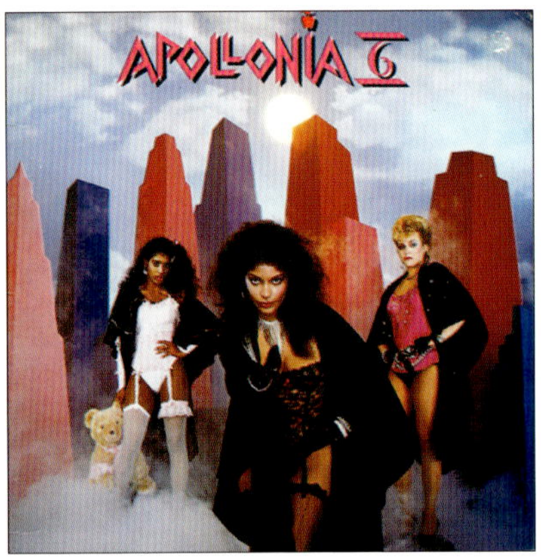

Prince wrote "Sex Shooter" for the girl trio **Apollonia 6** to sing in his seminal film *Purple Rain*, and his lingerie-clad protégés landed a Top 10 R&B smash.

Billboard Hot 100: "Sex Shooter" (#85)

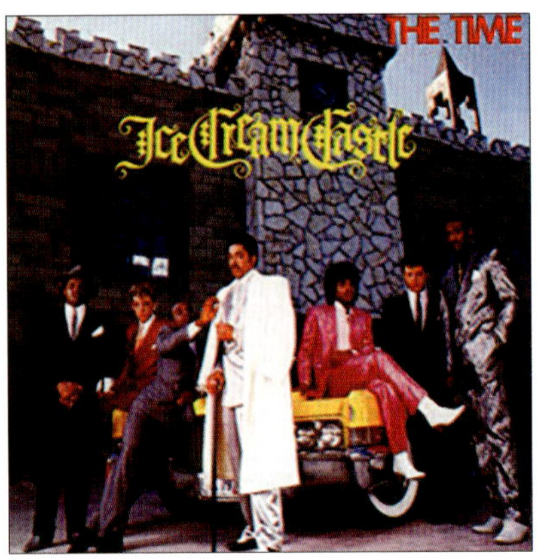

The Time, led by charismatic lead singer Morris Day, was played up performing the funk-rock hits "Jungle Love" and "The Bird" in Prince's *Purple Rain*.

Billboard 200: *Ice Cream Castle* (#24)
Billboard Hot 100: "Jungle Love" (#20); "The Bird" (#36)

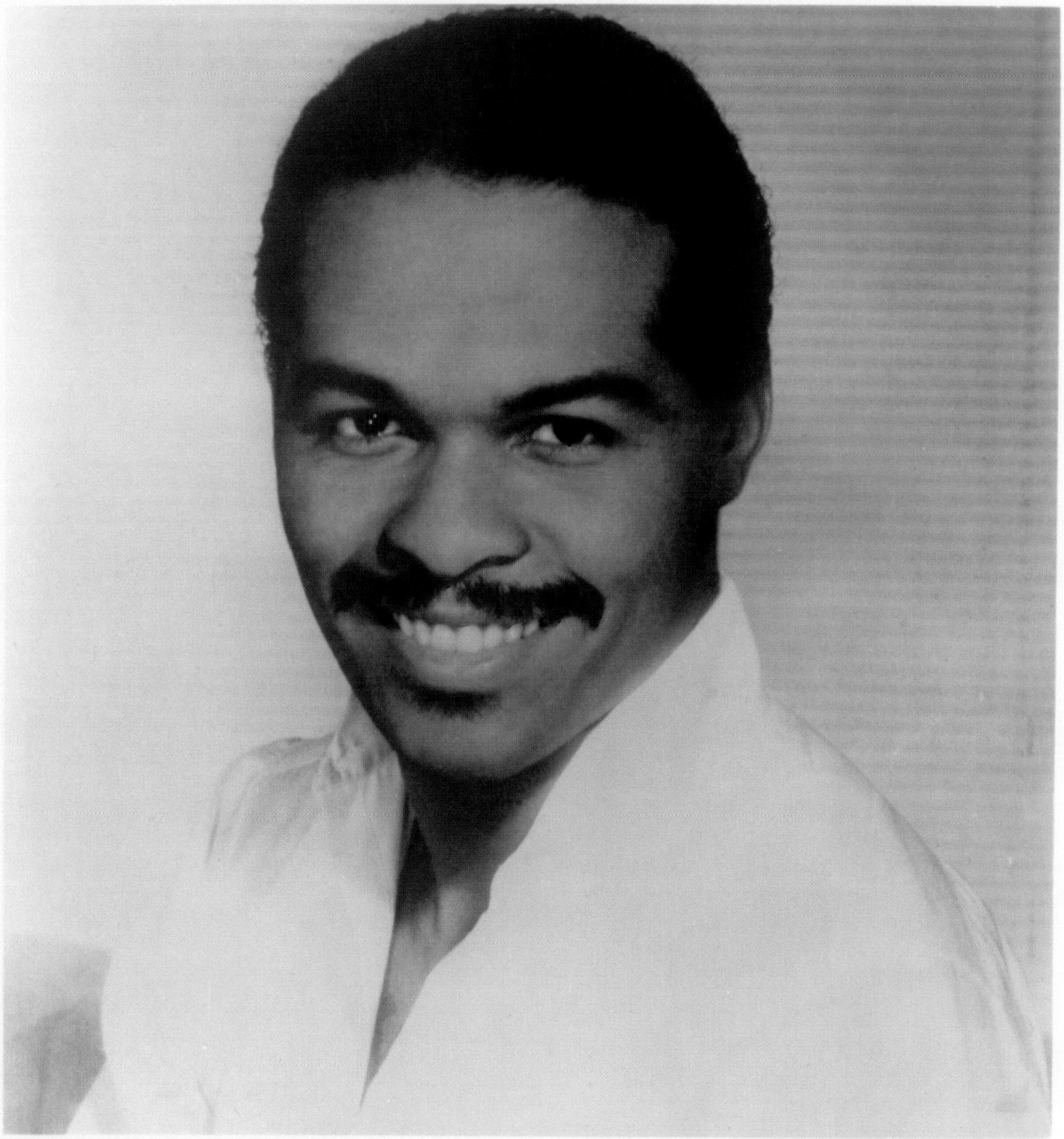

RAY PARKER JR.

EXCLUSIVE REPRESENTATION
CAVALLO, RUFFALO & FARGNOLI
(213) 473-1564

ARISTA™

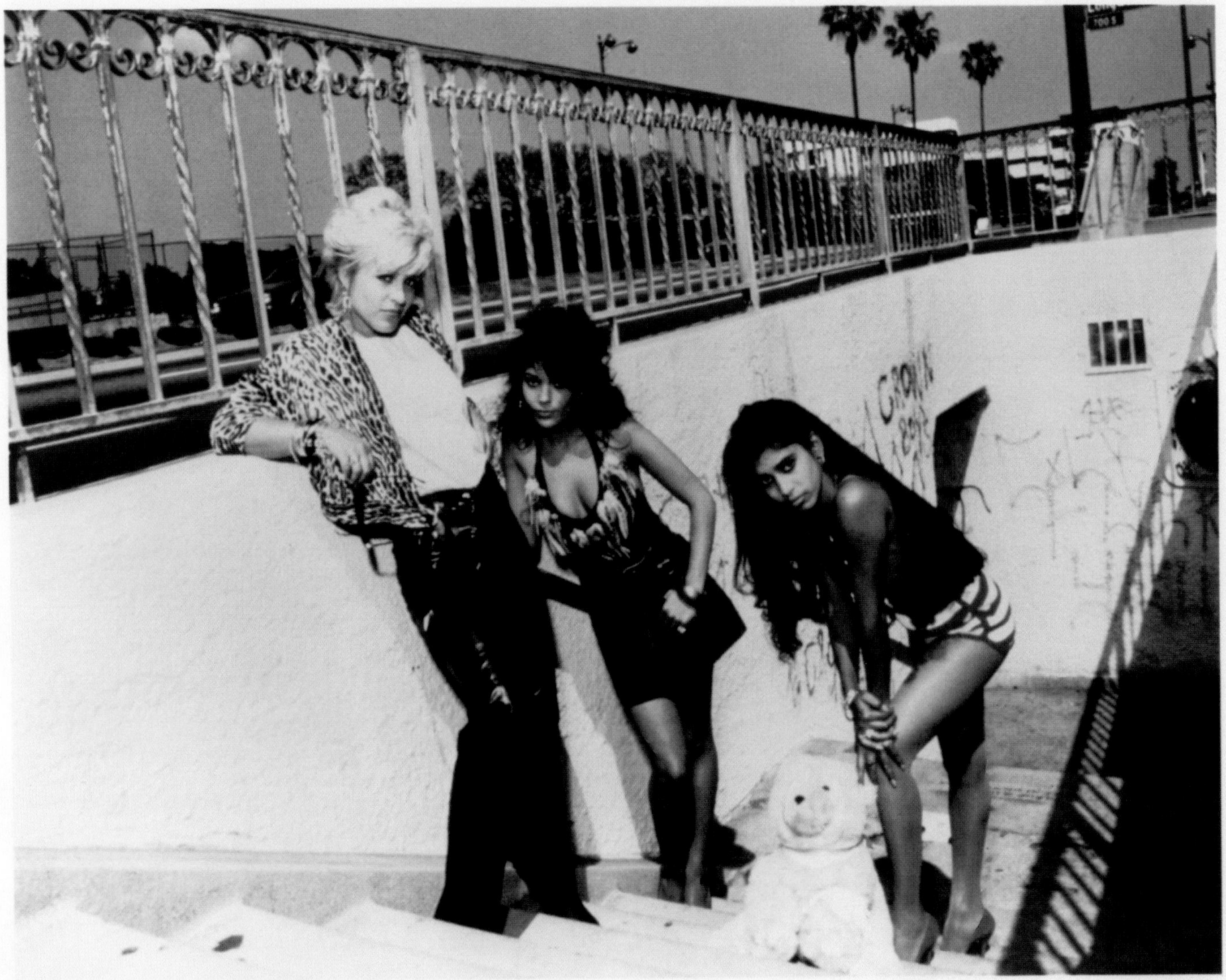

Photo Credit: Raúl Vega

APOLLONIA 6

WARNER BROS.

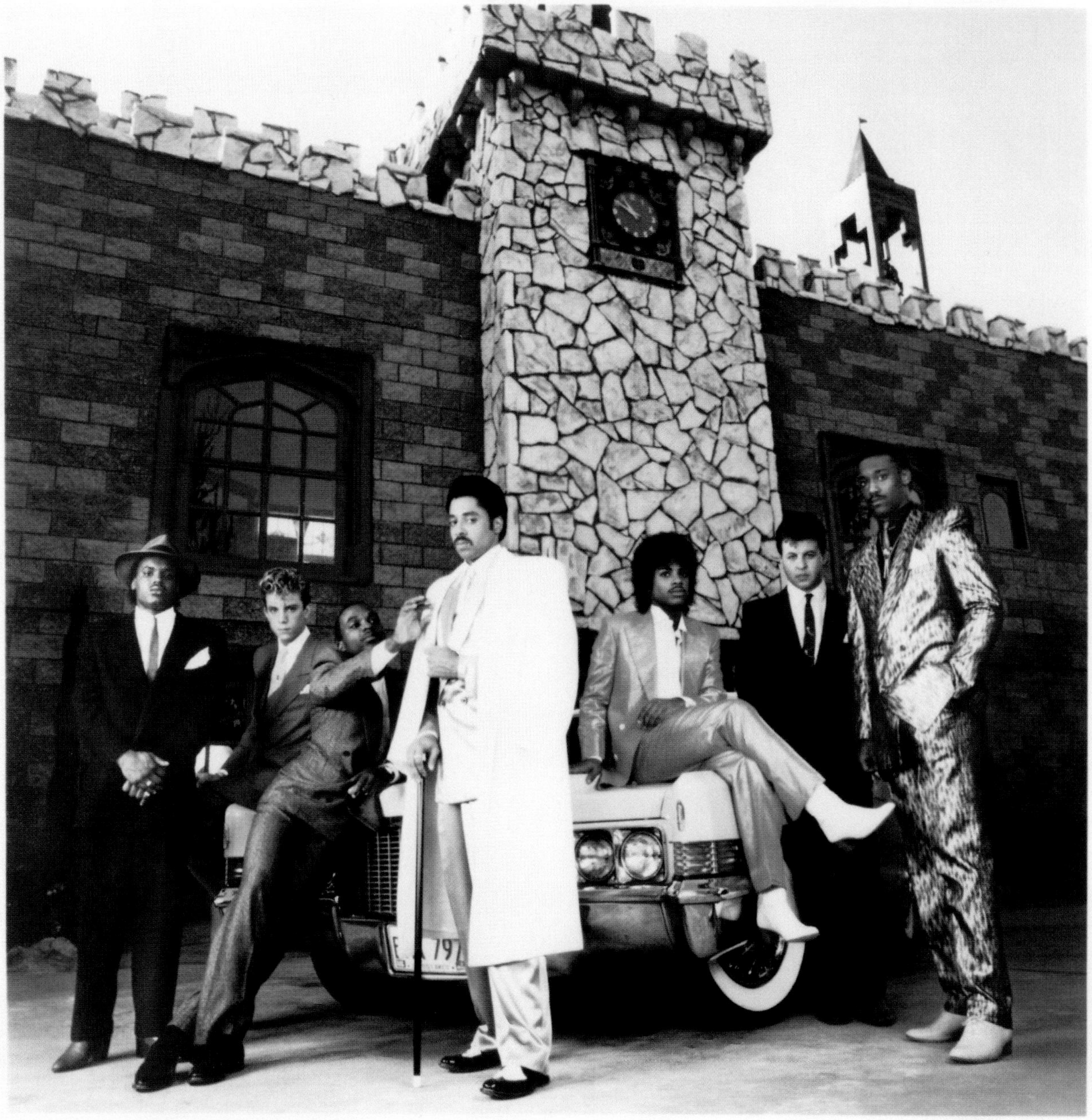

Photo Credit: Larry Williams

THE TIME

WARNER BROS.

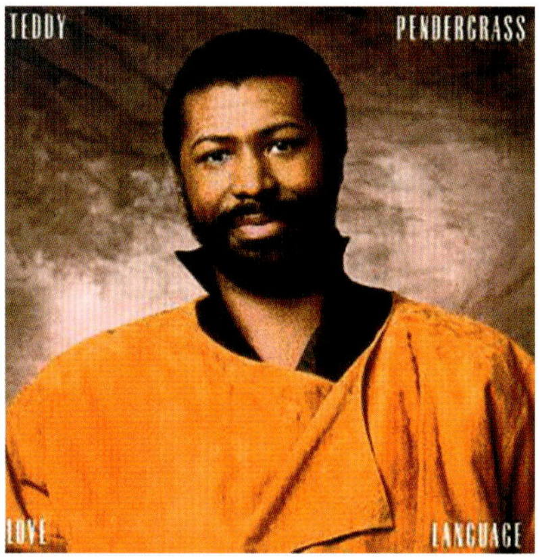

"Hold Me," a duet performed by **Teddy Pendergrass** with Whitney Houston, would later disqualify her from the Best New Artist category at the Grammys.

Billboard 200: *Love Language* (#38)
Billboard Hot 100: "Hold Me" (#46)

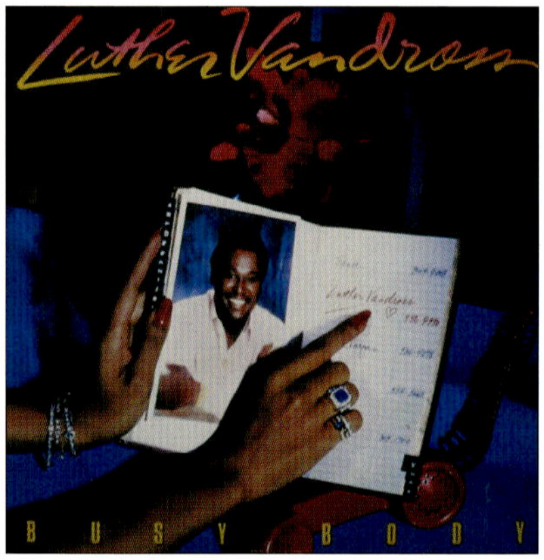

By virtue of "How Many Times Can We Say Goodbye" and a singular interpretation of "Superstar," **Luther Vandross**' *Busy Body* hit No. 1 on the R&B chart.

Billboard 200: *Busy Body* (#32)
Billboard Hot 100: "How Many Times Can We Say Goodbye" (#27); "Superstar" (#87)

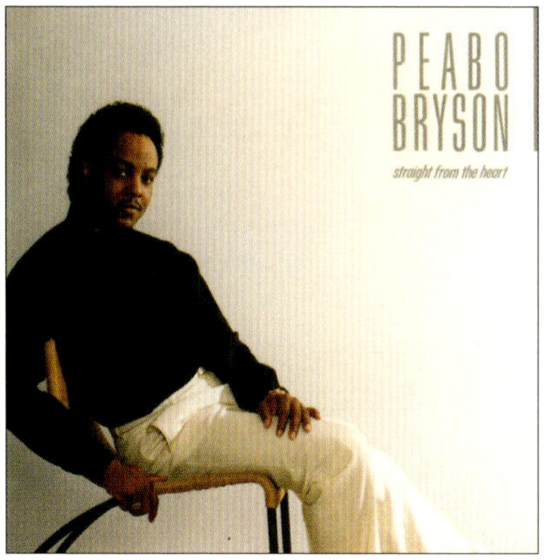

R&B balladeer **Peabo Bryson**'s first Top 10 pop hit, "If Ever You're in My Arms Again," did duty as a love theme on the television soap opera *Santa Barbara*.

Billboard 200: *Straight from the Heart* (#44)
Billboard Hot 100: "If Ever You're in My Arms Again" (#10); "Slow Dancin'" (#82)

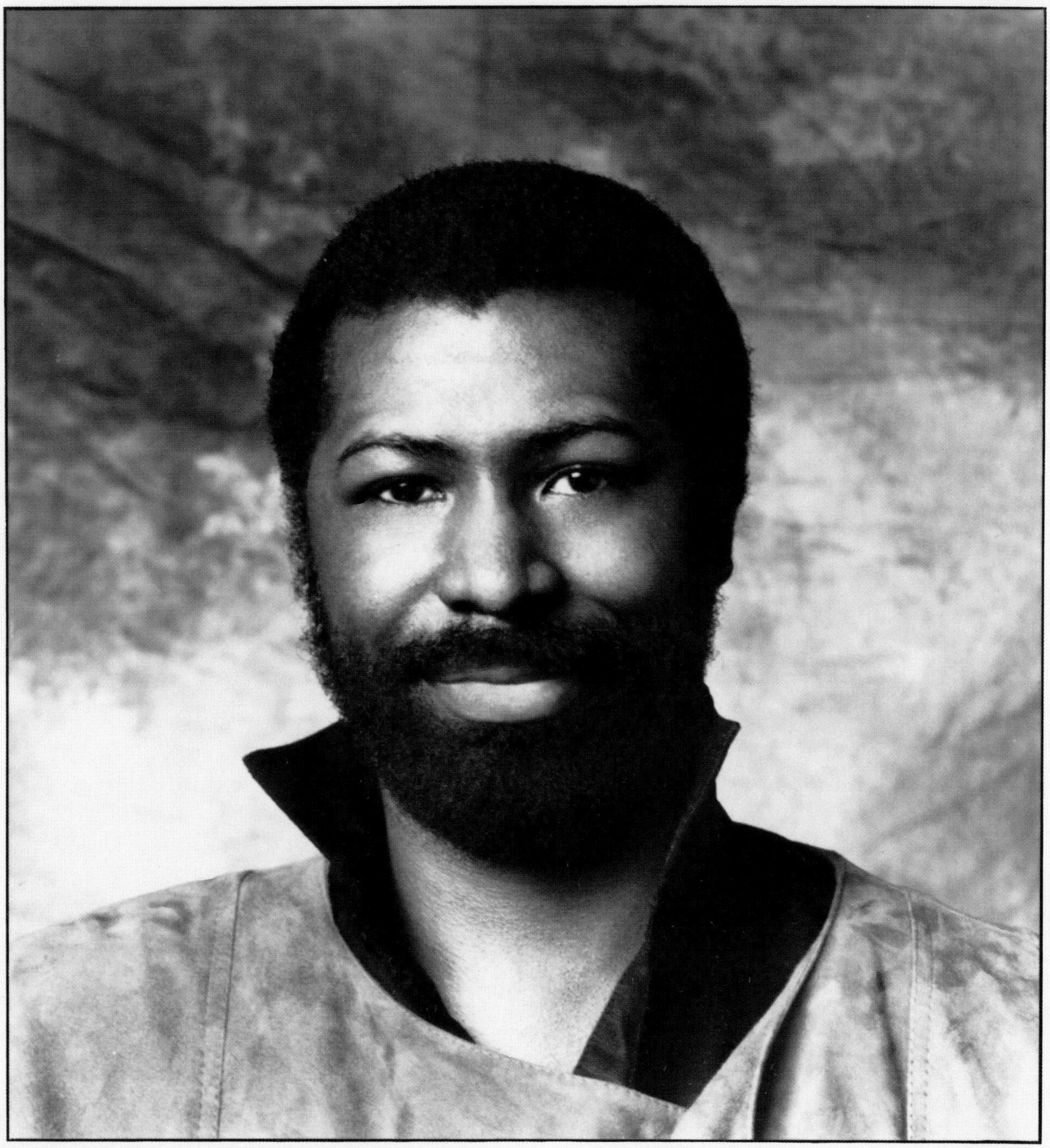

PHOTO CREDIT: ANNIE LEIBOVITZ/1984

TEDDY PENDERGRASS

ASYLUM

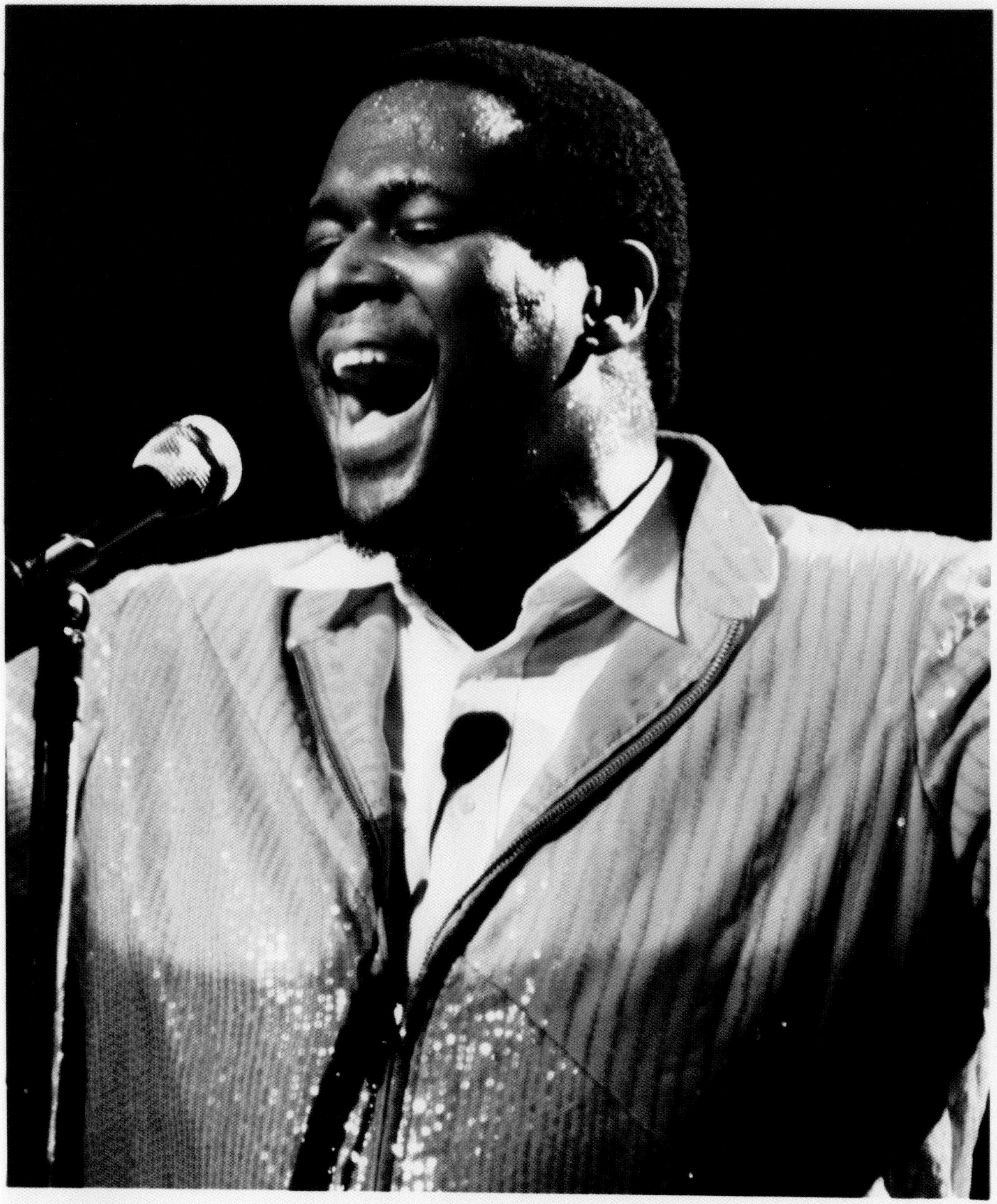

Epic
8405

LUTHER VANDROSS

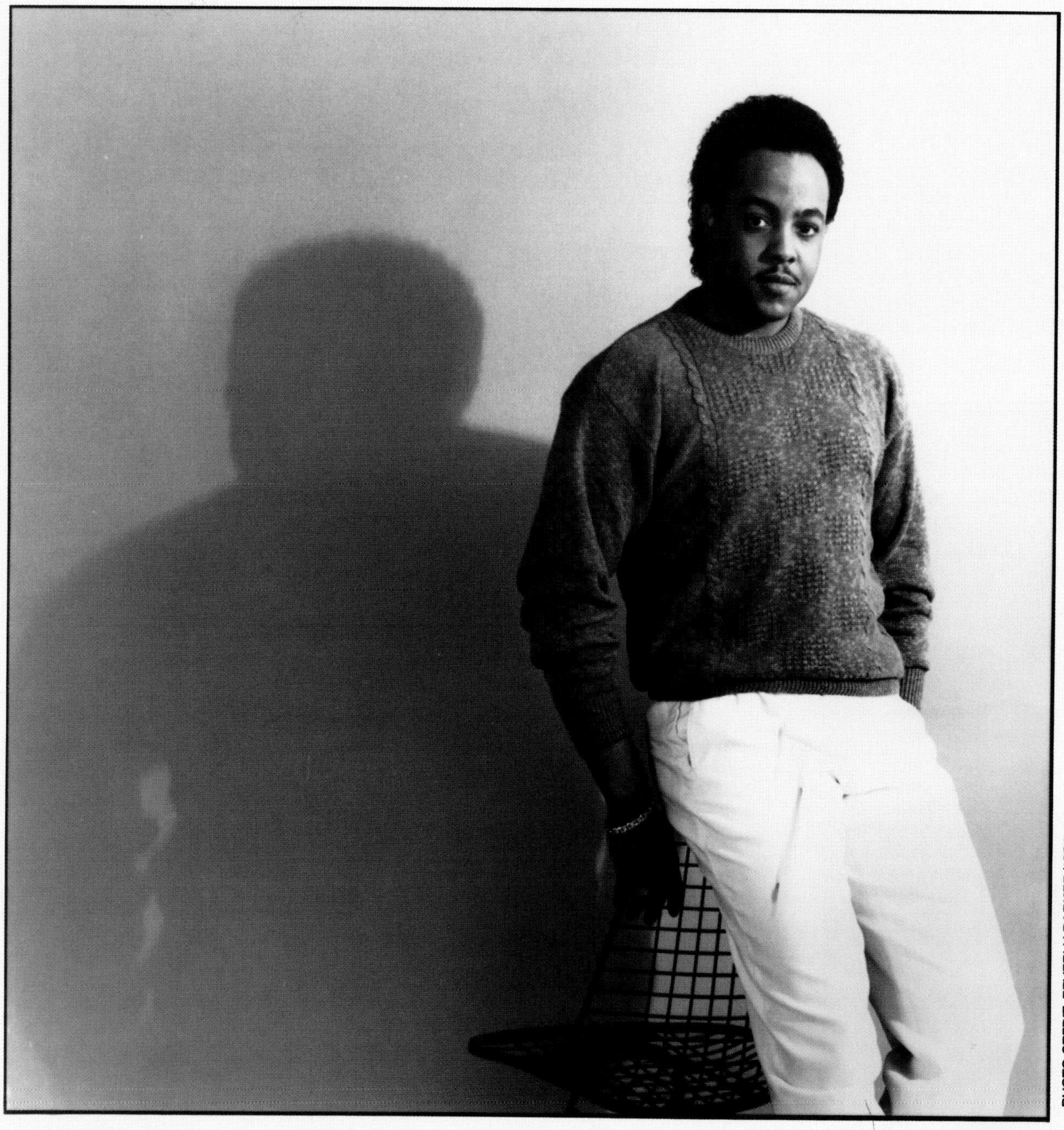

PHOTO CREDIT: BEVERLY PARKER/1984

PEABO
BRYSON

ELEKTRA

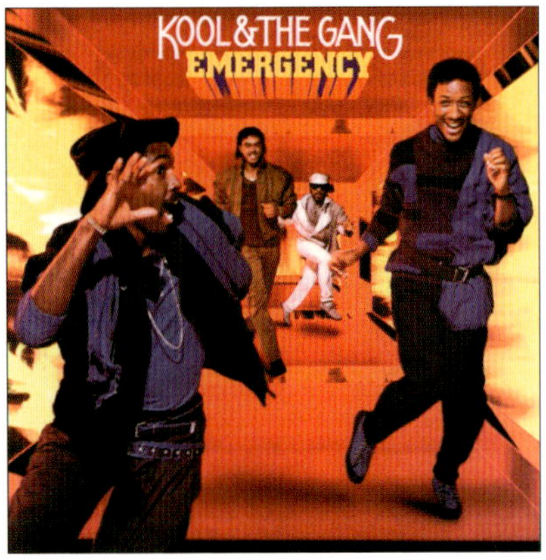

Emergency developed into **Kool & the Gang**'s biggest-selling album, producing the No. 1 adult contemporary hit "Cherish," a platinum-certified single.

Billboard 200: *Emergency* (#28)
Billboard Hot 100: "Misled" (#10); "Fresh" (#9); "Cherish" (#2); "Emergency" (#18)

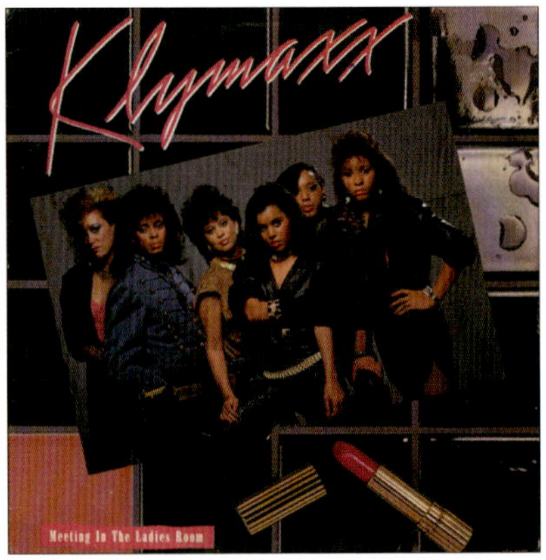

The campy singles "I Miss You," "The Men All Pause" and the title track elevated the all-female **Klymaxx**'s *Meeting in the Ladies Room* to platinum status.

Billboard 200: *Meeting in the Ladies Room* (#18)
Billboard Hot 100: "Meeting in the Ladies Room" (#59); "I Miss You" (#5); "The Men All Pause" (#80)

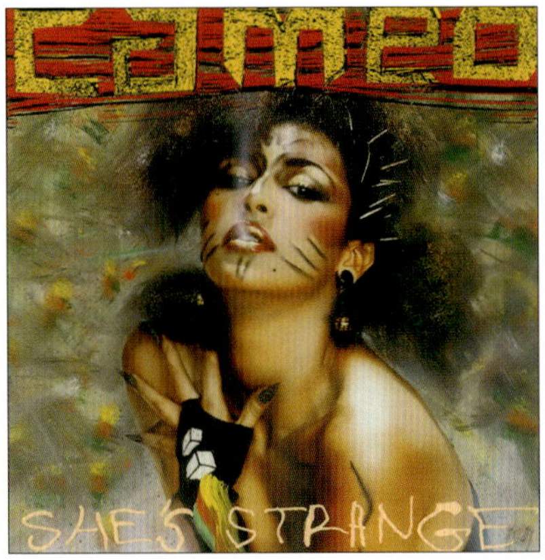

She's Strange, the simmering title track from funk ensemble **Cameo**'s tenth release, answered hip-hop's popularity by integrating a good deal of rapping.

Billboard 200: *She's Strange* (#27)
Billboard Hot 100: "She's Strange" (#47)

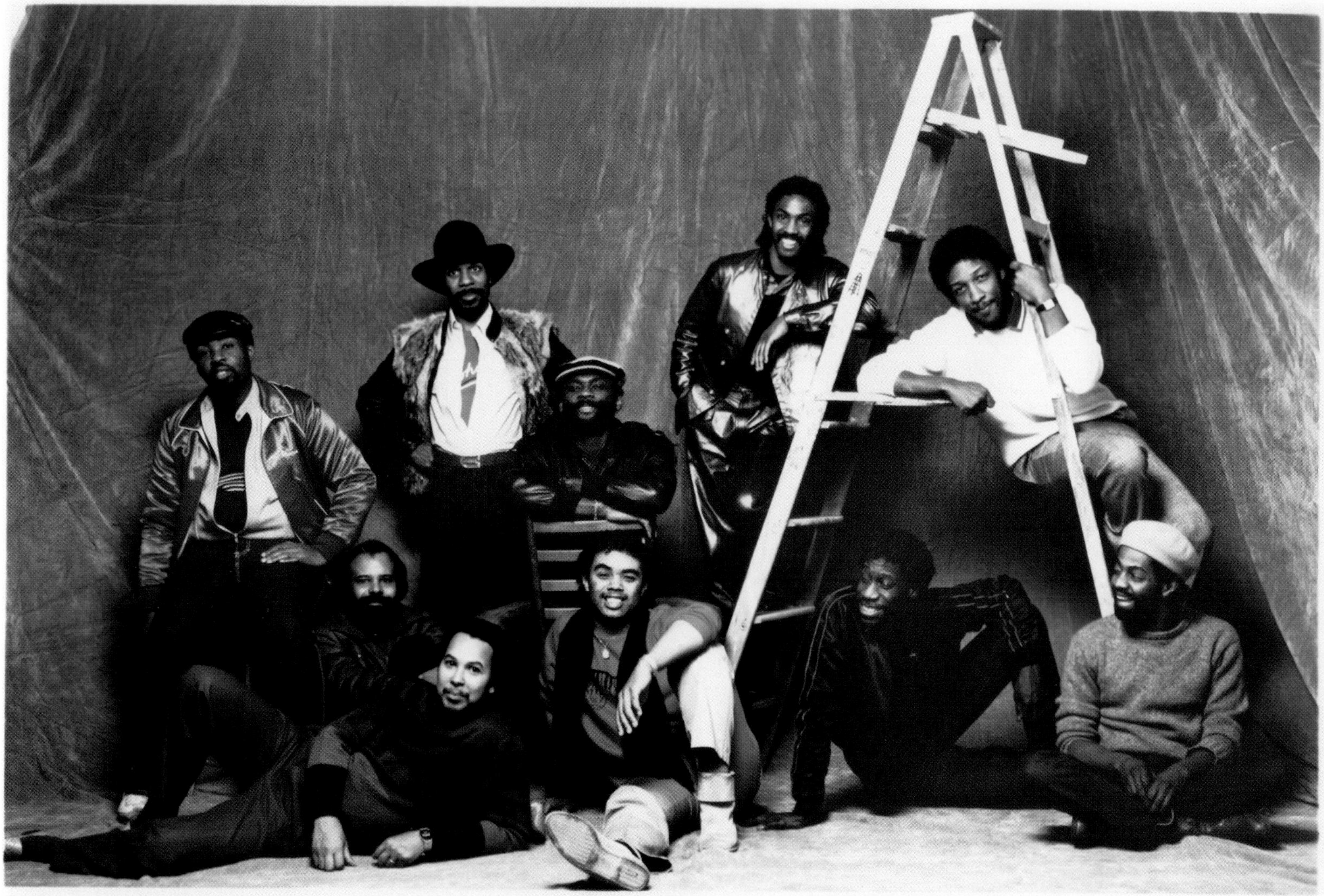

Management & Direction
Quintet Assoc. Ltd.
And TWM Management
641 Lexington Ave.
New York N.Y 10022
Bookings:
Norby Walters Assoc.

PolyGram Records

De-Lite Records

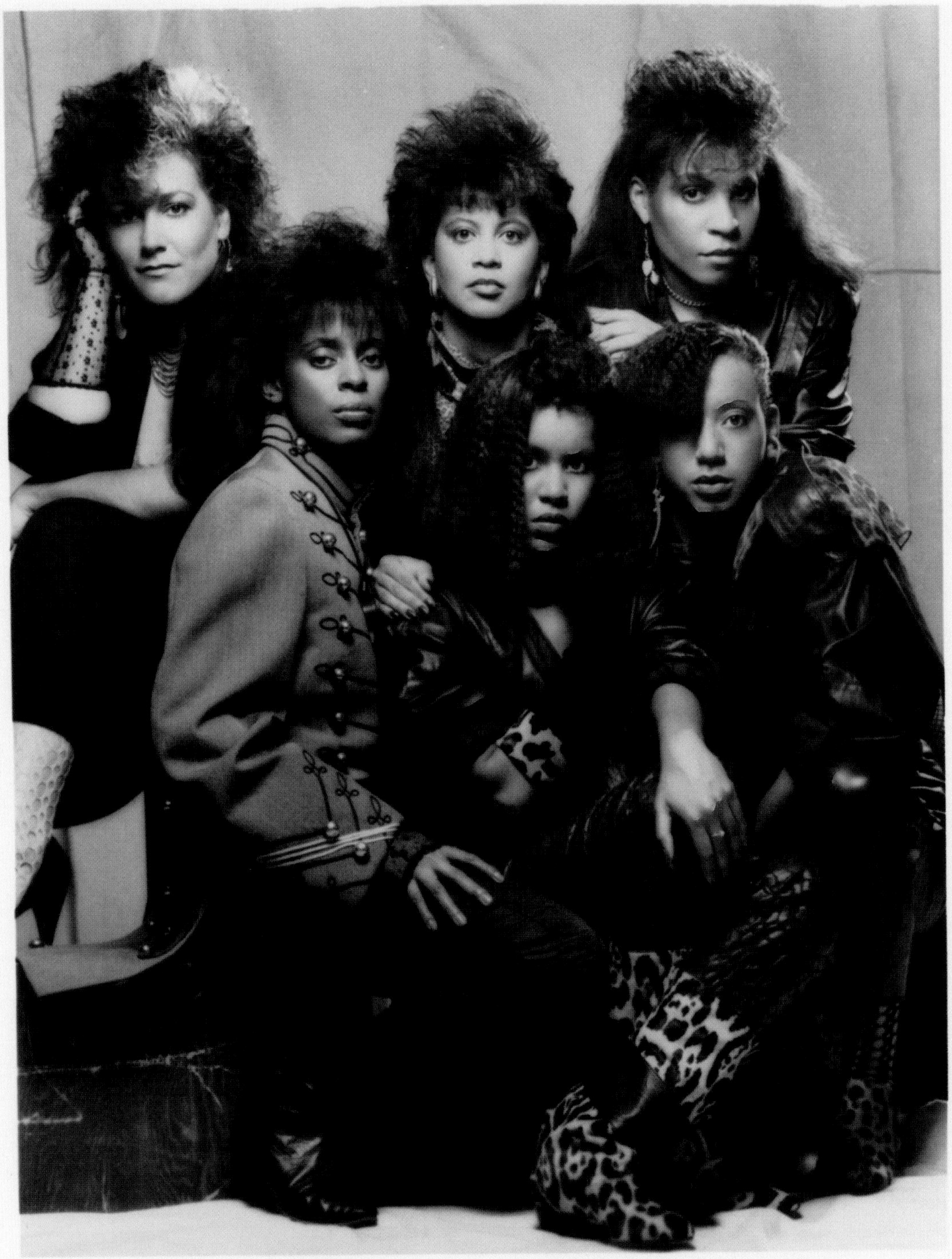

PHOTO CREDIT: DARIUS ANTHONY

.MCA RECORDS

Klymaxx

CONSTELLATION

LEFT TO RIGHT(BACK): LYNN MALSBY, CHERYL COOLEY, ROBBIN GRIDER
LEFT TO RIGHT(FRONT):JOYCE IRBY, LORENA PORTER, BERNADETTE COOPER

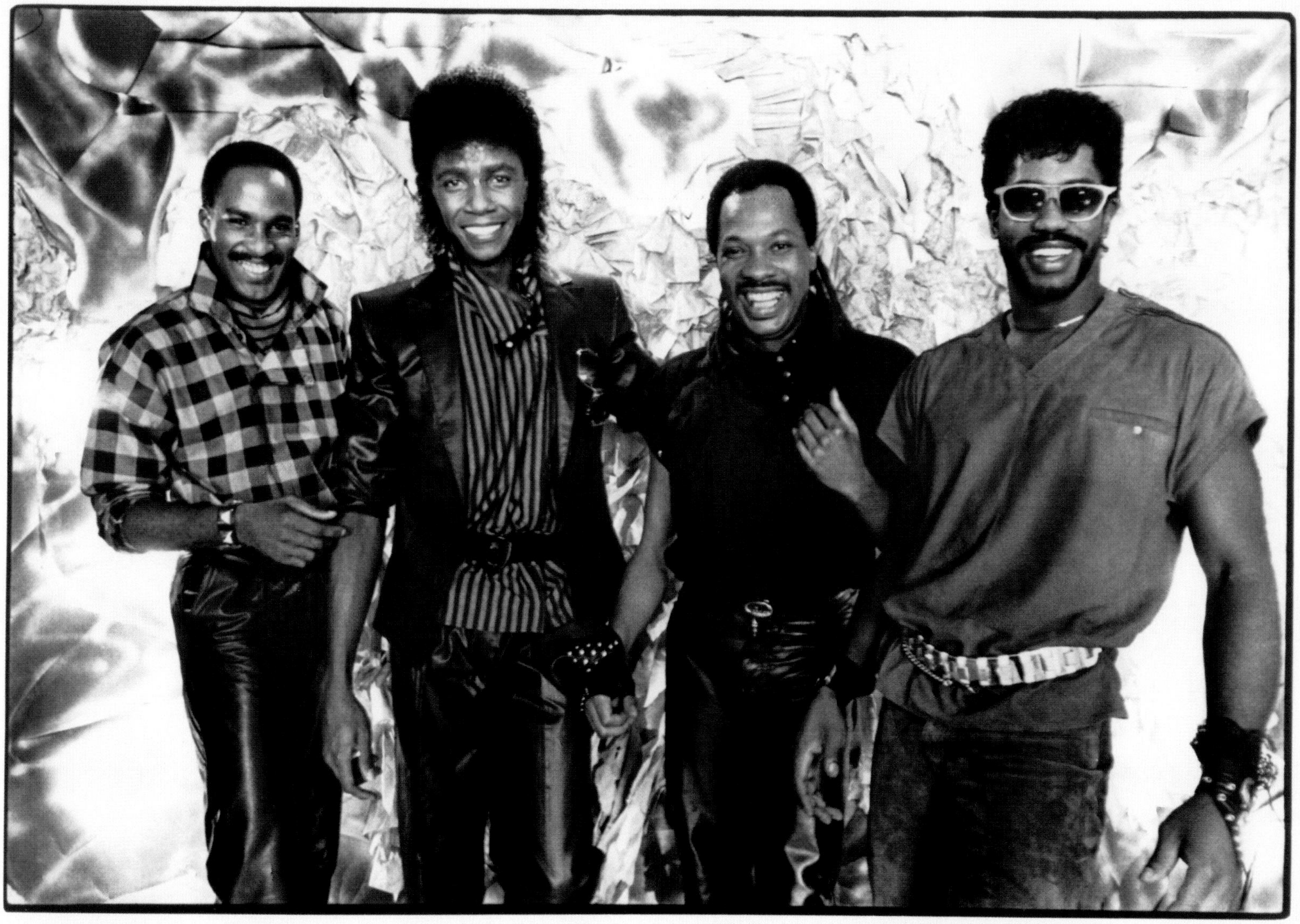

CAMEO

ATLANTA ARTISTS

PolyGram Records

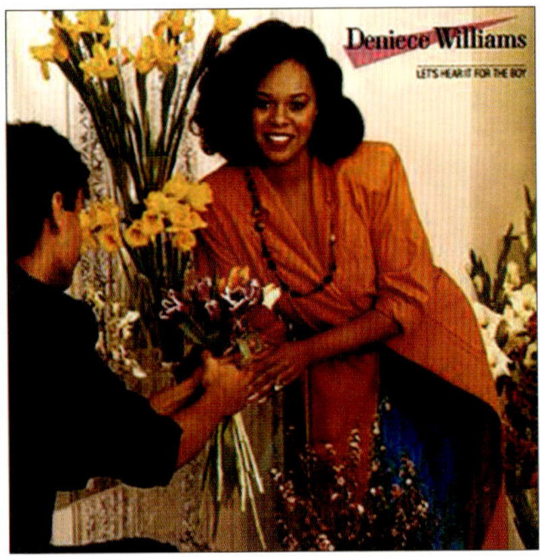

Produced by virtuoso musician George Duke, **Deniece Williams**' "Let's Hear It for the Boy" appeared on the soundtrack to *Footloose* and peaked at No. 1.

Billboard 200: *Let's Hear It for the Boy* (#26)
Billboard Hot 100: "Let's Hear It for the Boy" (No. 1);
"Next Love" (#81)

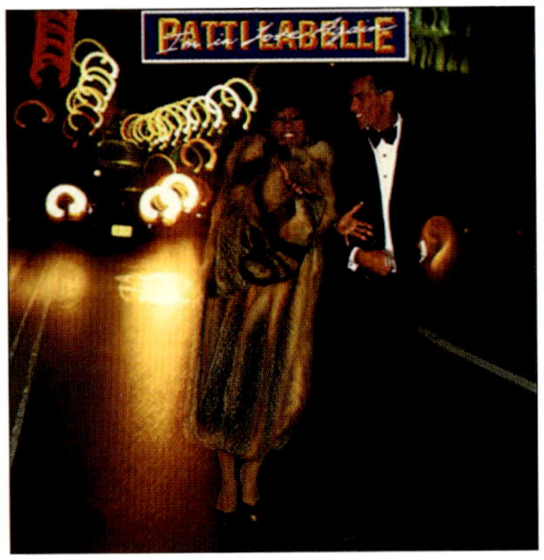

Patti LaBelle's "If You Only Knew" became her commercial breakthrough—her first No. 1 R&B single as a solo performer and her first crossover pop hit.

Billboard 200: *I'm In Love Again* (#40)
Billboard Hot 100: "If You Only Knew" (#46)

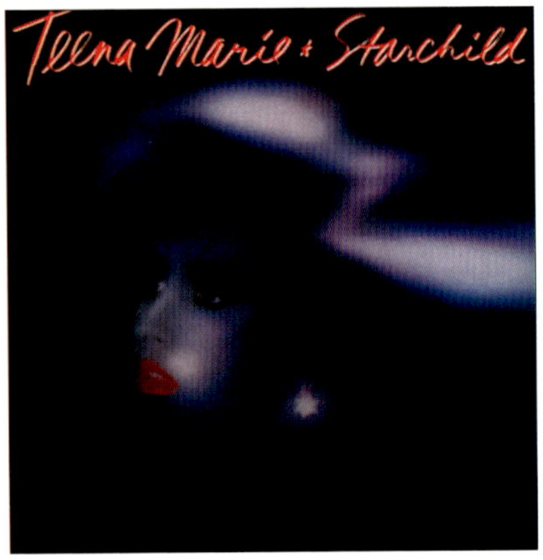

After a nasty legal battle with Motown, **Teena Marie** wrote and produced her album *Starchild*, yielding "Lovergirl," the soul singer's biggest pop hit ever.

Billboard 200: *Starchild* (#32)
Billboard Hot 100: "Lovergirl" (#4); "Jammin'" (#81)

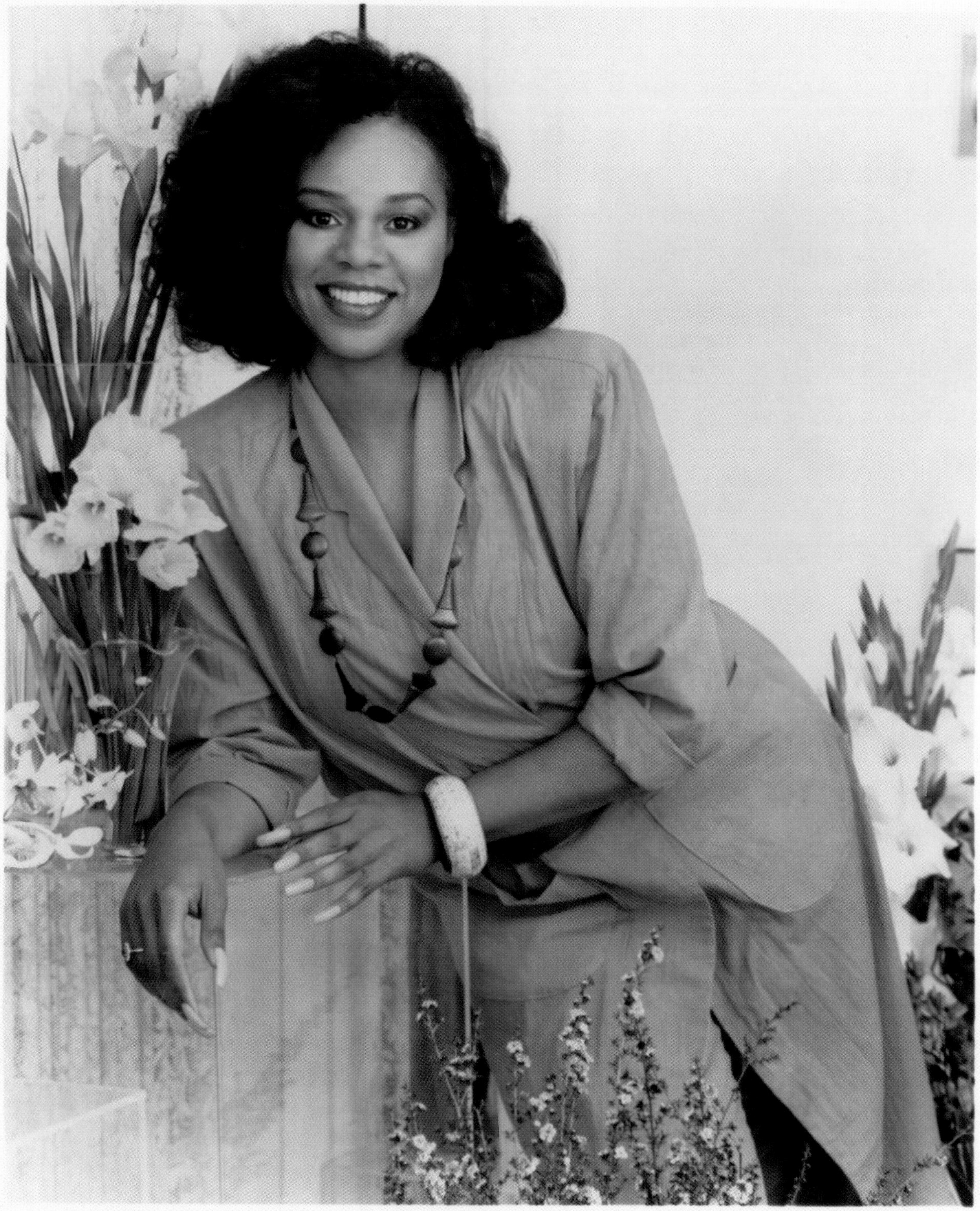

Photo Credit: Margaret MacFarland

DENIECE WILLIAMS

Columbia

8404

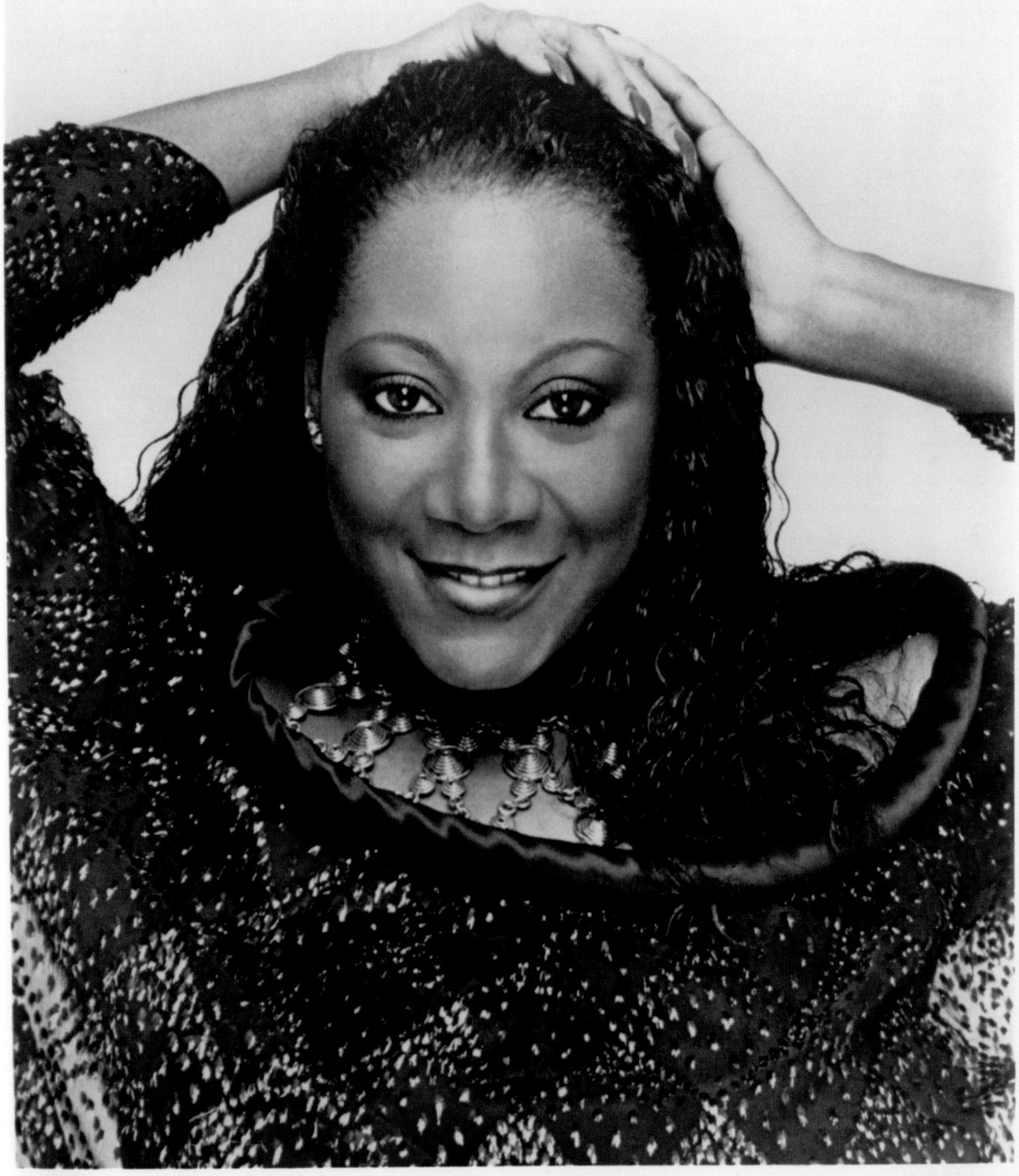

PATTI LABELLE

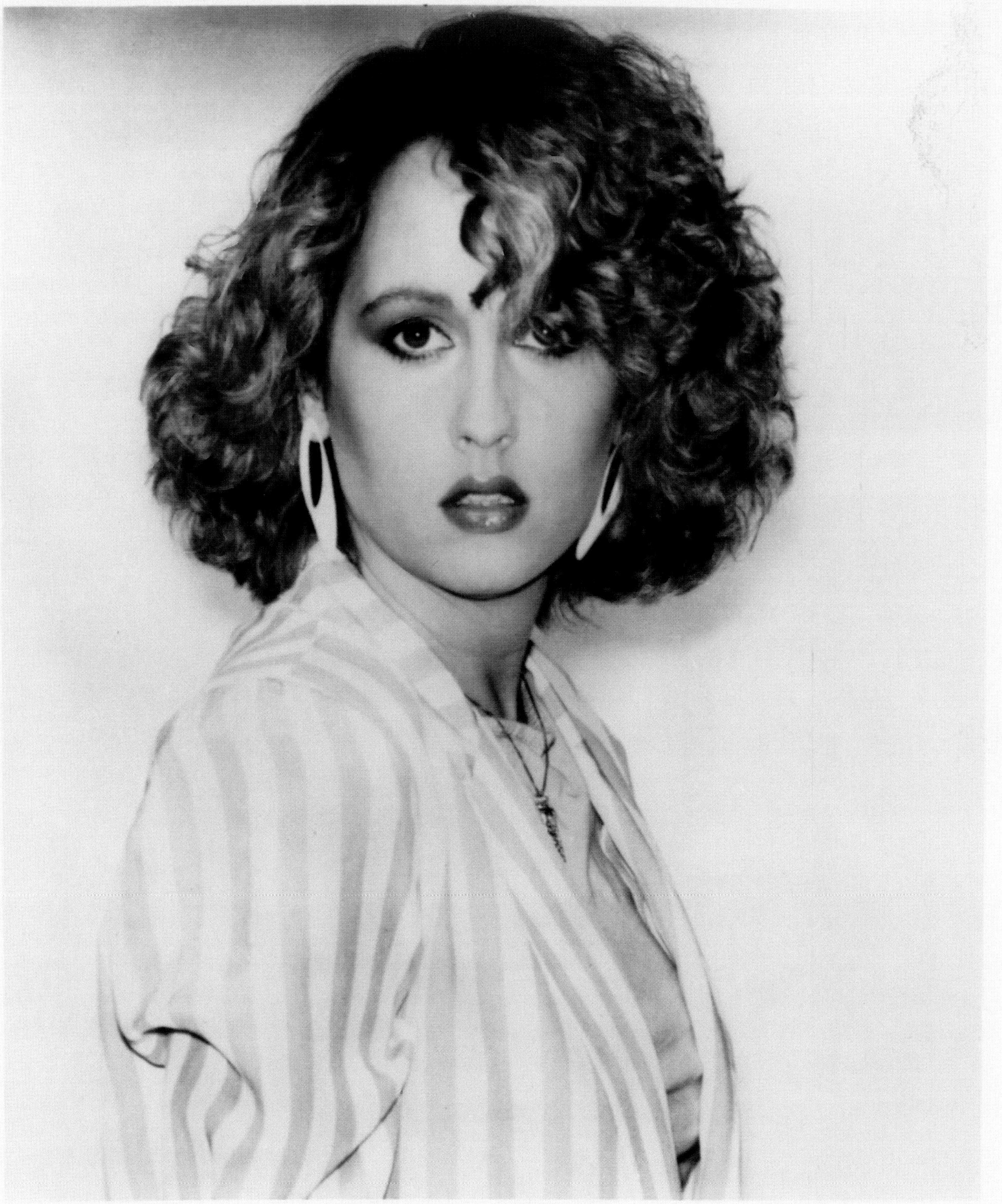

TEENA MARIE

TEENA MARIE ENTERPRISES
213-904-1292

Epic

8311

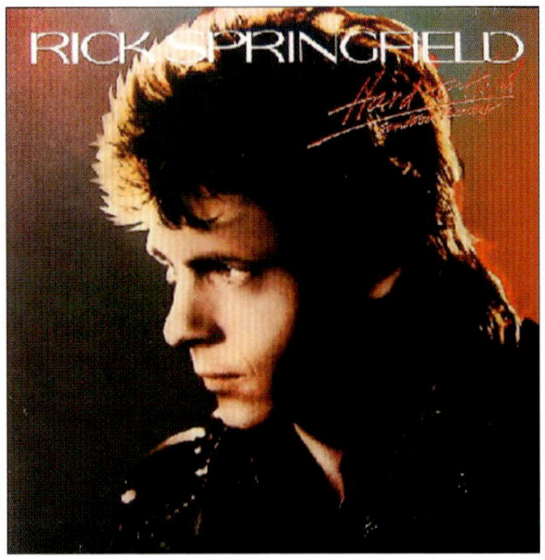

Rick Springfield starred in the feature film *Hard to Hold*, the soundtrack for which spawned three charting singles, including the Top 5 "Love Somebody."

Billboard 200: *Hard to Hold* (#16)
Billboard Hot 100: "Love Somebody" (#5); "Don't Walk Away" (#26); "Bop 'Til You Drop" (#20)

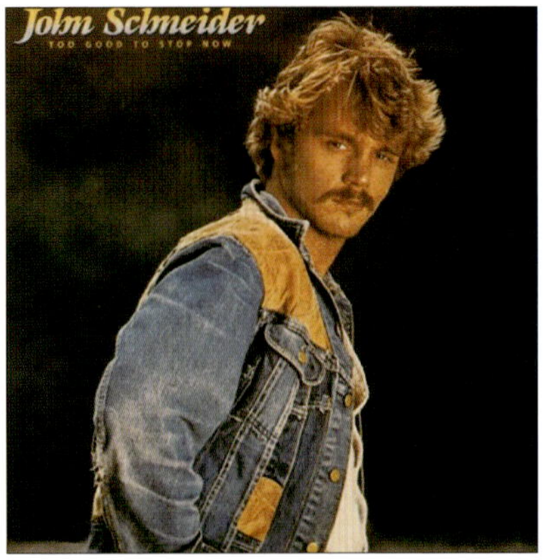

Actor **John Schneider**—Bo Duke of television's *The Dukes of Hazzard*—announced his appearance on the country music scene with a pair of No. 1 hits.

Billboard 200: *Too Good to Stop Now* (#111)

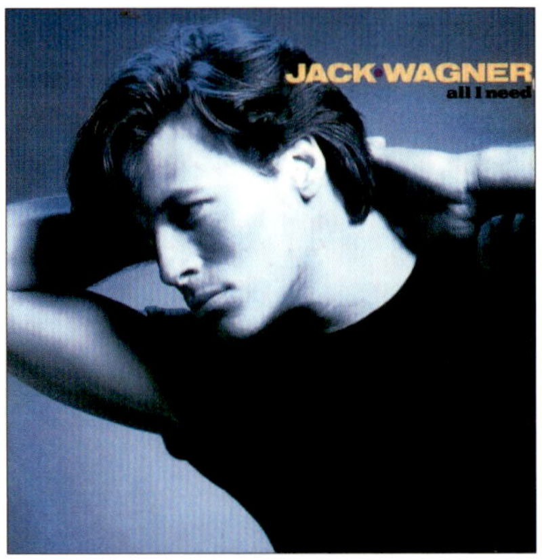

Known for his role as Frisco Jones on the soap opera *General Hospital*, **Jack Wagner** climbed to No. 1 on the adult contemporary charts with "All I Need."

Billboard 200: *All I Need* (#44)
Billboard Hot 100: "All I Need" (#2); "Lady of My Heart" (#76)

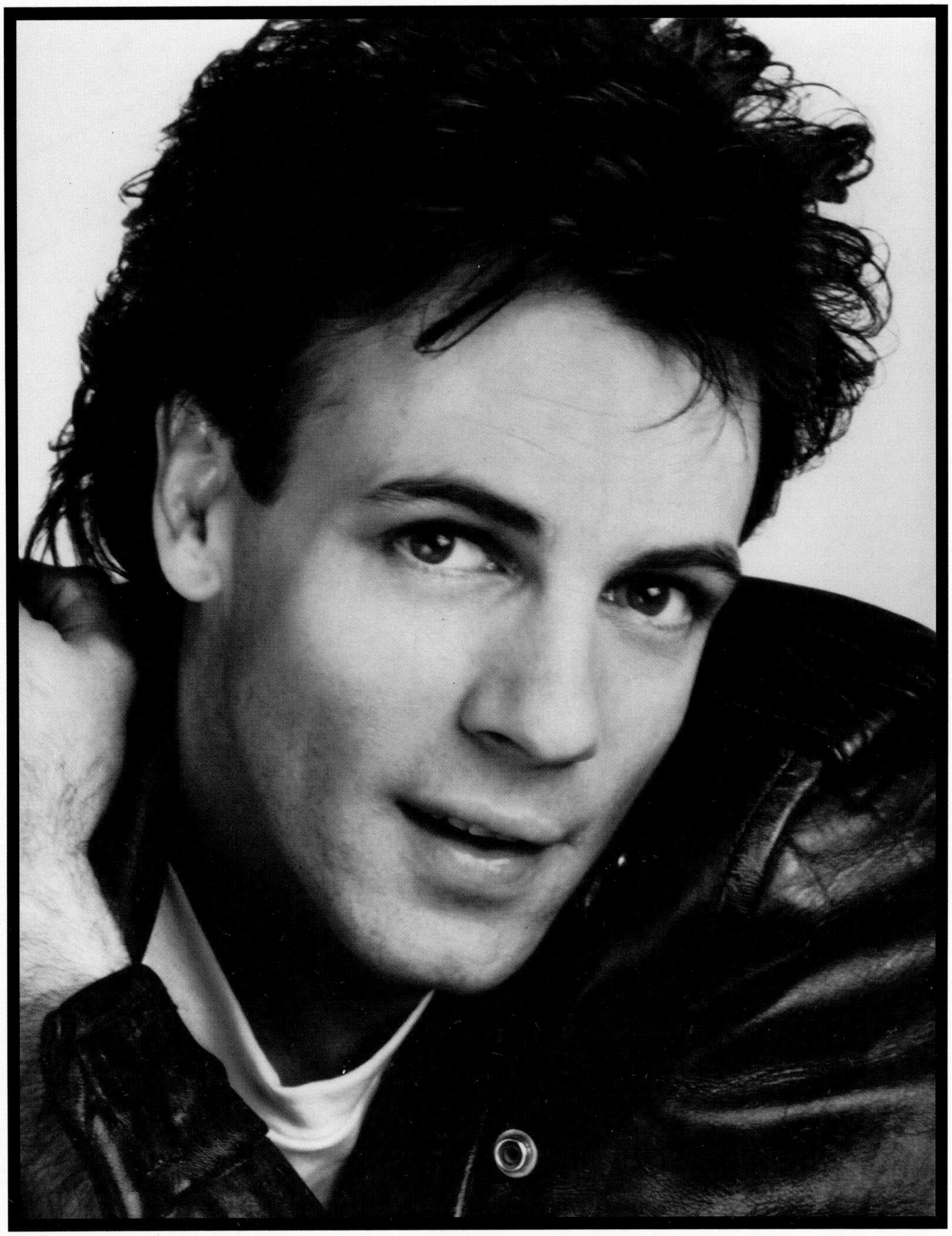

RICK SPRINGFIELD

RCA Records and Tapes

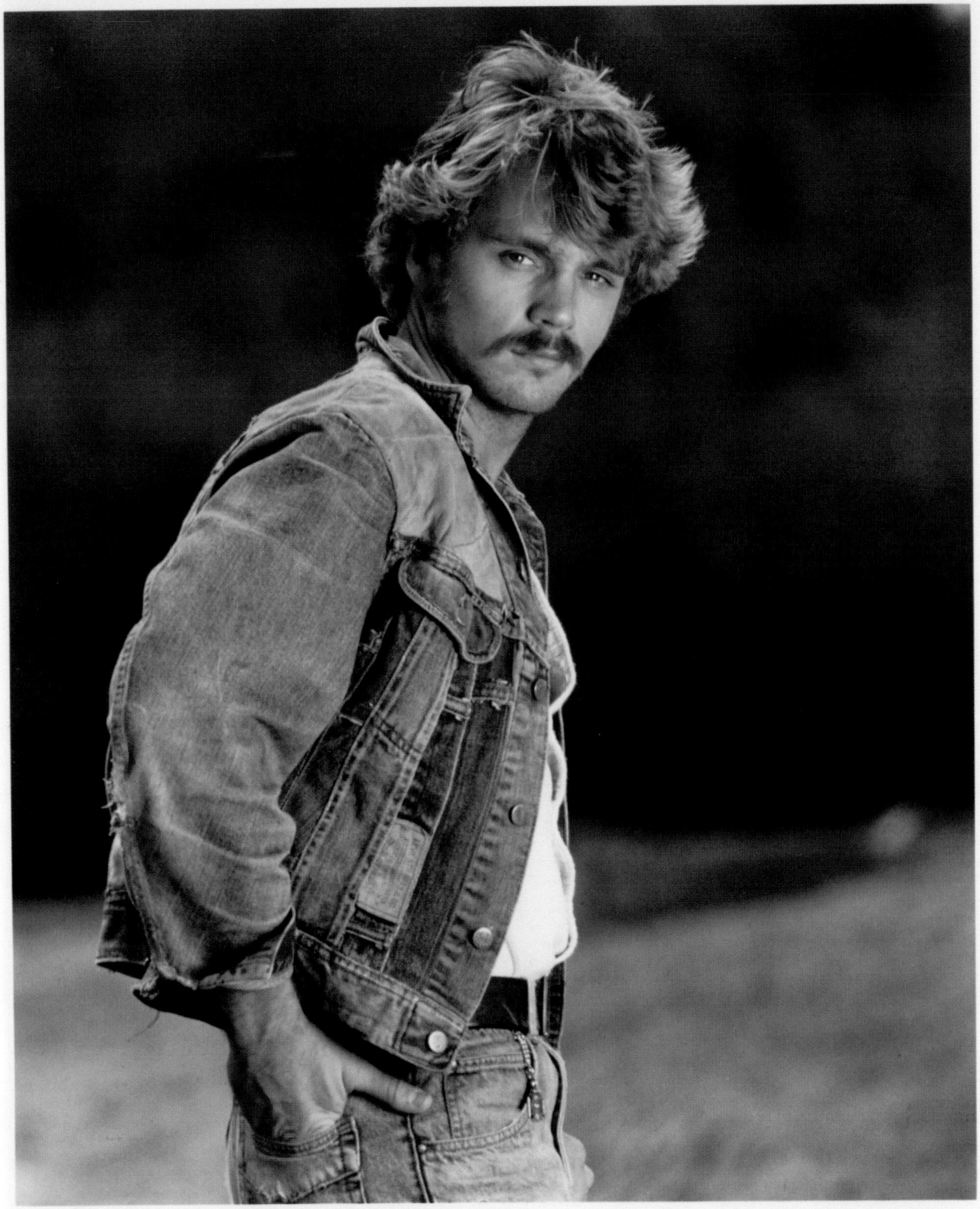

JOHN SCHNEIDER

MCA RECORDS

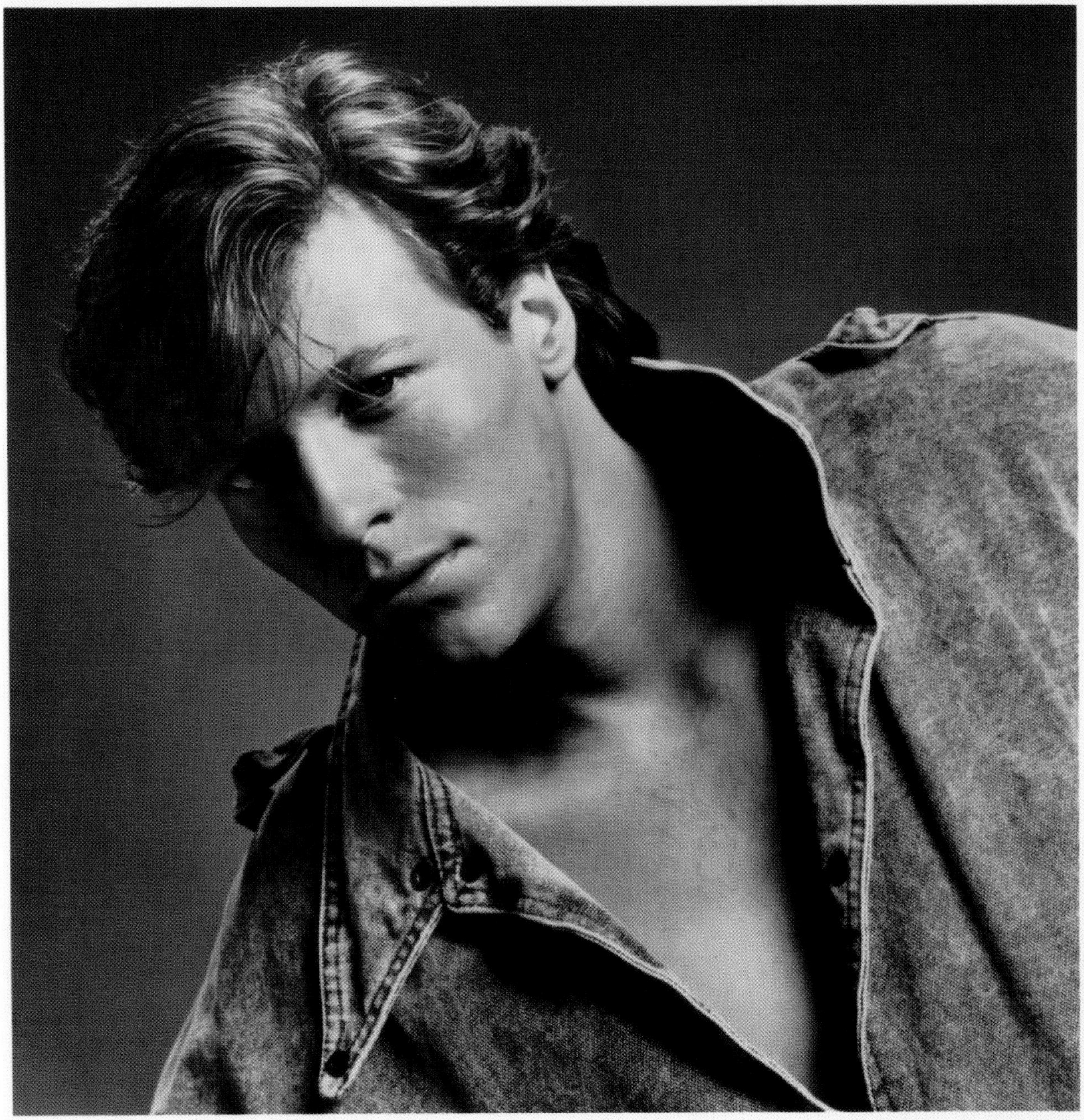

Photo Credit: Penny Wolin

JACK WAGNER

QWEST RECORDS ™

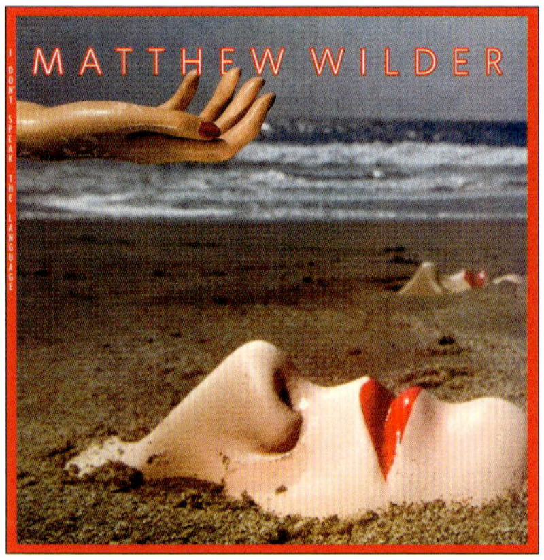

Singer-songwriter **Matthew Wilder** established a trademark hit ditty with "Break My Stride," his upbeat declaration of individuality in the music business.

Billboard 200: *I Don't Speak the Language* (#49)
Billboard Hot 100: "Break My Stride" (#5);
"The Kid's American" (#33)

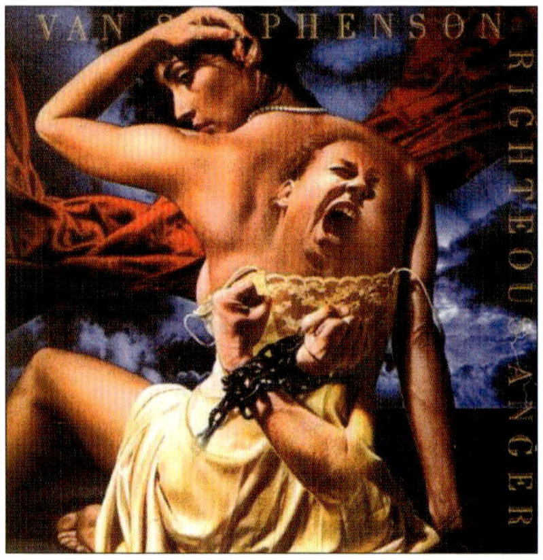

Concurrent with his success as a songwriter, **Van Stephenson** scored a big hit on the pop charts as a recording artist, releasing "Modern Day Delilah."

Billboard 200: *Righteous Anger* (#54)
Billboard Hot 100: "Modern Day Delilah" (#22);
"What the Big Girls Do" (#45)

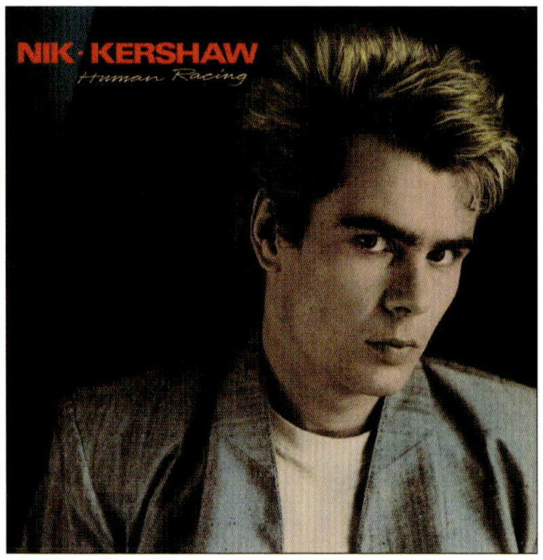

English singer-songwriter **Nik Kershaw** released his breakthrough single "Wouldn't It Be Good," resulting in pop stardom in the UK and a hit in the US.

Billboard 200: *Human Racing* (#70)
Billboard Hot 100: "Wouldn't It Be Good" (#46)

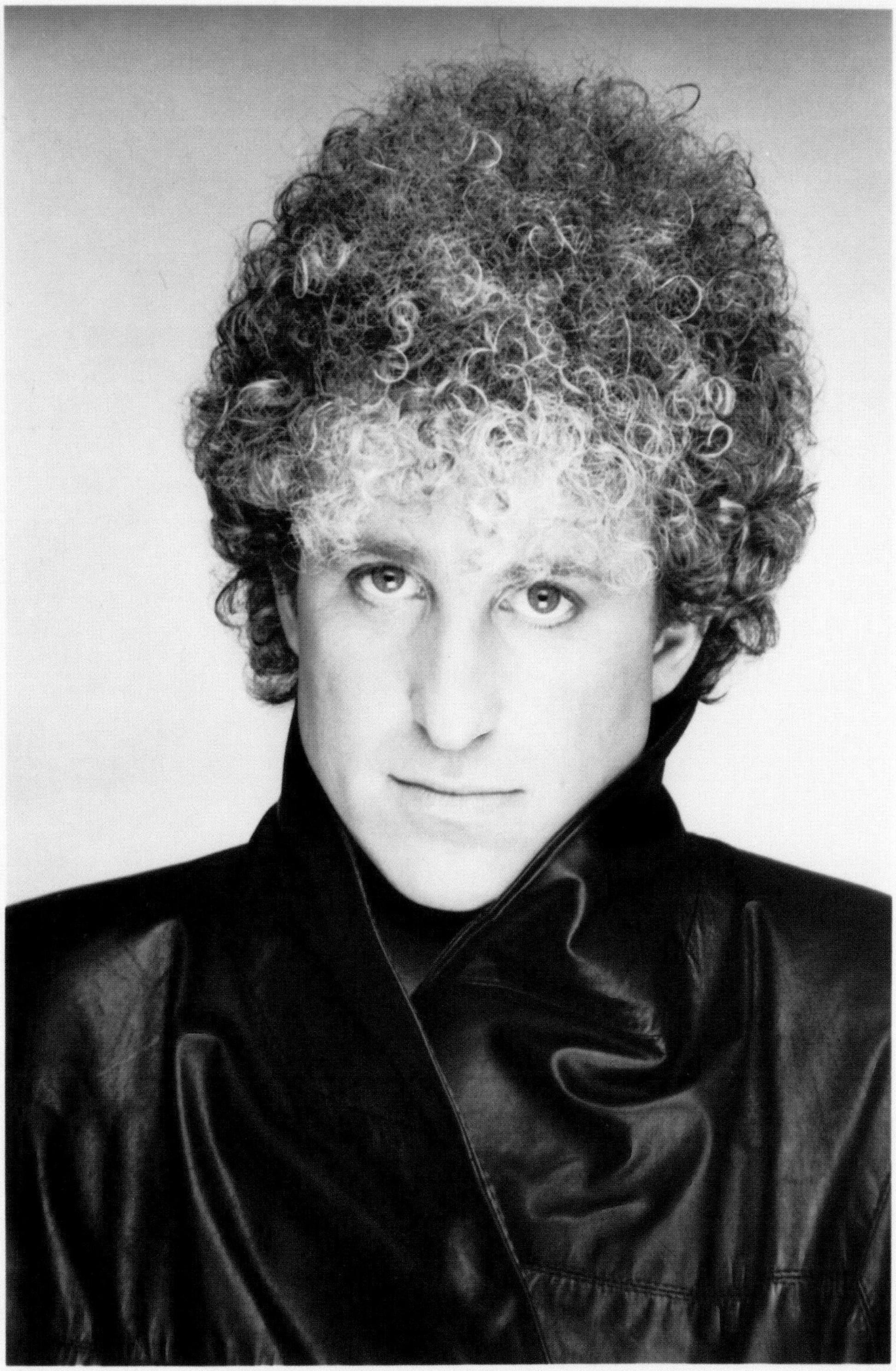

PRIVATE I RECORDS

MATTHEW WILDER

EPA
EPIC PORTRAIT ASSOCIATED
8408

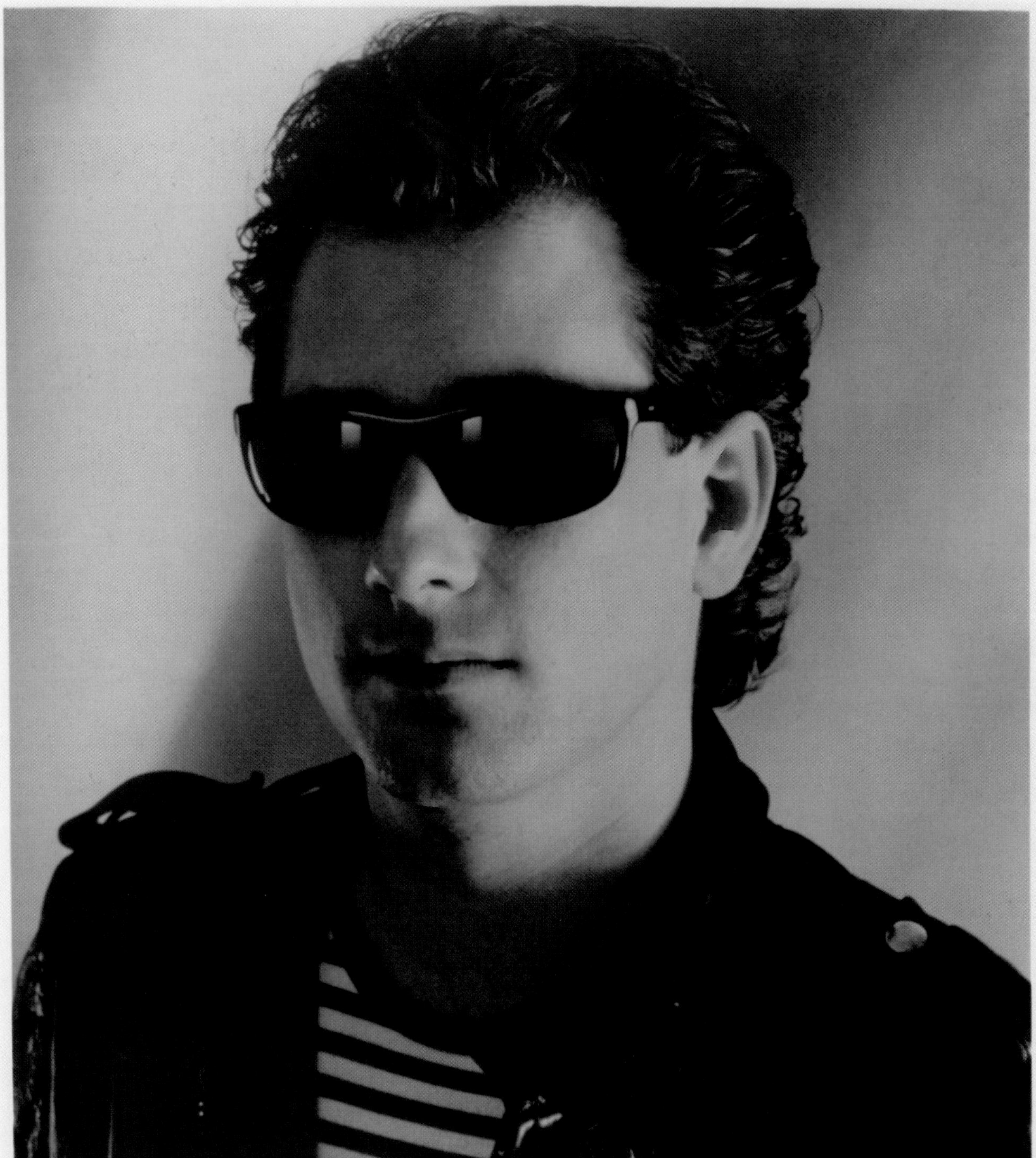

4/84

VAN STEPHENSON

MCA RECORDS

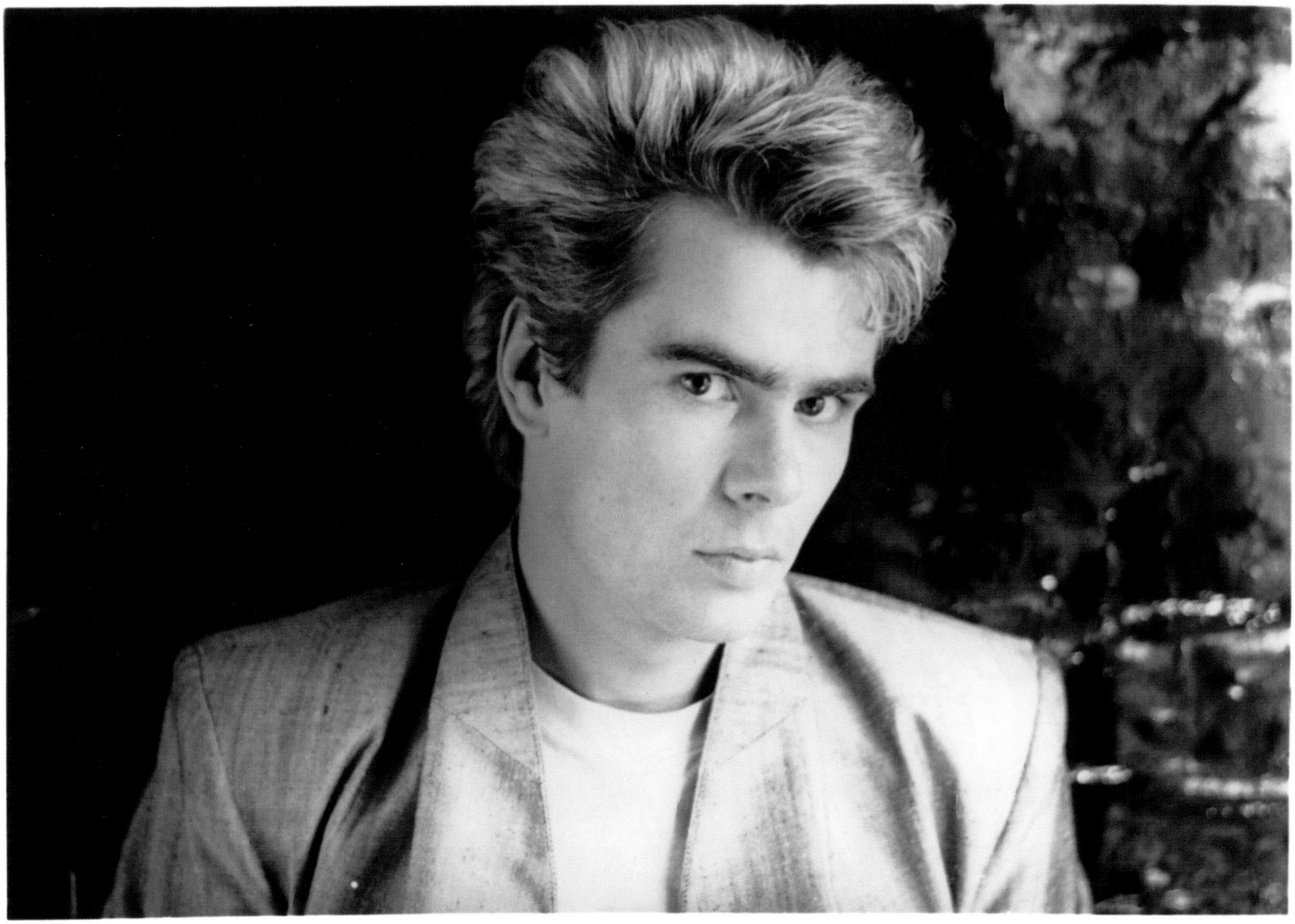

NIK · KERSHAW

MCA RECORDS

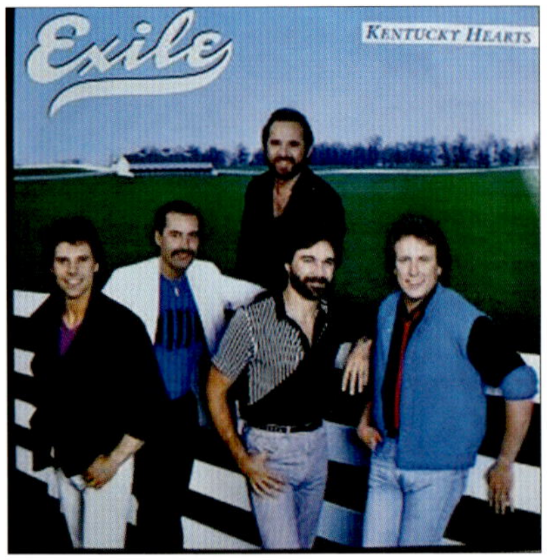

After reaching the pop charts in the late Seventies, **Exile** had switched to country music, landing a troika of No. 1 hits from the album *Kentucky Hearts*.

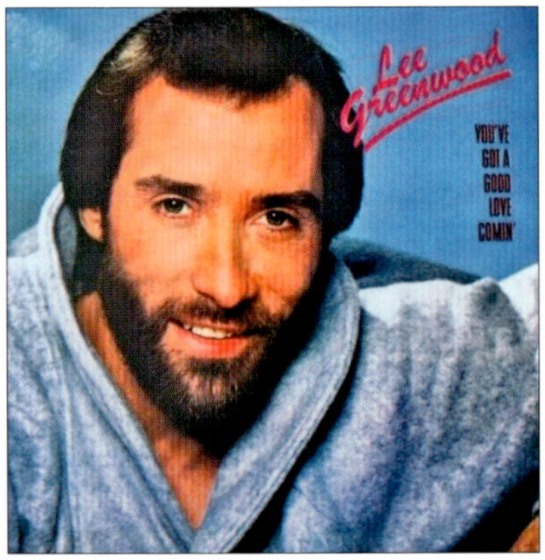

Lee Greenwood wrote and recorded his signature anthem, the patriotic "God Bless the USA," released on his third album, *You've Got a Good Love Comin'*.

Billboard 200: *You've Got a Good Love Comin'* (#150)

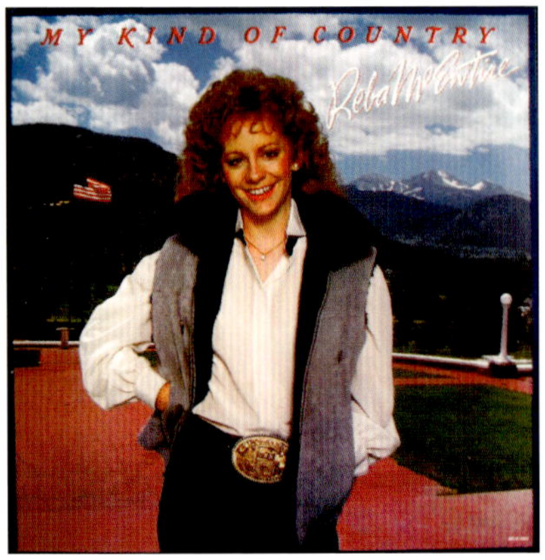

Two songs from **Reba McEntire**'s pointedly titled *My Kind of Country* rose to No. 1 on the country charts–"How Blue" and "Somebody Should Leave."

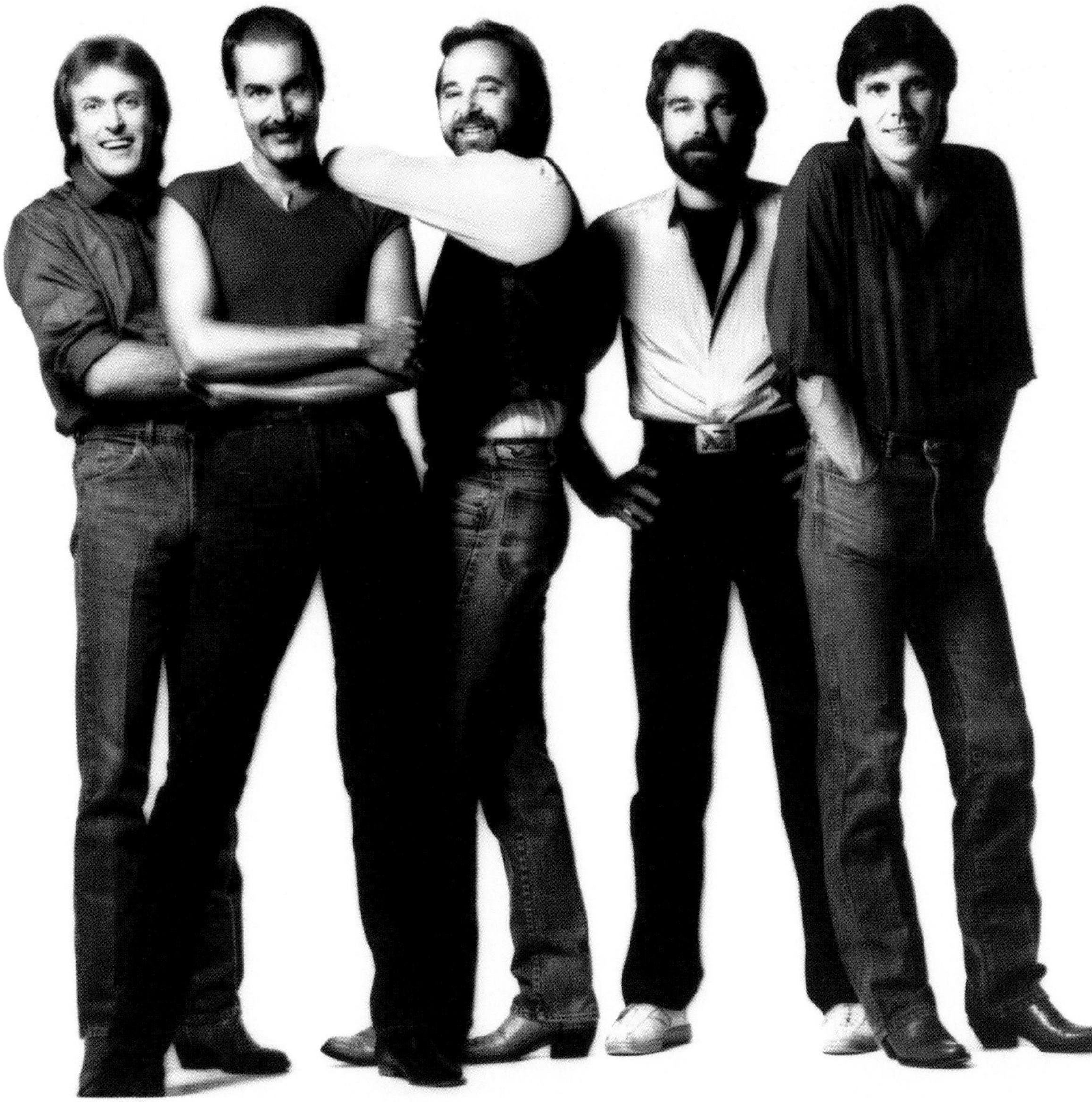

photo credit: NORMAN SEEFF

Epic

Exile

IN CONCERT INTERNATIONAL, INC.
P.O. Box 22419 Nashville, Tennessee 37202 Phone (615) 244-9550

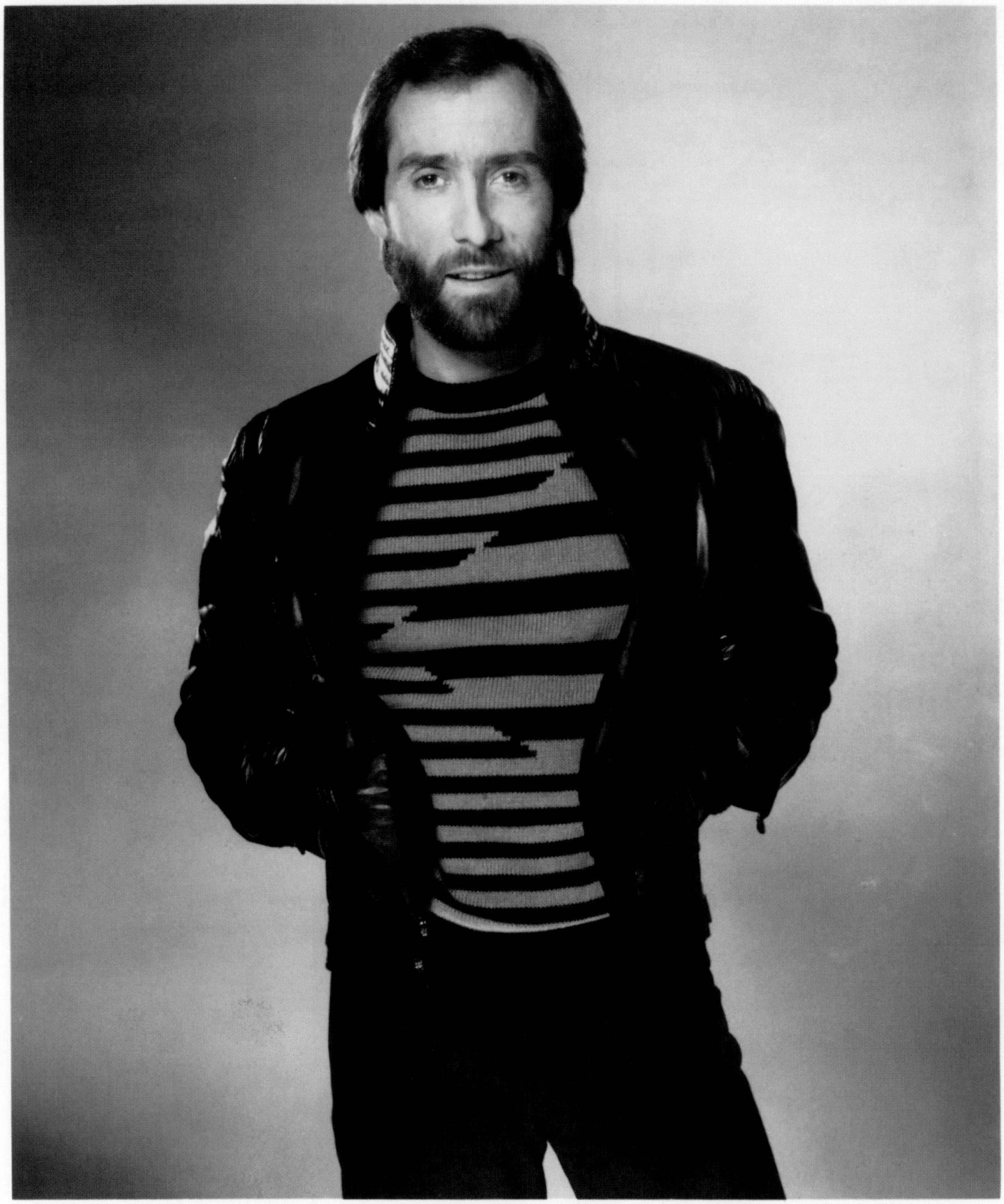

HARRY LANGDON PHOTOGRAPHY © 1984

KATHY GANGWISCH & ASSOC., INC.
(8 1 6) 9 3 1 8 0 0 0

Lee Greenwood

MCA RECORDS

THE JIM HALSEY CO. INC.
3225 S. NORWOOD
TULSA, OKLAHOMA 74135
(918) 663-3883

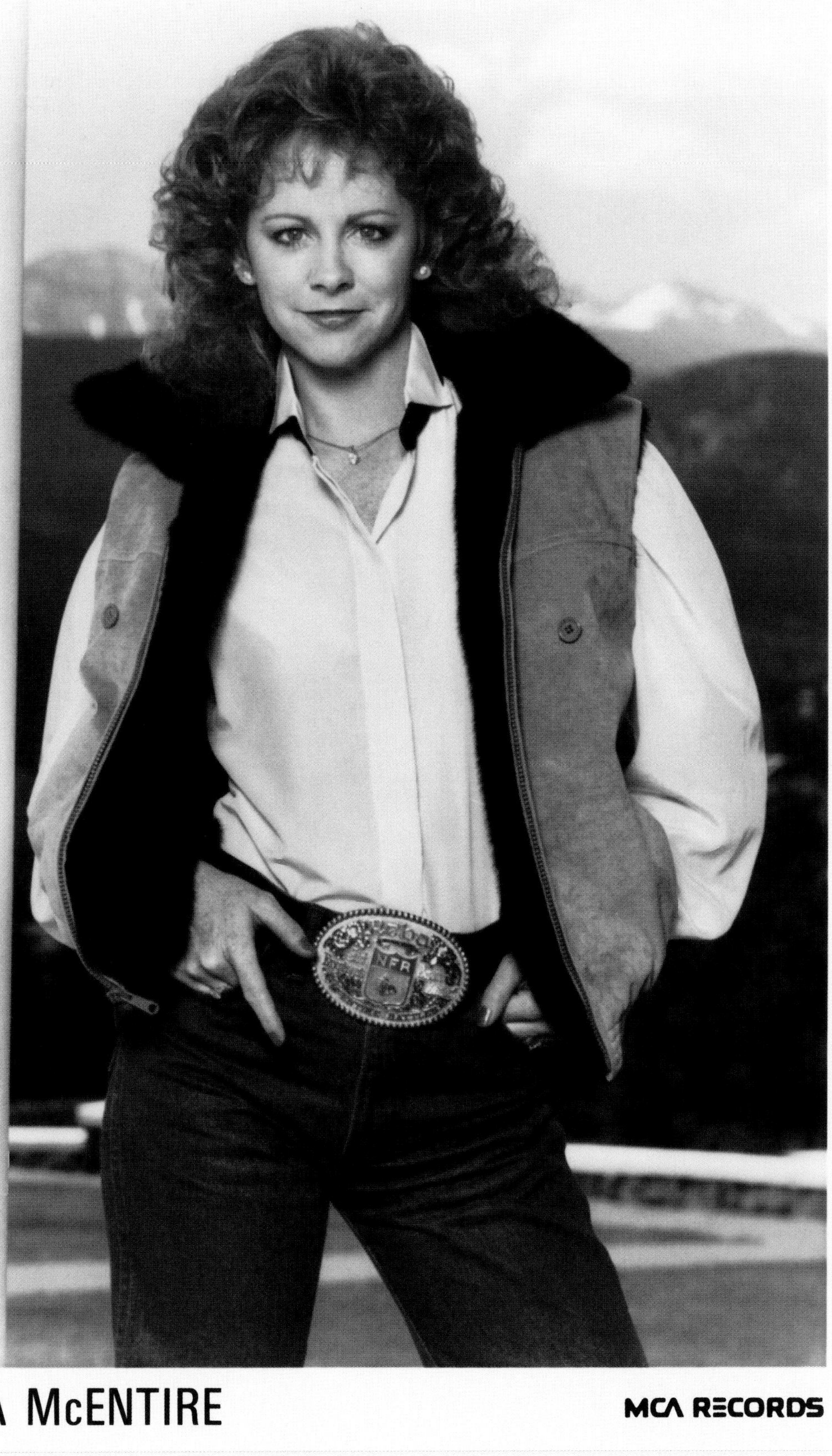

REBA McENTIRE

MCA RECORDS

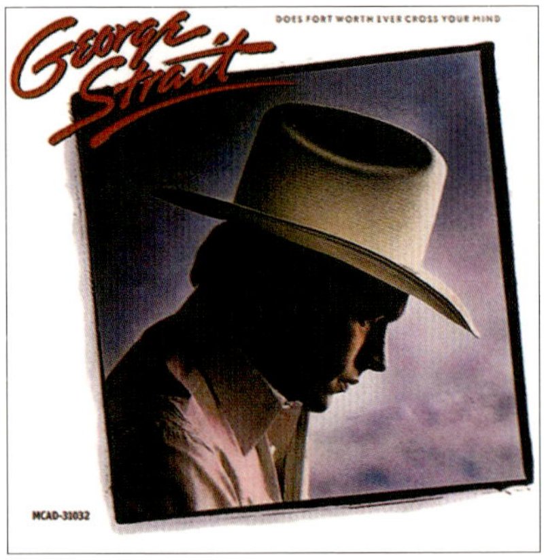

Traditionalist **George Strait**'s *Does Fort Worth Ever Cross Your Mind*, a CMA award winner, ascended to No. 1 on the country charts, as did the title track.

Billboard 200: *Does Fort Worth Ever Cross Your Mind* (#139)

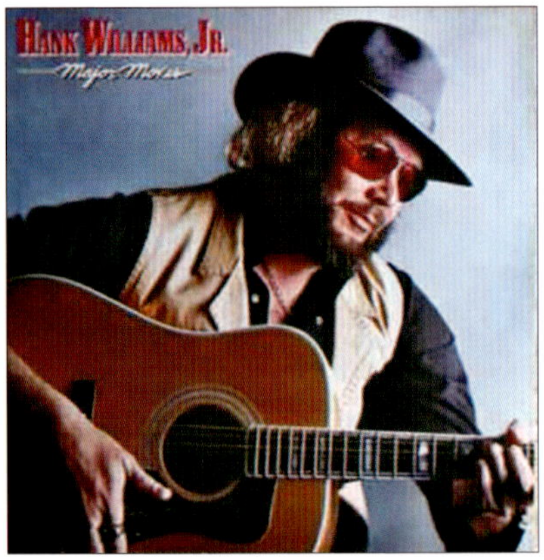

Major Moves, **Hank Williams Jr.**'s first No. 1 album on the country charts, generated a hell-raising anthem, "All My Rowdy Friends Are Coming Over Tonight."

Billboard 200: *Major Moves* (#100)

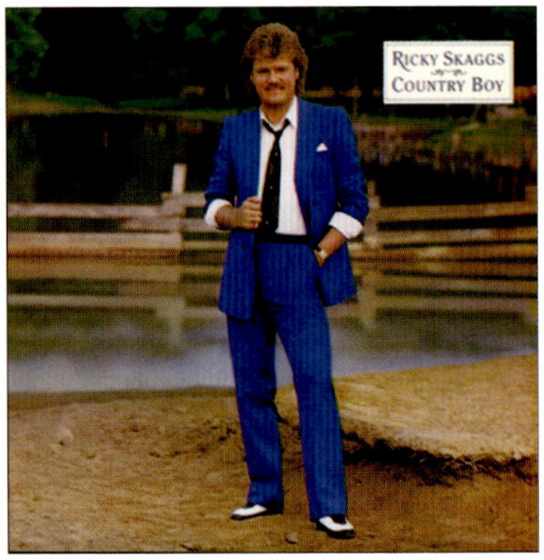

Bluegrass pioneer Bill Monroe appeared in the entertaining video for "Country Boy" by **Ricky Skaggs**, which peaked at No. 1 on the country singles chart.

Billboard 200: *Country Boy* (#180)

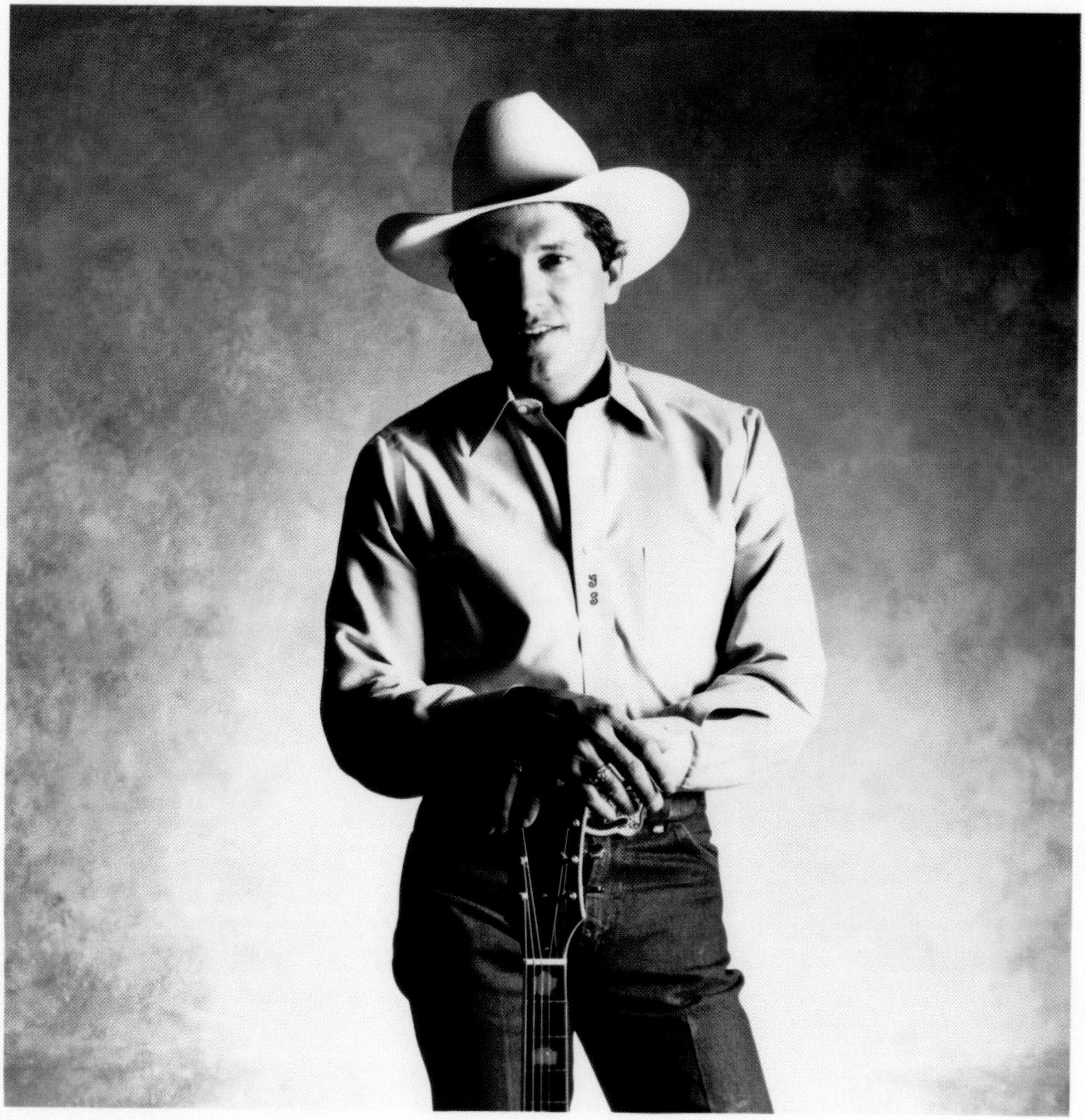

GEORGE STRAIT

MCA RECORDS

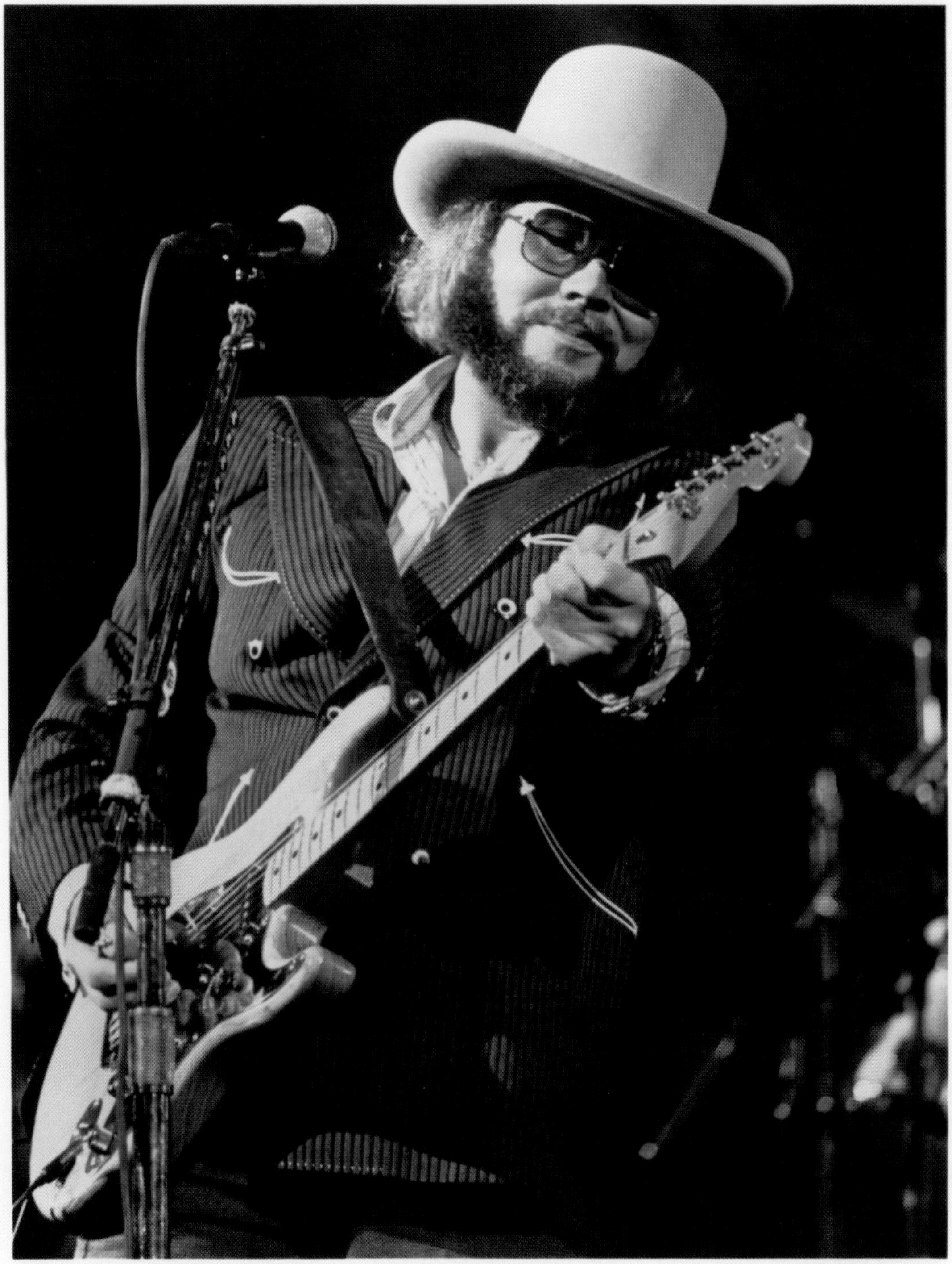

photo credit: Jacki Sallow/1984

HANK WILLIAMS JR.

CURB RECORDS

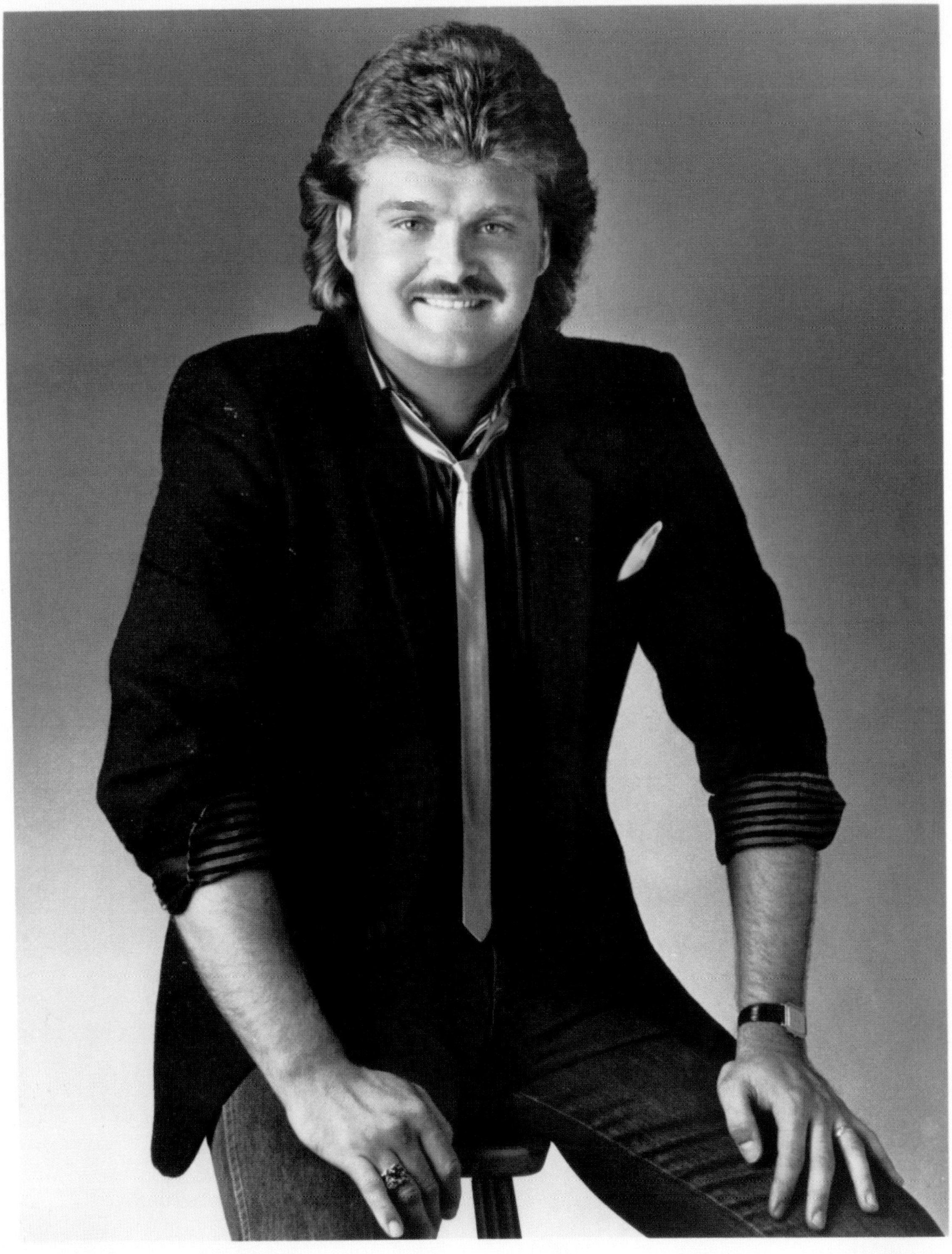

photo credit: LEONARD KAMSLER

RICKY SKAGGS

Epic
8409

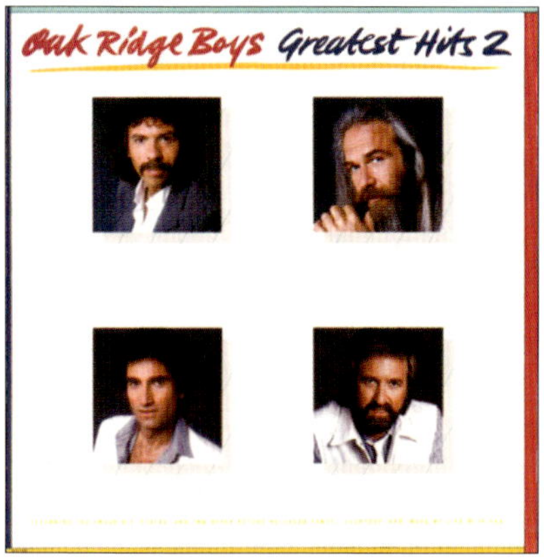

The Oak Ridge Boys' compilation *Greatest Hits 2* added the new songs "Everyday" and "Make My Life with You," their tenth and eleventh No. 1 country hits.

Billboard 200: *Greatest Hits 2* (#71)

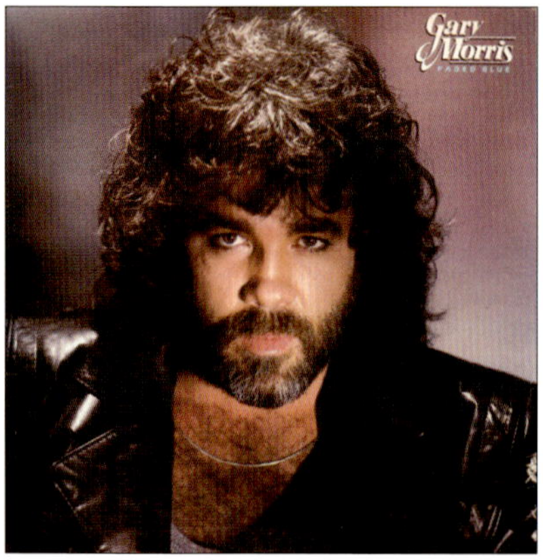

From the album *Faded Blue*, balladeer **Gary Morris** garnered his first chart-topping hit when "Baby Bye Bye" reached No. 1 on the country singles chart.

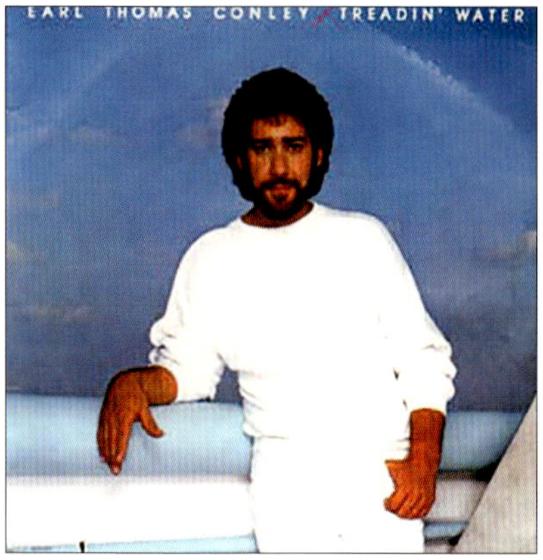

Earl Thomas Conley's *Treadin' Water* featured the No. 1 country hits "Honor Bound," "Chance of Lovin' You" and "Love Don't Care (Whose Heart It Breaks)."

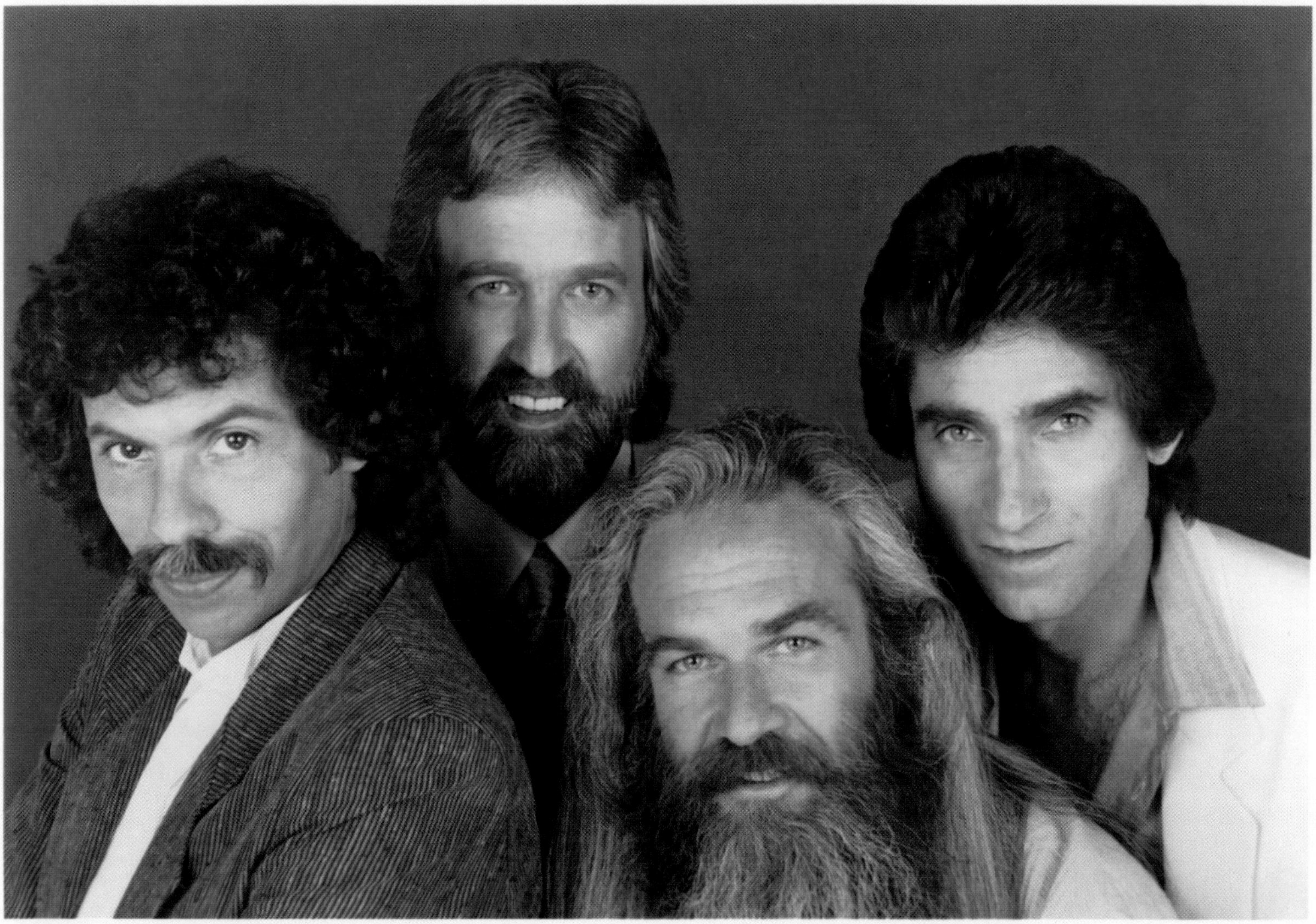

The Oak Ridge Boys

MCA RECORDS

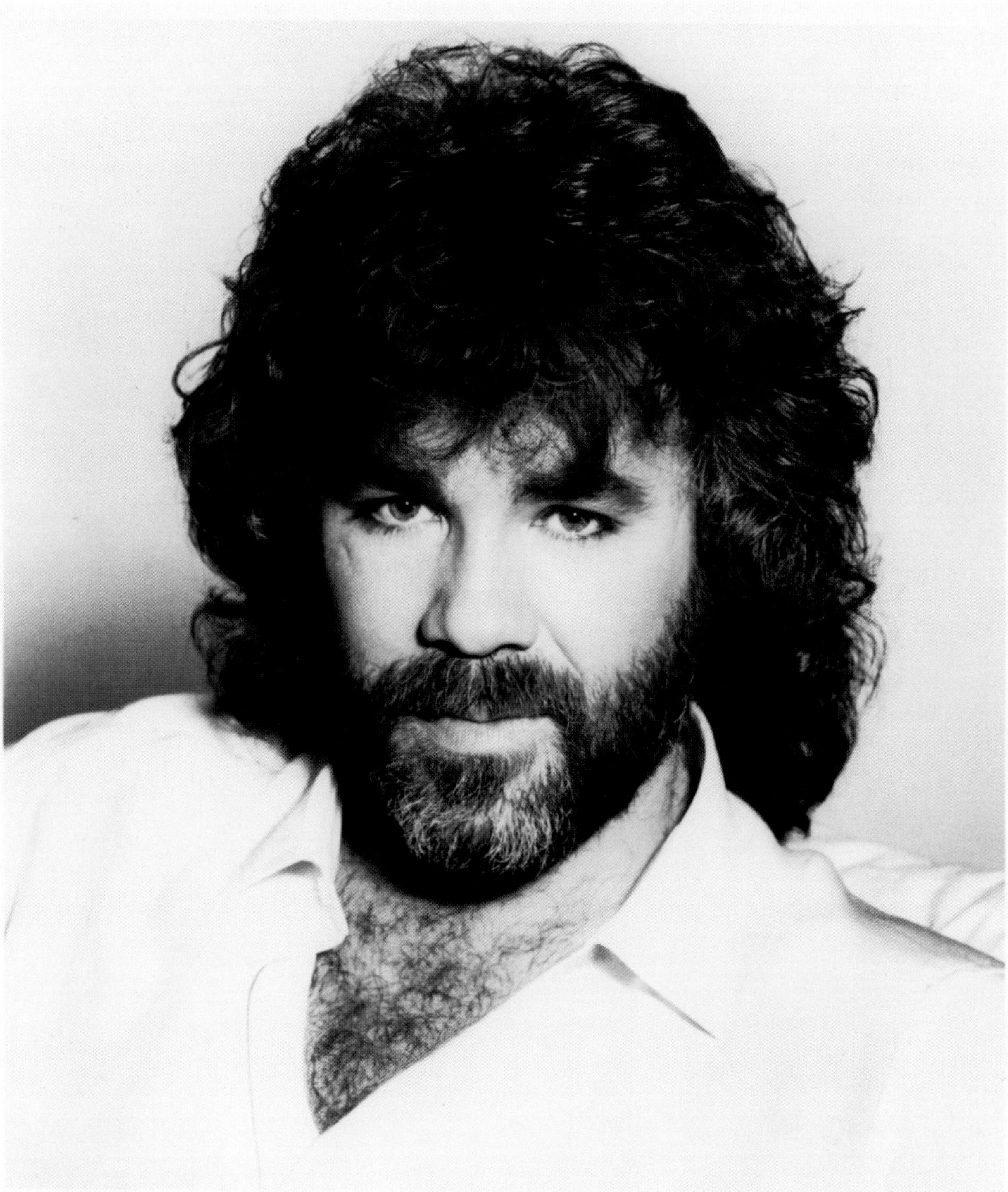

Photo Credit: Dick Zimmerman/1984

Gary Morris

WARNER BROS.

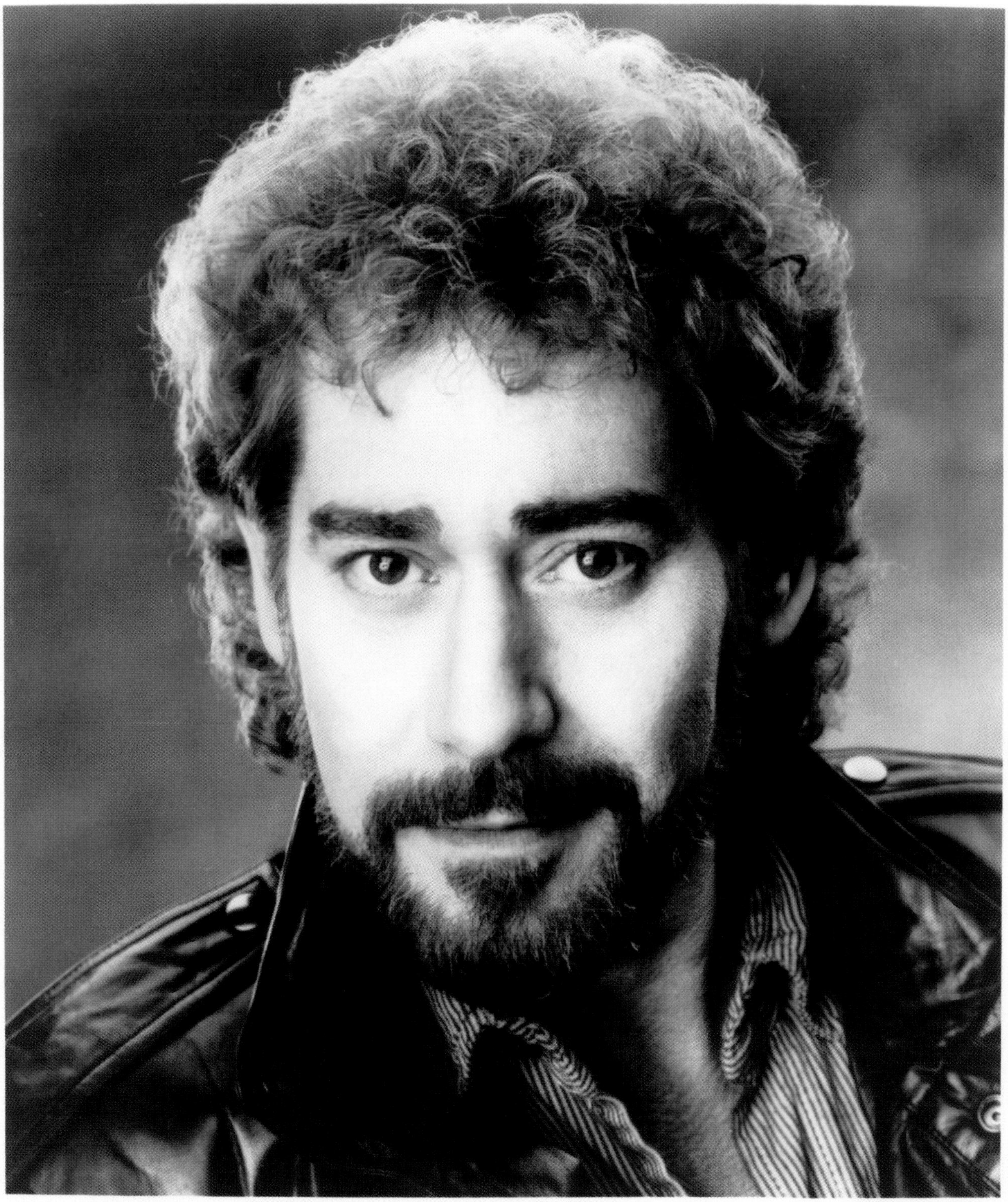

EARL THOMAS CONLEY

RCA Records and Cassettes

30 Music Square West
Nashville, TN 37203
Telephone (615) 244-9880

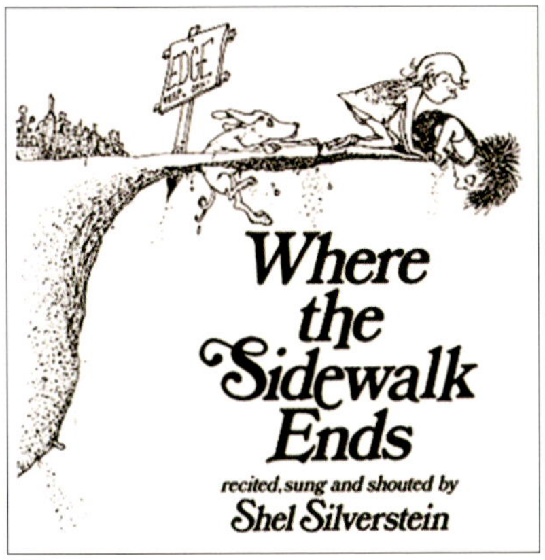

The audio edition of *Where the Sidewalk Ends*, an album based on **Shel Silverstein**'s best-selling book, earned the Grammy for Best Recording for Children.

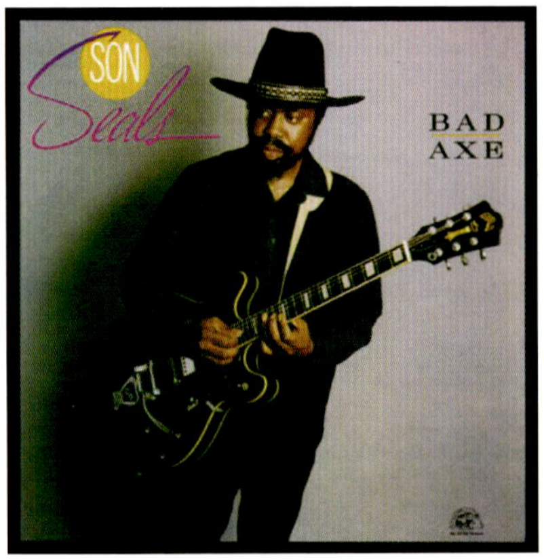

One of Chicago's greatest artists, **Son Seals** recorded *Bad Axe* for Alligator Records and won a W.C. Handy Award for Contemporary Blues Album of the Year.

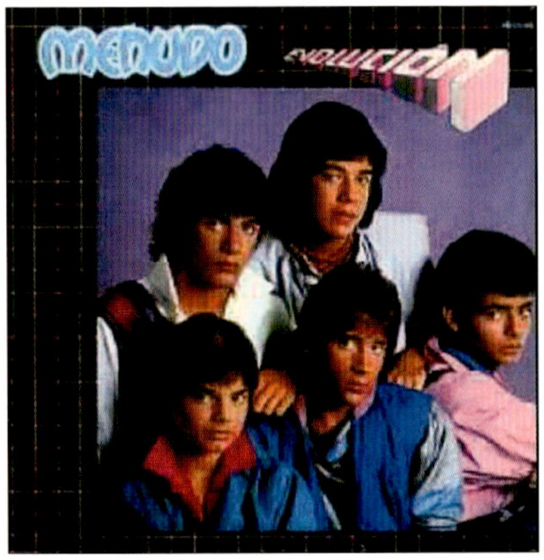

Menudo, Latin America's most popular teen group, issued the Spanish-language release *Evolución*, the starting point for new member Ricky Martin.

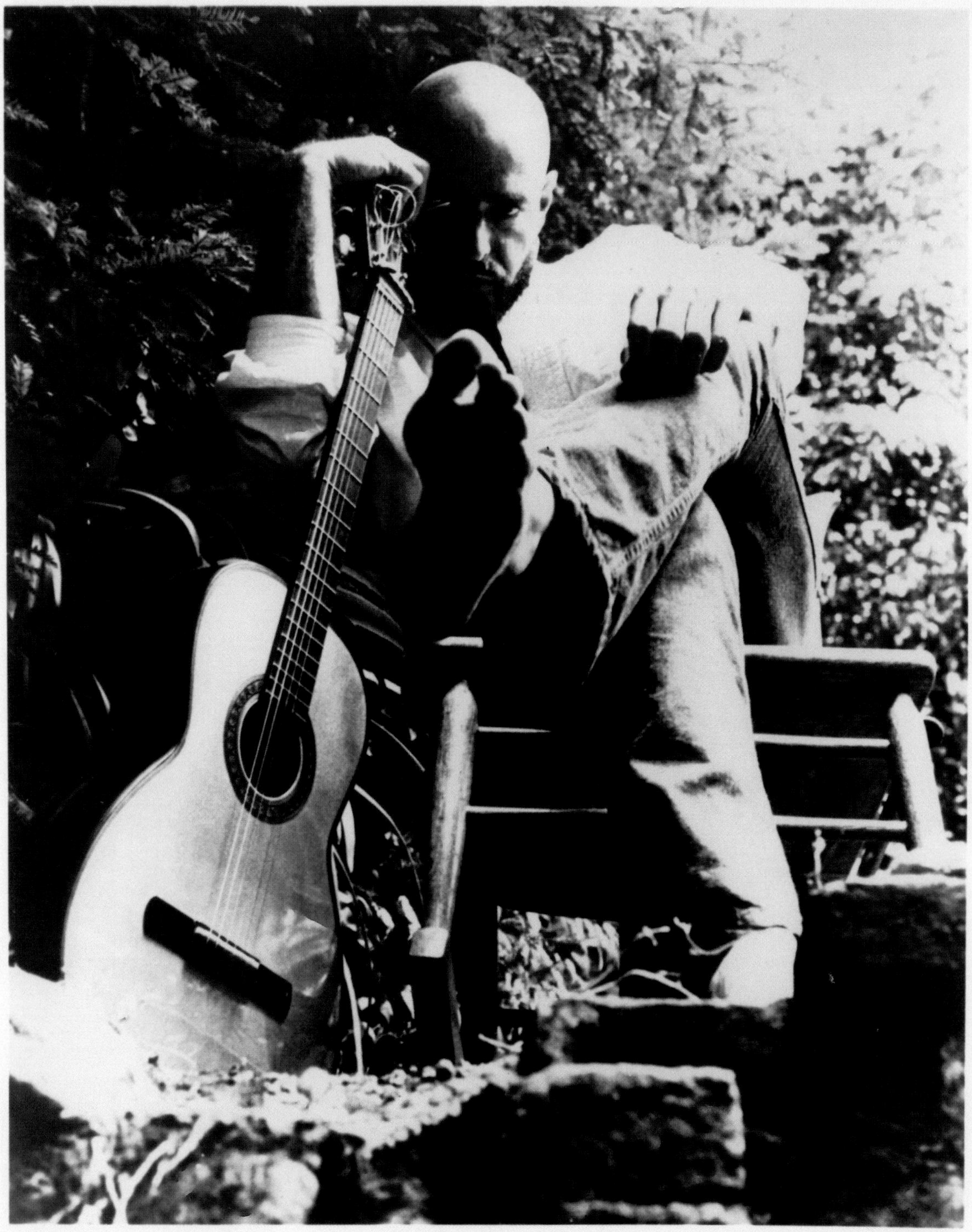

Shel Silverstein

Columbia
8408

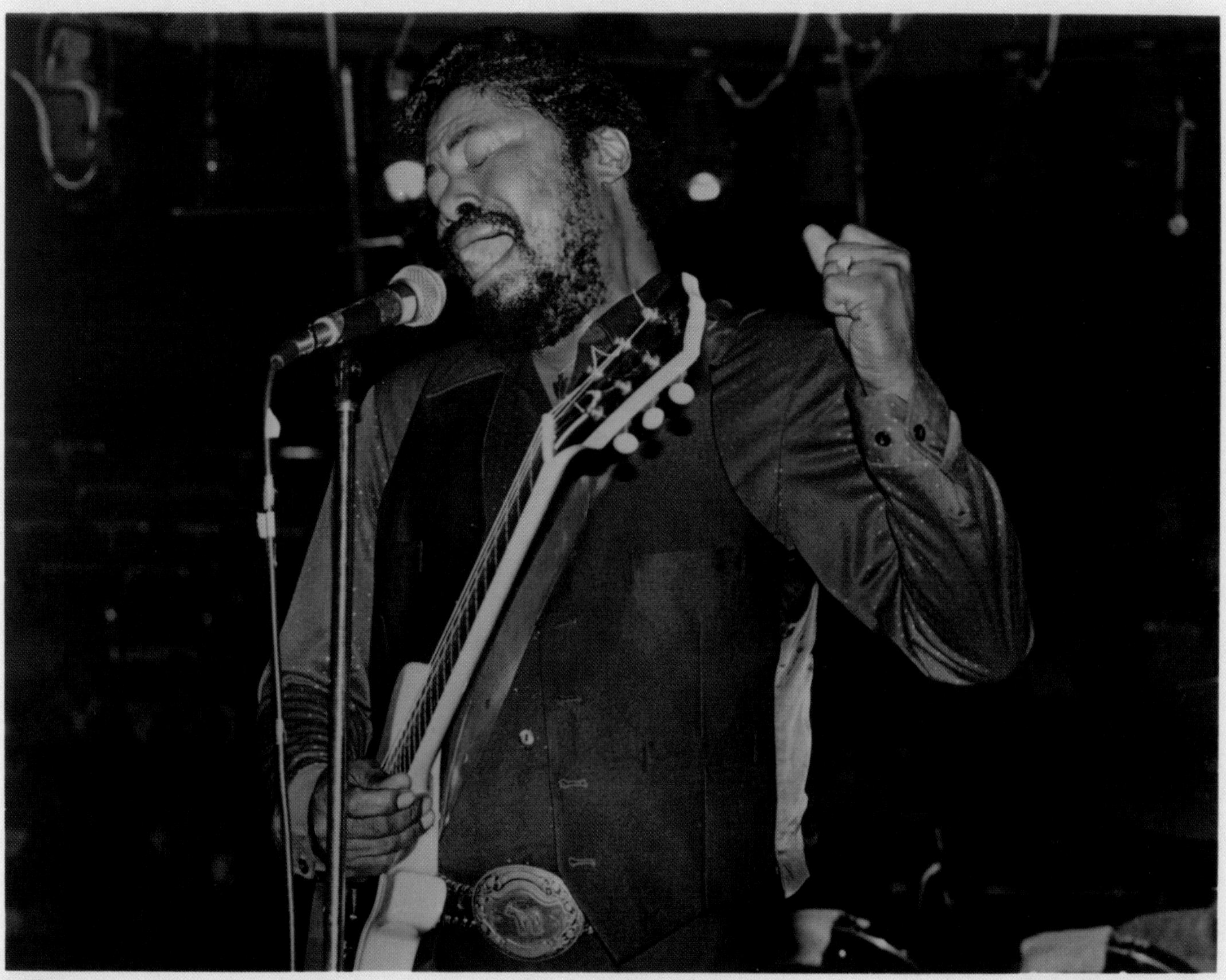

SON SEALS

PHOTO: STEVE KAGAN

MANAGEMENT:
ALLIGATOR PRODUCTIONS
BOX 60234
CHICAGO, IL 60660
(312) 973-7736

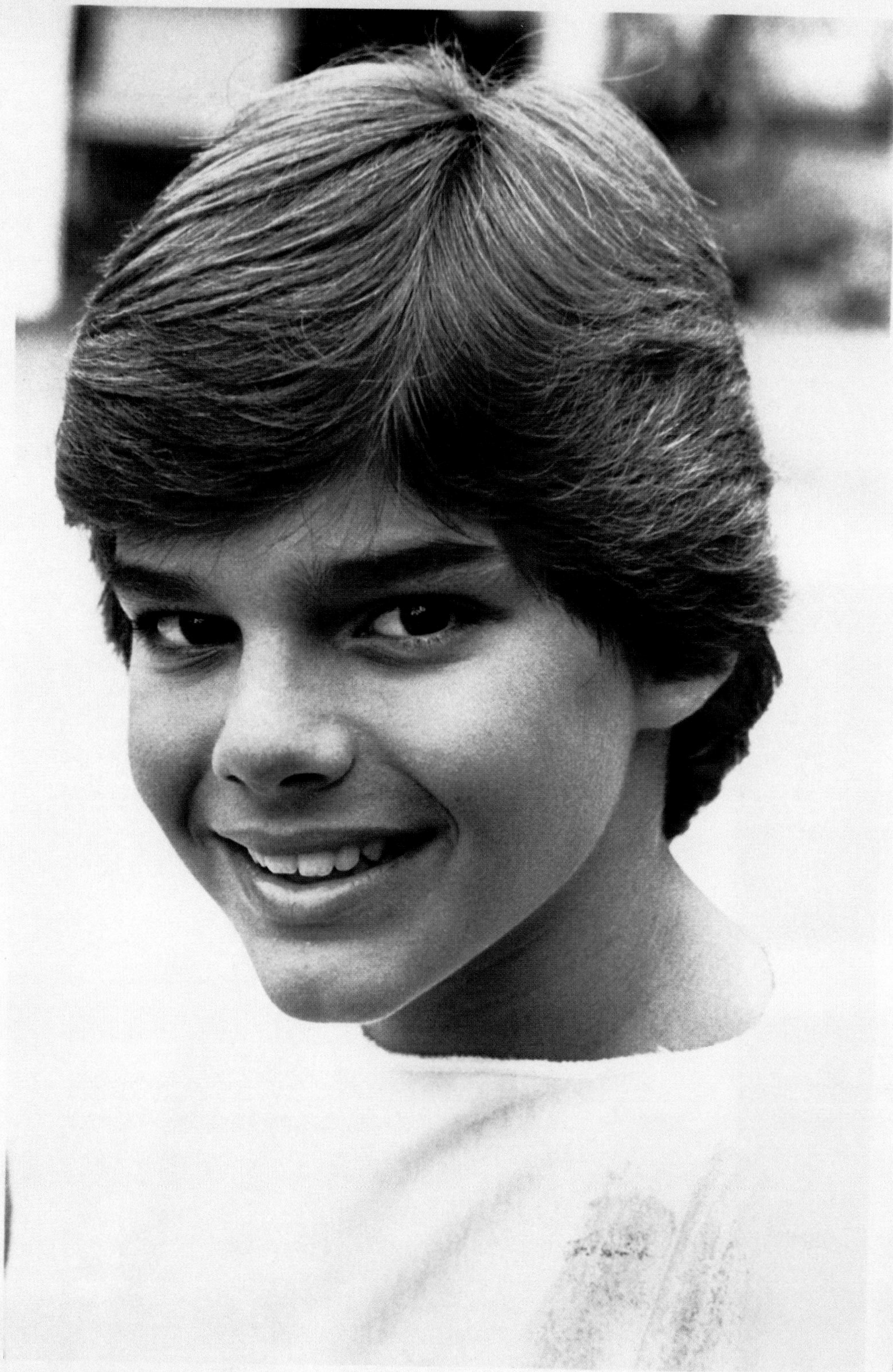

Photo: Rio Hernandez

MENUDO™ RICKY MARTIN RCA International

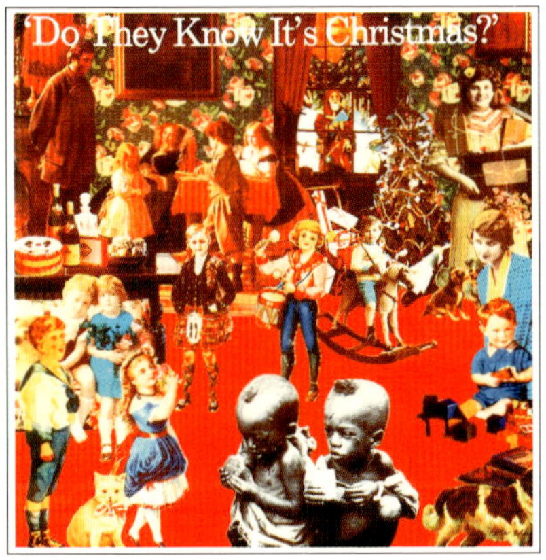

Band Aid, comprised primarily of British and Irish musicians, raised money to combat famine in Ethiopia through the single "Do They Know It's Christmas?"

Billboard Hot 100: "Do They Know It's Christmas?" (#13)

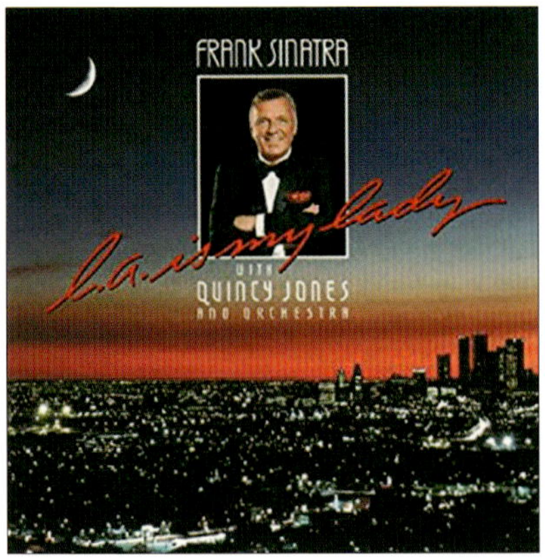

Mostly recorded in New York City, *L.A. Is My Lady*, arranged and produced under the direction of Quincy Jones, was **Frank Sinatra**'s last true solo release.

Billboard 200: *L.A. Is My Lady* (#58)

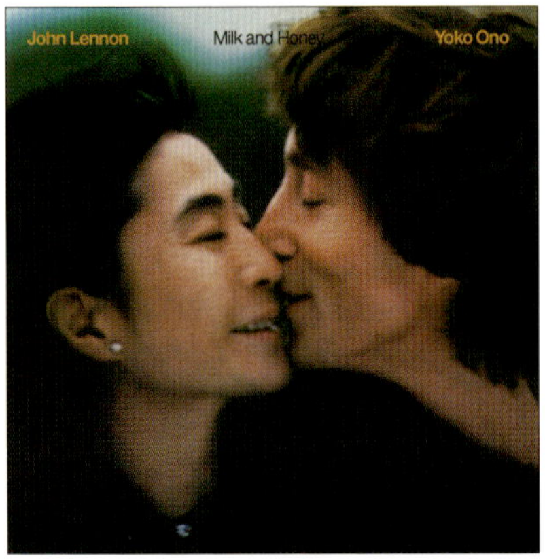

Milk and Honey by **John Lennon & Yoko Ono**, recorded in the last months of Lennon's life, featured the jaunty "Nobody Told Me," a posthumous worldwide hit.

Billboard 200: *Milk and Honey* (#11)
Billboard Hot 100: "Nobody Told Me" (#5);
"I'm Stepping Out" (#55)

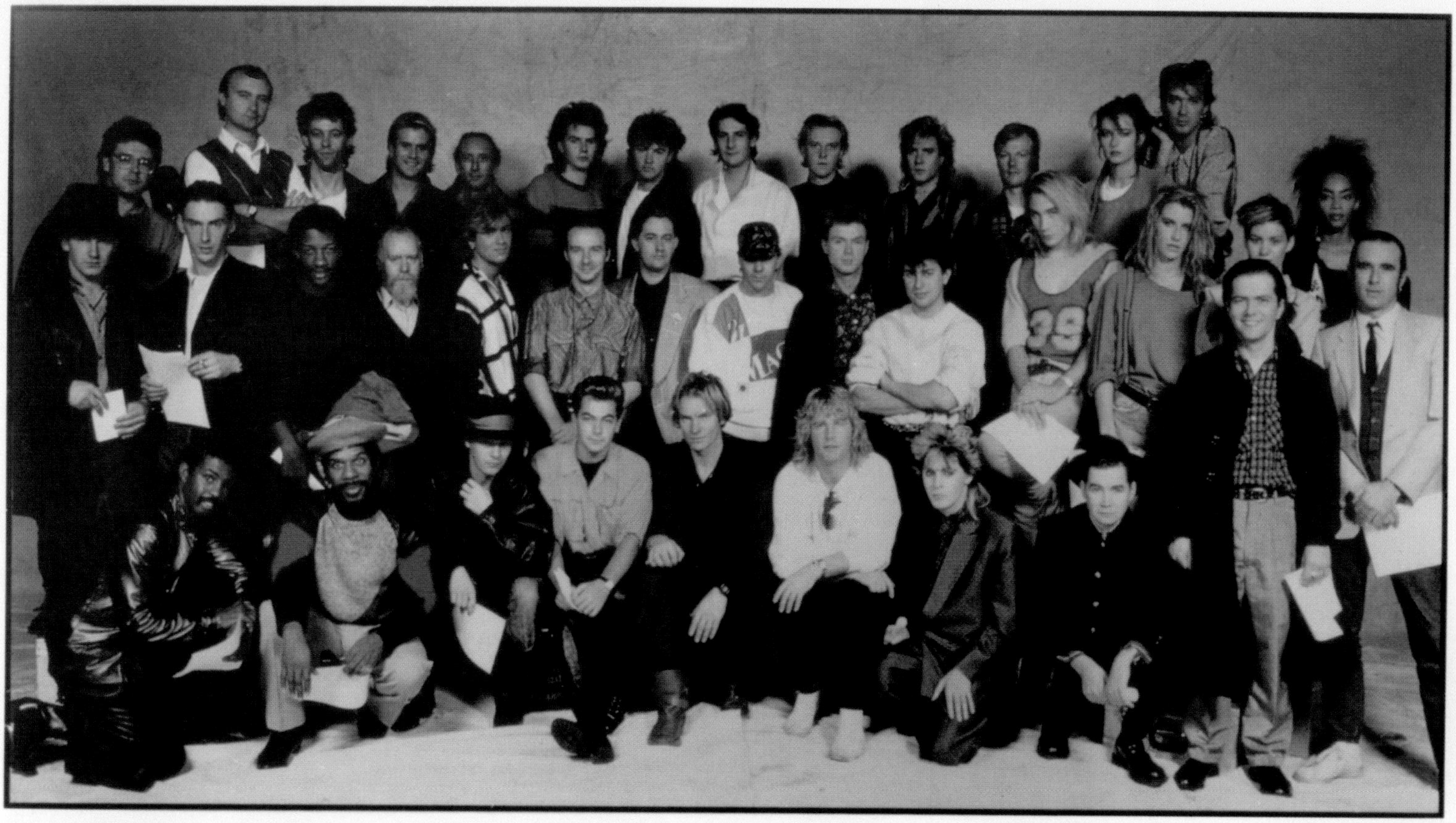

PHOTOGRAPH: BRIAN ARIS

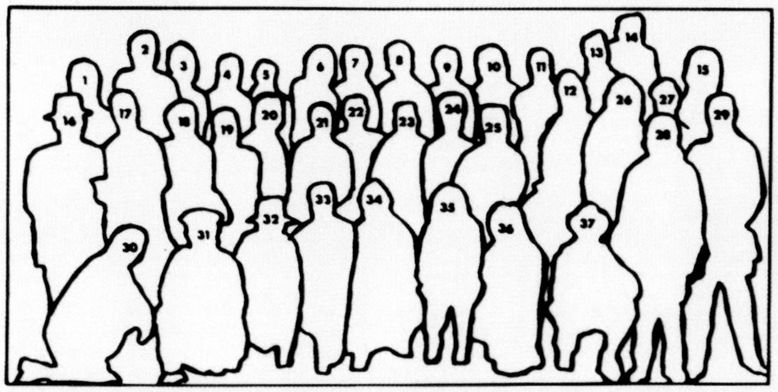

BAND AID are

1 Adam Clayton
2 Phil Collins
3 Bob Geldof
4 Steve Norman
5 Chris Cross
6 John Taylor
7 Paul Young
8 Tony Hadley
9 Glenn Gregory
10 Simon Le Bon
11 Simon Crowe
12 Marilyn
13 Keren
14 Martin Kemp
15 Jody Watley
16 Bono
17 Paul Weller
18 James Taylor
19 Peter Blake (sleeve artist)
20 George Michael
21 Midge Ure
22 Martin Ware
23 John Keeble
24 Gary Kemp
25 Roger Taylor
26 Sarah
27 Siobhan
28 Peter Briquette
29 Francis Rossi
30 Robert 'Kool' Bell
31 Dennis Thomas
32 Andy Taylor
33 Jon Moss
34 Sting
35 Rick Parfitt
36 Nick Rhodes
37 Johnny Fingers

ALSO FEATURING:
David Bowie
Boy George
Holly
Paul McCartney

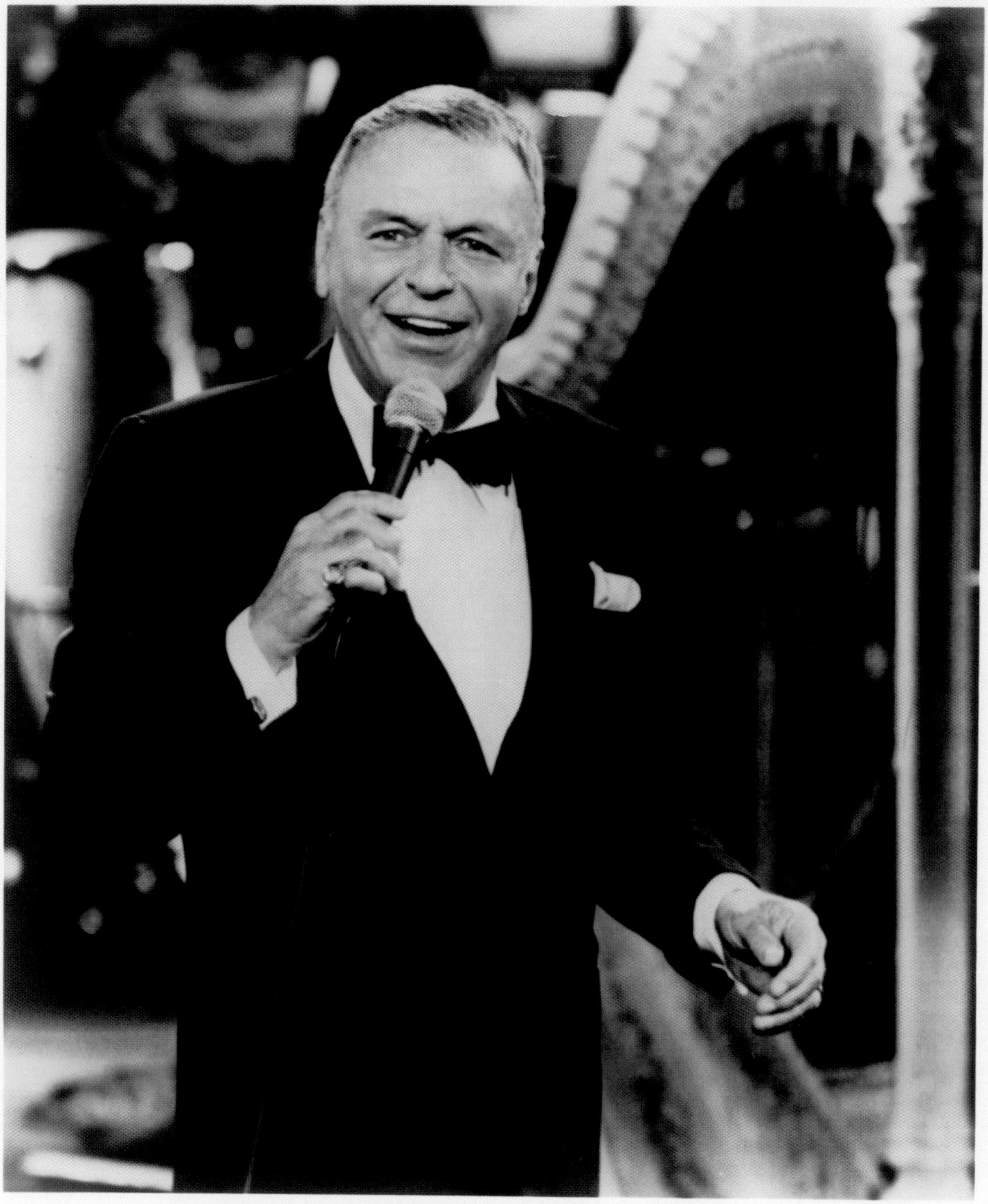

FRANK SINATRA

QWEST RECORDS ™

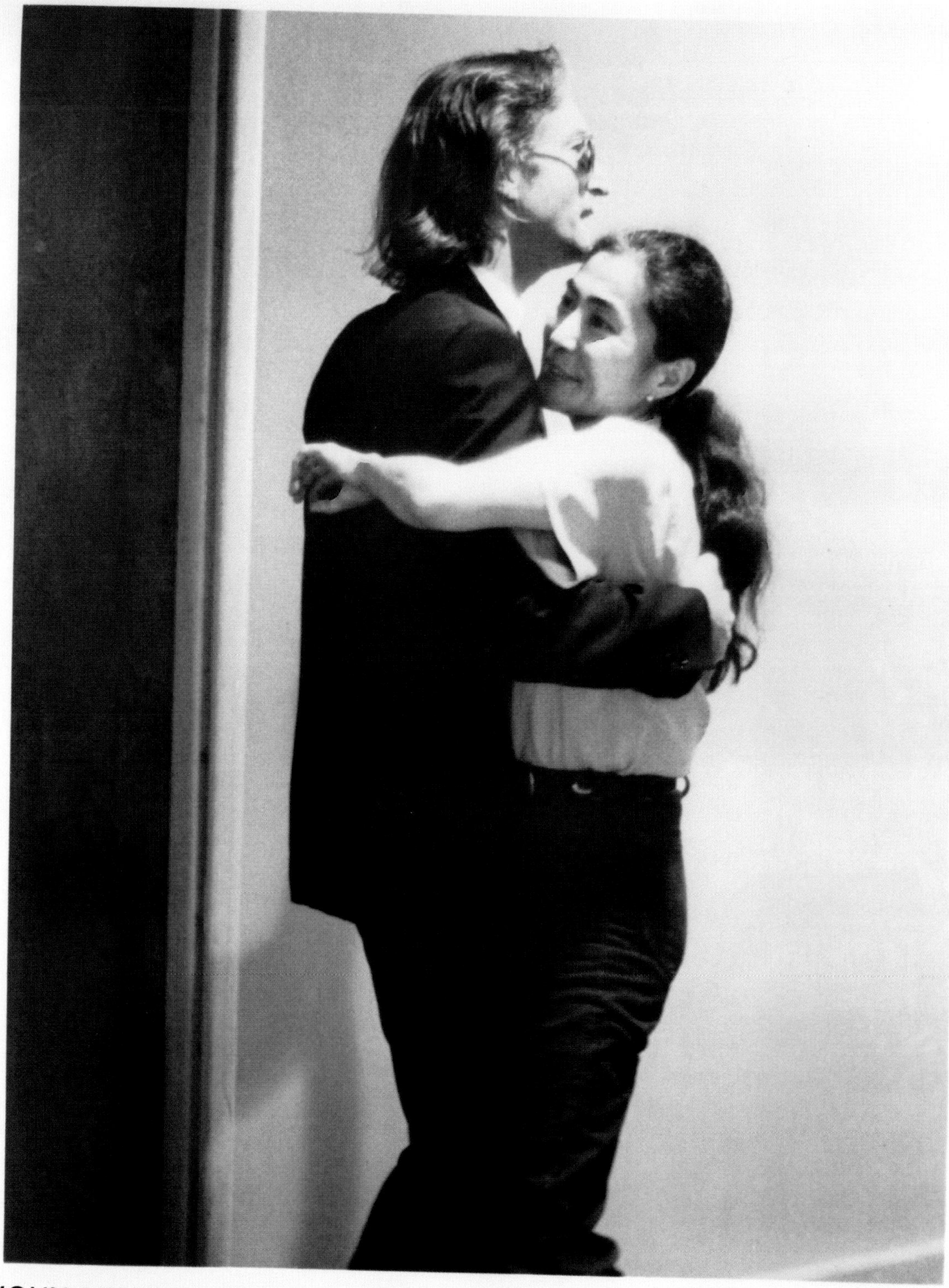

Photo by: BOB GRUEN

JOHN LENNON & YOKO ONO

ONO MUSIC™

polydor

PolyGram Records

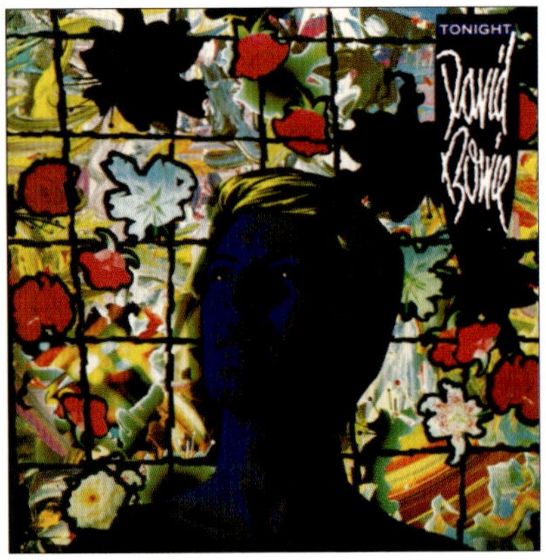

Following *Let's Dance*, his most commercially successful recording, and his "Serious Moonlight Tour," **David Bowie** delivered *Tonight* and the hit "Blue Jean."

Billboard 200: *Tonight* (#11)
Billboard Hot 100: "Blue Jean" (#8); "Tonight" (#53)

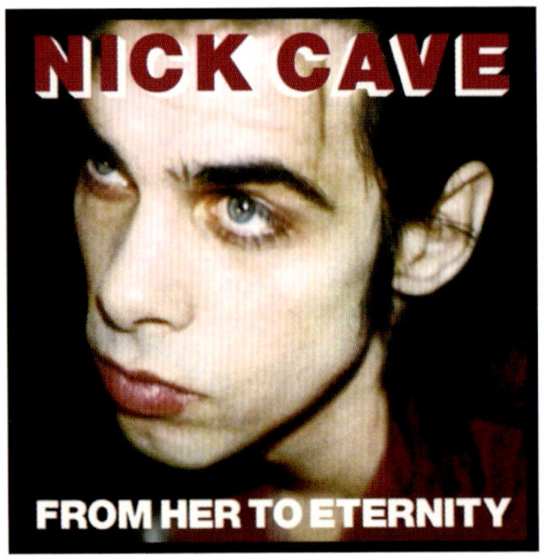

After the breakup of the Birthday Party, the Australian singer-songwriter **Nick Cave** emerged with the post-punk experimentalism of *From Her to Eternity*.

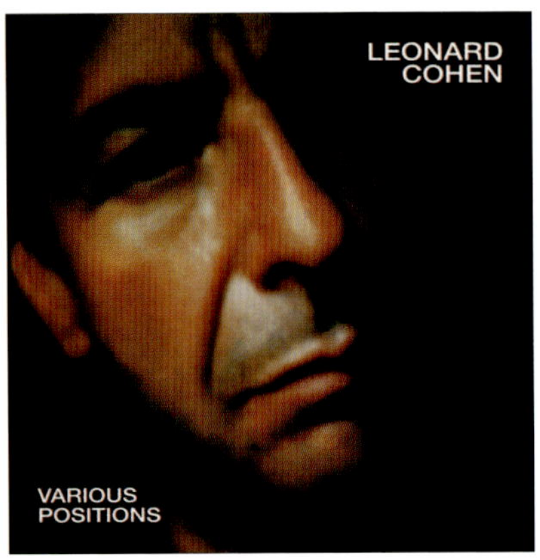

Achieving little initial success, **Leonard Cohen**'s classic "Hallelujah" first appeared on his album *Various Positions*, recorded with vocalist Jennifer Warnes.

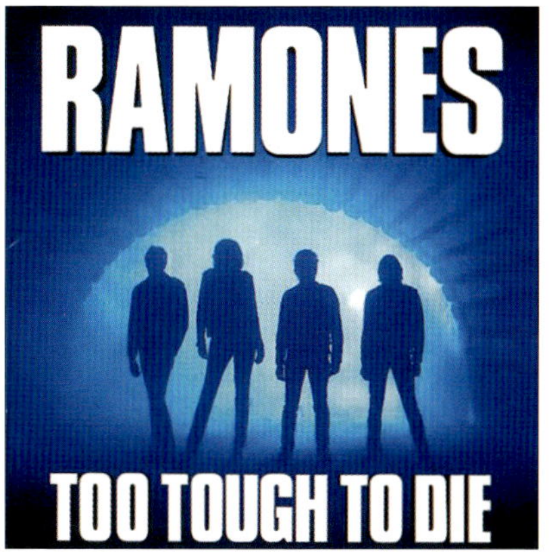

With original drummer Tommy Ramone producing, **Ramones'** *Too Tough to Die* turned to the band's prior approach to punk rock and revived its standing.

Billboard 200: *Too Tough to Die* (#171)

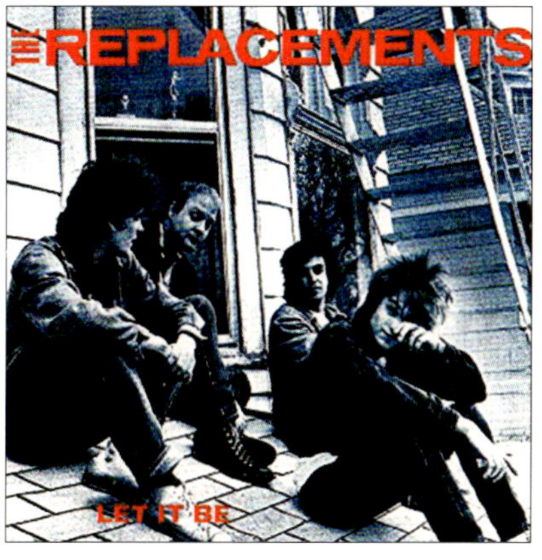

The Replacements successfully amplified their musical reach beyond hardcore rock with the coming-of-age album *Let it Be* and the single "I Will Dare."

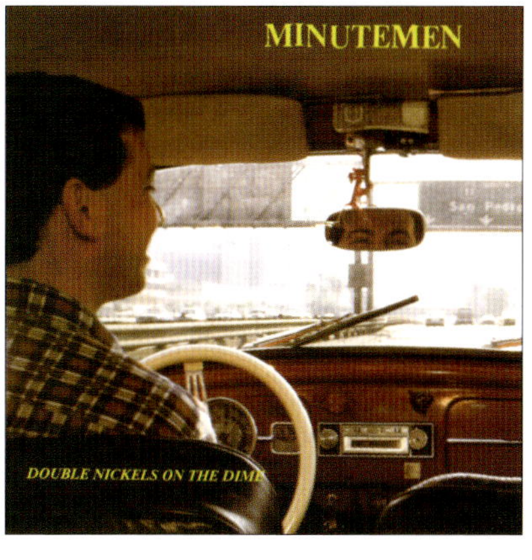

Formed by guitarist D. Boon and bassist Mike Watt, **Minutemen** delivered the wildly varied *Double Nickels on the Dime* to the American rock underground.

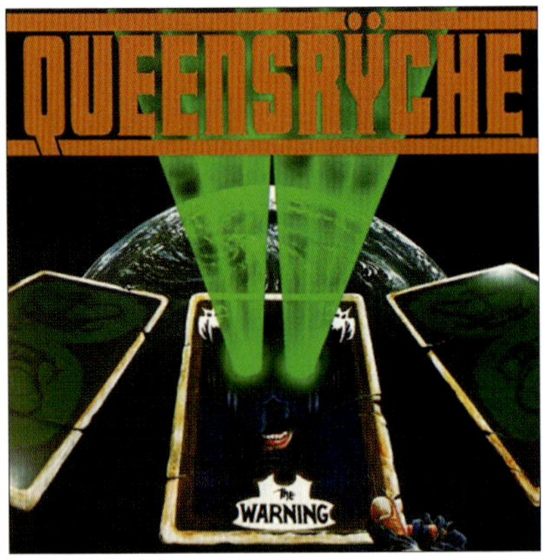

The Warning, **Queensrÿche**'s first album, revealed the Washington State ensemble's metal mindset, which informed the Japanese hit "Take Hold of the Flame."

Billboard 200: *The Warning* (#61)

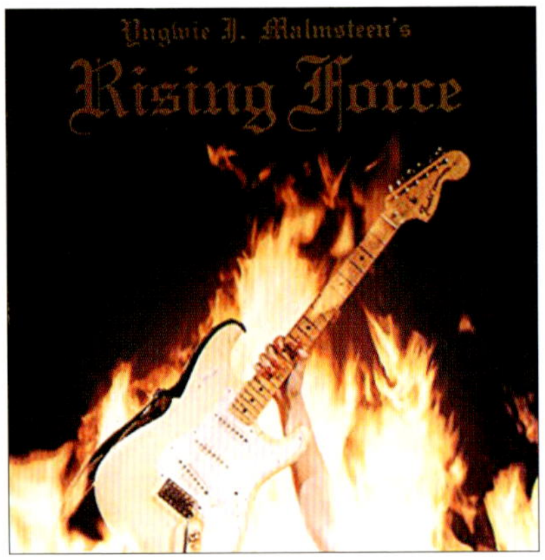

Rising Force, Swedish guitar virtuoso **Yngwie Malmsteen**'s first solo album, launched the age of "shredding"–challenging, incomprehensibly breakneck licks.

Billboard 200: *Rising Force* (#60)

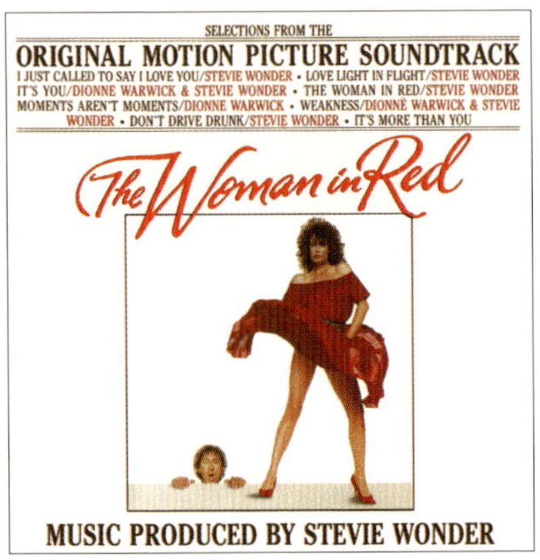

Stevie Wonder's soundtrack for *The Woman in Red* contained "I Just Called to Say I Love You," a ballad that won an Academy Award for Best Original Song.

Billboard 200: *The Woman in Red* (#4)
Billboard Hot 100: "I Just Called to Say I Love You" (No. 1); "Love Light in Flight" (#17)

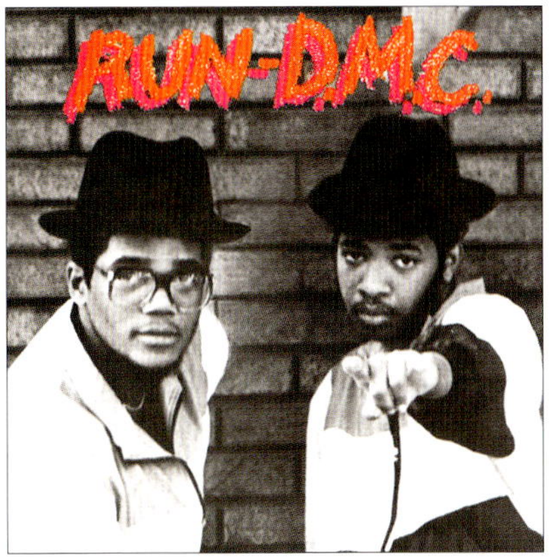

With **Run-D.M.C.**'s eponymous debut, the Hollis, Queens-based group became the first hip-hop act to earn a gold album and a Grammy Award nomination.

Billboard 200: *Run-D.M.C.* (#53)

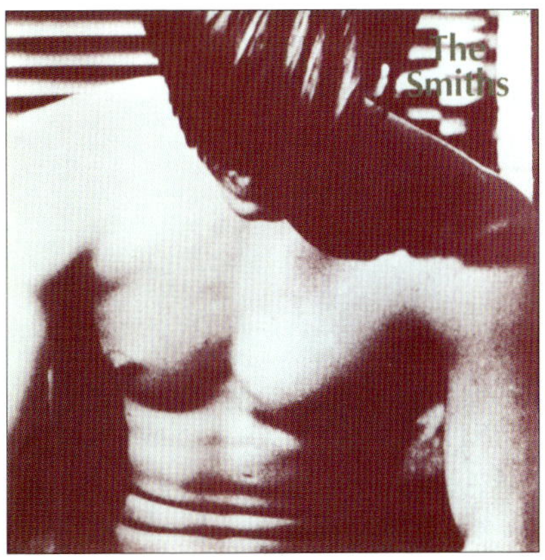

The Smiths' eponymous debut album peaked at #2 on the UK chart, establishing the writing partnership of guitarist Johnny Marr and lead singer Morrissey.

Billboard 200: *The Smiths* (#150)

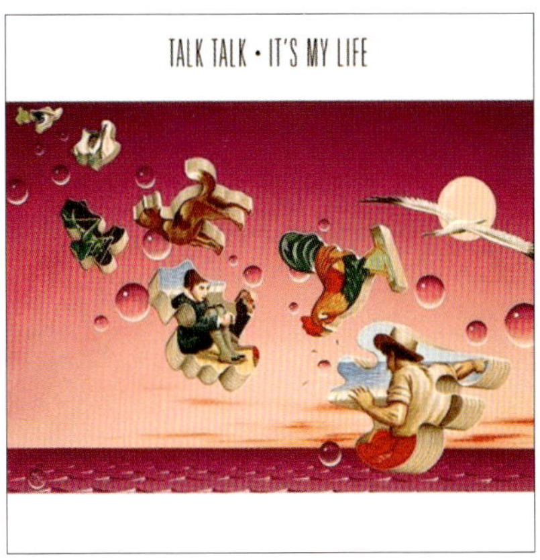

Refashioning its style to go beyond the synth-pop designation, the British group **Talk Talk** broke through in America with the vibrant single "It's My Life."

Billboard 200: *It's My Life* (#42)
Billboard Hot 100: "It's My Life" (#31); "Such a Shame" (#89)

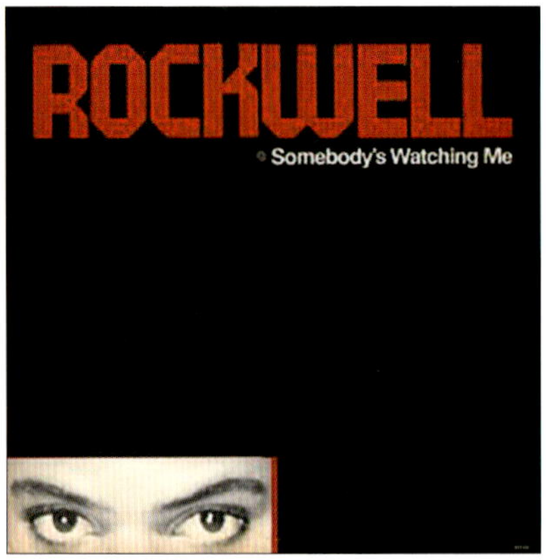

Rockwell, the son of Motown chairman Berry Gordy, released the hit "Somebody's Watching Me," featuring childhood pals Michael and Jermaine Jackson.

Billboard 200: *Somebody's Watching Me* (#15)
Billboard Hot 100: "Somebody's Watching Me" (#2); "Obscene Phone Caller" (#35)

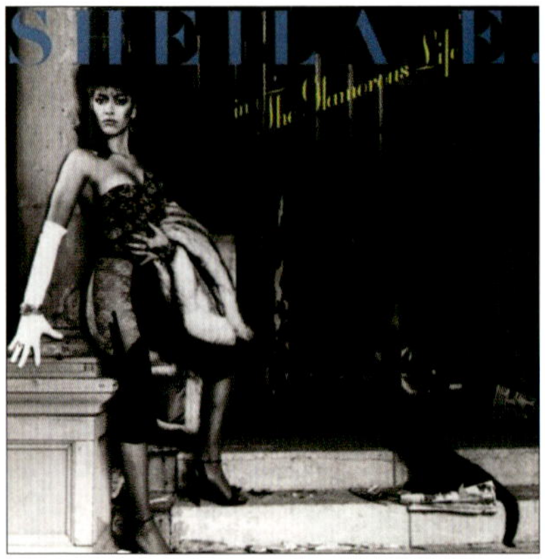

Written and co-produced by Prince, the title track from *The Glamorous Life*, singer and percussionist **Sheila E.**'s debut album, topped the dance charts.

Billboard 200: *The Glamorous Life* (#28)
Billboard Hot 100: "The Glamorous Life" (#7); "The Belle of St. Mark" (#34)

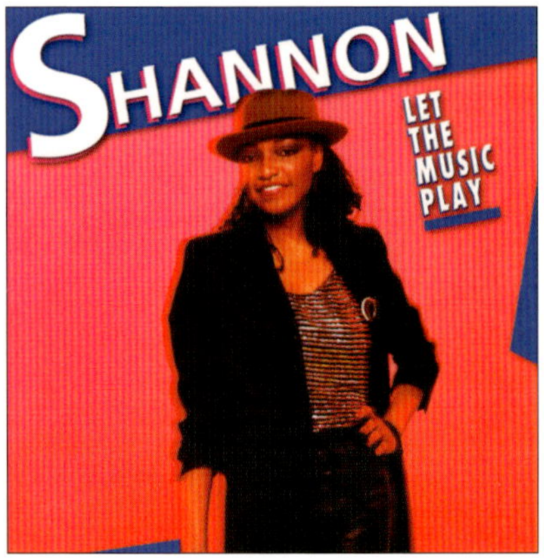

Shannon's "Let the Music Play," the singer's freestyle club classic from the album of the same name, pumped its way to No. 1 on *Billboard*'s dance chart.

Billboard 200: *Let the Music Play* (#32)
Billboard Hot 100: "Let the Music Play" (#8); "Give Me Tonight" (#46)

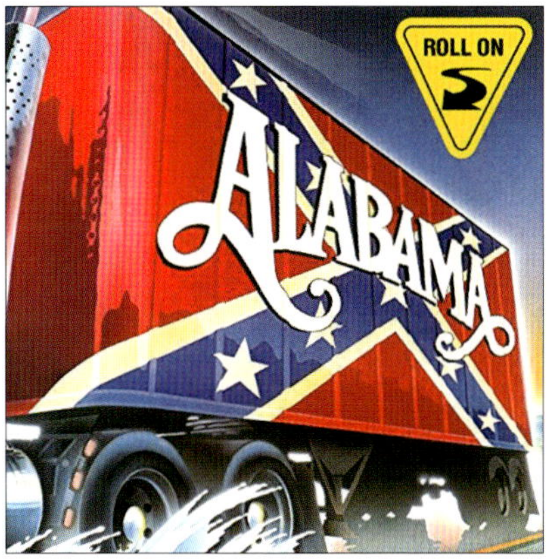

All four singles released from the quadruple-platinum album *Roll On* maintained **Alabama**'s streak of No. 1 hits on *Billboard*'s Hot Country Singles chart.

Billboard 200: *Roll On* (#21)
Billboard Hot 100: "When We Make Love" (#72)

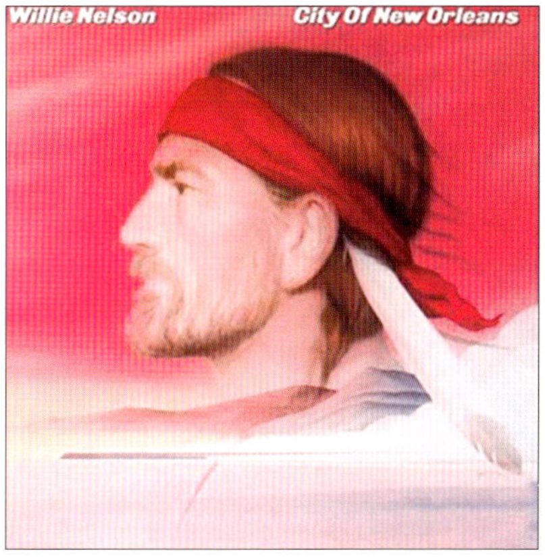

Willie Nelson's No. 1 version of the Steve Goodman-penned "City of New Orleans" earned Goodman a posthumous Grammy Award for Best Country Song.

Billboard 200: *City of New Orleans* (#69)

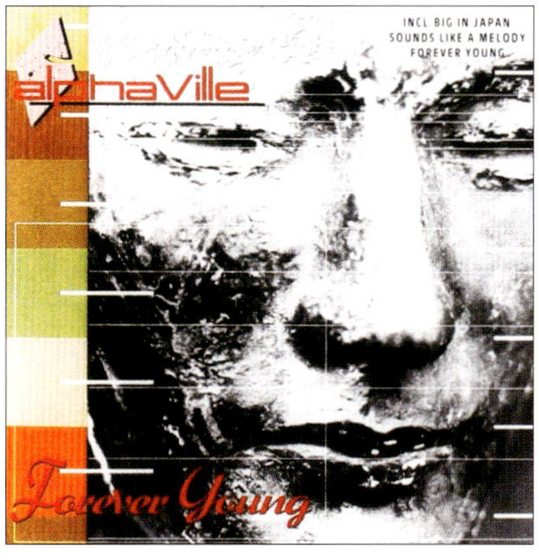

The German synth-pop outfit **Alphaville** delivered the debut album *Forever Young* and topped the dance chart with the international hit "Big in Japan."

Billboard 200: *Forever Young* (#180)
Billboard Hot 100: "Big in Japan" (#66);
"Forever Young" (#93)

{ IN MEMORY OF **MARY S. GLASSNER** }

ACKNOWLEDGMENTS

Many people were essential to the creation of this book. My first thanks go to my amazing publishing team—Jon Rizzi for bringing his special brand of editorial wit and intelligence, and Kate Glassner Brainerd for her design artistry and unflagging pursuit of excellence. Special appreciation goes to the Michael & Patricia Matthews Fund, whose facilitation was indispensable.

Chip Garofalo, Mark Zaremba, Jay Elowsky, Dave Zobl, Jennifer Soulé, Matt Rue, Sandra Jonas, Mark Lewis and Mike Dickson contributed expertise and resources. I am especially indebted to my dear friend Michael Jensen, as well as Sue Satriano, Janice Azrak, Bryn Bridenthal, Byron Hontas, Kathy Acquaviva, Shelly Selover, Sue Sawyer, Glen Brunman, Rick Ambrose, Bob Merlis, Bill Bentley, Heidi Ellen Robinson, Les Schwartz, Rick Gershon, Judi Kerr and Susan Blond—all of whom supported my efforts.

I specifically treasure the beneficence of Dave Rothstein, Greg Phifer, John Tope, Kevin Knee, Dick Merkle, Jeff Cook, Michael Brannen, Zak Phillips, Rich Garcia, Jason Minkler, Burt Baumgartner, Mitch Kampf, Don Zucker, Carl Walters, Charlie Reardon, Robin Wren, Jimmy Smith, Sharona White, John Ryland, Geina Horton, Michael Linehan, Mike Prince and Jeffrey Naumann, who all graciously furnished information and assistance.

I also salute Leland Rucker, Steve Knopper, David Menconi, Jon Iverson, Gil Asakawa, Mark Bliesener and Justin Mitchell, whose writings formed a vital index for the music-obsessed.

Finally, I would like to acknowledge with gratitude my beloved wife, Bridget, for her constant devotion and kindness. I cherish her—the love of my life.

EDITOR | **JON RIZZI**
ART DIRECTOR | **KATE GLASSNER BRAINERD**

ISBN 978-0-9915668-4-6 PRINTED IN CHINA | Asia Pacific Offset

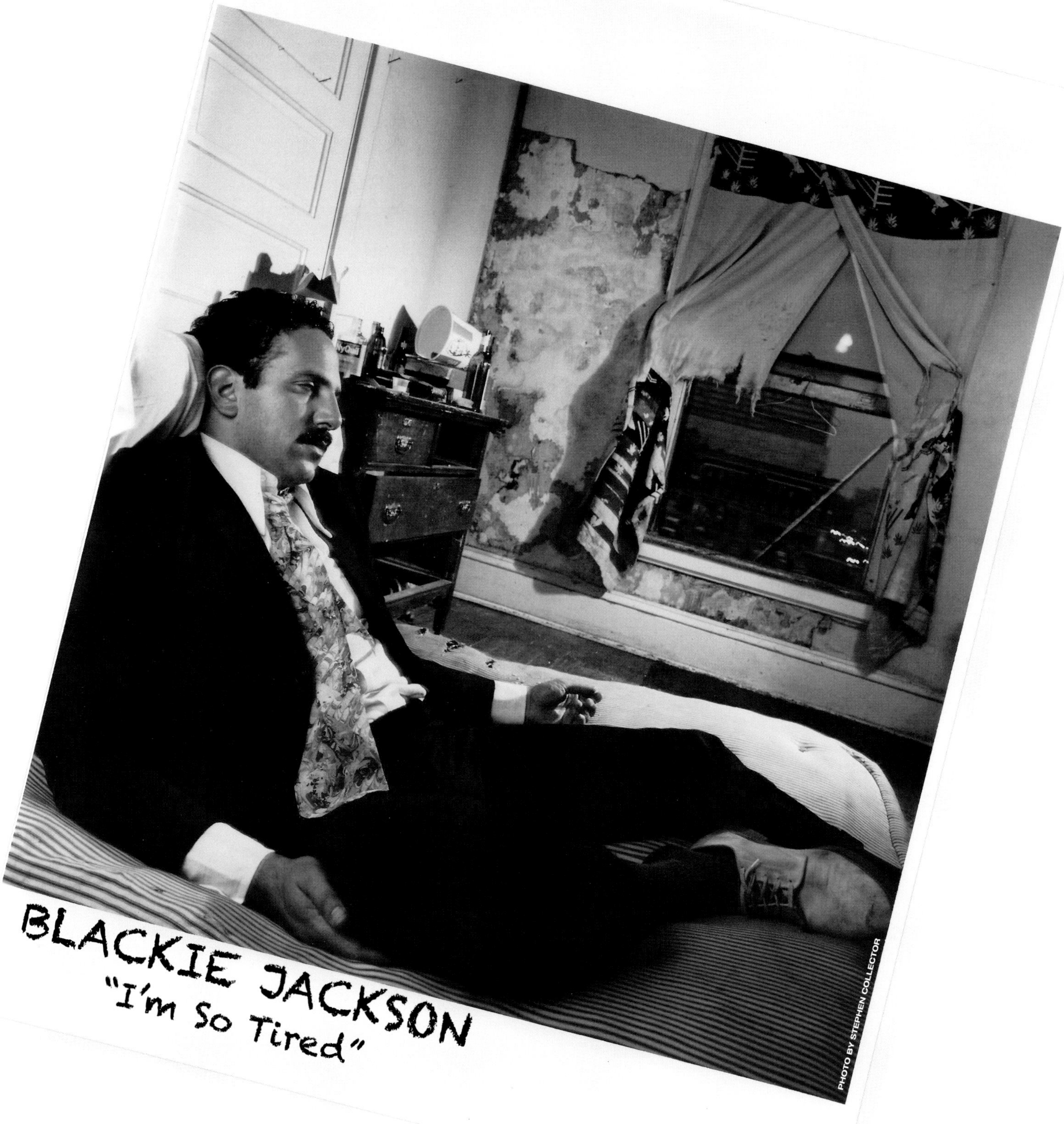
BLACKIE JACKSON
"I'm So Tired"
PHOTO BY STEPHEN COLLECTOR

Next in the *ON RECORD* book series

Vol.3 1991

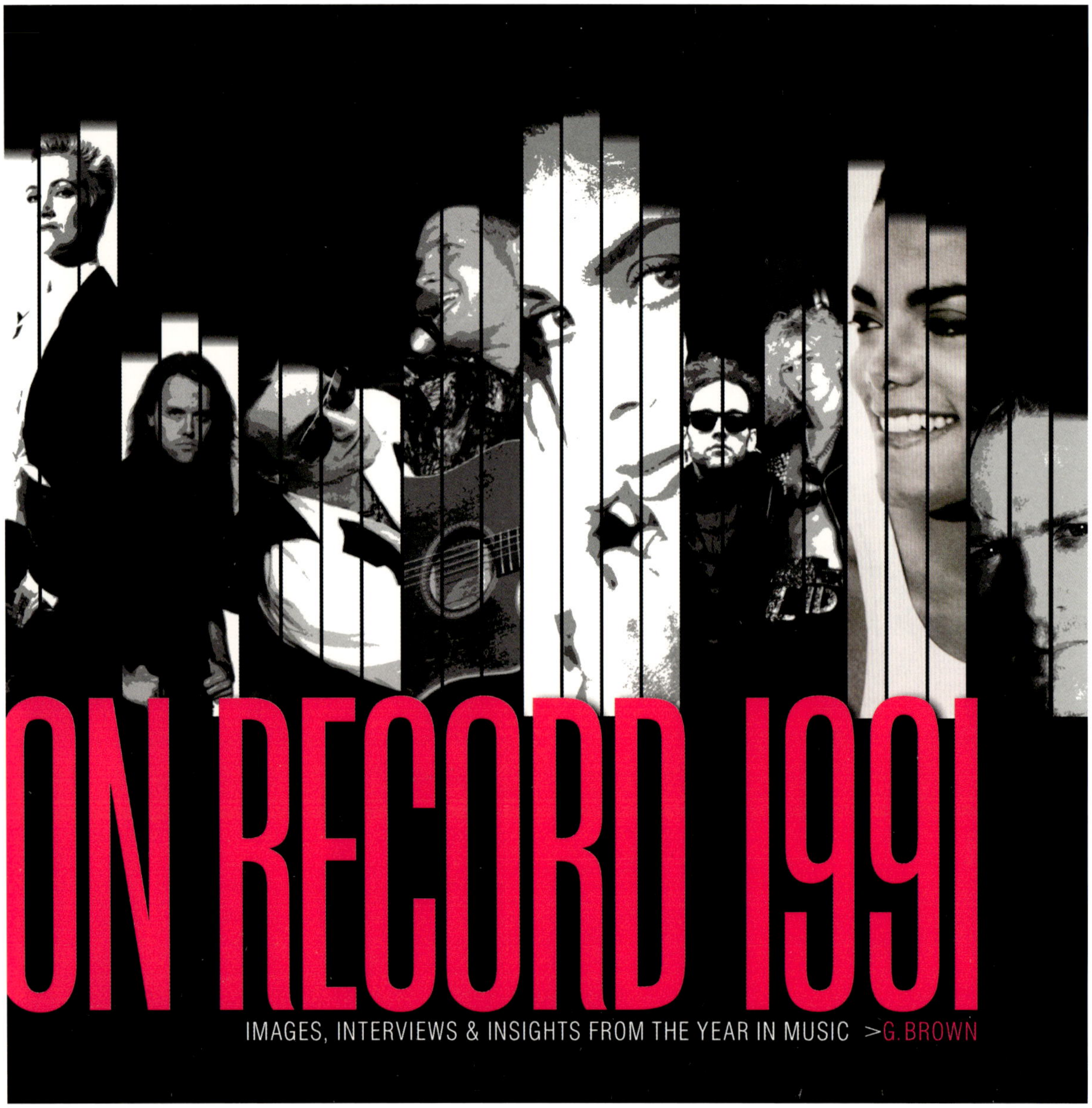